D1591868

For Reference

Not to be taken from this room

Sexual Harassment and Misconduct

Sexual Harassment and Misconduct

An Encyclopedia

Gina Robertiello, Editor

ABC-CLIO®

An Imprint of ABC-CLIO, LLC
Santa Barbara, California • Denver, Colorado

Library of Congress Cataloging-in-Publication Data

Names: Robertiello, Gina, editor.
Title: Sexual harassment and misconduct : an encyclopedia / Gina
  Robertiello, editor.
Description: Santa Barbara, California : ABC-CLIO, [2021] | Includes
  bibliographical references and index.
Identifiers: LCCN 2020052220 (print) | LCCN 2020052221 (ebook) | ISBN
  9781440866081 (hardcover ; alk. paper) | ISBN 9781440866098 (ebook)
Subjects: LCSH: Sexual harassment—United States—Encyclopedias.
Classification: LCC HD6060.3 .S494 2021 (print) | LCC HD6060.3 (ebook) |
  DDC 305.420973/03—dc23
LC record available at https://lccn.loc.gov/2020052220
LC ebook record available at https://lccn.loc.gov/2020052221

ISBN: 978-1-4408-6608-1 (print)
      978-1-4408-6609-8 (ebook)

25 24 23 22 21   1 2 3 4 5

This book is also available as an eBook.

ABC-CLIO
An Imprint of ABC-CLIO, LLC

ABC-CLIO, LLC
147 Castilian Drive
Santa Barbara, California 93117
www.abc-clio.com

This book is printed on acid-free paper ∞

Manufactured in the United States of America

Contents

Acknowledgments

When Kevin Hillstrom (the acquisitions editor for my second book, *Use and Abuse of Police Power in America*, which was published by ABC-CLIO in 2017) contacted me about this project, I could not pass it up, due to the very interesting, timely, and meaningful subject matter. When I mentioned the project to friends and family, I was amazed at how many people opened up to me about their own personal experiences or opinions in reference to the #MeToo Movement.

As with my previous two books, I have benefited enormously from those same family members and friends. My parents, Russ and Angela Pisano, have always been my biggest supporters (as a child and as an adult). My husband, Peter Robertiello, is my rock. He has so much confidence in my abilities that he believed in me when we were dating in high school, when I was in graduate school, when I was applying for teaching jobs, when I working on my dissertation, and when I was trying to get promoted. In August 2019 we were married for twenty-five years and have been together since we were seventeen years old. He has seen me at my best and my worst and has challenged me in more ways than I can count (or can mention here). But by being hard on me, he has taught me that I had it in me to be successful. He has always been supportive of my career and has never questioned my devotion to my work and my other kids (aka my students).

But I would particularly like to extend my gratitude to *my children*. They are my biggest accomplishment—pushing me to be the best at everything I do, as a mom, as an educator, and as a writer. I appreciate the time they gave me to devote to my scholarly interests, and I am enormously proud of the paths they are forging for themselves. As I write these words, my oldest, Brie, has already graduated college and is working for a magazine in the publishing industry. My middle child, Gigi, is a junior in college studying theater and communications. My son, Joey, is completing his senior year of high school and deciding what college to attend in the fall of 2021. All three of them are a daily inspiration to me. They spent enough time at work with me to understand what it entails to become a professor, and I am so proud of the young adults they have developed into. They are great kids and extremely smart and motivated. They actually motivate me to be a better person. I thoroughly enjoy their successes—from having the guts to travel abroad (not knowing one other person), to performing in school plays and musicals (in front of huge crowds), to running on the track team and never missing a day of school.

I am also grateful to my students at Felician University for being understanding if I was stressed out about meeting a deadline and for the endless times they had to hear me talk about "the book." My colleagues at Felician went out of their way to support me on this project. Finally, I thank my friends for putting up with me when I was tense and when I complained about how much work I had to do. Nights out to dinner and traveling with them always take the edge off and make me a better writer.

Introduction

This title provides a comprehensive, objective overview of the dimensions of sexual harassment and misconduct in the United States. The book includes significant historical coverage, but the main focus is on recent events that have made this issue so prominent today in the worlds of American entertainment, politics, business, and society.

As revelations of sexual harassment and misconduct have roiled Hollywood, Washington, DC, and workplaces across the country in recent years, these problems—and the underlying societal pressures and traditions that drive them—are being examined more closely than ever before. This encyclopedia contains approximately 150 entries that help readers understand not only the specific harassment and abuse scandals that have erupted across the United States in the wake of the emergence of the #MeToo Movement but also the historical factors and events that have led to this moment in American history. In addition, it will illuminate various types of sexual harassment and misconduct (e.g., quid pro quo, hostile work environment), explain different classifications of harassers (e.g., territorial, predatory), survey how sexual harassment and misconduct manifest themselves in different settings (e.g., workplace, school, military, entertainment industry), and explain various reforms, laws, and other responses that are being crafted to address these deeply entrenched problems. Each essay concludes with a further reading section that provides users with sources of additional information on the topic in question.

This encyclopedia was prepared to provide readers with an easy-to-use, accurate, up-to-date guide to the controversial past and current controversies facing our society as it grapples with the important and interrelated issues of sexual harassment, misconduct, and misogyny in American society. It also provides authoritative accounts of specific scandals and controversies in this area, exploring allegations made against everyone from presidents and Supreme Court nominees to famous actors, directors, journalists, singers, movie moguls, and chefs.

The encyclopedia provides a unique approach to presenting the events that have made it easier for offenders to take advantage of others. It allows readers to develop a sense of the "climate" over time in a clear, concise, and neutral manner, allowing them to increase their knowledge regarding previous and current events and understand why scandals, controversies, justifications, and claims pertaining to issues of sexual harassment and sexism are perceived the way they are—by both women and men.

The selection of topics was based on the most important and pressing issues, trends, and events shaping the efforts of contemporary American society to not only understand and confront the damage wreaked by sexual harassment and misconduct but also to chart a new path of gender equality and respect.

This book's wide-ranging topic list includes important laws, codes of conduct, legal principles, and court decisions pertaining to sexual harassment and misconduct. Influential advocates for women's rights and activists fighting against sexual harassment and abuse are also featured, including leading figures in the #MeToo Movement, such as Tarana Burke, Rose McGowan, and Susan J. Fowler. Readers will also find entries devoted to specific industries and sectors of American society, where sexual harassment and misconduct has been well documented as well as specific allegations and scandals that have rocked those industries over the past several years and orbited around powerful figures, ranging from Hollywood and media moguls (e.g., Harvey Weinstein and Roger Ailes) to celebrities (e.g., Bill Cosby and Matt Lauer) to Supreme Court justices (e.g., Clarence Thomas and Brett Kavanaugh). This work even explores how sexual harassment, assault, and gender norms have been—and continue to be—depicted in American popular culture, ranging from rap music to television shows and movies, such as *M*A*S*H*, *Sixteen Candles*, and *9 to 5*. Finally, this resource provides authoritative accounts of important events, ranging from the notorious Tailhook symposium of 1991 (in which male U.S. military officers sexually assaulted dozens of female officers in attendance) to the #MeToo and Time's Up movements.

This book is geared toward high school, undergraduate, and graduate students who want to increase their knowledge of sexual abuse, misconduct, and harassment in its many different forms, locations, and contexts. However, laypersons would also benefit from the general knowledge they can gain about the ways issues of power and control are so essential to understanding acts of sexual abuse and harassment. This book is dedicated to all those who have experienced sexual harassment and misconduct and to the women and men working to drain American relationships, families, businesses, and communities of those poisons.

A

Affirmative Consent Laws

INTRODUCTION

Sexual violence, particularly among college students, is an ongoing epidemic spanning many decades. A 2016 report prepared for the National Institute of Justice (NIJ), Bureau of Justice Statistics (BJS), found that 21 percent of women and 7 percent of men were victims of sexual assault during college. Most of the victims did not report the sexual assault to campus police, campus health services, or law enforcement. The most common reasons for not reporting were that they did not believe the assault was serious enough; they felt shame or guilt that they bore some responsibility for the encounter; or they feared retaliation from others.

The American public has criticized college and university campuses for encouraging sexist attitudes toward women and promoting a "rape culture" by mishandling sexual assault cases. In response to growing public concern over this issue, President Obama signed the Campus Sexual Violence Elimination Act (Campus SaVE Act) in 2013. This legislation requires private and public colleges and universities that receive federal funding to adopt and advertise policies consistent with Title IX of the Education Amendments of 1972. Sexual violence, including sexual assault and sexual harassment, are forms of discrimination prohibited by Title IX.

WHAT IS AFFIRMATIVE CONSENT?

Consent is a critical tool for distinguishing healthy sexual activity from sexual assaults. Many colleges and universities have revised their sexual misconduct/assault policies to include affirmative consent (AC) (i.e., "yes means yes"). The "yes means yes" feature of AC is a stark contrast to the previous and ever-present message of "no means no." AC communicates that a lack of protest or resistance does not equal consent, nor does one's silence. The standards of AC are intended to decrease any miscommunication that may lead to nonconsensual sex (i.e., rape or sexual assault).

In September 2014, California governor Jerry Brown signed Senate Bill 967. This law, which requires the state's public institutions of higher education to implement an AC policy, was the first state law of its kind. California's AC law requires students to not only verbally agree to initial sexual activity but also explicitly say yes to one another for each sexual activity they engage in. To date, thirty states have statewide AC laws that have been signed into law, and the remaining twenty states have AC laws under consideration.

WHY AFFIRMATIVE CONSENT IS NECESSARY

Surveys of college students have revealed that many do not verbally discuss consent (e.g., "yes" or "OK") prior to engaging in sexual activity. Instead, students tend to use nonverbal communication (i.e., body language) to communicate consent or nonconsent (e.g., resistance). However, overreliance on nonverbal communication can lead to miscommunication. Allegations of nonconsensual sex or sexual assault are sometimes the result of "misunderstanding" one's body language. Because sexual assault is often defined in terms of *nonconsent* ("no means no"), initiators of sex often rely on cues such as physical resistance or a verbal no to communicate whether to continue with sexual activity. Therefore, AC requires individuals to be more mindful and to obtain an affirmative yes *prior* to engaging in *any* sexual activity to reduce incidents of sexual assault.

PROBLEMS WITH AFFIRMATIVE CONSENT

AC laws are not without controversy, and some administrators, legislators, students, and victims question whether they will be effective in reducing sexual assaults. Although AC laws are written using gender-neutral language, some argue they assume traditional gender roles and sexual scripts in which men are the primary initiators of sex and women determine whether or not sex will actually happen. Such traditional sexual scripts reinforce men as sexual initiators, which may influence perceptions of how men and women should behave sexually. These perceptions may influence definitions of rape and reinforce stereotypes or myths regarding rape (e.g., victims are responsible for their rape if they were intoxicated or if they did not physically resist). The popular media, such as movies and television shows, have been complicit in depicting stereotypes of the "typical rape victim" and the "typical rapist," further perpetuating rape myths and misinformation about consent.

AC also assumes that individuals can willingly say yes or no to sexual activity. Individuals often find themselves pressured to consent. For example, one may consent to engage in some form of sexual activity but may not want to continue any further but agree to it anyway in fear of being labeled a "tease." Some feel pressured to consent to sex as a sort of compensation for expenditures of time, money, or attention spent on them.

AC also does not adequately address two common problems on college campuses: intoxication and predatory behavior. The 2007 report prepared for the NIJ found that the majority of campus sexual assaults against women occur when they are incapacitated, primarily by alcohol. Being under the influence of drugs or alcohol can make informed consent to sexual activity an impossibility. Sometimes victim intoxication is a factor in predatory behavior. Initiators of sex may use aggressive, coercive, or deceptive strategies to either obtain or perceive they have obtained consent.

Anthropologist Dr. Peggy Sanday brought worldwide attention to such predatory behavior among college males at Penn State University in her book *Fraternity Gang Rape: Sex, Brotherhood, and Privilege on Campus* (1990). Sanday provided an in-depth account of the daily life in the fraternity, the misogynistic attitudes toward women and sex, and the prevalence of rape and gang rape on campus. Although the accounts are from 1984, this rape culture and predatory behavior continues. In 2012, a flier titled "Top Ten Ways to Get Away with Rape" was found in the men's bathroom of an Ohio university dorm.

FUTURE DIRECTIONS

AC polices may be a step in the right direction for improved communication between parties and may reduce sexual assaults/unwanted sex due to miscommunications, but simply passing a law is not enough. The AC laws must be accompanied with a culture shift that not only includes students but also faculty, staff, administrators, athletic directors, coaches, and fraternity and sorority councils, particularly if these officials are sitting on committees that hear sexual assault cases. Sexual assault prevention education initiatives must be mandatory for all stakeholders, and training must be ongoing. Such programs must include, at a minimum, consent promotion (i.e., the Consent Is Sexy Campaign), how to monitor one's alcohol consumption, drug use, bystander intervention, and clear procedures to hold accountable all those responsible for the promotion of sexism, rape culture, and sexual assaults.

Melanie Clark Mogavero

See also: Campus Accountability and Safety Act; College Campuses; Equal Employment Opportunity Commission; Objectification of Women; Relationship Violence; Title IX; Victim Blaming

Further Reading

Affirmative Consent and Respect. 2017. "Affirmative Consent Laws (Yes Means Yes) State by State." Accessed January 26, 2019, http://affirmativeconsent.com/affirmative -consent-laws-state-by-state/.

Bogle, K. A. 2014. "'Yes Means Yes' Isn't the Answer." *Chronicle of Higher Education,* October 27. Accessed January 21, 2019, http://chronicle.com/article/Yes-Means -Yes-Isnt-the/149639/.

Jozkowski, K. N. 2015. "'Yes Means Yes'? Sexual Consent Policy and College Students." *Change: The Magazine of Higher Learning* 47: 6–23.

Jozkowski, K. N., Tiffany L. Marcantonio, and Mary E. Hunt. 2017. "College Students' Sexual Consent Communication and Perceptions of Sexual Double Standards: A Qualitative Investigation." *Perspectives on Sexual and Reproductive Health* 49: 237–244.

Keenan, S. 2015. "Affirmative Consent: Are Students Really Asking?" *New York Times,* July 28. Accessed January 21, 2019, http://www.nytimes.com/2015/08/02/education /edlife/affirmative-consent-are-students-really-asking.html.

Klement, K. R., B. J. Sagarin, and E. L. Lee. 2017. "Participating in a Culture of Consent May Be Associated with Lower Rape-Supportive Beliefs." *Journal of Sex Research* 54:130–134.

Krebs, C. P., C. H. Lindquist, M. Berzofsky, B. Shook-Sa, and K. Pearson. 2016. "Campus Climate Survey Validation Study Final Technical Report." Washington, DC: Bureau of Justice Statistics, U.S. Department of Justice.

Krebs, Christopher P., Christine H. Lindquist; Tara D. Warner, Bonnie S. Fisher, and Sandra L. Martin. 2007. "The Campus Sexual Assault (CSA)." National Institute of Justice. NIJ Grant No. 2004-WG-BX-0010.

Pugh, Brandie, and Patricia Becker. 2018. "Exploring Definitions and Prevalence of Verbal Sexual Coercion and Its Relationship to Consent to Unwanted Sex: Implications for Affirmative Consent." *Behavioral Sciences* 8: 1–28.

Roberts, Christine. 2012. "Flier Found at Miami University in Ohio Advises 'Top Ten Ways to Get Away with Rape.'" *Daily News*, October 15. Accessed January 21, 2019, https://www.nydailynews.com/news/national/flier-found-miami-university -ohio-advises-top-ten-ways-rape-article-1.1184009.

Sanday, Peggy R. 1990. *Fraternity Gang Rape: Sex, Brotherhood, and Privilege on Campus.* New York: New York University Press.

Silver, Nathan, and Shelly R. Hovick. 2018. "A Schema of Denial: The Influence of Rape Myth Acceptance on Beliefs, Attitudes, and Processing of Affirmative Consent Campaign Messages." *Journal of Health Communication* 23: 505–513.

Tinkler, Justine E., Jody Clay-Warner, and Malissa Alinor. 2018. "Communicating about Affirmative Consent: How the Threat of Punishment Affects Policy Support and Gender Stereotypes." *Journal of Interpersonal Violence* 33: 3344–3366.

Zimmerman, Eilene. 2016. "Campus Sexual Assault: A Timeline of Major Events." *New York Times*, June 22. Accessed January 27, 2019, http://www.nytimes.com/2016 /06/23/education/campus-sexual-assault-a-timeline-of-major-events.html.

Agriculture Industry

Sexual harassment is an ongoing threat to gender equality in the agriculture industry, which is predominately composed of males; women make up about one-quarter of those employed in the industry. This imbalance fosters a male-dominant culture, which can increase the risk of sexual harassment. The agriculture industry is an expansive and diverse area of work settings that range from farmwork, in which people perform manual labor, to careers in teaching agriculture. Researchers believe that the rural locations of many types of work that occur in fields and processing plants make it easier for perpetrators of sexual harassment to engage in these actions—and to conceal them from others. The lack of major labor laws to protect farmworkers has exacerbated the problem of sexual harassment in the agriculture industries.

Sexual harassment in the agriculture industry along with problems with gender discrimination and gender bias all contribute to what is known as a hostile work environment. This type of intimidating environment interferes with women's work and other areas of their lives. According to the Equal Employment Opportunity Commission (EEOC), in the agriculture industry, there is a greater power imbalance between the perpetrators of sexual harassment (employer or direct supervisors) and the victims (often farmworkers) than in other industries. The existence of this power imbalance facilitates sexual harassment.

In the agriculture industry, sexual harassment in the form of unwanted sexual behavior most often involves farmworkers working in fields. The type of physical labor that is involved in harvesting crops, such as bending over and crouching, makes women more vulnerable to stares, sexual comments, and physical assault than women in other occupations. Another aspect of unwanted sexual misconduct in farm fields is sexual coercion, in which a supervisor uses rewards or threats to obtain sexual favors from victims (e.g., easier responsibilities or better hours).

Gender discrimination and bias are present in all levels and occupations of the agriculture industry. The views of women's roles are largely shaped by traditional gender roles. In the agriculture industry, there is often an attitude among leaders that women do not possess adequate skills and abilities to be successful in leadership positions. The lack of female representation in leadership positions has also made it harder for problems of harassment and sexism to be effectively addressed.

In 2016, female farmworkers made up about 24 percent of the agricultural workforce, according to the U.S. Department of Agriculture. Across several studies, the number holds steady at around eight in ten women experiencing some type of sexual harassment in the agriculture workplace. As a comparison, sexual harassment estimation rates range from 25 percent to 50 percent of all women in the U.S. workforce.

The women who most often report sexual harassment are predominately African Americans, Latinas, and immigrant women of color—groups that account for the majority of women working in the industry. These are the best estimations, as low reporting rates remain a problem. Many women are afraid to disclose sexual harassment for fear of losing their jobs or being on the receiving end of other forms of retaliation, such as being assigned particularly exhausting, dangerous, degrading, or low-wage work. Additionally, language barriers often create an obstacle in reporting sexual harassment.

In 2018, a Tampa, Florida, jury awarded a victim of sexual harassment compensatory damages of $450,000 and punitive damages of $400,000 for an incident that occurred while she was employed by Favorite Farms. In 2015, the victim in the case reported to police and the management at Favorite Farms on the day of the assault that her supervisor had raped her. At that time, Favorite Farms allegedly sent her home without pay and let her supervisor continue supervising female employees.

In a California case, Maribel Ochoa was a seventeen-year-old migrant worker picking grapes at a California vineyard when a fellow worker began to sexually harass her. The man harassed her verbally and then approached her from behind and pressed his genitals against her. When Ochoa complained to her employer about the latter incident the next day, she and other family members working at the vineyard were fired and told to leave the property. This was a serious blow to Ochoa and her family, as they had been living at the vineyard in employer-provided housing. The EEOC filed a lawsuit against the vineyard, and Ochoa was paid $100,000 for her suffering and losses. The vineyard also spent $250,000 on sexual harassment training in the various languages spoken by workers at the vineyard.

Despite such high-profile cases, sexism and sexual harassment remain persistent problems in many sectors of the agriculture industry. A 2018 study by Corteva Agriscience found that 52 percent of women employed in the agriculture industry see gender discrimination as a continuing problem.

Melissa Inglis

See also: Equal Employment Opportunity Commission; Hostile Work Environment; Traditionally "Male" Workplaces; Workplace Gender Diversity

Further Reading

Corteva Agriscience. 2018. "Global Women in Agriculture: Research Findings." October 15. https://www.corteva.com/content/dam/dpagco/corteva/global/corporate/general/files/Global%20Women%20In%20Agriculture%20White%20Paper%20100318.pdf.

McGivern, K. 2018. "EEOC: Dover Farmworker Sexually Assaulted, Retaliated Against." ABC Action News, December 21. https://www.abcactionnews.com/news/local-news/eeoc-dover-farmworker-sexually-assaulted-retaliated-against.

Poo, A., and Mónica Ramírez. 2018. "Female Domestic and Agriculture Workers Confront an Epidemic of Sexual Harassment." American Civil Liberties Union, May 4. https://www.aclu.org/blog/womens-rights/womens-rights-workplace/female-domestic-and-agricultural-workers-confront.

Ramchandani, A. 2018. "There's a Sexual-Harassment Epidemic on America's Farms." *The Atlantic*, January 29.

United States Department of Agriculture. 2018. "Farm Labor." https://www.ers.usda.gov/topics/farm-economy/farm-labor/.

Ailes, Roger (1940–2017)

Roger Ailes was a media executive whose strategy to make Fox News an unapologetically conservative news outlet made it the most popular and powerful news network on television. But in the summer of 2016, he resigned as chairman and CEO of Fox News in response to allegations that he had sexually harassed several Fox News personalities and other female employees.

Ailes was born on May 15, 1940, in Warren, Ohio. He pursued his education at Ohio University in Athens, majoring in radio and television. Following his graduation in 1962, Ailes secured a job as a production assistant on *The Mike Douglas Show* and quickly rose up the ranks to executive producer. This early success led him to start his own advertising company in 1969, where he focused on showcasing businesses and politicians, and then he went a step further in creating a conservative-leaning network with Television News, Inc., which broadcast from 1973 to 1975. After a brief hiatus from television, Ailes returned in 1993 to launch an early iteration of MSNBC: America's Talking. His time with NBC was short lived, however, after Ailes met with News Corporation leader Rupert Murdoch to collaborate on a conservative news station. These discussions resulted in the creation of the Fox News Channel, which officially launched on October 7, 1996, with Ailes as its chairman and CEO. Over the next twenty years, Fox News grew exponentially, garnering a daily viewership of over two million people—more than the combined viewership of CNN and MSNBC.

Success did little to shield Ailes when his workplace misconduct was brought into public focus. In July 2016, former Fox News anchor Gretchen Carlson filed a sexual harassment lawsuit against Ailes, alleging that she had been fired from her position after refusing his sexual advances. Carlson's coming forward sparked a flurry of additional accusations against Ailes. On July 19, 2016, one of Fox News's biggest stars, Megyn Kelly, stated that Ailes had made unwanted sexual advances against her a decade earlier. Two days later, Ailes ended his twenty-year reign as chairman and CEO of the network.

Following the resignation of Ailes, even more women came forward with sexual assault allegations. On July 29, 2016, Laurie Luhn, a former Fox News staffer, alleged that she had been harassed by Ailes for more than twenty years and that Fox News had been aware of the harassment. Later, in the summer of 2016, Laurie Dhue, an anchor on Fox from 2000 to 2008, was paid in a settlement by Fox for her sexual assault claims regarding Roger Ailes and Fox News on-air personality Bill O'Reilly.

In August 2016, Andrea Tantaros also claimed that she had been sexually harassed by Ailes and O'Reilly. In September 2016, Fox paid a settlement to Juliet Huddy, a former Fox News host, who claimed O'Reilly had tried to kiss her. After all the allegations were made public, a federal investigation into the Fox News Channel was initiated. It examined the company's handling of the sexual assault allegations and the treatment of all the women who worked there.

Ashley Fundack

See also: Hostile Work Environment; #MeToo Movement; Power Dynamics; Sexism

Further Reading

Ellison, S. 2016. "Inside the Final Days of Roger Ailes's Reign at Fox News." *Vanity Fair*, September 22. https://www.vanityfair.com/news/2016/09/roger-ailes-fox-news -final-days.

Hong, N. 2017. "How Roger Ailes's Death Affects Lawsuits." *Wall Street Journal*, May 18. https://www.wsj.com/articles/how-roger-ailess-death-affects-lawsuits -1495150048.

Koblin, J., and J. Rutenburg. 2016. "Accused of Sexual Harassment, Roger Ailes Is Negotiating Exit from Fox." *New York Times*, July 19. https://www.nytimes.com/2016 /07/20/business/media/roger-ailes-fox-news-murdoch.html.

Sherman, Gabriel. 2014. *The Loudest Voice in the Room: How the Brilliant, Bombastic Roger Ailes Built Fox News—and Divided a Country*. New York: Random House.

Amateur Sports

Sexual harassment and abuse are among the most critical problems in sports today, in part because they can be so difficult to detect and address. Adolescent victims often feel that they cannot come forward because almost all aspects of their lives are under the control of adults who are either perpetrators of the abuse or have considerable emotional or financial investments in the young athletes' success. Feelings of shame and helplessness are often present as well. As a result, many accusations of sexual abuse in sports settings only come out after the victims are well into adulthood. Even then, the pressure to remain silent is strong, as survivors have to grapple with the possibility that their claims will be met with skepticism or disbelief.

Amateur sports embrace and depend on the involvement of many parties, including parents, coaches, officials, administrators, and athletes. The social commitments of these people (many of whom volunteer their time, talents, and energy) and their

demonstrations of responsibility are noteworthy. However, the very nature of ama-
teurism often makes regulation of these sports a difficult endeavor. As a result, controls against sexual harassment and abuse are often inadequate. While professional
sports can create better controlled environments and regulations against such behavior, it is not always easy to provide the same means of protection, oversight, and
appropriate intervention in amateur sports. In amateur settings, victims of harassment or assault may be even more reluctant to report or file a formal complaint
against their abusers. When the athlete has the potential to become a professional or
to secure a college scholarship and his or her success is dependent on maintaining
the abusive relationship with the perpetrator, it can become even more difficult to
cope with the issue.

Amateur sports are important activities that affect the psychomotor and physical development of individuals, especially the young. Engagement in sports activities plays an important role in the cognitive development and socialization
processes of an individual. Amateur sports can provide advantages to participating children in such varied areas as health, nutrition, self-confidence, discipline,
problem-solving, and focus.

Some of the practices and established cultures within sports can be risky for
athletes. Power, prestige, competitiveness, performance, power relations, success
orientation, and many other features have become endemic to the institution of
sports in an era and culture of consumption. These vulnerabilities, combined with
the fact that sport is an area where physical contact is common, can make it easier
for people—especially authority figures such as coaches—to abuse, harass, or
otherwise take advantage of children.

In addition, other forms of abusive behavior, such as screaming, humiliating
(and often sexist) language, and pushing and shoving of young players, have been
normalized and accepted by not only the coaches, administrators, and other professionals but also the athletes and their families. The perception that abusive
practices stem from the nature of sports—especially rough sports such as
football—has created environments rife with the potential for abuse. In some societies, the established culture conducive to abuse is further supported by the institutionalized patriarchal power, where the power of male coaches over female
athletes is not merely an individual relationship but a culturally established one.

Moreover, even some institutions that prioritize the health and well-being of
their amateur athletes have limited means to properly screen and monitor the volunteers and employees; many amateur sports organizations do not have the necessary tools for preventing sexual abuse.

STUDYING SEXUAL ABUSE IN AMATEUR SPORTS

Academic studies on sexual abuse started to emerge in the 1970s. The studies
in question showed that the patterns of abuse were similar, but the prioritization of
the problem and methods of addressing the issue were different in each studied
area of society As recognition of the problem increased, sexual abuse in sports
started to draw attention. In the 1980s, studies on the sport-specific characteristics

of sexual abuse began to be carried out, and evidence rapidly accumulated that abuse was a significant problem in most youth and amateur sports. Not surprisingly, these studies found that a large proportion of the perpetrators (98 percent) consisted of coaches, teachers or trainers—people in positions of power and authority who are directly involved in developing the skills and guiding the actions of the victimized athletes.

Some researchers believe that promising athletes are at a higher risk of victimization at the amateur level than those who are unlikely to pursue their sports at anything other than a recreational level after high school graduation. Such athletes spend much more time with coaches, trainers, and other authority figures, and in many cases, they establish close emotional bonds with these adults. In many cases, these relationships are healthy and productive and benefit the young athletes. But these dynamics may also give abusers more opportunities and increased leverage to pressure their victims into submitting to their predations and keeping silent about them. The athletes do so because they believe—often accurately—that their abusers hold the key to their future careers. The perpetrators know how dependent young athletes are and use this power during the grooming process.

It is also important to remember that sexually abusive behavior may be observed in both same-sex and cross-gender relationships. Only limited data has been collected about men's abuse of boys in sport, however, and relatively few women have positions of direct influence over boys in amateur sports, especially in the coaching ranks. The sexual abuse of young female athletes by adult male coaches in amateur sports is more common. Apart from the obvious and clearly defined acts of sexual abuse, some argue for looking at past incidents of sexual abuse and creating detailed classifications to better distinguish normal actions from actions of abuse.

MYTHS ABOUT SEXUAL ABUSE IN SPORTS

At the How Safe Is Your Sport conference hosted by the Coventry Sports Foundation and the NSPCC Child Protection in Sport Unit, Celia Brackenridge, the director of the Centre for Youth Sport and Athlete Welfare, addressed some of the most common myths in youth sports. The first one is that sports are a safe space for all young people. While this is the reality in many cases, there are predatory adults who see youth and amateur sports as an opportunity to engage in abuse. The second myth is that abuse does not happen in "our sport." Unfortunately, abuse happens in all sports, and it does not always have to be physical or sexual, as mental abuse can be quite damaging as well.

A third common misconception is that safeguarding against sexual misconduct by coaches, officials, trainers, and athletes is not necessary at the elite levels. Survey data from Australia, the Czech Republic, Norway, and Belgium show that the higher an athlete progresses up the sporting talent ladder, the greater the risks of being sexually exploited. There is also some research that shows that even at the amateur level, abuse is far too common and may be easier to hide (as most offenders are volunteers).

A fourth myth is that team sports do not need to worry because teams have a better chance of catching offenders. The reason the abuse continues in amateur sports is because the victims are usually emotionally linked with their abusers, who are often authority figures. In too many instances, a sport's primary stakeholders (i.e., athletes, parents, coaches, administrators) are uninformed about sexual abuse prevention policies and procedures or characteristics of an offender. Finally, local-level sports franchises are usually unaware of prevention measures implemented by their national or regional organizations (nays.org).

ATHLETES AS PERPETRATORS

Athletes are expected to represent their society, culture, and country within the scope of cooperation and competition. Sports are seen as a way of developing individuals with strong minds and bodies. However, events of the last decades have shown that sports are structured in ways that can increase the risk of sexual abuse. Various research has emerged on the relationship between team sports and expressions of misogyny by young male athletes. Debasing and objectifying language and attitudes toward girls and women are present on many youth sports teams, and researchers believe that marinating in these attitudes (and misogynistic messages in wider American culture) along with the sense of entitlement that sometimes accompanies athletics-related social status may increase the risk of sexual misconduct and harassment by young male athletes.

ATHLETES AS VICTIMS

Sports training is a long, tedious, repetitive, and sometimes tiresome process. Amateur athletes are expected to focus both psychologically and physically on achieving the maximum possible level in their respective fields. Similarly, many occupations focus on assisting athletes in these efforts. Therefore, athletes, their coaches, and other related professionals, such as trainers and therapists, often forge close relationships with the athletes under their care and supervision.

This interdependent relationship sometimes makes the connection between the coach and the athlete a personal one. On many occasions, these relationships can be healthy and affirming, with coaches serving as mentors both on and off the field. But some authority figures use their positions to abuse players, especially if the relationship in question does not have properly defined and drawn boundaries. Under such close relationships and without proper mental and social development, athletes at young ages are vulnerable to all kinds of abuse from parents, coaches, trainers, and peers.

There are vast social, political, and moral potentials attributed to sports organizations, and these potentials put those organizations under a lot of pressure to actualize what is expected of them. Yet, these pressures also lead to incidents in which sports organizations tend to conceal aberrant and deviant behavior for the sake of preserving their reputation and dignity, especially if discounting or concealing abusive behavior is seen as the price of winning.

Historically, relatively few studies have been conducted on the subject of sexual abuse and misconduct in organized sports settings. However, over time, sports scientists, sociologists, psychologists, and investigators in law enforcement have focused on this issue. As a result of these studies, the phenomenon of abuse has been observed in different dimensions and scales in sports, yielding four types of abuse: physical abuse, emotional abuse, sexual abuse, and neglect.

Abuse can occur in many forms in sports. Whether perpetrated by a coach, administrator, manager, parent, or a peer, some of these abusive behaviors may include psychological humiliation with regard to the gender, performance, or body type of the athlete; using authority to force the athlete to engage in sexual relations or favors in return for inclusion on team rosters, increases in playing time, and other privileges (a type of abuse commonly known as quid pro quo); subjecting athletes to cultural rituals for acceptance into the team involving sexual humiliation, abuse, or assault; and issuing verbal threats of a sexual nature.

The process of grooming (preparing the victim for victimization) is one of the important stages of abuse. The abuser prepares the victim for sexual abuse by various methods. High-level athletes are often isolated from typical group friendships; their only social contacts are those made through the sport itself. Consequently, young athletes who already suffer from low self-esteem, unmatured personality, and lack of experience find themselves facing social and emotional isolation during the preparation for an elite sports career. These conditions facilitate their involvement in the grooming process that precedes actual abuse.

The grooming process of the abuser involves four stages. Initially, the abuser targets a victim by observing various features of the potential victim, such as weaknesses, needs, the likelihood that he or she will report the abuse, and so on. In the second stage, the perpetrator establishes a relationship of trust and friendship by offering the target various gifts, privileges, recognition, and other things he or she needs, making him or her feel special. At the next stage, the abuser develops control and loyalty by isolating the victim. Finally, the abuser creates and maintains an environment of abuse through strategies ranging from emotional manipulation to blackmail.

SEXUAL ABUSE PREVENTION IN SPORTS

Developing preventive measures against sexual abuse in sports is predicated on removing protections utilized by abusive coaches, trainers, and other involved individuals at the expense of young athletes.

Feminist interpretations of gender and relational issues also offer alternative solutions to reducing sexual abuse in sports. This means identifying and rooting out toxic examples of cultural masculinity associated with sports. Increased representation of females in administrative or coaching positions would also be beneficial in this regard. Establishing processes whereby confidential complaints could be placed, triggering fair and careful investigations that protect the rights of both the accuser and the accused, have also been championed by experts and organizations devoted to reducing sexual abuse in society.

While researchers have focused on the inadequacy of legal instruments to protect the vulnerable against perpetrators in amateur sport settings, many incidents have shown that even when the necessary instruments are in place, the abusers find a way around them. Some observers assert that this situation exists because of unrealistic but persistent assumptions about the assumed "purity" of the sports activity. This assumed purity, and the long-standing exemption from legal sanctions and scrutiny stemming from that, may have delayed the systematic study of sexual abuse in sports organizations. However, after the emergence of the #MeToo Movement, no organization or institution has been off-limits to investigation. Moreover, events such as the Larry Nassar sexual abuse scandal, in which hundreds of young female gymnasts were assaulted by a single doctor within the U.S. national gymnastics program, underscored the need for increased oversight of amateur sports.

Youth advocates today agree that authorities must take decisive steps to make amateur sports safer for young athletes. They urge schools, programs, and leagues to implement meaningful precautionary measures and procedures to prevent sexual abuse and harassment from occurring and to handle allegations of sexual harassment and abuse incidents seriously and responsibly when they do occur.

Serhat Demir and Hasan Akin

See also: Hostile Work Environment; Office/Workplace Settings; Predatory Sex Offenders; Quid Pro Quo

Further Reading

Breeland, N. R. 2018. "'The Army You Created': Combating the Issue of Sexual Assault in College and Quasi-Professional Sports." *Mississippi Sports Law Review* 7: 1–33.

Koller, D. L. 2017. "A Twenty-First-Century Olympic and Amateur Sports Act." *Vanderbilt Journal of Entertainment & Technology. Law* 20: 1027.

Mirsafian, H. 2016. "Legal Duties and Legal Liabilities of Coaches toward Athletes." *Physical Culture and Sport. Studies and Research* 69(1): 5–14.

Morton, H. O. 2016. "License to Abuse: Confronting Coach-Inflicted Sexual Assault in American Olympic Sports." *William & Mary Journal of Women & Law* 23: 141.

The National Alliance for Youth Sports. "National Standards for Youth Sports." https://nays.org/resources/nays-documents/national-standards-for-youth-sports/.

Owton, H., and A. C. Sparkes. 2017. "Sexual Abuse and the Grooming Process in Sport: Learning from Bella's Story." *Sport, Education and Society* 22(6): 732–743.

Pacella, J. M., and M. Edelman. 2019. "Vaulted into Victims: Preventing Further Sexual Abuse in US Olympic Sports through Unionization and Improved Governance." *Arizona Law Review* 61: 463.

Solomon, A. 2017. "Preventing Recurrences of the Cover-Ups at Penn State & Baylor (and Now Michigan State): Where Does It End?" *Marquette Sports Law Review* 28: 379.

Authority Figures

Authority figures have existed since the dawn of humanity, and there is always the potential for people with authority to take advantage of their subordinates. Authority figures are at the core of feminist theories of sexual harassment. Academic studies and anecdotal reports alike support the belief that many instances of sexual harassment, abuse, and misconduct orbit around males in positions of authority who use that position of power to harass female subordinates. Also, power-threat theories are of the opinion that female authority figures are more frequent targets and victims of harassment, intimidation, and abuse.

AN ERA OF GROWING AWARENESS

However, the #MeToo Movement seems to have ushered in a major shift in society's sexual norms and workplace behavior. Many victims of sexual harassment have recently been empowered to speak out about their victimization by people who wield power over them, both in and out of the workplace. Victims of sexual victimization now enjoy more societal support and encouragement and are more likely to be taken seriously and believed.

The world is full of authority figures: parents, partners, teachers, school principals, school directors, supervisors, bosses, coaches, physicians, religious leaders, and so on. Dependents can be children, teenagers, partners, students, employees, patients, religious followers, or athletes, among many other forms. At the center of the relationship is a power imbalance and some sort of dependence. That dependence may be physical, financial, emotional, psychological, or spiritual.

Authority figures have also been linked to quid pro quo as a type of sexual harassment. *Quid pro quo* is a Latin term that translates to "something for something," for example, when a manager or other authority figure hints by his or her behavior or offers to reward the employee (with a desired work assignment, promotion, vacation, raise, etc.) in return for that employee's giving in to sexual demands. It can also occur when the authority figure says he or she will not terminate the appointment of employee if he or she cooperates with a sexual favor. Quid pro quo can also occur when an employment decision is dependent, positive or negative, on the result of the sexual demand. To show or prove quid pro quo in the workplace, the harasser must be an authority figure in the company who has indicated that the subordinate individual's advancement or security is conditional on providing sexual favors or submitting to harassment.

The power that comes with authority figures and the ensuing workplace sexual harassment culture disproportionally affects women. In October 2017, the *New York Times* and the *New Yorker* reported that dozens of women were accusing American film producer ("authority figure") Harvey Weinstein of harassment, rape, sexual assault, and sexual abuse over a period of at least thirty years. After these revelations, many other women in the American entertainment industry came forward with allegations that described a culture that permits widespread harassment and assault against women. Several men reported similar experiences at the hands of prominent, powerful men in the industry.

There are also authority figures in organized sports and the classroom environment who have been accused of sexual misconduct. It is important that greater accountability and enforcement be placed on those who are in teacher and coach roles and who establish rules and regulations to identify potential abuses. The confusion, intimidation, and fear surrounding a minor's experience as a result of abuse by an authority figure make it difficult to report the crime. Authority figure abusers often deny any allegations against them, and they can marshal their enormous resources to intimidate their accusers. When an authority figure abuses someone, it is considered an interpersonal violence in the form of sexual abuse, physical abuse, severe neglect, and violence.

Untreated abuse by an authority figure can lead to severe mental health problems. Most men and women treated in psychiatric settings have histories of physical or sexual abuse or both. Suicide and self-injury can also result from untreated abuse by authority figures. Alcohol and drug abuse and a wide variety of other dangerous behaviors and health problems have also been attributed to past abuse in some cases. Studies show that many violent criminals were physically or sexually abused by authority figures at some point in their lives. Severe social problems and developmental disabilities can also be the result of abuse. There is also a relationship between being a first-time victim and being revictimized.

SEXUAL HARASSMENT BY AUTHORITY FIGURES

Sexual harassment is a behavior that demeans, humiliates, or embarrasses someone. It is any behavior—physical, verbal, written, or otherwise—that is unwanted and unwelcomed and that offends or humiliates a person. It may happen in public, in school, at work, or at home and can take many forms: verbal or physical abuse, rumor spreading, repeated phone calls, demanding things, or sending and posting pictures, among others.

Harassment built into authority figure–dependent relationships has come under increased scrutiny in recent years. Current theories conceptualize and consequently criminalize such behaviors, either through a liberal conception of sexual autonomy or through feminist theories of gender inequality. Both theories do criminalize sexual harassment behaviors emanating from authority figures and dependent relationships.

Authority figure's harassment of subordinates may not entail the use of force or coercion; hence, it should be considered an abuse of office or authority, which may be grouped under anticorruption laws. Abuse of bureaucratic authority would fit into the criminal law concept. This would define "consensual" sexual relationships as wrongful and potentially criminal if the offender misuses his or her authority.

The first step in combating abuse from an authority figure is to report the situation to a higher authority figure (one that can be trusted). The second step is to seek legal and medical help. Authority figures who abuse their power and authority should be held accountable for their actions. An important step for society as well as the abuser himself or herself is to recognize it and call it what it is—"abuse."

Noel Otu and O. Oko Elechi

See also: #MeToo Movement; Sexism; *Time Magazine* "Silence Breakers"

Further Reading
Almukhtar, S., M. Gold, and L. Buchanan. 2017. "After Weinstein: 71 Men Accused of Sexual Misconduct and Their Fall from Power." *New York Times*, November 10.

McLaughlin, H., C. Uggen, and A. Blackstone. 2012. "Sexual Harassment, Workplace Authority, and the Paradox of Power." *American Sociological Review* 77(4): 625–647.

Schneebaum, G. 2015. "What Is Wrong with Sex in Authority Relations? A Study in Law and Social Theory." *Journal of Criminal Law and Criminology* 105(2).

B

"Baby It's Cold Outside"

The emergence of the #MeToo Movement and its corresponding revelations of alleged sexual misconduct and harassment have had a significant impact on American pop culture, specifically radio. One of the best examples of this is the controversy over radio play of "Baby It's Cold Outside." Factions were divided over whether this debate had merit or whether a song written in the 1940s could really be the object of such controversy. Regarding this specific debate, it might be relevant to consider the historical context of the time in which this song was written. Along those same lines, had it not been for the emergence of the #MeToo movement, it seems unlikely this popular standard song would have been viewed as controversial.

In October 2018, many major radio stations around the United States and Canada banned "Baby It's Cold Outside" from their playlists. Opponents of playing the song claimed that it promoted date rape and insensitivity to the #MeToo movement. On the other hand, proponents argued that historical context has been ignored and that a song written in 1944 could not symbolize date rape in any way. Maybe the larger question to answer is this: How can we explain how something as familiar as a popular holiday song could emerge as a symbol for the ways in which groups became divided politically and socially over sexual harassment and assault? To that end, the symbolic nature of this song provides some interesting contrasts and comparisons.

After the ban in December 2018, selective stations began to play the song in protest. Subsequent to that, there were several polls conducted in which listeners accused radio stations of caving to political correctness. Responding to the majority of listeners, radio stations removed the ban, and the holiday standard song was once again on the air.

Viewing this phenomenon through an historical context, it would be relevant to examine what social norms were evident after 1944. Generally, most women were expected to remain at home and take care of their families, and they had few opportunities to be independent. In fact, according to the *Washington Post*, when it was written, "Baby It's Cold Outside" was symbolic of progressive women rather than the more traditional women of that time. The song was composed by Frank Loesser (1910–1969) and sung with his wife at their housewarming. At the height of its popularity, the debate was actually about whether it should be considered a Christmas song.

"Baby It's Cold Outside" was an addition to the musical *Neptune's Daughter*. It even won an Academy Award in 1950 for Best Song. It is interesting that even before the #MeToo Movement, opponents expressed concern over the nature of the lyrics. In fact, the Urban Dictionary had listed the song as the "Christmas Date Rape Song." To clarify, the role of the male wolf toward the female mouse was viewed as predatory in nature. There was also a larger question to examine when reviewing the lyrics. How did the appropriateness of a single woman staying overnight in 1944 evolve into a debate about date rape? Given the social norms of 1944, it may have been more suitable to stay overnight simply because of the weather.

To opponents of the message, what seems more contentious was the way in which the female (the mouse) was subjectively perceived. Is she autonomous and rejecting the mores of the day or is she innocently lured by the more powerful wolf? Historical context is particularly significant, as gendered roles are far more flexible today. The role of the mouse and the wolf might be reversed today. In fact, Miss Piggy once attempted to lure the famous dancer Rudolf Nureyev to stay in her steam room.

Those who argue that the media, and particularly radio, is too focused on political correctness are challenged by feminist writers, who counter that real experiences of sexual assault should not be taken lightly. Thus, the significance of context and individual experience emerges. Additionally, the debate over playing the song is but one example of a more far-reaching social phenomenon. In other words, public discussion over whether the song is appropriate is a reflection of a larger debate about the prevalence of harassment and sexual assault in American society.

There are two emerging concepts in this analysis: patriarchy and autonomy. Patriarchy is evident in cultures where men are more likely to hold positions of power and, more importantly, moral authority over women. Of the three major traditions that have influenced the ways in which society treats women, all of them suggest that males are superior and advocate for patriarchy as the norm. The other concept that emerges from this debate is autonomy. Relative to this discussion, autonomy conveys the female ability of choice or self-determination. Both notions are evident in the way that this issue is perceived and why there is passionate debate between both camps.

One could argue that among the more powerful influences introduced to this debate was the emergence of social media and its ability to reach the public on a mass scale. More recent forms of modern communication, such as Facebook, Twitter, and Tumblr, can effectively create or contribute to mainstream controversy in unprecedented ways. For example, one tweet by Alyssa Milano created a worldwide phenomenon where nearly five million people used the #MeToo hashtag in one twenty-four-hour period. This does not change the perspectives of either side; rather it may have resulted in both camps becoming more entrenched in their positions.

In response to the question of the bigger issue, the controversy over airplay does seem to reinforce the conflict between the #MeToo movement proponents who maintain that the song crosses boundaries and those who argue that banning it is overreacting and taking the lyrics out of context. It is more likely that the song is merely symbolic of the ways in which society establishes its norms. With the emergence of the feminist movement, patriarchy is being challenged, and female autonomy is emerging.

In a somewhat circular fashion, the meaning of the song "Baby It's Cold Outside" has evolved. Once perceived to be progressive in nature by allowing women the opportunity for playful banter about spending the night, it reminds others about predatory practices in Hollywood and the emergence of the #MeToo Movement. Whether progressive or predatory, history and social context make all the difference.

Beverly Ross

See also: Gender Equality; #MeToo Movement; Milano, Alyssa; Power Dynamics; Predatory Sex Offenders

Further Reading

Bauman, A. 2018. "Is 'Baby It's Cold Outside' Really Too Offensive to Play in 2018?" CBS New York, December 4. https://newyork.cbslocal.com/2018/12/04/is-baby-its-cold-outside-really-too-offensive-to-play-in-2018/.

Hannun, M. 2014. "'Baby It's Cold Outside' Was Once an Anthem for Progressive Women. What Happened?" *Washington Post*, December 19. https://www.washingtonpost.com/posteverything/wp/2014/12/19/baby-its-cold-outside-was-once-an-anthem-for-progressive-women-what-happened/.

McDonnell-Parry, A. 2018. "'Baby, It's Cold Outside': A Brief History of the Holiday Song Controversy." *Rolling Stone*, December 13. https://www.rollingstone.com/culture/culture-news/baby-its-cold-outside-controversy-holiday-song-history-768183/.

White, M. 2018. "Drinking, Smoking, Carousing: Why 'Baby, It's Cold Outside' Is Actually a Feminist Anthem." *USA Today*, December 11. https://www.usatoday.com/story/opinion/2018/12/11/baby-its-cold-outside-christmas-song-feminist-anthem-column/2242568002/.

Zilles, C. 2018. "The #MeToo Movement Shows the Power of Social Media." *Social Media*, May 3. https://socialmediahq.com/the-metoo-movement-shows-the-power-of-social-media/.

Backlash against Allegations of Sexual Harassment and Assault

In the United States, *innocent until proven guilty* is a valued cornerstone of the nation's system of justice. On the other hand, instances of sexual abuse and exploitation are reported with alarming frequency. These outcries are sometimes unaccompanied by corroborating evidence because such crimes are commonly perpetrated covertly. Many also go unreported within the statute of limitations or in time for viable evidence, such as physical injury or DNA, to be ascertained within a verifiable chain of custody. In other cases, extenuating circumstances, such as the behavior of the victim leading up to the alleged attack, are cited to suggest that she or he bears some responsibility for the incident. Other alleged victims of sexual assault have been charged with mischaracterizing consensual sexual encounters or fabricating charges for reasons ranging from spite to psychological problems to the desire to seek advantage in child custody disputes. These and other accusations against people who come forward with claims of rape and other forms of sexual assault have spurred a contentious debate between those who advocate for victims' rights and those who support the legal needs and safety of the accused.

Victims of sexual assault sometimes experience the backlash, like the act of sexual assault itself, to be a power-based effort to exert control over the vulnerable that privileges the accused's narrative as more valid than the victim's. Meanwhile, those accused of sexual assault frequently assert there is bias against them that precedes adjudication, and even when there is a finding of not guilty, they reportedly continue to experience suspicion that interferes with their personal and work lives. Individuals accused of sexual assault commonly rely on defense strategies that disparage or defame their accusers. Empirically, false allegations do exist, but they are rare. According to the National Sexual Violence Resource Center, only about 2–10 percent of allegations of sexual assault have been found to be false.

VICTIM BLAMING

The most common tool in the backlash arsenal is victim blaming. In this scenario, the victim, regardless of age, physical appearance, or mental capacity, is at fault for whatever transgressions are visited upon her or him. People who promote such accusations—defense attorneys, friends and family of the accused, the defendant himself (or herself)—assert that the victim bears some or even most or all the responsibility for the event. They blame victims for becoming intoxicated with alcohol or drugs or for dressing provocatively. Victims have also been accused of changing their minds about consent in the midst of a sexual encounter or in its aftermath because of the guilt they allegedly feel about their own actions. In the victim blaming scenario, the victim's background, sexual history, mode of dress, educational or employment status, and character are open to criticism, whereas the accused perpetrator is portrayed as the true victim.

In 2010, an eleven-year-old girl was raped by twenty-one men and adolescent boys over a period of four months in Cleveland, Texas. Some of the incidents were videotaped. The victim did not make a complaint and was only identified when the videos surfaced. At the trial of one of the defendants, the defense attorney compared the victim to a spider who lured her assailants into her web. The eleven-year-old victim was blamed for her own assault because she wore makeup and "seductive" clothing.

This line of defense was unsuccessful, and all twenty-one assailants were found guilty. Seven minor defendants received one-year probation sentences in exchange for guilty pleas. Two of the accused adults requested jury trials, and both received life or sentences of ninety-nine years in prison. Eleven other adult males received fifteen-year sentences in exchange for pleading guilty to sexual assault of a child. The last assailant pleaded guilty after being positively linked to the assault by DNA. He received a reduced sentence of seven years for indecency with a child and will be required to register as a sex offender for ten years after his sentence is served.

RELATIVE VALUE OF ASSAILANT AND VICTIM

A second strategy is to use the alleged assailant's wealth, celebrity, reputation, and potential for future material success and cultural prominence to avoid punishment and censure. In this "relative value" calculation, the victim's societal value is framed as inferior to that of the accused and sometimes convicted assailant. A recent representation of this tactic is seen in the case against Brock Turner, a Stanford University swimming champion who was accused of sexually assaulting an intoxicated young woman. Turner was interrupted in the act of raping the unconscious victim and was subsequently arrested and convicted, but the sentencing judge, citing Turner's athletic achievements and potential for future success, sentenced him to only six months in jail and three years' probation. Turner was released after serving only three months. Turner's lawyers later appealed the conviction and the requirement that Turner register as a sex offender for the rest of his life. The appeal was denied. It was later confirmed that prior to sentencing, Turner's father had written a letter to the judge in which he asked for leniency on his son's behalf and suggested probation in lieu of jail time. The *Washington Post* (June 6, 2016) reported that Mr. Turner wrote, "His life will never be the one that he dreamed about and worked so hard to achieve. . . . That is a steep price to pay for 20 minutes of action out of his 20 plus years of life."

Many victims' rights advocates assert that a version of this approach was demonstrated during the confirmation hearing of now Supreme Court justice Brett Kavanaugh, wherein the allegations of his accuser, Christine Blasey Ford, were only superficially investigated, and those by other accusers were not investigated at all. Ultimately, all circumstantial evidence produced against Kavanaugh was disregarded, and he was elevated to a lifetime appointment to the court.

PARENTAL ALIENATION SYNDROME AND FALSE MEMORY SYNDROME

Another means of discrediting allegations of sexual violence is to claim or imply that allegations of abuse are rooted in the emotional or psychological problems of the victim. One of these is generally used when there are accusations of abuse directed against a parent, usually the father. This defense, parental alienation syndrome (PAS), was created by the late Richard Gardner, a child psychiatrist who asserted that many allegations of child sexual abuse are an artifact of contentious divorce proceedings concocted by vengeful women. Although not recognized by the American Psychiatric Association's *Diagnostic and Statistical Manual of Mental Disorders* (*DSM*), PAS has been successfully used in some child custody cases in which primary custody was conferred on the alleged abuser.

False memory syndrome (FMS) is another psychological diagnosis that has been used to discredit individuals who, as adults, allege incidents of sexual assault during their childhoods. An organization in support of this concept, the False Memory Syndrome Foundation (FMSF), was founded in 1992 by Peter and Pamela Freyd after their daughter, Jennifer Freyd, confronted them with memories of childhood sexual improprieties. The premise behind FMS is that unscrupulous or incompetent psychotherapists implant false memories of abuse in the minds of vulnerable patients. However, as in the case of Jennifer Freyd, memories of abuse may occur outside of psychotherapy and, in fact, may be the motivating factor driving individuals to obtain psychological treatment. The false memory defense has been used against complainants alleging sexual abuse by defendants ranging from Catholic priests to actor and comedian Bill Cosby.

Neither PAS nor FMS meet the criteria for inclusion in the *DSM*, although proponents have nominated their inclusion for some years since 1992. "It is important to note that False Memory Syndrome is not a diagnosis recognized in either the *DSM* of the American Psychiatric Association or the *International Classification of Diseases* published by the World Health Organization (WHO). It is a contrived term that doesn't actually describe a "syndrome," or collection of symptoms. Instead, it is a pejorative expression that reassigns blame (Noblitt and Noblitt 2014, 170–171). As Lowenstein (1992) stated, "I know of no clinical research or tradition of clinical description that empirically validates or supports that such a clinical condition exists as such. FMS is a syndrome without signs and symptoms (the defining characteristics of a syndrome)" (2).

One of the cofounders of the FMSF, Ralph Underwager, was also the founder of Victims of Child Abuse Laws (VOCAL), an organization that lobbied against state and national legislation that imposed mandatory reporting of abuse and other child protections. A contemporary proponent of FMS is Elizabeth Loftus, the author of *The Myth of Repressed Memory: False Memories and Allegations of Sexual Abuse* (1994). Loftus, a frequent expert witness in criminal and civil actions involving sex crimes, bases her opinion on her own "lost in the mall" study, in which she instructed trusted adults to tell children about an imaginary past traumatic event where the child was lost or a similar situation and persuaded the child to absorb that story as their reality (Dallam 2000). Loftus subsequently equated the experience of being briefly lost with sexual assault to support her claim that a false memory can be easily implanted.

Critics of Loftus dismiss such broad claims. They assert that although people sometimes have inaccurate recollections, they are typically about inconsequential details rather than entire events. These skeptics of repressed memory acknowledge that false allegations of abuse do occur, but only rarely, and it has never been proven that such false allegations are attributable to false memories.

Unfortunately, there is no entirely bias-free environment whereby sexual violence can be evaluated on the merits of each case. Witnesses to sexual assault (other than the victim) are rare and can typically only attest to proximate time, location, and relevant histories of the primary participants. But we can recognize the role of bias and its influence in the prosecution of sexual violence. Currently, there are backlash groups with agendas supporting accused perpetrators, and in some cases, their arguments are biased and based on false premises or are unsubstantiated by scientific evidence. Victims and the accused are owed a fair evaluative process in which each case rests on its own individual merits.

James Randall Noblitt and Pamela Perskin Noblitt

See also: Discrimination; Victim Blaming

Further Reading

Cabrera, A. 2018. "'Boys Will Be Boys and She Was Asking for It.' How the Media Perpetuates Victim Blaming and the Rape Myth in Rape Cases." *Alpenglow: Binghamton University Undergraduate Journal of Research and Creative Activity* 4(1). https://orb.binghamton.edu/alpenglowjournal/vol4/iss1/7.

Carbone, June, and Leslie J. Harris. 2008. "Family Law Armageddon: The Story of Morgan v. Foretich." In *Family Law Stories*, edited by C. Sanger, 1–23. New York: Foundation Press.

Dallam, S. J. 2000. "Crisis or Creation? A Systematic Examination of 'false memory syndrome.'" *Journal of Child Abuse & Neglect* 9(3–4): 9–36.

Felson, R. B., and C. Palmore. 2018. "Biases in Blaming Victims of Rape and Other Crime." *Psychology of Violence* 8(3): 390–399.

Klement, K. R., B. R. Sagarin, and J. J. Skowronski. 2018. "Accusers Lie and Other Myths: Rape Myth Acceptance Predicts Judgments Made about Accusers and Accused Perpetrators in a Rape Case." *Sex Roles: A Journal of Research* 81 (1–2): 16–33.

Noblitt, James Randall, and Pamela Perskin Noblitt. 2014. *Cult and Ritual Abuse: Narratives, Evidence, and Healing Approaches*. Santa Barbara, CA: Praeger.

Ballard, Sarah (1984–)

Sarah Ballard is a prominent scientist whose allegations of workplace sexual harassment cast a spotlight on the problem of sexual misconduct in academia and research institutions. Born in 1984, Ballard earned her bachelor's degree in astronomy from the University of California at Berkeley and completed her graduate studies at Harvard University. She became an exoplanetary astronomer and a Torres and a L'Oreal Fellow at the Massachusetts Institute of Technology. In addition to her academic expertise, she speaks about her experience as a victim of sexual harassment and gender and minority equity in science.

Ballard's disclosure was, like so many reports of victimization in higher education, an open secret. Like other victims of sexual harassment, her allegations were dismissed or discounted by administrators. Unlike many victims (who for privacy protection and other reasons are known only by their complainant number), Dr. Ballard went public with charges that she had endured an extended period of sexual harassment during her years of study at Berkeley. She became the face of sexual harassment in science departments by disclosing details of a highly regarded professor who had for many years engaged in inappropriate physical behavior with undergraduate and graduate students.

A six-month investigation by the Office for the Prevention of Harassment and Discrimination at the University of California at Berkeley disclosed that Professor Geoffrey Marcy violated the campus sexual harassment policies between 2001 and 2010 by groping, kissing, touching, offering unwanted massages, and making sexually suggestive comments to at least four former students. Three complainants detailed their personal harassment incidents, and one witnessed the professor's inappropriate behavior. One of the sexually harassed students was Ballard, who had been a student in Marcy's astronomy class—and who was flattered when the renowned scientist took an interest in her academic development and future career as a scientist.

Ballard had also started out as a gender studies major and helped organized an anti–sexual violence event on the Berkeley campus. Without her knowledge, Professor Marcy had attended the event. After learning of his attendance, she sent him an email thanking him for his support. He wrote back and asked her to call his home phone to talk about it in more detail. Emails were exchanged over a period of months, and they also met in cafés around campus. He acted professionally during this time, complimenting her academic and scientific abilities, and eventually became her adviser. Over time, however, the conversations changed, and he was more explicit about sexual topics. For example, he would offer her relationship advice or discuss his own sexual experiences when he was young.

The specific incident described in the sexual harassment complaint occurred in 2005 when Marcy offered to drive Ballard home after an off-campus meeting. As she was getting out of his car, he reached over and tried to give her a neck massage. She walked away and stopped meeting him outside of class. She did not report the incident and did not confront him, but she felt ashamed, afraid, and confused about what had happened. She did not want to speak up and hurt her chances of going to graduate school. She was a junior in college, and she needed letters of recommendation for graduate school.

For his violation of the campus sexual harassment policies, Professor Marcy received a warning about his future conduct. For example, for shaking hands with students, he could be sanctioned with a suspension or dismissal. Marcy might have kept his job and the official university report kept private, except a BuzzFeed News investigative article was published detailing the sexual harassment stories. One week after the news article came out, Marcy resigned.

Myrna Cintron

See also: College Campuses; Quid Pro Quo; *Time Magazine* "Silence Breakers"; Title IX

Further Reading

Ghorayshi, A. 2015. "Famous Berkeley Astronomer Violated Sexual Harassment Policies over Many Years." BuzzFeed News, October 9. https://www.buzzfeednews.com /article/azeenghorayshi/famous-astronomer-allegedly-sexually-harassed-students.

Hinckley, S. 2015. "Was UC Berkeley Too Easy on Professor Accused of Sexual Harassment?" *Christian Science Monitor*, October 14. https://www.csmonitor.com/USA /Education/2015/1014/Was-UC-Berkeley-too-easy-on-professor-accused-of -sexual-harassment.

Kleinfeld, Z. 2015. "Light Shed on a Dark Matter: Campus Professor Geoffrey Marcy's Resignation Comes after Concerns about Sexual Harassment in Sciences." *Daily Californian*, October 15. http://www.dailycal.org/2015/10/15/light-shed-dark -matter-campus-professor-geoffrey-marcys-resignation-comes-concerns-sexual -harassment-sciences/.

Scoles, S. 2016. "What Happens When a Harassment Whistleblower Goes on the Science Job Market." Wired, July 7. https://www.wired.com/2016/07/happens-harassment -whistleblower-goes-science-job-market/.

Barnes v. Costle (1977)

The case of *Barnes v. Costle* (1977) in the U.S. Court of Appeals for the District of Columbia Circuit (D.C. Circuit) considered and expanded the jurisprudence on sexual harassment by unanimously upholding Paulette L. Barnes's appeal on sexual harassment victimization at the workplace on grounds that the harassment qualified as discrimination under Title VII of the Civil Rights Act of 1964. The U.S. Equal Employment Opportunity Commission (EEOC) has defined sexual harassment as conduct amounting to "unwelcome sexual advances, requests for sexual favors, and other verbal or physical conduct of a sexual nature . . . when this conduct explicitly or implicitly affects an individual's employment, unreasonably interferes with an individual's work performance, or creates an intimidating, hostile, or offensive work environment."

Sexual harassment in the workplace takes various forms, hence making it difficult to articulate a concise definition that covers all the peculiar variations. However, there is a common understanding in regard to the current jurisprudence that any unwelcome sexual requests made in situations where there is an unequal power dynamic in the workplace would qualify as sexual harassment. This does not in any way suggest that harassment cannot also be carried out by nonsupervisory staff against work colleagues.

Jurisprudence on sexual harassment is novel because human society and cultures over the past several millennia never seriously contemplated legislation proscribing the variety of actions that today amount to sexual harassment. Basically, sexual harassment victims remained mute because there was no legal precedence to guide them in seeking redress. However, consideration of the psychological, economic, and social effects of sexual harassment in the workplace began to see the light of day in the 1970s with a flurry of complaints, investigations, media reports, and court cases.

Hitherto, cases entertained by the courts under Title VII of the Civil Rights Act could be summarized into three broad groups: actions that challenged the exclusion of one of either sex from certain occupations, actions that sought to address restrictions excluding women from employment, and actions against employers who engaged in discriminatory practices regarding pay, promotions, and other forms of treatment on the basis of gender. Cases involving an employer's policies in regard to employee pregnancy and sexual harassment in the workplace were construed to fall outside the purview of Title VII.

In the *Barnes v. Costle* case, the plaintiff, Paulette L. Barnes, a newly hired female employee with the U.S. Environmental Protection Agency, had sued her supervisor, Douglas M. Costle, under Title VII for sexual harassment after he repeatedly solicited dates and sexual favors from her as a quid pro quo or condition for professional advancement and other career considerations. Her refusal to comply with those demands led to her being fired by Costle. Barnes lost her lawsuit in the trial court but was availed on appeal to the D.C. Circuit. This decision was precedent setting in that it marked the first instance in which a U.S. court found a quid pro quo claim of sexual harassment to be unlawful discriminatory conduct.

The decision in the *Barnes* case opened a floodgate of sexual harassment cases based on claims of discrimination under Title VII. To a large extent, this was engendered by the omission to provide proper guidance as to the scope of the meaning of "sex" under the act. After *Barnes v. Costle*, sexual harassment case law generated confusion, especially with regard to homosexual sexual harassment in a hostile workplace.

This lack of clarity as to the meaning of "sex" and other aspects were to a large extent considered, and clarifying amendments were added in the Civil Rights Act of 1991. The law also paved the way for class action sexual harassment suits, which afforded opportunities for more potential claimants to seek legal redress if victimized. However, these advances notwithstanding, there are still voices advocating for a reconceptualization of the law and jurisprudence on sexual harassment.

Jude L. Jokwi Lenjo and Alaba Oludare

See also: Sexism; Title VII of the Civil Rights Act of 1964

Further Reading

Allegretti, J. G. 1981–1982. "Sexual Harassment of Female Employees by Nonsupervisory Coworkers: A Theory of Liability." *Creighton Law Review* 15: 437–476.

Cahill, Mia L. 2018. *The Social Construction of Sexual Harassment Law: The Role of the National, Organizational and Individual Context*. London: Routledge.

Green, Tristin K. 2018. "Was Sexual Harassment Law a Mistake? The Stories We Tell." *Yale Law Journal* 128: 152. https://www.yalelawjournal.org/forum/was-sexual-harassment-law-mistake.

Locke, S. S. 1995. "The Equal Opportunity Harasser as a Paradigm for Recognizing Sexual Harassment of Homosexuals under Title VII." *Rutgers Law Journal* 17: 3.

MacKinnon, C. A. 1979. *Sexual Harassment of Working Women: A Case of Sex Discrimination*. New Haven, CT; London: Yale University Press.

Piece, M. R. 1989. "Sexual Harassment and Title VII: A Better Solution." *Boston College Law Review* 30: 1071–1101.

Schultz, V. 2018. "Reconceptualizing Sexual Harassment." *Yale Law Journal* 22: 24–65.

Weiner, C. 2005. "Sex Education: Recognizing Anti-Gay Harassment as Sex Discrimination under Title VII and Title IX." *Columbia Human Rights Law Review* 37: 189–219.

Barnes v. Train (1974)

Barnes v. Train (retitled *Barnes v. Costle* on appeal) is considered the first sexual harassment case under Title VII of the Civil Rights Act of 1964. *Barnes* was a quid pro quo sexual harassment case in which the plaintiff complained that her supervisor requested sexual favors in return for favorable employment conditions. Originally, however, the plaintiff, an African American woman, filed her complaint based on race discrimination, not sex discrimination, because an U.S. Equal Employment Opportunity Commission (EEOC) employee advised her that her supervisor's request of sexual favors was not sex discrimination but rather a personnel matter. Barnes eventually amended her complaint to allege sex discrimination.

In the early 1970s, Paulette L. Barnes worked as an administrative assistant for the U.S. Environmental Protection Agency (EPA). Barnes's supervisor, an African American male, was the director of the EPA's Equal Employment Opportunity Division. According to Barnes, her supervisor repeatedly asked her to have a sexual affair with him outside of the workplace, and he told her that her employment status would be "enhanced" if she agreed to the affair. Barnes refused on numerous occasions. Eventually, her position was eliminated, and she was assigned to a position elsewhere in the EPA.

Barnes filed her complaint in the U.S. District Court for the District of Columbia, and the EPA (her employer) filed a motion for summary judgment asking the court to dismiss Barnes's complaint. Incredibly, the trial court dismissed the complaint, stating that "the substance of plaintiff's complaint is that she was discriminated against, not because she was a woman, but because she refused to engage in a sexual affair with her supervisor." The trial court further rationalized that "regardless of how inexcusable the conduct of plaintiff's supervisor might have been, it does not evidence an arbitrary barrier to continued employment based on plaintiff's sex." Barnes appealed the trial court's dismissal of her complaint to the U.S. Court of Appeals for the District of Columbia Circuit (D.C. Circuit).

The D.C. Circuit reversed the trial court's decision in 1977 and remanded the case for a new trial. The court noted that Title VII of the Civil Rights Act of 1964 originally only applied to private employers, but the 1972 amendment to Title VII applied the act to government employers as well. In support of its holding, the court pointed out that Congress, when enacting Title VII, was "deeply concerned" about employment discrimination based on gender, and Congress "intended to combat [gender discrimination] as vigorously as any other type of forbidden discrimination." The court stated that while the lower court may have been correct in asserting that Barnes's supervisor made her cooperation in the sexual affair a condition of her employment, her gender was also an indispensable factor absent a showing by the employer that the supervisor imposed a similar condition on a male coworker. Finally, the court stated that Title VII does not require a plaintiff to prove that the employer discriminated against all employees of the plaintiff's gender but rather that "the protections afforded by Title VII against sex discrimination are extended to the individual."

Elizabeth W. Marchioni

See also: Authority Figures; *Horrible Bosses*; Power Dynamics; Quid Pro Quo; Title VII of the Civil Rights Act of 1964

Further Reading

Baker, Carrie N. 2004. "Race, Class, and Sexual Harassment in the 1970s." *Feminist Studies* 30(1): 7–27.

Lareau, Craig. 2016. "Because of . . . Sex: The Historical Development of Workplace Sexual Harassment Law in the USA." *Psychological Injury and Law* 9(3): 206–215.

Batali, Mario (1960–)

One of the sexual misconduct scandals in the restaurant industry that grabbed great public attention in the late 2010s concerned famed chef Mario Batali. Batali was born September 19, 1960, in Seattle, Washington. He graduated from Rutgers University before attending Le Cordon Bleu, where he received his first formal culinary training. Batali dropped out of school to apprentice in London, and after that, he started his career as a chef and restaurant owner.

Batali was well known for being one of the most recognized and respected chefs worldwide. Starting his career in the early 1980s, Batali climbed to success and reached the peak of the restaurant industry. One of the keys to his rise was his starring role on *Molto Mario*, one of the Food Network's first hit television shows. In 2011, he also served as cohost of a new daytime show broadcast on ABC called *The Chew*. With his business partnerships, he created a restaurant chain that spanned New York, Los Angeles, Las Vegas, and Singapore. Moreover, Batali is the founder of the Mario Batali Foundation, which was established to fund educational programs for children and to support pediatric disease research, and he worked actively in another charity organization called the Food Bank for New York City. Batali authored eleven cookbooks during his career, further increasing his name recognition and influence. He also received many awards, including the 2001 D'Artagnan Cervena Who's Who of Food & Beverage in America, a prestigious lifetime achievement award in the food industry.

In 2017, however, four women, three of whom had worked for Batali in some capacity during their careers, accused him of sexual misconduct on the food industry website Eater. One of the allegations was made by a woman who had filed a police report accusing Batali of rape on January 29, 2004. She told police that Batali had both drugged and raped her, attesting that she had been drinking at the bar at Batali's Greenwich Village restaurant Babbo and then went upstairs to use the bathroom; the next thing she remembered was waking up to find Batali raping her.

Another woman alleged that she had been sexually assaulted by the chef and restauranteur in 2005 at a popular restaurant called Spotted Pig. She alleged that she blacked out while having drinks with Batali and then woke up with a scratched leg and semen on her skirt. Upon waking up, she called a rape crisis hotline and had a rape kit taken at a hospital. She later reported the incident to the police but did not file an official complaint. In a statement regarding this claim, Batali said, "I vehemently deny any allegations of sexually assaulting this woman." However, the chef issued an ambiguous apology in response to other sexual misconduct accusations leveled against him. He vaguely acknowledged that he had made many mistakes and that he was sorry to have disappointed his friends, his family, his fans, and his team. He stated that his behavior was wrong and that he took full responsibility for his actions.

However, after the original allegations surfaced and Batali had apologized, more women came out with allegations against him. The total number of women accusing Batali of sexual misconduct increased to more than ten. When the additional accusations surfaced, the Batali & Bastianich Hospitality Group released a statement indicating that Batali had agreed to step away from the company's operations, including the restaurants. ABC also asked Batali to leave *The Chew*. According to some sources, the restaurants of disgraced celebrity Mario Batali saw as much as a 30 percent decline in business.

In January 2019, investigators in New York City closed two alleged sexual assault claims against the chef without filing charges. The New York Police Department explained that it could not find any witnesses or evidence supporting claims made by the accusers. On the other hand, another investigation against

Batali was still pending by the Boston Police Department for a different woman's accusations in Massachusetts. This case was brought to court by the Office of the District Attorney, and Batali pleaded not guilty. In January 2020, a separate investigation was initiated against Batali by the attorney general of New York after uncovering information within the scope of a sexual harassment settlement regarding the Spotted Pig restaurant, where Batali was once an investor.

In March 2019, it was reported that Batali's ownership stake in Eataly, which was his gourmet Italian marketplace and a top restaurant chain, had been bought out by the other owners.

Serhat Demir and Hasan Akin

See also: Hostile Work Environment; Quid Pro Quo; Restaurant/Bar Industry

Further Reading

Equal Rights Advocates. 2019. "Sexual Harassment at Work: What Is Workplace Sexual Harassment?" https://www.equalrights.org/issue/equality-in-schools-universities/sexual-harassment/.

Jenkins, A. 2018. "175 Women Demand Change to Culture, Sexual Harassment Policies at Washington Legislature." *News Tribune of Tacoma*, March 1. https://www.knkx.org/post/175-women-demand-change-culture-sexual-harassment-policies-washington-legislature.

Maynard, M. 2018. "Celebrity Chef Mario Batali's Troubles Deepen as New Sexual Abuse Allegations Surface." *Forbes*, May 22. https://www.forbes.com/sites/michelinemaynard/2018/05/22/celebrity-chef-mario-batalis-troubles-deepen-as-new-sexual-abuse-allegations-surface/.

Moskin, J., and A. Southall. 2018. "Mario Batali Said to Face Second Sexual Assault Investigation." *New York Times*, May 21. https://www.nytimes.com/2018/05/21/dining/mario-batali-sexual-assault.html.

National Conference of State Legislatures. 2019. "Legislation on Sexual Harassment in the Legislature." February 11. http://www.ncsl.org/research/about-state-legislatures/2018-legislative-sexual-harassment-legislation.aspx.

Rao, J. 2018. "Woman Sues Mario Batali, Saying He Groped Her in Boston Bar." *New York Times*, August 23. https://www.nytimes.com/2018/08/23/dining/mario-batali-lawsuit.html.

Severson, Kim. 2018. "Disgraced by Scandal, Mario Batali Is Eyeing His Second Act." *New York Times*, April 2. https://www.nytimes.com/2018/04/02/dining/mario-batali-sexual-harassment.html.

Southall, A., and J. Moskin. 2019. "Police Close Sexual Assault Investigations of Mario Batali." *New York Times*, January 8. https://www.nytimes.com/2019/01/08/dining/mario-batali-sexual-assault-no-charges-nypd.html.

Title VII of the Civil Rights Act of 1964 (Title VII). https://www.eeoc.gov/statutes/title-vii-civil-rights-act-1964.

Blair, Selma (1972–)

American film, theater, and television actress Selma Blair was born in Detroit, Michigan, on June 23, 1972. She graduated from the University of Michigan in 1994 with a bachelor of fine arts in photography and a bachelor of arts in psychology. Blair is credited with starring roles in many popular movies, including *Cruel*

Intentions (1999), *Legally Blonde* (2001), and *Hellboy* (2004), among others, but she received more recent recognition during the first months of the #MeToo movement when she accused American film director James Toback of sexual harassment that took place in 1999, when she was starting her acting career.

Blair was part of a group of thirty-eight anonymous women who described their sexual victimization at Toback's hands in an October 2017 *Los Angeles Times* story. Within days, the number of victims grew to more than two hundred. The victims recounted similar stories and a pattern of behavior by the perpetrator. They disclosed that they met with the perpetrator to audition for an upcoming movie and that the meetings were arranged by their representatives. The meetings took place in a hotel room or a private place, and the conversations would start with general small talk before Toback turned it in a sexual direction. He would then masturbate in front of them, claiming that he had to do it several times a day. Then the meetings would abruptly end.

Blair requested anonymity when the story was first published. However, after the *Times* published the piece, she felt obligated to come forward after Toback called the victims liars, stated he did not recall the meetings ever taking place, and denied the accusations. He claimed it was physically impossible for him to do what he was accused of by the victims, citing diabetes and a heart condition. Infuriated by his denials, Blair asserted that someone had to come forward and become the face of Toback's victims. Since the incident in 1999, she had only told her story to two people, and she had remained silent until 2017. She finally came forward publicly about her victimization after other women accused producer Harvey Weinstein of sexual harassment and assault.

Blair's story fit the common pattern of Toback's behavior alleged by his other accusers. Her representatives arranged the meeting. They described him to her in advance of the meeting as interesting and odd, but someone who could do a lot for her career. Blair insisted on meeting him in the hotel restaurant. She arrived at the restaurant dressed for the movie part for which she was auditioning only to be told that he wanted her to come to his hotel room. Blair alleged that as soon as she arrived at his room, he made her feel uncomfortable. He asked about her relationship with her parents, told her she lacked confidence, and intimated that he could have people killed, all of which confused Blair. She recalled thinking that maybe his behavior was part of an acting technique, but then she alleged that he asked her to perform a monologue naked. When she asked why, he responded it was to build trust and to see how comfortable she was with her body and that it was part of the training for becoming a good actress.

Blair said that, against her best judgment, she took her sweater off. She remembered feeling ashamed when he made comments about her body needing a lot of work. Blair alleged that she got dressed and attempted to leave the room, but he told her she could not leave and proceeded to rub his penis through his pants and asked to have sex. She said that she reminded him that he was married and tried to leave the room again, only to be stopped by Toback. According to Blair's account, the director then walked her back to the bed, sat her down, got on his knees, and rubbed himself against her leg while forcing her to pinch his nipples while looking into his eyes. At this point, recalled Blair, she was worried that Toback was going to try to rape her. Instead, Blair said that he finished masturbating and then threatened to kidnap and kill her if she disclosed the incident to anyone. She was afraid, confused, disgusted, and ashamed. She did not go back for a second meeting with Toback and asked her representatives to not send any women actresses to him. Blair admitted, though, that she did not provide any details of the incident with Toback because of the threats he had made to her life.

In April 2018, authorities in Los Angeles County, where most of Toback's alleged assaults had occurred, said that it could not press charges against the director because the statute of limitations—a limit on the amount of time that parties have to file charges from the date of an alleged offense—for most of the alleged incidents had expired.

Blair, meanwhile, worked on several television series for much of the 2010s. She also remained actively involved in a number of charitable causes. In the fall of 2018, she announced she had been diagnosed with multiple sclerosis.

Myrna Cintron

See also: Harvey Weinstein Scandal; #MeToo Movement; *Time Magazine* "Silence Breakers"

Further Reading

Fernandez, M. 2017. "Selma Blair and Rachel McAdams Detail Sexual Harassment by James Toback." *Variety*, October 26. https://variety.com/2017/biz/news/selma-blair-rachel-mcadams-james-toback-sexual-harassment-1202600217/.

Friedman, M. 2017. "Rachel McAdams and Selma Blair Have Accused Director James Toback of Sexual Harassment: More Than 40 Women Have Accused Him of Harassment." *Elle Magazine*, October 26. https://www.elle.com/culture/celebrities/a13100508/rachel-mcadams-selma-blair-james-toback-allegations/.

Saad, N. 2017. "James Toback on New Allegations by Rachel McAdams, Selma Blair: 'I Have Nothing to Say about Anything.'" *Los Angeles Times*, October 27. https://www.latimes.com/entertainment/movies/la-et-mn-selma-blair-rachel-mcadams-james-toback-20171026-story.html.

Smith, K., and J. Miller. 2017. "Selma Blair and Rachel McAdams Share Their Stories of James Toback's Sexual Harassment." *Vanity Fair*, October 26. https://www.vanityfair.com/hollywood/2017/10/selma-blair-and-rachel-mcadams-share-their-stories-of-james-toback-sexual-harassment.

Whipp, G. 2017. "39 Women Have Come Forward to Accuse Director James Toback of Sexual Harassment." *Los Angeles Times*, October 22. https://www.latimes.com/entertainment/la-et-mn-james-toback-sexual-harassment-allegations-20171018-story.html.

Buddhism

Similar to all religions, Buddhism provides ethical standards meant to guide interpersonal conduct and sexual behavior. At the core of Buddhist ethics are five precepts. These precepts provide a framework of morality for lay followers of Buddhism. The five precepts include refraining from the following: harming living things, taking what is not given, sexual misconduct, lying, and intoxication from substances. Buddhists believe living according to the precepts will reduce suffering and enhance one's capacity for achieving enlightenment—the highest level of spiritual knowledge.

Unlike the Ten Commandments in Judaism and Christianity, these precepts are voluntary and not connected to a god, as there is no such being in Buddhism. The precepts provide general guiding principles for behavior. However, in Buddhism, each person is obligated to make the appropriate moral decision for each unique circumstance he or she encounters. Buddhists believe moral judgment is fluid and does not include following a fixed set of rules. Rather, living ethically requires each person to think critically about the moral judgment he or she should make within a given situation.

The third precept in Buddhism addresses sexual misconduct. To understand how Buddhists define sexual misconduct, it must be considered within the contexts of the other precepts. Sexual behavior must be honest and nonharming. In Buddhism, sexual misconduct includes any act that includes violence, deceit, or manipulation. Essentially, any sexual act that leads to pain or suffering is considered not permissible. Appropriate sexual conduct promotes positive outcomes for self and others, including love, happiness, and kindness.

If sexual activities are conducted honestly and without harm, then the third precept is upheld, and the individual is on a path toward enlightenment. Yet, Buddhists acknowledge this may be challenging at times given the strong energy force of sexuality. In fact, sexual desire is considered to be a primary cause of many damaging behaviors, such as betrayal, vanity, and violence. Therefore, sexual behavior must constantly be examined to determine whether it is being conducted in a moral or destructive way. In fact, Buddhists suggest that living in contradiction to the precepts across other domains of life will contribute to sexual deviance. On the other hand, living in friendliness, generosity, and wisdom contributes to a healthy sex life.

In Buddhism, each person should consider how much time and energy is being given to sex, even when sexual behavior is aligned with the five precepts. This is because the fleeting pleasure resulting from a sexual encounter distracts from an individual's spiritual growth.

Buddhism is well known for its belief in karma (getting what you give) and its teachings on nonviolence and compassion. However, procedures for addressing sexual abuse have not been clearly delineated. Buddhist understandings of sexual misconduct are more attuned to the spiritual implications of abuse rather than legal consequences. In 2018, one of the largest Buddhist organizations in the West, Shambhala International, was rocked by extensive sexual abuse allegations against teachers by their students. The organization admitted failure in addressing the abuse and reported a commitment to reevaluating its internal procedures to prevent sexual misconduct.

As Buddhism continues to expand globally, more Buddhist communities will likely require formalized procedures for dealing with sexual abuse. Whether and how the Buddhist community will address these issues is yet to be seen. There is no universal leadership structure in Buddhism, which can be a challenge in undertaking systemic change. However, the Dalai Lama, the head monk of Tibetan Buddhism, is considered the moral leader within the Buddhist community.

In 2018, 1,850 victims of sexual abuse by Buddhist teachers promoted the hashtag #MeTooGuru. The group requested that the Dalai Lama affirm that Buddhist teachers who commit sexual assault will be liable to prosecution and civil action. Subsequent to the petition, the Dalai Lama met with a small group representing the abuse survivors. During the meeting, he denounced the unethical behavior of the abusers and acknowledged that their actions constituted deviance from the Buddha's teachings. The Dali Lama encouraged all Tibetan spiritual leaders to join together and discuss the issue of abuse.

Megan Callahan Sherman

See also: Marital Violence; Sexism

Further Reading

Atwood, H. 2018. "An Expert on Faith-Based Abuse Talks about How Buddhists Can Address Sexual Misconduct." *Lion's Roar*, February 27. https://www.lionsroar.com/an-expert-on-faith-based-abuse-talks-about-how-buddhists-can-address-sexual-misconduct/.

Bao, H. 2012. "Buddhism: Rethinking Sexual Misconduct." *Journal of Community Positive Practices* 12(2).

Kaza, S. 2004. "Finding Safe Harbor: Buddhist Sexual Ethics in America." *Buddhist-Christian Studies* 24(1): 23–35.

Keown, D. 2013. "Buddhist Ethics." *International Encyclopedia of Ethics*. Wiley Online Library.

Burke, Tarana (1973–)

Tarana Burke is a cofounder of the #MeToo Movement whose public profile increased dramatically in the weeks following the Harvey Weinstein scandal. A longtime activist on behalf of organizations promoting racial and social justice, she has used her newfound celebrity status to advocate for victims of sexual harassment and assault and to promote feminist-intersectional social change.

Burke was born on September 12, 1973, in New York City. She grew up in the New York borough known as the Bronx in a poor neighborhood, where she herself was a victim of sexual assault as both a child and a teen. She attended Alabama State University before transferring to Auburn University. After graduating from Auburn, she moved to Selma, Alabama, where she worked for the 21st Century Youth Leadership Program and the National Voting Rights Museum. In 2008, she worked to promote African American arts, history, and culture with Art Sanctuary in Philadelphia, and she later became a consultant for the 2014 movie *Selma*.

In her extensive work with African American youth, Burke was troubled by girls' frequent reports of sexual exploitation and assault. In 2003, Burke developed Jendayi Aza, an extracurricular Afrocentric cultural and leadership program for girls. In 2006, she expanded the program to create the nonprofit JustBe, which is dedicated to the empowerment of girls and young women of color. That same year, she began using the phrase "Me Too" on social media to publicize the frequency with which girls and women in American society are subjected to sexual violence, intimidation, and harassment. Burke is now the senior director of Girls for Gender Equity in Brooklyn, and she maintains the advocacy website https:// metoomvmt.org/.

Burke's approach to healing the damage inflicted by the spectrum of sexual intimidation, exploitation, and assault experiences of her clients and students emphasizes empathy and resilience. The use of the "Me Too" phrase is a purposeful linguistic trope that implicitly challenges the profound shame and isolation typically experienced by victims in response to abuse and assault. Burke also advocated for replacing the term sexual assault "victim" with "survivor," which is now in common use.

The *New York Times* broke the story of Harvey Weinstein's long and sordid history of alleged sexual misconduct in Hollywood on October 5, 2017. Ten days later, the actress Alyssa Milano tweeted on October 15, 2017, that all women who had been sexually harassed or assaulted should tweet the reply "Me too." Within twenty-four hours, the tweet had received fifty-three thousand replies; within forty-eight hours, one million people had tweeted the hashtag. Twelve million responses in the first twenty-four hours were reported by Facebook. Milano learned her hashtag was a term already in use by Burke's program and contacted Burke on October 17. The actress and activist subsequently met in person on the set of the *Today* show on December 6, 2017, where they appeared together to describe the changes they saw as necessary to end sexual harassment and assault in American workplaces and in wider society.

Burke was quickly embraced by prominent women in Hollywood, and her rise to fame was swift. She released the New Year's Eve ball drop in Times Square in 2017, and in 2018, Burke was one of eight activists invited to the Golden Globe Awards as guests of actress Michelle Williams. At the event, many female actors wore black to express solidarity with the #MeToo Movement. In the red carpet interviews in which female actresses are traditionally required to name the designers of their gowns and jewelry, the celebrities instead explained their activism in #MeToo and #TimesUp to the journalists for the television audience. That year, Burke received the Voices of the Year Catalyst Award from SheKnows Media.

Burke continues to be in high demand as a public speaker on these issues. In 2017, Burke and other "Silence Breakers" at the forefront of the #MeToo movement were named *Time Magazine*'s Persons of the Year. One year later, she was named one of *Time*'s 100 Most Influential People of 2018.

Cynthia Ninivaggi

See also: Gender Equality; Harvey Weinstein Scandal; McGowan, Rose; #MeToo Movement; Milano, Alyssa; *Time Magazine* "Silence Breakers"; Time's Up Movement

Further Reading

Brockes, E. 2018. "#MeToo Founder Tarana Burke: You Have to Use Your Privilege to Serve Other People." *The Guardian*, January 15. https://www.theguardian.com /world/2018/jan/15/me-too-founder-tarana-burke-women-sexual-assault.

Garcia, S. E. 2017. "The Woman Who Created #MeToo Long before Hashtags." *New York Times*, October 20. https://www.nytimes.com/2017/10/20/us/me-too-movement -tarana-burke.html.

"Burn Book of Bad Men"

On the heels of allegations against Harvey Weinstein, women working in politics in the state of Texas came forward with information detailing allegations of inappropriate behavior, sexual harassment. and sexual assault that they had endured for twenty years or more. These allegations, gathered together in a collection called the "Burn Book of Bad Men," was publicized in an article published in the *Daily Beast,* an online newsmagazine, on November 7, 2017. The authors of the "Burn Book of Bad Men" spoke to the *Daily Beast* about the culture of intimidation and fear that they felt permeated the Texas State Capitol. They reported feeling as though they were unable to report their victimization due to the fear that they would lose their jobs or suffer other forms of retaliation.

The #MeToo Movement inspired the women to speak out. They hoped that by coming forward with their stories, perpetrators and potential perpetrators would be aware that their inappropriate behavior would become common knowledge and would not be tolerated. After the contents of the "Burn Book of Bad Men" became public, a new sexual harassment policy was approved through a Texas House committee to improve education and training of employees on sexual harassment issues as well as to provide information to all employees about the complaint process and their rights.

On November 7, 2017, the *Daily Beast* published an article detailing allegations against thirty-eight men, many of whom were politicians or otherwise worked in politics in the state of Texas. The spreadsheet that these women created became known as the "Burn Book of Bad Men." The list was started in 2016, and it details allegations against men who were mostly from the Democratic Party. The women who worked on creating the list reported that the information contained in the "Burn Book of Bad Men" was nothing new to them and had been spread person to person prior to the creation of the actual spreadsheet. The creators of the spreadsheet explained that they intended the information to be informative in nature and to be spread to women connected in politics in Texas as a way to share information and experiences. Specifically, the *Daily Beast* story detailed how female staffers, journalists, and other women professionals who had to interact with male lawmakers and public officials felt helpless to stop the harassment to which they were subjected. In most cases, they expressed concern that if they spoke out against their harassers or filed charges, their jobs would be in jeopardy.

The authors of the "Burn Book of Bad Men" detailed how the harassment and assaults these women experienced often started with seemingly innocent comments or actions that nonetheless had clear sexual undertones, simply to see how far the women could be pushed. When the victims kept quiet, usually to protect their careers, the harassers became more emboldened and subjected them to more severe forms of harassment, up to and including sexual assault.

The women were identified in the media after knowledge of the "Burn Book of Bad Men" was released. These women claimed that the toxic culture at the Capitol was well known and that politics in general in the state of Texas had a history of scandal and corruption. Those intimately involved were aware that the female victims of the sexual assaults and harassment had no one to turn to because a good portion of the behavior reported in the "Burn Book of Bad Men" came from individuals who had positions of authority and power in the state.

After the existence of the "Burn Book of Bad Men" became public knowledge, several men who worked in politics reported that they were aware of the bad behavior and culture within the Capitol and the state as a whole, but they feared retaliation if they came forward and reported what they had observed. Both the women who were victimized and the men who were sympathetic to their plights felt for many years that there was nothing that could be done.

The authors of the "Burn Book of Bad Men" stated that they gathered and distributed the information in an attempt to let the perpetrators known that the victims are communicating with each other and that a record existed of their unlawful and immoral behavior. They expressed hope that revelations about the existence of the "Burn Book of Bad Men" would make men think twice about engaging in inappropriate or criminal behavior and encourage victims of harassment to speak out.

Several media outlets reached out to politicians in Texas for comments after the "Burn Book of Bad Men" came to light. However, most of these inquiries elicited nothing more than "no comment" or denials that the problem existed. Some observers also pointed out that no formal complaints regarding workplace sexual harassment or assault had been filed against individuals in the House or Senate in Texas since 2011. But the authors of the "Burn Book of Bad Men" responded by asserting that the absence of formal complaints merely underscored the degree to which women subjected to harassment felt powerless to fight back.

Although sexual harassment policies have existed for members of the Texas House and Senate since 1995, many of the authors of the "Burn Book of Bad Men" report that they are drastically in need of revision. In December 2017, a new policy was adopted through a Texas House committee that listed increased protections for sexual harassment victims. The policy also required training for all employees regarding the policies and procedures in place, including specific information detailing the complaint process. To regulate the process, all staff and House members were required to complete the training by January 31, 2018.

Darla D. Darno

See also: Harvey Weinstein Scandal; Power Dynamics; State Legislatures; Traditionally "Male" Workplaces

Further Reading

Messner, O. 2017. "Women Expose the Secret Sexual Predators inside Texas Politics." *Daily Beast*, November 7. Accessed October 15, 2018. https://www.thedailybeast .com/women-in-texas-politics-started-their-own-shtty-men-list-a-year-ago.

Sadasivam, N. 2017. "Committee Approves New Sexual Harassment Policy for Texas House." *Texas Observer*, December 1. Accessed October 16, 2018. https://www .texasobserver.org/committee-approves-new-sexual-harassment-policy-texas -house/.

Ura, A. 2018. "Texas Senate Revises Anti–Sexual Harassment Policy Following Allegations of Misconduct." *Texas Tribune*, May 30. Accessed October 16, 2018. https:// www.texastribune.org/2018/05/30/texas-senate-revises-anti-sexual-harassment -policy/.

C

Campus Accountability and Safety Act (CASA)

The Campus Accountability and Safety Act (CASA) is a proposed law that proponents say would help combat the national problem of sexual violence on college campuses. Senator Claire McCaskill (D-MO) first introduced CASA to the U.S. Senate on February 26, 2015. McCaskill reintroduced a revised bill on April 5, 2017, and eleven additional senators joined her in cosponsoring the legislation. Also referred to as Senate Bill 856, CASA amends the Jeanne Clery Disclosure of Campus Security Policy and Campus Crime Statistics Act (Clery Act), introduced in 1990 as part of the Higher Education Act of 1965. CASA includes four main provisions: reporting requirements, campus security policies, sanctions for failure to comply, and a grant program for education and training programs.

Sexual assaults and the underreporting of these violent acts plague colleges and universities on a national scale. One in five women is a victim of sexual assault during her college career (White House Task Force to Protect Students from Sexual Assault 2014, 2), and studies indicate that an alarmingly low percentage (as few as 5.3 percent) of assault victims report the incidents to their institution (Fisher et al. 2003, 24). Equally alarming, in a study by the U.S. Senate Subcommittee on Financial and Contracting Oversight, 40 percent of colleges and universities failed to investigate the sexual assault cases reported to them over the last five years (Griffin et al. 2017, 404). Many legislators argue that improved national legislation, such as CASA, presents a path forward for addressing these troubling figures and trends.

HISTORY OF NATIONAL SEXUAL ASSAULT LEGISLATION

CASA represents the most recent attempt by the U.S. government to regulate how colleges and universities deal with sexual violence. Such legislation began with the introduction of Title IX of the Education Amendments of 1972. Title IX prohibits discrimination based on sex in recruitment, admissions, athletics, sex-based harassment, or employment and prohibits retaliation against those who oppose a discriminatory practice (U.S. Department of Education 2015). The U.S. Department of Education's (ED) Office of Civil Rights enforces Title IX.

The Clery Act was crafted in 1990 to increase institutional requirements for reporting campus crimes. In particular, higher education institutions must report information on campus crimes, including sexual assaults, to receive federal funding (Brubaker et al. 2017, 13). The vast majority of colleges and universities in the United States rely on this federal funding for student financial aid and research dollars, among other programs.

In 2013, President Barack Obama signed the Campus Sexual Violence Elimination Act (SaVE Act) into law as part of the Violence Against Women Reauthorization Act. The SaVE Act builds on the Clery Act through increased transparency in reporting, additional rights for victims of sexual violence, increased campus education and prevention requirements, and higher standards for campus disciplinary procedures (Griffin et al. 2017, 402).

As additional requirements emerge, the federal government issues "Dear Colleague" letters to advise institutions on how to implement legislation (Brubaker et al. 2017, 12). The most recent Dear Colleague letter related to sexual assault legislation was released in 2017 by the Trump administration in reference to Title IX. Even with this guidance and the current legal requirements, as many as 25 percent of colleges and universities are out of compliance with regard to sexual assault reporting policies (DeMatteo et al. 2015, 229). CASA represents an effort by concerned lawmakers to address this lack of compliance and improve campus safety for students.

DETAILS OF THE CAMPUS ACCOUNTABILITY AND SAFETY ACT

Many specific provisions exist within the four areas CASA seeks to address. First, and in clear expansion of the Clery Act, CASA requires broader reporting of sexual violence on college campuses. Additionally, it calls for additional fines to be levied against institutions that violate these reporting requirements. CASA relates to Title IX, too, as it provides clarification to current Title IX guidance, including training for university employees who may interact with victims. Under current legislation, colleges and universities may be investigated by the ED for violations of Title IX. Under CASA, those investigations would be publicly disclosed to increase transparency.

CASA also includes elements that would be brand-new for campus sexual assault legislation. Under the bill, campuses would be required to conduct campus climate surveys and to publish the results. These surveys would increase transparency and allow administrators to analyze the overall campus atmosphere. Additionally, CASA would require institutions to enter into a memorandum of understanding (MOU) with all local law enforcement agencies that have jurisdiction over campus. The MOUs would allow campus administrators and local law enforcement to investigate instances of sexual violence in tandem.

Finally, in a less punitive vein, CASA would authorize the ED to create a grant program to reward and support institutions with high levels of commitment for combating sexual violence. Altogether, each of the elements of CASA ties back to reporting requirements, campus security policies, or the ability of the ED to either reward or punish institutional behaviors.

REACTIONS TO CASA

Various stakeholders agree that CASA represents a substantial next step to addressing the problem of sexual violence on college campuses. However, the

American Council on Education (ACE) has expressed concern that stakeholders have not been adequately involved in the development of CASA. College administrators in particular, they argue, believe that the one-size-fits-all approach proposed by CASA may not be the most effective method for combating sexual assault on such a wide variety of college campuses (American Council on Education 2015, 2).

However, many researchers point to CASA as supporting proven solutions for combating sexual violence. Holland and Cortina (2017, 430) cite the importance of increased training for campus employees, as outlined in CASA. Increased fines and campus reporting audits have also led to more effective and accurate reporting of violence (Griffin et al. 2017, 421), just as CASA outlines. Lastly, many college campuses already issue campus climate surveys and have worked to improve their reporting and disciplinary procedures. Such behavior supports the idea that CASA, if passed, would effect positive change at colleges and universities across the United States.

Lindsay R. Davis

See also: College Campuses; Gender Equality; Sexism; Title IX

Further Reading

American Council on Education. 2015. "Comments on S.590 (CASA)." May 15. Accessed February 11, 2019. https://www.acenet.edu/news-room/Documents/Letter-Alexander-Murray-CASA2.pdf.

Brubaker, Sarah Jane, Brittany Keegan, Xavier L. Guadalupe-Diaz, and Bre'Auna Beasley. 2017. "Measuring and Reporting Campus Sexual Assault: Privilege and Exclusion in What We Know and What We Do." *Sociology Compass* 11(12): 11–29.

Campus Accountability and Safety Act, S.856, 115th Congress (2017).

DeMatteo, David, Meghann Galloway, Shelby Arnold, and Unnati Patel. 2015. "Sexual Assault on College Campuses: A 50-State Survey of Criminal Sexual Assault Statutes and Their Relevance to Campus Sexual Assault." *Psychology, Public Policy, and Law* 21(3): 227–238.

Fisher, Bonnie S., Leah E. Daigle, Francis T. Cullen, and Michael G. Turner. 2003. "Reporting Sexual Victimization to the Police and Others: Results from a National-Level Study of College Women." *Criminal Justice and Behavior* 30(1): 6–38.

Griffin, Vanessa Woodward, Dylan Pelletier, O. Hayden Griffin III, and John J. Sloan III. 2017. "Campus Sexual Violence Elimination Act: SaVing Lives or SaVing Face?" *American Journal of Criminal Justice* 42: 401–425.

Holland, Kathryn J., and Lilia M. Cortina. 2017. "The Evolving Landscape of Title IX: Predicting Mandatory Reporters' Responses to Sexual Assault Disclosures." *Law and Human Behavior* 41(5): 429–439.

U.S. Department of Education. 2015. "Title IX and Sex Discrimination." April. Accessed February 11, 2019. https://www2.ed.gov/about/offices/list/ocr/docs/tix_dis.html.

White House Task Force to Protect Students from Sexual Assault. 2014. "Not Alone: The First Report of the White House Task Force to Protect Students from Sexual Assault." U.S. Government Publishing Office, April. Accessed February 8, 2019. http://purl.fdlp.gov/GPO/gpo48344.

Campus Sexual Violence Elimination Act (SaVE Act)

Senator Bob Casey Jr. (D-PA) introduced the Campus Sexual Violence Elimination Act (SaVE Act) to Congress on January 24, 2013. The bill became law on March 7, 2013, when it was included as part of the Violence Against Women Reauthorization Act of 2013. The SaVE Act is enforced by the U.S. Department of Education's (ED) Office of Civil Rights and includes a number of provisions to protect victims of sexual assault and prevent further occurrences of violence.

The legislation also connects and enforces existing policy and guidance. First, the SaVE Act amends the Jeanne Clery Disclosure of Campus Security and Campus Crimes Statistics Act (Clery Act) and bridges a gap between the Clery Act and Title IX requirements. Also, the SaVE Act takes recommendations from the Obama administration's 2011 "Dear Colleague" letter—which was originally issued by the U.S. Department of Education's Office for Civil Rights—and makes them law. The ED issues Dear Colleague letters to help institutions appropriately interpret and apply pieces of legislation. These letters are not law and only serve as guidance for campuses. Therefore, the SaVE Act is significant in its turning Dear Colleague–inspired guidance into law.

The SaVE Act addresses a number of concerns related to sexual violence on college campuses. First, the legislation seeks to protect victims of sexual violence by requiring institutions to protect victim confidentiality when reporting crimes to campus constituents. The reporting rights of victims are also protected by the SaVE Act. Many victims of sexual violence fail to report the crimes committed against them because they do not want to pursue law enforcement proceedings due to the potential emotional toll on themselves and their families (DeMatteo et al. 2015, 228). Under the SaVE Act, victims have the right to elect to pursue internal campus investigation, external law enforcement investigation, or both.

On the policy side, the SaVE Act expands educational requirements for faculty, staff, and students to include prevention and bystander training. When instances of sexual violence do occur, the SaVE Act requires institutions to publish crime statistics on acquaintance rape, stalking, and cyberbullying as a part of the expanded Clery Act requirements. Colleges and universities must also write and publish clear, transparent policies on how sexual violence will be investigated on their campuses. Lastly, institutions that fail to comply with the SaVE Act face hefty fines and sanctions.

Experts and practitioners in the field of higher education have found strengths and weaknesses in the SaVE Act. In terms of strengths, the SaVE act excels in taking previously disjointed government-issued guidance and turning it into law. Codifying the 2011 Dear Colleague letter, expanding the Clery Act, and bridging gaps between the Clery Act and Title IX make the SaVE Act an inclusive and relevant piece of legislation. Additionally, the increased focus on bystander education for students and employees addresses the chronic underreporting of sexual assault on college campuses.

Concerns related to the SaVE Act connect to fears that the ED lacks the ability to stringently enforce the provisions of the law. For example, in 2014, 40 percent of institutions surveyed by the U.S. Senate Subcommittee on Financial and

Contracting Oversight failed to investigate any of the sexual assault cases reported to them over the last five years (Griffin et al. 2017, 404). If previously existing fines and sanctions did not encourage investigation, some worry merely increasing these measures will not encourage colleges and universities to conduct sexual assault investigations appropriately.

Following the passage of the SaVE Act, the Obama administration created the White House Task Force to Protect Students from Sexual Assault to further elucidate and enforce victims' rights and prevent escalating sexual violence on college campuses. In 2017, though, the Trump administration issued a new Dear Colleague letter calling for increased rights for accused perpetrators of sexual violence and loosening requirements for internal investigatory practices on college campuses. It is unclear as of late 2019 how the SaVE Act and the Trump administration's 2017 Dear Colleague letter work together, leaving the sexual assault landscape on colleges campuses unclear once more.

Lindsay R. Davis

See also: Campus Accountability and Safety Act; College Campuses; Gender Equality; Sexism; Title IX; Violence Against Women Reauthorization Act of 2013

Further Reading

Campus Sexual Violence Elimination Act, S.128, 113th Congress (2013–2014).

DeMatteo, D., Meghann Galloway, Shelby Arnold, and Unnati Patel. 2015."Sexual Assault on College Campuses: A 50-State Survey of Criminal Sexual Assault Statutes and Their Relevance to Campus Sexual Assault." *Psychology, Public Policy, and Law* 21(3): 227–238.

Griffin, V. Woodward, Dylan Pelletier, O. Hayden Griffin III, and John J. Sloan III. 2017. "Campus Sexual Violence Elimination Act: SaVing Lives or SaVing Face?" *American Journal of Criminal Justice* 42: 401–425.

Rape, Abuse & Incest National Network. 2019. "Campus SaVE Act." Last modified March 2019. https://www.rainn.org/articles/campus-save-act.

U.S. Department of Education, Office of Civil Rights. 2011. "Dear Colleague Letter: Sexual Violence." April 4. https://www2.ed.gov/about/offices/list/ocr/letters/colleague-201104.pdf.

U.S. Department of Education, Office of Civil Rights. 2017. "Dear Colleague Letter." September 22. https://www2.ed.gov/about/offices/list/ocr/letters/colleague-title-ix-201709.pdf.

White House Task Force to Protect Students from Sexual Assault. 2014. "Not Alone: The First Report of the White House Task Force to Protect Students from Sexual Assault." April. Accessed February 8, 2019. http://purl.fdlp.gov/GPO/gpo48344.

Carlson, Gretchen (1966–)

Gretchen Carlson, a former Miss America and a graduate of Stanford University, worked as a reporter and on-air host at CBS and Fox News before achieving fame as one of the cohosts of the show *Fox & Friends* on the conservative Fox News cable network. The defining moment of her ongoing career to date, however, was her successful 2016 lawsuit against Fox News CEO Roger Ailes for sexual harassment and retaliation. Carlson's legal victory triggered the end of Ailes's chairmanship at Fox.

Gretchen Carlson's suit and settlement against Ailes also marked the first of several widely publicized takedowns of powerful men (e.g., Bill O'Reilly, Matt Lauer, Les Moonves, and Harvey Weinstein) in the news media for sexual misconduct. Beginning in 2016, the collective scandals have ushered in a cultural shift in the United States around understanding the prevalence and consequences of sexual misconduct in the workplace.

After graduating from Stanford University in 1990, Carlson began her career as a local reporter. She steadily advanced to more high-profile jobs and eventually landed a position as cohost of CBS's *The Early Show* on Saturday mornings in 2002. In 2005, she accepted a higher-profile role at Fox News, and in 2006, she began cohosting the daily morning show *Fox & Friends* and appearing regularly on Bill O'Reilly's "Culture Warrior" feature during *The O'Reilly Factor*.

During her time at Fox News, Carlson was known as an outspoken critic of political correctness (Luscombe 2016). Unlike at CBS, which purportedly erased Carlson's Miss America pageant experience from its biographic profile of her, Fox CEO Roger Ailes encouraged her to reference her beauty pageant background in her work at the network (Weprin 2016). Prior to the lawsuit, she jokingly referred to this time in her career as her achieving "the 'bimbo trifecta': I was already a natural blonde, former Miss America, and now I'm at Fox!" (CBN News 2015). Carlson experienced the sexist environment at Fox News in different ways. For example, after one of her *Fox & Friends* cohosts joked in 2012 that "Women are everywhere. It's out of control. We're even letting them play golf," Carlson walked off the set after retorting, "You know what? *You* read the headlines since men are so great." Although she later characterized walking off the set as a joke, observers noted that Carlson's cohosts frequently made comments about her appearance on air.

CIVIL SUIT AGAINST ROGER AILES FOR SEXUAL HARASSMENT

In 2016, Carlson filed a lawsuit against Roger Ailes, citing an atmosphere of "deep and pervasive sexual harassment" at the network as well as acts of harassment and misconduct perpetrated by the executive himself. After filing the lawsuit, Carlson was depicted in some quarters as a proverbial David to Ailes's Goliath, as he was a figure of immense power in both politics (he worked with Richard Nixon, Ronald Reagan, Rudy Giuliani, and Donald Trump) and the news industry. Having helped to found and then lead Fox News to a position of unmatched influence in the American news media landscape, he was a key architect for conservative news media, shaping the narratives on which many Americans relied for their news.

Carlson's suit provided explicit details of the workplace culture she endured at Fox News. When she went to confront Ailes about her treatment, she claimed that he only further harassed her, telling her that "I think that you and I should have had a sexual relationship a long time ago and then you would be good and better and I would be good and better" (Grynbaum and Koblin, 2016).

She further claimed that when she rebuffed Ailes's unwanted advances, she was punished professionally. Carlson said that Ailes denied her guest appearances on Fox's prime-time shows and eventually fired her. She alleged that she was dubbed a "manhater" who should learn to "get along with the boys." She relayed feeling like a "blond female prop" (*Carlson v. Ailes* 2016). It was subsequently reported that Carlson had secretly taped some of her conversations with Ailes.

Several notable Fox News personalities quickly defended Ailes, questioning Carlson's motives. However, several other women at the network, including Megyn Kelly, another blonde news anchor/personality, came forward shortly thereafter to accuse Ailes of similar harassment over several decades. Andrea Tantaros, a former Fox host, also filed suit, alleging, "Fox News masquerades as a defender of traditional family values, but behind the scenes, it operates like a sex-fueled, Playboy Mansion–like cult, steeped in intimidation, indecency and misogyny" (Disis and Pallotta, 2017). These accusations from other women employees at the network made it more difficult for skeptics and critics to dismiss Carlson's charges.

Fox News opened an internal investigation almost immediately after Carlson filed suit and then moved to settle the case rather quickly: it took just two months for the network to settle the case with Carlson for $20 million. The corporation also issued an apology as part of the settlement: "We sincerely regret and apologize for the fact that Gretchen was not treated with the respect and dignity that she and all of our colleagues deserve" (Ellison 2016).

For his part, Ailes's position was less conciliatory, with some reporting that the Fox News leader considered countersuing Carlson for defamation (Ellison 2016). Ailes denied the allegations when the suit was filed, but he left his job in a cloud of scandal just a few weeks later. Leaving Fox was hardly his demise though: he quickly found work advising Republican nominee Donald Trump in his 2016 presidential campaign. Ailes died the following year.

Carlson's suit—and the nearly two dozen women who followed her example by making similar allegations against Fox News—may have opened the door for what became an even bigger sexual misconduct scandal the following year. In 2017, more than eighty women accused moviemaking mogul Harvey Weinstein of sexual harassment or assault. These accusations marked the unofficial beginning of the #MeToo Movement, in which a series of powerful men, mostly hailing from the worlds of entertainment, business, and politics, were professionally dethroned as a result of credible accusations of sexual misconduct. In 2017, Carlson reflected on the relevance of her lawsuit to CBS: "The gift of courage is contagious. It passes along one woman at a time. And look where we are. The hashtag metoo [is] trending" (*CBS This Morning* 2017).

In October 2017, Carlson published a memoir, *Be Fierce: Stop Harassment and Take Your Power Back*, in which she chronicled her experiences at Fox and urged women to stand up against sexism and sexual harassment. She also asserted that for women who feel harassed in the workplace, human resources is not always the best option, as employees in those departments are sometimes being paid by the harasser. She advocated on Capitol Hill to end forced arbitration clauses in contracts, which serve to silence victims, thereby enabling the abuser. She further promoted bystander training to educate others on being able to support and defend those being harassed or abused (Bond 2018).

After leaving Fox and settling her suit, Carlson was named CEO of the Miss America program. One of her biggest moves upon taking the position was to remove the swimsuit competition portion of the pageant. She also founded the Gretchen Carlson Leadership Initiative as well as the March of Dimes Gretchen Carlson Advocacy Fellows program.

In 2017, Carlson was named one of *Time Magazine*'s 100 Most Influential People. "I know that I have been a voice for so many women who never had one," she said in an interview with CBS. "And now I'm seeing that *something good* is coming of this. And I really hope I can change laws on Capitol Hill as well and get rid of this secrecy, so that we take this issue out of the shadows and help so many others" (*CBS This Morning* 2017).

Jennifer M. Balboni

See also: Harvey Weinstein Scandal; Lauer, Matt; #MeToo Movement

Further Reading

Bond, Shannon. 2018. "Gretchen Carlson Is on a Mission to End Secret Pacts." *Financial Times*, March 7. https://www.ft.com/content/3aff8560-0bcc-11e8-bacb-2958fde95e5e.

CBN News. 2015. "Gretchen Carlson Talks Faith and 'Getting Real.'" June 16. https://www1.cbn.com/cbnnews/us/2015/June/Gretchen-Carlson-Talks-Faith-and-Getting-Real.

CBS This Morning. 2017. "Gretchen Carlson on Harassment and the 'Excruciating Choice' to Speak Out." October 17. https://www.cbsnews.com/video/gretchen-carlson-on-harassment-and-the-excruciating-choice-to-speak-out/.

Concha, Joe. 2016. "Ex-Fox News Host Secretly Recorded Ailes: Report." *The Hill*, September 2. https://thehill.com/media/294338-ex-fox-news-host-secretly-recorded-ailes-report.

Disis, Jill, and Frank Pallotta. 2017. "The Last Year of Roger Ailes' Life Was Consumed by Scandal." CNN Business, May 18. https://money.cnn.com/2017/05/18/media/timeline-roger-ailes-last-year/index.html.

Ellison, Sarah. 2016. "Fox Settles with Gretchen Carlson for 20 Million—and Offers an Unprecedented Apology." *Vanity Fair*, September 6. https://www.vanityfair.com/news/2016/09/fox-news-settles-with-gretchen-carlson-for-20-million.

Grynbaum, Michael M., and John Koblin. 2016. "Gretchen Carlson of Fox News Files Harassment Suit against Roger Ailes." *New York Times*, July 6.

Luscombe, Belinda. 2016. "Gretchen Carlson's Next Fight." *Time Magazine*, October 21. http://time.com/4540095/gretchen-carlsons-next-fight/.

Weprin, Alex. 2016. "Gretchen Carlson's Old-Fashioned Career Path." *Politico*, July 7. https://www.politico.com/blogs/on-media/2016/07/gretchen-carlsons-old-fashioned-career-path-225240.

Casting Couch

The *casting couch* is a term used to describe the problem in Hollywood whereby directors, producers, and other men in positions of influence require women to perform sex acts or endure sexual harassment in exchange for roles in television or film. This predatory behavior is most frequently targeted at young actresses, who are made to feel, often with good reason, that rejecting such advances will be detrimental to their careers. Although the phenomenon had long been recognized as a real one in some parts of the entertainment industry—some attribute its origins to Darryl F. Zanuck, a powerful film studio executive from the 1930s through the 1950s—it received much greater scrutiny in 2017 after serious allegations of sexual assault and harassment were leveled against producer Harvey Weinstein, the cofounder of Miramax and the Weinstein Company, by dozens of actresses.

Many famous actresses have spoken out about the realities of the casting couch. Thandiwe Newton, Charlize Theron, Reese Witherspoon, Ashley Judd, Myleene Klass, Jennifer Lawrence, Gwyneth Paltrow, and Megan Fox, among others, have all claimed to have been victims of the casting couch. Famous actresses of earlier eras, such as Judy Garland, Marilyn Monroe, and Jane Fonda, also suffered. As Marilyn Monroe wrote in her memoir, *My Story*, "I met them all. Phoniness and failure were all over them. Some were vicious and crooked. But they were as near to the movies as you could get. So you sat with them, listening to their lies and schemes. And you saw Hollywood with their eyes—an overcrowded brothel, a merry-go-round with beds for horses."

In addition to Weinstein, talk show host Charlie Rose; the chief executive officer of CBS Corp., Leslie Moonves; and many others have faced similar allegations. Moonves was accused of sexual harassment by six women who claimed he sabotaged their careers when they declined his advances. As of August 2018, some 475 high-level executives and employees in numerous industries had been accused of sexual harassment in the previous eighteen months, including twenty-eight Hollywood directors, producers, and agents. Although most of the attention has been focused on females, men are also victims of the casting couch. A July 2018 report by the Center for Talent Innovation found that 40 percent of women and 20 percent of men in media have been harassed by a colleague.

The state of California, where the American film and television industries are concentrated, responded to the casting couch controversy by revising a 1994 sexual harassment law to ensure that producers and directors are included in the statute's coverage, to add regulatory oversight, and to make it easier for victims of sexual harassment to file complaints. The revised code will allow the California Department of Fair Employment and Housing to review complaints about the casting couch, as opposed to victims hiring lawyers to go to court.

Lawsuits are one way that victims of the casting couch are seeking renumeration. In New York, a judge ruled that an actress could sue Harvey Weinstein for violating state sex trafficking laws because the casting couch could be considered a "commercial sex act." The judge rejected Weinstein's lawyers' contention that nothing of value was exchanged when he saw a demo reel of one of Weinstein's accusers, Kadian Noble, being molested and then forced to watch Weinstein masturbate in a bathroom in Cannes, France, in 2014. Weinstein has also been indicted on criminal charges. He was fired from the company he cofounded in October 2017.

Shaming men who have been accused of such behavior as well as those who allegedly knew about it but stayed silent is another tactic. Actress Rose McGowan took some heat for publicly shaming Matt Damon and Ben Affleck for knowing about and doing nothing to address Weinstein's behavior. These accusations are often met with disbelief and disdain, as exemplified by McGowan being tempo-rarily suspended from Twitter after her comments. Opponents maintain that these women and men are overblowing the problem and that allegations are unfairly costing men their careers.

Laura Finley

See also: Harvey Weinstein Scandal; Hostile Work Environment; McGowan, Rose; #MeToo Movement

Further Reading

Adams, T. 2017. "Casting-Couch Tactics Plagued Hollywood Long before Harvey Wein-stein." *Variety*, October 17. Accessed December 18, 2018. https://variety.com/2017/film/features/casting-couch-hollywood-sexual-harassment-harvey-weinstein-1202589895/.

Associated Press. 2018. "Harvey Weinstein Scandal: Judge Cites Casting Couch's His-tory, OKs Weinstein Suit." *USA Today*, August 14. Accessed December 18, 2018. https://www.usatoday.com/story/life/people/2018/08/14/harvey-weinstein-scandal-judge-couch-history-suit/987680002/.

Green, J. 2018. "Hollywood Casting Couch Is Targeted in California Harassment Law Changes." *Los Angeles Times*, August 1. Accessed December 18, 2018. http://www.latimes.com/business/la-fi-casting-couch-law-20180801-story.html.

Pemberton, B. 2018. "What Is the Casting Couch and Which Hollywood Actresses Have Told Their Stories about It?" *The Sun*, January 8. Accessed December 18, 2018. https://www.thesun.co.uk/fabulous/5291359/casting-couch-hollywood-actresses-stories/.

Schager, N. 2017. "Hollywood's Heinous 'Casting Couch' Culture That Enabled Harvey Weinstein." *Daily Beast*, October 14. Accessed December 18, 2018. https://www.thedailybeast.com/hollywoods-heinous-casting-couch-culture-that-enabled-harvey-weinstein.

Catcalls

Catcalls are acts of unwelcome sexual harassment or advances in the form of crude or suggestive remarks aimed at strangers (usually girls or women) in public settings. Catcalls are most frequently heard on streets and sidewalks or at bus stops; the ges-tures are often sexual in nature and show the perpetrator's lack of respect for the victim. Catcalls involve the use of verbal and nonverbal cues, such as requests for one's name and phone number, leers, wolf whistles, staring, and the like, the aim of which is to evaluate a woman's physical appearance and force the victim to com-municate with the perpetrator. Men who engage in catcalling frequently describe the practice as harmless, but women on the receiving end of this form of harassment often report negative feelings of humiliation and even fear for their safety.

In some cases, victims of catcalls have reported that the harassment limits their movements and full self-expression in society. Catcalls may lead to sexual objec-tification, body shaming, fear of rape, self-blaming, and fear of public safety, but responses to being the target of catcalls vary; some women interpret mild forms of the practice as compliments to their physical attractiveness. In fact, the reaction of victims of catcalls is often determined by their perception of both the act and of themselves. It has been observed, however, that catcalls can often increase in intensity and crudeness when initial statements are perceived to be welcomed by the target. This suggests that the potential dangers of catcalls cannot be ignored and must be at the fore of gender-based harassment discourse.

Context plays an important role in the perception and interpretation of catcalling experiences, as it tends to involve no physical contact and can be open to interpretation (depending on context and perception of victim). Therefore, the fear or enjoyment of catcalls is a function of the perceived goals of the perpetrator (i.e., whether the remarks are intended as demeaning or flirtatious), the attractiveness and age of the targeted individual, the time of day, and whether the victim is alone or with friends, among many other factors.

Catcalls can elicit a variety of negative responses from victims, and they can have psychological consequences for victims and witnesses (Saunders et al. 2016). Women who are catcalled may experience emotions such as degradation, embarrassment, helplessness, shame, self-blame, and feelings of being unsafe. These emotions may lead to questions about the legitimacy of catcalling thereby leading to psychological trauma and feelings of inadequacy. Therefore, support groups and help centers may play important roles in assisting victims of catcalls.

The common strategies women use to manage catcalling include passive coping, victim blaming, careful consideration for their surroundings, avoiding eye contact with a potential catcaller, ignoring or staring at the catcaller, or running, moving, or walking away. Essentially, some victims of catcalling cope by doing nothing, considering it just ordinary flattery, and some blame themselves, thereby maintaining gender relation imbalances.

Olasunmbo Ayanfeoluwa Olusanya

See also: Gender Equality; Groping; Music/Video Settings; Objectification of Women; Victim Blaming

Further Reading

Farmer, Olivia, and Sara Smock Jordan. 2017. "Experiences of Women Coping with Catcalling Experiences in New York City: A Pilot Study." *Journal of Feminist Family Therapy* 29(4): 205–225.

Fisher Sophie, Danielle Lindner, and Christopher J. Ferguson. 2017. "The Effects of Exposure to Catcalling on Women's State Self-Objectification and Body Image." *Current Psychological Research* 38(6): 1–8. https://www.researchgate.net/publication /320259582_The_Effects_of_Exposure_to_Catcalling_on_Women's_State_Self -Objectification_and_Body_Image.

Saunders Benjamin, Crista Scaturro, Christopher Guarino, and Elspeth Kelly. 2016. "Contending with Catcalling: The Role of System-Justifying Beliefs and Ambivalent Sexism in Predicting Women's Coping Experiences with (and Men's Attributions for) Stranger Harassment." *Current Psychology* 36: 324–338. https://doi.org /10.1007/s12144-016-9421-7.

Code of Conduct

Navigating the cultural landscape of an organization can be challenging for an employee. Organizations need guidelines, including so-called codes of conduct, that outline inappropriate and appropriate behaviors to ensure organizational compliance and a healthy and productive environment for all members. The mission statement and vision a company abides by are the starting point of this process. In addition, organizations often create both a code of ethics and a code of conduct to address appropriate behavior in the workspace. The code of ethics and code of conduct are two distinct aspects within an organization, so the terms should not be used interchangeably.

The code of ethics is the theoretical outline of the mission and vision of the organization. It links the standard of professional conduct with both the mission and vision. This alignment ensures and articulates a sense of consistency as well as training venues for the employee that define the desired behavior for the employee during his or her employment. The code of ethics includes a broad sketch of a variety of situations void of specific examples. This lack of specificity is purposeful because this document's purpose is to provide a broad framework for understanding the values of the employer. It is essentially meant to provide a road map for employees to make decisions within the organization, especially when faced with an ethical dilemma. Employees' behavior within an organization should not be random but indicative of the mission and values of the organization.

The employees' behavioral or operational aspects of the code of ethics—how they behave in word and deed—make up the code of conduct. The code of conduct governs how the employee should act in a situation. Thus, the code of conduct is the day-to-day application of the philosophical aspects of the code of ethics. Provisions in the code of conduct are quite specific, and the document moves away from vague language. For example, the code of conduct will state a specific situation along with the protocol to address the prohibited behavior within the organization. The code of conduct provides explicit guidance for the employees to navigate the daily challenges of the workplace in an appropriate manner that reflects the stated values of the organization.

To ensure effective implementation of the code of conduct, experts urge organizations to establish and execute a process of constant and consistent assessment to ensure an inclusive culture. The learning process should also include updates of current information policies and training. The organization should move beyond fulfilling the requirement of having a code of conduct to striving for an environment in which the members feel safe to indicate an issue or concern. Problems can arise when an organization changes over time but does not change the code of conduct to reflect new operating realities or priorities.

Wider societal changes may dictate the need to adjust the code of conduct. What was applicable in one setting may be inappropriate or outdated within another setting as time goes on. The conundrum is when the code of conduct lags to the demands of the organization. For example, many correctional institutions do not have a code of conduct to address the transgender population. The lack of procedures increases the likelihood of vulnerability to this population and possible avenues of victimization.

Shauntey James

See also: Discrimination; Equal Employment Opportunity Commission; Hostile Work Environment; Title IX; Title VII of the Civil Rights Act of 1964

Further Reading

Bagnall, R. G., and S. Nakar, S. 2018. "A Critical Reflection on Code of Conduct in Vocational Education." *Journal of Moral Education* 47(1): 78–90.

Cawthray, T., T. Penzler, and L. E. Porter. 2013. "Updating International Law Enforcement Ethics: International Codes of Conduct." *Criminal Justice Ethics* 32(3): 187–209.

Lewis, A. 2017. "The Outcomes, Economics and Ethics of the Workplace Wellness Industry." *Health Matrix: Journal of Law-Medicine* 27: 1–58.

Tricco, A. C., P. Rios, W. Zarin, R. Cardos, S. Diaz, V. Nincic, A. Mascarenhas, S. Jassemi, and S. E. Straus. 2018. "Prevention and Management of Unprofessional Behavior among Adults in the Workplace: A Scoping Review." *PLoS ONE* 13(7): 1–25.

Whitman, C. N. 2017. "Transgender Criminal Justice Ethical and Constitutional Perspectives." *Ethics & Behavior* 27(6): 445–457.

College Campuses

The word *university* is derived from the Latin term *universitas magistrorum et scholarium*, which roughly means "community of teachers and scholars." Additional interpretation of the Latin word *universitas* refers to "a number of persons associated into one body, a society, or community." Essentially, the concept represents a group of people gathered together for a common purpose, and this certainly includes today's colleges and universities. Historically, colleges and universities organized for the common purpose to design and deliver instruction and learning. To be effective, they became places of sanctuary that substantially set aside a student's responsibility from the doldrums of daily life. Students were offered freedom from the distractions of physical labor, family responsibilities, and work. With such distractions removed, students were free to concentrate and focus on their instruction and learning.

Built into the design of the college and university experience are the concepts of *personal freedom* as well as *academic freedom*. This environment proscribed a common experience that prohibited restrictions on speech and distinctly encouraged freedom of thought. This educational process highly valued the individual and recognized personal growth. Students were free to explore new thoughts and ideas. However, this noble and respected ideal of freedom as a common and meaningful experience has its darker side. With so much freedom on college campuses, do some members take advantage of that freedom? Are campus communities uniquely positioned for sexual predators?

Currently, there is a vast litany of publications, research articles, and public policy efforts to address the serious concerns related to campus sexual harassment. One of the many struggles in attempting to accurately identify sexual harassment on a college or university campus is the multiplicity of contexts in which personal contact takes place. Relationships exist at all levels, including staff to staff, faculty to faculty, coach to coach, student to student, and any mingling of those combinations that also includes campus visitors. Scholars studying those relationships have learned that sexual victimization by women is more common than previously known. Researchers are also gathering more accurate information about the true levels of sexual victimization on our college campuses.

ASSESSING THE TRUE EXTENT OF SEXUAL HARASSMENT AND ASSAULT ON CAMPUS

Sexual harassment on college and university campuses may largely be under-reported due to its hidden dimensions, despite recent headlines related to the #MeToo Movement. It is quite challenging for the average person to accurately recognize the nuanced ways in which sexual harassment takes place.

Generally, there are two forms of sexual harassment. The first and perhaps the most prominent form on college and university campuses is the *quid pro quo*, which in Latin means "something for something." In this form of sexual harassment, a person in authority, such as a member of the faculty, pressures or requires a student to exchange sexual acts for preferred treatment or to avoid undesired sanctions, such as a failing grade. Campus communities are rife with examples of how this form of sexual violence is alive, well, and often overlooked. The second form of sexual harassment is the creation of a *hostile work environment*, in which an employer or person in authority fails to protect an employee from unwanted, inappropriate behaviors that are sexually explicit and offensive and meant to intimidate and control the victim.

It is often difficult to recognize, prevent, and resolve sexual harassment on college and university campuses due to the myriad contexts in which sexual harassment can take place. Campuses are places of employment as well as schools with faculty and students engaged in learning and research. There are classroom settings, offices, dormitories, laboratories, athletic and cultural events, travel, and much more. People on college campuses range in age from the typical first-year teenage student to a much older group of faculty and staff. As a whole, their experiences and perceptions in regard to the dangers of sexual harassment are varied, but young students and new employees are generally recognized as the most vulnerable. What contributes to their vulnerability is their inexperience combined with their comparative lack of power, influence, and community standing.

Such an unformulated understanding of sexual harassment does not go unnoticed by sexual predators outside the campus. These predators know how to operate on the fringe and will attempt to violate a victim's personal boundaries as well as any workplace policies prohibiting sexual harassment. Any member of a campus community may become the victim of sexual harassment while on campus, but students who are athletes or those involved in off-campus educational settings are often overlooked for risk of victimization. For example, well-known scandals, such as those at Pennsylvania State (Penn State) and Michigan State Universities, have highlighted the problem. Athletes have been vulnerable to sexual victimization from coaches, trainers, and medical staff. Students that are involved in practicum and field placement experiences are reluctant to report harassment due to the high stakes involved in successful completion of their placements. Female students lack confidence in reporting their experiences, while male students commonly believe that they can handle it on their own terms.

Institutions need to routinely assess whether they are adequately addressing this issue for students engaged in all institutionally sponsored off-campus experiences. Institutional policies as well as routine practices must be effective in reassuring students that if they should be victimized off campus, such policies will result in a swift investigation, and sanctions will be enforced if misconduct is determined. Additional awareness training should be undertaken for all students engaged in any off-campus activity or learning experience. Ultimately, colleges and universities are responsible for the sexual harassment of their students while off campus or when they are involved in any college-sponsored activity.

LAWS, POLICIES, AND REGULATIONS

Campuses can range in size from small private colleges that represent a village to the large public universities that resemble cities. All campuses have two important considerations when examining sexual harassment. First, they are all workplaces. Second, they are educational institutions that attract new students every year. Colleges and universities do prohibit sexual harassment and are regulated by local, state, and federal laws. Many campuses have engaged in formal training for staff, faculty, and specific student populations, such as student athletes. In addition, colleges and universities orient new students prior to the beginning of the academic year. During new student orientation, students are engulfed with so much information and so many activities that they are overwhelmed and numb. Despite this information and training, sexual harassment remains a serious problem on campuses.

How do members of a campus community sort out the terms *sexual assault* and *rape* from the term *sexual harassment*? Sexual harassment is a vicarious form of sexual violence due to its immediate and residual effects on its victims and should never be subsumed by the other definitions.

When an individual is sexually harassed in the workplace or in an educational setting, victims often feel they have been violated in the same way as the victims of physical violence. Victims often face the fear that sexual harassment may eventually lead to sexual assault or rape because it was not stopped in its early stages. Generally, sexual harassment consists of the following: propositions for sex; inappropriate sexual humor; sexually suggestive comments or gestures; sexual focus on gender-specific body parts; insults and threats based on sex, gender, gender identity, sexual orientation, or gender expression; oral, written, or electronic communications of a sexual nature that is unwanted and unwelcome; written graffiti or the display or distribution of sexually explicit drawings, pictures, or written materials; sexually charged name-calling; sexually suggestive body language, such as touching, patting, pinching, hugging, kissing, or brushing against an individual's body; or cyberstalking through email or social media.

Even though college and university communities are guided by ethics and egalitarian values, campuses are microcosms of the outside world and have the same problems. Sexual harassment is about *power* and *control* in every setting. Campuses are uniquely designed for predatory behaviors that can be masked within a campus culture that focuses on self-regulation and freedom of expression.

Is it reasonable to wonder whether colleges and universities would have addressed the crisis of sexual violence on their campuses if not compelled by the creation of federal laws? Did the enactment of federal laws such as Title VII and Title IX force campuses into taking action?

Thankfully, more and more colleges and universities have recognized the importance of formalized approaches in establishing protocols, policies, and responses to sexual harassment. They offer helpful information and reliable resources. In addition to reporting to campus authorities, victims of sexual harassment can also petition a court for protective action in the form of either a *stay-away order* or a *restraining order*, either of which legally prohibits someone from engaging in harassing behaviors. A stay-away order usually results from a current criminal case and is issued by a criminal court, while a restraining order is civil in nature and frequently involves domestic relations. Each state defines the type of connections that determine domestic relationships, so it is important for colleges to be well informed and up to date on these legal protections. Violations of these court orders constitute a separate criminal offense that results in the arrest of the violator, which may prevent future victimization.

There is significant variation in the degree of responsiveness from campuses as to how they address the issues of sexual harassment and assault. At some institutions, inadequate policies and responses from administrations negatively impact the willingness of reporters to come forward. Victims are often unsure whether the unwanted behaviors meet the standard of sexual harassment, so they will intuitively seek advice and counsel from a family member or friend. These informal conversations may result in the victim being urged to "just forget about it" or "deal with it" because "it's just not worth the hassle!" These responses interfere with addressing the problem and are based in the fatalistic attitude that "as long as there has been sexual attraction between humans there will be sexual harassment." Such beliefs create a closed loop culture on campuses in which victims become convinced that incidents are not worth reporting.

It is thus essential that victims receive substantive aid and clear support from their institutions to ameliorate the harmful effects of sexual harassment. Sexual harassment is more than a mere act and should never be ignored or tolerated. The less victims fear campus reactions and are confident they will receive support, the more likely they will make a formal complaint, thereby finding relief and improving the quality of employee work experiences and student life on campus.

Gary L. Berte

See also: Hostile Work Environment; #MeToo Movement; Quid Pro Quo; Title IX; Title VII of the Civil Rights Act of 1964

Further Reading

Abrams, Z. 2018. "Sexual Harassment on Campus." *American Psychological Association* 49(5): 68. https://www.apa.org/monitor/2018/05/sexual-harassment.

Boorstein, M. 2019. "What Caused the Clergy Sex Abuse Crisis? Catholic Universities Are Pushing for Debate on the Answer." *Washington Post*, March 27. https://www.washingtonpost.com/religion/2019/03/27/what-caused-clergy-sex-abuse-crisis-catholic-universities-are-pushing-debate-answer/.

Cantor, D. 2015. "Association of American Universities Climate Survey on Sexual Assault and Sexual Misconduct (2015)." September 3. https://www.aau.edu/key-issues/aau -climate-survey-sexual-assault-and-sexual-misconduct-2015.

Fedina, L., J. L. Holmes, and B. Backes. 2016. "How Prevalent Is Campus Sexual Assault in the United States?" *National Institute of Justice Journal*, June 2. https://nij.gov /journals/277/pages/campus-sexual-assault.aspx

Greaney, J., and J. Poindexter. 2019. "Sexual Harassment in Education in Massachusetts: Are Schools, Colleges, and Universities Strictly Liable for the Conduct of Their Staff?" *Massachusetts Law Review* 100(2): 44–49.

Komaromy, M., B. Bindman, R. Haber, and M. Sande. 1993. "Sexual Harassment in Medical Training." *New England Journal of Medicine* 328: 322–326. https://www.nejm .org/doi/full/10.1056/NEJM199302043280507

National Institute of Justice. 2018. "Study Finds Agencies Can React More Supportively Than Family and Friends to Victims' Disclosures of Sexual Assault." October 31. https://www.nij.gov/topics/crime/rape-sexual-violence/Pages/agencies-react -supportively-to-disclosures.aspx.

Stemple, L., and H. Meyer. 2017. "Sexual Victimization by Women Is More Common Than Previously Known." *Scientific American*, October 10. https://www.scientific american.com/article/sexual-victimization-by-women-is-more-common-than -previously-known/

College Campuses, Institutional Transparency

American colleges and universities rely on corporate structures to assign legal authority and responsibility to their employees. These corporate structures begin by organizing a governing board that sits at the top of the structure, with the remaining parts of the organization reporting upward to the board. An important function of the governing board is to ensure that institutional policies and procedures comply with federal, state, and local laws. These governing boards are referred to as either a board of trustees, a board of regents, or a board of visitors. Lines of reporting are crucial for institutional accountability and defining employee responsibilities. Is there evidence to suggest that corporate structures restrict the free flow of information? If so, can this interfere with the formal reporting, investigation, and criminal prosecution of campus sexual assaults and rapes?

These governing boards have a variety of legal responsibilities, such as supporting the institution's mission, fundraising, and budgeting. Perhaps the most important function is the hiring of a president, who is responsible for the institution's day-to-day operations. Once chosen, the president is responsible for raising funds and sustaining a healthy number of first-year students. These responsibilities require a considerable amount of time and energy and often take the president away from campus. Therefore, the president becomes profoundly reliant on others to provide accurate, timely, and relevant information regarding the operations of the institution.

When it comes to the reporting and the investigation of sexual violence on campuses, the lines of reporting and communication are critical and occasionally muddled. A random sample of the organizational structures of American colleges reveals that the chief of police often does not report directly to the president. Such a structure is an anachronistic leftover from the late 1800s and mid-1900s, when custodians provided campus security along with night watchmen.

A quick review of college organizational structures indicates that at one prestigious institution, the campus chief of police reports directly to the director of the physical plant, who reviews all police reports and then reports to the treasurer. Does this director who is responsible for the physical care of facilities have the training to recognize the difference between college misconduct and criminality? Does the treasurer, who is next in line, further filter reports?

On yet another campus, the chief of police reports directly to the dean of the college, whose primary function is student affairs. To many persons, it is inconceivable that the chief of police in any city or town would report directly to the maintenance director. Also, on another campus, the police are not allowed to interview student athletes without first going through the athletic department (Dick and Zierling 2016). Such structures fly in the face of modern police organizations in which the chief of police is given an executive role and reports directly to an elected public official, such as a mayor.

The Jeanne Clery Act is a federal law that requires colleges and universities to give an annual accounting of the number of reported sexual assaults and rapes on their campuses. A review of 2014 Clery reports indicates that of approximately eleven thousand reporting schools, 91 percent had no incidents of rape (American Association of University Women 2015). This is in complete contrast to the large body of research that indicates that about one-in-five students have been the victim of a sexual assault or rape on a college campus. How can sexually violent perpetrators be concentrated on only 9 percent of campuses? Such an outcome is extremely unlikely and may indicate a culture of nonreporting or inaccurate reporting. The extraordinarily low number of rapes should be worrisome to campus populations. How is misinformation helpful to any institution's mission?

It is generally understood that victims of sexual violence hesitate to report to the police. This is true for both college students and members of the general public. However, college students are bombarded with information about how to report sexual assault and rape. Such efforts begin day one with new student orientation and last throughout their college careers. The average noncollege person has the option to dial 911.

A 2018 study found that when a woman formally reported being a victim of sexual assault or rape to the police, she received greater support and more positive outcomes than when first sharing this information with family or friends (National Institute of Justice 2018). This finding seems to be counterintuitive to the commonly held belief that most victims will have negative outcomes when reporting to the police. This survey, however, found that informal support and reactions from family and friends provided less help and fewer measurable outcomes. The study also noted that sexual minorities, such as lesbians and bisexuals, were less likely to report to the police. The researchers noted that a community-wide response gets better results. When a rape is reported to the police, it results in a coordinated effort by multiple agencies. Researchers have reported that a small number of perpetrators on college campuses are repeat offenders and responsible for a large number of victims. If acts of assault by these perpetrators are promptly reported to the police, it is more likely that these predators can be stopped before they claim other victims.

Another concern regarding transparency in higher education is the lack of understanding by campus administrators of their institution's practices regarding Title IX reporting. Having a general understanding of a policy is not the same as confidently knowing how to apply it. One 2016 survey found that administrators who were polled regarding Title IX had a broad understanding of the purpose of the statute. However, there were many differing responses as to how, and to whom, to report violations (Brown 2018).

Some colleges define sexual assault as nonconsensual sexual contact that may include rape. Colleges thus may treat rape as though it was the same as sexual assault, a stance that makes for considerable variation and inconsistency in institutional sanctions (Dick and Zierling 2016). Due to federal definitions, college policies can categorize sexual assault and rape into one classification in their student conduct policies. Off college campuses, criminal statutes differentiate between sexual assault and rape. Rape is the outcome of a sexual assault, but not all sexual assaults meet the criminal definition of a rape. Combining these two crimes into one category does not help to inform the college community about the very serious differences between the two.

To determine the actual number of occurrences, and to protect the safety of all students, colleges should conduct a review of current and past incidents. Governing boards should utilize their leadership roles and self-initiate a review of their policies and procedures with a meticulous focus on the day-to-day practices for preventing, reporting, and investigating sexual violence on their campuses.

Gary L. Berte

See also: Campus Accountability and Safety Act; College Campuses; Relationship Violence; Sexism; Title IX

Further Reading

American Association of University Women. 2015. "91 Percent of Colleges Reported Zero Incidents of Rape in 2014." November 23. https://ww3.aauw.org/article/clery-act-data-analysis/.

Brown, Sarah. 2018. "Researchers, Posing as Students, Quizzed Campus Officials about Sexual Assault. How Did They Do?" *Chronicle of Higher Education*, August 14. https://www.chronicle.com/article/Researchers-Posing-as/244270.

Dick, Kirby, and Amy Zierling. 2016. *The Hunting Ground: The Inside Story of Sexual Assault on American College Campuses*. New York: Simon and Schuster.

National Institute of Justice. 2018. "Study Finds Agencies Can React More Supportively Than Family and Friends to Victims' Disclosures of Sexual Assault." October 31. https://nij.ojp.gov/topics/articles/study-finds-agencies-can-react-more-supportively-family-and-friends-victims.

Concerts

In the workplace, empirical research suggests that women in particular are subjected to unwanted sexual demands from their male superiors and sexist treatment and misconduct from male colleagues. Since the emergence of the #MeToo Movement in 2017, this problem has understandably become a subject of extensive discussion and research. However, other areas of American culture in which sexual harassment abounds have also received increased attention. For example, there appears to be increased recognition that sexual harassment at public entertainment events such as musical concerts and festivals is a significant and long-standing problem.

A concert is an event that showcases diverse musical entertainment, usually performed live. The events are intended to bring relaxation and pleasure to people of all ages, and they have a positive economic impact on smaller businesses within and around the concert venues. Many of these events draw younger people in particular. Musical concerts pull in large crowds, some of which have become the backdrop for sexual assaults, groping, and outright rape. Those problems are typically linked to the environment of concerts, which can and do feature the heavy consumption of alcohol and drugs and rowdy and unrestrained behavior in crowded settings that often provide concertgoers with a veneer of anonymity (Heen and Lieberman 2018).

In one 2017 study, 92 percent of female concertgoers experienced being harassed (Elias 2017). There were over 500 respondents, most of whom were female (379), but there were also 84 males and 57 nonbinary (those that do not identify as exclusively masculine or feminine) respondents. The survey was taken at the end of 2017, and it inquired about spoken and physical harassment, coercion, and violence. The female respondents mentioned "groping, sexual gestures, stalking, being yelled at and being photographed or videoed without permission." Of the male respondents, 31 percent of them experienced physical and nonphysical harassment, while 60 percent of transgender fans experienced physical homophobic or transphobic violence.

According to another study conducted by the market research and data analytics company YouGov, nearly half of female festival-going respondents (43 percent) under forty say they have faced unwanted sexual behavior at a music festival, and 22 percent of all festivalgoers have faced assault or harassment, rising to 30 percent of women overall. The most common forms were unwelcome physical contact and verbal sexual harassment.

Sexual harassment and sexual assault are problems at concerts outside the United States as well. At one particular festival in the United Kingdom (called a Secret Garden Party), a girl had allegedly been raped, which has been a common occurrence at festivals in the United Kingdom. There have been reports at house raves and arty folk-rock shows. Incidents occurred at the Reading Festival, Latitude, and Wilderness, all located in the United Kingdom. Assaults at these venues led to arrests in 2009, 2010, 2014, and 2015. At the third venue, a man assaulted two unconscious women in the medical tent. Another woman was grabbed by a group of at least three men while walking from her campsite to the toilet. Female victims have reported being spit at and threatened and have had to endure degrading language.

Data from the Crime Survey for England and Wales showed more than 80 percent of all victims of sexual assault did not report it to police. Yet, one in five women had experienced some form of sexual assault since they turned sixteen. In relation to concert experiences, YouGov surveyed 1,188 festivalgoers and found that only 2 percent of such incidents were reported to police (either before or after the event), though 19 percent of men did report their experience to staff.

Such survey results confirm the widespread belief that most serious sexual offenses at concerts and festivals are not reported. Victims feel they will not be believed if they have been taking drugs or drinking alcohol, and they are also afraid that they will not remember exactly what happened. In another UK study by the Office for National Statistics, in 2017, 85 percent of victims did not report the offenses against them. One victim said she felt like she was blamed (even by her friends) for an assault that occurred when she drank too much and blacked out in a friend's tent at a festival.

To reduce the occurrences of these crimes, there has been a joint effort between nonprofit organizations to promote a consensual music experience for concertgoers. OurMusicMyBody, for example, implemented policies at many major and local festivals (including Pitchfork, Lollapalooza, and Riot Fest) and also worked with Between Friends and Rape Victim Advocates to create anti-harassment policies and guidelines at music venues and festivals across Chicago.

When OurMusicMyBody surveyed concertgoers in November and December of 2017, it found 1,286 instances of harassment: "47 percent of respondents experienced unsolicited comments about their body, 41 percent were groped, and 45 percent were aggressively 'hit on.'" Of the females, 92 percent had experienced harassment. Of the male fans who identified as LGBTQ+, 31 percent had experienced both physical and nonphysical harassment. Of the fans who identified as transgender, 60 percent had experienced physical homophobic or transphobic violence ("Our Music My Body" n.d.).

Fans mentioned that they wanted the festivals and venues to support them and to create a safer environment for them. Further, they felt that artists with abusive pasts should not be booked to perform. The goal is to change the culture of these events so that the issues are addressed head-on and so that we as a society stop the current habit of trivializing or normalizing sexual assault. In one specific example, a man was wearing a shirt that read "eat, sleep, rape, repeat" at Coachella, an annual music festival held in California. An interviewer for *Teen Vogue* said she spent ten hours at Coachella to report her story on problems of sexual harassment in live music settings and was groped twenty-two times. She interviewed fifty-four festivalgoers about their experiences with sexual assault and found that all of them had some sort of story about either sexual harassment or sexual assault at Coachella in 2018.

Researchers and activists alike assert that if concert organizers can do a better job of creating an environment where women are respected, behavior will improve. Some suggest a zero tolerance policy, where all forms of sexual violence, even rape jokes and discriminatory comments made about women and their bodies, are not tolerated. Raising awareness that these attitudes lead to negative behavior is a step in the right direction. This is a societal problem (and does not just happen in the concert venues). Also, there have been campaigns to have music venues sign a pledge that they will not commit, condone, or remain silent about violence or assault at their locations.

A "consent campaign" called Reclaim the Night was introduced in the United Kingdom at Bestival. The council that runs it gives visitors a safe space to talk and discuss issues of consent and responsibility. Just because a woman is drunk or half naked does not mean she is responsible for a rape. Having an independent sexual violence adviser, domestic abuse experts, and sexual health nurses is one of their goals as well. The idea of this education campaign is to urge concert and festival organizers to include these services in their planning to give victims a chance to defend and express themselves.

Beginning in 2018 at Lollapalooza concert events, a huge digital sign (prompted by the anti–sexual harassment campaign of OurMusicOurBody) was displayed that told fans "You make Lolla great! Look out for each other!" It urged attendees to alert staff if they have felt threatened or harassed at the event. Similar information and anti-harassments procedures have been taken at different venues across the United States in the wake of the #MeToo movement.

One particular supporter of this movement is a singer for the punk band War on Women. Shawna Potter has become an activist in establishing new policies to prevent and punish harassment and assault at music venues and festivals. Potter founded a Baltimore chapter of Hollaback!, which is a national organization that was formed to end harassment through the Safer Spaces initiative (which began in academia, but she feels can be applied in the mainstream). Utilizing her knowledge, she also taught tactics to attendees at Vans Warped Tour in 2017 (Molina 2019). Basically, the signage at entryways and bathrooms as well as via social media and event pages can declare that the venues are harassment free and that certain behaviors will not be tolerated. She feels these events need to be clear about how they will handle violations by posting anti-harassment policies as well.

Concert venues could hold themselves accountable by outsourcing their security and violence prevention to organizations trained in combating harassment in public arenas. Almost all surveyed concertgoers on YouGov said they preferred enhanced security measures, with 84 percent preferring that staff and security be trained in violence prevention and crisis intervention. Also mentioned by 75 percent of respondents was that venues and festivals should increase signage that clarifies anti-harassment policies, and 62 percent mentioned the need for venues to create a designated safe space for those being harassed to go and still be able to enjoy the show. Preventive messages and information on-site are a great idea as well as working with specialist local services so that security staff know how to respond to victims with respect and empathy.

In the last two decades, research has shown a significant increase in the cases of sexual harassment reported at gigs and concerts. Between 2013 and 2014, a survey conducted by the staff of the Ottawa (Canada) Hospital revealed that 25 percent of all new cases of sexual harassment occurred at or around mass gatherings. Victims of these attacks suffer both emotional and physical trauma. A study released in 2018 by the University of Leeds found that most victims are left with a wide range of feelings, such as shock, fear, powerlessness, and anger. These feelings are often intensified by feelings of guilt or self-blame as well as doubts about the capacity of society in general or the justice system in particular to punish their harassers.

After past criticisms involving reports of rape, sexual harassment, and unwanted groping, Goldenvoice created an anti-assault initiative called Every One that mandates zero tolerance for any form of sexual, physical, or verbal assault or harassment at Coachella and Stagecoach to make music festivals safer. One step has been to station trained ambassadors throughout the grounds for assistance to victims as well as the distribution of marketing materials (posted to educate festival-goers on resources and rules). Unfortunately, there has not been a scientifically sound collection of harassment data at either of these music festivals, and most organizers do not collect or publish reported rape data related to their events. Thus, there is a gap in rape statistics reported by local police and health care providers versus those reported at the music venues. One reason may be that incidents that occur outside the Indio city limits are outside the jurisdiction of the Indio Police Department. However, it may also be that rapes in general are not likely to be reported to authorities. The overall numbers are probably much higher due to the underreporting of rape and sexual assault at any venue.

The Indio (Colorado) Police Department, which is the lead investigative agency for crimes at both of the events (Coachella and Stagecoach), said it only investigated one rape report and two groping incidents over the last year at these events. However, the lead forensic nurse and program coordinator for SAFE (the Sexual Assault Forensic Examiner team), which is responsible for every rape kit done in the Coachella Valley, said they had seven reported rapes (either at the festival campgrounds or at short-term rentals or private residences nearby). Rapes occurred either before or after one of the April 2019 music festivals, while walking back from the showers, or while staying in an Airbnb in town for the festival or they were committed by a friend after the festival.

It appears those who commit these acts take advantage of the alcohol-infused environment. Even though drugs and drug paraphernalia are not allowed at the festivals and its being a misdemeanor for someone to sell alcohol to any intoxicated person in the State of California, drugs and alcohol are readily available from many sources. Offenders may think their own use of alcohol excuses their behavior or entitles them to do something they would not do if they were not drunk. They may also think the survivor will be less likely to be believed or that they might not remember the encounter.

The campaign coordinator for OurMusicMyBody says that organizers of these music festivals are starting to take sexual assault more seriously and are starting to keep track of incidents. Experts agree that much more is required from both the legal system and the business community in terms of implanting strong policies to prevent victimization and encourage and treat victims.

Gina Robertiello and Bamidele Wale-Oshinowo

See also: Catcalls; Groping; Music/Video Settings; Popular Music; Victim Blaming

Further Reading

Crockett, E. 2016. "The History of Sexual Harassment Explains Why Many Women Wait So Long to Come Forward." Vox, July 14. Accessed March 24, 2019. https://www .vox.com/2016/7/14/12178412/roger-ailes-sexual-harassment-history-women-wait.

Damien, C., and N. Hayden. 2019. "We Reviewed Rape Statistics Surrounding Coachella, Stagecoach. Here Is What We Found: As Goldenvoice Rolls Out Anti-Assault Initiative, There's a Gap in Rape Statistics Reported by Local Police and Health Care Providers." *Desert Sun*, April 5. https://www.desertsun.com/story/life/entertainment /music/coachella/2019/04/05/rape-statistics-surrounding-coachella-stagecoach -heres-what-we-found/3228396002/.

Duca, L. 2017. "Coachella, Rape Culture and What You Can Do about It." HuffPost, December 6. https://www.huffpost.com/entry/rape-culture-coachella_n_7072836.

Elias, E. 2017. "Women and Sexual Assault at Concerts." *The Oarsman*, March 18. Accessed March 28, 2019. https://veniceoarsman.com/2835/opinion/women-and -sexual-assault-at-concerts/.

Heen, M., and J. D. Lieberman. 2018. "Sexual Harassment and Violence at Music Concerts and Festivals." UNLV Center for Crime and Justice Policy (Technical Report). https://doi.org/10.13140/RG.2.2.21767.04009.

Hill, R. L. 2018. "Sexual Harassment, Groping, and Assaults at Gigs and Concerts." University of Leeds Report, November 23. Accessed March 29, 2019. https://gender -studies.leeds.ac.uk/wp-content/uploads/sites/53/2018/11/Sexual-violence-at-gigs -prevention-and-response-guidelines-20181123.pdf.

Kruger, M., and M. Saayman. 2015. "Attendance at the U2 Concert: Is It a Case of 'This Is a Man's World?'" *Event Management* 19: 15–32.

Macaya-Andrés, L., and A. S. Andrés. 2018. "Protocol 'We Won't Keep Quiet' Campaign against Sexual Assault and Harassment in Private Night-Time Leisure Venues." https://bcnroc.ajuntament.barcelona.cat/jspui/bitstream/11703/109241/1/protocol %20oci%20nocturn%20ENG.pdf.

Molina, A. 2019. "Punk Lessons for Ending Harassment and Making Spaces Safer." Next City, July 10. https://nextcity.org/daily/entry/ending-harassment-and-making -spaces-safer.

"Our Music My Body." n.d. Resilience Empowering Survivors Ending Sexual Violence. https://www.ourresilience.org/get-involved/ourmusicmybody/.

Papisova, V. 2018. "Sexual Harassment Was Rampant at Coachella 2018." *Teen Vogue*, April 18. https://www.teenvogue.com/story/sexual-harassment-was-rampant-at -coachella-2018.

Roti, J. 2018. "Incidents of Sexual Harassment, Assault High at Music Festivals, New Survey Reveals." *Chicago Tribune*, March 29. Accessed March 24, 2019. https:// www.chicagotribune.com/lifestyles/ct-life-music-festivals-sexual-assaults-0328 -story.html.

Sexual Assault Network (SAN) Ottawa. 2015. "Project SoundCheck: Ending Sexual Violence at Mass Gatherings: A Guide to Safe and Effective Bystander Intervention for Music Festivals, Large Events, and Parties." Accessed March 30, 2019. http:// www.sanottawa.com/sites/default/files/pdf/FINAL-MANUAL-2016.pdf.

Steyger, I. P. 2017. "A Study Examining the Extent to Which Sexual Harassment and Assault Affect the Female Customer Experience at Music Events." A thesis submitted to Cardiff Metropolitan University (unpublished) in April 2017. Accessed March 24, 2019. https://repository.cardiffmet.ac.uk/handle/10369/8719.

Webster, E., M. Brennan, A. Behr, M. Cloonan, and J. Ansell. 2017. "Valuing Live Music: The UK Live Music Census 2017 Report." Accessed March 30, 2019. uklivemusiccensus.org/wp-content/uploads/2018/03/UK-Live-Music-Census -2017-full-report-LARGE-PRINT.pdf.

Congress

Lawmakers and staffers have consistently stated that sexual harassment is rampant in the U.S. Congress. This issue has been brought into the light regarding both congressional members and their staff, and there is now increasing awareness by the general public—the same taxpayers who are voting these people into political office. However, there is very little data to help shed insight on exactly how pervasive the issue of sexual harassment is among members of the U.S. Congress and their staff (hereinafter referred to collectively as Capitol Hill). The one thing that is known is that within a twenty-year period, there has been a total of 264 discrimination cases of various types (race, age, sex, etc.) brought against members of Capitol Hill, resulting in more than $17 million of settlement monies being paid out to discrimination victims, including victims of sexual harassment.

Changes have been implemented on Capitol Hill to stem the rise, or continuation, of sexual harassment, but it appears that more changes may be necessary. However, even with pressures being placed on Capitol Hill by some of its members and by members of the public, the burden remains on Capitol Hill to reform its own system to prevent sexual harassment.

SEXUAL HARASSMENT AND THE OFFICE OF CONGRESSIONAL WORKPLACE RIGHTS

In many employment situations, a sexual harassment claim is traditionally handled through a company's human resources department. There is no human resources department on Capitol Hill. The lack of a human resources department makes it quite confusing and challenging for individuals to determine how to file a sexual harassment complaint in their place of work.

In 1995, Congress passed the Congressional Accountability Act (Act), which incorporated thirteen statutes dealing with the potentiality of workplace harassment and discrimination on Capitol Hill. The Act, sponsored by Senator Charles Grassley, a Republican from Iowa, imposed a range of laws on Capitol Hill protecting civil, labor, and worker rights, including protections against sexual harassment. This was notably the first time any such implementation of rights was specifically applied to Capitol Hill.

The Office of Compliance (hereinafter referred to as the OOC) was established under the Act, and it is assigned to handle harassment claims. Since its creation in 1995, the OOC has paid out more than $17 million in settlements to victims of workplace harassment on Capitol Hill, although the specific amount paid to victims of sexual harassment is not known. It is not known because the OOC is not required to (nor does it) keep a breakdown of the individual cases of sexual harassment, as some of the workplace claims handled by the OOC may involve more than one type of harassment. The OOC is now known as the Office of Congressional Workplace Rights (OCWR).

PROCEDURES FOR FILING A SEXUAL HARASSMENT COMPLAINT

Under the Act, the twenty-person OCWR was established to adjudicate worker disputes on Capitol Hill, including sexual harassment allegations. Under the procedures, an alleged victim has 180 days from the time of the alleged offense in which to file a complaint with the OCWR. To file the complaint, the alleged victim must first agree to go through counseling for a period of 30 days. Then, after that 30-day period, the alleged victim has 15 days in which to decide whether she or he wants to pursue the next step, mandatory mediation.

If the alleged victim chooses to take the next step in the process, the alleged victim must enter a 30-day period of mediation. Mediation is a process in which two parties agree to meet with a third impartial person (a mediator), who will assist both sides in reaching a resolution or settlement of the matter. It should be noted that this mandatory mediation process has received criticism, as it contrasts from what the remainder of the federal government employees are required to do in such situations. Almost all the federal government groups allow mediation as an option, but they do not require it to be a mandatory process.

After the mediation, the alleged victim must then wait 30 days before she or he can continue in the process, that is, if the mediation was not successful. If the mediation is not successful, the alleged victim can then file a formal complaint with the OCWR or she or he may choose to file a federal lawsuit (although a federal lawsuit does not appear to be the normal route taken by the alleged victims). Once a formal complaint is filed with the OCWR, a hearing officer, who maintains subpoena power, will issue a decision on the matter within a 90-day period. However, historically, most matters appear to be resolved through settlements between the parties.

Once a settlement is reached, it must be approved by the chairperson of the House Administration Committee and that committee's ranking member. In other words, the top Democrat and Republic leaders on that committee vote to approve the settlement. The Senate has no such committee or member vote for settlement payment approval.

SETTLEMENT PAYMENTS

In general, once a settlement is reached, the settlement monies are not paid out of the accused individual lawmaker's office. Rather, the monies are paid from special funds set up within the U.S. Treasury. These special funds have been described by critics as a sort of congressional "slush fund." A slush fund, in its kindest interpretation, is a fund that does not have a designated purpose. Moreover, it is a fund that is used for payoffs regarding illegal or illicit behaviors. In regard to this particular slush fund, it is the U.S. taxpayers who are paying for these workplace sexual harassment settlements.

Some members of Capitol Hill have paid settlement monies out of their own office budgets rather than follow OCWR procedures. Thus, these Capitol Hill members can circumvent the OCWR by paying separate monies. However, the bottom line is that, whether paid through the special funding and the OCWR procedure or through the office budget of the congressperson in question, the monies being paid to sexual harassment victims are taxpayer-funded monies.

Many observers have expressed concern that these abuses will continue if members of Capitol Hill are not held publicly accountable for their actions. In its current state, the system does not appear to encourage true transparency that would allow for public accountability. One main factor is the fact that the alleged victims are usually required to enter into a nondisclosure agreement (NDA), also known as a confidentiality agreement.

VEIL OF SECRECY: NONDISCLOSURE AGREEMENTS

As noted earlier, the mandatory mediation process required under the OCWR for sexual harassment claims against members of Congress or their staff members does not exist with other federal agencies. The second notable difference between the OCWR procedures and those governing other federal agencies, which resolve their disputes under the Equal Employment Opportunity Commission (EEOC), is that resolution under the EEOC, if successful, results in public notification. Under the EEOC, if an accuser is successful in pursuing her or his claim of workplace harassment, the EEOC requires that information about the accused's behavior be publicly posted.

Under the OCWR procedures, alleged victims are subjected to confidentiality requirements during the mandatory periods of counseling and mediation. The mediation process itself applies strict nondisclosure rules that bar alleged victims from publicly speaking about the sexual harassment they have endured. Once an alleged victim begins the counseling process, if she or he violates the confidentiality agreement and chooses to speak publicly about the fact that she or he intends to file a complaint against a member of Capitol Hill, the alleged victim can be sanctioned, jeopardizing the case.

Any accuser wishing to file a complaint with the OCWR must also sign a nondisclosure agreement (NDA), which prohibits the accuser from publicly revealing the terms of the complaint and any monies received through a settlement. As noted by one news reporter, the NDAs require both parties to not talk about the matter in public or in private, the parties agree that neither is liable or accountable, and the accusers are paid to go away. So, throughout the entire process, including its conclusion or settlement, there is no disclosure of the actual allegations or settlement agreement terms reached between the accused and her or his accuser.

Throughout the process and thereafter, there is also no disclosure of the identities of the accused members of Capitol Hill. The troubling aspect of this type of secrecy is that it allows the accused members to continue their behaviors by failing to provide any transparency allowing for their public condemnation, and it does not provide any type of warning to other potential victims (interns, people seeking employment as members of the congressperson's staff, etc.) of such behavior. Indeed, even knowing that over $17 million has been paid out to workplace victims over a twenty-year period does not give us an indication of how widespread sexual harassment is on Capitol Hill. In fact, as is indicative in studies involving females as victims of sexual harassment and assault, generally fewer than half of all victims will ever report such instances.

POWER CULTURE

Power is the ability to accomplish a task that one chooses, or wishes, to do. But why does power allow members of Capitol Hill to believe that they are without repercussions or liability to do what they wish? The more power one has, the more that person can potentially accomplish. But power is not without moral obligation. People in power are seen at times as objectifying other people, relying on their individual motives to govern their own behavior, and applying moral standards on others that they do not place upon themselves. These factors allow them to engage in a moral hypocrisy, particularly if consequences from their actions are not disclosed to the general public.

Why do victims of sexual harassment committed by members of Capitol Hill not report such behaviors? It can be due to fear of retaliation, fear of a loss of work, or any number of factors. One must remember that when a lone individual attempts to seek reparation due to sexual harassment from a member of Capitol Hill, that individual is facing a member of one of the most powerful groups within the United States; in addition, almost all members of Congress are members of political parties that wield enormous influence in politics and media and many other aspects of American life.

It is true that instead of reporting the alleged sexual harassment through the OCWR, an accuser can also choose to file a federal lawsuit instead. However, Capitol Hill is still governed by powerful individuals who can make or break the careers of their staff members and other employees. By choosing to file a lawsuit, the alleged victim may begin an action that could end her or his ability to work not only on Capitol Hill but in government in general.

MANDATORY TRAINING

In a monumental stance against sexual harassment, in November 2017, both the U.S. House of Representatives and the U.S. Senate passed legislation requiring all the members of Capitol Hill and their staffs to undergo mandatory anti–sexual harassment training. All members must attend an initial training and then retrain at least once during every congressional session. Activists working against sexual harassment applauded this reform, but emphasized that much more needs to be done to improve the process of reporting sexual harassment on Capitol Hill.

With the 2020 election, the faces of the U.S. House of Representatives and the U.S. Senate have shifted. That election brought more females into these legislative bodies than ever before in the history of the United States. Perhaps this shift in the gender makeup, combined with the now mandatory sexual harassment training for all legislative employees, will have a positive effect in the reduction of sexual harassment incidents in the U.S. Congress. Time will tell.

George E. Coroian Jr.

See also: Equal Employment Opportunity Commission; Nondisclosure Agreements; Sexual Harassment Training

Further Reading

Dahl, R. A. 1957. "The Concept of Power." *Behavioral Science* 2(3): 201–215.

Georgeson, J. C., and M. J. Harris. 2000. "The Balance of Power: Interpersonal Consequences of Differential Power and Expectations." *Personality and Psychology Bulletin* 26(10): 1239–1257.

Lammers, J., and D. A. Stapel. 2009. "How Power Influences Moral Thinking." *Journal of Personality and Social Psychology* 97(2): 279–289.

Lovaglia, M. J. 1999. "Understanding Network Exchange Theory." *Advances in Group Processes* 16: 31–59.

Lucas, J. W., and A. R. Baxter. 2012. "Power, Influence, and Diversity in Organizations." *Annals of the American Academy* 639(1): 49–70.

Office of Congressional Workplace Rights website. https://www.compliance.gov.

Constand, Andrea (1973–)

Andrea Erminia Constand was born in Toronto and played basketball at Albert Campbell Collegiate Institute in the city. After high school, Constand earned a scholarship to play basketball at the University of Arizona and then spent several years pursuing a professional basketball career in Europe before accepting an offer to serve as director of operations of women's basketball at Temple University.

Constand was one of the first women to come forward during the #MeToo Movement, breaking her decade-long silence on being sexually assaulted by Hollywood's most famous television father, Bill Cosby. Constand claimed Cosby drugged her and subsequently sexually assaulted her at his Philadelphia home in 2004. Following Constand's original complaint, more than a dozen women came forward with similar complaints of sexual assault by Cosby.

Constand and Cosby met at a Temple University basketball game, and they became friends. Cosby, a Temple alum and former student athlete, kept in close contact with the school and its athletics program. By 2002, he was acting as a mentor to Constand. In January 2004, Constand was visiting Cosby at his home, seeking career advice, when she told Cosby she was feeling stressed. She alleged that he responded by giving her three pills, telling her they would take the edge off. When she asked whether they were herbal, he reportedly said, "Yes. Down them."

After taking the pills and drinking wine at Cosby's urging, Constand testified that her vision became blurry and her speech slurred. Cosby then went on to grope and digitally penetrate her and also guided her hand to touch his genitals. Hours later, according to Constand's account, she awoke in his house with her clothing askew. Cosby greeted her in a robe, gave her a muffin, and walked her out of his house.

Constand did not come forward with her accusations against Cosby until a year later, when she filed a civil lawsuit against the comedian and actor. When Cosby was questioned, he claimed the sexual acts were consensual. When the news of Constand's allegations first went public in early 2005, California attorney Tamara

Green appeared on the *Today Show* with a similar story about how Cosby gave her pills to help with a fever and then sexually assaulted her in her apartment.

Cosby denied both allegations, and Montgomery County district attorney Bruce Castor said Constand's case lacked enough evidence to move forward with criminal charges. Constand, who had moved back to Toronto, settled her civil lawsuit against Cosby for an undisclosed, confidential cash settlement (later revealed to be more than $3 million) in November 2006.

After settling with Constand, the actor dismissed questions about her accusations and tried to get his career back on track. But as the years passed, the country's general understanding of sexual assault, rape, consent, and power had evolved, and the public appeared less willing to ignore the idea that "America's dad" could be capable of sexual assault.

More than decade later, another woman came forward claiming sexual abuse by Cosby. In July 2015, the deposition from the January 2005 complaint filed by Constand was unsealed. The deposition included an admission from Cosby that he gave Constand quaaludes without her knowledge. Constand's original complaint thus laid the foundation for more than fifty women to come forward with claims of sexual abuse by Cosby—many of them with similar stories of being drugged and then subjected to sexual assaults.

The statute of limitations for most of these cases had expired, so Cosby could not be prosecuted. But the statute of limitations for the filing of criminal charges had not yet run out for the Constand case, and in December 2015, prosecutors in Montgomery County, Pennsylvania, filed three counts of aggravated indecent assault against Bill Cosby for his alleged attack on Constand in 2004. Cosby's first trial ended in a mistrial, as jurors could not reach unanimous agreement on a verdict. But prosecutors retried the case in April 2018, giving Constand another opportunity to tell the court what had happened to her. This time, Cosby was convicted on all three counts. He received a prison sentence of three to ten years and a $25,000 fine.

Tara A. Garrison

See also: Cosby, Bill; Groping; Movies, Depictions of Sexual Harassment

Further Reading

Calvert, C. 2017. "Counterspeech, Cosby, and Libel Law: Some Lessons about 'Pure Opinion' and Resuscitating the Self-Defense Privilege." *Florida Law Review* 69(1): 151.

Mandell, S. P., Steven L. Baron, Cristina M. Salvato, David E. Armendariz, Michelle K. Arishita, John P. Borger, Natalie A. Harris, et al. 2017. "Recent Developments in Media, Privacy, Defamation, and Advertising Law." *Tort Trial & Insurance Practice Law Journal* 52(2): 531.

Corrections System

According to the U.S. Department of Justice (DOJ), sexual harassment and misconduct are included in the overall definition of sexual victimization that exists in state and federal prisons. The DOJ's Bureau of Justice Statistics defines sexual victimization based on who the perpetrator is. Congress determined that the extent of the problems of sexual harassment, assault, and misconduct between inmates or staff and inmates was not widely known. As a result, Congress passed the Prison Rape Elimination Act (PREA) in 2003. This legislation authorized the development of the National Prison Rape Elimination Commission, which was charged with drafting standards for the elimination of prison rape. Those standards were published in June 2009 and were then turned over to the DOJ for review and passage as a final rule, which became effective August 20, 2012. The intent of the act has been to provide prisons, jails, community confinement, and juvenile detention facilities with specialized training for medical and mental health personnel on specific aspects of PREA. What PREA does not cover is a third problem: sexual harassment and misconduct between male and female correctional staff.

INMATE-ON-INMATE HARASSMENT AND ASSAULT

Inmate-on-inmate sexual victimization is defined as nonconsensual sexual acts or abusive contact with a victim without his or her consent or with a victim who cannot consent or refuse.

Regarding male inmate-on-inmate victimization, studies have shown that there are several differences between the perpetrator and the victim. Perpetrators tend to be Black, bigger, older, and violent offenders. They also tend to have more extensive criminal records. Victims tend to have the opposite characteristics. They are typically smaller, younger, and white. However, experts agree that incidents of sexual harassment and misconduct in prisons have historically been— and continue to be—significantly underreported because victims fear retaliation by the perpetrator or other inmates (Benya, Widnall, and Johnson 2018; Sutton and Sutton 2016).

Meanwhile, researchers believe that female inmate-on-inmate victimization is increasing. In the past, much of the violence has been attributed to men who express rage and dominance; however, there has been a rise in female crime over the years as well. The reporting of harassment and misconduct has risen since the PREA standards went into effect.

STAFF-ON-INMATE HARASSMENT AND ASSAULT

Staff-on-inmate sexual victimization includes sexual misconduct or sexual harassment perpetrated on an inmate by staff. Staff includes an employee, volunteer, contractor, official visitor, or other agency representative. Most sexual harassment and misconduct incidents involve female prisoners. Harassment by staff includes being viewed in the nude and being forced to submit to body cavity and pat searches in the presence of male guards, but it can also include guards and other staff who pressure inmates to engage in "voluntary" sexual relations with them in exchange for better living conditions (such as increased physical freedom during outdoor exercise periods) or extra products or necessities from the prison store. Some observers consider these actions by female prisoners to be voluntary bartering. However, because the staff have power over all inmates, the inmates cannot legally consent.

In the New Jersey Edna Mahan Correctional Facility, the only all-female facility in the state, specific corrections officers and a trade instructor were found guilty of sexual assault, sexual conduct, and official misconduct against prisoners. These cases occurred over a period of time from 2015 to 2016. Several inmates are also suing the Department of Investigations, and the federal government is also investigating civil rights violation at the facility. One officer, found guilty in November 2018, received a sixteen-year sentence. Two other corrections officers received three years in prison.

INMATE-ON-STAFF HARASSMENT AND ASSAULT

Another problem in U.S. correctional institutions concerns male inmates who sexually harass female guards and staff by groping them, exposing themselves to them, threatening rape, and masturbating in front of them. Historically, complaints from female staff to administrators about such incidents have often been ignored. Finally, female guards filed lawsuits against prisons and administrators in several states for failing to protect them against this harassment. In several cases, they won large awards for damages. For example, in 2017, the Bureau of Prisons agreed to pay $20 million to 524 female employees at the Coleman prison complex in Sumter County, Florida. The award stemmed from the Coleman administration's practice of ignoring female staff complaints and failing to protect them from inmates.

STAFF-ON-STAFF HARASSMENT AND ASSAULT

Staff-on staff victimization most often involves male staff and guards sexually harassing female staff and guards. Some victims say the harassment has included being propositioned, being subjected to sexually explicit messages, being groped, or worse. In Kentucky, four female guards at Little Sandy Correctional Complex filed a lawsuit against Sergeant Stephen Harper, Warden Joseph Meko, and the Kentucky Department of Corrections in 2014. They alleged that Harper masturbated where one woman could see him, touched female staffers' breasts and buttocks, rubbed his body against them, tried to force them to touch him, and attempted to rape one of the plaintiffs. The jury awarded the four guards $1.6 million in 2018. The accusations occurred over the time period of 2012–2014.

Since PREA was enacted, reports of sexual victimization in the nation's jails and prisons have increased. There were 24,661 allegations of sexual harassment and misconduct in prisons in 2015. However, only an estimated 1,473 allegations were substantiated. Of the latter cases, 58 percent were perpetrated by inmates, and 42 percent were perpetrated by staff members.

SEXUAL HARASSMENT AND MISCONDUCT IN LAW ENFORCEMENT

Police and fire departments are also taking steps to address sexual harassment and misconduct after years of ignoring the issue. This development is partly in response to growing willingness of victims of such treatment to fight back in the courts. In 2018, for example, five female paramedics in the Chicago Fire Department filed a complaint with the Equal Employment Opportunity Commission (EEOC) for alleged incidents of sexual harassment they endured from 2017 to 2018.

In particular, there have been significant numbers of police staff, including women from every age group, reporting their supervisors for initiating behavior perceived as harassment. Most often, the instigator was a colleague (either police or support staff).

According to one report, 75 percent of those who experienced sexual teasing and jokes reported that it was not a onetime event, and 54 percent of those pressured for sexual favors said that occurred more than once. Much of the harassment in U.S. law enforcement includes sexualized or sexist remarks as the most common form. Other studies show that staff experience sexually suggestive jokes or comments, intrusive questions about their private life, inappropriate leering or staring, and unwelcome touching, hugging, or kissing. They also experience repeated requests for unwanted dates, sexual gestures, and sexually explicit emails and texts or have been pressured for sex. Staff often witness sexually harassing behaviors (i.e., bystander harassment) as well.

According to research from Bowling Green State University, police officers in the United States were charged with forcible rape 405 times between 2005 and 2013, which is an average of 45 a year, and there were 636 incidents of forcible fondling over this time frame. Victims include both suspects and citizens the police are supposed to protect. However, any data collected on the prevalence of these crimes in civil service are not going to be reliable or comprehensive. In fact, data on sexual assaults by police are almost nonexistent due to their positions of power, the way police protect each other, and fear of retaliation by victims.

It is interesting to note that when someone from the public is victimized, those individuals tend to be targeted because they are vulnerable or not trusted. Some have criminal records, drug or alcohol problems, or are homeless. Others are sex workers, who are not likely to report a police officer having assaulted them.

Police sexual misconduct and violence are referred to as hidden offenses. Arrest rates are low because they are dependent on the victim reporting the offense and the law enforcement agency making that report public. When inappropriate behavior is reported, a number of cases simply result in an officer resigning or retiring before being asked to appear before any disciplinary body.

Overall, there needs to be a better system for reporting this behavior, especially in certain lines of work, where doing so can be extremely intimidating or where the personnel involved in the behavior represent the law. Instead, some states utilize "shield laws" to hide the identities of police officers accused of crimes, and some include nondisclosure agreements (NDAs) in victim settlements.

A number of reforms to address these problems have been suggested, from the development of anonymous online reporting systems to increased investment in officers specifically trained to deal with alleged victims and allegations. Officers should be mandated to activate their bodycams and dashcams (for their own protection as well as for accountability). Further, GPS tracking devices could be used to see where officers are spending their time. In this way, it could be determined whether officers are spending too much time in a place they should not be, such as a victim's home, or spending time in an alley or apartment for too long.

One important way to avoid abuse, assault, harassment, and misconduct of any kind is to hire quality officers. National standards of behavior must be followed in recruitment policies and procedures. Reformers assert that if a department (or officers within a department) violate the law, the department must be subject to disciplinary action (such as losing certifications or being put under receivership with the county or state). They also urge the implementation of rules forbidding departments from hiring officers who were fired from other agencies. This is called "passing the trash," and it happens in school systems and with the clergy as well.

Cathie Perselay Seidman and Gina Robertiello

See also: Equal Employment Opportunity Commission; Hostile Work Environment; "Passing the Trash"; Quid Pro Quo; Retaliation

Further Reading

Benya, F. F., S. E. Widnall, and P. A. Johnson, eds. 2018. *Sexual Harassment of Women: Climate, Culture, and Consequences in Academic Sciences, Engineering, and Medicine.* Washington, DC: National Academies Press.

Bureau of Justice Statistics. 2018. "PREA Data Collection Activities, 2018." June. https://www.bjs.gov/content/pub/pdf/pdca18.pdf.

Dickerson, C. 2018. "Hazing, Humiliation, Terrorism: Working While Female in Federal Prison." *New York Times*, November 17.

Egan, D. 2018. "Female Officers Face Widespread Sexual Harassment in Michigan Prison System." *Detroit Free Press*, April 20.

Estep, B. 2017. "Kentucky Jury Awards $1.6 Million to Four Female Prison Guards in Sex Harassment Case." *Lexington Herald Leader*, March 27.

Rantala R. R. 2018. "Sexual Victimization Reported by Adult Correctional Authorities, 2012–15." Bureau of Justice Statistics Special Report, July.

Silvestri, M. 2017. "Police Culture and Gender: Revisiting the 'Cult of Masculinity.'" *Policing, Journal of Policy and Practice* 11: 289–300.

Sullivan, S. P. 2019. "Another Corrections Officer from N.J. Women's Prison Arrested amid Ongoing Sex Abuse Inquiry." NJ.com, April 5. https://www.nj.com/crime/2019/04/another-corrections-officer-from-nj-womens-prison-arrested-amid-ongoing-sex-abuse-inquiry.html.

Sutton, J., and J. Sutton. 2016. "Male Inmate-on-Inmate Sexual Assault: Characteristics Associated with Risk." *Criminology, Criminal Justice, Law and Society* 17(3): 57–73).

Cosby, Bill (1937–)

Bill Cosby, born William H. Cosby Jr. in Philadelphia in 1937, enjoyed a tremendously successful career that spanned over fifty years in the entertainment field. He was a highly influential creative force within television, film, and comedy. His bemused observational humor influenced a generation of performers and entertained fans of all ages. His status as a living comedic legend, however, was shattered when he was charged with (and ultimately convicted of) multiple counts of sexual assault in 2018. The uproar surrounding the disturbing details of that case as well as additional accusations from other victims that emerged over time exemplify the kind of reckoning faced by various public figures during the rise of the #MeToo and Time's Up Movements, when allegations of past sexual assault and impropriety surfaced and victims stepped forward to offer statements of support and cooperation in ongoing legal proceedings. Cosby's case was unusual, however, due to the breadth of his celebrity and the warmly paternal image he had fashioned for himself in American popular culture; his fall from grace was particularly shocking.

Affectionately referred to in the media as "America's dad," Bill Cosby enjoyed a career that spanned five decades. His early forays into stand-up comedy in the early 1960s led to steady work in television and movies and evolved over time into a family-friendly entertainment empire. As an African American actor, he broke racial barriers in 1965 with his first major television role, starring in the dramatic series *I-Spy*; he went on to win several Emmy Awards for his work on the program. During the course of his varied career, he recorded comedy albums, starred in both comedic and dramatic films, created and voiced character roles in the influential children's cartoon series *Fat Albert and the Cosby Kids* (which served as the basis of his doctoral dissertation at the University of Massachusetts, Amherst), and hosted child-centered game shows.

Cosby's status in the entertainment industry reached its pinnacle with his creation of the immensely popular and critically lauded sitcom *The Cosby Show*, which aired from 1984 until 1992. His persona as a dedicated family man was cemented by his role as Dr. Cliff Huxtable, a prosperous obstetrician married to a devoted and professionally successful wife and blessed with five spirited children. Cosby himself had been married for many years and had five children of his own. During this same period, he published numerous books in which he shared his droll perspectives on fatherhood and family life. Even his work as a commercial spokesperson for Jell-0, among other products, emphasized his wholesome parental image.

Cosby's creative output in the 1990s and beyond did not achieve the same level of success as *The Cosby Show*, but he remained active in television, working on sitcoms, game shows, and children's programming. Throughout this period, he was awarded dozens of honorary doctorates from universities around the country and was a sought-after commencement speaker. He also positioned himself as a social observer who was vocal in his critiques of the African American community, reserving his harshest observations for young men and single mothers. His statements later came back to haunt him; he was condemned as a hypocrite as the staggering scope of the allegations against him slowly emerged.

During the course of Cosby's career, there had been occasional whisperings of questionable sexual behavior, and he had at one point admitted to an extramarital affair in the 1970s with Shawn Thompson Upshaw (who later claimed their sexual activity had been nonconsensual). This encounter possibly produced a daughter (although her paternity was never publicly established). As became a pattern, Cosby threw money at the problem to try to make it disappear, and he ultimately paid tens of thousands of dollars to try to keep the incident quiet. It was not until a lawsuit filed by Andrea Constand in 2005, however, that Cosby became the target of legal action stemming from a sexual assault allegation.

Andrea Constand was the director of operations for Temple University's women's basketball team. Bill Cosby had attended Temple University as an undergraduate and was an ardent booster of the school and its athletic programs. He served on its board of trustees, welcomed incoming freshmen at convocation, and frequently spoke at commencement. Constand and Cosby met in 2002, and their relationship developed to the point where she viewed him as a mentor, relying on him for career guidance. She had visited his home outside Philadelphia on multiple occasions, including one evening in January 2004. During that visit, she expressed uncertainty about the direction of her career and described experiencing stress and anxiety stemming from the responsibilities of her current position. In response, Cosby offered her pills, which he claimed were "herbal" and would help her relax. She took the pills and, afterward, as she found herself semiconscious and unable to move, Cosby assaulted her.

A year later, having left Temple University and returned to her native Canada, Constand revealed details of the assault to her mother, and, together, they confronted Cosby. Cosby admitted to offering Constand pills (which he would not identify) and initiating sexual activity but claimed it was consensual. Constand reported the incident to police in Canada, who brought it to the attention of authorities in Montgomery County, Pennsylvania. In February, the district attorney of Montgomery County, Bruce Castor, determined that there was not enough evidence to prosecute, but Constand decided to pursue a lawsuit against Cosby. The lawsuit accused Cosby of assault and battery against Constand and sought monetary damages. Constand's attorney had identified over a dozen women who had similar complaints against Cosby who would be willing to testify at a trial.

During his deposition in the case, Cosby admitted to having obtained quaaludes from a gynecologist friend back in the 1970s for the purpose of supplying them to sexual partners (a practice that itself would have been illegal) but insisted that all his sexual activities (including those with Constand) had been consensual in nature and that Constand had in fact maintained an ongoing friendly communication with him in the aftermath of their encounter. Constand and Cosby ultimately settled out of court for a substantial sum ($3.38 million) that was not publicly disclosed until years later, thus avoiding a trial; Cosby's deposition was sealed, so the public was not made aware of the details of his statements.

Meanwhile, other women (including those who were named as witnesses in the lawsuit) began to publicly come forward with their own allegations against Cosby. Two described their experiences stemming from their contacts with him during the mid-1980s, during the height of his *Cosby Show* success. One woman, Beth Ferrier, had been in a sexual relationship with him; the other, Barbara Bowman, had been an aspiring teenage actress who had contacted him for mentorship and career guidance. Another woman, Tamara Green, a former model who had known Cosby in the 1970s, claimed he had offered her career advice. All three women had stories similar to Constand's: Cosby had earned their trust and then violated it by drugging them and either sexually assaulting them or attempting to do so. The women's accounts, however, did not gain much traction and received relatively little media attention at the time. Although entertainment industry insiders were aware of stories involving Bill Cosby's questionable behavior, the public seemed to forget that any claims of wrongdoing had ever been made.

It was not until many years later—a decade after Constand's alleged assault—that the accusations that had previously swirled around Bill Cosby earned renewed attention. Comic Hannibal Burress was recorded in October 2014 by a member of the audience as he performed a stand-up comedy set in which he ridiculed Cosby. Burress mocked Cosby's public criticisms of perceived failures within the African American community and accused him of hypocrisy: "'Pull your pants up, Black people. I was on TV in the '80s. I can talk down to you because I had a successful sitcom.' Yeah, but you raped women, Bill Cosby. So brings you down a couple notches." The video footage of the routine went viral, and there was suddenly renewed attention focused on Bill Cosby and the prior allegations of sexual misconduct.

Over the course of the next few months, a large number of women came forward to share their stories of sexual assault at the hands of Bill Cosby. Unlike previously, when accusations received relatively little media coverage, there was an interest in hearing their stories. The sheer volume of victims who were now willing to speak publicly, the advent of social media (and its ability to expose and widely share stories that in the past might have been buried), and the twenty-four-hour news cycle coalesced to produce a shocking barrage of allegations against Cosby that dated back to the 1960s.

What emerged was a dramatic picture of serial assault and rape involving dozens of victims, who varied in age and personal circumstances but who shared many common threads. Most of the women had met Cosby in a professional context, either working with him on a project or contacting him for career advice and mentorship; he would offer his assistance, and given his celebrity and his image as a wholesome and trustworthy father figure, it was not difficult to earn their trust. He would at some point have the opportunity to have the women alone and offer them either pills or, in many cases, a drink that had possibly been spiked. Rendered immobile or unconscious, Cosby would assault them, and they were left with only fleeting memories of the incident. Women who were able to fight off his sexual advances or assault attempts reported suffering retaliation by losing job opportunities over which he had some influence.

From a legal standpoint, almost none of these allegations could be pursued in a criminal prosecution because the statute of limitations had expired, but the cumulative weight of the accusations threatened to irreparably damage Bill Cosby's reputation and legacy. He and his public relations team struggled to keep up with the flood of accusations, and he continued to deny all wrongdoing. Meanwhile, in 2015, as a result of a complex series of legal maneuverings, Cosby's deposition from Andrea Constand's lawsuit was unsealed. His admission of pursuing sexual relationships with women who sought him out as a mentor and his proclivity for offering quaaludes to sexual partners (while insisting that all sexual contacts were consensual) became public record. Career-wise, Cosby started experiencing repercussions. A planned new series was canceled, *Cosby Show* reruns were yanked from syndication, and universities rescinded his honorary degrees. The man who was once one of the most beloved public figures in the world was becoming a pariah.

There was at least one potential case in which the statute of limitations to file criminal charges had not expired—Andrea Constand's. In December 2015, prosecutors in Montgomery County, Pennsylvania, filed three counts of aggravated indecent assault against Bill Cosby stemming from the incident at Cosby's home in January 2004. Cosby, who admitted no wrongdoing and persisted in his claim that their sexual encounter was consensual, was released pending trial on a $1 million bail. His attorneys' efforts to dismiss the charges were unsuccessful, and jury selection commenced in May 2017, with arguments beginning the following month.

The jurors were deeply divided during deliberations and struggled with the evidence and their interpretation of the charges; ultimately, they were unable to come to a unanimous agreement on any of the counts, and the judge declared a mistrial. Prosecutors immediately announced their intention to retry Cosby on the same charges. Following jury selection, the case went to trial once again in April 2018. The retrial incorporated more testimony from other victims (very little corroborating testimony of this type was presented by the prosecution in the earlier trial, with only one of Constand's fellow accusers taking the stand). This time, the jury convicted Cosby on all three counts, and he was sentenced to three to ten years in prison and ordered to pay a $25,000 fine and court costs.

In December 2018, Cosby's attorneys filed an appeal, challenging the earlier conviction on the basis of various trial errors. In the meantime, he continued to serve his prison sentence and faced a multitude of lawsuits that were filed by former victims.

Miriam D. Sealock

See also: Constand, Andrea; #MeToo Movement; Quid Pro Quo; Retaliation; *Time Magazine* "Silence Breakers"; Time's Up Movement

Further Reading

Bowley, Graham. 2018a. "Bill Cosby Assault Case: A Timeline from Accusation to Sentencing." *New York Times*, April 15. https://www.nytimes.com/2018/04/25/arts /television/bill-cosby-sexual-assault-allegations-timeline.html.

Bowley, Graham. 2018b. "Bill Cosby's Appeal Cites 11 'Errors' by Trial Judge." *New York Times*, December 13. https://www.nytimes.com/2018/12/13/arts/television/bill -cosby-jail-appeal.html.

Eagan, Nicole. 2019. *Chasing Cosby: The Downfall of America's Dad*. New York: Seal Press.

Seal, Mark. 2016. "The One Accuser Who May Bring Bill Cosby Down for Good." *Vanity Fair*, July 6. https://www.vanityfair.com/news/2016/07/bill-cosby-andrea -constand-sexual-assault-trial.

Svrluga, Susan, and Mary Pat Flaherty. 2015. "Does Temple University Still Have a Bill Cosby Problem?" *Washington Post*, July 23. https://www.washingtonpost.com /news/grade-point/wp/2015/07/23/does-temple-university-still-have-a-bill-cosby -problem.

Whitaker, Mark. 2014. *Bill Cosby: His Life and Times*. New York: Simon and Schuster.

Williams, Timothy. 2018. "Did the #MeToo Movement Sway the Cosby Jury?" *New York Times*, April 26. https://www.nytimes.com/2018/04/26/us/cosby-jury-metoo-nassar.html.

Crews, Terry (1968–)

Terry Crews is a former professional football player turned successful actor who added a new dimension to the #MeToo Movement when he revealed that he had been a victim of sexual harassment earlier in his Hollywood career.

Terry Alan Crews was born July 30, 1968, in Flint, Michigan. His early life was marked with abuse by his father, who Crews reports was an alcoholic. Having excelled in sports at an early age, Terry earned a football scholarship to Western Michigan University, where he starred at defensive end. He was drafted into the National Football League (NFL) in 1991 and played professional football for the next six years for four different teams. Upon his retirement from the NFL, Crews and his family moved to Los Angeles, California, so that he could pursue a career in acting. Crews's career steadily picked up over the next several years, leading to roles in several comedy and action films. He then extended his acting career to sitcoms, including *Everybody Hates Chris* and *Brooklyn Nine-Nine* (in which he continues to star).

On October 10, 2017, amid media attention directed toward Hollywood mogul Harvey Weinstein concerning allegations of sexual assault and harassment spanning several decades, Crews revealed through his Twitter account that he had also experienced sexual assault. He claimed that a Hollywood agent, Adam Venit, from William Morris Endeavor Entertainment, sexually assaulted him at a party in 2016 by making suggestive gestures and grabbing his genitals. Crews reported the incident to officials at the agency soon after but stated that the claims were ignored. Venit denied any such interaction occurred. Terry filed charges against Venit in November 2017, and one month later, he filed a formal lawsuit against the talent agent. Crews reported that the courage of the women who came forward during the Harvey Weinstein case encouraged him to take action.

Crews's lawsuit against Venit claimed sexual assault, sexual battery, emotional distress, and negligence and demanded unspecified financial damages. In March 2018, both the Los Angeles County district attorney and the Los Angeles city attorney dismissed his criminal case against Venit. This decision was not due to any judgment about the truthfulness of Crews's accusation but rather because the incident occurred outside the statute of limitations to criminally prosecute. Meanwhile, in September 2018, a settlement was reached in Crews's lawsuit against Venit. The settlement corresponded with Venit's announcement that he was leaving William Morris Endeavor Entertainment. In the aftermath of the settlement and resignation, Crews also revealed that Venit had written him an apology letter in March 2018.

Crews was featured as one of the Silence Breakers in the *Time* magazine Person of the Year December 2017 issue. Crews, one of the first men to share his experiences about being a target of sexual harassment and assault, emphasized the importance of men advocating for women in regard to sexual harassment and assault. Crews revealed that he was skeptically questioned regarding his response to the incident. For example, he was asked why he—a still-imposing former NFL veteran—did not respond physically to his assault when it happened. He stated that he feared being ostracized by those who had more power and influence in Hollywood and acknowledged that he struggled to overcome fears about the unfair stigma and shame sometimes heaped on victims of sexual assault and harassment.

Since coming forward with his story, Crew has been a steadfast supporter of victims of sexual assault and harassment. In June 2018, he shared his story before the Senate Judiciary Committee in support of the Sexual Assault Survivor's Bill of Rights. During his testimony, Crews revealed that he was pressured to not view his assault as abuse but to treat it as a joke. He shared that he chose to come forward with his story to stand in solidarity with other survivors and to encourage others to do the same.

Darla D. Darno

See also: Harvey Weinstein Scandal; *Time Magazine* "Silence Breakers"

Further Reading

Dockterman, Eliana. 2017. "Terry Crews: 'Men Need to Hold Other Men Accountable.'" *Time*, December 6. Accessed October 12, 2018. http://time.com/5049671 /terry-crews-interview-transcript-person-of-the-year-2017/.

Kindeland, Katie, and Sabina Ghebremedhin. 2017. "Terry Crews Names Alleged Sexual Assaulter: 'I Will Not Be Shamed.'" ABCNews.com, November 15. Accessed October 12, 2018. https://abcnews.go.com/Entertainment/terry-crews-names -alleged-sexual-assaulter-shamed/story?id=51146972.

Zacharek, Stephanie, Eliana Dockterman, and Haley Sweetland Edwards. 2017. "The Silence Breakers." *Time*, December 18. Accessed October 10, 2018. http://time .com/time-person-of-the-year-2017-silence-breakers/.

Denhollander, Rachael

Rachael Joy Denhollander (née Moxon) was born on December 8, 1984, in Kalamazoo, Michigan, to Paul and Camille Moxon. She was homeschooled and practiced gymnastics at a local club. She went to law school at Oak Brook College of Law and Government Policy, where she graduated in 2008. Denhollander holds a juris doctor (JD) from Oak Brook College of Law, and she is a member of the California Bar Association. Denhollander is actively involved in the research of teaching a biblical worldview, and she writes articles about Christian legal philosophy and provides legal assistance to attorneys and students. She is married with four children.

Denhollander is best known, however, for being the first person to publicly reveal the sexual abuse incidents that she endured from USA Gymnastics Olympic team doctor Larry Nassar. Following her lead, more than three hundred women announced that they were also sexually assaulted by Nassar when they were young athletes. Charges filed against Nassar for these crimes ultimately led to his life imprisonment. Denhollander is also known for her famous quote, "How much is a little girl worth?" The question was posed to the crowd in the courtroom for the Nassar hearing. With her courage, she inspired others to follow her example and to come forward to report their own accounts of the abuses they had suffered. Her testimony at Nassar's court hearing not only accounted in detail what she had gone through but also laid out the mistakes and shortcomings of relevant authorities who had had the power to stop the abuses in the first place.

On August 4, 2016, the *Indianapolis Star* newspaper published an investigative report titled "Out of Balance" about claims that USA Gymnastics (USAG) had buried sexual abuse complaints against a number of its coaches. Later that morning, the reporters who wrote the story received an email from Denhollander, who told them that she had been molested by Dr. Larry Nassar, the team doctor for USAG, when she was fifteen years old. The thirty-one-year-old Denhollander stated that the abuse took place under the guise of medical treatment for her back.

Denhollander also stated that when the *Indianapolis Star* story came out she decided that the time had come for her to publicly speak out about the abuses, victims, and the rampant cover-up at USAG. The fact that she was willing to go on the record and speak about her abuse inspired many other victims of Nassar's abuse to follow suit and step forward and relate their own experiences of victimization.

Rachael Denhollander filed a criminal complaint with the Michigan State University Police against Nassar in August 2016, and Nassar lost his job the following day. As the investigation into Nassar deepened, investigators uncovered evidence that he had assaulted hundreds of other girls and that he was involved in child pornography. On January 24, 2018, Nassar was finally sentenced to 175 years in prison for the sexual assault charges.

During Nassar's sentencing hearing, Denhollander emphasized to Judge Rosemarie Aquilina that the sentence she was about to impose on Nassar would not only put him behind bars for the crimes he had committed but also send a message across the nation to every victim and every perpetrator about the pursuit of justice and the importance of protecting the innocent.

In 2018, Rachael Denhollander was named to *Time* magazine's list of the 100 Most Influential People of the year. Along with other survivors of the USAG sexual abuse scandal, she was awarded the Arthur Ashe Courage Award at the 2018 ESPY Awards (Excellence in Sports Performance Yearly Award). Denhollander was announced as the winner of the Sports Illustrated's Inspiration of the Year Award, which she received on December 12, 2018. She was also selected as one of the 2018 Michiganians of the Year by the *Detroit News*, for which she was praised as a sexual assault survivor whose bravery inspired major institutional change at USAG and brought a sexual predator to justice.

In April 2018, Rachael Denhollander was given the Integrity and Impact Award founded by Dow Jones Sports Intelligence for exemplary levels of ethics, integrity, transparency, and trust in sport. She was also honored with the 2018 *Glamour* Women of the Year Award. Additionally, Denhollander is a recipient of the Heart Ambassadors Lifetime Achievement Award for Contributing to Social Justice, and she was a panelist on a United Nations Peace Messenger Organization at the UN's 62nd Commission on the Status of Women.

Serhat Demir

See also: Larry Nassar Scandal; *Time Magazine* "Silence Breakers"

Further Reading

Alesia, Mark, Marisa Kwiatkowski, and Tim Evans. 2018. "Rachael Denhollander's Brave Journey: Lone Voice to 'Army' at Larry Nassar's Sentencing." *Indianapolis Star* (*IndyStar*), January 24. https://eu.indystar.com/story/news/2018/01/24/larry-nassar -usa-gymnastics-sexual-abuse-rachael-denhollander-mckayla-maroney-aly -raisman/1060356001/.

CNN. 2018. "Read Rachael Denhollander's Full Victim Impact Statement about Larry Nassar." https://www.cnn.com/2018/01/24/us/rachael-denhollander-full-statement /index.html.

Fisher, L. A., & Anders, A. D. 2020. "Engaging with Cultural Sport Psychology to Explore Systemic Sexual Exploitation in USA Gymnastics: A Call to Commitments." *Journal of Applied Sport Psychology* 32 (2): 129–145.

Kwiatowski, M. 2016. "Out of Balance: An IndyStar Investigation into USA Gymnastics." *IndyStar*, December 22. https://www.indystar.com/story/news/investigations/2016 /10/05/indystar-investigation-usa-gymnastics-failed-report-cases-compilation /91626182/.

Snider, M. 2018. "Investigation by 'Indianapolis Star' Hailed as Proof of Local Journalism's Impact." *USA Today*, January 26. https://www.usatoday.com/story/money/media /2018/01/25/investigation-indianapolis-star-hailed-proof-local-journalisms-impact /1066040001/.

Discrimination

Discrimination involves treating individuals differently as a result of their group membership in a protected category. Sex discrimination is the act of treating someone unfavorably on the basis of gender identity, including transgender status, sexual orientation, or pregnancy status. In addition to making discrimination illegal, federal legislation prohibits retaliation against workers who complain, file a charge, or participate in an employment discrimination investigation or lawsuit.

Discriminatory practices can be carried out by individuals, organizations, and social institutions. With respect to sex, these practices are inclusive of sexual harassment, hostile and offensive work environments, differential treatment in any aspect of education or employment, and employment or educational policies that have a negative impact on the success of students or workers of a specific sex. Organizational policies and practices that apply to everyone but systematically result in unequal group outcomes can be particularly difficult to detect and exemplify a way that discrimination can be "baked into" social structures. Discrimination does not require intentionality to be unlawful, and it may result from unconscious or implicit bias as well as policies that appear neutral on their face. Victims of discrimination are more likely to come from less powerful socioeconomic groups.

Employer policies and practices are considered discriminatory under Title VII of the Civil Rights Act of 1964 if those policies or practices have a disproportionately negative effect on workers (or applicants) of a protected category, are not job-related, and are not necessary for the operation of the business. Under Title VII, charges of discrimination typically fall into two categories: disparate treatment and disparate impact.

In cases involving disparate treatment, plaintiffs must demonstrate that a work-related disparity in treatment between groups resulted from intentional discrimination. Disparate impact cases do not require proof of intentional discrimination by employers. For example, in the 1970s, many fire departments had minimum height and weight requirements for firefighters. These requirements had a disparate impact on women candidates and failed the standards of Title VII. When the New York City Fire Department (FDNY) was forced to allow women into its ranks in the 1970s, it created a substantially more arduous physical ability test (compared to prior tests taken by male applicants) for the first class of female cadets in 1977. None passed. This is an example of disparate treatment (the test was intentionally made more difficult for women applicants) and resulted in a successful class action lawsuit and the entrance of the first women firefighters into the NYC Fire Academy in 1982.

In the United States, federal legislation has made employment and education discrimination illegal on the basis of sex (i.e., gender, gender identity, sexual orientation, and pregnancy), race, color, religion, age, national origin, disability, and genetic information. This legislation includes Title VII, Executive Order 11246 of 1965, the Equal Pay Act of 1963 and the Lilly Ledbetter Fair Pay Act of 2009, Title IX of the Education Amendments of 1972, the Pregnancy Discrimination Act of 1978, the Civil Rights Act of 1991, the Age Discrimination in Employment

Act of 1967, the Rehabilitation Act of 1973, Title I of the Americans with Disabilities Act of 1990, and the Genetic Information Nondiscrimination Act of 2008. States and municipalities have also enacted more comprehensive laws against discrimination.

Federal legislation is limited in some important ways. Antidiscrimination laws enforced by the Equal Employment Opportunity Commission (EEOC) only cover employers with at least fifteen employees, require a charge be filed within 180 days with the EEOC (this is extended within some states) or 45 for federal employees to request a meeting with an EEOC counselor. All laws enforced by the EEOC, except the Equal Pay Act, require charges to be filed before a job discrimination lawsuit can be filed against an employer. Moreover, the EEOC is required to notify the employer that a charge has been filed. These rules limit the coverage and ability of workers to file suit under antidiscrimination laws.

Michelle J. Budig

See also: Hostile Work Environment; Sexism; Sexual Harassment Training; Title IX; Title VII of the Civil Rights Act of 1964

Further Reading

Bishu, S. G., and M. G. Alkadry. 2017. "A Systematic Review of the Gender Pay Gap and Factors That Predict It." *Administration & Society* 49: 65–104.

England, P. 2017. *Comparable Worth: Theories and Evidence.* New York: Routledge.

U.S. Equal Employment Opportunity Commission. 2019. "Sex-Based Discrimination." March 28. https://www.eeoc.gov/laws/types/sex.cfm.

E

Equal Employment Opportunity Commission (EEOC)

Sexual harassment laws address cases of workplace sex discrimination pursuant to Title VII of the Civil Rights Act of 1964. The act prohibits employment discrimination based on race, color, religion, sex, and national origin as amended by the Civil Rights Act of 1991 (Pub. L. 102-166) (CRA) and the Lily Ledbetter Fair Pay Act of 2009 (Pub. L. 111-2). The courts have interpreted the act in light of various sets of facts. In *Burlington Industries, Inc. v. Ellerth* (1998) and *Faragher v. City of Boca Raton* (1998), the U.S. Supreme Court held that employers are liable for harassment by supervisory workers unless the employer took immediate and appropriate steps to correct the conduct (George 2019).

The Equal Employment Opportunity Commission (EEOC) is the federal government agency responsible for the enforcement of sexual harassment laws. It provides guidelines for determining employer liability for harassment by supervisors based on sex, race, color, religion, national origin, age, disability, or protected activity. According to the EEOC (2019a) Guidelines on Sexual Harassment,

> Unwelcome sexual advances, requests for sexual favors, and other verbal or physical conduct of a sexual nature constitute sexual harassment when this conduct explicitly or implicitly affects an individual's employment, unreasonably interferes with an individual's work performance, or creates an intimidating, hostile, or offensive work environment.
>
> Sexual harassment can occur in a variety of circumstances, including but not limited to the following: the victim and the harasser may be of the same sex; the harasser can be the victim's supervisor, an agent of the employer, a supervisor in another area, a co-worker, or a non-employee; the victim does not have to be the person harassed but could be anyone affected by the offensive conduct; unlawful sexual harassment may occur without economic injury to or discharge of the victim; the harasser's conduct must be unwelcome. (Equal Employment Opportunity Commission 2019a)

In examining the EEOC guidelines on sexual harassment, it is important to discuss the elements of the law. The first is the element of *prohibition against harassment*. Employers are charged with a duty of prevention of sexual harassment in the workplace. Employers must have a published policy in their workplace to disseminate a clear warning that any form of harassment will not be tolerated pursuant to the Civil Rights Act. The policy should encourage employees to report harassment before it becomes serious and violates federal law.

The next element is *protection against retaliation*. Employers should provide clear assurance to employees that adverse treatment of complainants and witnesses will not be tolerated. Complainants and witnesses should not have to fear retaliation that may include loss of job, promotion, or wages; denial of leave; or any negative impact. Management must monitor employment decisions affecting complainants and witnesses during and after investigations.

An *effective complaint process* is also required. Employers should implement effective procedures for complaints that not only encourage victims to report them but are also flexible, with an accessible contact person for the initial complaint other than the erring supervisor. Management must assure employees that complaints will be handled impartially. An officer outside the employee's chain of command may be delegated to receive the complaints. Employer policies should provide time limits for filing charges with the EEOC or state fair employment practice agencies and explain that the deadline starts from the last date of harassment rather than the date the employer resolved the complaint. An employee may not have to wait until the complaint with the employer is resolved before filing with the EEOC.

A necessary additional element is *confidentiality.* Employers are required to inform employees that case information and records will be protected except to the extent necessary to conduct a successful investigation through interviews. An employer may set up an informal telephone line to discuss issues with employees anonymously.

Employers must set up an *effective investigative process* for a prompt, thorough, and impartial investigation. However, a detailed fact-finding investigation is not required when the harasser admits to the charges. In cases where an investigation is necessary, some interim measures should be taken to separate the parties. The alleged harasser might be transferred or placed on administrative leave with pay pending the outcome of the investigation, but the victim should not be put in a position where his or her interest is jeopardized, as this would amount to retaliation. The investigators must be well trained and not subject to the alleged supervisor. The EEOC provides a list of appropriate questions that may be directed to the complainant, alleged harasser, and third parties during the investigation, including "who, what, when, where, and how."

To determine the credibility of evidence in sexual harassment investigations, the EEOC requires a consideration of factors, including the inherent plausibility of testimonies, demeanor of testifiers, motive to falsify, corroboration by witnesses and physical evidence, and history of similar behavior. The investigation should end with a determination of whether the harassment happened, and appropriate steps should be taken to correct the wrong. If a determination cannot be reached for any reason, the employer should still conduct preventive training and monitoring.

Finally, employers should create the awareness that immediate and corrective measures will be undertaken, including reprimand, transfer, suspension, demotion, wage reduction, training, monitoring, or even discharge of the erring supervisor, and restoration of leave, expungement of negative records, reinstatement, an apology, and monitoring might also be undertaken in benefit of the victim. This is called *assurance of immediate and appropriate corrective action.*

It is easier to define sexual harassment laws than to apply the principles to specific circumstances. In determining what constitutes a hostile environment, the courts will consider various factors, including the frequency and severity of the behavior, conduct of the victim, context of the allegation, the size of the employer's business, and whether a reasonable person would have thought the environment was hostile. Agreeably, the U.S. Supreme Court in both *Ellerth* and *Faragher* upheld the principles that (1) employers are liable for the actions of supervisors resulting in tangible employment action and (2) employers should prevent harassment and employees should be encouraged to avoid or limit damages resulting from harassment.

However, employers can avoid liability or limit damages if the supervisor's action does not end in tangible employment impact and an affirmative defense can be established to the extent that (1) the employer exercised reasonable care to immediately prevent and correct the conduct and (2) the employee unreasonably failed to take advantage of any preventive or corrective measures provided by the employer.

In *Vance v. Ball State University* (2013), the U.S. Supreme Court rejected in part the EEOC's definition of supervisor for construing a hostile work environment. It held that an employer is liable for harassment by employees who are not supervisors but who wield certain degrees of authority. For example, where the employer was negligent in monitoring, responding, or failing to provide a system for complaint and effectively discouraged complaints from being made, that employer could be held liable for the harassing conduct of its employees and agents against coworkers or clients, but only if the employer can be shown to be negligent in allowing the harassment to occur or continue (Herbert 2020).

Meanwhile, *Oncale v. Sundowner* (1998) established that discrimination based on sex is actionable as long as it results in a disadvantaged working environment for the victim irrespective of the gender of either the victim or harasser (Boudreau, Rao, and Adhikari 2019).

The laws on sexual harassment are available for prevention and mitigation of damages related to discrimination in the workplace provided employers and employees follow the guidelines. Employers are required to provide solid procedures for reporting, investigating, and redressing cases of harassment. Employees are expected to take advantage of mechanisms provided by the employers to prevent or reduce damages related to sexual harassment cases in the workplace. The U.S. Supreme Court laid the foundation in *Ellerth* and *Faragher* for vicarious liability of employers and subsequently shed more light on the definition and application of the law on sexual harassment.

Alaba Oludare

See also: Faragher v. City of Boca Raton; Hostile Work Environment; *Oncale v. Sundowner*; Title VII of the Civil Rights Act of 1964; *Vance v. Ball State University*

Further Reading
Boudreau, D., S. U. Rao, and D. R. Adhikari. 2019. "Implications of the Tax Reform Act of 2017 on Sexual Harassment in the Workplace." *Journal of Applied Business and Economics* 21(5).
Burlington Industries, Inc. v. Ellerth, 118 S. Ct. 2257 (1998).
Faragher v. City of Boca Raton, 118 S. Ct. 2257 (1998).

George, B. 2019. "Legal Aspects of Ethical Decision-Making in the Event of Sexual Harassment and Discrimination in the Workplace." *Business Ethics and Leadership* 3(4): 34–42. http://doi.org/10.21272/bel.3(4).34-42.2019.

Harris v. Forklift Systems, Inc., 510 U.S. 17 (1993).

Hebert, L. Camille. 2020. "How the 'MeToo' Movement Is Reshaping Workplace Harassment Law in the United States." Ohio State Public Law Working Paper No. 523, January 13.

Meritor Savings Bank, FSB v. Vinson, 477 U.S. 57, 72 (1986).

Oncale v. Sundowner Offshore Services, Inc., 118 S.Ct. 998, 1002 (1998).

U.S. Equal Employment Opportunity Commission. 1990. *Policy Guidance on Current Issues of Sexual Harassment.* Section E, 8 FEP Manual 405 (March 19): 6699.

U.S. Equal Employment Opportunity Commission. 2019a. "Facts on Sexual Harassment." https://www.eeoc.gov/laws/types/sexual_harassment.cfm.

U.S. Equal Employment Opportunity Commission. 2019b. "Harassment." https://www.eeoc.gov/laws/types/harassment.cfm.

Vance v. Ball State University, 570 U.S. 421 (2013).

Equal Protection Clause

After the Civil War, several amendments were added to the U.S. Constitution, including the Fourteenth Amendment. The Fourteenth Amendment states in part, "No state shall make or enforce any law which shall abridge the privileges or immunities of citizens of the United States; nor shall any state deprive any person of life, liberty, or property, without due process of law; nor deny to any person within its jurisdiction the equal protection of the laws." The last part of the sentence, known as the *equal protection clause*, prohibits state governments (and by extension local governments) and government agencies from discriminating against people based on characteristics such as race or sex. The Fourteenth Amendment only applies to the states and not the federal government. However, federal courts, including the U.S. Supreme Court in *Bolling v. Sharpe*, 347 U.S. 497 (1953), have interpreted the Fifth Amendment to the U.S. Constitution as (1) pertaining to the federal government and (2) implicitly containing an equal protection clause similar to that in the Fourteenth Amendment.

Due to the equal protection clause, the government, with very few exceptions, cannot treat men and women differently. The most obvious violation of the equal protection clause would occur if a state were to pass a law that on its face treats people differently based on their sex. For instance, if a state were to pass a law prohibiting men under the age of twenty-one from consuming alcohol and prohibiting women under the age of nineteen from consuming alcohol, the men could sue because the law treats them differently from women.

However, many equal protection cases are not that obvious. They do not involve laws passed by the states but rather alleged actions by state employees against the plaintiff. When a government employee such as a police officer, for instance, sexually harasses someone, the victim may be entitled to bring a lawsuit under the equal protection clause. Plaintiffs who bring lawsuits against governmental authorities for alleged violations of their civil rights under the equal protection clause file what is known as a Section 1983 claim. Section 1983 refers to the part of the U.S. Code (Title 42) that codified the Civil Rights Act of 1871.

The U.S. Constitution, including the equal protection clause, protects people from the government violating their civil rights, but it does not protect against actions by private employers or other private entities. A person who works for a private employer rather than the government cannot bring a sexual harassment lawsuit using the equal protection clause. Instead, he or she must use civil rights guarantees contained in other laws, such as Title VII of the Civil Rights Act of 1964, to seek redress from the employer. A person employed by the government who is sexually harassed at work may be able to sue under both Title VII and the equal protection clause, depending on the nature of the alleged harassment.

Finally, the equal protection clause may provide a remedy for a nonemployee (member of the public) who was sexually harassed by a government employee. Thus, while there may be some overlap between Title VII and the equal protection clause, they are very distinct from each other not only in who may bring a lawsuit but also in what the plaintiff is required to prove. Another sex discrimination law that somewhat overlaps with the equal protection clause is Title IX of the Education Amendments of 1972, which prohibits sex discrimination in education programs or activities that receive federal funding.

In early cases, defendants attempted to argue that sex discrimination statutes such as Title VII and Title IX were exclusive remedies for sexual harassment and therefore prevented plaintiffs from also bringing Section 1983 sexual harassment claims under the equal protection clause along with their Title VII or Title IX claims. However, in 2009, the U.S. Supreme Court held that plaintiffs could bring both Title IX and Section 1983 claims because Title IX's protections are narrower in some respects and broader in other ways than those guaranteed under the equal protection clause. Although the U.S. Supreme Court has not ruled explicitly on a case involving Title VII and the equal protection clause, lower courts have consistently held that a plaintiff who works for the government and who has been sexually harassed at work can bring both Title VII and equal protection claims.

Individuals who are sexually harassed outside of an employment or educational situation do not have a cause of action under statutes such as Title VII or Title IX, but if the harasser was a government employee, the victim may be able to file a Section 1983 claim based on the equal protection clause. In one case, for example, an independent contractor in Michigan sued Ogemaw County and several county employees for sexual harassment. The contractor alleged that a county employee grabbed her, kissed her, and otherwise sexually harassed her while she was cleaning offices in the county's municipal building. In another case, an employee of a towing and wrecker service company sued a Tennessee Highway Patrol lieutenant and his superiors, alleging that the lieutenant verbally sexually harassed her when he came out to inspect her employer's premises for compliance with state rules and regulations. However, these types of cases are not that common, most likely because they are more difficult to win than Title VII and Title IX cases and government employees often have legal immunity from lawsuits. More often, equal protection clause cases are brought together with Title VII and Title IX claims by plaintiffs who experienced sex discrimination on the job while working for government entities or those who suffered sex discrimination in an educational setting.

Elizabeth W. Marchioni

See also: Corrections System; Title IX; Title VII of the Civil Rights Act of 1964

Further Reading

Araiza, William D. 2015. *Enforcing the Equal Protection Clause: Congressional Power, Judicial Doctrine, and Constitutional Law.* New York: NYU Press.

United States Courts. n.d. "The 14th Amendment and the Evolution of Title IX." https://www.uscourts.gov/educational-resources/educational-activities/14th-amendment-and-evolution-title-ix.

U.S. Equal Employment Opportunity Commission. n.d. "Sex-Based Discrimination." https://www.eeoc.gov/laws/types/sex.cfm.

F

Factory and Manufacturing Settings

Sexual harassment can occur in any setting, with victims from varying gender, race, income, and religious and socioeconomic backgrounds. However, the victimization of those in vulnerable positions is most likely to occur because their position makes it difficult for them to reject advances or complain to authorities. Many people who work in factory or manufacturing settings are lower-wage workers with limited formal education. For women who work in these settings, securing reparations (compensation or damages) when they have been harassed or abused on the job is often difficult.

Women comprise fewer than 3 percent of workers in occupations such as electricians, machinists, transit vehicle mechanics, and welders, so they are the minority in an atmosphere of the "boys will be boys" mentality. Their working environment may condone sexualized conversations, jokes, and stories. Men who work in these fields are not used to working beside a woman. They may refer to equipment, tools, and parts in sexual terms. Females in these fields are judged as not qualified for "men's work" and may feel unwelcome. They struggle to break through stereotypes about their capabilities when they work in traditionally male-dominated occupations, which is where some of the highest rates of sexual harassment tend to occur.

Some key factors that increase the likelihood of workplace victimization are careers where women are isolated, such as domestic care workers, janitors, hotel workers, and agriculture workers, because there are few witnesses. Those working for tips (hotel workers and waitstaff), account for 14 percent of harassment victims. Those lacking legal immigration status (undocumented workers or those on temporary work visas) are particularly at risk. Sexual harassment is more common among Black women (though very unlikely to be reported).

When women work in male-dominated, blue-collar occupations, there is much less gender balance. Women find themselves isolated, perhaps the only representative of their gender, and this can make them feel like outsiders. Yet, if they complain, they are seen as too sensitive. They also may become easy targets. They may be threatened or put in harm's way. The stress of fitting in or becoming a target also puts a strain on the psyche of these women. It jeopardizes their employment opportunities in regard to pay and advancement. It also restricts their learning opportunities, and because they are not working in a salaried position, they do not get benefits and sick time. If women complain about being harassed, they run the risk of jeopardizing their chances at career advancement—or even of losing their jobs.

Ultimately, it is hard for women to challenge this workplace culture that has been typically male for so long. In extreme cases, this treatment can also be life-threatening. Tradeswomen have experienced environments in which they must contend with threats of physical harm, sabotaged work, and being placed in dangerous situations by male coworkers and supervisors. If it is a hostile work environment, supervisors or coworkers may withhold training, assistance, and safety information or equipment.

Further, the costs of these crimes can be enormous. There are costs (for the victim) associated with lost wages if the victim feels so uncomfortable that she cannot work (e.g., calling in sick). There are also costs to the companies themselves (e.g., poor work performance, decreased productivity, or the need to pay for mental and psychological counseling). One in ten victims who experience this abuse are likely to develop health problems, including workplace accidents and PTSD. Harassment in these industries lowers the motivation to work and affects the quality of work. It also leads to high turnover rates (which can be costly to companies). Targets are also 6.5 times more likely to change jobs (McLaughlin, Uggen, and Blackstone 2017).

There are also legal costs, if there are formal charges, and financial settlements. Thus, it is in the best interests of companies to follow proper procedure to avoid lawsuits. It is incumbent upon employers to assess (and decrease) risk factors and to include proper training and community policies in orientation and department meetings. It is important to enforce these procedures if breaches are discovered and to discipline offenders immediately.

When there are significant power differentials between the workers and the employers, there is a high risk of victimization and a low likelihood of reporting.

EXAMPLES OF HARASSMENT IN FACTORY SETTINGS

The Mattress Factory is a contemporary art museum and experimental artist lab located in Pittsburgh, Pennsylvania. In 2018, four current and former female employees filed a lawsuit alleging that the Mattress Factory discriminated against employees who engaged in activities as a group to protect themselves from sexual harassment that dated back to as early as 2012. They were confronted with hostility, intimidation, and threats of losing their jobs after they voiced concerns about the museum's response to multiple reports of sexual harassment and assaults allegedly inflicted by a coworker who no longer worked there. The National Labor Relations Board (NLRB) investigated, and an internal probe by the nonprofit board that oversaw the museum led to a settlement in December 2018 that included policy changes and new training requirements. After the NLRB complaint, the company acknowledged that some of the procedures that were in place were inadequate and that its response to the complaint was ineffective.

Because of this case, the museum made plans to hire an in-house human resources officer to prevent situations like this one from happening again or to at least immediately intervene if a situation occurred. It also established clear and direct policies and procedures that meet the Equal Employment Opportunity

Commission (EEOC) requirements and took advice from legal counsel as well as recommendations from the charging parties. One of the suggestions that will be utilized is additional training for all employees and management on these new policies. The Mattress Factory art museum did reach a settlement with the former and current employees who accused supervisors of downplaying their concerns and retaliating against them.

Elsewhere, incidents of harassment directed at minority employees at a manufacturing plant in Kansas City, Missouri, rocked the Harley-Davidson motorcycle company. Most of the harassment and discrimination—and at least one assault—was focused on racial minorities and employees of Jewish descent. Swastikas and nooses were posted in the plant, and racial epithets were used. These deplorable workplace conditions were revealed when contract workers with Syncreon.US Inc., who had been contracted out to the Harley-Davidson plant, issued formal complaints about their treatment. Although Harley-Davidson said it does not tolerate any form of harassment or discrimination and insisted that it maintained well-established processes for employees to report harassment, victims said that when the offenses were reported, images were left up for days before being covered. They also reported that management claimed that they were investigating the incidents, but no disciplinary measures were ever handed down to the perpetrators. Yet another victim, who was a union representative for the steelworkers at the plant for many years before she was fired, said that each time she tried to file a grievance, she had difficulty. An investigation was subsequently launched by the company at the request of the NAACP civil rights organization to determine whether her treatment was an isolated incident or part of the culture at Harley-Davidson.

The car and truck industry is another type of work dominated by males in which sexual harassment allegations have been made. At the Ford Dearborn Truck Plant, a victim sued the company in November 2018 because of the behavior of her male supervisor, alleging that it was so persistent that it gave her PTSD (posttraumatic stress disorder). She said he sexually harassed her and showed her photos of a sexual encounter he had had with a female coworker at the plant. She also said he groped her and that he would ask her to expose her breasts while he was teaching her and assessing her performance. He told her he wanted to have sex with her and sent her sexually suggestive and inappropriate texts as well as a picture of his genitals and pictures of himself in his underwear.

When the victim complained, her manager told her to "just" have sex with him to get it done with. Not only was her situation not taken seriously, but she was treated poorly. Her cell phone was confiscated by human resources, even though she found out that her supervisor refused to give his up. Unfortunately, the problem at the Dearborn location was not an isolated incident at Ford assembly plants. There were complaints in 2017 that women in the company's Chicago Assembly Plant experienced similar victimization. A few women complained that not only were they victims of sexual harassment but also that their complaints were met with hostility and that management did not handle their complaints correctly.

Since these incidents, the CEO of Ford has stated that the company does not tolerate sexual harassment or discrimination, and he played a video on a loop in all U.S. plants denouncing sexual harassment. Further, the United Auto Workers (UAW) stated that there is no place for discrimination in the workforce, and that its goal is to make all its members feel safe. To accomplish this, the UAW has created a number of ways for members to address allegations of discrimination, including through its civil rights committee, procedures in the UAW Constitution, the grievance process, and other workplace mechanisms.

In another factory, Atlantic Caps Fisheries, in Fall River, Massachusetts, reached a $675,00 settlement with workers in 2019. Five Spanish women who packed shellfish at the company made allegations about *quid pro quo* ("this for that") sexual harassment that they endured from 2013 to 2019. (In a sexual harassment context, quid pro quo means that a supervisor might have said that if an employee agrees to perform a sexual act, the employee will get a better schedule or different perks associated with the job.) In one case, a supervisor rubbed his crotch against a victim while she packed shellfish. Since the settlement, there have been efforts to improve conditions, and improved training to combat sexual harassment was instituted at the plant.

In the construction industry, another male-dominated field, there are similar problems. As positions are not permanent, a layoff might be used as a way to retaliate against a victim. The work involves heavy objects and equipment, and women might feel the need to overcompensate to prove their worth. This can affect their safety (as might the lack of support from male coworkers). Besides the physical risk, if female employees feel uncomfortable, they may become distracted or unable to focus. To protect victims (and run a company correctly), industries need to have an inclusive workforce and understand what circumstances create a working environment where females (or those of minority status) are marginalized or intimidated. This is critical for any industry, because no matter where the sexual harassment occurs, it is a violation of Title VII of the Civil Rights Act.

HARASSMENT IN FACTORIES OVERSEAS

Garment factories are an example of where a high level of victimization can occur. Those who work in this industry may be undocumented and will not bring charges for fear of deportation. According to Human Rights Watch (HRW), sexual intimidation is extremely common in clothing factories, particularly in "Bangladesh, Cambodia, India and Pakistan, where many international fashion brands have their apparel manufactured." According to HRW, fifty-nine countries in the world "have no laws at all against sexual intimidation at work, [and] even where such regulations do exist (like in Pakistan and India), many employees are not aware of their rights, or they are afraid of retaliations" (Human Rights Watch 2019).

Unfortunately, the sexual harassment may even extend beyond the workplace itself. For example, one female textile worker in India (who was cited in the report) said her supervisor called her after work hours to request sexual favors. If she complied, he promised her lighter work and more breaks. Instead, she complained about his behavior to her Human Resources Department, who told her to learn to deal with it.

REFORMS

For factory and manufacturing industries to ensure that their workplaces are harassment free, there needs to be collaboration and clear-cut policies, both public and private. Strategies need to be in place that are equitable to all workers, and the goals must be to protect the most vulnerable workers and train the supervisors and bystanders. It is suggested that all industries establish clear steps that must be taken when there is a complaint (who to report to as a victim or as a witness) on its processing, investigating, and disciplinary process. One newer tactic has been the Be That One Guy campaign, which challenges sexism and addresses workplace hazing, harassment, and discrimination. Another is the bystander intervention training, Green Dot, and then the Respectful Workplace Training sponsored by the EEOC.

To be effective, the language concerning sexual harassment policies must be clear and understandable. There should be no confusion on what qualifies as sexual harassment, as it can be any unwelcome sexual advance (verbal or physical) or any behavior that interferes with one doing his or her job. Policies must be clear to prevent it from happening and to effectively deal with it if it does happen. The workplace supervisors need to periodically investigate the workplace setting to examine whether there is violence and intimidation, and steps should be taken to investigate a company's buying practices as well. The bottom line is that the safety and security for all victims must be upheld and without fear of retaliation.

Gina Robertiello

See also: Agriculture Industry; Equal Employment Opportunity Commission; Hostile Work Environment; Quid Pro Quo; Retaliation; Stalking; Title VII of the Civil Rights Act of 1964

Further Reading

Coalition of the Immokalee Workers. 2018. "'A Movement, Not a Moment': Lessons from the Fair Food Program for the Growing Fight against Sexual Harassment and Assault in the Workplace." January 2. Accessed September 19, 2018. http://ciw -online.org/blog/2018/01/in-these-times-sexual-harassment/.

Durana, A., A. Lenhart, R. Miller, B. Schulte, and E. Weingarten. 2018. *Sexual Harassment: A Severe and Pervasive Problem.* Washington, DC: New America Foundation. Accessed September 26, 2018. https://www.newamerica.org/better-life-lab /reports/sexual-harassment-severe-and-pervasive-problem/summary-of-findings.

Feldblum, C., and V. Lipnic. 2016. *EEOC Select Task Force on the Study of Harassment in the Workplace: Report of Co-Chairs Chai R. Feldblum & Victoria A. Lipnic.* https://www.eeoc.gov/eeoc/task_force/harassment/.

Fernández Campbell, A. 2018. "Housekeepers and Nannies Have No Protection from Sexual Harassment under Federal Law." *Vox.* https://www.vox.com/2018/4/26 /17275708/housekeepers-nannies-sexual-harassment-laws.

Fitzgerald, L. F., and L. M. Cortina. 2017. "Sexual Harassment in Work Organizations: A View from the 21st Century." In *Handbook of the Psychology of Women*, edited by C. B Travis and K. W. White, 1–12. Washington, DC: American Psychological Association. http://www.apa.org/pubs/books/4311534.aspx.

Frye, J, 2017. "Not Just for the Rich and Famous." Center for American Progress, November 20. https://www.americanprogress.org/issues/women/news/2017/11/20/443139/not-just-rich-famous/.

Hegewisch, A., and B. O'Farrell. 2015. *Women in the Construction Trades: Earnings, Workplace Discrimination, and the Promise of Green Jobs: Findings from the IWPR Tradeswomen Survey.* Washington, DC: Institute for Women's Policy Research.

Human Rights Watch. 2019. "Combating Sexual Harassment in the Garment Industry." February 12. https://www.hrw.org/news/2019/02/12/combating-sexual-harassment-garment-industry#.

McLaughlin, H., C. Uggen, and A. Blackstone. 2017. "The Economic and Career Effects of Sexual Harassment on Working Women." *Gender and Society* 31(3): 333–358.

Sugerman, L. 2018. "#MeToo in Traditionally Male-Dominated Occupations: Preventing and Addressing Sexual Harassment." Chicago Women in the Trades, June. http://womensequitycenter.org/wp-content/uploads/2017/10/CWIT-MeToo-in-Male-Dominated-Jobs-003.pdf.

Yeung, B. 2015. "Rape on the Night Shift: Under the Cover of Darkness, Female Janitors Face Rape and Assault." *Frontline*, June 23. https://www.pbs.org/wgbh/frontline/article/rape-on-the-night-shift/.

Faragher v. City of Boca Raton (1998)

In *Faragher v. Boca Raton* 524 U.S. 775 (1998), the U.S Supreme Court decided on whether an employer may be held liable under Title VII of the Civil Rights Act of 1964 for the actions of supervisory employees whose sexual harassment of subordinates create a hostile work environment, thus resulting in employment discrimination. The plaintiff in the case, Beth Ann Faragher, was one of three female ocean lifeguards in a squad of about forty-five members employed by the city of Boca Raton, Florida. Though proficient and capable, these female lifeguards were constantly subjected to sexual harassment by two male supervisors. The supervisors made sexually related jokes and lewd comments about their physical appearance. They also used physical gestures to mimic the act of oral sex. Faragher was also physically tackled by one of the supervisors, who said he would have sex with her in a minute but for the size and shape of her breasts. The other supervisor grabbed, touched, and stroked various body parts of Faragher and the other female lifeguards. Faragher reported these incidents to a supervisor, only to be advised to keep quiet or risk losing her job or even greater levels of harassment.

Faragher resigned and later sued, claiming that the conduct of the supervisors produced a sexually hostile work environment that resulted in employment discrimination and violated her rights under Title VII of the Civil Rights Act of 1964. She also claimed that she was never given a copy of the city's sexual harassment policy. The district court found that the city should be held liable for the supervisors' conduct that created a hostile work environment resulting in employment discrimination.

The U.S. Court of Appeals for the Eleventh Circuit, however, reversed the trial court's decision. It held that the city had no actual knowledge of the harassment, that the supervisors were not acting within the scope of their employment, and that knowledge of the harassing conduct could not be imputed to the city. As a result of these factors, the city could not be held liable for negligence in failing to prevent the actions of the supervisors.

In a majority decision, the U.S. Supreme Court rejected the appeals court's decision. The Supreme Court held that an employer is vicariously liable under Title VII of the Civil Rights Act of 1964 for actionable discrimination caused by supervisors subject to an affirmative defense based on the reasonableness of the employer's and plaintiff's conduct. According to the court, the City of Boca Raton totally failed to disseminate its policy against sexual harassment among the employees. The court also found that officials made no attempt to keep track of the conduct of supervisors. Hence, it was held as a matter of law that the city could not be found to have exercised reasonable care to prevent the supervisors' harassing conduct.

Some scholars question whether the standard in *Faragher* is sufficient to reduce workplace discrimination, arguing that the existing standards of affirmative defense are flawed and need to be updated (Medina 2017). They assert that the defense holds a potential loophole for employers to avoid liability because the requirements for affirmative defense are not specific. Sexual harassment laws must specify requirements for employers to train employees as well as set and observe procedures for grievance and disciplinary actions to claim affirmative defense and be absolved of vicarious liability for the discriminatory actions of employees.

Alaba Oludare and Jude L. Jokwi Lenjo

See also: Equal Employment Opportunity Commission; *Harris v. Forklift Systems*; *Meritor Savings Bank v. Vinson*

Further Readings

Faragher, B. A. 2004. "*Faragher v. City of Boca Raton*: A Personal Account of a Sexual Discrimination Plaintiff." *Hofstra Labor and Employment Law Journal* 22: 417.

Faragher v. City of Boca Raton. n.d. Oyez. Accessed December 21, 2018. https://www .oyez.org/cases/1997/97-282.

Medina, K. F. 2017. "Workplace Discrimination and the Inefficiency of the Ellerth/Faragher Defense." *Brigham Young University Prelaw Review* 31(1), article 8.

U.S. Equal Employment Opportunity Commission. 1999. "Enforcement Guidance on Vicarious Employer Liability for Unlawful Harassment by Supervisors." Accessed December 21, 2018. https://www.eeoc.gov/policy/docs/harassment.html.

Faragher-Ellerth Defense

The Faragher-Ellerth defense is an affirmative defense against harassment claims under Title VII of the Civil Rights Act of 1964 that makes it unlawful to discriminate against a job applicant or employee based on the person's race, color, religion, sex, or national origin. Pertaining to sexual harassment, there are generally two categories: quid pro quo harassment and a hostile work environment claim. Quid pro quo harassment is when an employer (supervisor or superior) conditions an employee's job status or takes a tangible employment action based on an employee's submission to harassing actions of a supervisor. A hostile work environment occurs when an employee is severely or pervasively harassed by a supervisor, contributing to a "hostile" workplace, but the supervisor takes no action against an employee. There are two U.S. Supreme Court decisions, *Faragher v. City of Boca Raton* and *Burlington Industries, Inc. v. Ellerth*, both of which were handed down in 1998, that established the basis for the Faragher-Ellerth defense.

In *Faragher v. City of Boca Raton*, Beth Ann Faragher, the plaintiff, attended college and worked during the summer as a lifeguard for the Marine Safely Section of the Parks and Recreation Department in the City of Boca Raton, Florida. She claimed that from 1985 to 1990, when she was employed as a lifeguard, she and other women worked in "a hostile work environment." Faragher's immediate supervisors were Bill Terry, David Silverman, and Robert Gordon. In June 1990, Faragher resigned, accusing Terry, Silverman, and Golden of creating a "hostile work environment." Two years later, Faragher took action against Terry, Silverman, and the City of Boca Raton. Faragher claimed under Title VII, 42 U.S.C. Section 1983, and Florida law that Terry and Silverman specifically created a "sexually hostile atmosphere" by committing unwanted gestures (i.e., unwanted and offensive touching) and making offensive and lewd remarks toward her and other women. For example, according to Faragher, Terry said that he would never promote a woman to the rank of lieutenant, and Silverman stated, "Date me or clean the toilets for a year."

In the case of *Burlington Industries, Inc. v. Ellerth*, Kimberly Ellerth, the plaintiff, quit her employment in June 1994 after working as a salesperson for Burlington Industries, Inc., for about a year and three months because of a hostile work environment. Ellerth alleged that she had been subjected to constant sexual harassment in the form of offensive remarks and gestures by Ted Slowik, who was one of her supervisors and had the authority to hire and promote employees. Ellerth recounted at least three incidents when Slowik's comments could have been taken as threats to deny her tangible job benefits. Ellerth did not accept any advances made by Slowik, and she was nonetheless promoted. Therefore, the court held that she did not suffer "tangible retaliation." Ellerth never reported Slowik's advances toward her to anyone in authority. Also, she did not adhere to the harassment policy in place by Burlington Industries, Inc. Ellerth knew the company had a sexual harassment policy, but she chose not to inform her supervisors or other authority figures regarding Slowik's conduct because her husband advised her not to say anything to anyone. He thought it would jeopardize her job.

The U.S. Supreme Court rulings on the abovementioned cases established the Faragher-Ellerth affirmative defense that is used by employers to defend against employees who file claims of hostile work environment sexual harassment acts committed by members of management (supervisors or other superiors). The court ruled in both *Faragher* and *Ellerth* that if supervisors or superiors create a sexually hostile work environment that results in a tangible employment action against the employee, such as termination, demotion, or failure to promote, the employer is vicariously liable for the behavior of the offending supervisor. The court's rationale was that when a supervisor uses his or her workplace authority to take an action against the employee, the supervisor acts as the agent of the employer.

When an employee suffers no tangible employment action, as in *Burlington Industries, Inc. v. Ellerth*, the court established a different standard of liability. In such a case, an employer may not be liable under the Faragher-Ellerth affirmative defense. Faragher-Ellerth established a two-pronged affirmative defense. First, the employer must show that a harassment policy exists and that complaint procedures are in place for employees to follow to report alleged behavior that may constitutes harassment. The second prong of the affirmative defense, which focuses on the harassment policy, requires that the employer proves "that the plaintiff employee unreasonably failed to take advantage of any preventive or corrective opportunities provided by the employer or to avoid harm otherwise."

However, the court also ruled that if the employee fails to follow the complaint procedures established by the employer, that is enough to show the unreasonable behavior of the employee. The court also ruled that the employer can present other evidence to support the claim of the employee's unreasonableness, but it did not specifically describe what the evidence may entail; the employer must also be in compliance with its own established procedural process for complaints and promptly investigate and terminate unwanted behavior (harassment) committed by its supervisors. The employer must also provide periodic training on the established harassment policy. Establishing such standards constitutes that the employer has exercised reasonable care to prevent all sexual harassment.

Rochelle McGee-Cobbs

See also: Faragher v. City of Boca Raton; Hostile Work Environment; Quid Pro Quo; Title VII of the Civil Rights Act of 1964

Further Reading

Cornell University Law School. 2018a. "Supreme Court of the United States: *Burlington Industries, Inc. v. Ellerth*." Accessed April 13, 2019. https://www.law.cornell.edu/supct/html/97-569.ZS.html.

Cornell University Law School. 2018b. "Supreme Court of the United States: *Faragher v. City of Boca Raton*." Accessed April 13, 2019. https://www.law.cornell.edu/supct/html/97-282.ZO.html.

Garrison, C. W. 2012. "Once Is Enough: The Need to Apply the Full Ellerth/Faragher Affirmative Defense in Single Incident and Incipient Hostile Work Environment Sexual Harassment Claims." *Catholic University Law Review* 61(4), article 5. Accessed April 13, 2019. https://scholarship.law.edu/lawreview/vol61/iss4/5/.

Henry, A. M. 1999. "Employer and Employee Reasonableness Regarding Retaliation under the Ellerth/Faragher Affirmative Defense." *University of Chicago Legal Forum* 1999(1), article 14. Accessed April 14, 2019. https://chicagounbound.uchicago.edu/uclf/vol1999/iss1/14/.

Farley, Lin (1942–)

American journalist and feminist activist Lin Farley was born December 14, 1942, to working-class parents and was raised in New Jersey. Farley received a journalism scholarship from the University of Southern California and went to work for the Associated Press in New York (1973), right before she started teaching at

Cornell University. Lin returned to school in the 1980s and earned a master's in psychology and a PhD in Eastern psychology in 1993 from the California Institute of Integral Studies.

In 1974, Cornell University, which was the first American university to teach a course in women's studies, hired Farley to teach a course on women in the workplace. Farley quickly learned that men were making unwanted sexual advances toward women at this liberal university. Farley's students felt safe in her class, however, and they disclosed a variety of incidents of sexual harassment and intimidation that they had experienced or seen in the workplace and at the university. In 1975, Carmita Wood, a staff member of the Physics Department, confided in Farley that her well-known boss had been subjecting her to unwanted kissing and groping and other forms of harassment for several years. Wood's mental and physical health had suffered, and she eventually quit her job. When she filed for unemployment, her claim was denied. She told Farley she wanted justice.

Farley and a few of her feminist colleagues gathered to discuss what to call these experiences. They knew that if they wanted it to stop, it needed to be named, defined, and consistent. They settled on the term *sexual harassment*. The women also formed the group Working Women United (WWU) to bring together women from different organizations to discuss how to combat sexual harassment. Working Women United started organizing rallies on university campuses to educate more women and explain their rights in the workplace. Farley was invited to testify at the New York City Human Rights Commission Hearings on Women and Work in April 1975; this was the first time the term *sexual harassment* was used and defined in a public space. Farley described the term to encompass unwanted sexual advances toward women by their male bosses, supervisors, or managers. Farley further developed the concept to include women who were hired because they were pretty or not hired because they were not pretty and also to include women whose job security hinged on their bosses' satisfaction often including sexual companionship rather than the quality of their work. Farley's testimony was reported by the *New York Times* and was soon being discussed across the country.

Farley and her colleagues believed that their efforts to publicize the problem of sexual harassment had the potential to change the way women were treated in the workplace. The Equal Employment Opportunity Commission (EEOC) created guidelines for sexual harassment lawsuits, and women began suing employers. Susan Meyer and Karen Sauvigne, colleagues of Farley's and organizers of WWU, developed a survey on sexual harassment. In 1976, *Redbook* published their disturbing findings, including the fact that 80 percent of respondents reported suffering sexual harassment on the job.

In 1978, Farley published her book *Sexual Shakedown: The Sexual Harassment of Women on the Job.* The book was well received by some and criticized by others. A major criticism of the book focused on Farley's assertion that an integrated workplace and women unions would solve the problem. Farley's theory was that patriarchy was threatened by women in the workplace, and men's sexual harassment was a method used to protect the patriarchy. Farley believed that sexual harassment would stop when women took control of their work environments using collective bargaining and striking.

After writing her 1978 book, Farley went on to earn an MA and PhD. In 1981, she collaborated on a thirty-three-minute documentary, *The Workplace Hustle*; she was a consultant and also appeared in the film. She took a break from her research and moved to China, where she worked with the *Free China Journal* for a few years. She also began writing a book about caring for her aging parents.

In 2017, Farley wrote an op-ed in the *New York Times* in which she acknowledged that despite growing recognition of sexual harassment as a significant social problem and the growth of the feminist movement in the United States, many American workplaces had not changed for women like she had hoped. Farley admitted that sexual harassment as a term was successful; companies wrote policies and created training programs to quash any potential sexual harassment. However, the culture in the workplace was not transformed in the way the feminists in the 1970s believed it would or should. Sexual harassment should not be about policies and training, she wrote, but rather a cultural shift.

Lisa Bell Holleran

See also: Equal Employment Opportunity Commission; Wood, Carmita

Further Reading

Blakemore, E. 2018. "Until 1975, 'Sexual Harassment' Was the Menace with No Name." History.com. Accessed February 2019. https://web.unican.es/unidades/igualdad /SiteAssets/guia-de-recursos/acoso/Acoso%20Sexual_History.pdf.

Cohen, S. 2016. "A Brief History of Sexual Harassment in America before Anita Hill." *Time*, April 11. Accessed February 21, 2020. http://time.com/4286575/sexual -harassment-before-anita-hill/.

Farley, L. 1978. *Sexual Shakedown: The Sexual Harassment of Women on the Job*. New York: McGraw-Hill.

Farley, L. 2017. "I Coined the Term 'Sexual Harassment.' Corporations Stole It." *New York Times*, October 18.

Gertner, N. 1980. Book Review of Sexual Shakedown: The Sexual Harassment of Women on the Job. *Harvard Women's Law Journal* 3: 205–207.

Fashion Industry

Sexual harassment has been a problem in the fashion industry since its earliest days. The fashion industry revolves around beauty and sex and is a predominantly male-run industry. It is also competitive and filled with eager, young, vulnerable models intent on securing a place in the fashion world. Manipulation, distrust, and sexual harassment are not uncommon between members of the fashion industry, but it is rarely discussed because of the wealthy, powerful, and high-profile leaders of the industry. These conditions provide a ripe environment for inappropriate behavior.

Models are more likely to experience sexual harassment in the workplace at the beginning of their careers, when they are not well known and are still learning about the industry and how it operates. This makes them open targets for abuse by those in positions of authority. Models who experience sexual abuse or harassment at this stage often do not report it because they do not want to jeopardize their careers. Moreover, it is not uncommon for a model to not know where she can seek help.

Sexual harassment of models in the fashion industry can take place at any time, including photoshoots, fittings, interviews, and even during fashion shows. Models have been taught that sexual harassment is common in their field of work, and they work toward coping with this mistreatment by ignoring the sexual advances made toward them.

Before his death, Karl Lagerfeld, a fashion designer and photographer, revealed that being sexually harassed comes along with being part of the fashion industry and that if you cannot handle that, then it is not the industry for you.

Some models who have made sexual harassment accusations over the years have seen their careers ruined. As a result, aspiring and established models alike often keep quiet if they are faced with sexual harassment because of the fear that speaking out could ruin what they have worked for.

Critics assert that sexual harassment has become normalized in the fashion industry and that the trend toward freelance modeling—in which models work without agents or other representation—has created even more opportunities for unscrupulous people to engage in harassing behavior. Freelancing leaves young models in situations where they are alone with people who have greater clout in the industry, a dynamic that makes it easier for them to be taken advantage of. One of the biggest reasons why this behavior continues to occur in the industry is that many young models will not report its occurrence. They do not want to "rock the boat." They will endure being harassed if it means that they will get the job they desire. This teaches more and more young men and women to be okay with this kind of behavior because they see the well-known models who have been successful and know that many are likely to have experienced harassment, abuse, or other inappropriate behavior but were unwilling to speak up about the issue or report their situation to anyone in order to get ahead.

In recent years, members of the fashion industry have been willing to reveal their experiences with sexual harassment. When the #MeToo Movement shone a spotlight on issues of sexual harassment and sexism in American workplaces in 2017, many famous models finally came forward and talked about the sexual harassment they had endured over the years from stylists, photographers, and other fashion professionals.

One model that broke her silence about the sexual harassment she endured as a young model was Kate Upton. In an interview with *Time*, she spoke about times she was groped by photographers and kissed without permission by designers and stylists. Upton also opened up about her fears of losing her job because of sharing her story.

Becoming a model means that your face and body will be recognized across numerous platforms, including print and online media. With so much prominence in media, many models fear that aspects of their personal lives will be leaked and linked together if they speak up about harassment they are facing. Whomever they speak out against may have leverage against them, including images and personal details about them that can be used for defamation and could ultimately end their career. While many of these fears exist in any workplace harassment situation, models are in the limelight, making it easier for information to leak—and for the resulting controversy to bring upheaval to their personal lives and careers.

The #MeToo Movement has been encouraging people to talk about the harassment they endured without fearing repercussions. Having more models and actresses speak up about what they have experienced has allowed changes to occur in the fashion industry. Regulations have already been set out to deny modeling work for those ages sixteen and under, and more brands are providing private changing areas for models and more protection for models in the workplace.

Sexual harassment will always exist in the fashion industry because not everyone is brave enough to tell the authorities about what they have experienced and not all authorities are willing to expose what complaints have been made. However, members of the fashion industry hope that reforms prompted by the #MeToo Movement and increased awareness of legal protections available to victims of harassment and abuse have the potential to dramatically decrease incidents of sexual harassment and misconduct throughout the industry.

Brianna Robertiello

See also: Burke, Tarana; Harvey Weinstein Scandal; #MeToo Movement; Objectification of Women; Social Media

Further Reading

Bernstein, J., V. Friedman, and M. Schneier. 2018. "Many Accusations, Few Apologies: Sexual Harassment Complaints Buffet the Fashion Industry." *New York Times*, March 4: 1–2.

Dockterman, E. 2018. "Kate Upton Shines a Light on Fashion's Biggest Problem with Her #MeToo Story." *Time International (Atlantic Edition)* 191(6): 18.

Dumenco, S. 2018. "When #MeToo Came into Fashion." Ad Age, March 20. https://adage.com/article/the-media-guy/metoo-fashion/312776.

Pressler, J., and A. Tsoulis-Reay. 2018. "Can Fashion Ever Be an Ethical Business? A Notorious Industry Gets Its #MeToo Moment. Sort of." *New York Magazine*, February 5. https://www.thecut.com/2018/02/will-fashion-have-a-metoo-moment.html.

Federal Express Sexual Harassment Scandal

On February 24, 2004, a federal jury awarded Marion Shaub, a former Federal Express truck driver, over $3 million in a case involving sexual harassment, a hostile work environment, and retaliation against Shaub when she complained to her supervisor about the treatment she was receiving.

Shaub was employed from 1997 to 2000 as the only female tractor trailer driver in a Federal Express facility near Harrisburg International Airport in Pennsylvania. During that period, her male coworkers engaged in frequent and severe verbal harassment. Much of the harassment was sexual in nature. Shaub was called derogatory names and subjected to offensive language. She was told that "women should be pregnant." Witnesses corroborated that in his efforts to distress and intimidate Shaub, one coworker engaged in a number of behaviors: grabbing his genitals in front of her, describing sex with his wife in coarse terms, and speculating on potential sexual intercourse he was going to have with Shaub and with other women. Shaub was told that she "looked like a porn star," and on another occasion, she was told by a male coworker that if she were his daughter, he "would abort her."

When Shaub complained of the sexual and verbal harassment to her supervisor in January 2000, the abuse escalated. Shaub soon found her truck was not being loaded at all by coworkers employed to do so. A coworker permitted a heavy package to collide with Shaub on a loading ramp. Shaub's truck was sabotaged, her brake cables cut, and the lines filled with dirt. She was then demoted to another job with lower hourly pay. Four months after her complaint, her driving route was put up for bid.

The Equal Employment Opportunity Commission (EEOC) sued on Shaub's behalf in 2002, with Shaub joining the suit as an intervenor two weeks later. The EEOC chose to pursue the Shaub case in part because hers was not the only significant sexual harassment allegation that had been lodged against the company. The Shaub case followed a similar case in which a Philadelphia jury awarded Kathleen Talbot-Lima, a Federal Express supervisor who had reported sexual harassment and was also retaliated against, $2.3 million, a settlement that was later renegotiated out of court.

The Shaub trial commenced in U.S. district court on February 9, 2004. The jury concluded that Shaub was not discriminated against on account of gender. However, it did find Federal Express liable for a hostile working environment, for retaliation against Shaub when she complained about her working conditions to management, and for intentional infliction of severe emotional distress.

Shaub received $2.5 million dollars in punitive damages, $391,000 in back and front pay, and $350,000 in compensation for the pain and suffering she had endured. The case is notable due to the size of the award and because the intentional infliction of emotional distress on the part of an employer is difficult to establish. Employers have been able to disparage employees publicly or deprive them of privileges without those sanctions rising to the level of "outrageous" found in the Shaub case. In her case, sexual harassment accompanied by retaliation was found by the jury to meet this high burden of proof.

Also notable in this case is its clear illustration of disparate treatment to exclude coworkers who integrated a formerly all-male job category. Workers who are judged by virtue of their gender, race, age, or other characteristics may receive messages that they are unwelcome in the workplace—messages that may be tolerated or even encouraged by lower management. Coworkers or supervisors engaged in this behavior, sometimes called "boundary heightening," will intensify their own behaviors in ways intended to ostracize and exclude the targeted employee. Such workplace bullying often includes the type of gendered sexual harassment experienced by Shaub.

Historically, business and management literature has been slow to recognize sexual harassment as motivated by power rather than "natural" (usually) male desire. Early business and management literature addressed the purported problem of lowered productivity and morale when workplace love affairs took place and ignored the issue of consent. Media accounts of sexual harassment as well as business and management literature seldom specifically describe victims' experiences. This refusal to clearly describe the pattern of behaviors involved, how they escalate when victims resist, and how devastating to victims they may be even though no direct sexual demands are made or sexual touching is experienced was documented in view of the large settlement that drew public interest in the Shaub case.

Cynthia Ninivaggi

See also: Equal Employment Opportunity Commission; Hostile Work Environment; Stalking

Further Reading

Equal Opportunity Employment Commission and Marion Shaub, Plaintiff/Intervenor *v. Federal Express Corporation*, Defendant. Civil Action No. 1:02-CV-1194. 537 F. Supp. 2d 700 (2005).

Scolforo, Mark. 2004. "3.2 Million Verdict for FedEx Driver Who Alleged Sexual Harassment." Associated Press State and Local Wire, February 25.

U.S. Equal Employment Opportunity Commission. 2004. "Federal Express to Pay over $3.2 Million to Female Truck Driver for Sex Discrimination, Retaliation." Press release, February 25. https://www.eeoc.gov/eeoc/newsroom/release/2-25-04.cfm.

Fine Arts

In the aftermath of the Harvey Weinstein scandal and the related #MeToo Movement, many sectors of American society long thought to be insulated from the scourge of sexual harassment have been found to have deep problems in that area as well. One such area is the fine arts, which was rocked in the late 2010s by allegations of sexual misconduct and assault against young artists, especially in the world of classical music.

Sexual harassment in the fine arts, as in any other workplace or social setting, may take the form of unwanted sexual advances or sexual comments, or it may exacerbate into sexual abuse or assault. Though this type of control is carried out sexually, it also controls an individual in other ways. People who are looking for career advancement are fearful that if they reject sexual advances or report sexual harassment, they will not receive roles they are auditioning for or will not have the favor of the producer, conductor, or others in positions of power.

Young artists across several venues have reported sexual harassment perpetrated by teachers, mentors, famed artists, and conductors. While empirical research on the topic of sexual harassment in the fine arts is limited, many journalistic outlets have found the problem to be widespread. In interviews conducted by the *Washington Post* over a six-month period in 2018, more than fifty classical musicians disclosed that they had been victims of sexual harassment. During the six-month period of interviews, musicians disclosed they had been subjected to sexual harassment such as unwanted sexual advances and offers of lessons in exchange for sexual favors. Additionally, many disclosed sexual assaults that had occurred in dressing rooms and inappropriate touching during lessons.

As an example, James Levine, once a famed Metropolitan Opera conductor, was fired in March 2018 after accusations of sexual abuse and harassment of musicians arose. Levine's alleged sexual abuse and harassment of young musicians spanned decades, beginning as early as 1968. Several alleged victims detailed abuse that had occurred at summer camps while they were as young as seventeen years old. They alleged that Levine had used his power as an accomplished conductor to sexually harass young musicians who were afraid of losing their careers. Levine's career ended amid credible evidence that he had sexually abused and harassed musicians for decades while he held the position of director of the Metropolitan Opera's young artists program.

William Preucil, a renowned violinist, concertmaster, and former instructor at the Cleveland Institute of Music, was accused of sexual harassment and assault by several women who were students of his from 1998 to 2007. Accusations against Preucil included requesting sexual favors for lessons, exposing himself, and forcing himself upon women who were afraid to reject him due to his prominent position in the music community. The youngest woman he allegedly sexually harassed claimed that she was seventeen years old at the time.

Another famed conductor, Charles Dutoit, was accused of sexual harassment or sexual assault by ten women in incidents spanning from 1985 to 2010. In a particularly stunning account, one woman who was assaulted by Dutoit in his dressing room was told by the Boston Symphony Orchestra management that women are advised not to enter Dutoit's dressing room alone, as they had received previous complaints. This alleged incident was cited as evidence that such outrageous behavior, when it came from men in positions of power, was accepted in the classical music community.

Daniel Lipton, formerly the conductor of several prestigious orchestras, was also accused by numerous women of sexual harassment and assault that spanned decades in two countries. In 2017, Opera Tampa bought out his contract (a way of letting him go) because of his rumored behavior toward women under his direction. Allegations ranged from inappropriate comments to sexual assault.

Reports of sexual harassment also rocked other sectors of the fine arts world in the late 2010s. For example, renowned painter and photographer Chuck Close was accused of sexual misconduct and harassment by several women in late 2017 and 2018. They accused Close of asking them to serve as nude models for his work and then making lewd comments to them. Most of the women who accused Close of sexual harassment were student interns and aspiring artists who had once admired Close. The controversy over the allegations—for which Close later apologized—led the National Gallery of Art to cancel a planned exhibition of his work that had been scheduled to open in May 2018.

Melissa Inglis

See also: Authority Figures; Casting Couch; Harvey Weinstein Scandal; #MeToo Movement

Further Reading
Cooper, M. 2018. "James Levine's Final Act at the Met Ends in Disgrace." *New York Times*, March 12. Accessed February 11, 2019. https://www.nytimes.com/2018/03/12/arts/music/james-levine-metropolitan-opera.html.

Lonsway, K., A., and W. Patrick. 2018. "Sexual Harassment and Sexual Assault: Understanding the Distinctions and Intersections." *Sexual Assault Report* 21(6): 85–95.

Midgette, A., and P. McGlone. 2018. "Assaults in Dressing Rooms. Groping during Lessons. Classical Musicians Reveal a Profession Rife with Harassment." *Washington Post*, July 26.

Pogrebin, R. 2017. "Chuck Close Apologizes after Accusations of Sexual Harassment." *New York Times*, December 20. Accessed February 11, 2019. https://www.nytimes.com/2017/12/20/arts/design/chuck-close-sexual-harassment.html.

Fowler, Susan J. (1991–)

Susan J. Fowler was raised in Yarnell, Arizona. Susan was homeschooled by her mother, and her father was a preacher and a salesman. Susan graduated from the University of Pennsylvania with a physics degree and worked as an engineer and writer. She made news headlines in February 2017 when she published a blog post that condemned her own employer, the popular ride-sharing service Uber, for maintaining a company culture rife with sexual harassment and gender discrimination against women.

Susan Fowler was hired by Uber, the ride-hailing service headquartered in San Francisco, California, in November 2015 as a site reliability engineer. Over the ensuing months, however, she became a target of sexual harassment and found that her decision to report the issue was jeopardizing her career. In 2017, Fowler posted a blog entry of about three thousand words describing her "strange" and "slightly horrifying" experiences. Her blog post was shared many times throughout various news outlets and Twitter, and before long, Uber and its leadership were engulfed in controversy about their allegedly hostile actions and attitudes toward women. Specifically, Fowler's blog post led to outrage about how Travis Kalanick, the cofounder and chief executive officer (CEO) of Uber, ignored various reports of sexual harassment by employees of the company.

The blog post detailed a culture that was pervasively hostile to women in the workplace of Uber. During Fowler's first official day of work, her manager sent her messages on the company chat about wanting to have sex with women and emphasizing to Fowler that he was in an open relationship. She immediately reported the harassment to the company's Human Resources Department, only to be told that her harasser was a highly valued employee. Rather than punish or fire him, the company told Fowler that she should either find another department in Uber to work in or be prepared for her manager to give her a negative job performance review. Faced with these choices, Fowler changed teams within Uber. As the months passed, however, she learned that many other women working at Uber had been victims of sexual harassment. Fowler also learned that her harasser was doing the same to other women in the workplace and that neither human resources nor any supervisors were taking steps to protect women in the company. Fowler continued to press Uber management to make changes to end the sexism and sexual harassment riddling the company, but her efforts went nowhere. Instead, she started receiving negative job reviews for vague and unspecified "performance" issues.

After Fowler's blog post reached the news media, however, everything changed. "Her essay set into motion a series of events that ultimately resulted in the ouster of notoriously combative . . . Kalanick, as well as the termination of 20 or so employees who'd been accused of harassment or other issues," wrote journalist Johana Bhuiyan. "I feel a sense of relief, and a great deal of optimism for our future," Fowler told Bhuiyan. "It seems to me that this year, our country finally stood up and said that awful treatment of women will not be tolerated" (Bhuiyan 2017).

The blog post also led to a lawsuit targeting Travis Kalanick that was initiated by one of the company's leading investors as well as two separate internal investigations that confirmed Fowler's account. Her essay thus became a prominent part of the #MeToo Movement and helped inspire others who have faced sexual harassment in the business and tech industries.

Fowler's public profile rose to the point that she was offered several book and film deals. She was also named *Financial Time*'s Person of the Year in 2017 and made the cover of *Time Magazine's* Person of the Year issue that same year. In April 2017, Fowler left Uber to work at the company Stripe as editor in chief for a new magazine called *Increment*. A year later, she was hired away by the *New York Times* to write about high-tech issues and industries in Silicon Valley and around the world.

Angelo Brown

See also: Backlash against Allegations of Sexual Harassment and Assault; Health Effects; #MeToo Movement; Sexism; *Time Magazine* "Silence Breakers"

Further Reading

Bhuiyan, Johana. 2017. "With Just Her Words, Susan Fowler Brought Uber to Its Knees." Vox: Recode, December 6. Accessed January 16, 2020. https://www.vox.com/2017/12/6/16680602/susan-fowler-uber-engineer-recode-100-diversity-sexual-harassment.

Fowler, Susan. 2017. "Reflecting On One Very, Very Strange Year at Uber." *Susan Fowler* (blog), February 19. Accessed January 26, 2019. https://www.susanjfowler.com/blog/2017/2/19/reflecting-on-one-very-strange-year-at-uber/.

Hall, J. D., C. Palsson, and J. Price. 2018. "Is Uber a Substitute or Complement for Public Transit?" *Journal of Urban Economics* 108: 36–50.

Harris, Duchess, and Morris, Rebecca. 2018. *The Silence Breakers and the #Metoomovement*. Essential Library.

Levin, Sam. 2018. "Susan Fowler's Plan after Uber? Tear Down the System That Protects Harassers." *The Guardian*, April 11. Accessed January 26, 2019. https://www.theguardian.com/technology/2018/apr/11/susan-fowler-uber-interview-forced-arbitration-law/.

Franken, Al (1951–)

Al Franken is a well-known progressive figure in the worlds of both American politics and entertainment who reluctantly resigned his U.S. Senate seat in 2017 after sexual misconduct allegations from years before came to light.

Alan Stuart Franken was born in 1951 to Joseph and Phoebe Franken in New York City. His father was a printing salesman and his mother a real estate agent.

Both of his parents were Jewish. Franken graduated from Harvard College, where he majored in political science, with a bachelor of arts in 1973.

Franken came to prominence in the 1970s for his comedic performances and writing abilities on *Saturday Night Live* (*SNL*). He ultimately received numerous Emmy nominations and awards for producing and writing scripts for new characters on *SNL*. Franken also wrote several best-selling books in which he used comedy to criticize Republican president George W. Bush, media personality Rush Limbaugh, and other conservatives.

In the early 2000s, Franken hosted a liberal talk show on Air America Radio. He broadcast his final appearance in 2007, after which he announced his candidacy in 2008 for the U.S. Senate.

Franken was subsequently elected as the nominee for the Minnesota Democratic-Farmer-Labor Party, which is associated with the Democratic Party. However, Franken's Republican opponent, Norm Coleman, filed an appeal regarding absentee ballots, and the results of the election were not decided until 2009, after a Minnesota Supreme Court verdict dismissed Coleman's claims. Franken went on to be reelected in 2014 by defeating his Republican opponent, Mike McFadden. However, several years later, during the highly publicized #MeToo Movement, numerous elected officials were called to task for allegations of sexual misconduct, and an unexpected turn of events derailed Franken's career.

In November 2017, radio news personality Leeann Velez Tweeden alleged in an interview and blog post that Franken forcibly kissed her in 2006. The alleged incident took place while they were on a United Service Organizations (USO) tour in Iraq, Afghanistan, and Kuwait. The USO is a nonprofit organization that has provided entertainment for military personnel and their families since 1941. Franken had also been photographed with his open hands touching (or at least pretending to touch) Tweeden's breasts as she slept on a military airplane flight back to the United States. When the photograph was first made public, Franken claimed that it was supposed to be funny, but he admitted that it was not and apologized to Tweeden. He stated that he understood how she might have felt violated by his actions. Moreover, he requested and claimed that he would cooperate with an ethics investigation.

A few days after the Tweeden revelation, another woman, Lindsay Menz, claimed that, in 2010, while posing for a photo with Franken at a Minnesota State Fair, he allegedly touched her buttocks. Franken claimed he did not remember the incident but felt badly that Menz believed he had disrespected her. Four subsequent victims alleged incidents of groping and unwanted sexual advances against Franken during November 2017.

Some of Franken's colleagues in the U.S. Senate requested that he resign from his position. Complaints against Franken were forwarded to the Senate Ethics Committee for investigation. Nevertheless, in December 2017, Franken announced that he would resign from the Senate because he could no longer be an "effective senator" for the people of Minnesota. But he also insisted that some of the allegations made by his accusers were not true or reflected different memories of events than his own. He also reiterated in his defiant resignation announcement that he remained a strong supporter of women's rights and that sexual harassment and misogyny had no place in American society. Franken officially resigned on January 2, 2018.

Brian L. Royster

See also: Hostile Work Environment; #MeToo Movement

Further Reading

Ball, Molly. 2017. "Al Franken Is Not Sorry." *Time*, December 9. Accessed January 10, 2019. http://time.com/5057462/al-franken-resignation-sorry/.

Harding, Kate. 2017. "I'm a Feminist. I Study Rape Culture. And I Don't Want Al Franken to Resign." *Washington Post*, November 17. Accessed January 10, 2019. https://www.washingtonpost.com/news/posteverything/wp/2017/11/17/im-a-feminist-i-study-rape-culture-and-i-dont-want-al-franken-to-resign/.

McGann, Laura. 2018. "The Still-Raging Controversy over Al Franken's Resignation, Explained." Vox, May 21. Accessed January 10, 2019. https://www.vox.com/2018/5/21/17352230/al-franken-accusations-resignation-democrats-leann-tweeden-kirsten-gillibrand.

G

Gamergate

In August 2014, a quickly deleted blog post about a relationship gone sour went viral and turned from an attack on one person to an industry and a social media campaign that shined a stark light on questions about ethics in gaming and journalism, feminism, and the role of nontraditional gamers and games.

On August 16, 2014, gaming community member Eron Gjoni wrote a lengthy blog post about his ex-girlfriend, independent game developer Zoë Quinn. In his post, he accused Quinn of engaging in infidelity, emotional abuse, and unethical behavior (with gaming journalist Nathan Grayson) to obtain positive reviews about *Depression Quest*, a game that Quinn had designed. Quinn vehemently denied all these allegations, which were widely seen by journalists and most members of the industry as ugly character assassination from a spurned suitor. Nonetheless, Gjoni's post, which he eventually deleted, became a catalyst for an avalanche of misogynistic and threatening attacks against Quinn from a subset of the gaming community—heterosexual white males—that were already incensed about the perceived intrusion of more nontraditional gamers (i.e., women, people of color, and nonbinary individuals) into the industry.

Although Quinn was the original target of this anonymous online mob, over time, several other high-profile women involved in the gaming industry were targeted for their outspoken criticism of the primarily male gaming community. Harassment tactics included threatened rape and death threats against the women; the release of private information about them, such as the home addresses of the women and their friends and family (known a *doxing*); and the stalking of friends and family members.

Accounts vary about how one personal spat could have set off such a frenzy, but the general agreement is that the reaction was due to a perfect storm of events in a rapidly changing industry that was experiencing growth in the form of new ideas and new members. Gaming has progressed from playing Pac-Man in the local arcade to technologically sophisticated gaming systems and online multiplayer universes and from simple sketches to amazingly colorful and realistic artwork. The gaming industry pulled in $91.95 billion in sales in 2015 (Salter 2017). According to the Entertainment Software Association, over 155 million Americans play video games, and over 80 percent of American households have at least one gaming device. Of particular interest is the demographic profile of gamers, which was long been viewed as being dominated by young white males. Women are the most rapidly growing group of gamers. According to the PEW Research Center, 42 percent of females and 37 percent of males reported that they had a gaming console (such as an Xbox or PlayStation). Gaming has become so popular that the fifth edition of the *Diagnostic and Statistical Manual of Mental Disorders* (*DSM-5*) is even considering adding gaming as an addiction.

In this context, Quinn's game, *Depression Quest*, which had players go on a journey with a woman and her experiences with depression, was an example of the new generation of both games and gamers, which some credit as being the reason it (and she) was so easy to target. Once Gjoni's post went viral, several of her critics worked together to discredit Quinn and threaten her personal safety. This was exacerbated by the anonymous nature of the internet, with no one individual or group yet claiming responsibility for the many acts involved in the Gamergate scandal. Individuals used the internet, specifically sites such as Reddit, 4chan, and Twitter, to work together to terrorize Quinn and the other victims. Their efforts were originally termed a "quinnspiracy"; however, actor Adam Baldwin coined the hashtag #gamergate in a Twitter post supporting the harassment campaign against Quinn.

According to Twitter analytics, "in the first week, the hashtag was tweeted over 244,000 times. By November 2014, the hashtag had been tweeted just over 1.8 million times in the prior month, with an average of 50,000 tweets per day" (RandomMan 2014). At the time, there were few guidelines for law enforcement investigating online harassment, often due to jurisdictional issues, so police were not able to stop the abuse. The leaderless nature of the internet attacks exacerbated the problem, with internet trolls often using pseudonyms or creating fake accounts, with little hope of identifying the actual users. When websites such as 4chan attempted to put in place restrictions to end the attacks, users then moved to less supervised spaces, such as 8chan.

Although the Gamergate attacks originally started as an attack on Quinn and her game, it quickly pulled together several fractured groups into a bigger complaint about independent gamers and game designers. Many critics who were pro-Gamergate claimed that the attacks were primarily focused on the ethics of gaming, or lack thereof. They asserted that independent gamers were too close with journalists, which was negatively changing the industry. Proponents of a more inclusive gaming space were soon targeted as a result; these targets were most often women.

Such was the case for Brianna Wu, a fellow game developer. A pseudo Twitter handle was created entitled "Death to Brianna" that posted tweets threatening to brutally rape and kill her. On October 10, 2014, Wu's address and other personal information was posted on 8chan. The FBI eventually apprehended four gamers who had sent the threats. Those gamers claimed that the threats were not to be taken seriously, and no further action was taken. Media critic Anita Sarkeesian spoke up about the absurdity of Gamergate, describing it as a cynical fake controversy used to harass and marginalize women under the guise of protecting the gaming industry. She was also sent multiple death and rape threats (including threats to bomb her and those around her at events she spoke at) and was doxed (her personal information was searched for and published, with malicious intent).

Much of the Gamergate harassment took place on Twitter, which at the time did not have strong anti-harassment policies. After becoming embroiled in the scandal, Twitter made changes to its terms of service and to its platform to make blocking accounts more user-friendly and the process of reporting abuse much easier. Before Gamergate, reporting harassment was difficult, which made users frustrated and deterred some from continuing with the process. Twitter also banned pornographic images, specifically revenge porn. Lastly, the company banned hate speech that was threatening or promoted violence based on demographic or other factors, such as race, gender, or sexuality. As a result of Gamergate, several female game designers and game critics did back out of the industry. Quinn is still in the gaming community, however. She has written a book and created a nonprofit to help other victims of online harassment.

Ellen Repeta, Bryan M. Blaylock, and Nadine Marie Connell

See also: Objectification of Women; Quinn, Zoë; Sarkeesian, Anita

Further Reading

Anderson, M. 2015. "The Demographics of Device Ownership." Pew Research Center, October 29. http://www.pewinternet.org/2015/10/29/the-demographics-of-device -ownership/.

Entertainment Software Association. 2015. "2015 Sales, Demographic and Usage Data: Essential Facts about the Computer and Video Game Industry." https://www .coursehero.com/file/14808553/essential-facts-about-the-video-game-industry-2015/.

RandomMan. 2014. "Gamergate." https://knowyourmeme.com/memes/events/gamergate.

Salter, M. 2017. "Gamergate and the Subpolitics of Abuse in Online Publics." In *Crime, Justice and Social Media*, edited by Michael Salter. New York: Routledge.

Gelser, Sara (1973–)

Sara Gelser is a Democratic politician in Oregon who has been influential in setting an example for female lawmakers and public officials to stand up and discuss their experiences with sexual harassment. Born on December 20, 1973, Gelser earned a BA in history and education from Earlham College and a master's degree from Oregon State University. She was a Council on State Governments Henry Toll Fellow, a Marshall Memorial Fellow, and a participant in an American Council of Young Political Leaders international exchange program. She is also the mother of five children.

Sexual harassment is evident and has come under increased scrutiny in many specific workplaces as well as American society in general. However, it was not until Gelser reported her experiences that the problem of sexual harassment in state legislatures and the U.S. Congress received much notice. Gelser claimed that when she was a young, elected member of the Oregon State Legislature, representing District 8, fellow legislator Jeff Kruse touched her inappropriately. She filed a formal complaint in 2017 after an informal complaint to the legislative human resources office appeared to go unnoticed. Her complaint detailed incidents in both the state House of Representatives and state Senate (Gelser moved from the House to the Senate in 2014) during legislative sessions in 2011, 2013, 2015, 2016, and 2017. Senator Kruse continued his advances even after it was brought to his attention that Gelser did not want him to approach her. Gelser went through efforts to avoid Kruse, such as taking the stairs to her office so that she would not encounter him in elevators, avoiding committees where he was a member, and forbidding her female staff to go to his office alone.

A state investigation found "substantial evidence" of sexual harassment at the Oregon State Capitol and determined that the legislature did not take appropriate action to stop it. The findings were released by the Bureau of Labor and Industries in February 2019, more than a year after Gelser filed a formal complaint against Kruse. Kruse resigned in 2018 but denied the allegations against him. In the findings, documents showed that after Gelser came forward, other senators retaliated. Senate president Peter Courtney was overheard yelling at her when she pointed out that it was his job to enforce policy.

The investigation supported Gelser's claims and the claims of harassment and abuse that had been made by other employees. The documents stated that the legislature failed to take immediate and appropriate corrective action, which led other victims of harassment to conclude that the risk of reporting harassment at the capitol was "too great." The investigation showed that those victims experienced a fear of retaliation for coming forward and that there was no confidence in the processes in place to protect them. Investigators also found substantial evidence of unlawful employment practices by the state assembly over several years. Her formal complaint triggered the public investigation into the allegations of the many women who had accused Kruse of similar behavior. Following Gelser's claim, dozens of women came forth with accusations of sexual harassment by members of the lawmaking body. A culture of harassment existed in the very place where laws are made to prevent harassment. Gelser's persistence paved the way for the next generation of women. She stated, "This is really the (start) of a culture change" (Zacharek, Dockterman, and Edwards 2017).

The Oregon legislature ultimately reached a settlement with the state Bureau of Labor and Industries and eight women who had alleged sexual harassment. The women received a combined $1.1 million, the largest settlement for workplace harassment cases in the United States. This settlement also required the legislature to implement a new reporting system to handle complaints of workplace harassment as well as increased sexual harassment training for lawmakers and staff.

Tara A. Garrison

See also: Congress; Hostile Work Environment; *Time Magazine* "Silence Breakers"; Workplace Gender Diversity

Further Reading

Dake, L. 2017. "Oregon State Senator Calls for Public Investigation, Says 15 Other Women Inappropriately Touched by Kruse." OPB, November 15. https://www.opb.org/news/article/oregon-sexual-harassment-sara-gelser-jeff-kruse-formal-complaint/.

KGW8 News. 2017. "Oregon Sen. Sara Gelser One of Time Magazine's 'Silence Breakers.'" December 6. https://www.kgw.com/article/news/politics/oregon-sen-sara-gelser-one-of-time-magazines-silence-breakers/283-497439963.

Zacharek, S., E. Dockterman, and H. S. Edwards. 2017. "Time Person of the Year 2017: The Silence Breakers." *Time*, December 17. https://time.com/time-person-of-the-year-2017-silence-breakers/.

Gender Competency

The workplace may serve as an excellent laboratory for the analysis of gender-oriented behaviors. As most of the sensational episodes of sexual harassment revealed in the opening months of the #MeToo Movement (Matt Lauer, Harvey Weinstein, Bill O'Reilly, and so on) occurred in the workplace, it may be best to examine the subject of gender competence, what that is, and, if achieved, what effect it may have. *Gender competence* has been defined as "the ability of people to recognize gender perspectives in their work and policy fields and concentrate on them towards the goal of gender equality" (Gender Competence Center 2010). When it is functioning optimally, it must have a balanced, equitable, and dedicated work culture that demands and reinforces a comprehensive understanding of how the opposite sex works. However, experts acknowledge that achieving this state in workplace settings is difficult, as long-standing gender-based expectations and traditional constructs in American society will not change overnight.

Empirically, much of the dialogue and protest along with the many calls to change the predominately patriarchal culture of work have emanated from women. Men may join the chorus, but according to Amy Stevens, a published expert and lecturer on gender studies, most will remain silent. Is the effort being made by women to disrupt the male-dominated workplace producing unintended consequences? Because gender is seen not just as an experience but as a social institution as well, this is one of the most significant ways in which people organize and structure their lives. Yet, separating the gender-specific roles, tasks, and expectations that may be surviving intact at home from work is critical if progress is to be made for both genders. Progress, for the sake of this treatment, means recognition of abilities, equitable distribution of tasks, and assignments or promotions that are fulfilled without the influence of gender. For this to occur, both men and women need to be gender competent (Amy Stevens, personal interview, February 15, 2019).

This may occur in any venue and should work toward the goal of gender equality. It has also been said to be a key qualification for job-related as well as political equality of the genders and represents an essential prerequisite for the successful implementation and realization of gender-related equality strategies. If all men were gender competent, would that eliminate the need for women to protest against sexual harassment and sex-based discrimination? Experts believe so, because it would dismantle consciously and subconsciously held perceptions and beliefs that drive such behaviors. In theory, universal gender competence among men would eliminate misogynistic and unwanted sexual behaviors (Niederle and Vesterlund 2011).

For progress to be made in this regard, scholars assert that men will have to be keenly aware of the differing gender-based perceptions of acceptable and unacceptable behaviors. Either one may be unclear if the contexts in which they occur have not received formal parameters, such as workplace policies that are understood and reinforced. However, if the lines are blurred, the rules may be weak or unenforceable. Tangibly, gender-based differences in perceptions of sexual harassment continue to inform legal discourse and workplace law. The problem, say some observers, lies with the American legal system's use of a "reasonable person standard" instead of a "reasonable woman standard" to evaluate sexual harassment claims. The courts have recognized that the reasonable woman standard relies on the *assumption* that men and women differ in their perceptions of which behaviors constitute sexual harassment. Applying legal weight to "assumptions" is precarious, and the fact that women perceive a broader range of behaviors as harassing may compound the confusion. Finding common ground in assessing and perceiving unwanted behaviors may thus be quite difficult, although men and women may not always differ in their perceptions of social sexual behaviors (Nguyen and Rotundo 2001).

In assessing an act that results in a formal accusation of sexual harassment or other form of misconduct, it may be necessary to examine historical workplace attitudes and behaviors that may have been ignored, accepted, or perhaps tolerated. Communication is often contextual, influenced by tone, inflection, and circumstance. For instance, if a male supervisor asks a female subordinate to meet him in his office before she departs for the day, her comfort levels may be influenced by a wide variety of factors: tone, facial expressions, body language, prior conversations, acceptance of requests such as these by others, a lack of job security, and so on. In addition, one must consider his ability to recognize the female's perceptions of what this request may mean to her and how she feels. Failure to consider her perceptions may be viewed as a direct affront to her value in the workplace and, thus, diminishment of equality. Sexual banter, jokes, or remarks made by either gender could also affect perceptions (Albrecht 2014).

Sexual harassment policies, regulations, and laws abound. Rather than bring the behavioral referees into the discussion, drawing from research devoted to cultural competency, we may begin to apply recommendations devoted to creating gender-competent men and women. The objective of any workplace devoted to gender equality should be to seek a deep, unabridged understanding of gender-based perceptions of how interactions may be interpreted. The ultimate goal should be a workplace where all are gender competent. This includes (1) *gender knowledge* (which means that all members of the organization possess some general knowledge of characteristics, history, values, beliefs, and behaviors of gender); (2) *gender awareness* (being open to the idea of changing attitudes and acceptable behaviors of the opposite sex); (3) *gender sensitivity* (the knowledge that differences exist in gender perceptions without assigning attendant values to those differences); and (4) *gender competence* (the aggregate of the previous stages; it can be operationalized for effectiveness). If an organization is gender competent, it should have the capacity to bring into the workplace a variety of different attitudes and perceptions to work effectively in cross-cultural settings (Brownlee and Lee 2017).

What would gender-competent workers be like? They would be able to distinguish between the benefit of socialization that promotes cohesive actions that focus solely on productivity and socialization for the sake of recreation. They would be able to consistently and accurately interpret context of work interactions and relationship dynamics, which would allow for careful assessment of communication before it occurs. It would be the ability to recognize situations that if left uncontrolled may lead to complaints of unwanted behavior. Overall, wholesale adaption may prevent the development and perpetuation of a culture of disrespect, abuse, and retreat into an intolerable work environment.

Jeffrey Czarnec

See also: Corrections System; Gender Equality; Popular Music; Victim Blaming

Further Reading

Albrecht, Steve. 2014. "Sexual Bantering in the Office." *Psychology Today*, January 17. www.psychologytoday.com/us/blog/the-act-violence/201401/sexual-bantering-in -the-office.

Brownlee, T., and K. Lee. 2017. "Building Culturally Competent Organizations." Accessed February 10, 2019. https://ctb.ku.edu/en/table-of-contents/culture/cultural -competence/culturally-competent-organizations/main.

Gender Competence Center. 2010. "Gender Competence." February 1. Accessed February 10, 2019. http://www.genderkompetenz.info/eng/gender-competence-2003 -2010/Gender Competence.html.

Nguyen, D., and M. Rotundo. 2001. "A Meta-Analytic Review of Gender Differences in Perceptions of Sexual Harassment." *Journal of Applied Psychology* 86(5): 914– 922. https://doi.org/10.1037//0021-9010.86.5.914.

Niederle, M., and L. Vesterlund. 2011. "Gender and Competition." *Annual Review of Economics* 3: 601–630. https://doi.org/10.1146/annurev-economics-111809-125122.

Gender Equality

Gender equality is defined by the World Health Organization (WHO) as "equal treatment of women and men in laws and politics, and equal access to resources and services within families, communities, and society at large." The concept of equality of the sexes is relatively new, as women have been treated as inferior not only in society but also in terms of basic legal rights for much of American history. It was not until 1920, for example, that women even secured the right to vote. Women were excluded from participating in politics, education, and certain professions, and they were viewed as "property." They had no voice, faced many forms of discrimination, and were deprived of their civil rights. Changes in this regard can be attributed to the hard work and sacrifice of many women's rights activists who challenged the status quo in all spheres of life, including the social, sexual, reproductive, educational, political, and economic areas. This history is intricately tied to the feminist movement, which is identified as occurring in three waves.

The first wave began with the women's suffrage movement in the late nineteenth to the early twentieth centuries. This culminated with two landmark triumphs. The Representation of the People Act of 1918 gave women in the United Kingdom who were thirty years old and older and owned a house the right to vote. Two years later, the Nineteenth Amendment to the U.S. Constitution was ratified, giving women voting rights. Pioneers in this era included Elizabeth Cady Stanton, Susan B. Anthony, Lucy Stone, and Lucretia Mott.

The second wave of changes continued with the feminist movement in the early 1960s to the late 1980s and is known as the women's liberation movement. The movement focused its attention on ending all forms of discrimination against women in the areas of employment, equal pay, access to education, reproductive rights, and household and family gender roles. This wave saw many changes in the area of gender equality, such as the Equal Pay Act of 1963 and Title VII of the Civil Rights Act of 1964; in 1966, the creation of the U.S. National Organization for Women (NOW), who fought for the Equal Rights Amendment (ERA); Title IX and the Women's Educational Equity Act of 1972 and 1975; and the Family Planning Services and Public Research Act of 1970 (which is often called Title X Family Planning Program). Other acts were also influential, including the Equal Credit Opportunity Act in 1974, the Pregnancy Discrimination Act in 1978, and the landmark decision in the *Roe v. Wade* case in 1973, in which the U.S. Supreme Court made it legal for women to get abortions.

On the international level, committees and conferences were dedicated to fighting this cause as well. In 1946, the United Nations established the Commission on the Status for Women, with the mandate to raise the status of all women relative to men and to eliminate all discrimination against women in the law. Through this commission, the following conventions aimed at furthering gender equality were adopted by the General Assembly: in 1952, the Convention on the Political Rights of Women; in 1957, the Convention on the Nationality of Married Women; in 1962, the Convention on Consent to Marriage, Minimum Age for Marriage and Registration of Marriage; and in 1965, the Recommendations on Consent to Marriage, Minimum Age for Marriage and Registration of Marriages. Other notable initiatives during this period included the UN world conferences on women held in 1975, 1980, 1985, and 1995 in Mexico, Copenhagen, Nairobi, and Beijing, China, respectively. The UN General Assembly declared the period 1976–1985 as the Women's Decade. In 1979, the General Assembly furthered the cause of gender equality by adopting the first international bill on women's rights, the Convention on the Elimination of All Forms of Discrimination against Women (CEDAW). This bill was initially signed by sixty-four countries on September 3, 1981.

Other notable changes promoting gender equality included trailblazing milestones for women. In 1969, Shirley Chisholm became the first African American woman to serve in the U.S. House of Representatives. Three years later, Katherine Graham became the first woman CEO of a Fortune 500 company. In 1980, Paula Hawkins was the first woman elected to represent Florida in the U.S. Senate. One year later, Sandra Day O'Connor became the first woman sworn in to serve as a justice on the U.S. Supreme Court. In 1983, twenty-seven-year-old astronaut Sally Ride became the first American woman to fly into space. In 1986, the U.S. Supreme Court ruled that the work environment can be declared hostile or abusive because of discrimination based on sex.

The third wave of feminism and the fight for gender equality continued into the 1990s and is very prominent in the twenty-first century. In this era, the emphasis is placed on creating greater awareness for marginalized women, including minority women, women of different sexual orientations, and lower-class women. Changes were observed at both the international and national levels and include the following at the international level: in 1993, the United Nations World Conference on Human Rights was convened in Vienna, Austria, and the General Assembly adopted the Declaration on the Elimination of Violence against Women; in 1996, the UN Expert

Group met and developed guidelines on gender mainstreaming in programs, and the first UN International Agencies Meeting on Women and Gender Equality (IAM-WGE) was held; and in 2000, Beijing +5 campaign for the equality between men and women and the improvement of women's status was held, followed by the twenty-third UN General Assembly Special Session on gender equality.

On the national level, the 1994 Gender Equity in Education Act included provisions for the training of teachers in gender equity in the areas of math and science and in the prevention of sexual harassment. In 1996, the landmark decision in the *United States v. Virginia* was written by Justice Ruth Bader Ginsburg, allowing the admission of women in the Virginia Military Institute. In 2013, the U.S. military issued new regulations permitting women to serve in combat positions, and the Violence Against Women Act was reauthorized. This period also saw many firsts for women: in 1997, Madelene Albright became U.S. Secretary of State; in 2005, this honor was given to an African American woman, Condoleezza Rice; in 2007, Nancy Pelosi was named Speaker of the House; in 2009, the first Hispanic American, Sonia Sotomayor, was named a U.S. Supreme Court justice; and in 2016, Hillary Rodham Clinton became the first female presidential nominee of one of the nation's two major political parties.

Despite all the accomplishments of these women and progress made in terms of gender equality, there is still a long way to go to achieve true equality in the United States. According to the 2018 Global Gender Gap Report, the United States is ranked 51st of 149 countries and has closed 72 percent of its overall gender gap. In terms of the four key areas assessed in the report, the United States is ranked 46th in terms of educational attainment, 71st in terms of health and survival, 19th in economic participation and opportunity, and 98th in terms of political empowerment for women.

The fight to promote gender equality continues today, especially in the workplace. Policies are now in place banning sexual harassment, as recognized by the Equal Employment Opportunity Commission (EEOC) in 1980. Women are now taking the fight further, as seen in 2017 when millions of women gathered to march in support of women's rights and against misogyny and sexual abuse in American society. This gave rise to several new movements (#MeToo and Time's Up), giving voice and power to women in their continuing quest for the same rights, resources, opportunities, and protections under the law that men enjoy.

Sherill V. C. Morris-Francis

See also: Congress; Equal Employment Opportunity Commission; #MeToo Movement; Time's Up Movement; Title IX; Title VII of the Civil Rights Act of 1964

Further Reading

Committee on Elimination of Discrimination against Women. 2003. "Experts in Women's Anti-Discrimination Committee Raise Questions Concerning Reports of Switzerland on Compliance with Convention." Press release, January 14. https://www.un.org/press/en/2003/WOM1373.doc.htm.

"Convention on the Elimination of All Forms of Discrimination against Women (CEDAW)." 29th Session. https://www.un.org/womenwatch/daw/cedaw/text/econvention.htm.

Coontz, S. 2013. "Why Gender Equality Stalled." *New York Times*, February 16. https://nytimes.com/2013/02/17/opinion/sunday/why-gender-equality-stalled.html.

Milligan, S. 2017. "Stepping through History: A Timeline of Women's Rights from 1769 to the 2017 Women's March on Washington." *US News*, January 20. https://www .usnews.com/news/the-report/articles/2017-01-20/timeline-the-womens-rights -movement-in-the-us.

Raday, Frances. 2012. "Gender and Democratic Citizenship: The Impact of CEDAW." *International Journal of Constitutional Law* 10 (2): 512–530.

United Nations. 1948. "Universal Declaration of Human Rights." wwda.org, December 16. https://wwda.org.au/wp-content/uploads/2013/12/undechr1.pdf.

United Nations. 1993. "Declaration on the Elimination of Violence against Women." United Nations General Assembly, December 20. http://www.un-documents.net /a48r104.htm.

United Nations. n.d.a. "The Convention on the Elimination of All Forms of Discrimination against Women (CEDAW)." UN Women. https://www.un.org/womenwatch /daw/cedaw/text/econvention.htm.

United Nations. n.d.b. "Goal #3 Gender Equity." United Nations Millennium Campaign. https://www.un.org/millenniumgoals/gender.shtml.

United Nations Population Fund. n.d. "Gender Equality." https://www.unfpa.org/gender -equality.

World Bank. 2006. "Gender Equality as Smart Economics: A World Bank Group Gender Action Plan (Fiscal Years 2007–10)." September.

World Economic Forum. 2018. "The Global Gender Gap Report 2018." http://www3 .weforum.org/docs/WEF_GGGR_2018.pdf.

World Health Organization. 2001. *Transforming Health Systems: Gender and Rights in Reproductive Health*. Geneva, Switzerland: WHO.

Gillibrand, Kirsten (1966–)

Democratic U.S. senator Kirsten Gillibrand of New York is a leading advocate at the national level against sexual misconduct. Gillibrand has been a proponent of legislative reform to address sexual harassment and sexual assault in the military, on college campuses, and in the U.S Congress, and she is prominent among Democratic politicians.

Born Kirsten Elizabeth Rutnik on December 9, 1966, in upstate New York, Gillibrand was raised in a politically active family. Her grandmother was a member of the Democratic machine in Albany, New York. Gillibrand's parents were both lawyers, and her father was a political adviser. Gillibrand attended law school at the University of California, Los Angeles, and worked in private practice before entering public service. In 2006, she ran for a Republican-held congressional seat in upstate New York and won, and she was reelected in 2008. Gillibrand served as a member of the House of Representatives from January 3, 2007, until January 26, 2009, when she resigned to fill Hillary Clinton's U.S. Senate seat. Gillibrand was elected to that seat in the 2010 special election and reelected in 2012 for the term ending January 3, 2019.

In Congress, Gillibrand's signature issues include paid family leave and a living minimum wage. In 2018, *60 Minutes* pronounced Gillibrand "the #MeToo Senator," recognizing her role in combating sexual assault and sexual harassment. Her engagement on these issues long predated the October 2017 allegations against

Harvey Weinstein. In response to the high rate of sexual assault in the military, Gillibrand campaigned to enact legislation that would remove the authority for adjudicating and prosecuting sexual misconduct from superiors, allowing allegations to be handled by trained military prosecutors. She worked extensively with the Obama administration on federal policy governing sexual assault on university campuses. More recently, she proposed procedural changes for sexual harassment cases on Capitol Hill. She argues that institutions protect the powerful within those institutions with procedures that lack transparency and accountability and that work in favor of predators and are biased against accusers. In an interview with *The New Washington*, she claimed that there were no conversations more important than the #MeToo Movement. Gillibrand is also a proponent of increasing women in national and local politics.

On November 16, 2017, Gillibrand was the first leading Democrat to state that former president Bill Clinton should have resigned during the Monica Lewinsky scandal. The position was significant because Gillibrand had been closely aligned with the Clintons, and she considered Hillary Clinton a key political role model. Weeks later, on December 6, 2017, Gillibrand was at the forefront of political conversations again when she led a group of senators calling for the resignation of Senator Al Franken after allegations of sexual misconduct. She was also among politicians who announced on May 7, 2018, that New York attorney general Eric Schneiderman should resign in the hours after the *New Yorker* published allegations that Schneiderman had physically assaulted four women.

Gillibrand has her critics. Some on the left argue that she too easily denounces those accused of misconduct before facts have been established under a system of due process. In calling for individuals such as Franken to resign, they claim she equated incidents of misconduct with more serious forms of violence, attacking an ally while some Republican politicians remained unscathed by sexual scandals. Those on the right have disparaged Gillibrand for previously accepting support from the Clintons.

Gillibrand's defenders hail her stance as principled, resisting temptations to identify some forms of sexual misconduct as acceptable or to treat allies differently than political opponents. Moreover, they claim that her positions do not foreclose investigations and due process.

Marny Requa

See also: Congress; Franken, Al; Military Settings; Presidential Scandals; Schneiderman, Eric

Further Reading

Alfonsi, Sharyn. 2018. *60 Minutes.* "Kirsten Gillibrand: The #MeToo Senator." Produced by Howard L. Rosenberg and Julie Holstein. CBS News, February 11.

Gillibrand, K. 2014. *Off the Sidelines: Raise Your Voice, Change the World.* New York: Ballantine Books.

Gillibrand, Kirsten. 2017a. "'The New Washington': Senator Kirsten Gillibrand." Interview with Jennifer Steinhauer. *New York Times* (audio podcast), November 18. https://www.nytimes.com/2017/11/18/podcasts/kirsten-gillibrand-sexual-harassment-new-washington.html.

Gillibrand, Kirsten. 2017b. "Senator Franken Should Step Aside." Kirsten Gillibrand's Facebook page, December 6. https://www.facebook.com/KirstenGillibrand/posts

/senator-franken-should-step-asidei-have-been-shocked-and-disappointed-to
-learn-o/10155471770513411/.

Killough, A. 2013. "'Their Patience Had Worn Incredibly Thin': How the Dam Broke on
Al Franken." CNN, December 7.

"Kirsten Gillibrand: United States Senator for New York." Official Senate website.
Retrieved July 30, 2018, from www.gillibrand.senate.gov.

Olson, A. 2017. "Gillibrand vs. McCaskill: Fighting the Invisible War." *Women Leading
Change: Case Studies on Women, Leadership, and Feminism* 1(3): 9–21.

Osnos, E. 2013. "Strong Vanilla: The Relentless Rise of Kirsten Gillibrand." *The New
Yorker*, December 16.

Steinhauer, J. 2017. "Bill Clinton Should Have Resigned over Lewinsky Affair, Kirsten
Gillibrand Says." *New York Times*, November 16.

Glenn Thrush Scandal

Glenn Thrush is a journalist and reporter for the *New York Times*. He was born in
Brooklyn, New York, in 1967 and went to Brooklyn College. He was formerly a
White House correspondent and a senior staff writer for *Politico Magazine*. He is
a book author and contributor for MSNBC.

On November 20, 2017, Vox, an American news and opinion website, reported
that Thrush had a history of inappropriate behavior with young female staffers.
Four women publicly recounted their allegations of inappropriate behavior, adding their voices to the growing #MeToo Movement that was revealing and publi-
cizing incidents of sexual harassment and assault across the country. According to
Vox, Thrush was one of 263 high-profile men accused of sexual misconduct from
April 2017 to January 2019.

The first reported incident occurred in June 2017. A twenty-three-year-old
woman reporter encountered Thrush, who was fifty at the time, in a bar at a "going
away" party. She reported that after sharing drinks, he twice attempted to kiss her.
Bianca Padró Ocasio, a friend of the woman and also a journalist, confronted
Thrush via text message that evening and the next day. Reportedly, Thrush claimed
he would never "lure anyone ever," but he also apologized and acknowledged the
imbalance of power between him—as an older, more powerful male journalist—
and the young female reporter.

In the text exchange, Thrush claimed to have been an advocate for women and
female journalists for twenty years. In October 2017, months after the incident
occurred but before it was reported, Thrush posted a Facebook message, writing,
"Young people who come into a newsroom deserve to be taught our trade, given
our support and enlisted in our calling—not betrayed by little men who believe
they are bigger than the mission." This post linked to a news report about accusations of sexual harassment by another well-established male political journalist,
Mark Halperin.

Two additional young female journalists later detailed similar experiences
with Thrust, reporting behavior that ranged from unwelcome touching, groping, and kissing to sexual advances. There were several commonalities between
the reports of each of the three women. They were all in their twenties and relatively new to journalism, and these encounters generally occurred at events

involving alcohol. There was also a power imbalance between the women and Thrush, particularly due to his status as a senior correspondent. All the women said they felt the need to be cordial with Thrush because of his influence in the industry.

Laura McGann, the author of the Vox exposé, recounted her own experience with Thrush when they were journalistic colleagues at *Politico*. The incident mirrored that of the others: McGann and Thrush were at a bar, sitting next to each other in a booth, when he put his hand on her thigh. She quickly got up and left. McGann says, when she returned to the office the following week, she noticed a change in behavior from her male colleagues. A colleague later alleged that Thrush had spread rumors of her being sexual aggressive toward him and that he had declined her advances.

In the aftermath of the Vox article, Thrush was suspended from the *New York Times* pending the completion of an internal investigation. He sought substance abuse treatment and wrote an apology letter, which stated that he had been responding to personal and health crises by drinking heavily. He then stated that he had brought hurt to his family and friends by participating in things he was ashamed of doing over the years while inebriated.

The *New York Times* concluded its investigation on December 20, 2017. The newspaper permitted Thrush to continue as a reporter but not as a White House correspondent and required him to complete workplace conduct training. Dean Baquet, the executive editor of the *Times*, said that although Thrush had acted offensively, he did not deserve to be fired. Thrush was also removed from a book publishing project with Random House that he had been lined up to write with Maggie Haberman, another White House correspondent with the *New York Times*.

Lauren Moton and Kwan-Lamar Blount-Hill

See also: Groping; Hostile Work Environment; #MeToo Movement; News Media Coverage; Power Dynamics

Further Reading

Ember, S. 2017. "Glenn Thrush, Suspended Times Reporter, to Resume Work but Won't Cover White House." *New York Times*, December 20. Accessed February 11, 2019. https://www.nytimes.com/2017/12/20/business/media/glenn-thrush-suspension -white-house.html.

Farhl, P. 2017. "Glenn Thrush Is Suspended and Reassigned by the New York Times, but Not Fired." *Washington Post*, December 20. https://www.washingtonpost.com /lifestyle/style/glenn-thrush-is-suspended-and-reassigned-by-the-new-york-times -but-not-fired/2017/12/20/9eb1b8f4-e5ce-11e7-833f-155031558ff4_story.html.

McGann, L. 2017. "Exclusive: NYT White House Correspondent Glenn Thrush's History of Bad Judgment around Young Women Journalists." Vox, November 20. Accessed February 11, 2019. https://www.vox.com/policy-and-politics/2017/11/20/16678094 /glenn-thrush-new-york-times.

Wemple, E. 2017. "Why the New York Time's Investigation of Glenn Thrush Is Particularly Tricky." *Washington Post*, December 5. https://www.google.com/amp/s/www .washingtonpost.com/blogs/erik-wemple/wp/2017/12/05/why-the-new-york-timess -investigation-of-glenn-thrush-is-particularly-tricky/%3foutputType=amp.

Groping

Groping is a sexual assault crime committed by invading the sanctity of someone's body without permission or consent. It is a form of sexual harassment that involves unsolicited touch, or fondling, of someone's body part by another person. The most common forms of groping are grinding; grabbing of buttocks, the chest area (breast), thighs, or vulva; touching or fondling other areas of another person's body; and pressing one's body against another without permission. Groping is more likely to occur at public events that attract a large number of people, such as musical concerts, festivals, and public transportation (such as trains and buses). There are also statistics suggesting a significant occurrence of groping of women involved in certain sectors of the economy and professions (e.g., agriculture, the military, and aid and relief work).

In the Western world, public entertainment is seen as a way of life. Consequently, the creative industry thrives due to the value placed on lives shows, concerts, outdoor theaters, orchestras, festivals, and clubs/pubs. The large audiences that these types of events attract allow shrouded sexual crimes such as groping to be more prevalent and with few consequences for the perpetrators.

In 2018, the British Broadcasting Corporation (BBC) reported that approximately 43 percent of females under forty years of age have experienced unwanted/uncomfortable touching at musical festivals in the United Kingdom. This significant statistic questions the effectiveness of the strong institutional policies against sexual crimes. The critical consideration underscores the role of value systems stemming from the environmental conditioning of young persons in regard to appropriate behavior at public events. Are unwelcomed touches unconsciously consented to at public events through the silence of the victims? Does the law adequately classify groping as a sexual offense?

Some of the elements of sexual assault include whether a person intentionally touches another person sexually, whether the person did not consent to the touching, and whether the person does not reasonably believe that he or she consented. The 10 U.S. Code § 920, Art. 120, dealing with rape and sexual assault states in section B that "sexual assault is when someone commits a sexual act upon another person without the consent of the other person."

Reports show that majority of groping victims are women. At the 2018 Coachella Valley Music and Arts Festival, all the fifty-four women interviewed in a quick survey reported experiencing at least one form of sexual harassment; one female attendee reported being groped on twenty-two separate occasions at the event. In Sweden, at the Bråvalla Festival in 2017, twenty sexual assaults (mostly groping) were reported by mostly female victims. Generally, over 90 percent of females who attend public entertainment events are groped indiscriminately. However, despite these high suspected cases of groping, very few victims make formal reports to the appropriate authorities. In the United Kingdom, the outcome of a 2018 survey suggests that over 80 percent of sexual assault victims did not report the assault to the police (BBC 2018).

Unfortunately, the prevailing culture of public entertainment and festivals, combined with a rationalization that groping is not as serious an offense as many other forms of sexual misconduct, tends to allow this behavior to continue. These behavioral patterns also continue due to the prevalence of silence among the victims. Further, groping of minors may even be more prevalent because they may not understand what has happened to them or might not regard it as a crime. When they do feel violated and victimized, they may choose to keep silent due to fear, embarrassment, or guilt—or the belief that perpetrators are never held accountable for groping behavior. This experience can have profound and lasting psychological effects on the victims.

Bamidele Wale-Oshinowo

See also: Concerts; Music/Video Settings; Objectification of Women

Further Reading

Bates, L. 2017. "It's Not Groping or Fondling—It Is Sexual Assault." *The Guardian*, January 13. Accessed March 20, 2019. https://www.theguardian.com/lifeandstyle/2017/jan/13/its-not-groping-or-fondling-it-is-sexual-assault.

British Broadcasting Corporation (BBC). 2018. "'Shocking' Level of Sexual Harassment at Music Festivals." BBC News, June 18. Accessed February 19, 2020. https://www.bbc.com/news/entertainment-arts-44518892.

Clegg, S., M. Kornberger, and T. Pitsis. 2016. *Managing and Organizations*. 4th ed. London: Sage Publications.

Papisova, V. 2018. "Sexual Harassment Was Rampant at Coachella 2018." *Teen Vogue Report*, April 18. Accessed February 19, 2020. https://www.teenvogue.com/story/sexual-harassment-was-rampant-at-coachella-2018.

Roti, J. 2018. "Incidents of Sexual Harassment, Assault High at Music Festivals." *Chicago Tribune*, March 29. Accessed February 19, 2020. https://www.chicagotribune.com/lifestyles/ct-life-music-festivals-sexual-assaults-0328-story.html.

H

Harris v. Forklift Systems (1993)

In *Harris v. Forklift Systems*, 510 US 17 (1993), the U.S. Supreme Court delved into the definition of a discriminatory, abusive work environment, considering whether sexual harassment must affect an employee's psychological health to the point of creating a hostile work environment—which would qualify as a violation of Title VII of the Civil Rights Act of 1964, 78 Stat. 253, as amended, 42 U.S.C. § 2000e et seq. (1988 ed., Supp. III). Under Title VII of the Civil Rights Act of 1964, it is unlawful for an employer to discriminate against any person with respect to his compensation, terms, conditions, or privileges of employment because of such person's race, color, religion, sex, or national origin (42 U.S.C. § 2000e-2(a)(1)).

The case in question concerned sexual harassment allegedly suffered by Theresa Harris, a manager at Forklift Systems, Inc., an equipment rental company. Harris alleged that the company president, Charles Hardy, frequently insulted her and directed sexual innuendo at her because she was female. For example, Harris accused Hardy of calling her a "dumb ass woman" and asked if she could go to the Holiday Inn with him to renegotiate her salary. He also threw objects on the floor for the females to pick up in front of him, asked them to get coins from his front pants pockets, and frequently made suggestive comments about their clothing.

When Harris complained to the employer about his conduct, he claimed he was surprised that Harris was offended, stated that he was only joking, apologized, and promised to stop engaging in the offensive behavior. Based on this assurance, Harris stayed on the job. About a month later, however, Harris claimed that Hardy asked her, in front of other employees, whether she promised a customer sex in exchange for his business. Thereafter, Harris vacated the employment after she received her paycheck.

She subsequently filed a lawsuit claiming that her employer's sexual harassment created a hostile work environment that violated her rights under Title VII of the Civil Rights Act of 1964. The district court decided, and it was consequently affirmed by the U.S. Court of Appeals for the Sixth Circuit, that the harassment Harris endured was not severe enough to create an abusive work environment under Title VII.

On appeal to the U.S. Supreme Court, however, the justices unanimously held that Title VII undoubtedly bars any employer's conduct that seriously affects a reasonable employee's psychological well-being, albeit the law is not limited in application to such circumstances alone. According to the court, a Title VII violation occurs whenever the work environment would reasonably be perceived as hostile or abusive, as was perceived by Harris in this case.

According to the Supreme Court, the harassing conduct did not have to have seriously affected the employee's psychological health nor made him or her suffer injury. It qualified as a Title VII violation if both the victim and a reasonable person would perceive the behavior as having created an abusive or hostile work environment.

Alaba Oludare and Jude L. Jokwi Lenjo

See also: Equal Employment Opportunity Commission; Sexual Harassment Training; Title VII of the Civil Rights Act of 1964

Further Reading

Burns, S. E. 1993. "Evidence of a Sexually Hostile Workplace: What Is It and How Should It Be Assessed after Harris v. Forklift Systems, Inc." *New York University Review of Law and Social Change* 21: 357.

Harris v. Forklift Systems, Inc. n.d. Oyez. Accessed December 26, 2018. https://www .oyez.org/cases/1993/92-1168.

Harris v. Forklift Systems, Inc., 510 U.S. 17, 114 S. Ct. 367, 126 L. Ed. 2d 295 (1993).

Levy, A. C. 1994. "The United States Supreme Court Opinion in Harris v. Forklift Systems: Full of Sound and Fury Signifying Nothing." *University of Kansas Law Review* 43: 275.

Roy, M. 1995. "Employer Liability for Sexual Harassment: A Search for Standards in the Wake of Harris v. Forklift Systems, Inc." *Southern Methodist University Law Review* 48: 263.

Schultz, D. 1993. "From Reasonable Man to Unreasonable Victim: Assessing Harris v. Forklift Systems and Shifting Standards of Proof and Perspective in Title VII Sexual Harassment Law." *Suffolk University Law Review* 27: 717.

Harvey Weinstein Scandal

Up until 2017, Harvey Weinstein (1952–) was publicly known for being the head of two successful movie production companies (Miramax and the Weinstein Company) and was one of Hollywood's most prominent power brokers. Amid this success, however, some members of the movie industry privately spoke of rumors that Weinstein routinely preyed on women in his professional path, engaging in various acts that ranged from sexual harassment to outright assault. Although there were persistent rumors about his dark side over the decades, the open secret in Hollywood never managed to stand in the way of his business, and by all accounts, Miramax and the Weinstein Brothers—under Weinstein's (and his brother's) control—achieved great success.

This state of affairs changed with the publication in October 2017 of two stories—one by the *New York Times* and the other in the *New Yorker*—that chronicled an extensive and frightening pattern of sexual abuse by Weinstein. The behavior ranged from hounding and harassing aspiring young actresses (and others) into having sex with him or risk career ruin to physically forcing them into sexual acts, including forcible rape. Victims recounted that the incidents were often followed by threats of retaliation if the victim were to tell anyone. As the scandal exploded, other victims reported that Weinstein's legal team bullied them into signing nondisclosure agreements (NDAs). In the months following those initial stories, many actresses and other professional women in the industry stepped out of the shadows to claim Weinstein had abused them, and in doing so, they risked their personal and professional reputations. Perhaps even more importantly, the bombshell disclosures not only sparked outrage about Weinstein's specific abuses, but coming as they did on the heels of allegations against several other powerful men in the media, including Bill Cosby, Bill O'Reilly, and Roger Ailes, the Weinstein allegations ushered in the #MeToo era. This Movement was led by women who publicly came forward to disclose they had been sexually assaulted, shed the shame of their past, find power in their solidarity, and demand changes to misogynistic aspects of American society.

WEINSTEIN'S YEARS AS A HOLLYWOOD MAGNATE

Starting in 1979, Harvey Weinstein and his brother built Miramax from the ground up. Within a few years, the company had achieved considerable success on the strength of *Sex, Lies and Videotape* and several other critically acclaimed films. In 1993, the Weinstein brothers sold Miramax (named after their parents, Miriam and Max) for $60 million to the Walt Disney Company (in 1993), although they continued to run the company. Miramax continued to churn out hit films, such as *Shakespeare in Love*, *Good Will Hunting*, *The English Patient*, and *Silver Linings Playbook*.

In 2005, the Weinstein brothers left Miramax to form their own film studio, the Weinstein Company, which quickly emerged as a powerhouse in its own right. In 2015, *Forbes Magazine* estimated the new company to be valued at nearly $150 million. By this time, Harvey Weinstein had been involved in movies that had yielded several hundred Oscar nominations; he had effectively built a movie-making empire in Hollywood. Weinstein's sphere of influence reached far beyond movies; he came to be known as a champion of liberal causes, donating large sums of money and mingling with powerful individuals in politics and the media. In October 2017, however, his empire quickly came crashing down.

FIRST ALLEGATIONS OF SEXUAL ASSAULT

On October 5, 2017, the *New York Times* broke the first story in what some came to describe as Hollywood's biggest ever sexual abuse story. After months of scrupulous investigative journalism, Megan Twohey and Jodi Kantor chronicled a pattern of abuse, harassment, and sexual violence on the part of Weinstein that spanned decades. A second story by Ronan Farrow, which detailed additional allegations against Weinstein, followed in the *New Yorker* just a few weeks later. Many women recalled Weinstein seemed incapable of accepting "no"—no matter how forcefully or how many times they said it—in these traumatic encounters. These stories allege his predatory behavior was generally followed by threats he issued against his victims to either continue to submit to his demands or to remain silent.

The allegations detailed a clear modus operandi: Weinstein would invite a young actress, employee, or reporter to a meeting under the guise of his interest in giving them a role or some other career opportunity. These encounters often took place at hotels, and a second female employee would be invited, only to be dismissed or to leave shortly after the "meeting" began. These accounts detail little pretense once the third person had left. It is alleged that Weinstein would often disrobe and then reenter the room in a bathrobe, ask for a massage, or quickly advance on the women sexually. The women reported feeling overwhelmed physically and emotionally; not only was Weinstein physically large, but he would often alternately compliment or insult the women in what appeared to be a clear power play to disorient them. One woman, detailing a frightening physical encounter, stated, "I could feel, the more I was freaking out, the more he was excited" (Farrow 2017).

Weinstein's initial reaction to the published reports was to issue a carefully crafted nonapology that denied the behavior: "I appreciate the way I've behaved with colleagues in the past has caused a lot of pain, and I sincerely apologize for it." He further offered to go into a facility to "dig deep . . . [to] learn more about myself." A spokesperson subsequently followed up by stating Weinstein asserted that all instances of sexual contact alleged by his accusers were "consensual" (Farrow 2017). His statement of contrition was roundly criticized as evasive and inauthentic. Around this time, Weinstein's team threatened the *New York Times* with a lawsuit and allegedly tried to intimidate potential witnesses in the industry to remain quiet. But the story could not be contained: actresses came forward in droves to make accusations over the next few days and weeks.

While most members of the general public—who only knew Weinstein by his reputation as a movie mogul—were surprised when the story broke, many close to Weinstein were not. They had either heard rumors of his behavior or had themselves been part of what one witness referred to as the "complicity machine," an army of "enablers, silencers, and spies" (Twohey et al. 2017). Given the sheer number of allegations that came forward—by late 2018 the number had reached eighty-seven women—it was clear that Weinstein must have had help in setting up these encounters and then subsequently in keeping the women quiet. A number of assistants came forward (on and off the record), and his chauffeur, Mickael Chemloul, later admitted to witnessing several instances of nonconsensual sex by Harvey Weinstein as well as instances in which he had driven around "tearful aspiring actresses" who had been victimized by his employer.

Weinstein's fall happened more swiftly than many could have expected: within just a few days of the first story in the *Times*, Weinstein was fired from the Weinstein Company. His wife left him a few days later. Within a week, the Academy of Motion Picture Arts and Sciences expelled him from the organization (as did many other groups, foundations, and organizations in the months to come), and a series of awards, medals, and fellowships that he had received were rescinded. Inside of just a few weeks, Weinstein went from one of the most powerful men in Hollywood to social pariah. Within a few months, his former company had to file bankruptcy.

CHARGES AGAINST WEINSTEIN

With more than eighty women coming forward in just a few short months with stories of sexual assault and harassment, it was only a matter of time before Weinstein was charged. In May 2018, with the help of a New York City grand jury, Weinstein was charged with first- and third-degree rape and first-degree criminal sexual act against two unnamed women stemming from attacks alleged to have taken place in 2004 and 2013. The news of his arrest brought out cheers: people gathered to celebrate as he walked into the New York Police Department First Precinct. He was released on $1 million bail. In July, more charges were filed related to an incident with a third woman (also unnamed) from a case in 2006. Now in his mid-sixties (at the time of this writing), if found guilty, Weinstein potentially faces prison for the rest of his life. He is also under investigation in three other areas: Los Angeles, London, and by the U.S. federal authorities. He continues to maintain his innocence against these accusations.

Given the number of allegations against him, some confusion arose as to why more criminal charges were not filed against Weinstein. Due to constraints imposed by the statute of limitations, some of the acts Weinstein is accused of can no longer be criminally charged. These statutes, which determine how long the state has to prosecute criminal offenses after an offense has taken place, differ by state. Further, although the journalists have amassed what seems to be a mountain of evidence against Weinstein, winning these types of criminal cases (even within the statute of limitations) may be difficult because many witnesses are unwilling to testify, there is often a lack of forensic evidence, and sometimes the women had subsequent complicated interactions with Weinstein (including signing NDAs as well as continued professional contact). Further, because many years have passed in most of these cases, memories may fade, and proving guilt beyond a reasonable doubt—which is the legal standard in criminal cases—becomes difficult. The legal standard for responsibility in civil cases is considerably lower, and Weinstein is currently being sued in several different jurisdictions.

WEINSTEIN'S ENCOUNTER WITH SALMA HAYEK

Many of the women who ultimately spoke out were reluctant to share what they went through for various reasons, including feeling embarrassed, fearing ridicule of others, fearing damage to their careers, or worrying about the reactions of their loved ones after hearing such disclosures. Salma Hayek was one of these women. An American and Mexican film actress, producer, and former model, she is well known for many popular movies, such as *From Dusk Till Dawn*, *Grown Ups*, and *Desperado*. She came into contact with Weinstein when she was trying to produce the film *Frida*, which was a project she had been working on for years. Weinstein agreed to bankroll the film.

At the outset, Hayek was enthusiastic to work with Weinstein, and she signed a deal to do several other films with Miramax. Hayek later reported, though, that this dream quickly turned into a nightmare when Weinstein made repeated unwanted sexual advances against her. When she refused him, she alleges she had to incur his "rage." During the filming of *Frida*, she reported that he made angry phone calls in the middle of the night regarding the legality of her agents, and on one occasion, he physically removed her from an event for her to attend a private party with himself and high-paid prostitutes. She also alleges that he verbally threatened her, stating, "I will kill you, don't think I can't" (Hayek 2017). She stated she was terrified of him. Hayek reported that when she refused his sexual demands, he refused to carry out his duties as the producer of *Frida*: he did not hire a director, raise money for the film, cast actors, or rewrite the script. Despite this, Hayek was able to raise the money to support the film.

Still, because Weinstein had to produce a movie that he no longer wanted to be involved with, she reported that he harassed her and insulted her acting skills. Further, she claims he demanded that she film a "senseless" lesbian sex scene with her costar, actress Ashley Judd (who was also one of Weinstein's alleged victims). Because she felt that if she refused this request he would tank the film, Hayek agreed to do the scene. She felt physically ill the morning the scene was set to be filmed and reportedly took a tranquilizer to calm her nerves. Weinstein still attempted to prohibit the movie from reaching major theaters. Despite his alleged attempts to sabotage the film, the movie went on to win two Oscars.

BROADER IMPACT OF THE SCANDAL

Since the first stories became public in the *New York Times* and the *New Yorker*, Harvey Weinstein has gone from being one of the most powerful to one of the most reviled men in Hollywood. His legacy, however, reaches far beyond his immediate circle, as these allegations were the linchpin that began the #MeToo era. Just a few weeks after the widespread and long-standing allegations against Weinstein finally became public, actress Alyssa Milano posted #MeToo on social media, and the hashtag spread like wildfire on social media platforms. It was a message to women (and men) that the person claiming #MeToo was a survivor of sexual assault and that she stood with other victims coming forward. The message quickly went viral, with thousands of women coming forward to claim their pasts in an effort to shed the shame of sexual abuse and to support those coming forward to disclose their own painful experiences.

Where the movement will go next is hard to predict. However, Harvey Weinstein's fate is clear. In February 2020, he was convicted of third-degree rape and first-degree criminal sexual act, and one month later, he was sentenced to twenty-three years in prison for his crimes.

As far as the impact on culture in the United States, at the very least, the national conversation has turned decidedly to focus on women's issues at this point in history. This scandal and those that followed in its wake have prompted some deepening of understanding that women have been oppressed by sexual abuse and harassment throughout society and that change is necessary for a more fair and just society.

Jennifer M. Balboni and Samyah Williams

See also: Ailes, Roger; Bill O'Reilly; Cosby, Bill; #MeToo Movement; Nondisclosure Agreements

Further Reading

Farrow, Ronan. 2017. "From Aggressive Overtures to Sexual Assault: Harvey Weinstein's Accusers Tell Their Story." *New Yorker*, October 23.

Hayek, Salma. 2017. "Harvey Weinstein Is My Monster Too." *New York Times*, December 13.

Kantor, Jodi, and Megan Twohey. 2017. "Harvey Weinstein Paid Off Sexual Harassment Accusers for Decades." *New York Times*, October 5.

Moniuszko, Sara, and Cara Kelly. 2017. "Harvey Weinstein: A Complete List of the 87 Accusers." *USA Today*, October 27.

Twohey, Megan, Jodi Kantor, Susan Dominus, Jim Rutenberg, and Steve Eder. 2017. "Weinstein's Complicity Machine." *New York Times*, December 5.

Health Care Industry

Sexual harassment is common in the health care industry, with the majority of women and a significant minority of men reporting harassment at least once in their careers Much of this harassment is recent; in a 2015 study of home health workers, 25 percent of respondents say it happened in the past year, as did 58 percent of a national survey of female surgeons in 2018. The health care industry is typical of those industries that put workers at high risk for sexual harassment: it has a strong top-down authority structure, and men hold the majority of positions of authority. It also has a history of tolerating or hiding errors rather than reporting them. The risk of harassment starts during school and residencies/internships and remains as workers transition into the workplace. Harassment can come from supervisors, instructors, peers, and even patients.

Health care workers typically do not report sexual harassment—a fear of losing their job is among the top reasons for not reporting (as it is in many other industries). Fear of ostracism from colleagues is another frequently cited reason for deciding not to report harassment. Although most schools and health care organizations have sexual harassment policies in place, critics assert that these are often crafted to prevent lawsuits rather than to prevent incidents and help victims.

Sexual harassment occurs more frequently during training in health care than in other professional fields. In 2018, a national study by the National Academies of Sciences, Engineering, and Medicine found that the prevalence of sexual harassment in academic medicine is almost double that of other science specialties. Additionally, a 2014 meta-analysis of fifty-one studies found that 60 percent of medical students had experienced harassment during their training. Among nurses and allied health care workers, the rates are similar. The majority of this harassment takes the form of sexually explicit remarks, unwanted sexual overtures, and inappropriate touching. Other forms of harassment were also reported, albeit less frequently, including quid pro quo harassment in which victims are offered better job placements, grades, or help with massive student loan debt in return for sexual favors.

Health care workers are at risk of sexual harassment from both coworkers and supervisors. In a well-known 2017 lawsuit, the NYC Health and Hospitals Corporation faced charges because a senior vice president conducted a poll of his colleagues that asked which female employees they would sleep with. This type of toxic atmosphere in which inappropriate and sexualized comments are made is all too common in the health care setting according to industry critics. Sexual harassment from supervisors can also involve unwanted touching and offers of job advancement for sexual favors. Harassment from coworkers is likely to consist of unwanted sexual attention, repeated requests for dates, and inappropriate sexualized comments.

Sexual harassment of health care providers by patients is common; a 2018 Medscape survey found that 47 percent of physicians and 71 percent of nurses experienced it. The same survey found that women were more likely to report such incidents than men (73 percent of female nurses versus 46 percent of male nurses). Further, 58 percent of female physicians and 39 percent of male physicians reported experiencing sexual harassment.

Those working directly with patients for long periods of time, such as home health aides, are at especially high risk. Harassment from patients is difficult to address, as health care providers are taught to care for patients, not confront them. The harassment is often from a patient whose judgment may be impaired because of a health condition, such as dementia, but patients who are fully cognizant can also sexually harass providers and caregivers. Few workplaces have clear policies in place for addressing this type of harassment. Most interventions are informal and involve job shifts, such as changing the provider assigned to the patient.

Sexual harassment, abuse, and assault of patients by health care providers also occurs, although this phenomenon is not well studied or documented. In 2017, USA Gymnastics team doctor Larry Nassar was convicted of sexually abusing over three hundred patients over more than twenty years while working at Michigan State University (MSU). He was sentenced to 175 years in jail, and MSU agreed to pay out a $500 million settlement. Nassar is not alone; a 2016 *Atlanta Journal-Constitution* investigation identified more than twenty-four hundred cases of physicians across the country who have sexually assaulted their patients, and many are still licensed to practice.

Cases of nurses sexually assaulting patients have also been reported in the media; in one case, a male nurse impregnated a comatose woman, and in another, a male nurse was convicted of sexually assaulting multiple anesthetized patients.

Sexual harassment is associated with poor health and employment outcomes. A number of studies have found that victims report worse physical and mental health outcomes, including anxiety, anger, depression, and hypertension. Victims of sexual harassment who work in health care are likely to experience job dissatisfaction, burnout, increased stress, and poor job performance. There can be economic costs to victims as well. Numerous studies report that sexual harassment is associated with forced job changes; the loss of opportunities for training, advancement, or specialty choices; and job loss.

Workplace sexual harassment is expensive for health care organizations as well. This expense can come from legal settlements, which often exceed $100,000 per case. In 2017, the Equal Employment Opportunity Commission (EEOC) obtained $46 million from employers for sexual harassment victims (this is a small part of the number of sexual harassment lawsuits won each year). Health care organizations also face costs from reduced productivity, increased absences, and employee turnover due to the effect of sexual harassment on employees. Despite these costs, health care organizations do not always take action when harassment is reported. In a 2019 survey of health care workers by Modern Healthcare, 35 percent of respondents who experienced sexual harassment said no action was taken when they reported it to their employer.

The #MeToo and Time's Up Movements have pushed the health care industry to address sexual harassment prevention in the workplace. However, effective sexual harassment prevention requires transformational leadership and a top-down approach with a strong enforcement mechanism. A top-down approach is one in which the highest levels of management set, clearly communicate, and enforce a zero tolerance approach to sexual harassment. Reformers say that it is not enough to use piecemeal approaches such as training, written policies, and zero tolerance to stamp out harassment, although all those efforts are worthwhile. A comprehensive approach that creates a culture of accountability and equity in the health care setting is needed.

Such a comprehensive approach to sexual harassment for health care organizations involves several steps, including assessments of existing levels of sexual harassment in the organization, formulation of specific policies to address and prevent sexual harassment, creation of a secure method of reporting harassment, and following through with meaningful and appropriate penalties and other actions when harassment occurs. These best practices are recommended by numerous experts to reduce sexual harassment in the health care industry (Van Dis, Stadum, and Choo 2018).

Stacey B. Plichta

See also: Larry Nassar Scandal; #MeToo Movement; Quid Pro Quo; Time's Up Movement

Further Reading

Castellucci, M. 2019. "Workplace Harassment Often Ignored Say Women Healthcare leaders." Modern Healthcare, August 10. https://www.modernhealthcare.com /labor/workplace-harassment-often-ignored-say-women-healthcare-leaders.

Fnais, N., C. Soobiah, M. H. Chen, L. Perrier, M. Tashkhandi, S. E. Straus, M. Mamdani, M. Al-Omran, and A. C. Tricco. 2014. "Harassment and Discrimination in Medical Training: A Systematic Review and Meta-Analysis." *Academic Medicine* 89(5): 817–827.

Gartland, M., and M. Jaeger. 2017. "Hospital Boss Polled Colleagues on Which Female Employees They'd Sleep With: Suit." *New York Post*, October 16. https://nypost .com/2017/10/16/hospital-boss-polled-colleagues-on-which-female-employees -theyd-sleep-with-suit/.

Hanson, G. C., N. A. Perrin, H. Moss, N. Laharnar, and N. Glass. 2015. "Workplace Violence against Homecare Workers and Its Relationship with Workers Health Outcomes: A Cross-Sectional Study." *BMC Public Health* 15, article 11. https://doi.org /10.1186/s12889-014-1340-7.

Kane, L. 2018. *Sexual Harassment of Physicians: Report 2018.* Medscape, June 13. https:// www.medscape.com/slideshow/sexual-harassment-of-physicians-6010304.

National Academies of Sciences, Engineering, and Medicine. 2018. *Sexual Harassment of Women: Climate, Culture, and Consequences in Academic Sciences, Engineering, and Medicine.* Washington, DC: National Academies Press.

Strauss, S. 2019. "Overview and Summary: Sexual Harassment in Healthcare." *OJIN: The Online Journal of Issues in Nursing* 24(1). http://ojin.nursingworld.org /MainMenuCategories/ANAMarketplace/ANAPeriodicals/OJIN/TableofContents /Vol-24-2019/No1-Jan-2019/OS-Sexual-Harassment-in-Healthcare.html.

Van Dis, J., L. Stadum, and E. Choo. 2018. "Sexual Harassment Is Rampant in Health Care. Here's How to Stop It." *Harvard Business Review*, November 1. https://hbr .org/2018/11/sexual-harassment-is-rampant-in-health-care-heres-how-to-stop-it.

Health Effects

Sexual harassment consists of unwanted sexual attention that can take physical, verbal, visual, written, and online forms. It is often a dehumanizing experience for the survivor in which the desires of the perpetrator are prioritized over the survivor's right to safety, comfort, and agency. Experiences of sexual harassment typically begin at puberty and continue through schooling, vocational training, and work. These dehumanizing experiences can result in depression, anxiety, general psychological distress, poorer physical health, disengagement from work or school, and even suicidal urges. The health effects of sexual harassment are typically worse when the harassment is chronic and in locations where the victim cannot easily avoid the abuser(s), such as at work or school. Although sexual harassment more commonly affects girls and women, boys and men can also be harassed and may suffer similar health effects, although the research literature in this area is quite limited. The effects can last long after the harassment has ended. Sexual harassment survivors can best recover from the effects of the harassment when they feel they have social support from their peer group, their organization (work/school), and society. Mindfulness-based therapy, reframing, group therapy, and talk therapy have all been found to be helpful.

It is clear from published research that experiences of sexual harassment strongly relate to poorer health and functioning among victims. Numerous studies conducted in the United States, Europe, and other parts of the globe since the 1990s confirm these findings. Studies also find that the health effects are usually worse when the harassment continues over a period of time, when it involves physical contact, when it is perpetrated by someone with a higher socioeconomic or cultural status, when it occurs by someone the survivor trusts (or should be able to trust), and when the harassment creates fear. The health effects are also often worse when sexual harassment is entangled with other forms of oppression, such as racial harassment or homophobia. Studies carried out over time (longitudinal studies) find that the sexual harassment predates the physical health symptoms.

Sexual harassment survivors are at higher risk for poor physical and mental health, riskier health behaviors, and impaired social functioning. Sexual harassment is largely associated with poorer physical health through somatic symptoms. These include gastrointestinal distress (e.g., stomach pain, diarrhea), chronic pain, headaches, sleep disorders, and cardiovascular symptoms. It is also associated with high blood pressure, diabetes, and other chronic diseases.

Poorer mental health and emotional distress is also associated with being a survivor of sexual harassment. Depression, anxiety and post-traumatic stress disorder (PTSD) are common responses to sexual harassment, particularly when it is chronic; suicidal ideation is also higher in survivors. Some authors suggest that the link between the onset of puberty in girls and the development of depression/low self-esteem may actually be due to the increase in sexual harassment that occurs when girls sexually mature. Eating disorders, riskier sexual behavior, and lower self-esteem are also linked to sexual harassment. Additionally, the social functioning of survivors may be impaired, as they may avoid situations (e.g., school, work, going out) and change travel routes to avoid the harasser.

The research on recovering from sexual harassment is limited, but the findings are consistent. In general, the strongest predictor of recovery is that the survivor perceives he or she has social support. This social support can be at the family level, the community level, or at the workplace. Strong school, workplace, and union support for survivors of sexual harassment is shown to buffer the potential negative health effects. Additional interventions for individuals may include talk therapy, support groups, and a focus on self-care.

Stacey B. Plichta

See also: Objectification of Women; Power Dynamics; Sexism

Further Reading

Bates, S. 2017. "Revenge Porn and Mental Health: A Qualitative Analysis of the Mental Health Effects of Revenge Porn on Female Survivors." *Feminist Criminology* 12(1): 22–42.

Bryant-Davis, T., ed. 2011. *Surviving Sexual Violence: A Guide to Recovery and Empowerment.* Lanham, MD: Rowman & Littlefield.

Gallegos, A. M., W. Cross, and W. R. Pigeon. 2015. "Mindfulness-Based Stress Reduction for Veterans Exposed to Military Sexual Trauma: Rationale and Implementation Considerations." *Military Medicine* 180(6): 684–689.

Lean In. n.d. "Self-Care after Sexual Harassment." https://leanin.org/meeting-guides/self-care-after-sexual-harassment.

Puente, M., and C. Kelly. 2018. "How Common Is Sexual Misconduct in Hollywood?: National Study Reveals Extent of Sexual Abuse." *USA Today.* February 23. https://www.usatoday.com/story/life/people/2018/02/20/how-common-sexual-misconduct-hollywood/1083964001/.

Singh, J., and F. I. Ullah. 2017. "Role of Perceived Social Support in Determining the Psychological Well-Being of Victims of Eve Teasing." *Indian Journal of Positive Psychology* 8 (3): 309–314.

Skoog, T. S. Bayram Özdemir, and H. Stattin. 2016. "Understanding the Link between Pubertal Timing in Girls and the Development of Depressive Symptoms: The Role of Sexual Harassment." *Journal of Youth and Adolescence* 45(2): 316–327.

Thurston, R. C, Y. Chang, K. A. Matthews, R. von Känel, and K. Koenen. 2019. "Association of Sexual Harassment and Sexual Assault with Midlife Women's Mental and Physical Health." *JAMA Internal Medicine* 179(1): 48–53.

Hill, Anita (1956–)

Anita Faye Hill grew up in a rural black farming community in Oklahoma as the youngest of thirteen children. She earned a BA at Oklahoma State University and her JD at Yale University. Early in her career, she worked in Washington, DC, for Clarence Thomas. Today, she is a Brandeis University law professor; however, she is most noted for her testimony on October 11, 1991, at the Senate confirmation hearings of U.S. Supreme Court justice Clarence Thomas. Hill's nationally tele-vised testimony, in which she alleged suffering sexual harassment from Thomas, sparked intense debate and heightened public awareness of the problem of sexual harassment in the workplace.

Like many accusers, Hill found her character vilified by supporters of the accused. In the case of Thomas, who had been nominated by Republican president George H. W. Bush, Republican senators and conservative pundits alleged that she was mentally unstable and promiscuous. Conservative columnist David Brock famously called her "a little bit nutty and a little bit slutty" in a 1992 *American Spectator* article and for similar attacks on her character and motivations in a best-selling book, *The Real Anita Hill*. Brock later apologized and retracted these statements and claims. During the Harvey Weinstein scandal of 2017, Democratic senator Joe Biden, who presided over the tense 1991 hearings, expressed public regret for his inability to protect Hill from his Republican colleagues' hostile questioning during the hearing. However, some of Biden's critics remained dis-satisfied. They asserted that it was not an inability to protect Hill as much as it was an unwillingness to take her claims seriously.

The hearings were broadcast live and drew record television audiences. Public discussion led to subsequent feminist demands for workplace policies and training that would hold both organizations and individual perpetrators accountable for sexual harassment. At the same time, it was alleged that Hill's public mistreatment by powerful men, whose own political careers suffered no damage then or now, stood as a warning of how easily male power in the workplace can be exercised with impunity through sexual intimidation.

Certainly, Thomas's nomination enjoyed vigorous support in Washington. Upon the retirement of U.S. Supreme Court justice Thurgood Marshall in 1991, President Bush sought to fill the post with another African American. Thomas's vehement opposition to affirmative action made him an attractive Republican nominee to the court, as did his libertarian, originalist judicial philosophy. Civil rights and feminist groups opposed his confirmation, however, for these same reasons.

Thomas had acted as Hill's supervisor from 1981 to 1983, first in his appoint-ment as assistant director at the Department of Education and again as chair of the Equal Employment Opportunity Commission (EEOC). In Hill's statement to the Senate Judiciary Committee and to the FBI, she described a pattern of periodic verbal sexual harassment from Thomas. The behavior consisted of persistent and unwelcome requests for dates, repeated and inappropriate comments on her appearance and sexual attractiveness, and disturbing graphic descriptions of scenes and characters in pornographic films.

Bush nominated Thomas to fill Marshall's seat on July 1, 1991. In early September, various staffers connected with Democratic senator Howard Metzenbaum, a member of the Senate Judiciary Labor Subcommittee, contacted Hill for verification of rumors of sexual harassment by Thomas at the EEOC. On September 23, she was interviewed at her home by FBI investigators concerning the harassment. In agreeing to come forward, Hill had insisted that she also be allowed to present a statement in her own words to the committee, which she wrote and sent on the same day.

On September 28, 1991, the Senate Judiciary Committee deadlocked 7–7 on a recommendation to the full Senate on Thomas's nomination. The committee subsequently sent the nomination to the Senate without a recommendation. The Senate vote was scheduled for October 8, 1991. The statement by Hill alleging sexual harassment was already in the possession of the committee, but it had apparently played little role in the decision to send Thomas's name forward.

However, the story of the allegation was leaked to the press. Timothy Phelps of *Newsday* and Nina Totenberg of National Public Radio both published the story on October 6, 1991. Despite an exhaustive investigation in the months following the fraught proceedings, the source of the leak was never identified.

Two days after the story broke, on October 8, 1991, seven female members of Congress marched from the House to the Senate to demand a delay in the confirmation vote to investigate the charges. Other spontaneous responses from women and women's groups were swift. Individual constituents contacted their representatives in great numbers, with many recounting stories of harassment experiences. A letter signed by two hundred women lawyers was delivered to the Senate on October 8 urging delay and investigation. On October 14, 1991, just days after the hearing, a group of five hundred women scholars signed a petition urging Judiciary Committee chair Joe Biden and the Senate to seriously consider the allegations of sexual harassment and to vote against the confirmation of Clarence Thomas. The petition stated that many women who experience sexual harassment, like Hill, do not immediately come forward with complaints.

On October 8, 1991, the outcome of a confirmation vote was very uncertain. The Senate therefore voted to delay. It then fell upon the committee to direct the process by which the allegations would be heard, and Thomas would be given an opportunity to respond to his accuser. The process decided upon has been subsequently criticized as ad hoc and even ultimately damaging to the institution as well as to the dignity of the two parties whose reputations were now so urgently at stake: Hill and Thomas. Because the hearing's purpose was so different from that of a courtroom, the process lacked the traditional safeguards that protect the adversarial parties' interests in a court of law.

Thomas was permitted to present first as well as to rebut the charges after Hill testified. Thomas was not required to hear Hill's testimony, so efforts to question him about specifics were impeded. After Hill gave her testimony, four corroborating witnesses for Hill were called, but two other women who had also allegedly experienced harassment from Thomas were never invited to testify before the committee. Witnesses in support of Thomas included a group of twenty women who had worked with or under him over the years. They contended that based on their own experiences of Thomas's behavior toward them in the workplace, he could not have engaged in harassing behavior.

Because Clarence Thomas and Anita Hill are African Americans, the allegations infused volatile issues of sexism into a process already fraught with racial overtones. The tense hearing consisted of an all-white, all-male committee directing embarrassing questions of a sexual nature to Hill. Footage of the hearing was carried live on all three major networks of the time, with record-breaking viewership. In 1991, inexpensive handheld video cameras and cable access were disrupting traditional media practices and the tone of media discourse on sensitive issues.

Though the process was not acknowledged as adversarial, the Republicans on the committee saw their role as a partisan one in defending their party's nominee against Hill and unnamed liberal special interest groups who expressed support for her and her claims. Democrat Dennis DeConcini as well as Republican senators Orrin Hatch, Alan Simpson, and Arlen Spector were particularly adversarial in their approach to questioning Hill. Senator (later vice president) Joe Biden saw his role as chair of the committee as one of impartial facilitator. Other Democrats on the committee were perhaps muted in their questioning of Thomas by his impassioned speech in his own defense—including a claim that he was a victim of a "high-tech lynching." The reference to lynching heightened an already racially tense proceeding. It is the best remembered quotation of any in the history of the court's confirmation proceedings. Thomas's adamant denials of ever asking Hill out or engaging in any inappropriate behavior as well as his veiled accusation of racism in the "high-tech lynching" reference proved effective enough for him to win confirmation to the Supreme Court by the narrowest margin in history: 52–48. Meanwhile, Hill took and passed a polygraph the following day on the advice of Charles Ogletree, her attorney, the results of which were released in a press statement.

Due to a number of factors, following the confirmation, the Bush administration lifted its veto of legislation that allowed victims of sexual harassment to sue for damages (up to $300,000). Previously, victims could only receive back pay if they prevailed in a suit. Organizations, schools, and businesses, including Congress itself, were urged (and pressured) to institute sexual harassment policies for the first time.

Cynthia Ninivaggi

See also: Congress; Equal Employment Opportunity Commission; Harvey Weinstein Scandal; Hostile Work Environment; Kavanaugh, Brett; Office/Workplace Settings; Sexism; Thomas, Clarence

Further Reading

Danforth, J. C. 1994. *Resurrection: The Confirmations of Clarence Thomas*. New York: Viking.

Hill, A. 1997. *Speaking Truth to Power*. New York: Doubleday.

Hill, A. F., and Emma Coleman Jordan. 1995. *Race, Gender, and Power in America: The Legacy of the Hill-Thomas Hearings*. New York: Oxford Press.

Kuczinsky, A., and William Glaberson. 2001. "U.S. Book Author Says He Lied in His Attacks on Anita Hill in Bid to Aid Justice Thomas." *New York Times*, June 27.

https://www.nytimes.com/2001/06/27/us/book-author-says-he-lied-his-attacks
-anita-hill-bid-aid-justice-thomas.html.

Mayer, J., and Jill Abramson. 1994. *Strange Justice: The Selling of Clarence Thomas*. Los Angeles: Graymalkin Media.

McNamara, B. 2017. "Joe Biden to Anita Hill: I Owe Her an Apology." *Teen Vogue*, December 13. https://www.teenvogue.com/story/joe-biden-anita-hill.

Morrison, T. 1992. *Race-Ing Justice, En-Gendering Power: Essays on Anita Hill, Clarence Thomas, and the Construction of Social Reality*. New York: Pantheon Books.

Smitherman, G. 1995. *African American Women Speak Out on Anita Hill–Clarence Thomas*. Detroit, MI: Wayne State University Press.

Horrible Bosses

Sexual harassment can look different to different people, but if there has been any form of sexual coercion, unwanted sexual attention, or gender harassment, then sexual harassment has occurred. When one thinks of sexual harassment in the workplace, the typical scenario is one in which hostile behaviors or degrading attitudes are being directed toward a female employee from a male employee. But men can be sexually harassed at work as well, and societal norms deter men from reporting instances when they have been sexually harassed. For instance, in 2017, when actors Terry Crews, Anthony Rapp, James Van Der Beek, Brendan Fraser, and Alex Winter, as well as some male models, came forward with sexual assault allegations against Hollywood talent agent Adam Venit and some high-profile entertainment industry photographers, some were condemned, ridiculed, and questioned as to whether the actions actually occurred. These reactions are not shocking, as men are typically viewed as perpetrators, not victims.

Horrible Bosses, a movie released in 2011, is a dark comedy directed by Seth Gordon and written by Michael Markowitz, John Francis Daley, and Jonathan Goldstein. A dark comedy refers to a comedic style that makes light of a topic that is considered to be controversial, sensitive, or painful to discuss. Although the film's intent was to make light of murder, it subsequently made light of male victims of sexual harassment as well. The movie depicted the lives of three different men: Nick Hendricks (played by Jason Bateman), Dale Arbus (played by Charlie Day), and Kurt Buckman (played by Jason Sudeikis). All three men had a difficult relationship with their respective bosses, and they decided that the best way to get rid of their problems would be to murder them. With the help of Dean "MF" Jones (played by Jamie Foxx), the three men devise a plan to get rid of their bosses for good.

In this film, one of the men, Dale, is a dental assistant to a female dentist named Julia (played by Jennifer Anniston). Julia makes inappropriate comments to Dale on a number of occasions in regard to his looks and his body. Julia has made the workplace a hostile environment for Dale. At several points in the movie, Julia forcefully expresses sexual attraction to him. She sprays water on his crotch, traps him against his will in her office as she wears nothing but lingerie, and grabs his private parts while he is against the wall. Dale verbally and physically expresses his disinterest and disapproval of her actions (and outright accuses her of raping him), and by the end of the movie, he states that he wishes to work in a "rape-free environment."

When Dale speaks to his male friends on the matter, however, they show no sympathy for him. They view the predatory behavior of his boss as an honor and not a gross violation of his sexual rights. Nick and Kurt constantly tease him and tell him he should be grateful that his beautiful boss is attracted to him.

Although the actions of Julia are overdramatized for comedic purposes, they draw attention to the not so discussed sexism when it comes to women perpetrators. This film exemplifies how easily sexual harassment committed by a female can be dismissed. The male victim in this movie tried reaching out for help from his friends, but they were unconcerned about his plight. In contrast, a film glorifying a middle-aged male hygienist harassing and molesting his young dental assistant might not be viewed as comical. Certainly, if a young woman was raped or molested by her boss and told her friends, they would not say that she should be grateful that such an attractive man wanted to sleep with her. This is because rape or sexual harassment of a female is considered serious and tragic in society, while the sexual harassment of a man is considered something that happens to weak men. Dale himself is portrayed as small, nervous, and cowardly, further perpetuating the idea that only a weak man can be a victim of sexual abuse.

By the end of the movie, one boss has been killed, one is in jail, and Julia is simply blackmailed into stopping the behavior, suffering no real consequence for her actions. At the end of the film, Dale blackmails her as she is about to perform oral sex on a patient assumed to be under anesthesia. Julia is clearly a serial rapist. However, because her victims are male, the movie does not portray her as a predator, but instead as an older woman crossing boundaries to have sex with younger men.

Although not as common, these gender expectations are contributing factors as to why men and women may not feel validated. Many men may be going through variations of sexual harassment or worse but will not speak up due to societal "norms." In this current climate, where mental health is discussed more than in the past, we are more open to nullifying the patriarchal gender role norms. This Westernized psychology of men and masculinity can be tackled through acknowledging the fact that men can be victims of unwanted sexual attention just as women can be. The validation and relief those men achieve when they have laid out their insecurities and experiences is contagious, and the more men that come forward with their experiences, the closer society can get to striking down these damaging views of male masculinity. The rape and sexual harassment of men is overshadowed by the film's comedic dialogue, despite its blatant display of abuse.

M'Balu P. Bangura and Ajaratu Alghali

See also: Hostile Work Environment; #MeToo Movement; Music/Video Settings; Quid Pro Quo; Retaliation

Further Reading

Holland, K. J., V. C. Rabelo, A. M. Gustafson, R. C. Seabrook, and L. M. Cortina. 2016. "Sexual Harassment against Men: Examining the Roles of Feminist Activism, Sexuality, and Organizational Context." *Psychology of Men & Masculinity* 17(1): 17–29. https://ezproxy.tcnj.edu:2083/10.1037/a0039151.

Walsh, K. 2018. "Commentary: Some Stereotyped Women's Film Roles We'd Like to Do Away With." *Los Angeles Times*, March 16. www.latimes.com/entertainment/movies /la-ca-mn-women-stereotyped-roles-20180316-story.html.

Hostile Work Environment

More than a half century after *hostile work environment* became popularized in the American lexicon, the occurrence and adverse effects created by the phenomenon persist. According to the U.S. Equal Employment Opportunity Commission (EEOC), the federal agency instituted by Title VII of the Civil Rights Act of 1964, a hostile work environment is one in which a culture of offensive, abusive, retaliatory, intimidating, or harassing behavior severely or pervasively alters conditions of employment (29 C.F.R. § 1604.11(a)). Criteria to establish grounds of a hostile work environment include a workplace containing fifteen or more employees that has violations of federal laws and other protections against discrimination based on race, age (forty years and older), color, national origin, gender, or religion.

Today, a hostile work environment is one of two types of workplace sexual harassment recognized by law. The other type is quid pro quo. The Latin term literally means "something for something."

The 1986 U.S. Supreme Court ruling *Meritor Savings Bank v. Vinson* (1986) set a precedent for the EEOC and extended protections against sexual harassment in the workplace. In this case, the court ruled that sexual harassment was a violation of Title VII of the Civil Rights Act of 1964. Michelle Vinson, an African American woman who worked as a bank teller and assistant branch manager, reported that she was sexually discriminated against and sexually harassed by her supervisor. The U.S. Supreme Court determined that Vinson was subject to sexually stereotyped insults and demeaning propositions and that these actions had created a hostile work environment.

Despite this historic ruling, studies reveal that many women remain reluctant to report sexual harassment for fear of job-related consequences, concerns that the assaults will be trivialized, and fears that their credibility will be impugned.

ASPECTS OF HOSTILE WORK ENVIRONMENTS

A hostile work environment is often characterized by discriminatory intimidation, the circulation of damaging rumors, ridicule, an undermining of one's work efforts, and hurled insults that sufficiently alter the conditions of the victim's employment. Depending on a variety of factors, including the identity of the abuser and the nature of the abuse, these behaviors may be referred to as bullying, incivility, moral harassment, psychological harassment, mobbing, systemic maltreatment, microaggressions and macroaggressions, or sexual harassment. Regardless of the terminology, the effects are pervasive, detrimental, and long-lasting.

According to the EEOC's 2019 data on charges alleging sex-based harassment, there were 12,739 claims filed, of which 692 lawsuits resulted in settlements. During the same year, the EEOC also reported recovering approximately $68.2 million for victim-survivors of sexual harassment through litigation and administration enforcement, an increase of $11.6 million from the previous year.

The enduring problem of sexual harassment as a form of hostile work environment has garnered increased attention through the work of women such as Tarana Burke, the creator of the #MeToo Movement; Nina Shaw, the cofounder of the Time's Up Movement; and Kenyette Barnes, the founder of the #MuteRKelly Movement. Victim-survivors and silence breakers who have leveled sexual harassment and abuse allegations against powerful politicians, celebrities, and business executives have greatly increased recognition that hostile work environments remain commonplace. Despite the national visibility of these cases, legislation strengthening the prohibition against sexual harassment, and a plethora of EEOC claims, some victim-survivors still endure abuse in silence rather than risk their jobs or reputations.

ANALYSIS OF SOCIAL JUSTICE AND SOCIAL LEARNING THEORIES

According to Crenshaw (2015) and Collins (2017), a hostile work environment takes diverse theoretical frameworks into account. Carbado and Harris (2019) contend that there are fundamental differences in regard to race and challenging hierarchy. Whereas women who experience sexual harassment based on their gender may share a sameness when measured against men, there are significant historical differences based on race.

From the view of Fredrickson and Robert's objectification theory, socialization in the United States leads to women and girls being treated as sex objects. That links to societal messaging with interlocking forms of behavior and oppression. Cheney et al. (2015) reported that servicewomen employed protective strategies to reduce the threat of sexual harassment and sexual assault, such as wearing nonfeminine clothing to minimize violence exposure and not challenging the social hierarchy of the military culture.

In another study, Chmielewski (2017) found that sexual harassment among adolescents was correlated with their identities (e.g., gender, race, sexuality). These oppressive perspectives reinforce power structures that view women as subordinate. Schulz and Braekkan's (2017) study indicated that consumers with low levels of perceived behavioral control tended to justify their consumer behaviors, as they did not believe they could make a difference. In the context of sexual harassment, it is plausible to say that the harasser's behavior toward his or her victim is both calculated and impulsive. Planned or unplanned, the harasser's actions result in the same outcome for the victims—isolation, invisibility, marginalization, and limited access to social mobility.

HOSTILE WORK ENVIRONMENTS IN DIFFERENT INDUSTRIES

Studies have found that hostile work environments have been most frequently alleged in the American service industry, including the retail, food services, and hospitality sectors, accounting for 30 percent of all such allegations. Following the service industry are manufacturing, health care, and social assistance workers (Paquette 2017). Observers note that all these industries boast a high number of women employees with few women in leadership roles. Regardless of industry, this dynamic contributes to organizational climates that foster a hostile work environment and fears that reporting such problems will result in retaliation. Organizational employers invested in supporting victim-survivors can no longer view themselves as neutral or innocent bystanders.

The psychological effects of being employed in a hostile work environment can be profound. In severe cases, researchers have found that victims exhibited symptoms similar to post-traumatic stress disorder (PTSD). Studies also revealed that the effects of a hostile work environment include decreased job satisfaction, increased psychological distress, and organizational withdrawal behaviors. Victims may express additional withdrawal behaviors, such as lowered morale and productivity, despondency, tardiness, absenteeism, depression, disruption in sleep, and reduced appetite. Notwithstanding these similarities, survivors who challenge systems that uphold hostile work environments also tend to endure social isolation. It is imperative to make their narratives visible.

GOALS

Literature affirms that the laws in regard to sexual harassment primarily focus on the victim-survivor's perceptions rather than on the offender's intention. Seeking solutions for victim-survivors must include holding so-called innocent bystanders accountable. The twenty-first century has seen a steady growth of sexual harassment and misconduct incidents across industries and postsecondary institutions. Adapting an intersectional approach to understanding policies (e.g., the Checklist for Campus Sexual Misconduct) and oppressive practices can help to create safe work and learning environments for victim-survivors.

Selena T. Rodgers, Erzulie Vica Mars, and Sebrena Kearns

See also: Equal Employment Opportunity Commission; #MeToo Movement; Objectification of Women; Quid Pro Quo; Time's Up Movement; Title VII of the Civil Rights Act of 1964; Unions

Further Reading

Carbado, D. W., and C. I. Harris. 2019. "Intersectionality at 30: Mapping the Margins of Anti-Essentialism, Intersectionality, and Dominance Theory." *Harvard Law Review* 132(8): 2193–2239.

Cheney, A. M., H. S. Reisinger, B. M. Booth, M. A. Mengeling, J. C. Torner, and A. G. Sadler. 2015. "Servicewomen's Strategies to Staying Safe during Military Service." *Gender Issues* 32(1): 1–18.

Chmielewski, J. F. 2017. "A Listening Guide Analysis of Lesbian and Bisexual Young Women of Color's Experiences of Sexual Objectification." *Sex Roles: A Journal of Research* 77(7–8): 533–549.

Collins, P. H. 2017. "On Violence, Intersectionality and Transversal Politics." *Ethnic and Racial Studies* 40(9): 1460–1473.

Crenshaw, K. 2015. "Why Intersectionality Can't Wait." *Washington Post*, September 24.

Hooks, B. 1981. *Ain't I a Woman: Black Woman and Feminism.* New York: South End Press.

MacKinnon, C. A. 1979. *Sexual Harassment of Working Women: A Case of Sex Discrimination.* New Haven, CT: Yale University Press.

Meritor Savings Bank v. Vinson, 477 U.S. 57 1986.

Paquette, D. 2017. "The Industries with the Worst Sexual Harassment Problem." *Washington Post*, November 24. https://www.washingtonpost.com/news/wonk/wp/2017/11/24/the-industries-with-the-worst-sexual-harassment-problem.

Schulz, M., and K. F. Braekkan. 2017. "Social Justice Attitudes and Concerns for Labor Standards: An Empirical Investigation of the Theory of Planned Behaviors and Consumer Actions." SAGE Open (January). https://journals.sagepub.com/doi/full/10.1177/2158244016688135.

U.S. Department of Education Office of Civil Rights. 2017. "Campus Sexual Misconduct." https://www2.ed.gov/about/offices/list/ocr/docs/qa-title-ix-201709.pdf.

U.S. Equal Employment Opportunity Commission (EEOC). 2018. "Facts about Sexual Harassment." https://www.eeoc.gov/eeoc/publications/fs-sex.cfm.

U.S. Equal Employment Opportunity Commission (EEOC). 2019. "Charges Alleging Sex-Based Harassment (Charges Field with the EEOC) FY 2010–FY 2019." https://www.eeoc.gov/eeoc/statistics/enforcement/sexual_harassment_new.cfm.

Human Trafficking

According to the U.S. Department of Homeland Security (DHS), human trafficking involves the use of force, fraud, or coercion to obtain some type of labor or commercial sex from victims. Over different time periods in history, human trafficking has been called by many different names. In its purest form, human trafficking is slavery; hence, scholars in recent years have termed human trafficking as modern-day slavery. Numerous federal laws have been passed to define human trafficking, with the most recent laws starting after the passage of the Trafficking Victims Protection Act 2000 (TVPA). There is a great disparity in the estimated number of incidents of human trafficking and the cases that are prosecuted in court proceedings. This is a cause for concern for governments struggling to fulfill their civic duties to protect the basic human rights of their citizens.

Every year, trafficking claims millions of victims worldwide and involves victims of all ages, races, genders, and nationalities. According to one report, human trafficking generates global profits of about $150 billion a year, with about two-thirds of that stemming from forced prostitution and other sexual exploitation (Gallucci 2019).

In rural areas, human trafficking is one of the most underpoliced and underresearched crimes. The main focus on human trafficking is set in urban areas or at the international level. Reports suggest that although human trafficking is primarily seen as an urban phenomenon, Polaris and other human trafficking tip line services illustrate something that is quite to the contrary. "The general public thinks that trafficking of girls occurs in inner cities," stated Dr. Sharon Cooper, who treats sexually traumatized children and adults trying to recover from their trafficking experiences. "We've seen cases where girls were taken to farms and sold to migrant farmers, drugged in order to become compliant. We've seen girls who have been living in homeless shelters, and who come out of the homeless shelter just to walk down the street, but that homeless shelter has been cased by traffickers who will then drive down the street and say, 'Hey I have a job for you, and you can get the tips'" (Gallucci 2019).

This disparity may be due to human trafficking's trait as an elusive crime that is further compounded by the isolation that is characteristic of rural areas. In addition, a compilation of human trafficking cases released by the United States Attorney's Office (USAO) suggests that there is a higher prevalence of extreme behaviors that accompany rural human trafficking cases.

In one case example, the defendants, Edward Bagley and Marilyn Bagley, recruited minor females from 2004 to 2009 to their trailer home in a rural area in the Western District of Missouri. The Bagley's used recruitment methods often used by sex offenders. They evaded the law and abused victims for long periods— during which time they subjected the girls to numerous forms of torture and other sadistic acts—because they were not strangers to their victims and their families. Instead, they were close to the family members, friends, or well-respected individuals in the community, and they used their positions to groom their victims into trusting them. The minor girls they recruited suffered from mental health issues and came from troubled childhoods. Findings also suggest that traffickers use violence, manipulation, or false promises of well-paying jobs or even romantic relationships to lure victims.

Future research is needed to investigate the different dynamics of human trafficking regardless of the nation, region, or setting in which it occurs. Because some victims are of different nationalities, language barriers may make it difficult for them to report the crimes. There is also fear of their traffickers and fear of law enforcement, which keeps them from seeking help. These factors make human trafficking more likely to be a hidden crime.

There are policies and programs that have been created to help address these types of issues when it comes to certain populations of victims of human trafficking. This is especially important for those that are marginalized in some manner from mainstream society, inhibiting them from reporting their captors. Some of the simpler programs that help to overcome language barriers are flyers, billboards, victim advocates, and victim services. Many of these are in different languages, which enables victims to communicate and be more comfortable in reaching out for help.

One of the major policies that some cities have enacted to address the victims' fear of law enforcement due to deportation is the concept of "sanctuary cities." The sanctuary city initiative (starting in Berkeley and Los Angeles, California) has established a policy where local law enforcement is prohibited from working with U.S. Immigration and Customs Enforcement (ICE). This helps to ameliorate the concerns of people who may have problems with their immigration status (and may be of interest to ICE) from going forward to report or cooperate with local law enforcement.

Consequently, due to local law enforcement's noncooperation with ICE, the policy helps to ease fears of deportation of individuals that may have otherwise had this concern. This engenders a community environment where these individuals would be more open and willing to work with police on matters concerning human trafficking. Therefore, sanctuary cities subsequently create a local police force that can work more closely with the communities they serve to better address their needs.

There has been forward progress in developing initiatives to combat human trafficking; however, there is still more room for development and improvement of existing programs. Practitioners need to be more aware of better ways to prevent and treat victims of this crime. Strategies that focus on better identifying the most likely locations where human trafficking could occur, developing more tailored approaches for treating victims, and identifying conditions that engender environments conducive to human trafficking are some of the areas that need to be improved to more effectively address human trafficking. Some of this progression to grasp a firmer understanding of human trafficking to produce effective initiatives may be hindered by the limited availability of data. This is an area where governments have to step up to fund initiatives to collect comprehensive data on human trafficking so that authorities can (1) better understand its operations and effects and (2) develop effective programs to address the root causes of human trafficking and care for its victims.

Wendy Dressler and Brent Blakeman

See also: Predatory Sex Offenders; Violence Against Women Reauthorization Act of 2013

Further Reading

Gallucci, J. 2019. "Human Trafficking Is an Epidemic in the U.S. It's Also Big Business." *Fortune*, April 14. https://fortune.com/2019/04/14/human-sex-trafficking-us-slavery/.

Kakar, S. 2017. *Human Trafficking.* Durham, NC: Carolina Academic Press.

Polaris Project website. https://polarisproject.org/.

Taylor, H., and L. Mickelwait. 2017. "The Fight against Sex Trafficking in the U.S." Ethics and Religious Liberty Association, Southern Baptist Convention, October 13. https://erlc.com/resource-library/articles/the-fight-against-sex-trafficking-in-the-u-s.

Incel

The term *involuntary celibacy*, later shortened to "incel," is thought to have first been coined in the 1990s to refer to the experience of those people who are unable to engage in a romantic or sexual relationship, despite their desire to find one. It is thought that this online subculture first developed as part of a website that was created by a young woman in Canada, known only as Alana. The online community, titled "Alana's Involuntary Celibacy Project," was first developed for lonely people to discuss their experiences and find support. Over time, this community moved to message boards and social media, and it began to draw participation from resentful, angry, and even aggressive (mostly male) individuals.

Presently, the term *incel* is used to broadly refer to a radicalized online subculture associated with other hate groups, including patriarchal, alt-right, and other hate groups. This form of extremism has been identified as playing a role in multiple violent acts, including rape and murder. Most notoriously, in 2014, a young man in California named Elliot Rodgers uploaded a video to YouTube explaining that he wished to punish those he blamed for his involuntary celibacy, including the women who rejected him and the males who were sexually active. He then went on a rampage, first with a knife and then with a gun, killing six and injuring fourteen people near a college campus in Isla Vista, California, before he took his own life with police closing in. Following this incident, hashtag campaigns such as #YesAllWomen emerged, where women described experiences of harassment and violence when refusing sexual advances by men. These stories demonstrated the danger posed by angry and resentful males who felt entitled to sex.

Incel narratives make the valid point that sexual desire is not equally distributed and follows the lines of other forms of power and oppression, including wealth, weight, and norms of male attractiveness. Srinivasan (2018) identified that "no one has a right to be desired, but also that who is desired and who isn't is a political question." As such, gender role expectations play an important part in the incel subculture. Gender discrepancy stress, which refers to the stress experienced due to self-perception of not conforming to prescribed gender roles in a given community, is an issue with some incels (Reidy et al. 2015). Males who experience stress for feeling "submasculine" have been found to engage in risky and violent behavior, including sexual violence, to demonstrate their masculinity. Importantly, all people have the potential to experience gender-related stress and its negative consequences because many gender norms are an impossible ideal to achieve.

Despite perceptions that hook-up culture and promiscuous sexuality are on the rise, national data suggests that youth and young adults are engaging in sex later, less frequently, and with fewer partners than prior generations (Finer and Philbin 2014; Twenge, Sherman, and Wells 2017). However, popular media representations promote an image that other people are engaging in a lot of sex, further promoting a sense of inequity among individuals who are unsuccessful in their efforts to engage in sexual relations with people to whom they are attracted. The incel subculture responds to this perceived or real inequity through resentment and rhetoric that has the potential to incite violence.

Ultimately, though, the violent side of involuntary celibacy is not about a desire for sex. Instead, it brings together beliefs about male superiority and entitlement. Some of the central tenets of rape culture are that males need and are entitled to sex with women. Further, rape culture shames women who are sexually active and blames women who have been raped for allegedly provocative behavior. These attitudes equate rape with sex instead of a violent act meant to exert power. Attitudes such as these are also attributed to other forms of violence, such as stalking, in which rejection is identified as a primary motivator for the most dangerous and common form. As such, they normalize and excuse sexually aggressive and violent behavior, forming a foundation for the incel subculture.

Poco Kernsmith

See also: Gender Equality; Power Dynamics; Relationship Violence; Stalking

Further Reading

Finer, L. B., and J. M. Philbin. 2014. "Trends in Ages at Key Reproductive Transitions in the United States, 1951–2010." *Women's Health Issues: Official Publication of the Jacobs Institute of Women's Health* 24(3): 271–279.

Reidy, D. E., J. P. Smith-Darden, K. S. Cortina, R. M. Kernsmith, and P. D. Kernsmith. 2015. "Masculine Discrepancy Stress, Teen Dating Violence, and Sexual Violence Perpetration among Adolescent Boys." *Journal of Adolescent Health* 56(6): 619–624.

Srinivasan, A. 2018. "Does Anyone Have the Right to Sex?" *London Review of Books* 40(6): 5–10.

Twenge, J. M., R. A. Sherman, and B. E. Wells. 2017. "Declines in Sexual Frequency among American Adults, 1989–2014." *Archives of Sexual Behavior* 46(8): 162.

Iwu, Adama (1977–)

Adama Iwu is the cofounder and board president of the We Said Enough Foundation, an organization devoted to combating sexual harassment and bullying in American culture. Born on January 1, 1997, Iwu received her bachelor of arts degree in political science from the University of San Diego and later obtained her master's degree in public administration. Following her graduation, she began working for Governor Arnold Schwarzenegger's administration in California in 2005 as an executive fellow. Between 2010 and 2015, she worked as the head of California's Government Affairs for Farmers Insurance. In January 2015, she became the senior director of State and Local Government Relations for Visa and continues to work there today.

In October 2017, Iwu was standing outside the state capitol building with several work colleagues following a work event. They were discussing the role of men in serving as allies for sexually harassed women when a drunk colleague inappropriately touched her. Although Iwu repeatedly said no to his advances and pushed the man away, none of her other male colleagues she had been chatting with stepped in. This was not the first time she had been sexually harassed; however, the circumstances of this particular event inspired her to speak out for the first time.

In response to the incident, Iwu sent an open letter to the *Los Angeles Times* discussing the climate in California politics regarding sexual harassment, assault, and discrimination. The letter was not just from Iwu, though; 140 women signed it to send the same message regarding the toxic culture of sexism and sexual harassment that was present in many areas of California politics. Iwu's leadership in calling attention to the issue brought her national attention, including inclusion in *Time Magazine*'s 2017 list of "Silence Breakers"—female and male survivors who were speaking out against sexual harassment and misconduct. Since then, she has been working to change the climate of tacit acceptance that has traditionally surrounded sexual harassment in politics.

Sexual harassment in politics has been an issue since women first entered the political stage. As men found themselves working side by side with women, some welcomed them, some tolerated them, and some objectified them. Even though this has been a problem for a long time, it is just now receiving significant attention from the media as public awareness has increased. Historically, sexual harassment has been underreported by women in positions of power because of the fear of repercussions, such as losing their jobs. But emboldened by the #MeToo movement, women have started speaking up about the sexual harassment they have faced in politics and other careers.

Following the publication of the letter, more women started coming forward with their stories. Iwu and some of her friends set up a website where they could do just that in a safe space. However, it grew into something much bigger; it led to the creation of the We Said Enough Foundation, which serves as a platform to discuss and end workplace sexual harassment and to give women a voice. Iwu herself serves on the foundation's board as its president.

Since Iwu stepped to the forefront of the battle against sexual harassment, the City and County of San Francisco's Commission on the Status of Women has passed a resolution recognizing her efforts. She has worked closely with the commission to create new recommendations for addressing and preventing sexual harassment. Some of the recommendations include requiring city and county employees to undergo sexual harassment training and mandating that the Department of Human Services (DHS) publish statistics on anti-harassment training and harassments.

Adama Iwu is just one of many women in recent years who has courageously spoken about the issue and their personal experiences in the public sphere. She has made herself a strong advocate for women and a role model for those in similar situations.

Gemini Creason-Parker and Jennifer Edwards

See also: #MeToo Movement; Sexism; *Time Magazine* "Silence Breakers"

Further Reading

City and County of San Francisco. 2018a. "New Recommendations on Strengthening Sexual Harassment Prevention and Response." Department on the Status of Women, March 1. https://sfgov.org/dosw/new-recommendations-strengthening-sexual-harassment-prevention-and-response.

City and County of San Francisco. 2018b. "Resolution Recognizing Adama Iwu." San Francisco Commission on the Status of Women, February 28. https://sfgov.org/dosw/resolution-recognizing-adama-iwu-2-28-2018.

Crawley, Edmund. 2018. "Adama Iwu: Time's Person of the Year 2017 on the Fight against Sexual Harassment." *Cambridge Student*, July 1. https://www.tcs.cam.ac.uk/adama-iwu-time-s-person-of-the-year-2017-on-the-fight-against-sexual-harassment/.

Luna, Taryn, and Alexei Koseff. 2017. "Campaign Grows against Sexual Harassment at California Capitol." *Sacramento Bee*, October 20. https://www.sacbee.com/news/politics-government/capitol-alert/article179882956.html.

Mason, Melanie. 2017. "California Lobbyist Who Spoke Out against Sexual Harassment in the Capitol Featured on Time's 'Person of the Year' Cover." *Los Angeles Times*, December 6. https://www.latimes.com/politics/essential/la-pol-ca-essential-politics-updates-california-lobbyist-who-spoke-out-1512586211-htmlstory.html.

Megerian, Chris, Melanie Mason, Dakota Smith, and Jack Dolan. 2017. "In Her Own Words: Women of California Politics Tell Their Stories of Sexual Harassment and Unwanted Touching." *Los Angeles Times*, October 29. https://www.latimes.com/politics/la-pol-ca-sexual-harassment-sacramento-2017-htmlstory.html.

Professional Business Women of California. 2018. "Adama Iwu." http://pbwconference.org.

Tahirih Justice Center. 2018. "Adama Iwu Calls on Us All to Join the Ranks." March 19. https://www.tahirih.org/news/adama-iwu-calls-on-us-all-to-join-the-ranks/.

J

Jenson vs. Eveleth Taconite Co. (1997)

Widely regarded as the first class action sexual harassment lawsuit to be litigated in the United States, *Jenson vs. Eveleth Taconite* (filed in August 1988) determined that Eveleth Mines condoned a culture that was hostile to women and that discriminated against women in hiring and promotion. In addition to providing a hard-won (but in some ways hollow) victory for harassed miners, *Jenson vs. Eveleth Taconite* illustrates the severe difficulties imposed by corporate, union, cultural, and court processes on employees who seek justice for claims of sexual harassment.

The complaint against the mine originated with an employee, Lois Jenson, who joined the organization's overwhelmingly male workforce in 1975 along with a few other women. The company opened its workforce to women only after it was directed by a federal mandate to offer a handful of well-paid union jobs to women. Jenson's first days at the mine served as a crash course in the patterns of harassment that would become familiar to her and other women working in the mine. In both subtle and bold ways, male employees of the mine acted to ensure that women felt unappreciated and unwelcomed. For example, there were reports of men entering the women's locker room during work shifts and ejaculating on unattended clothing and personal belongings. Harassment regularly included pornographic graffiti, lewd comments, unwanted sexual and romantic advances, and open displays of a variety of handmade props intended to emulate genitals or sex toys. Male employees frequently told women miners they were not wanted as coworkers and urinated in plain sight of female coworkers during work shifts. Women not comfortable doing the same were required to summon a portable bathroom to be delivered (with harassing fanfare) to their job site. Favoritism of men was the rule. Assertions that women "didn't belong" in mining jobs was common. The occasional extensions of what resembled good will toward women were mostly confined to men interested in dating or having sex with the miners. Jenson even received harassing letters from her supervisor.

According to the court's findings, this hypersexualized and hostile-to-women work atmosphere was created collectively by the community of men working at the mine. Its existence, the court found, was largely ignored by mine management and union leadership. An additional obstacle faced by victims of sexual harassment at Eveleth Mines was the lack of full trust and comradery among the women of the mine. Many women were inclined against making waves about the harassment for fear of losing their jobs or being singled out for retaliation or extra harassment. Harassed miners also did not want to lose what little support they had from their male coworkers—support that was earned, in part, by not complaining about harassment.

Another aspect of mine culture that presented a challenge to fighting harassment was the union, which enforced a strong social norm against complaining about another union member. The overwhelmingly male union leadership did not prioritize protection of the women's interests in the workplace. Language was eventually added to the union contract in the late 1980s, noting that harassment was against company policy, but the resulting policy was largely unenforceable, as it did not indicate a point person or mechanism for reporting or counteracting sexual harassment.

Attorney Paul Sprenger served as lead counsel on the case, officially known as *Lois E. Jenson and Patricia S. Kosmach v. Eveleth Taconite Co.*, filed in August 1988 in the U.S. district court in Minneapolis. Class action status was granted by Judge James M. Rosenbaum on December 16, 1991. Although the court eventually ruled in favor of the women miners, the victory came at high cost and after a significant passage of time. During litigation, Jenson and other miners associated with the class action endured protracted depositions wherein intimate details of their personal lives were probed and their medical histories were disclosed. The payout received (averaging $10,000 per harassed miner) was viewed by many observers as inadequate compensation, given what the plaintiffs had endured. The special master appointed to determine financial damages owed to victims in this case was later found to have committed legal errors in his report. After laying the burden of proof of harassment on the plaintiffs, he refused to allow the expert testimony that could have demonstrated the emotional harm caused by the sexual harassment.

The original monetary judgment was appealed and reversed by the U.S. Court of Appeals for the Eighth Circuit on December 5, 1997. Marking a decade of litigation, a final settlement was reached on December 1998, wherein fifteen miners received a total of $3.5 million from Eveleth Mines. *Jenson vs. Eveleth Taconite* was later dramatized in the 2005 feature film *North Country*, starring Charlize Theron and directed by Niki Caro.

Anne Cross

See also: Factory and Manufacturing Settings; Retaliation; Workplace Gender Diversity

Further Reading

Bingham, C., and L. L. Gansler. 2003. *Class Action: The Story of Lois Jenson and the Landmark Case That Changed Sexual Harassment Law.* New York: Doubleday.

Crain, M. 1995. "Women, Labor Unions, and Hostile Work Environment Sexual Harassment: The Untold Story." *Texas Journal of Women & Law* 4: 9.

Fitzgerald, L. F. 2003. "Sexual Harassment and Social Justice: Reflections on the Distance Yet to Go." *American Psychologist* 58(11): 915–924. https://doi.org/10.1037/0003-066X.58.11.915.

Hart, M. 2002. "Litigation Narratives: Why Jenson v. Eveleth Didn't Change Sexual Harassment Law, but Still Has a Story Worth Telling." *Berkeley Women's Law Journal* 18: 282. http://scholar.law.colorado.edu/articles/524/.

O'Brien, M. 1993. "Jenson v. Eveleth Taconite Co.: A Legal Standard for Class Action Sexual Harassment." *Journal of Corporate Law* 19: 417.

Judd, Ashley (1968–)

American actress and political activist Ashley Judd was born April 19, 1968, in Granada Hills, California. Judd grew up in a family of famous performers as the daughter and half-sister of country music stars Naomi Judd and Wynonna Judd, respectively. Her family moved around frequently during her youth, and she was enrolled in twelve schools over a span of thirteen years before entering college. She was a member of the sorority Kappa Kappa Gamma and elected to Phi Beta Kappa at the University of Kentucky. Before graduating, however, Judd dropped out of college and moved across the country to start an acting career in Hollywood. She landed a few small parts on television and in motion pictures during the 1980s, but in the following decade, she emerged as a genuine movie star on the strength of critically praised performances in films that included *Ruby in Paradise* (1993), *Kiss the Girls* (1997), *Simon Birch* (1998), and *Double Jeopardy* (1999).

Judd was named one of "The 50 Most Beautiful People in the World" by *People* magazine in 1999. She speaks French fluently and has been married and divorced once. She has also used her stardom to bring attention to a variety of political and humanitarian causes. In 2005, for example, she testified to the U.S. Senate Foreign Relations Committee on "Stopping Cross Generational Sex and Sexual Violence to Protect Young Women from AIDS in Developing Countries: A Call to Action." She also served as the global ambassador for Youth AIDS International and as a member of the board of directors of Population Services International (PSI). In 2007, Judd completed her degree at the University of Kentucky and went on to earn an MBA from Harvard University.

Ashley Judd made headlines in 2017 when she became the first in a long line of entertainment industry workers to make public allegations of sexual misconduct against Hollywood producer Harvey Weinstein. She recounted how, in 1997, Weinstein, the head of Miramax Studios, had invited her to a meeting in his Beverly Hills hotel room. According to Judd, Weinstein attempted to force her into the bed, but she got away. Judd did not stay quiet about the encounter and immediately started telling everyone that would listen (Zacharek, Dockterman, and Edwards 2017).

Judd revealed that a friend who was a screenwriter told her that Weinstein's sexual misconduct was well known by those in the industry but that no one felt they could openly challenge the powerful producer's predatory behavior. In October 2017, Judd went on the record about Weinstein's behavior in the *New York Times*. She was the first star to expose Weinstein, and the world listened. However, Weinstein denied Judd's allegations and claimed that he had never had nonconsensual sex with other accusers (Zacharek, Dockterman, and Edwards 2017). After Judd made her allegations, Rose McGowan and more than forty other actresses and entertainment industry workers came forward with their own accusations against Weinstein. This rapid turn of events was an important factor in the rise of the #MeToo Movement.

Subsequently, Ashley Judd and five other plaintiffs filed a lawsuit seeking class action status against Harvey Weinstein, Miramax, the Weinstein Company, and members of its board. The suit claimed that these entities worked to "perpetuate and conceal Weinstein's widespread sexual harassment and assault," a cover-up that amounted to civil racketeering. In a joint statement, the plaintiffs claimed, "We are but six women representing hundreds" who had been harassed or assaulted by Weinstein (Salam 2017).

The lawsuit was filed in the U.S. District Court for the Southern District of New York. It stated that "actresses and other women in the film industry were lured to industry events, hotel rooms, Mr. Weinstein's home, office meetings or auditions to discuss projects, only to be victimized" by the film producer (Salam 2017). By Judd naming Weinstein, she both put an end to his career and laid bare the manipulative and abusive conditions that women were facing when trying to make it in the entertainment industry.

Weinstein was charged in New York with two counts of predatory sexual assault, one count of criminal sexual act in the first degree, and one count each of rape in the first and third degree. These charges stemmed from allegations that he raped a woman he knew in a hotel room in March 2013 and forcibly performed oral sex on another woman in 2006 at his Manhattan apartment. Weinstein denies all allegations of nonconsensual sex (Linton 2019).

In March 2020, he was found guilty of two of these counts: criminal sexual assault in the first degree and rape in the third degree. He was sentenced to twenty-three years in prison.

Carolyn Dennis

See also: Harvey Weinstein Scandal; McGowan, Rose; #MeToo Movement; Predatory Sex Offenders

Further Reading

Bernstein, J. 2017. "From Family Feuds to Taking Down Harvey: How Ashley Judd Learnt to Fight Back." *Telegraph*, October 26. Accessed February 7, 2019. https://www.telegraph.co.uk/films/0/family-feuds-taking-harvey-weinstein-ashley-judd-learnt-fight/.

Linton, C. 2019. "Ashley Judd's Sexual Harassment Lawsuit against Harvey Weinstein Dismissed." CBS News, January 9. Accessed February 9, 2019. https://www.cbsnews.com/news/ashley-judd-sexual-harassment-lawsuit-against-harvey-weinstein-dismissed-today-2019-01-09/.

Salam, M. 2017. "6 Women Sue Harvey Weinstein and His Former Businesses in Proposed Class Action." *New York Times*, December 6. Accessed February 7, 2019. https://www.nytimes.com/2017/12/06/business/harvey-weinstein-class-action.html?partner=bloomberg.

Zacharek, S., E. Dockterman, and H. S. Edwards. 2017. "*Time* Person of the Year 2017: The Silence Breakers." *Time*, December 18. Accessed February 7, 2019. http://time.com/time-person-of-the-year-2017-silence-breakers/.

K

K–12 Education, Peer-to-Peer

Peer-to-peer sexual harassment in K–12 education is a significant and growing social problem. Such encounters can have extremely negative consequences for students, teachers, parents, and schools. Students may suffer poor mental health or a decrease in overall well-being, while teachers struggle daily to provide a healthy learning environment. Parents are looking for ways to protect their children, and schools are facing increasing liability through ongoing changes to Title IX of the Education Amendments of 1972 regarding its implementation in the K–12 educational setting.

EXTENT OF SEXUAL HARASSMENT IN K–12 EDUCATION

It is almost impossible to determine the true amount of peer-to-peer sexual harassment occurring in K–12 education in the United States each year. Researchers, national gender equity organizations, and the Centers for Disease Control and Prevention (CDC) have released many findings that report how such harassment negatively impacts K–12 students, but violations are very often underreported by students due to embarrassment and fear of retaliation. Most researchers also believe that schools underreport such incidents to protect their reputations and school rankings. They note that national studies often show a clear disconnect between the small number of schools reporting incidents of sexual harassment and the large number of students stating they have experienced such incidents.

Research and national surveys support the belief that many K–12 students have been affected by peer-to-peer sexual harassment but rarely seek help. Unfortunately, schools frequently discount or dismiss reports of sexual harassment and assault or students are discouraged from reporting incidents. Obviously, by failing to properly address sexual harassment, schools may foster an environment where sexual harassment can continue and potentially lead to other types of assault.

The concept of school climate involves myriad aspects of a student's total educational experience. A positive school climate is most often the result of concentrated efforts by everyone involved to offer students a supportive academic program, a fair disciplinary structure, and a safe physical environment. Such a climate will generally foster physical and psychological development and safety. Research supports that such an environment will improve attendance, achievement, retention, and rates of graduation and reduce incidents of bullying, harassment, violence, and child suicide.

Peer sexual harassment is a significant threat to a positive school climate and can negatively impact student learning. Such harassment can weaken or destroy the relationships that connect them with fellow students, teachers, families, and their schools. It can make students question their safety as they try to participate in both educational and school-related extracurricular activities.

TITLE IX ISSUES

The basic element of Title IX is that it protects K–12 students from sexual harassment and discrimination as they participate in any and all academic, educational, extracurricular, and athletic programs at their schools. These protections are in place whether an activity occurs in the facilities of the school, on a school bus, or at any school-sponsored event. Ongoing debate exists, however, as to how this protection should be legally applied in real-life situations.

Directives from the Trump administration's U.S. Department of Education have allowed K–12 schools to shift the threshold (i.e., level of proof needed) that school officials use to decide whether an "incident" happened from the "preponderance of evidence" standard set under the Obama administration or a "clear and convincing evidence" standard, which is inherently a higher level of proof requirement. These changes also involve defining sexual harassment more narrowly as sexual assault or "unwelcome conduct on the basis of sex that is so severe, pervasive and objectively offensive that it denies a person access to the school's education program or activity." Under the previous guidance offered from the U.S. Department of Education, it was defined as "unwelcome conduct of a sexual nature."

These changes also impact the potential liability that K–12 schools will have regarding dealing with sexual harassment reporting. Currently, schools are to be held responsible for addressing a complaint if they have "actual knowledge" that an offense occurred, a higher level of proof than under prior guidance, which stated they were required to intervene if they "reasonably" should have known about a violation. The new guidance requires schools to respond to "conduct within its education program or activity," leading some institutions to pay little attention to incidents that occur off campus. This also places online harassment and misconduct, such as sending explicit photos or sending sexually inappropriate messages, in a gray area.

The new guidance also fails to properly address the rights of transgender students. Under separate Title IX guidance, the Obama administration asserted that the federal law requires schools to allow transgender students to use the pronouns, restrooms, and locker rooms that correspond with their gender identity. However, that policy changed under the Trump administration. In early 2017, U.S. Secretary of Education Betsy DeVos worked with U.S. Attorney General Jeff Sessions to revoke that guidance.

There are many ways in which K–12 education is trying to address peer-to-peer sexual harassment. All schools want to provide a healthy learning environment and try to maintain a positive school climate. They desire a climate that can potentially reduce the likelihood of harassment, bullying, and violence. Through a coordinated effort using evidence-based strategies, schools can create such a positive school climate.

A large part of any school's climate is the quality of peer-to-peer relationships among its students. There are many ways in which schools can enhance such relationships, including increasing students' competencies in self-awareness/ management, social awareness, relationship skills, and responsible decision-making. Healthy relationships between students are the foundation for preventing sexual and other forms of harassment, bullying, and other types of violence.

Students must be taught how to identify and avoid bullying, harassment, and teen-dating violence. Such instruction can help students learn positive relationship skills while they develop their own social-emotional skills. Children also learn characteristics of positive relationships and interactions by seeing them modeled by adults, including teachers and school administrators in the K–12 school educational setting.

Finally, researchers urge all school administrations to see peer-to-peer sexual harassment in K–12 American education as a significant issue that must be taken seriously. The mental and physical damage that is done to victims of such harassment can cause them to drop out of school, fail academically, or even commit self-harm and suicide. The repercussions of such victimization can follow a child into adulthood and negatively impact the child for the rest of his or her life. Efforts to determine the true extent of peer sexual harassment will continue as well as debates on how such incidents should be handled. Title IX implementation in the K–12 educational setting will continue as schools work to maintain positive school climates and healthy learning environments. While debates continue regarding proper approaches, most agree that solutions will be found through teaching children how to have positive relationships with themselves, their families, their schools, and with each other.

Gordon A. Crews

See also: Equal Employment Opportunity Commission; Relationship Violence; Title IX

Further Reading

Allnock, D., and R. Atkinson. 2019. "Snitches Get Stitches: School-Specific Barriers to Victim Disclosure and Peer Reporting of Sexual Harm Committed by Young People in School Contexts." *Child Abuse & Neglect* 89: 7–17.

Barnett, A., S. Molock, K. Nieves-Logo, and M. Zea. 2019. "Anti-LGBT Victimization, Fear of Violence at School, and Suicide Risk among Adolescents." *Psychology of Sexual Orientation and Gender Diversity* 6: 88–95.

Dobson, A. S. 2019. "'The Things You Didn't Do': Gender, Slut-Shaming, and the Need to Address Sexual Harassment in Narrative Resources Responding to Sexting and Cyberbullying." *Narratives in Research and Interventions on Cyberbullying among Young People* 10: 147–160.

Espelage, D. L., et al. 2018. "A Longitudinal Examination of Homophobic Name-Calling in Middle School: Bullying, Traditional Masculinity, and Sexual Harassment as Predictors." *Psychology of Violence* 8(1): 57–66.

Espelage, D. L., J. Sung-Hung, S. Rinehart, and N. Doshi. 2016. "Understanding Types, Locations, & Perpetrators of Peer-to-Peer Sexual Harassment in U.S. Middle Schools: A Focus on Sex, Racial, and Grade Differences." *Children and Youth Services Review* 71: 174–183.

Forber-Pratt, A., and D. L. Espelage. 2018. "Sexual Violence in K–12 Setting." In *The Wiley Handbook on Violence in Education: Forms, Factors, and Preventions*, edited by H. Shapiro, 375–392. Hoboken, NJ: John Wiley & Sons, Inc.

Leemis, R., D. Espelage, K. Basile, L. Kollar, and J. Davis. 2019. "Traditional and Cyber Bullying and Sexual Harassment: A Longitudinal Assessment of Risk and Protective Factors." *Aggressive Behavior* 45(2): 181–192.

Melnick, R. S., 2019. "Rethinking Federal Regulation of Sexual Harassment: The Need for Deliberation, Not Demagoguery, in the Age of Trump." *Education Next* 18(1): 8–15.

Meyer, E. J., A. Somoza-Norton, N. Lovgren, A. Rubin, and M. Quantz. 2018. "Title IX Coordinators as Street-Level Bureaucrats in U.S. Schools: Challenges Addressing Sex Discrimination in the #MeToo Era." *Education Policy Analysis Archives* 26(68): 1–19.

Vega-Gea, E., R. Ortega-Ruiz, and V. Sanchez. 2016. "Peer Sexual Harassment in Adolescence: Dimensions of the Sexual Harassment Survey in Boys and Girls." *International Journal of Clinical and Health Psychology* 16(1): 47–57.

Kavanaugh, Brett (1965–)

Prominent conservative attorney and judge Brett Kavanaugh was confirmed as a U.S. Supreme Court justice in October 2018 despite controversial allegations from several accusers that he had committed acts of sexual assault and harassment as a young man.

Shortly after Supreme Court justice Anthony Kennedy announced his retirement in June 2018, President Donald Trump nominated federal (appellate) court judge Brett Kavanaugh to fill the seat. Kavanaugh had served in a series of high-profile legal and political positions, starting as a clerk to Supreme Court justice Anthony Kennedy after his graduation from Yale Law School in 1990. Later, he served as a key investigator for Special Counsel Kenneth Starr, who investigated President Clinton's sex scandal in the 1990s. During the course of that investigation, Kavanaugh argued for the president's impeachment on the grounds that he had lied to the public and members of his staff about his secret sexual relations with a White House intern. Kavanaugh later went to work in the White House for President George W. Bush, and in 2006, he was confirmed as an appellate judge for the U.S. Court of Appeals for the District of Columbia Circuit. By 2018, Judge Kavanaugh had established himself as a solidly conservative jurist, known in particular for his opinions and writings in favor of restrictions on abortion rights.

At first glance, Kavanaugh appeared to be a well-qualified conservative candidate. His nomination, however, became highly controversial after serious and credible allegations of sexual misconduct during his high school and college days became public. Despite these claims, Judge Kavanaugh was sworn in as an associate justice of the U.S. Supreme Court after a rancorous and deeply partisan confirmation hearing in the U.S. Senate.

What appeared most controversial, early in the nomination process, was that he had authored a law review article in 2009 arguing that a sitting president should not face criminal or civil liability while in office. This gave critics pause about whether Kavanaugh could be impartial, as the Trump administration at that time was being investigated by Special Counsel Robert Mueller on a wide range of issues, including the Trump campaign's possible involvement in Russian efforts to influence the 2016 presidential election. The concerns raised by Kavanaugh's critics about his views of presidential power, however, were soon eclipsed by allegations of sexual misconduct made by Christine Blasey Ford.

Ford, now a research psychologist and professor of psychology, alleged that in high school, at the age of fifteen, she attended a party where Kavanaugh (then age seventeen) and a few other friends were in attendance. Ford stated that Kavanaugh sexually assaulted her at the party, holding her down on a bed, pressing himself on her, and covering her mouth so she could not call for help. Ford recalls thinking that he might accidentally kill her. She stated she was eventually able to escape the room as Kavanaugh fumbled to remove her clothes. Although she did not report this incident to anyone at the time, Ford did supply supporting evidence (notes from a therapist whom she had told and results from a lie detector test).

Within weeks of this allegation becoming public, two additional women (Julie Swetnick and Deborah Ramirez) came forward to make other accusations of sexual violence by Kavanaugh during high school and college. Under political pressure, the Republican-led Senate Judiciary Committee agreed to hold an additional day of hearings to allow Ford to testify and for Kavanaugh to respond to the allegations. The hearing, however, was severely limited in scope in that neither Ramirez or Swetnick were invited to testify, nor were any potential corroborating or character witnesses.

Ford appeared before the Senate Judiciary Committee on the morning of September 27, 2018. During the course of her testimony, which was broadcast nationally, Ford stated that she was "one hundred percent certain" that the person who attacked her was Kavanaugh. Ford also drew upon her medical training to explain to the senators the physiological impact trauma has on the brain and why there were some gaps in her memory. By the time her appearance was over, even conservative pundits on Fox News who supported Kavanaugh's nomination acknowledged that her testimony was credible.

The second half of the hearing, however, gave Kavanaugh the opportunity to respond to the allegations. He offered fiery and tearful denials of all charges and asserted that the allegations amounted to "a calculated, orchestrated political hit." Kavanaugh also insisted that "I'm not questioning that Dr. Ford may have been sexually assaulted by some person in some place at some time. But I have never done this, to her or to anyone."

When Democratic senator Amy Klobuchar asked him whether he had ever blacked out or forgotten events after drinking, he retorted sarcastically, "I don't know, have you?" Republican senators were supportive of Kavanaugh as well, with Republican senator Lindsey Graham using his allotted time to loudly excoriate the Democratic senators for engaging in what he characterized as irresponsible character assassination.

Aside from Ford's allegations, the hearing also touched on accusations of generally boorish and offensive sexual behavior by Kavanaugh during high school and college as well as glorification of excessive drinking. Democrats on the committee, for example, asked Kavanaugh about several passages from his high school yearbook, such as one claim that he was a "Renate alumnus"—which many interpreted as a veiled boast that he had had a sexual encounter with a particular female friend. His yearbook entry also included references to the "devil's triangle" and "boofing," which several classmates claimed were offensive sexual references frequently used at the school (Abad-Santos 2018).

For his part, Kavanaugh claimed the references were merely juvenile references to drinking games or flatulence. Unfortunately, because of the way the hearing had been structured by the committee's Republican majority, no other witnesses were allowed to testify to either substantiate or refute these claims—or the more serious allegations of sexual assault.

Like the Clarence Thomas/Anita Hill hearings more than two decades earlier, the hearing both riveted and polarized much of the country. In the days following the hearing, support for Kavanaugh dropped, and several significant parties withdrew earlier support for his nomination. More than twenty-four hundred law professors signed a letter to Senators Mitch McConnell and Chuck Schumer (later published as an op-ed in the *New York Times*), objecting to Kavanaugh's potential confirmation: "We are united, as professors of law and scholars of judicial institutions, in believing that he did not display the impartiality and judicial temperament requisite to sit on the highest court of our land" (Aaronson et al. 2018).

Even the American Bar Association, which had initially rated Kavanaugh as "well qualified," hedged on its endorsement just before the confirmation vote, stating it would "re-evaluate" the rating. The prominent Jesuit magazine *America* formally rescinded its endorsement as well, asserting that "for the good of the country and the future credibility of the Supreme Court in a world that is finally learning to take reports of harassment, assault and abuse seriously, it is time to find a nominee whose confirmation will not repudiate that lesson" (Editors 2018).

Conservative allies for Kavanaugh dug in, however, coalescing around a few different points. Many dismissed the allegations as confused, politically motivated, or untrue. Defenders of Kavanaugh also expressed outrage that allegations from so long ago were ruining a man's life. In the end, fifty senators (forty-nine Republicans and one Democrat, Joe Manchin of West Virginia) voted to confirm Kavanaugh, narrowly elevating him to the court (forty-seven Democrats and Republican Lisa Murkowski of Alaska cast "no" votes). On October 6, 2018, at a small swearing-in ceremony, Kavanaugh became the 114th Supreme Court justice of the United States.

The events that took place in the fall of 2018 will not soon be forgotten by the country. The emotions of both supporters and opponents of Kavanaugh's nomination remained raw in the aftermath of the confirmation battle. In addition, some legal scholars, lawmakers, and other members of the legal profession fear that the controversial hearings and Kavanaugh's eventual confirmation did lasting damage to the reputation of a Supreme Court already seen in many quarters as beholden to partisan political interests (Edelman 2018). In addition, Ford's testimony dredged up many painful memories for victims of sexual violence. Rape crisis hotlines reported a surge in calls after the hearing. Even C-SPAN, which often provides fairly dry coverage of legislative affairs, had a deluge of callers to their hotline, relaying their own stories of abuse.

Meanwhile, Ford went into hiding during and after the hearing. The decision stemmed in part from a desire to escape the crush of media attention she received, but it was also a response to death threats and other harassment aimed at her and her family.

Just a few weeks after Kavanaugh's confirmation, President Trump mocked Ford during a campaign rally, mimicking her testimony by exaggerating her lack of memory around the alleged assault. When asked later about this taunt, he stated to *60 Minutes*, "We won. It doesn't matter. We won."

Jennifer M. Balboni

See also: Backlash against Allegations of Sexual Harassment and Assault; Hill, Anita; Presidential Scandals; Thomas, Clarence

Further Reading

Aaronson, Mark N., Richard L. Abel, David Abraham, Susan Abraham, Nancy S. Abramowitz, Jamie R. Abrams, Kathryn Abrams, et al. 2018. "The Senate Should Not Confirm Brett Kavanaugh: Signed 2,400+ Law Professors." *New York Times*, October 3. https://www.nytimes.com/interactive/2018/10/03/opinion/kavanaugh-law-professors-letter.html

Abad-Santos, Alex. 2018 "Brett Kavanaugh's Questionable Definition of 'Boof' and 'Devil's Triangle,' Explained." Vox, October 3. https://www.vox.com/2018/9/27/17911728/brett-kavanaugh-boof-definition-supreme-court.

Bever, Lindsay. 2018. "This Brings Back So Much Pain: Hear the Wrenching C-SPAN Call from a Sexual Assault Survivor." *Washington Post*, September 27. http://www.washingtonpost.com/news/arts-and-entertainment/wp/2018/09/27/kavanaugh-c-span-calls-sexual-assault-survivors-share-stories-during-christine-blasey-ford-hearing/.

Cillizza, Chris. 2018. "Amy Klobuchar's Moment in the Brett Kavanaugh Confirmation Hearings." CNN, October 1. https://www.cnn.com/2018/10/01/politics/amy-klobuchar-brett-kavanaugh-supreme-court/index.html.

Da Silva, Chantal. 2018. "It Doesn't Matter. We Won." *Newsweek*, October 15. https://www.newsweek.com/donald-trump-dismisses-treatment-christine-blasey-ford-1169330.

Edelman, Adam. 2018. "'Cloud.' 'Legitimacy Crisis.' 'Taint.' Legal Experts on Kavanaugh joining the Court." NBC News, October 7. https://www.nbcnews.com/politics/supreme-court/cloud-legitimacy-crisis-taint-legal-experts-kavanaugh-joining-court-n916731.

The Editors. 2018. "It's Time for the Kavanaugh Nomination to Be Withdrawn." *America Magazine*, September 27. https://www.americamagazine.org/politics-society/2018/09/27/editors-it-time-kavanaugh-nomination-be-withdrawn.

Fox News Insider. 2018. "Chris Wallace on Christine Blasey-Ford Testimony: 'This Is a Disaster for Republicans.'" September 27. https://insider.foxnews.com/2018/09/27/chris-wallace-christine-blasey-ford-testimony-rachel-mitchell-disaster-republicans.

Horton, Alex. 2018. "Citing His Temperament, American Bar Association Will Re-Evaluate Kavanaugh's High Rating." *Chicago Tribune*, October 5. https://www.chicagotribune.com/news/nationworld/politics/ct-aba-re-evaluate-kavanaugh-rating-20181005-story.html.

Kavanaugh, Brett. 2009. "Separation of Powers during the Forty-Fourth Presidency and Beyond." *Minnesota Law Review* 93: 1454–1486.

"Kavanaugh Hearing: Transcript." 2018. *Washington Post*, September 27. https://www
.washingtonpost.com/news/national/wp/2018/09/27/kavanaugh-hearing-transcript/.

Phillips, Amber. 2018. "Brett Kavanaugh's Explicit Clinton Memo Shows How Much He
Despised a President Accused of Behaving Badly." *Washington Post*, August 20.

Ungun-Sargon, Batya. 2018. "Americans Are Divided over Ford and Kavanaugh, but Not
as Much as You May Think." *Los Angeles Times*, September 30. https://www
.latimes.com/opinion/op-ed/la-oe-ungar-sargon-kavanaugh-case-unites-us-on
-treatment-of-women-20180930-story.html.

Kelly, R. (1967–)

Robert Sylvester Kelly, who uses the stage name R. Kelly, is a recognizable name
in show business in the United States. He is a notable singer, songwriter, actor,
and music producer whose career has been overshadowed by multiple sexual
abuse allegations and scandals spanning more than a quarter century.

R. Kelly was born in Chicago on January 8, 1967, and raised in impoverished
circumstances. He reportedly was a victim of child sex abuse from a female family member for several years, beginning at age eight. He dropped out of high
school, and after several years of struggling to launch a music career, he managed
to obtain a record deal. In 1991, he released his first album. Since then, Kelly has
sold more than seventy-five million records worldwide and released twelve solo
albums. He has also won three Grammys. His other musical awards include Soul
Train, BET, NAACP, American Music, and Billboard Awards. He has collaborated and recorded with other music icons of our time, such as Lady Gaga, Celine
Dion, Jay-Z, Aretha Franklin, and Michael Jackson.

R. Kelly's musical stardom, however, was tarnished by numerous rumors of sexual misconduct and assault. In January 2019, a docuseries titled *Surviving R. Kelly*
was aired by Lifetime. The docuseries brought renewed attention to the sexual abuse
scandals and allegations against him. The video relayed accounts by four women
that Kelly manipulated and took advantage of their innocence to sexually abuse
them. Based on this account, the Cook County State's Attorney Office in Illinois
filed ten counts of aggravated sexual abuse against Kelly. According to the court filings, between 1998 and 2010, Kelly was alleged to have sexually abused four underaged females, which he completely denies. He is out on bail pending trial.

In 1995, Kelly's marriage to Aaliyah Haughton was annulled. Aaliyah was Kelly's musical protégé. The marriage, which was registered in Cook County, Illinois,
on August 31, 1994, was annulled because Aaliyah was said to have been fifteen at
the time of the marriage (Kelly was twenty-seven years old at the time). However,
the marriage certificate stated Aaliyah's age to be eighteen at the time of the
marriage.

In 1996, another woman, Tiffany Hawkins, filed a lawsuit against Kelly, claiming the singer sexually assaulted her. She claimed that she had an ongoing sexual
relationship with Kelly when she was fifteen, and the relationship continued until
she was eighteen years old. The case was reportedly settled out of court.

In 2000, the *Chicago Times* reported that Kelly was having sexual relationships
with girls as young as fifteen. The newspaper recounted the sexual assault lawsuit

by Tiffany Hawkins and Kelly's annulled marriage to Aaliyah. The newspaper further reported that the Chicago Police had on more than two occasions investigated Kelly for having inappropriate relationships with underage girls. However, the Chicago Police could not pursue the case because the girls at the center of the sexual allegations would not cooperate with the prosecution. As with all the other sexual allegations made against him, Kelly denied any wrongdoing.

In 2001, a videotape was anonymously sent to Jim DeRogatis, a music critic who writes for many newspapers and magazines. He forwarded the video to the Chicago Police upon seeing what appeared to be Kelly having sex with underage girls. Later that year, an aspiring rapper named Tracy Sampson filed a lawsuit against Kelly, claiming he engaged in a sexual relationship with her when she was seventeen years old. That suit was eventually settled out of court. The *Chicago Sun-Times* reported in 2002 that the police were investigating Kelly for sexual misconduct based on the anonymous tape from 2001. At the time the report was filed, the identified girl in the video was seventeen years old. However, the girl's aunt claimed the girl must have been about fourteen years old at the time the video was made. Kelly firmly denied the allegations, claiming it was a frameup orchestrated by disgruntled former employees. Pirated copies of the sex tape were sold on the streets of Chicago.

Later in 2002, a woman named Patrice Jones sued Kelly, claiming she started a sexual relationship with him when she was sixteen years old. She even alleged to have been impregnated by Kelly but was persuaded by him to terminate the pregnancy. Kelly vehemently denied the allegations. This matter was also settled out of court. In the same year, a thirty-three-year-old dancer named Montina "Tina" Woods sued Kelly for secretly taping their sexual encounter without her consent. The case was once more settled out of court with an undisclosed sum paid to the accuser.

In 2002, Kelly was charged by the Chicago Police with child pornography and sexual abuse based on a video that showed him engaging in sex and urinating on an underaged girl. The charges emanated from a second anonymous sex videotape of Kelly sent to the press and subsequently to the Chicago Police. In June 2008, the Chicago jury acquitted Kelly of all fourteen counts of child pornography and abuse with which he had been charged. The jury only deliberated for seven and a half hours. A key witness in the trial, the alleged victim of the child pornography and abuse, refused to testify against Kelly.

In this era of the #MeToo Movement, many are wondering whether the docuseries depicting R. Kelly of sexual abuse of underage girls will be his nemesis. Many activist groups, including the powerful Time's Up group, have intensified their campaigns to end his career—or as they put it, #MuteRKelly.

O. Oko Elechi and Noel Otu

See also: #MeToo Movement; Music/Video Settings; Quid Pro Quo; Time's Up Movement

Further Reading

CBS News. 2019. "R. Kelly Accuser Lanita Carter Breaks Her Silence after 16 Years: 'I'm Not Ashamed.'" CBS News, March 28. https://www.cbsnews.com/news/r-kelly-accuser-lanita-carter-speaks-out-im-not-ashamed-of-what-naysayers-say/.

DeRogatis, J., and A. M. Pallasch. 2002 "Chicago Police Investigate R. Kelly in Sex Tape." *Chicago Sun Times*, February 8. https://chicago.suntimes.com/2002/2/8/18432320/chicago-police-investigate-r-kelly-in-sex-tape.

Fortin, J. 2019. "'Surviving R. Kelly' Documentary on Lifetime Details Sex Abuse Accusations." *New York Times*, January 4. https://www.nytimes.com/2019/01/04/arts/music/surviving-r-kelly.html.

Kelly, R. 2013. *The Soulacoaster: The Diary of Me*. With contributions by David Ritz. Wolfeboro, NH: Smiley Books.

Kesha (Kesha Rose Sebert, Ke$ha) (1987–)

Kesha is an American singer, songwriter, rapper, and actress. She was born on March 1, 1987, in Los Angeles, California. Her singing and songwriting talent was likely inherited from her mother, singer-songwriter Rosemary Patricia "Pebe" Sebert. In 2005, Kesha signed a contract with Kemosabe Records (later part of Sony Records), and Dr. Luke (Lukasz Sebastian Gottwald) became her record producer. Her first major success was in 2009, when she was featured in rapper Flo-Rida's record "Right Round." In 2010, her debut album, *Animal*, reached the top of the charts in the United States. Many of her songs and albums have reached the top of the hit charts worldwide. Between 2014 and 2017, however, Kesha filed a series of lawsuits against Dr. Luke, alleging a wide range of shocking sexual crimes. He quickly countersued. Collectively, these lawsuits are known as *Kesha v. Dr. Luke*.

The first lawsuit was filed in California in October 2014. In it, Kesha sued Dr. Luke for sexual assault and battery, sexual harassment, gender violence, infliction of emotional abuse, forcing her to take drugs to rape her, and violation of California's fair business practices. She alleged that these incidents occurred over the ten-year period they had worked together. The lawsuit lasted almost one year, and in February 2015, she sought a preliminary injunction. It requested the court to release her from her music contract—which required her to make no fewer than six new albums produced by Dr. Luke—as compensation for the damages she suffered. Four months later, she amended the injunction to include Sony Music Entertainment, claiming the company knew about the alleged incidents. She also submitted a motion requesting the New York litigation launched by Dr. Luke be placed on hold to allow her California lawsuit to continue. Dr. Luke filed an opposing motion, which he was granted.

On February 19, 2016, Justice Shirley Kornreich of the New York Supreme Court ruled against the injunction. On April 6, 2016, the same judge dismissed all other claims, stating that even if the allegations of sexual assault were true, the five-year statute of limitations had run out on the rape allegations. One was said to have occurred in 2005 and another in 2008. In August 2016, Kesha dropped all other charges against the producer in California. In October 2016, Dr. Luke filed a countersuit charging Kesha with breach of contract and defamation (he argued that her rape and abuse allegations stemmed from her desire to renegotiate her contract).

Throughout her legal ordeal, Kesha's fans carried "Free Kesha" signs at her concerts, and a GoFundMe campaign was started to raise money to buy her out of her music contract. In this time before the #MeToo Movement, Kesha's attorneys argued that the expansion of the defamation lawsuit would have a chilling effect on rape and domestic violence victims reporting or filing complaints.

In January 2017, Kesha filed a request to amend her New York lawsuit to include claims that Dr. Luke failed to report or pay her music royalties. Judge Kornreich denied her request in March 2017. This decision upheld the legality of the existing contract and thus prevented Kesha from releasing music to other record companies. In addition, Justice Jennifer Schecter of the New York Supreme Court authorized an expansion of the defamation lawsuit filed by the music producer against Kesha by allowing him to present documents alleging that she planned a smear campaign against him. In 2017, Kesha dropped her lawsuit against Dr. Luke and released twenty-eight new songs recorded at her own expense to the Sony and Kemosabe recording companies.

Myrna Cintron

See also: Hostile Work Environment; #MeToo Movement; Music/Video Settings; Popular Music; *Time Magazine* "Silence Breakers"

Further Reading

Gardner, E. 2018. "Kesha Faces Expanding Defamation Lawsuit upon Judge's Decision." *Hollywood Reporter*, September 4. https://www.hollywoodreporter.com/thr-esq /kesha-faces-expanding-defamation-lawsuit-judges-decision-1139415.

Johnson, M. 2016. "Kesha and Dr. Luke: Everything You Need to Know to Understand the Case?" *Rolling Stone*, February 22. https://www.rollingstone.com/music/music -news/kesha-and-dr-luke-everything-you-need-to-know-to-understand-the-case -106731/.

Rindner, G. 2017. "How Kesha's 3-Year Legal Battle with Dr. Luke Shaped Her New Album Rainbow: The Singer Is Still Struggling to Get Out of Her Contract after a Sexual Assault Claim against Her Producer." Vox, August 14. https://www.vox .com/culture/2017/8/14/16135214/kesha-new-album-lawsuit.

Sanchez, D. 2018. "Dr. Luke Scores a Major Victory in His $40 Million Defamation Lawsuit against Kesha." *Digital Music News*, September 5. https://www.digital musicnews.com/2018/09/05/dr-luke-kesha-defamation-lawsuit-victory/.

Stutz, C. 2019. "Kesha's Attorneys Argue Dr. Luke & Katy Perry's Denials Are Not Proof Rape Did Not Occur." *Billboard*, January 29. https://www.billboard.com/articles /columns/pop/8495669/kesha-dr-luke-katy-perry-rape-denials-not-proof-lady -gaga-lawsuit.

Tsioulcas, A. 2018. " Kesha Loses Appeal to Break Deals with Dr. Luke." National Public Radio, May 30. https://www.npr.org/sections/therecord/2018/05/30/615433776 /kesha-loses-appeal-to-break-deals-with-dr-luke.

L

Larry Nassar Scandal

Lawrence "Larry" G. Nassar, MD, was born on August 16, 1963, and became an athletic trainer and medical doctor for the USA Gymnastics Olympic team from 1986 to 2016. Nassar was first accused of sexual misconduct in 2014 and has since been accused of sexual abuse and assault by upward of 160 athletes. He was convicted of ten counts of criminal sexual misconduct, and in January 2018, he was sentenced to between 40 and 175 years in prison. The sexual misconduct involved the sexual abuse of minors and other female athletes. When the allegations first arose, the #MeToo Movement had begun to enter the spotlight of mass media (such as news broadcasting and social media), and it helped to bring forth the numerous allegations against Nassar.

FIRST ACCUSATIONS

The first athlete to report Nassar's sexual misconduct was gymnast Rachael Denhollander. She claimed that Nassar sexually assaulted her five times when she was fifteen years old. Denhollander reported these incidents to the Michigan State University police. The officer assigned to the case, Lt. Det. Andrea Munford, initiated the criminal investigation into Denhollander's allegations of sexual assault against Nassar. The investigations soon uncovered other victims, many of whom were under the age of thirteen when the assaults took place and some who were as young as six years of age. Several of these victims came forward during the course of the trial to report Nassar engaging in acts that ranged from sexual harassment to sexual assault. Nassar's behaviors have been classified into one specific term: *sexual misconduct.*

Many news articles refer to Nassar's behaviors as "sexual misconduct." This appears to be in accordance with the laws of Michigan, where Nassar was tried and convicted. While still sexual misconduct, Nassar's behaviors and actions constitute child sexual abuse and sexual assault. Many of Nassar's behaviors were described by his victims as the most severe form of sexual assault, known as rape (forced sexual penetration). Nassar, as a medical practitioner assigned to the U.S. Olympic Women's Gymnastics Team, sexually exploited the female children under his medical care. He engaged in fondling of their breasts and genitals. He penetrated the genitals of the minors digitally, with and without force. He also engaged in lewd sexual acts in their presence. Nassar did not have consent from any of these females. In fact, minors under the age of sixteen are not legally empowered to give consent for sexual relations in Michigan.

In the United States, the age of consent in various states ranges from sixteen to eighteen, depending on a number of factors. In Michigan, where Nassar offended, the age of consent is sixteen (limited by relationship). This means that the younger partner is deemed able to consent to sex with the older one as long as the older one is not in a position of trust or authority. Thus, even if the victims were sixteen or older, the law was already violated by Nassar due to his position of authority. Most were much younger when Nassar's abuse began. In Michigan, one is deemed able to consent to sex with anyone at the age of eighteen.

Nassar would not have had access to the minor female athletes if not for his professional standing as a medical professional. Being a medical doctor for the USA Gymnastics Olympic team, he was in the unique position to have access to female athletes, and Dr. Nassar used his medical practice to commit sexual abuse and to assault female athletes in his care. The female athletes (and their parents) reported having trust in the team's medical doctor. Due to being minors, however, many of the victims lacked the knowledge that Nassar's behaviors were not medically necessary or were illegal.

Often, perpetrators of child sexual abuse will target specific minors who are believed by the perpetrator to be less likely to report the abuse. The perpetrators will often "groom" the child before engaging in the sexual abuse/assault. This grooming is a process in which the perpetrator gradually engages in a continuum of sexual behaviors toward the child that includes both physical contact and non-physical contact to ensure the child will be complicit and not report the perpetrator's behaviors to his or her parents or another adult.

Nassar used his professional position as a medical doctor with authority to physically touch his patients' bodies and to claim that his actions were medically legitimate. Perpetrators of sexual crimes are often motivated to use their position of power and authority to pressure, deceive, or otherwise manipulate victims into cooperation with the sexual misconduct. Perpetrators may rely on their position of power and authority to ensure that victims of sexual misconduct do not report the behaviors or ensure that others will not believe the victims' reports of sexual misconduct.

MICHIGAN STATE/USA GYMNASTICS SCANDAL

Many of the victims were not believed when they first disclosed Nassar's sexual misconduct. This is often the case when the victims are minors. Parents are often shocked and disbelieving of the child's allegations, instead concluding that the child does not have the intellectual development to comprehend the differences between medical treatment and sexual misconduct. Meanwhile, officials at USA Gymnastics and the U.S. Olympic Committee were slow to react to the allegations. In fact, some authorities took no action whatsoever, including coaches and trainers. Many of these individuals ultimately resigned from their positions after the scale and severity of Nassar's abuse finally came into focus This includes the president and the entire board of directors for USA Gymnastics.

The Nassar scandal also implicated officials at Michigan State University (MSU), where Nassar was a faculty member with clinical responsibilities. One female athlete, Amanda Thomashow, reported Nassar's sexual misconduct directly to Michigan State University in 2014. Thomashow filed a Title IX complaint against Nassar when he was practicing medicine as a sports doctor on MSU's campus. Title IX is the federal regulation that prohibits discrimination (including harassment and assault) based on a person's sex within education institutions and provides remedies for the victim of such discrimination. Thomashow alleged that Nassar sexually assaulted her during a medical examination in his office on the MSU campus. Nassar served a temporary suspension during the investigation. However, the MSU administration ultimately determined that Nassar did not engage in sexual misconduct. No criminal charges were brought forth at that time.

During the criminal investigation and trial of Nassar in 2016 for alleged sexual abuse of other female athletes, the MSU investigation was reexamined. It was found that the Title IX investigator at MSU, Kristine Moore, wrote two separate reports. Moore gave one version of the report to Thomashow and a different report to the MSU administration. The report to Thomashow was said to have withheld key information about Nassar's behavior and cleared him of sexual harassment. The report to MSU, which until that point had remained internal, also cleared Nassar of harassment. However, it did include the assessment that his methods were inflicting "unnecessary trauma" on his patients. It also stated that he put the university at risk. Thomashow never saw that version of the document.

Some critics have argued that the inaction of the MSU administration in 2014 enabled the victimization of dozens of female athletes between 2014 and 2016. As a result of the negative publicity that ensued, MSU's president and several other administrators resigned.

Despite this initial report of a Title IX violation by Nassar in 2014, it was not until 2016 that Nassar was investigated by an independent law enforcement agency. The investigation determined that Nassar engaged in the sexual abuse and sexual assault of ten different minor children. Ultimately, Nassar was found guilty of ten counts of first-degree criminal sexual conduct in the state of Michigan. This means the courts found Nassar guilty of engaging in the sexual penetration of another person under the age of thirteen years as well as the sexual penetration of another person at least thirteen years of age but less than sixteen years of age in which the perpetrator is in a position of authority over the victim and used this authority to coerce the victim to submit. During the sentencing hearings for Nassar, more than 160 female victims came forward to testify about being sexually abused by Nassar. These victims included dozens of gymnasts as well as softball players, a figure skater, a swimmer, and runners. Nassar's sexual misconduct toward these female athletes spanned a time frame of over twenty years.

NASSAR'S PATTERN OF SEXUAL MISCONDUCT

Nassar's sexual misconduct occurred as a pattern of predatory behavior. Simply defined, predatory sexual behavior involves using a position of authority or power to repeatedly take advantage of vulnerable individuals who are less informed and knowledgeable due to their developmental stage (compared to the perpetrator) for sexual gratification. In Nassar's case, he used his position as a medical professional assigned to an athletic team of minor female athletes who were significantly younger in age, many of whom were not of legal age to consent. Due to the age, intellect, and overall life experience differences, Nassar was in a position of power over these female athletes. Being a medical doctor, he was trusted and believed to have engaged in legitimate medical procedures. However, the judge concluded differently. The judge opined that Nassar used his position of power and authority, including his credentials as a medical professional, to perpetrate nonconsensual sexual acts against the minor females and that these sexual acts occurred as a pattern of behaviors over time.

At the same time Nassar was being investigated and prosecuted for the sexual misconduct of female minor athletes, he also pleaded guilty to child pornography charges. The Federal Bureau of Investigation (FBI) revealed that Nassar was in possession of at least thirty-seven thousand images of child pornography. It is believed that this collection of pornography occurred over the course of ten years. In addition to the images, the FBI recovered video that showed Nassar sexually assaulting female minors.

The stories of the female athletes who experienced sexual misconduct at the hands of Nassar are consistent with the stories of other women who have begun to share their experiences of men using their positions of power and authority to engage in sexual harassment, sexual abuse, and sexual assault. These experiences became part of numerous news media stories and are considered by some to be the mainstream beginnings of the #MeToo Movement.

Aimée X. Delaney

See also: Amateur Sports; Authority Figures; Backlash against Allegations of Sexual Harassment and Assault; Denhollander, Rachael; #MeToo Movement; Olympics; Title IX

Further Reading

Benjamin, C. 2018. "First Victim to Publicly Accuse Larry Nassar: Grace and Mercy 'Will Be There for You.'" CBS Sports. https://www.cbssports.com/olympics/news/first -victim-to-publicly-accuse-larry-nassar-grace-and-mercy-will-be-there-for-you/.

Bureau of Justice Statistics. 2019. "Rape and Sexual Assault." https://www.bjs.gov/index .cfm?ty=tp&tid=317.

Casarez, J., E. Grinberg, and S. Moghe. 2018. "She Filed a Complaint against Larry Nassar in 2014. Nothing Happened." CNN, February 1. https://www.cnn.com/2018/02 /01/us/msu-amanda-thomashow-complaint-larry-nassar/index.html.

Correa, C., and M. Louttit. 2018. "More Than 160 Women Say Larry Nassar Sexually Abused Them. Here Are His Accusers in Their Own Words." *New York Times*, January 24. https://www.nytimes.com/interactive/2018/01/24/sports/larry-nassar -victims.html.

Crosson-Tower, C. 2014. *Understanding Child Abuse and Neglect*. 9th ed. Upper Saddle River, NJ: Pearson.

Hauser, C., and K. Zraick. 2018. "Larry Nassar Sexual Abuse Scandal: Dozens of Officials Have Been Ousted or Charged." *New York Times*, October 22. https://www .nytimes.com/2018/10/22/sports/larry-nassar-case-scandal.html.

Michigan Judicial Institute. 2019. *Sexual Assault Benchbook*. Rev. ed. https://mjieducation .mi.gov/documents/benchbooks/28-sabb/file.

National Public Radio. 2018. "Larry Nassar's Survivors Speak, and Finally the World Listens—and Believes." https://www.npr.org/2018/12/07/674525176/larry-nassars -survivors-speak-and-finally-the-world-listens-and-believes.

Lauer, Matt (1957–)

Matt Lauer was a television news personality who served as anchor of NBC's popular *Today* show for twenty years. His career came to an abrupt end when he was fired in 2017 amid multiple accusations of sexual misconduct.

Matthew Todd Lauer was born in New York City on December 30, 1957. His mother, Marilyn Lauer, owned a boutique, and his father, Jay Robert Lauer, was a business executive for a bicycle company. Lauer's parents divorced when he was a child.

Lauer's career in television began in 1979 after he dropped out of Ohio University's Scripps College of Communications. Lauer started as a television producer for WOWK-TV in Huntington, West Virginia, but quickly moved up within the station. By 1980, Lauer was serving as an on-air reporter for the station. He eventually returned to Ohio University and earned an undergraduate degree in 1997.

Early in his career, Lauer moved through multiple television stations. He hosted talk programs for stations in several states, including Pennsylvania, Massachusetts, Rhode Island, and Virginia. He joined NBC in 1992 as cohost of *Live at Five* and *Today* in New York. In 1994, he joined Katie Couric as cohost of the popular *Today* show. He also married and started a family in the late 1990s.

Lauer's charismatic on-air personality quickly made him one of NBC's premier talents. He secured several high-profile interviews for the network, including Presidents Bush and Obama, members of the royal family, and numerous celebrities and athletes. Lauer hosted the 2014 Winter Olympics in Sochi, Russia, and in 2016, he interviewed presidential candidates Hillary Clinton and Donald Trump.

On the *Today* show, Lauer was well known for the news segment "Where in the World Is Matt Lauer?" NBC aired this program annually from 1998 to 2009 during TV sweeps season. The segment took Lauer to multiple locations around the world. At each site, he would speak with locals and educate viewers about the fascinations of the location. Some of the destinations Lauer visited for this popular segment included Easter Island, the Panama Canal, Iran, Hong Kong, and the Great Wall of China.

On November 30, 2016, Lauer signed a new two-year contract with NBC. His salary was reportedly $20 million per year. Lauer celebrated his twentieth anniversary with the *Today* show on January 6, 2017. Less than a year later, however, NBC News announced Matt Lauer's termination. In a public statement released on November 29, 2017, the network reported the decision was the result of a sexual harassment complaint filed by a female employee of NBC. The unidentified female employee reported she had been sexually harassed by Lauer during the 2014 Winter Olympics and that the harassment continued upon their return to New York.

Since Lauer's 2017 termination, at least three other women have accused the former television personality of sexual misconduct. Additionally, several reports speaking to the extent of Lauer's sexual harassment and inappropriate behavior have surfaced. One account stated that Lauer had a button under his desk that allowed him to lock his door from the inside. Allegedly, Lauer used this to ensure privacy during sexual encounters.

Several other reports have surfaced describing Lauer's inappropriate behavior with female employees of NBC. Articles by the *New York Times* and *Variety* magazine allege he would invite female NBC employees to his hotel room while covering the Olympics in various cities over the years. A former *Today* show production assistant, Addie Zinone, also accused Lauer of "abuse of power" during a consensual sexual relationship in June 2000. Zinone reported being afraid her career would be damaged if she turned down Lauer's advances.

In 2019, new allegations against Lauer surfaced. Journalist Ronan Farrow revealed the full story in regard to the "unnamed former NBC News employee" whose complaint was what contributed to his original firing. Those allegations were never made public, but in Farrow's book *Catch and Kill*, the coworker, Brooke Nevils, reportedly alleged that she was anally raped by Lauer in his hotel room in 2014 (while attending the Sochi Olympics).

There have been no criminal or civil charges brought against Matt Lauer. Since his public firing and multiple allegations of sexual misconduct, Lauer has remained relatively silent and out of public view, and he has only addressed the allegations minimally. In doing so, he has acknowledged his failures as a husband and father but denies any allegations of abuse.

Lauer and his wife, Annette Roque, were married for twenty years but separated in 2018 after the allegations against him were made public and NBC terminated his employment. They share custody of their three children.

Megan Callahan Sherman

See also: Hostile Work Environment; #MeToo Movement; Quid Pro Quo; Time's Up Movement

Further Reading

Bibbs, D. 2017. "Matt Lauer Is No Longer at NBC, but Will He Face Legal Repercussions?" *Berkeley Law* 510: 7095.

Carlsen, A., M. Salam, C. Miller, D. Lu, A. Ngu, J. K. Patel, and Z. Wichter. 2018. "MeToo Brought Down 201 Powerful Men. Nearly Half of Their Replacements Are Women." *New York Times*, October 23.

Desta, Y. 2017. "Graphic, Disturbing Details of Matt Lauer's Alleged Sexual Misconduct." *Variety*, November 29.

Setoodeh, R., and E. Wagmeister. 2017. "Matt Lauer Accused of Sexual Harassment by Multiple Women." *Variety*, November 29.

Usborne, D. 2018. "The Peacock Patriarchy." *Esquire*, August 5.

Louis C.K. (1967–)

Louis Szekely, better known as Louis C.K., is an Emmy-winning comedy writer, producer, and stand-up comedian, who rose to a premier position of influence in comedy and earned millions as one of the country's most popular comedy acts before revelations of sexual misconduct derailed his career in 2017. He is best known for the television series *Louie* and his role in the 2013 film *American Hustle*. His semiautobiographical FX television series *Louie* (2010–2015) featured himself as a divorced comedian grappling with issues of sexual and family relations. Much of his work at that time revolved around self-deprecating humor involving male sexual ineptitude and masturbation.

On November 9, 2017, the *New York Times* published a story detailing the accusations of five women who described episodes in which Louis C.K. forced them to watch him masturbate. Psychologists describe this act as a form of aggressive sexual exhibitionism expressing dominance and control over the witness. It is greatly distressing and can be traumatic for victims. As additional victims of C.K. came forward, most reported they feared the influential comedian would hurt their careers in comedy if they reported the incidents. C.K. admitted guilt about the accusations the following day and apologized in a statement released to the press: "These stories are true. At the time, I said to myself that what I did was O.K. because I never showed a woman my d— without asking first, which is also true. But what I learned later in life, too late, is that when you have power over another person, asking them to look at your d— isn't a question. It's a predicament for them. . . . There is nothing about this I forgive myself for."

The repercussions of these revelations for the comedian's career were immediate and significant. After the comedian issued his apology, the distribution company the Orchard canceled Louis C.K.'s latest film, *I Love You, Daddy*, which had been scheduled to premiere that afternoon. The plot of the film concerned a teenage daughter seduced by a much older film director, an apparent homage to Woody Allen, who married his stepdaughter and was accused of molesting another. TBS also terminated its contract with the comedian for an animated television series, *The Cops*. HBO and Netflix deleted the comedian's prior work from their streaming services, including popular stand-up specials. Universal Pictures and Illumination announced Louis C.K. would not be reprising his character in the planned sequel to the children's film *The Secret Life of Pets*. The comedian was removed from several television series in which he had a production role, such as *Baskets*, *One Mississippi*, and *Better Things*. The influential comedy talent company 3Arts Entertainment Company, which was accused of ignoring reports of the comedian's behavior, also dropped the comedian as a client.

By August 2018, however, Louis C.K. had embarked on an effort to revive his comedy career. He resumed unannounced public appearances at comedy clubs, including Greenwich Village's Comedy Cellar. On October 28, 2018, a Louis C.K. appearance at the Comedy Cellar was advertised in advance. This prompted angry demonstrations outside the club and editorials by female media critics denouncing the venue. Comedy Cellar's owner, Noam Dworman, defended the booking in an interview on *The Daily*, a *New York Times* podcast. Host Michael Barbaro posed the question of whether and how soon it would be appropriate for Louis C.K. and other prominent media figures whose reputations had been damaged by sexual misconduct allegations to resume their careers.

Just as club owners like Dworman and audiences welcomed the comedian back on stage nine months after he admitted the sexual misconduct, however, Louis C.K's popularity again declined sharply. Many observers who saw his new comedy material indicated that it had an angrier and more callous edge than before. During a stand-up routine on December 29–30, 2018, for example, he mocked survivors of the Parkland, Florida, school shooting from earlier that year. That mass shooting claimed the lives of seventeen students and faculty and injured fourteen others.

Cynthia Ninivaggi

See also: Harvey Weinstein Scandal, #MeToo Movement

Further Reading

Deb, S. 2018. "Louis C.K. Mocks Parkland Shooting Survivors in Recent Set." *New York Times*, December 31. https://www.nytimes.com/2018/12/31/arts/louis-ck-mocks -parkland-school-survivors.html.

Dworman, N. 2018. "Letting Louis C.K. Back Onstage: Who Gets Second Chances in the #MeToo Era, and Who Gets to Decide?" Interview by Michael Barbaro, *The Daily* (podcast), *New York Times*, October 18. Audio 29:22. https://www.nytimes.com /2018/10/18/podcasts/the-daily/louis-ck-comedy-cellar-metoo.html.

Izadi, E. 2017. "Louis C.K. Responds to Allegations: 'These Stories Are True.'" *New York Times*, November 10. Accessed August 9, 2018. https://www.nytimes.com/2017/11 /10/arts/television/louis-ck-statement.html.

Ryzik, M., C. Buckley, and J. Cantor. 2017. "Louis C.K. Is Accused by 5 Women of Sexual Misconduct." *New York Times*, November 8. https://www.nytimes.com/2017 /11/09/arts/television/louis-ck-sexual-misconduct.html.

M

MacKinnon, Catharine A. (1946–)

Catharine A. MacKinnon (1946–) is an academic, lawyer, and feminist activist whose work led to the recognition of sexual harassment as a form of sexual discrimination in employment and education. She is a long-standing opponent of pornography and an international advocate for women's equality rights. MacKinnon, a law professor at the University of Michigan and Harvard, is the author of more than a dozen books and countless journal articles. She is among the most cited legal scholars in the United States and a passionate public figure.

MacKinnon was born in Minneapolis, Minnesota, on October 7, 1946. She earned a BA from Smith College, a JD from Yale Law School, and a PhD in political science from Yale. In her early academic work, MacKinnon developed the legal argument that sexual harassment was a form of sex discrimination and therefore a violation of federal law. Previously, sexual harassment had been considered a private harm, outside the realm of most legal claims. Adept at connecting the theoretical with the practical, MacKinnon's first book, *Sexual Harassment of Working Women: A Case of Sex Discrimination* (1979), is the foundational text on the subject. In the book, MacKinnon differentiated between quid pro quo harassment and what is commonly known as a hostile environment harassment as two distinct but closely aligned forms of harassment. MacKinnon was cocounsel for the plaintiff in *Meritor Savings Bank v. Vinson*, in which the U.S. Supreme Court unanimously held in 1986 that a hostile work environment was indeed sex discrimination in violation of Title VII of the Civil Rights Act of 1964.

Subsequently, MacKinnon maintained a focus on sex equality. She argued that "the law sees and treats women the way men see and treat women" (MacKinnon 1983, 644). Even when law is reformed, many problems of inequality are difficult to dislodge as a result of social hierarchies and misogyny. MacKinnon's work has covered biases in rape legislation, college campus sexual abuse and Title IX, and gender crime in international law. Pornography, according to MacKinnon, feeds the subordination of women in society and is a type of sex discrimination. Her anti-pornography advocacy earned her the consternation of many feminist activists and scholars, who claim that MacKinnon's stance presumes pornography victimizes women and can violate the First Amendment of the U.S. Constitution. More generally, commentators critique MacKinnon's work for failing to account for the role females play in our culture and being oriented around the powerlessness of women in society. She is most associated with second-wave feminism (which began in the 1960s and lasted approximately two decades after the end of World War II), a movement dedicated to, among other things, increasing equality for women in the workplace.

MacKinnon has worked on behalf of female victims of atrocities at the international level, including advocating on behalf of Croatian and Bosnian Muslim women targeted for rape and other sexual abuse by Serbian soldiers in the former Yugoslavia. She served as cocounsel in the case *Kadic v. Karadzic* (2000), the first in which a U.S. court recognized rape as an act of genocide. MacKinnon's work has shaped societal understanding of harassment, pornography, equality, and human rights.

Marny Requa

See also: Hostile Work Environment; *Meritor Savings Bank v. Vinson*; Pornography; Quid Pro Quo; Title IX; Title VII of the Civil Rights Act of 1964

Further Reading

Dinner, D. 2006. "A Firebrand Flickers." *Legal Affairs* (March/April).

MacKinnon, C. A. 1979. *Sexual Harassment of Working Women: A Case of Sex Discrimination*. New Haven, CT; London: Yale University Press.

MacKinnon, C. A. 1983. "Feminism, Marxism, Method, and the State: Toward Feminist Jurisprudence." *Signs* 8(4): 635–658.

MacKinnon, C. A. 2017. *Butterfly Politics: Changing the World for Women*. Cambridge, MA: Belknap Press of Harvard University Press.

MacKinnon, C. A. 2018. "#MeToo Has Done What the Law Could Not." *New York Times*, February 4. Accessed August 3, 2018. https://www.nytimes.com/2018/02/04/opinion/metoo-law-legal-system.html.

Strebeigh, F. 1991. "Defining Law on the Feminist Frontier." *New York Times Magazine*, October 6.

Mad Men

The television drama *Mad Men* tells the fictional story of the advertising executives and underlings working on Madison Avenue in New York City in the 1960s. The central character among these "Mad Men" is Don Draper (played by actor Jon Hamm), the creative director of Manhattan's Sterling Cooper advertising agency. Critics have described *Mad Men* as an examination of an era in American life when patriarchal attitudes and rigid gender roles were dominant. As the show progresses, history leaves its mark on the men and women of Madison Avenue, challenging and changing them with the Kennedy assassinations, the civil rights movement, the Vietnam War, and the women's movement.

In the late 1950s, real-life "Mad Men" reigned supreme as New York's executive elites. In 1958, *LIFE* magazine did an article to reveal fact from fiction, as the advertising industry became as well known for martini-laden lunches and interoffice affairs as for famous ad campaigns that revolutionized the industry. In the public imagination, advertising executives played as hard if not harder than they worked when in the office.

Despite the public eye centering on interoffice scandals, the Mad Men of the 1950s and 1960s drastically changed American culture. With the end of World War II, there came a time of American prosperity that led to an increase in shopping and consumerism. Catchy and competitive product promotion became integral to a business's success, positioning advertising agencies in a fast-paced world and vying for an unprecedented number of new clients. The new era generated the "creative revolution," a time when successful companies were spending millions of dollars on advertising campaigns. An ad agency would often charge a service fee of 15 percent or more on top of the cost of the advertising, meaning that the success of an ad campaign could make or break an agency, especially if it came with the addition (or loss) of new clients.

Mad Men is famous for illustrating this bygone era. The Mad Men of advertising were infamous for three-martini lunches, glamorous clothing, and, of course, casual sexism. As witnessed in the *Mad Men* drama, the rampant sexism was typical of the 1960s, when the outlook for women in the United States was just beginning to change. The attitudes of sexism carried over into advertising, which frequently portrayed women as simple and shallow creatures who mostly cared about pleasing their men (Harrison and Edwards 2014).

Carolyn Dennis

See also: Gender Equality; #MeToo Movement; Sexism

Further Reading

Handy, B. 2009. "Don and Betty's Paradise Lost." *Vanity Fair*, September. Accessed February 13, 2009. https://media.vanityfair.com/photos/55563651b80bcc99383a6b31/master /w_1580,c_limit/mad-men-jon-hamm-january-jones-september-2009-vf.jpg.

Harrison, J., and J. Edwards. 2014. "26 Sexist Ads of the 'Mad Men' Era That Companies Wish We'd Forget." *Business Insider*, May 8. Accessed February 13, 2019. https:// www.businessinsider.com/26-sexist-ads-of-the-mad-men-era-2014-5#how-does -mad-men-compare-to-reality-27.

Langley, W. 2014. "Mad Men: They Don't Make Them Like Don Draper Anymore." *Sunday Telegraph*, April 13. Accessed February 13, 2019. https://www.telegraph.co .uk/culture/tvandradio/10762227/Mad-Men-They-dont-make-them-like-Don -Draper-any-more....html.

Marital Violence

Marital violence is a form of domestic violence that specifically refers to violence or abuse between two people who are married, including both heterosexual and same-sex marriages. This type of violence can include physical, emotional, verbal, economic, or sexual abuse. It is more common for women to be the victims of marital violence, but men can also be abused, often verbally or emotionally.

Physical abuse includes hitting, slapping, strangling, throwing objects, or using a weapon, among other actions. Although people often think of violence as being physical, numerous forms of psychological and emotional abuse can also be enormously traumatic and detrimental. Emotional abuse can take a toll on someone's well-being, causing the victim to fear that he or she cannot leave the relationship or exist without his or her partner. Emotional abuse includes blaming, intimidation, yelling, and other controlling behaviors.

In cases of economic abuse, one of the partners may control finances, withhold credit cards, prevent the other partner from working, or withhold necessities such as food or shelter. Marital violence can also include sexual abuse. Even if two people are married and have consensual sex, any unwanted sexual activity is considered sexual abuse. This includes sexual assaults, rapes, sexual coercion, sexual harassment, and groping.

Abusers often exert dominance and force to feel in charge of the relationship. They may try to isolate the victim from the outside world so that the victim is dependent upon the abuser. Similarly, batterers are often emotionally dependent on their partners for validation. When they sense rejection, they feel threatened and may become violent—especially if they believe there is a possibility of their partner leaving.

Marital violence can involve factors at the biological, cognitive, and interpersonal levels. At the biological level, abusers may have abnormal levels of testosterone that contributes to their aggressiveness. Cognitively, the abuser may misread social cues and become unnecessarily hostile toward the victim. At the interpersonal level, abusers may not be able to deescalate conflicts that arise in their relationships.

Not all batterers are alike. Some engage in situational couple violence, whereby one or both partners react to a stressful event at home. These individuals infrequently engage in violence at home and are rarely violent outside of the home. Other batterers engage in intimate terrorism, frequently using control tactics and physical abuse to have power over their partners. This type of batterer can be verbally abusive, belligerent, or demeaning and is more likely to be violent outside of the home.

Many people wonder why victims remain in a violent relationship. However, the answer is not straightforward. Even though the relationship between the batterer and victim can be violent, it may also feature peaceful periods. In other cases, one of the partners may rely on the other financially, have substance abuse issues, or stay in the belief that keeping the household intact is best for any children involved.

Furthermore, marital violence often is marked by a familiar cycle of abuse. In this cycle, the abusive partner displays aggressive or violent behavior. Afterward, the abuser feels guilt for his or her actions—and sometimes expresses fear that the behavior will be noticed by people outside the relationship. The abuser then comes up with excuses or blames the victim to avoid responsibility for his or her violent actions. Next, the abuser tries to regain control of the relationship by apologizing and charming the victim, who often welcomes the abuser back. The cycle of violence then starts over again. However, domestic violence experts indicate that even this pattern of abuse tends to change over time; the excuses and feelings of guilt tend to disappear over time, as do the apologies.

Francesca Spina

See also: Relationship Violence; Stalking

Further Reading
Help Guide. 2018. "Domestic Violence and Abuse." Accessed July 12, 2018. https://www.helpguide.org/articles/abuse/domestic-violence-and-abuse.htm.

Marano, H. E. 2016. "Inside the Heart of Marital Violence." *Psychology Today*, June 9. Originally published November 1, 1993. https://www.psychologytoday.com/us/articles/199311/inside-the-heart-marital-violence.

Riedel, M., and W. Welsh. 2016. *Criminal Violence: Patterns, Explanations, and Interventions*. 4th ed. New York: Oxford University Press.

M*A*S*H

In 1972, Americans were preoccupied with the bad news coming out of Vietnam. Watergate was just beginning to raise eyebrows. African Americans were struggling to secure the rights that they had fought to obtain during the civil rights movement of the 1960s. The Apollo space program was coming to an end. It was in this turbulent environment that a new television show premiered on CBS that mixed comedy with the deadly serious business of warfare and other pressing social issues.

Set in a U.S. mobile army field hospital in Korea during the Korean War, *M*A*S*H* was welcomed into living rooms across the United States thanks to such memorable characters as Hawkeye, Trapper, Radar, Hot Lips, and Klinger. The humor was quick-witted and cutting. Authority figures were skewered. Martinis and hijinks took place one minute and then, in the next, the whole camp might be running to save wounded soldiers. Lazy poker games in the Swamp—the tent where the surgeons lived—were punctured by moments of wide-eyed adrenaline. War was boring, yet war was busy. Many viewers understood this contradiction, especially since the first episode of *M*A*S*H* flickered onto television screens long before an end to the Vietnam War was in sight.

M*A*S*H was one of the most popular TV shows ever— nearly 106 million viewers tuned in to the series finale in 1983—but it often treated sexist attitudes and acts of sexual harassment as fodder for comedy rather than serious social issues. "Those kinds of jokes probably wouldn't fly today," Yahoo Entertainment editor in chief Kristen Baldwin stated. "Hawkeye was hitting on everything that moved. Everyone [was] sort of sexually harassing Margaret 'Hot Lips' Houlihan every day." It was not just *M*A*S*H* that trafficked in such storylines and punch lines, but the 1970s comedy was one of the worst offenders and at the same time one of the nation's most popular television programs.

For some observers, however, the tidal wave of sexual misconduct allegations against some of Hollywood's most famous figures that took place from 2017 to 2020 has turned many favorite old shows into cringeworthy viewing. Sexual harassment and assault actually served as running gags on TV for decades—with lecherous men and office sleazebags a sitcom staple—but in this post–Harvey Weinstein era, what once had audiences rolling in the aisles now makes viewers shake their heads in dismay. For example, in an early episode of the long-running show, *Trapper John, M.D.*, one of the talented male surgeons around whom the show revolves upbraids a nurse who is slow to respond when he asks for instruments, telling her, "It's a good thing you have a nice body; otherwise, we'd get rid of you quick."

Parts of the show are difficult for viewers to watch today, even adjusting for the context and the era. For example, the show's early seasons featured a Black character named "Spearchucker," antigay jokes, and the sexually charged treatment of Margaret and other nurses and female characters. In later seasons, though, the program had evolved into a key social agent for fairness and sensitivity.

The program was a product of its times, and it sometimes also portrayed other issues, such as homosexuality, in ways that may strike modern viewers as insensitive or unrepresentative of prevailing American attitudes today. Pierce was often the first one to point out racism when it came up, and it happened frequently. Moreover, the character of Margaret evolved over the course of the show from a shrill, hypocritical figure who was frequently the target of sexist jokes to a proud, competent woman who demanded respectful treatment from her male colleagues. Attitudes about sexual orientation also changed as the years passed. In one of the later seasons, for example, a patient comes under risk of being drummed out of the military for being gay. Pierce and B. J. Hunnicutt, a fellow surgeon played by actor Mike Farrell, respond by declaring that it is none of their business and that he should be allowed to stay (Bertsch 2017). This was a fairly progressive attitude for the era in which the episode first aired.

Tara A. Garrison

See also: #MeToo Movement; Movies, Depictions of Sexual Harassment; Objectification of Women; Television

Further Reading

Bertsch, C. 2017. "M*A*S*H after #METOO." *Souciant*, November 30. http://souciant .com/2017/11/mash-after-metoo/.

Freedman, C. 1990. "History, Fiction, Film, Television, Myth: The Ideology of MASH." *Southern Review* 26(1): 89.

Innocenti, V., and G. Pescatore. 2016. "15 TV Series, Convergence Culture, and the Davy Crockett Hat." In *The Politics of Ephemeral Digital Media: Permanence and Obsolescence in Paratexts*, 1st ed. edited by S. Pesce and P. Noto, 228–240. New York: Routledge.

Kalter, S., and L. Gelbart. 1984. *The Complete Book of M*A*S*H*. New York: Abradale Press.

McGowan, Rose (1973–)

Rose McGowan was born September 5, 1973, in Certaldo, Tuscany. Her father and mother were active members of the Children of God. McGowan grew up living in religious communes while in Italy with her parents and became a child model while in Tuscany. At the age of ten, she returned to the United States, settling with her parents in Seattle, Washington. When her parents separated, she stayed with her father. As a teenager, she had a history of running away from home. In light of her penchant for running away, McGowan had to attend to an alternative high school for truants, where she studied ballet.

At the age of fifteen, McGowan left for Los Angeles, where her career in Hollywood began with a short role in the comedy *Encino* (1992) followed by parts in

the dark comedy *The Doom Generation* (1995) and *Scream* (1996). Her performances in these roles gave her greater recognition in Hollywood. She has since
appeared in many independently produced films, including *Devil in the Flesh*
(1998), *Jawbreaker* (1999), *The Black Dahlia* (2006), and *Grindhouse* (2007).
McGowan is also known for her starring role in the television series *Charmed*
from 2004 to 2006 (she was cast midway through the show's six-season run, from
2001 to 2006).

However, despite her successful acting career, McGowan is best known as one
of the first and most outspoken women to raise questions about the sexual misconduct of Hollywood mogul Harvey Weinstein. When the first troubling allegations
about Weinstein became the subject of newspaper reports in 2017, McGowan
came forward with her own shocking allegation: she had been raped by Weinstein
back in 1997, when she was a young actress still struggling to make a career for
herself in Hollywood.

According to McGowan, while attending the Sundance Film Festival in 1997,
she was summoned to Weinstein's suite. At the recommendation of her manager,
McGowan went to visit Weinstein, only to be raped by the movie industry executive. According to McGowan, Weinstein then hired a firm to spy on her and make
certain that she did not divulge any information to journalists about the events at
the film festival.

After McGowan and others made allegations of sexual harassment and assault,
Weinstein was forced to step down from his company. According to the *New York
Times*, Weinstein reached a $100,000 settlement with McGowan based on the
allegation.

As a result of McGowan's decision to verbalize concerns about sexual harassment in the workplace, she and other "silence breakers" on the subject of sexual
abuse and harassment were recognized as *Time Magazine*'s Person of the Year for
2017. Since then, McGowan has become an outspoken activist for women's rights,
expressing concerns about salary disparities and generally speaking out about the
importance of equal rights for women in the film industry. Most notably, she also
leveled major criticisms at politician Hillary Clinton and famed actress Meryl
Streep for allegedly remaining silent about their knowledge of Weinstein's misconduct. McGowan asserted that their silence contributed to the pervasiveness of
sexual harassment in the movie industry.

It is also worth noting that on the day Rose McGowan went public about the
allegation against Weinstein, Amazon Studios dropped her project called "Brave,"
about her childhood and growing up, and Twitter interfered with her account for
several hours. All this suggests a calculated effort to silence McGowan, who
would then become a part of the #MeToo Movement.

In October 2018, McGowan was arrested at Dulles International Airport in
Washington, DC, after a search revealed narcotics in her personal belongings.
She later tweeted, "Are they trying to silence me?" while her attorney maintained
that "these charges would have never been brought if it weren't for her activism
as a voice for women everywhere." She also claimed that her purse had been left
in the restroom. It was suggested that maybe someone connected with the movie
had planted the evidence, but in the end, McGowan pleaded no contest to the

charge of misdemeanor possession of a controlled substance. Usually possession of any amount of cocaine is considered a felony in Virginia. However, she was a first time offender and was allowed to plead guilty to a reduced misdemeanor charge. She was ordered to pay a $2,500 fine and serve a twelve-month suspended sentence.

Rose McGowan is not without controversy. She made some remarks about how gays should play a greater role in the sexual harassment movement and was criticized for those remarks. She later apologized for them, stating that she was making a gross generalization, but she also stood by her assertion that gay men were more misogynistic than their straight counterparts.

Ultimately, though, McGowan has encouraged all Americans to play a greater role in the movement to end sexual harassments; more specifically, she helped to launch the #MeToo Movement and create a greater awareness about the scourge of sexual harassment in the movie industry and throughout society. Her new role has been as a director of short films, and she released both a memoir and a documentary about her life in 2018.

Robert L. Bing III

See also: Harvey Weinstein Scandal; #MeToo Movement; *Time Magazine* "Silence Breakers"

Further Reading

Bekiempis. V. 2019. "Harvey Weinstein's New Legal Team Includes Rose McGowan's Former Lawyers." *Vulture*, January 25. https://www.vulture.com/2019/01/harvey -weinstein-new-lawyer-attorney-rose-mcgowan.html.

Dockterman, E. 2017. "Rose McGowan: 'They Really F--ed with the Wrong Person.'" *Time Magazine*, December 6.

Goldberg, M. 2018. "In 'Brave,' Rose McGowan Exposes Hollywood Exploitation." *New York Times*, January 29.

Hatchett, K. 2017. "Rose McGowan Explains Why She Quit Acting (Hint: Hollywood Sexism)." The Mary Sue, January 29. https://www.themarysue.com/rose-mcgowan -on-quitting-acting/.

Matheson, A. 2018. "Rose McGowan Speaks Out after Former Manager Jill Messick's Death." NME, February 11. https://www.nme.com/news/2240071-2240071.

Saner, E. 2018. "Rose McGowan: Hollywood Is Built on Sickness. It Operates Like a Cult." *The Guardian*, June 1. https://www.theguardian.com/film/2018/jun/01/rose -mcgowan-interview-hollywood-is-built-on-sickness-it-operates-like-a-cult.

Media Men's List

In 2017, a crowdsourced Google spreadsheet known as the "Shitty Media Men" list started circulating online. Directly following the sexual assault allegations made against film producer Harvey Weinstein, the list seemed as if it was poised to take down even more high-profile, powerful men in the U.S. entertainment and media industries. The editable spreadsheet was filled with anonymous accusations of inappropriate behavior, ranging from sexually explicit messages to rape, involving well-known individuals in the journalism and publishing industries.

The creator of the list was Moira Donegan, a young New York–based journalist. When Donegan first published the list in 2017 on an online website called The Cut (an offering of *New York* magazine), she was never identified as the creator of the list. Donegan had created it as a private list to share with her female friends in the media, allowing them to add the names of men who engaged in misogynistic or harassing behavior—and their personal experiences with those men. The list was published for twelve hours before Donegan took it down, overwhelmed by the response from women who wanted to add names to the list. After the list was taken down, word began spreading on social media that a writer for *Harper's Magazine* was going to publish a story that would credit Donegan as the creator of the list.

In an essay for The Cut, Donegan outed herself as the creator of the list, coming forward before any article could be written. She explained that she had created an editable Google spreadsheet that allowed those who accessed it to add anonymous warnings, rumors, and personal stories about sexual harassment and assault committed by their coworkers and superiors. The final version of the spreadsheet included the names of more than seventy men, a number of them affiliated with well-known publications such as the *Paris Review*, the *New Yorker*, and the *New York Times*. Some of the men were famous, and they were accused of a wide range of offenses that ranged from creepy messages to sexual assault, sexual harassment, and even rape.

Donegan has since compared her Google list to the "whisper networks" that served as a precursor to the modern #MeToo Movement, which involved women sharing names of men who had victimized them or someone they knew. The Google list was created and meant to be a warning and a protection mechanism for women so they would not find themselves in those kinds of situations. Donegan also added a disclaimer to the document, confirming that it collected misconduct allegations and rumors. She told readers to take everything with a grain of salt. She also added that if readers saw a man they knew or were friends with on the list, they should not "freak out." These cautions were emphasized by Donegan's defenders. They said that her "Media Men" list was a good faith effort to protect women from harm and give women a safe space to share their experiences without judgment or dismissal. In addition, the list provided women with a forum for warning other women about dangerous individuals without fear of being "found out" by their offenders. The sheet was organized by offense, with each accusation meticulously detailed. Repeat offenders and violent assaults were highlighted in red.

In October 2017, as the world was reeling from the numerous sexual misconduct allegations being leveled against Hollywood mogul Harvey Weinstein, women fired up by the #MeToo Movement saw the "Media Men" list as a weapon that could be wielded against predatory men with histories of sexual harassment and violence as well as an educational tool to highlight the extent to which sexual misconduct and misogyny is a reality in American society.

Ashley Fundack

See also: Harvey Weinstein Scandal; #MeToo Movement; Publishing

Further Reading

Blair, E. 2019. "When the Whisper Network Goes Public: The S****y Media Men's List 2 Years On." NPR, September 4. https://www.npr.org/2019/09/04/757282973/when -the-whisper-network-goes-public-the-s-y-media-men-list-2-years-on.

Ciampaglia, D. 2018. "Who Is Moira Donegan? Woman behind 'Shitty Media Men' List Comes Forward." *Newsweek*, January 11. https://www.newsweek.com/who-moira -donegan-woman-behind-shitty-media-men-list-was-little-known-writer-777682.

Donegan, M. 2018. "I Started the Media Men List: My Name Is Moira Donegan." *The Cut*, January 10. https://www.thecut.com/2018/01/moira-donegan-i-started-the -media-men-list.html.

Grady, C. 2018. "The 'Shitty Media Men' List Explained: How the Argument over an Anonymous Spreadsheet Encapsulates the Debates of the Post Weinstein Era." Vox, January 11. https://www.vox.com/culture/2018/1/11/16877966/shitty-media -men-list-explained.

Meritor Savings Bank v. Vinson (1986)

Meritor Savings Bank v. Vinson (1986) is an important U.S. Supreme Court case that established that sexual harassment that creates a hostile work environment is actionable under Title VII of the Civil Rights Act of 1964. While lower courts prior to this decision had found that sexual harassment leading to a hostile work environment was actionable under Title VII, *Meritor Savings Bank v. Vinson* marked the first time the Supreme Court agreed, provided that the sexual harassment in question created a hostile work environment. In this ruling, the Supreme Court provided standards for judging sexual harassment claims, but it did not create "a definitive rule on employer liability." It rejected a lower court ruling that employers are automatically liable for sexual harassment by their supervisors, paving the way for future court cases to determine the parameters for when employers are responsible for sexual harassment in their places of business.

Is sexual harassment a form of sex discrimination? Initially, sexual harassment was not considered a form of sex discrimination actionable under Title VII of the Civil Rights Act. Early lower court rulings had found that firing an employee for refusing to engage in sexual demands was not a violation of Title VII because it was not based on gender but on the individual's willingness to engage in these demands. It was not until the late 1970s and early 1980s that lower courts in the United States began to find that sexual harassment was a form of sex discrimination and addressable under Title VII. However, many early cases determined that sexual harassment was only actionable if there was a "tangible loss" due to the harassment. In other words, the sexual harassment had to lead to a job loss, demotion, or other clear economic loss.

Although *Bundy v. Jackson* (1981) was the first case that found sexual harassment that leads to a hostile work environment is illegal under Title VII, *Meritor Savings Bank v. Vison* was the first time the U.S. Supreme Court had addressed sexual harassment. In *Meritor*, the Supreme Court officially declared that sexual harassment is illegal under Title VII and that a tangible loss is not the only criteria for determining whether sexual harassment has taken place.

In the *Meritor* case, Mechelle Vinson accused Sidney Taylor, the assistant vice president and branch manager of Meritor Savings Bank, of sexual harassment. According to Vinson, Taylor made inappropriate sexual remarks and sexual demands, and he threatened to fire her if she did not comply. She complied with these demands out of fear of losing her job. She also claimed that she was raped by Taylor while working in the bank. Vinson eventually stopped complying with the demands, took indefinite sick leave, and filed suit against Taylor and Meritor Savings Bank. Vinson said that she never reported the harassment to authorities because she was afraid of losing her job. Both Taylor and Meritor Savings Bank denied any sexual harassment had occurred.

COURT RULINGS

The case was first heard at the district court level. At this trial, the bank presented testimony concerning Vinson's dress habits and sexual fantasies in an effort to cast doubt on her claims. The district court eventually ruled that Vinson did not experience sexual harassment because she had voluntarily entered into a sexual relationship with Taylor and that she did not experience any tangible loss (i.e., suspension, firing, demotion) due to Taylor's behavior. The court also found that the bank was not liable because it had sexual harassment policies in place and the alleged harassing behavior by Taylor was not reported to the bank by Vinson.

The appellate court overturned the district court decision. The appellate court found that the bank was liable for a supervisor engaging in sexual harassment of an employee (even if the institution did not know about it), that the admittance of evidence concerning Vinson's dress habits and fantasies should not have been allowed, and that her submission to Taylor's sexual demands did not mean that a hostile work environment did not exist.

The appellate court's findings were mostly upheld by the Supreme Court. For the first time, the Supreme Court unanimously declared that sexual harassment is a violation of Title VII. The Supreme Court found that sexual harassment that is severe enough to create a hostile work environment is actionable under Title VII, not just actions that lead to an economic loss. However, the Supreme Court also ruled that evidence of Vinson's clothing choices and sexual fantasies were allowable. The Supreme Court disagreed with the appellate court that employers were strictly liable, although the court did not provide specific guidance on when employers were liable for sexual harassment of employees (Robinson, Kirk, and Stevens 1987).

THE IMPACT

How did *Meritor* impact future sexual harassment claims? Women's groups, including the National Organization for Women (NOW), hailed the decision as a victory for women. They also recognized that the decision brought national attention to the issue of sexual harassment. The Supreme Court's ruling that the sexual harassment had to be pervasive enough to create a hostile work environment led to future court cases determining whether behavior was pervasive or severe enough to create a hostile work environment and thus a violation of Title VII. The Supreme Court's decision not to define employer liability, however, also led to a wave of other cases focused on determining when employers are responsible for sexual harassment against their employees.

Season Hoard

See also: Equal Employment Opportunity Commission (EEOC); Hostile Work Environment, Title VII of the Civil Rights Act of 1964

Further Reading

Bartols, V. T. A. 1987. "Meritor Savings Bank v. Vinson: The Supreme Court's Recognition of the Hostile Environment in Sexual Harassment Claims." *Akron Law Review* 20: 575–589. https://www.uakron.edu/dotAsset/e4ef57bd-5bd9-4b86-8bf5 -0bcab16ddc43.pdf.

Brown, D. L. 2017. "She Said Her Boss Raped Her in a Bank Vault. Her Sexual Harassment Case Would Make Legal History." *Washington Post*, October 13. https://www .washingtonpost.com/news/retropolis/wp/2017/10/13/she-said-her-boss-raped-her -in-a-bank-vault-her-sexual-harassment-case-would-make-legal-history/.

Robinson, R. K., D. J. Kirk, and E. C. Stephens. 1987. "Hostile Environment: A Review of the Implications of *Meritor Savings Bank v. Vinson.*" *Labor Law Journal* 38(3): 179.

Taylor, S. T. 1986. "Sex Harassment on Job Is Illegal." *New York Times*, June 20. https:// www.nytimes.com/1986/06/20/us/sex-harassment-on-job-is-illegal.html.

#MeToo and Environmental Abuse

Some people who study gender discrimination and misogyny in society, from women's rights activists to researchers and scholars, have asserted that domination, abuse, and violence against girls and women by men is not unlike human "domination" over the planet Earth. Our stories, narratives, politics, and even certain interpretations of religious writings and philosophies can play into our understandings and use of power over others and over Earth, as well. The difference, according to some activists in both the women's rights and environmental protection camps, is that nature and its ecosystems cannot declare, "I have been abused," much less, "me too."

When someone is viewed as subservient or of lesser value or is objectified for whatever reason, it becomes easier to treat that person with less respect and agency. The person is looked upon as an object, not with the fullness of a human being. This creates a situation whereby a person in a position of power and control can more easily abuse and take advantage of the one who is objectified, as in situations of sexual abuse and violence. However, there is another dimension to objectification, and this concerns the natural world and the views that some humans hold toward it.

Natural systems such as oceans, rivers, forests, and plains—and the species of flora and fauna that reside within those systems—have historically been resilient in the face of environmental destructiveness caused by human ignorance or greed. That is because human population numbers grew slowly, not reaching one billion until around 1900 CE. Time and space gave regions the opportunity to recuperate from destructive practices such as deforestation, overfishing, the burning of wood and coal, and the flow of sewage into rivers. However, Earth's diminished capacity to carry the current human population, now nearing eight billion, brings glaringly to the forefront the effects of harmful human domination beliefs and practices toward the planet.

Over the centuries, researchers have learned more about human development and what fosters and nurtures human well-being. Scientists have also learned more about what it takes to support healthy natural systems and environments for humans, nonhuman species, and natural systems. However, attention to nature-related research and programing, not to mention environmental laws and enforcement, can be hampered, if not derailed, when there is a counter human desire to exploit nature for short-term financial gain, military advantage, or recreational pleasure.

Beliefs, interpretations, customs, and practices in the social, economic, and legal realms have not necessarily integrated new learnings and information at a pace similar to the rapid growth of the human population in the last century. A frontier mindset that still thinks nature has to be "conquered" is still a prevalent mindset among many people.

Meanwhile, attachment to the idea of male domination over other humans, particularly over women, has to some degree lessened for some women, but not for many others. However, in terms of Earth, the consequences of destructive domination practices now leave all inhabitants and natural systems of Earth with a questionable future. A swath of issues related to the degradation of the planet, including climate change, pollution, water contamination, the potential for gross nuclear and biological warfare and accidents, and exhaustion of natural resources, are growing in severity with each passing year.

The degradation of nature and nature's systems is the result, say some observers, of a worldview that discounts the value of other humans, other species, and natural systems. This stance too often leaves those in positions of power and influence the means to use Earth for their own short-term economic gain or for pleasure and entertainment, dismissing the needs, value, dignity, and integrity of all others, including future generations.

The #MeToo Movement is providing a collective swell of increasing awareness of the ways that women (and men) are violated, degraded, violently injured, and sometimes even killed by people who distort their proper use of power. These perpetrators do not respect the dignity and rights of others, nor do they know how to be in healthy and just relationships, personally and professionally.

Many of our human systems, like economic and legal systems, emerge out of enduring patriarchal, domination worldviews, which justice movements steadily confront, but often slowly and with limited funds, as with #MeToo, women's rights, and race issues. Part of facing situations and cultures of abuse is to recognize unjust social environments and to hear the cry of suffering, especially where people are particularly vulnerable and afraid to speak up, as in sexual abuse.

Earth has no "voice," but researchers contend that dying oceans, polluted air, unclean water, and the dying off of species and natural systems are sending a clear message of environmental peril.

Mary-Paula Cancienne

See also: #MeToo Movement; Objectification of Women

Further Reading

Community Environmental Legal Defense Fund. n.d. "Champion the Rights of Nature." Accessed December 29, 2018. https://celdf.org/rights/rights-of-nature/.

Intergovernmental Panel on Climate Change. 2018. "Summary for Policymakers of IPCC Special Report on Global Warming of 1.5 Centigrade Approved by Governments." October 8. Accessed December 29, 2018. https://www.ipcc.ch/2018/10/08/summary-for-policymakers-of-ipcc-special-report-on-global-warming-of-1-5c-approved-by-governments/.

Lee, Darlene. 2017. "Rights of Nature at the International Level." Earth Law Center (blog post), October 26. Accessed December 29, 2018. https://www.earthlawcenter.org/blog-entries/2017/10/rights-of-nature-within-the-un-and-iucn.

UN Women. n.d. "Women and the Environment." Accessed December 29, 2018. http://beijing20.unwomen.org/en/in-focus/environment.

#MeToo Movement

In the fall of 2017, articles published by the *New York Times* and the *New Yorker* exposed multiple allegations of decades-long abuse of female employees by entertainment mogul Harvey Weinstein. What followed was a fury of subsequent allegations and media descriptions about pervasive abuses of power and sexual misconduct. The broadcasting frenzy marked the beginning of a momentous cultural shift within the United States, as women across the country joined forces to speak out against unbridled abuses of power and privilege by men, both inside and outside the workplace.

Harvey Weinstein originally found fame and fortune as a film producer and as the cofounder of the entertainment group Miramax. He later established the Weinstein Company with his brother, Bob Weinstein. For many years, Harvey Weinstein was revered as one of the most powerful film producers in the entertainment industry, even though dark rumors that Weinstein routinely abused his power to sexually harass and assault female employees and colleagues percolated beneath the surface of his public persona.

Within one month of the publication of revelations of misconduct by the *New York Times*, nearly eighty women had come forth with allegations against Weinstein (Kantor and Twohey 2017a). At the forefront of the accusations were American film actresses Ashley Judd and Rose McGowan. Judd accused Weinstein of sexual harassment in his room after being invited there by the producer to discuss an upcoming film project. McGowan stated Weinstein raped her in a hotel room in 1997.

On October 15, 2017—ten days after the initial *New York Times* report on Weinstein—American actress and activist Alyssa Milano tweeted a message encouraging survivors of sexual assault to respond with #MeToo (Sayej 2017). Within twenty-four hours, the hashtag reached number one on Twitter, and within two months, it had been posted eighty-five million times on Facebook (Sayej 2017). Milano's tweet vitalized a global conversation about sexual assault and contributed to the emergence of a so-called #MeToo Movement dedicated to uncovering and combating pervasive sexual assault and sexual misconduct in the United States.

In the wake of Weinstein's public disgrace and subsequent fall from power, it quickly became evident that sexual misconduct, harassment, and abuses of power did not stop with Weinstein. In the months following the initial exposé, numerous other men of power and privilege were faced with accusations. These previously formidable men spanned the industries of politics, journalism, entertainment, academia, and business. News personality Bill O'Reilly was fired from his high-profile place at Fox News, journalist Matt Lauer's twenty-year reign as cohost of the *Today* show was terminated, actor-turned-politician Al Franken resigned from his Senate seat amid groping allegations, and actor Kevin Spacey's career plummeted in the wake of multiple allegations of assault against young men. These are just a few of the numerous men who were removed from positions of power for alleged acts of sexual assault or harassment as the #MeToo Movement gathered additional momentum.

The presence of social media provided the #MeToo Movement with an immediate and expansive platform to publicly discuss the endemic nature of sexual assault in American culture as well as the stigma sometimes attached to girls and women who report harassment, assault, or other forms of sexual misconduct. Indeed, Milano's 2017 tweet sparked a viral global conversation. However, as that conversation progressed, growing numbers of participants emphasized that the #MeToo Movement was actually rooted in responses to sexual assault and victimization that had been launched more than a decade earlier (Lafuente 2018).

HISTORICAL EVOLUTION OF THE MOVEMENT

Scholars today identify Tarana Burke as the spiritual founder of the #MeToo Movement in recognition of her 2006 establishment of a support program in New York City—actually called Me Too—for survivors of sexual violence. Burke's earliest work focused on assisting young women of color and low socioeconomic status whose voices were predominantly unheard. Burke framed her "empowerment through empathy" approach as one that helped survivors know they are not alone in their assault experience (Lafuente 2018). The goal was to offer sexual assault survivors mutual support through the sharing of abuse experiences (Zarkov and Davis 2018).

Burke contends that the #MeToo Movement she established has a different focus than that of the social media campaign that spread across the nation more than a decade later (Lafuente 2018). While the nucleus of #MeToo seems to focus on legal justice and perpetrator prosecution, Burke's Me Too efforts were primarily concerned with survivor support and healing (metoomvmt.org). Additionally, Burke's work reflected a recognition of significant disparities in outcomes for sexual assault survivors, depending on their financial resources and access to legal assistance. An overarching goal of the initial #MeToo Movement was to assist the most marginalized survivors who have, in many ways, been revictimized by systemic societal issues that impair equal access to support and advocacy.

Assault experiences are not universal. Each survivor's narrative is unique and requires an individualized response and system of support. To effectively understand survivor experience, public education efforts must emphasize this reality. All women can be victimized differently, and they are likely to respond in a variety of ways. Burke's MeToo initiative sought to support survivors through mutual aid interventions and knowledge dissemination.

IMPACT OF #METOO

One year after the #MeToo social media campaign's inception—and the subsequent relaunch of Tarana Burke's MeToo initiative—the impact of what can be considered the #MeToo Movement continued to be widespread. After years of accusations and legal battles, Bill Cosby was found guilty of sexual assault. In September 2018, the eighty-one-year-old actor and comedian, once revered as a cultural icon for challenging and transcending racial barriers, was sentenced to ten years in prison. This felony conviction made him the first celebrity of the $MeToo era to be sent to prison (Love 2018). In July 2018, Harvey Weinstein, after being expelled from the Academy of Motion Picture Arts and Sciences for alleged sex crimes against women in the film industry, was indicted in a court of law on sexual assault charges.

However, the enduring ripples of the #MeToo Movement were not just felt in Hollywood. In the fall of 2018, a follow-up *New York Times* article identified more than two hundred men in power who had been terminated from their positions amid accusations of sexual misconduct. Also noteworthy is that about half of the positions vacated by men were subsequently filled by women (Carlsen et al. 2018).

The influence of the #MeToo Movement has also been experienced politically. Sexual assault accusations have been responsible for several resignations of political office at both the state and federal levels. These resignations necessitated the establishment of special elections throughout the country, with many women seeking election to the newly vacated positions (Gabriel and Bidgood 2018).

Yet, despite the vast progress made toward survivor rights and gender equity, the #MeToo movement also endured some setbacks. In the fall of 2018, one of the sexual assault charges against Harvey Weinstein in New York was dropped due to alleged police misconduct (Noveck 2018). In October of the same year, the United States was contentiously divided by President Donald Trump's nomination of Judge Brett Kavanaugh to the U.S. Supreme Court. During the confirmation hearings, Christine Blasey Ford accused Kavanaugh of sexual assault three decades earlier. Numerous national protests ensued, and an abbreviated FBI investigation into the incident was conducted.

Despite the allegations against Kavanaugh, the nomination was confirmed by the full Senate along partisan lines. Kavanaugh's confirmation was viewed by many supporters of the #MeToo Movement to be an affront to survivor rights and a setback for gender equality. Additionally, despite the progress made by the #MeToo movement, supporters say that the rights of sexual assault survivors continue to be limited. They contend that police investigations and the litigation process remain stacked against the victims and that sexual harassment and assault protections in the workplace are inadequate and have standards of proof considerably outweighing potential damages for the victim (Noveck 2018).

These variables pose challenges for survivors seeking support from the criminal justice system.

In response to the #MeToo Movement, a number of states have begun to develop and enact legislation addressing workplace sexual harassment, with much of the emphasis on "limiting or banning non-disclosure agreements or forced arbitration; several states have already enacted such legislation. Legislation has also been introduced in some states that would require sexual harassment training for employers and employees" (Noveck 2018).

Perhaps the paramount component of the #MeToo Movement is the sustained effort to destigmatize and deshame survivors of sexual assault. Trauma often accompanies sexual assault. What often perpetuates the trauma experience for survivors is the concept of victim blaming and the erroneous assumption that the survivor's actions somehow contributed to the assault. In the United States, there has been a long-standing history of victim blaming, as evidenced by the pervasive and long-term abuses apparent in both the Weinstein and Cosby cases.

RECOGNITION OF #METOO LEADERSHIP

In the months following the explosive arrival of the #MeToo Movement, the individuals who tirelessly fought to facilitate a culture of anti-abuse and anti-assault within the United States and globally received a host of accolades. In December 2017, *Time* magazine awarded its Person of the Year recognition to a collection of social activists associated with the Movement. The group, which *Time* referred to collectively as the "Silence Breakers," included activist Tarana Burke, movie stars Ashley Judd and Rose McGowan, singer-songwriter Taylor Swift, and several other sexual abuse awareness advocates.

In April 2018, the Pulitzer Prize in Public Service was awarded to Jodi Kantor and Megan Twohey of the *New York Times* and Ronan Farrow of the *New Yorker* for their diligent reporting that exposed the sexual abuses by Weinstein and other "wealthy predators" (Ellingson 2018). This honor marked a public commendation of the tireless efforts journalists contribute to expose truth, fight injustice, and oppose abuses of power, even against the most powerful.

While these public acknowledgments are important, only time will tell what long-term impact the #MeToo Movement will have for survivors of sexual harassment and assault. The longevity of the cultural shift to fight against unencumbered abuses of power and privilege is yet to be known. Perhaps one of the most significant impacts of the #MeToo social media campaign is that it has brought into public awareness what has been isolated in secrecy for too long—the lived experiences of survivors of sexual assault. In doing so, it has also sparked a global conversation about human equity and justice.

MOVING FORWARD

It is yet to be seen how the movement will push forward through this equity lens both in the United States and globally. For example, some observers have questioned the #MeToo Movement's ability to transcend the attractions of the wrong done in Hollywood to truly advocate for victims of sexual assault who come from traditionally marginalized and oppressed communities (Zarkov and Davis 2018).

For many years before the social media campaign sparked by Milano erupted, Tarana Burke worked tirelessly to ensure the voices of woman of color were heard. Yet, much of her work was relatively unknown until those of privilege in the entertainment industry spoke out. To be genuinely inclusive, the #MeToo movement must ensure every survivor's experience is considered. Universal justice will not prevail until it is secured for all victims of sexual assault, regardless of gender, race, or socioeconomic status.

Perhaps this acknowledgment contributed to the establishment of the Time's Up campaign. Organized by more than three hundred prominent professional women within the entertainment industry, this social advocacy initiative seeks to combat systemic sexual harassment by pooling resources to assist all survivors (Buckley 2018). To do so, the Time's Up campaign has partnered with the National Women's Law Center to establish a $13 million legal defense fund to assist working-class women in pursuing justice (Buckley 2018).

Social justice initiatives such as the Time's Up campaign are an example of the impact the #MeToo Movement has had on a national and global level. They represent a cultural shift away from victim blaming and silencing toward transparency and survivor support. According to its supporters, the #MeToo movement represents a "no more" mindset: No more to unbridled privilege, no more to abuses of power, and no more to gender marginalization.

Megan Callahan Sherman

See also: Burke, Tarana; Hostile Work Environment; Social Media; Time's Up Movement

Further Reading

Campbell, Rebecca, Emily Dworkin, and Giannina Cabral. 2009. "An Ecological Model of the Impact of Sexual Assault on Women's Mental Health." *Trauma, Violence, & Abuse* 10(3): 225–246.

Buckley, Cara. 2018. "Powerful Hollywood Women Unveil Anti-Harassment Action Plan." *New York Times*, January 1. https://www.nytimes.com/2018/01/01/movies/times-up.

Carlsen, Audrey, Maya Salam, Claire Cain Miller, Denise Lu, Ash Ngu, Jugal K. Patel, and Zach Wichter. 2018. "MeToo Brought Down 201 Powerful Men. Nearly Half of Their Replacements Are Women." *New York Times*, October 23.

Ellingson, Annlee. 2018. "Weinstein Exposés Win Pulitzer for New York Times, New Yorker." *L.A. Biz*, April 16.

Gabriel, Tripp, and Jess Bidgood. 2018. "Sexual Misconduct Spurs New Elections: The #MeToo Races." *New York Times*, February 20.

Izadi, Elahe. 2018. "Harvey Weinstein Indicted on New Sexual Assault Charges, Could Face Life in Prison." *Washington Post*, July 2.

Kantor, Jodi, and Megan Twohey. 2017a. "Harvey Weinstein Paid Off Sexual Harassment Accusers for Decades." *New York Times*, October 5.

Kantor, Jodi, and Megan Twohey. 2017b. "Sexual Misconduct Claims Trail a Hollywood Mogul." *New York Times*, October 6.

Lafuente, Cat. 2018. "Who Is The Woman Behind The #MeToo Movement?" *The List*, February 19.

Love, David. 2018. "Bill Cosby's Fall Ripples through the #MeToo Movement." NBC News, September 26.

Me Too Movement. metoomvmt.org

Noveck, Jocelyn. 2018. "A Year into #MeToo, What's Next for the Movement?" *Washington Post*, October 23.

Sayej, Nadja. 2017. "Alyssa Milano on the# MeToo Movement: 'We're Not Going to Stand for It Any More.'" *The Guardian*, December 1.

Zacharek, Stephanie, Eliana Dockterman, and Hayley Sweetland Edwards. 2017. "Time Person of the Year 2017: The Silence Breakers." *Time*, December 18.

Zarkov, Dubravka, and Kathy Davis. 2018. "Ambiguities and Dilemmas around #MeToo: #ForHow Long and #WhereTo?" *European Journal of Women's Studies* 25(1): 3–9.

Milano, Alyssa (1972–)

Alyssa Milano is an actress and social activist. Regarding her acting career, Milano is primarily known for her roles on the American television shows *Who's the Boss?* (1984–1992) and *Charmed* (1998–2006). Since that time, however, she has become better known for her social activism, including her work to fight sexual harassment and sexism in American society.

Using social media such as Twitter, Milano engages in public support and awareness for a variety of causes. She primarily focuses on women's experiences and social movements for gender equality and sets herself apart from some other white feminist activists by specifically including the need for racial and sexual minority representation in discussions about gender equality.

Milano is closely associated with both the Time's Up and #MeToo movements. The purpose of Time's Up is to bring about social awareness and promote legislation surrounding sexual assault, harassment, and inequality experienced in the workplace. In an open letter to the *New York Times* (2018), Milano and others describe how they had worried about sharing their stories of victimization. They feared that they would be shamed, allegations would be dismissed, and they would be fired or never hired again in the workplace. Milano and others explained how people in power are the ones typically victimizing women—and that many women in low-wage occupations are particularly vulnerable to such predatory behavior. Powerful individuals are partially able to avoid punishment because low-wage workers lack financial and social resources to fight back. Milano claims that Time's Up will create social change in which victims feel empowered to fight against the systems that promote sexism in the workplace.

Milano is also actively involved in the #MeToo Movement. Originally created by Tarana Burke as a way to change a private conversation about sexual assault victimization into a public one, the #MeToo Movement has encouraged survivors to come forward and not remain silent. Another goal of the #MeToo Movement is to switch the public discourse of sexual assault so that terms of discussion are not dictated by perpetrators and victims have a voice. Milano started to use the #MeToo hashtag after reports of sexual assault and misconduct against Harvey Weinstein began to surface in 2017. Milano also shared her own story of victimization in which at age nineteen she was repeatedly punched in the genitals during a crowded concert.

Beyond being a social activist, Milano has harshly criticized President Donald Trump and other politicians for social policies that she views as taking away or not promoting women's rights. She is also vocal about how culture and social policy play into gender equality and encourages others to show support through voting and protest. Milano attended the September 2018 confirmation hearings for U.S. Supreme Court nominee Brett Kavanaugh. Kavanaugh's nomination to the high court had been jeopardized after he was accused by Christine Blasey Ford, Deborah Ramirez, and Julie Swetnick of inappropriate sexual behavior and assault. Blasey Ford, for example, testified during the Kavanaugh hearings that he attempted to sexually assault her at a party when she was fifteen years old in the early 1980s. Despite these accusations, Kavanaugh was confirmed as a Supreme Court justice due to strong support from Trump's fellow Republicans.

Beyond her activism related to sexual assault and harassment, Milano is also a prominent advocate for net neutrality and gun control legislation. She has expressed support for government legislation to prevent internet providers from charging customers more for select websites. Milano claims this is a civil rights issue, asserting that banning net neutrality would restrict internet access and the free flow of information for low-income groups. Milano has also protested against the National Rifle Association (NRA) and has been an outspoken supporter of gun control reform by creating the No Rifle Association (NoRA).

Outside of social media, Milano has implemented her focus on women's issues and gender equality within her professional life. Milano launched a feminine clothing line called Touch, primarily for female sports fans. Milano claims that she launched the business after attending a Los Angeles Dodgers baseball game and finding no fashionable, feminine clothing for fans available in their team store. As a television producer, Milano claimed in *Rolling Stone* (2018) to have an agreement with CBS Studios that any programming she produces will have a 50/50 gender ratio for the entire operation. Lastly, Milano has called for others to increase their representation of LGBTQ, women of color, and people with disabilities in Hollywood.

Chastity Blankenship

See also: Concerts; Harvey Weinstein Scandal; Kavanaugh, Brett; #MeToo Movement; Time's Up Movement

Further Reading

Glow, Kory, and Alyssa Milano. 2018. "Alyssa Milano on Joining Time's Up: 'Women Are Scared; Women Are Angry.'" *Rolling Stone*, January 4. Accessed February 1, 2019. https://www.rollingstone.com/culture/culture-news/alyssa-milano-on -joining-times-up-women-are-scared-women-are-angry-204035/.

Hauser, Christine, and Melissa Gomez. 2018. "The Women Who Have Accused Brett Kavanaugh." *New York Times*, September 26. Accessed February 1, 2019 https:// www.nytimes.com/2018/09/26/us/politics/brett-kavanaugh-accusers-women .html.

Me Too. 2018. Accessed February 1, 2019. https://metoomvmt.org/.

Milano, Alyssa. 2018. "Alyssa Milano: Kavanaugh's Confirmation Doesn't Mean We're Giving Up." *Variety*, October 9. Accessed February 1, 2019. https://variety.com /2018/biz/news/alyssa-milano-brett-kavanaugh-guest-column-1202973036/.

Milano, Alyssa. 2019. "Alyssa Milano." Accessed February 1, 2019. http://alyssa.com/.
"Open Letter from Time's Up." 2018. *New York Times*, January 1. Accessed January 15, 2019. https://www.nytimes.com/interactive/2018/01/01/arts/02women-letter.html.

Military Settings

Sexual harassment is not a uniquely military problem; it is a societal problem. According to the most recent data from the National Sexual Violence Resource Center 2020 (NSVRC), sexual victimization is prevalent in our society. The available statistics show that, globally, one out of five women and one out of every seventy-one men will be sexually assaulted in their lifetime. In the United States, according to the NSVRC 2020 report, one out of three women and one out of six men will experience sexual victimization. This problem pervades every sector of American life—up to and including every branch of the U.S. Armed Forces.

A survey conducted and reported by the U.S. Department of Defense in its *Fiscal Year 2018 Annual Report on Sexual Assault in the Military* included accounts of harassment and abuse from 20,500 active service members (about 13,000 women and about 7,500 men). The sexual victimizations that the military personnel reported experiencing at the hands of fellow members of the armed forces included rape, attempted rape, and sexual touching without consent. The report further noted an increase in reported sexual victimizations from 14,900 as estimated in the *Fiscal Year 2016 Report* to 20,500 in the *Fiscal Year 2018 Report* (Department of Defense 2018).

One major implication of this discrepancy between the number of military officers who reported sexual victimization during the survey and the number that actually filed a sexual victimization report is that an overwhelming majority of victims of sexual victimization in the military do not report it. Another important lesson to learn from the Department of Defense survey is that a sizable number of military men also experience sexual victimization; however, the rates at which women experience sexual victimization in the military are steadily increasing. According to the *2018 Workplace and Gender Relations Survey of Active Duty Members* (WGRA), approximately 6.2 percent of women and 0.7 percent of men indicated experiencing sexual victimization in 2017. This indicates a significant increase from the estimated rates of sexual assault of 4.3 percent measured in 2016 (Department of Defense 2018). If conventional practice holds steady, men are less likely to report their sexual victimization than women. It is also important to point out that sexual assault is not uniquely a problem in the United States. In 2015, the British Army reported that almost four out of every ten women enlisted in the military experienced sexual victimization at the hands of other military officers. Such sexual victimization included unwanted sexual gestures and remarks, forced exposure to pornography, and other forms of harassment.

What factors drive sexual harassment and assault in the military? Younger people have a tendency to be single and to express their sexual desires in a more aggressive manner. Furthermore, military bases are more often than not located in remote areas and far away from the city. This makes it difficult for military personnel to find friends and sexual partners outside the military base. Social and sexual deprivation can therefore be a contributing factor. Childress (2013) further observes that "one reason sexual assault festers in the military is its leadership structure, according to former service men and women who have been assaulted in the military and advocates who work with them."

In early 2019, Arizona senator Martha McSally, a retired air force colonel who was the first American woman to pilot a plane in combat, told a Senate hearing that she was a victim of rape by superior air force officers. She thus became the second GOP senator to report her sexual victimization in the military in 2019, joining Iowa senator Joni Ernst, who also reported being sexually victimized while serving in the U.S. military (Cochrane and Steinhauer 2019). Neither of these senators reported the sexual victimization to the relevant authorities during her tenure in the military. They did not do so because they did not trust the system enough to report it.

Again, women constitute a small percentage of the military personnel. According to military data from 2018, only about 16 percent of U.S. military personnel are women. This can intensify the competition among male military personnel for the attention of these women, and some men are willing to abuse their powers and authority to take advantage of them. Furthermore, only about 18 percent of women in the military hold senior positions. This makes women in the military vulnerable to being easily preyed upon by the men in positions of authority. The military's rigid command structure, which emphasizes conformity and obedience, makes it difficult for women and junior male officers to resist the advances of the senior officers who have power and authority over them.

Many factors account for why an overwhelming number of military officers who are victims of sexual assault fail to report their victimization to the relevant authorities. The administrative structure and culture in the military discourage victims of sexual harassment from filing reports with the appropriate authorities. Reports show that, in some cases, commanders have been discouraged by the military leadership from investigating sexual abuse complaints, with some risking future promotions if they aggressively pursue sexual misconduct allegations.

Furthermore, sexual assault complaints are handled by the military commanders who have the power to decide whether to investigate, stop an investigation, or even set aside the conviction of sexual assault. "In the military, sexual assaults are handled within the chain of command. That means that a victim's commanding officer has the ability to intervene at any point: to stop an investigation, reduce a sentence or even set aside a conviction" (Childress 2013). Sexual harassment in the military can be reduced with the necessary reforms undertaken, including enacting the legislation with reforms that abrogate the hierarchical administrative command structure in the military. More women should also be encouraged to enlist in the military, and an enabling environment for their promotion to leadership positions should be created.

O. Oko Elechi and Ifeoma Okoye

See also: #MeToo Movement; Sexism; *Time Magazine* "Silence Breakers"

Further Reading

Childress, S. 2013. "Why the Military Has a Sexual Assault Problem." Frontline, May 10. Accessed March 8, 2019. https://www.pbs.org/wgbh/frontline/article/why-the-military-has-a-rape-problem/.

Cochrane, Emily, and Jennifer Steinhauer. 2019. "Senator Martha McSally Says Superior Officer in the Air Force Raped Her." *New York Times*, March 6. https://www.nytimes.com/2019/03/06/us/politics/martha-mcsally-sexual-assault.html.

Department of Defense. 2018. "Annual Report on Sexual Assault in the Military, Fiscal Year 2018." Accessed March 5, 2020. https://www.politico.com/f/?id=0000016a-794c-d79f-adfb-fb4c003a0000.

Ferdinando, L. 2018. "Department of Defense Releases Annual Report on Sexual Assault in Military." Accessed April 8, 2019. https://www.defense.gov/Explore/News/Article/Article/1508127/dod-releases-annual-report-on-sexual/not_exists.aspx.

Gallagher, K. E., and D. J. Parrott. 2011. "What Accounts for Men's Hostile Attitudes towards Women? The Influence of Hegemonic Male Norms and Masculine Gender Role Stress." *Violence Against Women* 17(5): 568–583.

Morral, A. R., T. L. Schell, M. Cefalu, J. Hwang, and A. Gelman. 2014. "Sexual Assault and Sexual Harassment in the U.S. Military: Estimates for Installation- and Command-Level Risk of Sexual Assault and Sexual Harassment from the 2014 RAND Military Workplace Study." RAND. Accessed April 8, 2019. https://www.rand.org/pubs/research_reports/RR870z7.html.

National Sexual Violence Resource Center (NSVRC). 2020. "Sexual Assault in the United States." https://www.nsvrc.org/node/4737.

Orchowski, L. M., C. S. Berry-Caban, K. Prisock, B. Borsari, and D. M. Kazemi. 2018. "Evaluations of Sexual Assault Prevention Programs in Military Settings: A Synthesis of the Research Literature." *Military Medicine* 183(Suppl 1): 421–428. Accessed April 8, 2019. https://www.ncbi.nlm.nih.gov/pmc/articles/PMC5991094/.

Thomsen, C., D. R. McCone, and J. A. Gallus. 2018. "Conclusion of the Special Issue on Sexual Harassment and Sexual Assault in the US Military: What Have We Learned, and Where Do We Go from Here?" *Military Psychology* 30(3): 282–293.

Wood, E. J., and N. Toppelberg. 2017. "The Persistence of Sexual Assault within the US Military." *Journal of Peace Research* 54(5): 620–633.

Minassian, Alek (1992–)

Alek Minassian (1992–) is a former software developer from Richmond Hill, Ontario, Canada, who in April 2018 purposely drove a van onto a crowded Toronto sidewalk in a murderous action likely motivated by misogynistic attitudes and beliefs. Minassian's "vehicle-ramming" killed ten pedestrians and injured sixteen others. Prior to his infamous attack, Minassian attended Toronto's Seneca College, and he was briefly (for sixteen days) a member of the Canadian Army.

On April 23, 2018, at approximately 1:30 p.m. (EDT), Minassian drove a white Ryder rental van onto the sidewalk at the intersection of Yonge Street and Finch Avenue in North York City Centre of Toronto, Ontario, Canada, and proceeded approximately 2.2 kilometers (1.37 miles), targeting, hitting, and running over pedestrians—primarily women—before the van stopped with severe front-end damage. Once the vehicle stopped, Minassian exited holding a cell phone as if it were a handgun and entered into a standoff with Canadian police. During the standoff, Minassian repeatedly yelled, "Shoot me in the head!" He also claimed to have a gun in his pocket. After a brief period, Minassian was taken into custody with no shots fired.

The entire incident, from the initial 911 emergency call to Minassian's arrest, took approximately seven minutes. In total, Minassian left ten dead, eight of whom were women, and sixteen wounded. Minassian was charged with ten counts of first-degree murder and sixteen counts of attempted murder. Minassian's trial was originally scheduled for February10, 2020, but it was delayed until November 2020 due to problems obtaining his psychiatric assessment from Saint Joseph's Health Center and COVID-related delays. If convicted, Minassian faces an automatic sentence of life imprisonment without the possibility of parole for up to 250 years.

Just prior to committing the alleged attack, Minassian posted the following cryptic message on Facebook: "The Incel Rebellion has already begun! We will over throw all the Chads and Stacys! All hail the Supreme Gentleman Elliot Rodger!" This declaration suggested a misogynistic motivation for the attack, as the term *incel* refers to someone who is involuntarily celibate—an angry young man unsuccessful in finding romantic or sexual relationships. Incels were known for gathering on Reddit and other websites to vent about their sexual frustrations, dismiss mainstream conceptions of gender inequality, and blame women for their problems in their lives. Minassian's note also references "Chads" and "Stacys"— slang terms used by incels to reference men and women with more active, healthy sexual lifestyles and aesthetically pleasing appearances.

Further suggesting a misogynistic link to his alleged offense, Minassian praised Elliot Rodger. On May 23, 2014, Rodger killed six people in a stabbing and shooting spree in Isla Vista, California, before taking his own life. Prior to his attack, Rodger uploaded a video on YouTube and emailed a 141-page manifesto entitled "My Twisted World" to almost two dozen people. In both the video and the manifesto, he proclaimed his extreme hatred of women based on an intense frustration over not being able to lose his virginity and repeated rejection by women. During his murderous rampage, Rodger targeted the Alpha Phi sorority at the University of California at Santa Barbara because their members were, according to him, the "hottest" and the least likely to have sex with him. Yet, despite his misogynistic massacre, Rodger declared in the final section of the manifesto, "I am the true victim in all of this. I am the good guy."

While some incel websites disavowed Rodger and, similarly, Minassian, many posters on these sites idolize both men. Regarding Minassian, one post noted, "I hope this guy wrote a manifesto because he could be our next new saint." Another proclaimed, "I will have one celebratory beer for every victim that turns out to be a young woman between 18–35" (BBC 2018).

Canadian police and Minassian's attorneys have been tight-lipped about Minassian's possible motives for the attack, but the fact that most of the victims in the attack were female (ranging from their mid-twenties to their early eighties) comes as no surprise to former acquaintances of Minassian, who portrayed him as troubled and with such fear and resentment toward women that he would run away if a woman approached him, even in a friendly context.

Daniel N. Clay

See also: Incel; Predatory Sex Offenders; Sexism

Further Reading

BBC. 2018. "Elliot Rodger: How Misogynist Killer Became 'Incel Hero.'" April 26. Accessed February 15, 2019. https://www.bbc.com/news/world-us-canada-43892189.

Bilefsky, Dan, and Ian Austen. 2018. "Toronto Van Attack Suspect Expressed Anger at Women." *New York Times*, April 24. Accessed February 15, 2019. https://www.nytimes.com/2018/04/24/world/canada/toronto-van-rampage.html.

Dempsy, Amy. 2018. "Inside the Life of Alek Minassian, the Toronto Van Rampage Suspect No One Thought Capable of Murder." *Hamilton Spectator*, May 14. Accessed February 15, 2019. https://www.thespec.com/news-story/8605039-inside-the-life-of-alek-minassian-the-toronto-van-rampage-suspect-no-one-thought-capable-of-murder/.

Gillis, Wendy, and Betsy Powell. 2018. "Most Victims in Van Rampage on Yonge St. Were Women, Police Say." *The Star* [Toronto], April 24. Accessed February 15, 2019. https://www.thestar.com/news/gta/2018/04/24/van-attack-suspect-alek-minassian-due-in-court-tuesday-morning.html.

Global News Staff. 2019. "Alek Minassian, Man Charged in Toronto Van Attack, Has Case Put Over to Late February." Global News, January 31. Accessed February 15, 2019. https://globalnews.ca/news/4910686/alek-minassian-van-attack-put-over/.

Hayes, Molly, and Jeff Gray. 2018. "Investigators Turn Attention to Motive as Toronto Van Attack Suspect Charged with 10 Counts of Murder." *Global and Mail* [Toronto], April 24. Accessed February 15, 2019. https://www.theglobeandmail.com/canada/article-alek-minassian-faces-multiple-counts-of-first-degree-attempted-murder/.

McLaughlin, Amara, and Kate McGillivray. 2018. "All 10 of Those Killed in Toronto Van Attack Identified." CBC, April 28. Accessed February 15, 2019. https://www.cbc.ca/news/canada/toronto/van-attack-victims-identified-1.4638102.

Tait, Amelia. 2017. "Spitting Out the Red Pill: Former Misogynists Reveal How They Were Radicalised Online." *New Statesman*, February 28. Accessed February 15, 2019. https://www.newstatesman.com/science-tech/internet/2017/02/reddit-the-red-pill-interview-how-misogyny-spreads-online.

Tait, Melissa. 2018. "Toronto Van Attack: How You Can Help and What We Know So Far." *Globe and Mail* [Toronto], April 30. Accessed February 15, 2019. https://www.theglobeandmail.com/canada/toronto/article-toronto-van-attack-what-we-know-so-far/.

Movies, Depictions of Sexual Harassment

Movies produced in the United States and other parts of the world have long featured scenes of sexual harassment, and they have historically portrayed such scenes in ways that glorify sexual harassment as something sexy or trivialize it as a source of humor. Most frequently, the object of the harassment is a female, as is true in real life, although there are some films that show males being sexually harassed (though, again, frequently for comedic value).

Both casual sexism and acts of sexual harassment have long been staples of American action films, which tend to have hypermasculine characters. The early James Bond films, for example, show the title character casually engaging in sexual harassment and even outright assault. For instance, in *Goldfinger* (1964), Bond not only meets the provocatively named Pussy Galore, but he corners her in a barn, grabs her when she tries to leave, and then grapples with her as she attempts to get away. Bond ends up on top of her, and in what is always a troubling portrayal, she succumbs to his advances. Similarly, Bond has a long-standing relationship with Miss Moneypenny, whom he behaves with inappropriately, given that she is his employee. His comments and behavior toward her are dismissed as flirting. In later films, though, Moneypenny does remind Bond of sexual harassment legislation, which is an improvement. Other Bond films have him forcibly kissing women and slapping them on the backside.

Another action film, Ridley Scott's *Blade Runner* (1982), contains a disturbing scene in which Harrison Ford's Rick Deckard tells Rachael (Sean Young) that she is not human but instead an android. He then aggressively kisses her before he hits her. He then punches the door, grabs her, pins her down and kisses her violently again. Like many films, changes in music are intended to indicate emotion, so at this time, the music becomes romantic. When he tells her to say, "Kiss me," she eventually does and seems to enjoy it, making the harassment and abuse seem romantic.

Romance films have also depicted sexual harassment in ways that seem to justify or excuse the perpetrator's actions. *Last Tango in Paris* (1972) largely focuses on the sexual relationship between Paul (Marlon Brando) and Jeanne (Maria Schneider). One of the most troubling aspects of the film is that prior to filming a graphic rape scene, Brando and director Bernardo Bertolucci privately discussed technical aspects of what the rape scene would entail but failed to tell Schneider. The rationale was that they wanted the scene to feel like a real rape. Schneider, in later interviews, expressed anger at both Brando and Bertolucci, saying that she did, in fact, feel raped in that scene, even though actual intercourse did not take place. Brando was nominated for an Academy Award for Best Actor in a Leading Role and Bertolucci was nominated for an Academy Award for Best Director for the film.

The wildly popular film *The Notebook* (2004) features Ryan Gosling's Noah as scoring a date with Allie (Rachel McAdams) by harassing her and telling her he will commit suicide if she does not say yes. Even highly acclaimed films often depict sexual harassment or misconduct with indifference—or implicitly praise it as evidence that the perpetrator is virile or manly. *Wolf of Wall Street* (2013) was nominated for the Academy Award for Best Picture. In one scene, Leonardo DiCaprio's Jordan Belfort learns that after a night of drug use, he forcibly kissed a flight attendant and then humped and licked the face of another.

Comedies are not immune from depicting sexual harassment in trivializing ways. *Tootsie* (1982) has been praised as a movie with an essentially feminist outlook. It tells the story of a man, played by Dustin Hoffman, who is a talented actor but cannot land roles due to having a reputation as being difficult to work with. He decides to dress as a woman and audition for women's roles and subsequently lands a part on a soap opera as the matronly "Dorothy Michaels." He immediately sees how preposterous roles for women are and must routinely fend off unwanted advances by male costars. For example, George Gaynes's John Van Horn forcibly kisses Hoffman's Dorothy Michaels and then later tries to force her to have sex with him during scenes on the set. While the film did indeed showcase stereotypical gender roles and the workplace struggles faced by some female actors, some critics claimed that mining these topics for comic value trivialized the very serious issues of sexual harassment and assault. While the debate over the film's attitude toward sexual harassment and misconduct in the entertainment industry has been inconclusive, there is no debate about the film's popularity. *Tootsie* was tremendously successful at the box office and was nominated for ten Oscars (Knott 2013). In *Ghostbusters* (1984), Peter Venkman (Bill Murray) tricks his young female student into spending time with him by administering false ESP tests and then makes sexually suggestive comments while in Dana's (Sigourney Weaver) apartment. *Clue* (1985) features many sexual harassment jokes and unwanted touching of Miss Scarlet's (Lesley Ann Warren) behind within the first ten minutes.

In *Bridget Jones's Diary* (2001), starring Renée Zellweger in the title role, one of her love interests is her boss, Hugh Grant's Daniel Cleaver. Grant's character repeatedly sexually harasses her, emails her inappropriate messages about her clothing, and then when they break up, corners her in the office and badgers her until she decides to quit. In the classic comedy, *Revenge of the Nerds* (1984), the film casually glosses over issues such as rape and revenge porn. In the movie, Lewis (Robert Carradine) tricks Betty (Julia Montgomery) into having sex with him. By definition, this would be considered rape by deception. However, in the movie, Betty is so impressed with his sexual skills that she becomes his girlfriend. In another scene, members of a fraternity that are portrayed as the "heroes" of the movie engage in a fundraising activity that consists of selling naked photos of cheerleaders that were taken without their knowledge or consent. No consequences were administered to the fraternity, and the incident was largely dismissed as normal fraternity behavior.

In *There's Something about Mary* (1998), Cameron Diaz's Mary is pursued by three men, with Ben Stiller's Ted, a stalker, eventually winning the woman. He has hired a detective to track her down thirteen years after they dated in high school, and Mary forgives him for lying to her about it because she says it shows his love. The raunchy comedy *Ted* (2012) shows the bear pantomiming sex in front of a new coworker he thinks is attractive. These examples are a small sampling of the American comedy films that mine leering, groping, crude sexually charged remarks, and other sexist behavior for laughs.

A few films depict sexual harassment perpetrated by females against males. *Disclosure* (1994) took in $83 million domestically and $131 million internationally. A thriller based on a novel by Michael Crichton, it features Demi Moore as Meredith Johnson. She is the boss of Tom Sanders, played by Michael Douglas. She sues him for sexual harassment, but it turns out she is the real aggressor, especially once she becomes his boss. In *Horrible Bosses* (2011), Jennifer Aniston plays a dentist who aggressively harasses her male hygienist. It earned $118 million domestically and positions the harassment as desirable because she is an attractive woman. Interestingly, these "reverse discrimination" cases do better at the box office than some very serious and more accurate depictions of sexual harassment. *North Country* (2005), which stars Charlize Theron and shows men harassing women in an iron mine, earned $25 million.

More often than not, the movies that do address the issue of sexual assault border on exploitation films that sensationalize sexual trauma. *The Girl with the*

Dragon Tattoo (2011) focuses on Lisbeth Salander (Rooney Mara), who is brutally raped and subsequently exacts vicious revenge on her attacker. Although it had five Oscar nominations, critics have argued that the sexual violence depicted within the film is more for shock value than for enhancing the narrative.

It is all too common in films that address rape or sexual assault that the depiction of the rape is filled with rape myth stereotypes (e.g., committed by a stranger or with extreme violence), and the only "acceptable" response for a "strong" female character is to exact an equally, if not greater, violent revenge. Not all rapes are the same, and not all victims process trauma in the same way. However, when Hollywood shows one-dimensional views of sexual trauma, it creates powerful stereotypes and narratives that can be difficult to overcome, especially when one's victimization experience is not consistent with the Hollywood version.

As of January 9, 2019, of the reported 263 politicians, celebrities, CEOs, and others who have been accused of sexual harassment since April 2017, 101 are in arts and entertainment, the largest group. Many prominent film directors have been accused of sexual harassment. As of December 2018, a total of nine women had accused French film director Luc Besson of sexual harassment. Besson is known for *The Professional, The Fifth Element,* and *La Femme Nikita.* Although some of the allegations focus on harassing comments and coercion, others allege that Besson committed sexual assault.

Since 1997, director Bryan Singer has faced accusations of sexual misconduct involving minors. The allegations started when the parents of an underage extra sued him for filming their son and other boys on the set of the movie *Apt Pupil.* Singer was later sued by model Michael Egan for sexual assault of a minor in 2014, although the case was withdrawn. An anonymous plaintiff sued him for sexual assault the same year, although it was dismissed. In 2017, Cesar Sanchez-Guzman filed a lawsuit in Washington and alleged that Singer had raped him when he was a teenager. Singer was fired from directing the film *Bohemian Rhapsody* because of the many allegations.

In December 2017, director Morgan Spurlock admitted to a history of sexual misconduct. This included rape allegations in college, settling a sexual harassment suit, and infidelity in all his relationships. Spurlock is best known for his documentary *Supersize Me.* Spurlock tweeted, "As I sit around watching hero after hero, man after man, fall at the realization of their past indiscretions, I don't sit by and wonder 'Who will be next?'" Spurlock wrote. "I wonder, 'When will they come for me?'"

The case receiving the most attention to date has been the litany of allegations against film mogul Harvey Weinstein. Public attention was focused on Weinstein after the *New York Times* published a story on October 5, 2017, describing decades of allegations. Shortly thereafter, many actresses spoke out. Among the earliest to do so were Rose McGowan and Ashley Judd. Women alleged that Weinstein made inappropriate comments and propositions, forced women to massage him and watch him naked, and promised career advancement in exchange for sexual favors. Weinstein issued an apology for "causing a lot of pain," and his lawyers claimed he planned to sue the *Times.* He announced a leave of absence from the Weinstein Company the same day as the *Times* report. Three days later, the board of the

Weinstein Company announced it had fired him. Many other actors denounced Weinstein, including Meryl Streep, George Clooney, and Dame Judi Dench. On October 10, 2017, the *New Yorker* magazine issued a report with thirteen more allegations, three of which included accusations of rape. Mira Sorvino, Gwyneth Paltrow, and Angelina Jolie all alleged that he had propositioned them. That same day, Weinstein's wife, Georgina Chapman, announced she was leaving him.

Over the next several days, many others came forward, and on October 15, 2017, the organization behind the Oscars, the Academy of Motion Picture Arts and Sciences, announced it was expelling Weinstein. British law enforcement was also investigating Weinstein, as there were numerous allegations of sexual misconduct in Great Britain as well. The following day, the Producers Guild of America expelled Weinstein, and on October 30, it announced Weinstein was banned for life. Several actors and directors were accused of knowing about Weinstein's behavior and doing nothing to stop it, among them Quentin Tarantino. Meryl Streep was criticized for staying silent about Weinstein for too long, although she claims she knew nothing. Several staff members who had worked with Weinstein also levied allegations.

In the next several months, even more actresses came out with allegations, including Lupita Nyong'o, Cara Delevingne, Brit Marling, Daryl Hannah, Annabella Sciorra, Salma Hayek, and Uma Thurman. On February 11, 2018, New York prosecutors announced they were filing a lawsuit against the Weinstein Company, alleging that it failed to protect its employees from sexual harassment, and on March 20, 2018, the company filed for bankruptcy. On May 25, 2018, Weinstein turned himself in to the New York police, where he was charged with rape and several other counts of sexual assault against two women. He pleaded not guilty on June 5, 2018. Another rape allegation was added in July, and Weinstein pleaded not guilty to that charge as well. A trial date was set for May 2019, and additional allegations continued to emerge in the case. Finally, in March 2020, Weinstein was sentenced to twenty-three years in prison.

Several women have accused actor Morgan Freeman of sexual harassment, ranging from suggestive comments to unwanted touching. The alleged behavior occurred on sets, during meetings, and in office environments, and the accusations came from production staff and reporters. Freeman has denied the allegations to date. Other actors who have faced allegations include Kevin Spacey, comedian Louis C.K., Michael Douglas, Sylvester Stallone, Tom Sizemore, and Richard Dreyfuss. Susan Braudy, a journalist and author who worked for Douglas's production company in the 1980s, alleged that Douglas once masturbated in front of her during a meeting and repeatedly made inappropriate comments about her appearance. Douglas has denied the allegation. Allegations first emerged against Spacey in October 2017, when actor Anthony Rapp alleged that Spacey made sexual advances toward him when he was fourteen. Spacey responded by saying he did not recollect the incident and chose that moment to come out as gay. The International Academy of Television Arts and Sciences announced it would no longer give Spacey a special Emmy award at the upcoming award ceremony that year.

Additional claims by actors and nonactors came in the days thereafter. Netflix said it would no longer be involved with *House of Cards* if Spacey was involved, and the show continued without him. Spacey was also under investigation for sexual misconduct in the United Kingdom. Spacey appeared in court for a charge of indecent assault and battery, for which he pleaded guilty.

Laura Finley and Gina Robertiello

See also: Harvey Weinstein Scandal; *Horrible Bosses*; Judd, Ashley; McGowan, Rose; #MeToo Movement; Spacey, Kevin; *Tootsie*

Further Reading

Cooney, S. 2017. "Here Are All the public Figures Who've Been Accused of Sexual Misconduct after Harvey Weinstein." *Time*, September 9. Accessed February 11, 2019. http://time.com/5015204/harvey-weinstein-scandal/.

Deb, S., and B. Barnes. 2018. "Morgan Freeman is Accused of Sexual Harassment by Several Women." *New York Times*, May 24. Accessed February 11, 2019. https://www.nytimes.com/2018/05/24/movies/morgan-freeman-sexual-harassment.html.

Glamour. 2018. "Post-Weinstein, These Are the Powerful Men Facing Sexual Harassment Allegations." December 1. Accessed February 11, 2019. https://www.glamour.com/gallery/post-weinstein-these-are-the-powerful-men-facing-sexual-harassment-allegations.

Grow, K. 2018. "Filmmaker Luc Besson Accused of Sexual Misconduct by More Women." *Rolling Stone*, November 28. Accessed February 11, 2019. https://www.rollingstone.com/movies/movie-news/luc-besson-sexual-misconduct-760959/.

Harper's Bazaar Staff. 2018. "A Video of James Bond's Most Inappropriate Moments Raises the Questions: Is 007 Outdated Post #TimesUp?" *Harper's Bazaar*, January 31. Accessed February 11, 2019. https://www.harpersbazaar.com/uk/culture/a15939555/video-of-james-bonds-most-inappropriate-moments/.

Knott, M. 2013. "Heroines of Cinema: 'Tootsie' and Feminism the Hollywood Way." *Indiewire*, August 22. Accessed April 8, 2020. https://www.indiewire.com/2013/08/heroines-of-cinema-tootsie-and-feminism-the-hollywood-way-35694/.

McCausland, P. 2017. "Filmmaker Morgan Spurlock Admits to History of Sexual Misconduct." NBC News, December 15. Accessed February 11, 2019. https://www.nbcnews.com/storyline/sexual-misconduct/filmmaker-morgan-spurlock-admits-history-sexual-misconduct-n829581.

Moyer, J. 2017. "A Look Back at 'Disclosure': Does Hollywood Prefer Films about Women Sexually Harassing Men?" *Washington Post*, December 22. Accessed February 11, 2019. https://www.washingtonpost.com/entertainment/a-look-back-at-disclosure-does-hollywood-prefer-films-about-women-sexually-harassing-men/2017/12/21/cb52df6e-d156-11e7-9129-83c7078d23cb_story.html.

Sanghani. R. 2018. "Ten Times Pop Culture Romanticized Sexual Harassment." BBC, March 7. Accessed February 11, 2019. https://www.bbc.co.uk/bbcthree/article/55b92fda-d9f0-436d-a1f6-674e9e3504c6.

Music/Video Settings

Like many social movements, the #MeToo Movement has extended its influence to the music industry and its partner, the music video industry. There are different ways in which females are characterized in this genre. Given the seemingly widespread acceptance of the message of the #MeToo Movement, there is an interesting paradox that has been exposed in music videos that represent women both favorably and unfavorably. From a feminist perspective, a sexualized or objectified representation of females is considered misogyny, whereas favorable representations are seen as philogyny.

Music can have a major impact on its listeners. In particular, adolescents' attitudes about sexuality and gender are influenced by what they see and hear. Artists with varied experiences or orientation convey personal messages that may explain why females are portrayed and written about in such dissimilar ways. One of the more controversial or negative ways to illustrate the female identity is through sexual objectification. Sexual objectification, or *misogyny*, reinforces that the primary function for women is sexual in nature, and she is valued for physical and sexual prowess.

In nearly all musical genres, there is an excess of misogynistic lyrical content. Rap and hip-hop, for example, have been condemned for reinforcing misogynist stereotypes. Depictions follow different stereotypes, but the majority marginalize women as sexual objects. The gold digger stereotype would illustrate this objectification. However, rap and hip-hop are not the only genres that objectify females in a misogynistic way. Rock, country, and pop musicians are also guilty of it. When young women accept the characterizations of women as subordinate and valued based on their sexual attractiveness and availability, they may also normalize other behaviors that correspond with misogynistic practices, such as coercion, aggression, and physical assault.

It is difficult to determine the extent of the influence of the #MeToo Movement on the music video industry, but it is reasonable to expect that it would have an impact on the artists who compose the music or collaborate on the videos. This is evident in the music videos where women are adored rather than objectified. A true fondness or admiration for women, also known as philogyny, challenges the stereotype of misogyny. Rather than characterizing women in music videos as sexual objects, some music videos characterize women in a positive way. These alternative images seem to represent admiration for women as human beings equal to men and also fully capable of expressing their own sexuality on their own terms and not dictated by male perspectives. The greatest difference between these two depictions is the ability of women to control the message.

Because a music video is a cultural phenomenon, it makes sense that the #MeToo Movement has had a particular impact on the entertainment industry and is therefore likely to influence the music video medium as well. This could explain why the messages are mixed. The mixed messages, or paradoxes, can be interpreted in different ways. The first explanation is that artists and producers believe their audiences embrace misogyny or female objectification; therefore, they deliver that content. There is a second explanation for a different projection of females in music video, and that is feminism.

For example, Black American feminism arose from the need to address negative racial portrayals of Black girls and women in media. Those that are called hip-hop feminists constructed their identity based on the second wave of American feminism—the wave associated with the civil rights movement. If hip-hop feminists embrace an ideology that calls traditional treatment of females into question, it seems likely that this would affect the narratives of their music. A final explanation for the mixed messages in music videos is that the personal stories of artists, male or female, in the music video industry have been influenced by the #MeToo Movement, and rather than objectify women, they glorify them.

It seems likely that the narratives and images displayed in music videos result from the mindset and experiences of the artists. Therefore, the messages will differ, and this may explain why the counternarratives to misogyny are evident in some of today's music videos. Specifically, this indicates that rather than objectify women in video portrayals, some video producers may actually promote women's rights and help to challenge sexual objectification. Those individual narratives (lyrics) and depictions also reinforce and represent many of the changing values and norms of modern society. While early hip-hop was ingrained in political and social consciousness that was dominated by male artists, there is an emerging group of women who may have been influenced by the second and third waves of feminism as well as the #MeToo Movement and its predominant message. What remains to be seen is whether the traditional power structures of this industry will support their alternative message.

Beverly Ross

See also: Gender Equality; #MeToo Movement; Objectification of Women

Further Reading

Aubrey, J., and C. Frisbey. 2011. "Sexual Objectification in Music Videos: A Content Analysis." *Mass Communication and Society* 14(4): 475–501.

Herd, D. 2015. "Conflicting Paradigms on Gender and Sexuality in Rap Music: A Systematic Review." *Sexuality and Culture* 19: 577–589.

Tyree, T., and M. Jones. 2015. "The Adored Woman in Rap: An Analysis of the Presence of Philogyny in Rap Music." *Women's Studies* 44(1).

Zilles. C. 2018. "The #MeToo Movement Shows the Power of Social Media." Social Media HQ, May 3. socialmediahq.com/the-metoo-movement-shows-the-power-of-social -media/.

N

National Sexual Assault Awareness and Prevention Month

Since April 1, 2001, the month of April has been designated as National Sexual Assault Awareness and Prevention Month (SAAPM) in the United States. The goal of SAAPM is to show support for victims of sexual assault and to educate communities about preventing this type of violence. Every April, individuals and organizations, including rape crisis centers, government agencies, and private businesses, plan events to raise awareness about sexual assaults. Although April is designated as SAAPM, the hope is that these events will provide opportunities to create new programs, establish partnerships, and implement prevention strategies that can continue throughout the year.

Throughout April, the Rape, Abuse & Incest National Network (RAINN), the nation's largest anti–sexual violence organization, encourages people to learn more about the nature and extent of sexual assaults. In addition, the National Sexual Violence Resource Center (NSVRC) arranges a campaign for SAAPM and provides resources for members of the public about how to start a campaign of their own. In 2018, the theme of NSVRC's SAAPM was Embracing Your Voice, and topics included consent, communication, and understanding sexual violence. For 2019, the SAAPM theme was I Ask. In 2018, the national conference was entitled Ending Sexual Violence in One Generation, and for 2019, it was entitled Beyond the Breakthrough.

The NSVRC encourages people to use their voices to promote respect and safety to prevent sexual violence. Embracing your voice involves teaching others not to blame victims or to minimize sexual violence. The NSVRC stresses that victims are never to blame, no matter how they were acting, whether they were under the influence of drugs or alcohol, or whether they knew the offender. The center also highlights the importance of consent. Consent is not only about sex; it also involves respecting emotional and personal boundaries and valuing the choices of others. If someone does not consent to sex, the act is considered a sexual assault.

The NSVRC also provides resources during April so that the public can gain a better understanding of rape and other sexual violence, intimate partner violence, sexual exploitation, and sexual harassment, among other unwanted sexual activities or behaviors. The center stresses how both children and adults can be the victims of sexual violence. Furthermore, NSVRC emphasizes that people can be sexually abused by family, friends, romantic partners, acquaintances, or strangers.

Individuals and organizations engage in coordinated efforts and events during SAAPM. For example, awareness events allow people to share information about sexual violence and establish new relationships within the community. Advocates often set up tables at community events, providing literature and resources to inform the public about sexual violence. Moreover, there are also fundraising events to raise money for the prevention of sexual assaults and to provide services for victims. There are also healing events so that survivors of sexual assault can share their stories and connect with other survivors.

Throughout April, advocates are encouraged to wear clothing or accessories that support survivors of sexual assault. The official color of SAAPM is teal, and people often wear teal ribbons or clothing to signify sexual violence prevention. In addition, they can also post pictures, supportive messages, or ideas to raise awareness about sexual violence prevention on social media.

Devoting a month to sexual violence awareness and prevention indicates that society takes sexual violence more seriously than it has in the past. Individuals, communities, and organizations are having more conversations and creating additional programs and policies that promote the safety and respect of everyone. Unfortunately, sexual assaults are rarely reported for numerous reasons, including the fear of not being believed, fear of retaliation, feelings of shame, or distrust of law enforcement. Even if the victim does not report the sexual assault to the police, it is essential to ensure that victims feel safe and understood and that their victimization is recognized.

Francesca Spina

See also: Rape, Abuse & Incest National Network (RAINN); Victim Blaming

Further Reading

National Sexual Violence Resource Center. 2018. "Sexual Assault Awareness Month." Accessed July 11, 2018. https://www.nsvrc.org/saam.

RAINN. 2018. "Your 2018 Guide to Sexual Assault Awareness and Prevention Month." Accessed July 11, 2018. https://www.rainn.org/SAAPM2018.

News Media Coverage

With the proliferation of twenty-four-hour news programming and the rapid expansion of internet information outlets, news media has never played a more substantial role in shaping public opinion and policy as it does today. Unfortunately, critics often complain that news media outlets' priorities and biases have colored their coverage of sexual misconduct and sexual harassment in numerous problematic ways.

Several factors shape reporting on intimate partner violence, abuse, rape, harassment, and misconduct in general and thereby influence public perception on the issue. One of the predominate factors affecting public perception and approaches to addressing sexual violence is the news media's tendency toward sensationalizing and reporting on single events in an overly simplified and distorted manner instead of contextualizing them as consequences of a broader social environment. This bias, according to critics, leads to a presentation of sexual violence and misconduct as isolated and inevitable facts of life.

Although there have been improvements in news coverage of violent and inappropriate behavior since the 1990s, increasing societal awareness and understanding of the issue, there is still significant room for improvement. Media coverage of harassment, misconduct, and sexual abuse cases holds a strong influence over legal and public policy responses. Indeed, as the public mostly relies on journalistic reporting and garners much of its information about any violence from news coverage, there becomes an added layer of filtering that obscures the reality and scope of the crimes. Dissipating myths and underpinning information about the true nature and extent of these wide-ranging social issues is of crucial importance.

Presenting harassment and misconduct as one-off incidents outside of a broader sociopolitical context helps to maintain gender norms and hierarchies and stifles potential solutions. Furthermore, news media's framing of incidents is both a cause and consequence of gender inequality, as coverage often depicts survivors and perpetrators as inherently different and explicitly or implicitly blames victims or survivors while excusing perpetrators, describing "real" and "deserving" victims and "provoked" or "desperate" perpetrators (e.g., the victim continued to have a business or personal relationship with the accused or the victim should have reported the victimization years earlier, when it occurred).

Although harassment, misconduct, sexual crimes, and abuse can be found across all racial and socioeconomic lines, media coverage often stereotypes both victims and perpetrators. Survivors tend to be described in terms such as "vulnerable" and "naive." It was also often implied by the media, at least before the #MeToo Movement, that women were at least partially responsible for the victimization they experienced. The displacing of responsibility is indicative of how media within a patriarchal culture, the social context in which violence against women is so overwhelmingly prevalent, enables men to shirk responsibility for violence and has the effect of normalizing physically or sexually violent behaviors in men. In addition, the use of language by media that disguises acts of physical violence, such as "altercation" or "dispute," additionally reduces women's experiences of physical and sexual violence to a matter of disagreement rather than embodied trauma. Media outlets ought to consider how the selective reporting of details in harassment and misconduct cases may be perpetuating misnomers about what constitutes a hostile work environment or a quid pro quo relationship as well as its far-reaching physical and psychological consequences.

Blaming the victim is a popular tactic used to dispel the systemic nature of some of these crimes. News coverage routinely provides depictions of cases that focus on the mundane details of interpersonal relationships rather than addressing sexual harassment as societally systemic. This approach to reporting stories as individualized, emphasizing the minute or sensationalistic details of relationships, distorts the broader nature of the treatment of women and promotes a lack of collective response. While media reporting often offers salacious aspects of a woman's intimate life and experiences of abuse, the perspective is often more provocative and works to undermine the highly traumatic reality of her ordeal.

When sexual harassment and misconduct take place, journalists should discuss the perpetrators' violent history, because when journalists address perpetrators' histories of violence and highlight their consistent patterns of abusive conduct, the narrative of who is responsible for the action and consequences of the abuse shifts and centers perpetrators of violence as the problem rather than the survivors. The selection of details and the terminology should be considered carefully so as not to excuse men's violence or blame the victim. Finally, journalists should also provide more holistic coverage that sheds light on existing research of the risk factors, myths, and stereotypes and the local resources available that provide reliable information to the public and assistance for victims and their loved ones.

Laurence Cobbaert

See also: Gender Equality; Hostile Work Environment; Quid Pro Quo; Rape, Abuse & Incest National Network (RAINN); Violence Against Women Reauthorization Act of 2013

Further Reading

Flood, M. 2014. "Preventing Violence against Women and Girls." In *Gender in Organizations: Are Men Allies or Adversaries to Women's Career Advancement?*, edited by R. J. Burke and D. J. Major, 405–427. Cheltenham, UK: Edward Elgar Publishing Ltd.

Lindsey, L. L. 2018. *Gender Roles: A Sociological Perspective.* London: Routledge.

National Domestic Violence Hotline. Accessed March 4, 2019. https://www.thehotline.org/.

Palazzolo, K. E., and A. J. Roberto. 2011. "Media Representations of Intimate Partner Violence and Punishment Preferences: Exploring the Role of Attributions and Emotions." *Journal of Applied Communication Research* 39(1): 1–18. https://doi .org/10.1080/00909882.2010.536843.

Smith, S. G., X. Zhang, K. C. Basile, M. T. Merrick, J. Wang, M. Kresnow, and J. Chen. 2018. *The National Intimate Partner and Sexual Violence Survey (NISVS): 2015 Data Brief—Updated Release.* Atlanta, GA: National Center for Injury Prevention and Control, Centers for Disease Control and Prevention.

9 to 5

The American comedic film *9 to 5* was produced by Bruce Gilbert and cowritten (with Patricia Resnick) and directed by Colin Higgins. The film was released in 1980 and starred Jane Fonda, Lily Tomlin, and Dolly Parton as three working women who make and execute a plan to get even with their company's "sexist, egotistical, lying, hypocritical bigot" of a boss, portrayed by Dabney Coleman.

When the movie was released in 1980, the women's liberation movement was still a new concept for many Americans. Revisiting the comedy, one will notice that the clothing and office technology has changed since its release, but much of the message about unhealthy and sexist dynamics between men and women in the workplace remains sadly relevant today. Second-wave feminism—a period in the 1960s and 1970s marked by a concerted push for employment equality for women—served as a catalyst for millions of middle-class white women to enter the American workforce while simultaneously exiting their marriages of the 1950s and 1960s. As the gender composition of the workforce changed, reports of workplace sexual harassment soared. The film *9 to 5* was grounded in the experiences of members of the 9 to 5 National Association of Working Women, an organization that was founded in 1973 and still exists today.

The working conditions of the women portrayed in the film have deep roots in American culture. Men have earned higher pay for identical jobs since the early nineteenth century, a time when teachers' unions were founded to right the misconception that working women were unable to adequately provide for their children. Women and men continue to earn unequal paychecks in nearly every area of employment. Although women were experiencing the blatant sexual harassment depicted in *9 to 5*, the concept of sexual harassment would not enter the American public's consciousness as a legitimate legal issue until Anita Hill testified at Clarence Thomas's Supreme Court confirmation hearings, eleven years after the release of the film (Traister 2015). The themes of the movie were timely in 1980, the year the U.S. Equal Employment Opportunity Commission (EEOC) issued guidelines clarifying that sexual harassment is unlawful under Title VII.

Although the film *9 to 5* is almost forty years old, the sexual harassment and gender inequality experienced by women that it depicts is still a reality in many workplaces, as the #MeToo Movement has documented (Blaschke 2018). Jane Fonda, one of the stars of the film, does not think things have improved much since the film's release. However, she predicts that the increased public awareness of the issue as a result of the #MeToo Movement—and the consequences that per-petrators of harassment and sexism have faced as a result of that movement—could bring about a drop in incidents of sexual harassment and assault in years to come (Blaschke 2018).

Before the movie *9 to 5*, there was a real-life clerical workers' advocacy group at Harvard University named 9 to 5. Throughout the 1970s, this group expanded around Boston as its members worked to achieve improved employment condi-tions and fairer pay for women in the workforce (Blaschke 2018). In 1992, Wiley and Sons published *The 9 to 5 Guide to Combating Sexual Harassment: Candid Advice from 9 to 5, the National Association of Working Women*, by Ellen Bravo and Ellen Cassedy. The National Association of Working Women also provided counseling and referral services to sexually harassed women in Boston; at the Cambridge Women's Center and Vocations for Social Change in Cambridge, Mas-sachusetts; and at Cleveland Women Working in the 1980s and 1990s.

Today, the organization 9 to 5 is one of the largest and most respected national organizations of working women in the United States. It is dedicated to putting the issues of working women on the public agenda and has been heavily involved in the passage of major laws, including the 1978 Pregnancy Discrimination Act, the Civil Rights Act of 1991,the Family Medical Leave Act, and the Lilly Ledbetter Fair Pay Act of 2009. The Lilly Ledbetter Fair Pay Act holds businesses accountable for their previous pay discrimination. It also forced employers to disclose their wage and salary statistics by gender and race beginning in 2016 (Blaschke 2018).

Although wage earnings have improved for most working Americans, there are massive salary and wage gaps that persist across gender, race, and ethnic lines. Efforts to reduce the salary and wage gaps still face challenges (Blaschke 2018).

Carolyn Dennis

See also: Equal Employment Opportunity Commission (EEOC); Hill, Anita; #MeToo Movement; Movies, Depictions of Sexual Harassment; Objectification of Women; Sexism

Further Reading

Blaschke, A. 2018. "Why This Is the Moment for a '9 to 5' Sequel?" *Washington Post*, August 6. Accessed February 5, 2019. https://www.washingtonpost.com/news

/made-by-history/wp/2018/08/06/why-this-is-the-moment-for-a-9-to-5-sequel /?noredirect=on&utm_term=.3d682bdcf778.

Bravo, Ellen, and Ellen Cassedy. 1992. *The 9 to 5 Gide to Combating Sexual Harassment: Candid Advice from 9 to 5, the National Association of Working Women.* New York: John Wiley & Sons, Inc.

Murtha, T. 2015. "9 to 5 Turns 35, and It's Still Radical Today." *Rolling Stone.* Accessed February 5, 2019. https://www.rollingstone.com/music/music-country/9-to-5-turns -35-and-its-still-radical-today-50499/

Omojola, F. 2018. "A '9 to 5' Sequel Is Coming—because Little Has Changed for Work-ing Women." MarketWatch, July 27. Accessed February 5, 2019. https://www .marketwatch.com/story/a-9-to-5-sequel-is-coming----because-little-has-changed -for-working-women-2018-07-27.

Staley, O. 2017. "The Screenwriter of the Film '9 to 5' Says We Are Finally Facing Reality." Quartz at Work, December 10. Accessed February 4, 2019. https://qz.com/work /1150399/a-lot-has-changed-for-working-women-since-1980s-9-to-5-even-more-hasnt/.

Traister, Rebecca. 2015. "If You Want to See What Revolutionary Workplace Policies Really Look Like, Watch '9 to 5.'" *New Republic*, May 13. Accessed February 4, 2019. https://newrepublic.com/article/121785/enduring-relevance-9-5.

Nondisclosure Agreements

In the wake of the #MeToo Movement, the use of nondisclosure agreements (NDAs) to silence victims of sexual harassment and assault has received national and international attention. These agreements, often used to prevent parties from disclosing their accusations and compensation when settling sexual harassment and sexual assault complaints, can lead to substantial penalties when women and men violate NDAs and come forward with their experiences. Several prominent figures accused of sexual harassment and assault, including Harvey Weinstein and Michael Bloomberg, used NDAs to prevent their accusers from sharing their experiences or disclosing their settlements. In light of these women and men com-ing forward, the United States and several other countries are beginning to exam-ine the use of NDAs in these cases, and some critics are proposing laws to stop or limit this practice.

In 2018, a bipartisan bill was introduced in the U.S. Congress to require compa-nies to report the number of sexual harassment claims they settle each year and the amount paid to settle these claims. Due to the #MeToo Movement, several other bills were introduced in Congress to deal with sexual harassment, including the Ending Forced Arbitration of Sexual Harassment Act, the EMPOWER Act, and Combat Sexual Harassment in Housing Act. None of these bipartisan bills became law.

The #MeToo Movement not only brought to light issues of sexual harassment in the workplace but also brought attention to the number of women unable to come forward with their experiences of sexual harassment without risking significant financial injury due to their signing confidentiality clauses and NDAs. Several women on the USA Gymnastics team (who accused Larry Nassar of sexual abuse) and Gretchen Carlson (who accused Roger Ailes) signed confidentiality clauses and NDAs. Harvey Weinstein, Larry Nassar, Roger Ailes, Bill Cosby, and Kevin Spacey were all protected by these agreements.

NDAs have long been used by companies to protect proprietary (not public) information, such as sales lists, codes, and business strategies. These agreements are often designed to protect company information from competitors. Employees typically sign these agreements when they are hired, and they must be carefully worded because if they are too broad, they can be overturned by the courts. However, the purpose of these agreements is to protect the company's confidential information through a signed agreement that can lead to substantial fines for violations.

NDAs and confidentiality clauses are also used in settlement agreements. A settlement agreement (a contract signed by two parties) is often used to resolve court disputes without going to trial, which is a very expensive process. It can be cheaper for both the plaintiff and the defendant to settle. Settlements can prevent both parties from revealing the amount of the settlement, the initial accusation, and other details of the case, which can make it more difficult to combat sexual harassment.

During the #MeToo Movement, several women came forward about their experiences with sexual harassment despite having signed NDAs stipulating that they would not discuss their cases. One woman, Zelda Perkins, accused Harvey Weinstein of attempted rape. She left his film production company after signing an NDA that prevented her from ever discussing Weinstein's attempted sexual assault. When she did come forward, the issue of NDAs to silence sexual harassment and sexual assault victims started to receive attention from both the media and lawmakers. The women who came forward after signing NDAs were opening themselves up to significant legal action.

The punishment for violating NDAs varies but could include significant fines, paying back the entire settlement, and paying the other party's attorney fees—the latter of which can often be higher than the initial settlement. For instance, McKayla Maroney, a former USA Olympic gymnast who accused team doctor Larry Nassar of sexual abuse, settled with USA Gymnastics and signed an NDA. If she testified against Nassar, she could have been fined $100,000 under the agreement. USA Gymnastics waived the agreement, however, so she could provide a victim impact statement at Nassar's trial.

It is unknown how many companies have nondisclosure or confidentiality agreements that prevent employees from coming forward publicly with sexual harassment claims or disclosing settlements for sexual harassment. Critics of NDAs and confidentiality in sexual harassment cases state that it enables serial harassment to continue and too often gives perpetrators continued power over the individuals they have abused. Critics point to the case of Harvey Weinstein, who used NDAs to prevent several of his victims from coming forward, thus enabling him to repeatedly harass and assault other women over several years. The United States is not the only country where NDAs can prevent sexual assault and harassment victims from coming forward; the United Kingdom, Canada, Australia, and several other countries are also dealing with this issue.

NONDISCLOSURE AGREEMENTS IN THE FUTURE

There have been several laws introduced in the U.S. Congress to deal with the issue of sexual harassment as a result of the #MeToo Movement. The EMPOWER

Act would not have made the use of NDAs illegal, but it required companies to report their settlements for sexual harassment. Although federal laws have not moved forward, several states have proposed their own laws to deal with sexual harassment and the use of NDAs to prevent victims from coming forward. During the late 2010s, a number of states proposed bills to limit the use of NDAs. As of 2020, these bills had become law in seven states: Washington, Vermont, Tennessee, New York, Maryland, Arizona, and, most recently, New Jersey. The impact of these new laws on the use of NDAs for sexual harassment and sexual assault cases, and ultimately their impact on sexual harassment and sexual assault in the workplace, will need to be examined over time.

Season Hoard

See also: Ailes, Roger; Carlson, Gretchen; Cosby, Bill; Harvey Weinstein Scandal; Larry Nassar Scandal; McGowan, Rose; Spacey, Kevin; *Time Magazine* "Silence Breakers"

Further Reading

The Associated Press. 2018. "States Move to Limit Workplace Confidentiality Agreements." CBS News, August 27. https://www.cbsnews.com/news/states-move-to-limit-workplace-confidentiality-agreements/.

Campbell, A. F. 2018. "A New House Bill Would Bar Companies from Using Nondisclosure Agreements to Hide Harassment." Vox, July 7. https://www.vox.com/2018/7/18/17586532/sexual-harassment-bill-ban-nondisclosure-agreements-ndas-congress-metoo.

Levinson, J. 2018. "Non-Disclosure Agreements Can Enable Abusers. Should We Get Rid of NDAs for Sexual Harassment?" Think, January 24. https://www.nbcnews.com/think/opinion/non-disclosure-agreements-can-enable-abusers-should-we-get-rid-ncna840371.

Perman, S. 2018. "#MeToo Law Restricts Use of Nondisclosure in Sexual Misconduct Cases." *Los Angeles Times*, December 31. https://www.latimes.com/business/hollywood/la-fi-ct-nda-hollywood-20181231-story.html.

Roth, E. J. 2018. "Is a Nondisclosure Agreement Silencing You from Sharing Your 'Me Too' Story? 4 Reasons It Might Be Illegal." ACLU (Spring). https://www.aclu.org/blog/womens-rights/womens-rights-workplace/nondisclosure-agreement-silencing-you-sharing-your-me-too.

Taulli, T. 2018. "What to Do before Signing an NDA (Non-Disclosure Agreement)." *Forbes*, July 29. https://www.forbes.com/sites/tomtaulli/2018/07/29/what-to-do-before-signing-an-nda-non-disclosure-agreement/#259cd7f6c363.

Norton, Eleanor Holmes (1937–)

Eleanor Holmes Norton was born June 13, 1937, in the District of Columbia. She is the nonvoting delegate to the House of Representatives for the District of Columbia. She was also the first African American woman to chair the Equal Employment Opportunity Commission (EEOC). Norton is an advocate for women's rights, and she developed pioneering regulation that defines what constitutes sexual harassment.

Norton grew up in Washington, DC, and she graduated from Antioch College in 1960. She earned her master's degree from Yale in 1963 and graduated from Yale Law School in 1964. She became active in civil rights in college. She was deeply involved in the civil rights movement of the 1960s, serving as an organizer for the Student Nonviolent Coordinating Committee (SNCC) and later volunteering with the Mississippi Freedom Summer Movement. After graduating from law school, she worked on the Mississippi Freedom Democratic Party's protests at the Democratic National Convention in 1964.

Norton later served as the assistant legal director for the American Civil Liberties Union (ACLU). Her work included taking a case on behalf of the National States Rights Party, a white supremacist group that alleged its free speech had been violated. She ultimately successfully argued for the group in front of the U.S. Supreme Court. Norton also successfully represented female employees of *Newsweek* in their claim of sexual discrimination at the magazine.

Norton's work at the ACLU and her community advocacy resulted in her nomination for the position of New York City's civil rights commissioner in 1970. Under her tenure, New York City held the first hearings in the United States about sex discrimination. In 1975, Norton's coauthored law textbook, *Sex Discrimination and the Law: Causes and Remedies*, was published. The book was one of the first to examine laws related to sex discrimination in the United States.

In 1977, President Jimmy Carter nominated Norton to chair the EEOC. In this role, Norton created a more cohesive organization by focusing on rooting out discrimination that existed within the commission itself. During her time at the EEOC, she pursued a "worst first" policy, targeting companies for enforcement that had the worst records given the demographics for the area.

Norton also pushed the EEOC to issue guidelines regarding sexual harassment. The EEOC's guidelines ultimately defined the behaviors that constitute sexual harassment in the workplace and named sexual harassment as a form of sexual discrimination. Prior to this, the legal definition of sexual harassment was not clear, and the Supreme Court had issued no decisions defining this discrimination. A significant number of women were harassed but unwilling to file suit. The guidelines developed under Norton put the responsibility on employers to take steps to prevent sexual harassment. Ultimately, the Supreme Court's decisions on sexual harassment utilized the EEOC's definition.

When Ronald Reagan assumed the presidency in 1981, Norton resigned as EEOC chair. She later earned tenure at Georgetown University as professor of labor law. She continued to advocate for many political causes, including the Free South Africa Movement and feminism.

Norton became the District of Columbia's delegate to Congress on January 3, 1991, and remained in this position as of early 2020. Norton has the same staff and duties as other members of the House and can vote in committee, but she cannot vote on the House floor. Yet, despite this limitation, Norton has extended her reach far. In the realm of combating sexual harassment, for example, she was a cosponsor of the Campus Accountability and Safety Act, an adamant supporter of Professor Anita Hill during the 1991 Supreme Court nomination hearings for Clarence Thomas, and an adamant supporter of Brett Kavanaugh's accusers, including Professor Christine Blasey Ford, when Kavanaugh's nomination to the Supreme Court went before the Senate for approval in 2019.

Sarah F. Fischer

See also: Campus Accountability and Safety Act (CASA); Congress; Discrimination; Equal Employment Opportunity Commission (EEOC); Hill, Anita; Kavanaugh, Brett

Further Reading

Lester, Joan. 2003. *Fire in My Soul*. New York: Atria Books.

Norton, Eleanor Holmes. 2019. "Congresswoman Eleanor Holmes Norton." Accessed February 13, 2019. https://norton.house.gov/.

Objectification of Women

The objectification of the female body is present in popular culture across a variety of settings. In beauty pageants, judges directly assess the appearance and physique of female contestants. At professional sporting events, cheerleaders and dance teams are enlisted to provide additional entertainment to predominantly male spectators and television viewers. Top-selling video games feature females as heroes as well as sex objects in revealing clothing. Once a year, a sports-oriented magazine turns its primary focus from athletic achievements to the female figure in the *Sports Illustrated Swimsuit Issue*. At some chain restaurants, marketing campaigns emphasize the attractiveness of the waitresses above the quality or affordability of the cuisine. Each of these examples across the popular culture landscape highlights this enduring phenomenon.

The two most successful national beauty pageants in the United States, Miss America and Miss USA, are contested on a yearly basis. Both pageants have been in existence for well over a half century, with Miss America beginning in 1921. The televised pageants consist of several categories that have historically included evening gown and swimsuit competitions. Although contestants are provided an opportunity to answer important questions, they are given extremely limited time to answer complex inquiries. In the age of social media, this portion of the program allows for the viral spread of occasional unclear or confused responses. Much of the remainder of the commentary on the event focuses exclusively on the visual appearance of the young women.

The majority of professional sports teams in the National Football League and the National Basketball Association employ low-paid, scantily clad cheerleaders or dance teams to entertain the fans during time-outs and other breaks in the action. While the competitive sport of cheerleading involves balance, coordination, timing, and routine, recent reports from former cheerleaders have exposed an exploitative process that has included consistent weigh-ins, topless photo shoots, and applicants without any prior dance or cheer experience getting hired strictly on the basis of their physical appearance. Most performers wear far less clothing in this setting than high school or collegiate cheerleaders. The focus on the female body as an addition to male sport is not isolated to team sports. There is a lengthy history of using "ring girls" to carry signs between rounds at boxing matches and "podium girls" to congratulate winners at major auto racing or bicycling events.

In video games, which have become part of popular culture, females play several sexualized roles. In some games, scantily clad women with figures regarded as conventionally attractive to men are the main characters, while in others, women take on the more traditional role of a visually attractive but nonessential addition to the central activity. Lara Croft, the protagonist in *Tomb Raider*, is perhaps the most recognizable female character from a video game. The initial debut of the game took place in 1996, and the franchise has had several follow-up releases and film adaptations. Croft presents an image of an young, athletic female with a sensationalized body, who is often shown with a bare midriff and tight shorts. Her portrayal has become the subject of cultural and academic debates about gender and sexuality for more than two decades.

The first swimsuit issue in *Sports Illustrated* magazine was published in 1964 with a single model at one location. Today, the annual issue features numerous women from photo shoots held around the world. The publication of this issue presents several concerns to critics. The swimsuit issue mainly features supermodels rather than athletes. The magazine rarely chooses female athletes for its cover in other issues and refuses to include men in the swimsuit version. With the decline of print media in the twenty-first century, *Sports Illustrated* has turned to electronic options, with photo shoot videos and an active social media presence, to showcase the women and their bodies.

Several chain restaurants have established a pop culture phenomenon by marketing the presence of female waitresses in minimal attire. Hooters, Twin Peaks, and Tilted Kilt Pub & Eatery are three of the well-known establishments colloquially known as "breastaraunts." The servers at nearly all locations are female, and they wear a standard uniform designed to draw attention to their bodies. Hooters, the most famous of the group, was founded in 1983. The chain became a part of popular culture by expanding its operations beyond food service. For a period of time, Hooters ran an airline and sponsored a professional golf tour. Today, the company operates a casino hotel, sponsors a NASCAR race car, and produces yearly calendars featuring Hooters waitresses in swimsuits.

Although it is unarguable that females are objectified in a number of different settings, the actual impact of this process is difficult to assess in a quantitative format. Studies on the topic often follow one of two directions. One type of research explores the influence on those who spend time or work in sexually objectifying environments. These studies have found negative implications, such as increases in substance abuse and anxiety. Another type of research assesses the impact of exposure to sexually objectifying content. This research has revealed complex conclusions about the impact of viewing sexually objectifying material on norms, values, and behaviors. It is difficult to generalize any of these results toward the broader effect of sexual objectification on societal views of gender and progress toward gender equality.

There have been reforms in several of these areas, however, indicating that significant change is possible. The Miss America Organization announced in June 2018 that it would drop the swimsuit portion of the competition. The San Antonio Spurs replaced their Silver Dancer dance team with a more family friendly, coed performance group. Meanwhile, the Tour de France eliminated "podium girls," and Formula One Racing has made strides to cease use of "grid girls" in races. Although *Sports Illustrated* continues to publish a swimsuit issue, *ESPN the*

Magazine, a competitor to *Sports Illustrated*, has published a "Body Issue" since 2009 that contains the athletic physiques of both male and female athletes.

Steven Block

See also: Objectification of Women in Media, Songs, Video; Objectification of Women in Movies, Books; Olympics; Publishing; Restaurant/Bar Industry

Further Reading

Davis, L. R. 1997. "The Swimsuit Issue and Sport: Hegemonic Masculinity in Sports Illustrated." *Communication* 19(2): 167–170.

Jansz, J., and R. G. Martis. 2007. "The Lara Phenomenon: Powerful Female Characters in Video Games." *Sex Roles* 56(3–4): 141–148.

Rasmusson, S. L. 2011. "We're Real Here: Hooters Girls, Big Tips, & Provocative Research Methods." *Cultural Studies/Critical Methodologies* 11(6): 574–585.

Szymanski, D. M., L. B. Moffitt, and E. R. Carr. 2011. "Sexual Objectification of Women: Advances to Theory and Research." *Counseling Psychologist* 39(1): 6–38.

Weaving, C. 2016. "Examining 50 Years of 'Beautiful' in Sports Illustrated Swimsuit Issue." *Journal of the Philosophy of Sport* 43(3): 380–393.

Objectification of Women in Media, Songs, Video

In much of American popular media, women are often objectified, or presented in a sexualized or hypersexualized way. This refers to the woman being presented in a manner that primarily focuses on her sex appeal to others or her sexual desire as if those are the most important criteria for ascertaining her value. Sexual objectification of women (and girls) has long been a hallmark of popular media, and even though many observers believe that awareness of this problem is growing and portrayals of the full humanity of the female gender are more common than they once were, objectification of women remains prominent in many cultural realms today.

Mass media is commonly defined as social applications, websites, magazines, television, and the entertainment industry. Mass media remains very influential in creating and promoting megatrends that shape what many people define as success. Through the metamorphosis of mass communication into more explicit forms, the media's depiction of women has become increasingly more objectified and sexualized in some areas, such as popular music.

Objectification of women in advertising can lead to higher sales through strategic marketing, global attention, fame, and fortune. Women sexualized through photos, films, and other media outlets can serve to maximize their exposure, thus garnering more attention. This attention often translates to higher sales of movie tickets, concert tickets, or designer lines of products.

Many desire to emulate the perceived image of the woman, and any added attention drawn to the woman creates a larger audience for the products she may endorse or peddle. However, what many see as the objectification of women, others interpret as empowerment and success. Many women claim their sexuality as control over their image and physical attractiveness. Some interpret this as a woman's right to capitalize on this "control" of her image in whatever fashion she sees fit. This could be through monetary advancement, fame, or both. What contribution, if any, do these portrayals make to the culture of sexual harassment, and at what cost?

HOW MASS MEDIA HAS CHANGED

With the onset of personal cell phones, there came a wave of change in how information is imparted to the public. Cell phones now act as mobile computers, giving the user instantaneous access to information. Users are bombarded with images, news, emails, text messages, and every form of information in an immediately accessible manner. The public is in a constant state of being subjected to many forms of information, advertisements, and sales pitches. Due to the competition, each industry strives to grab the viewer's attention by using scandalous and shocking headlines, photos, and images to sell their products.

This strategy is also true of the music and video industry. With the birth of accessing music videos outside of broadcasting regulations, there came an era of unlimited possibilities. As videos became available on different platforms, there also came the need for rating scales for songs and videos. For example, parental controls are now available for most devices that attempt to block access to dangerous sites and monitor online activity. With the growing accessibility to platforms of differing levels of regulations, there was (among other things) increased sexualization, nudity, and adult content.

Within the discipline of psychology, there is a theory about how people learn called generalization. Simply put, generalization is when a person learns to behave a certain way under certain circumstances and then shows that same behavior under different circumstances. How would this principle apply here? In this application, a viewer is consistently exposed to images of women that are objectified and sexualized in various media. According to this process, viewers would then *generalize* their reaction and apply a devaluing objectification to all women.

When the consumer is presented with a high volume of images of objectified women, this creates a generalized reaction to women, which would be of a sexual, dehumanizing nature. These images "teach" the audience that women are available for the pleasure of the user and are devoid of intelligence and insight.

Because the images and lyrics are ever present, the viewer constantly receives messages about the value—or lack thereof—of women and girls. Over time, the audience will fall prey to generalizing their negative feelings about the female gender. These negative feelings, warn experts, often ultimately manifest themselves in words and actions that devalue women.

Many young women along with the entertainment industry create an image that is used to bolster their success and sales. Since the early 2000s alone, we have seen an acceleration in the intensity of sexualized lyrics, images, and videos in the music industry. With every new level, some artists strive to reach a new shock value and outdo the last sensation. The competition for attention leaves many artists resorting to the use of highly sexualized videos, lyrics, and songs.

Another theory is a counterpoint to the first. It states that a woman is in control of her sexuality and has the choice to wear, look, and portray any image she chooses.

That choice should reflect empowerment and not the objectification of women. It should reflect intelligence and worth, because a woman's choice to portray herself in a sexualized manner could represent power and control on her terms.

Specifically, many women in the music industry have reached iconic levels of success by shattering prior images of women as being sexualized and objectified by parroting such ideals in biting sarcastic commentaries through their lyrics and videos. Some women in the music industry claim to command control of their sex appeal through irony and satire.

Under both theories, the end product may be the same. Whether empowering or not, some observers worry that women who leverage their sexual image for career gain contribute to the weaponization of sex and equate sex with power and control. The damage may be done because the resulting reaction is the same. The audience perceives the woman as an object that is highly sexualized, regardless of the intent with which it was put forth.

If the consumer is continually presented with images of women objectified by and through the media (in songs, videos, and other media outlets), the objectification becomes internalized. Consumers start to devalue women and associate them with being objects.

When women in the media are objectified and sexualized, they are often portrayed not only as objects for the viewer's pleasure but also as an image that is largely unrealistic for women to achieve. That leaves women chasing a ghost of an image. With the prolific presentation of women being objectified through the media, men often generalize these unrealistic appearances to all women. Women also use these unrealistic prototypes as a yardstick with which to measure their appearance and the appearance of other women.

When women, from a very early age, begin to compare their appearance to an unrealistic goal, it creates the pursuit of an endless journey filled with frustration, anxiety, and body shaming. Constant devaluing can produce long-term effects of poor self-image, low self-esteem, and self-destructive choices. Eating disorders and compulsive behavior can often be associated with young women's desperate attempts to reach the unreachable appearance. Women also develop maladaptive habits that require high levels of self-evaluation and preoccupation with one's physical appearance. Less time can be spent on the development of adaptive skills when a greater effort is being spent on perpetual self-monitoring.

Men and women (and boys and girls) subjected to a steady stream of messages that the value of women and girls is directly related to their attractiveness to the male sex are more likely to internalize a belief that women and girls can and should be treated like objects. They are more likely to be seen as objects that are available for the viewer's pleasure, to be gawked at and dehumanized, while stifling the intellect and personality development of young women. In some cases, these are views that translate to lesser opportunities, pay, and advancement. In other extreme cases, this can lead to a culture of violence, abuse, harassment, and the complete degradation of the culture of womankind.

Theresa Fanelli

See also: Objectification of Women; Objectification of Women in Movies, Books

Further Reading

Cherry, K. 2018. "How the Stimulus Generalization Process Is Conditioned." *Very Well Mind*, December 27. Accessed December 29, 2018. https://www.verywellmind .com/what-is-stimulus-generalization-2795885.

Chiara Rollero, S. T. 2016. "The Effects of Objectification on Stereotypical Perception and Attractiveness of Women and Men." *Psihologija* 49(3): 231–243. https://doi .org/10.2298/PSI1603231R.

Kyrölä, K. 2017. "Music Videos as Black Feminist Thought—from Nicki Minaj's Ana-conda to Beyoncé's Formation." *Feminist Encounters: A Journal of Critical Studies in Culture and Politics* 1(1), article 08. https://doi.org/10.20897/femenc.201708.

Rotem Kahalon, N. S. 2018. "Experimental Studies on State Self-Objectification: A Review and an Integrative Process Model." Edited by K. Corcoran. *Frontiers in Psychology* 9(1268): 27. https://doi.org/10.3389/fpsyg.2018.01268.

Objectification of Women in Movies, Books

Objectification is the act of viewing a person as an inanimate object lacking feelings, purpose, and insight. At no point during the objectification process is any consideration given to the person apart from his or her sexuality. No other traits, abilities, or feelings associated with that individual garner attention because they are thought to lack interest and appeal.

Literature traced as far back as Greek mythology depicts women as sexualized and having caused conflict between men and their gods. Largely, women have been portrayed as enticers who have manipulated men with their sexual prowess.

Throughout history, a woman's role in both movies and books has primarily been in support of her male counterpart. Women's roles in movies and books have not been as central characters but rather used to enhance and add to that of their male costars. Typically, females fit into a few narrow categories that limit their roles to attractive conquests or smart and capable characters devoid of sex appeal. It is unusual to see strong women characters, or those who are both strong and physically attractive. It is also unusual to see women have a storyline that is not dependent upon that of their male counterparts. It is even more disturbing to see women portrayed in a highly objectified manner, where their sexuality becomes weaponized as they manipulate and deceive their way through storylines. The message becomes that women must use their sexuality to achieve their goals due to the absence of more adaptable and functional skills.

The illustration of women in books and the animation of women in movies have also been highly sexualized. These images have perpetuated stereotypes that have haunted women for decades. Animated and illustrated female characters typically have disproportionately small waists, large breasts, flowing hair, and other physical characteristics typical with unrealistic standards for women's appearances. These images even appear in many children's books and movies.

Movies and books often reflect the issues and culture of the times. Frequently, highly debated topics, controversial figures, and shifts in societal norms make their way into books and onto the big screen. By exploring these cultural shifts through the symbolism of movies and literary works, the consumer can experience many aspects of society's ideals.

One can look at the literary works and cinema productions of an era and piece together the emotional issues, political climate, and plights of the marginalized. Movies and books of an era most certainly reflect emotions, triumphs, and struggles encapsulated during a generation. The same logic would then follow for depictions of women's roles in society and the dynamics of interpersonal relationships.

SOCIAL LEARNING THEORY

Social or observational learning is a process by which people learn new behavior by watching others and seeing the consequences of their behavior. Furthermore, this theory, coined by Albert Bandura, proposes that people are more likely to imitate a person's behavior if the consequences are favorable. Learning in this vicarious fashion can occur through both movies and books.

When women face degradation, undermining, or violations (either through mainstream movies or pornography), the consumer may imitate or learn from this behavior. The viewer may model that behavior toward women and reproduce the dynamics of dysfunctional relationships after having seen such content in movies or read about it in books. When movies and books show maladaptive and abusive relationships based on the objectification of women, this behavior can parallel real life.

PROBLEMS AND LONG-TERM EFFECTS OF OBJECTIFYING WOMEN

Modeling abusive and dysfunctional relationships will result in the imitation of these personal dynamics. People attempt to recreate relationships and the interactions between men and women portrayed in movies and books. These relationships are unrealistic and often based on stereotypes and images only present in fantasy and fiction. Women's roles, place in society, and contributions can become based on sexuality. If so, these roles can be used to define their worth. This dynamic then plays out in women wages, opportunities, and their perceived level of competence.

Even more dangerous are the notions that women invite violence, abuse, and humiliation. When the degradation and dehumanization of women become commonplace through roles in books and movies, that message seeps into the present-day culture. The more mainstream the dehumanization of women becomes the more desensitized people get to its existence. These realities may explain why, despite many of the advances made in human rights, harassment and violations toward women continue to increase at exceedingly high rates.

Theresa Fanelli

See also: Discrimination; Gender Equality; Movies, Depictions of Sexual Harassment; Sexism

Further Reading

Bandura, A. 2014. "Personality—Theories of the Whole Person." In *Psychology Core Concepts*, 7 ed., edited by R. L. Philip G. Zimbardo, 442–444. Upper Saddle River, NJ: Pearson.

Biernacki, L. 2013. "The Sexual Objectification of Woman in Literature." Prezi, March 4. https://prezi.com/-sdst1qxc6pv/the-sexual-objectification-of-woman-in-literature/.

Fredrickson, B. L., and T.-A. Roberts. 1997. "Objectification Theory: Toward Understanding Women's Lived Experiences and Mental Health Risks." *Psychology of Women Quarterly* 21(2): 173–206.

Murphy, J. N. 2015. "The Role of Women in Film: Supporting the Men—An Analysis of How Culture Influences the Changing Discourse on Gender Representations in Film." Journalism Undergraduate Honors Theses 2. Fayetteville, AR: Scholarworks@ UARK. https://scholarworks.uark.edu/jouruht/2/?utm_source=scholarworks.uark .edu%2Fjouruht.

Smith, K. 2008. "Stereotypical Roles of Women in Films." *Women in Hollywood* (blog), December 8. ksmith-hollywoodwomen.blogspot.com/2008/12/stereotypical-roles -of-women-in-films.html.

Thompson, T. L., and E. Zerbino. 1995. "Gender Roles in Animated Cartoons: Has the Picture Changed in 20 Years?" *Sex Roles* 32: 651–673. https://link.springer.com /article/10.1007%2FBF01544217.

Walsh, K. 2018. "Commentary: Some Stereotyped Women's Film Roles We'd Like to Do Away With." *Los Angeles Times*, March 16. www.latimes.com/entertainment/movies /la-ca-mn-women-stereotyped-roles-20180316-story.html.

Weebly.com. 2018. "Female Objectification in Movies." Growing Up Gendered. https:// growingupgendered.weebly.com/female-objectification-in-movies.html.

Office/Workplace Settings

Sexual harassment in the workplace has been around for as long as workplaces themselves. For ages, some employees—both women and men—have endured toxic office environments filled with sexual harassment in the forms of sexual innuendo and comments, unwanted sexual advances, and in some cases even sexual abuse or assault.

The first serious discussions of workplace/office sexual harassment—and about potential reforms to reduce the frequency of such incidents—came in the late 1960s and early 1970s, amid women's rising workforce participation and burgeoning feminist consciousness. According to U.S. Equal Employment Opportunity Commission (EEOC), this behavior violates Title VII of the Civil Rights Act of 1964. Title VII applies to employers with fifteen or more employees, including state and local governments. It also applies to employment agencies and to labor organizations as well as the federal government. However, despite the Civil Rights Act and other legal efforts, its proscription in legal jurisdictions around the world, and through social movements, sexual harassment continues to be experienced by many women and some men in industries of all shapes, sizes, and business sectors.

In "Findings on Workplace Sexual Harassment from the 2018 Empire State Poll," a report issued by the Industrial and Labor Relations (ILR) School's Worker Institute, researchers reported that quid pro quo (an exchange of service for something of equal value) workplace sexual harassment impacts about one in ten New York State residents. Social movements such as Time's Up and #MeToo as well as recent high-profile allegations in the media, government, Congress, and prominent firms have brought the often hidden and not talked about issue of sexual harassment to the forefront. However, it persists despite social awareness.

According to the Center for Employment Equity Report, which was issued in 2018, approximately five million employees are sexually harassed at work every year. The overwhelming majority (99.8 percent) of people who experience sexual harassment at work never file formal charges. Of those who file formal charges, very few (less than fifteen hundred per year), go to court. This report also indicates there is a fear that reporting or filing a case in court can backfire and lead to retaliation or other negative consequences for victims. The report stated that most employers react punitively toward people who file formal sexual harassment charges, with 68 percent of sexual harassment charges including an allegation of employer retaliation. This rate is highest for Black women, and 64 percent of sexual harassment charges are associated with job loss. The report documents that 68 percent of sexual harassment charges include an allegation of employer retaliation, and 64 percent of sexual harassment charges are associated with threats of job loss. Employer retaliation was reported most often by Black women, while threats of job loss were highest for white women and white men.

Two U.S. Supreme Court decisions made in 1998 regarding sexual harassment changed the landscape of workplace harassment and the laws against sexual harassment. *Faragher v. City of Boca Raton* and *Burlington Industries v. Ellerth* both played significant roles in determining how sexual harassment cases are handled today. In the *Faragher* case, municipal lifeguard Beth Ann Faragher alleged that during her time working near Miami in the late 1980s, her male supervisors sexually harassed and assaulted her and other female lifeguards by groping them, entering the women's locker room without knocking, asking women to shower with them, and miming oral sex. The court decided that the city was not liable for the harassment or assault, as City Hall had been unaware of the offenses when they were happening. In the case of *Burlington Industries*, Kimberly Ellerth alleged that a high-ranking executive at her company made comments about her physical appearance and said that he could make her job "very hard or very easy," implying that Ellerth's corporate success depended on her willingness to sleep with her boss. Although Ellerth was promoted by her own merit, a lower court decided that she had experienced quid pro quo harassment, even though the threatened retribution never materialized.

Since the #MeToo Movement, there have been some very public examples of sexual harassment in the office setting. Broadcast personality Bill O'Reilly, for example, was ousted from Fox News in April 2017 after multiple sexual harassment allegations against him came to light. The Fox News host was said to have agreed to a $32 million settlement with a former network analyst, in addition to paying, with the help of Fox News, an alleged $13 million to stop five other women from publicly accusing him of harassment.

Matt Lauer was fired from his job as the cohost of NBC's *Today* show in late November 2017 after a female subordinate reported inappropriate sexual behavior by him during the 2014 Sochi Olympics. Soon, more women came forward, including one who said he sexually assaulted her in his office. Lauer's accusers alleged that his harassment continued after the games. The *New York Times* reported that two more women lodged accusations against Lauer following his dismissal from NBC, which the network confirmed.

Another prominent case concerned UBS Financial, which paid out a massive settlement to a female employee who was sexually harassed in its offices. That case involved Carla Ingraham, who was a senior client service associate at UBS Financial Services in Kansas City, Missouri. Ingraham claimed that in 2003, a male broker called her his "work wife" and made comments about getting "laid" on a specific weekend. The male broker also commented on her physical appearance, conversed about favorite sexual positions, and suggested that she perform oral sex on a client. UBS Financial fired Ingram in 2009, one week after she filed her amended sexual discrimination suit. After Ingraham sued, a state court jury awarded her $10,592,000 in damages, agreeing that she had been sexually harassed and finding that UBS had retaliated against her. A judge reduced the award to $8,439,941, including attorney fees and other expenses, but the award was vacated in January 2012 when attorneys reached a "confidential resolution" of the case.

Suman Kakar

See also: Ailes, Roger; Equal Employment Opportunity Commission (EEOC); *Faragher v. City of Boca Raton*; Lauer, Matt; #MeToo Movement; Quid Pro Quo; Time's Up Movement; Title VII of the Civil Rights Act of 1964

Further Reading

Catt, M. 2019. "ILR Study: Workplace Sexual Harassment Impacts 1 in 10 in N.Y." *Cornell Chronicle*, February 21. https://news.cornell.edu/stories/2019/02/ilr-study -workplace-sexual-harassment-impacts-1-10-ny.

McCann, C., D. Tomaskovic-Devey, and M. V. Badgett. 2018. "Employer's Responses to Sexual Harassment." Center for Employment Equity, December. https://www .umass.edu/employmentequity/employers-responses-sexual-harassment.

McCoy, K. 2017. "Sexual Harassment: Here Are Some of the Biggest Cases." *USA Today*, October 25. https://www.usatoday.com/story/money/2017/10/25/sexual-harassment -here-some-biggest-cases/791439001/.

Ortiz, E., and C. Siemaszko. 2017. "NBC News Fires Matt Lauer after Sexual Misconduct Review." NBC News, November 19. https://www.nbcnews.com/storyline/sexual -misconduct/nbc-news-fires-today-anchor-matt-lauer-after-sexual-misconduct -n824831.

Steel, E., and M. S. Schmidt. 2017. "Bill O'Reilly Settled New Harassment Claim, Then Fox Renewed His Contract." *New York Times*, October 21. https://www.nytimes .com/2017/10/21/business/media/bill-oreilly-sexual-harassment.html.

Waxman, O. B. 2018. "The Surprising Consequences of the Supreme Court Cases That Changed Sexual Harassment Law 20 Years Ago." *Time*, June 26. http://time.com /5319966/sexual-harassment-scotus-anniversary/.

Olympics

In 2018, former Michigan State University (MSU) and U.S. Olympic doctor Larry Nassar was found guilty of sexually abusing hundreds of athletes in his care, including numerous Olympic gymnasts. After weeks of testimony from over one hundred women, including Olympic stars McKayla Maroney, Aly Raisman, and

Gabby Douglas, he was sentenced to serve 40 to 175 years in prison (he was also sentenced in 2017 to 60 years in prison on child pornography charges). The Nassar case was highly publicized, but it was not the first instance of sexual misconduct within the Olympics. However, this highly publicized case led Congress to introduce legislation to strengthen abuse prevention measures throughout Olympic sports organizations.

The Olympic Committee acted immediately by firing the entire USA Gymnastics (USAG) board, and then it began to completely overhaul the organization's bylaws to increase the board's accountability. After forcing out the new CEO, who some observers felt was slow to make necessary changes to the organization, the Olympic Committee began taking steps to decertify the USAG. This ultimately means that the USAG will continue to exist as a company organization for gymnastics across the country; however, it will not have any Olympic affiliation or funding associated with it.

In the aftermath of the Nassar scandal, the Olympic Villages in Pyeongchang, South Korea, were updated to include sexual assault centers in advance of the 2018 Winter Olympics. Each of these centers offers physical health care, mental health counseling, legal advice, and safe avenues to report sexual assault to law enforcement agencies. More importantly, these resources are available to anyone in the area who needs access to them, not just the athletes. All resources have counselors on staff who speak many different languages and are able to greet visitors, provide services, or answer the hotline phones. Additionally, the International Olympic Committee (IOC) gave out awareness-raising material about how to prevent harassment and abuse to the athletes and associated staff in the Olympic Village.

The IOC also added a Safe Sport section to its Athlete 365 website—a site that unites all athlete-focused IOC initiatives and communication (International Olympic Committee 2017). On this page, there are definitions of different types of harassment and abuse that can occur—psychological abuse, physical abuse, neglect, and sexual harassment and abuse—so that individuals are more aware of what abuse or harassment looks like. More importantly, they stress that the harassment does not have to be strictly physical; it can also be verbal, in person, online, a onetime event, or a repeated incident. These incidents can be reported on the hotline, by speaking to the IOC safeguarding officer at the Safe Sport booth, or by notifying the athlete role model, who can locate the IOC safeguarding officer.

The Safe Sport website also includes links to a quiz, a sexual harassment section, a reporting section, an online course, and a place to find additional resources. The Draw the Line quiz presents ten scenarios that allow individuals to learn the forms that harassment can take, what it means to be harassed in sports, how to identify it, and how they can protect themselves. The sexual harassment section provides overviews of different types of harassment and abuse—homophobia, sexual abuse, hazing, bystanding, and gender harassment—through definitions, describing the behaviors that exemplify the harassment or abuse, and explaining how they affect athletes as an individual and as part of a team as well as providing case studies with real-life examples.

Even though many people believe that sexual abuse only impacts the individual, there are also effects on the teammates of that individual. For example, sexual abuse can undermine team cohesiveness because it sets up jealousies and apparent favoritism, thus negatively affecting team performance. Think about this scenario: a young athlete on a team is being abused by his or her coach. The coach pays more attention to that particular athlete and starts to let that athlete play more and more at the expense of other deserving teammates. The teammates start to resent the athlete who appears to be receiving preferential treatment, even though they do not know about the abuse, and teamwork starts to falter. Meanwhile, teammates who are aware that a coach is engaging in inappropriate or abusive behavior often feel powerless or fearful to intervene. They may suffer from psychological stress that can lead them to drop out of the sport all together.

The sexual harassment section of the Safe Sport website also provides examples of abusive relationships by outlining types of power within the sports. Some examples include coercive power, which it defines as physical or emotional force applied to make athletes compliant, such as bullying or shouting at an athlete. These types of power are important to understand because they allow athletes to better understand their situation and know when they are being taken advantage of or being abused in any way.

THE CASE THAT ROCKED USA OLYMPICS

Larry Nassar joined the USA Gymnastics national team medical staff as an athletic trainer in 1986 and received his osteopathic medical degree from MSU in 1993. No one suspected that Nassar would cross the line with any of the gymnasts. Even after a young athlete named Larissa Boyce told her coach that Nassar has penetrated her with his hand without warning, her coach flatly denied that he could have done such a thing. According to Boyce, her coach stated, "He would never do anything inappropriate" (Howley 2018). Other gymnasts were even brought in by the coach to explain to Boyce that Nassar had touched that area of their bodies as well, but that it was never inappropriate. Eventually, Boyce conceded that she must have made a mistake and swore to tell no one else.

In 2018, victims supposedly started to "break their silence." However, that is not the case at all. Boyce and many other young girls under Nassar's care told parents, coaches, the MSU police, physicians, psychologists, university administrators, and USAG long before this time period. But even with all these outlets aware of the allegations made against Nassar, no meaningful action was taken. For the adults in the position of power, it seemed highly unlikely that this man, who was so nice, awkward, and helpful, would ever cross the line. Nassar's neighbor, Jody Rosebush, said Nassar would do anything in the world for anyone and that everybody loved him. Nassar's "nice guy" mask thus enabled him to get away with these horrific acts for years.

Although the Nassar case brought the issue of sexual assault in the Olympics into the spotlight, it was not the only event like this to have occurred. In 2000, at the Summer Olympics in Sydney, a Ugandan swimmer was accused of sexually assaulting a teenage girl. Joe Atuhaire, age twenty-two, was charged with sexual intercourse without consent with a seventeen-year old girl in Sydney's western suburb, near the Olympic Village.

At the 2002 Winter Olympics in Salt Lake City, an Olympic student volunteer and village staff reported incidents of sexual assault and harassment. Omar Sami

Qaradhi and Motaz Al Junaidi were dismissed from the 2012 London games for alleged incidents of voyeurism, indecent exposure, and sexual assault. Then, at the 2016 Summer Olympics in Rio de Janeiro, an Olympic boxer from Namibia named Jonas Junias Jonas was accused of grabbing, kissing, and attempting to solicit a housekeeper at the hotel in which he was staying. That same year, Moroccan boxer Hassan Saada was placed in jail for attempted rape after allegedly attacking two waitresses in the Olympic Village.

IOC DEFINITIONS OF HARASSMENT AND ABUSE

The IOC now identifies four main forms of harassment and abuse: (1) psychological abuse, which involves isolation, verbal assault, humiliation, intimidation, or infantilization; (2) sexual harassment or abuse, which is any unwanted and unwelcome conduct of a sexual nature; (3) neglect, which is the failure of a coach or another person with a duty of care toward the athlete to provide a minimum level of care to the athlete, causing harm; and (4) physical abuse, which is any deliberate and unwelcome act, such as punching, beating, kicking, biting, or burning, causing physical trauma or injury.

These terms are not new; however, the definitions that the IOC adopted and placed on its website are new and in response to the recent revelations. The website and these definitions came about in direct response to the Nassar case.

Cheryl Laura Johnson

See also: Authority Figures; Gender Equality; Groping; Larry Nassar Scandal; #MeToo Movement

Further Reading

Brackenridge, C. 2010. "Myths and Evidence—Learning from Our Journey." Paper presented at the Excel Sports Centre, Coventry, February 2010.

Fasting, K., C. H. Brackenridge, and J. Sundgot-Borgen. 2000. *Females, Elite Sports and Sexual Harassment. The Norwegian Women Project 2000.* Oslo, Norway: Norwegian Olympic Committee.

Fasting, K., and N. Knorre. 2005. *Women in Sport in the Czech Republic: The Experiences of Female Athletes.* Oslo, Norway; Prague, Czech Republic: Norwegian School of Sport Sciences and Czech Olympic Committee.

Howley, K. 2018. "Everyone Believed Larry Nassar." *The Cut*, November 19. Accessed February 1, 2019. https://www.thecut.com/2018/11/how-did-larry-nassar-deceive -so-many-for-so-long.html.

International Olympic Committee 2017. "IOC Session, Lima Peru." September 13–15.

Leahy, T., G. Pretty, and G. Tenenbaum. 2002. "Prevalence of Sexual Abuse in Organized Competitive Sport in Australia." *Journal of Sexual Aggression* 8(2): 16–36.

Peterson, M. 2019. "Abuse and Misconduct in Youth Sport Organizations." Nays.org. https://www.nays.org/default/assets/File/What%20Happens%20When%20Abuse %20Happens%20presented%20by%20Michelle%20Peterson.pdf.

Robinson, L. 1998. *Crossing the Line: Sexual Harassment and Abuse in Canada's National Sport.* Toronto, ON: McClelland and Steward Inc.

Safe Sport. 2019. "You Have the Right to Respect and Safety!" Accessed February 1, 2019. https://www.olympic.org/athlete365/safe-sport-yog/.

Oncale v. Sundowner (1998)

The landmark case *Joseph Oncale v. Sundowner Offshore Services, Inc.* (1998) was an appeal from the Fifth Circuit to the U.S. Supreme Court involving a same-sex sexual harassment claim under Title VII of the Civil Rights Act of 1964. In its opinion, the Fifth Circuit held that a male coworker had no cause of action for sexual harassment against a fellow male in the workplace under Title VII. This contention was overruled in a precedent-setting opinion by the U.S. Supreme Court. The Supreme Court argued that the appellant's claim of sexual harassment was actionable under Title VII, as nothing in the law's language sets out different rules or considerations if the plaintiff is of the same sex as the potential defendant.

The plaintiff, Joseph Oncale, was a low-level employee of the defendant, Sundowner Offshore Services, Inc., working on an oil rig off the coast of Louisiana as part of a crew of eight men. In his claim, the plaintiff alleged that he was regularly subjected to unwanted ignominious and sexually charged harassment and sexually explicit verbal mocking from some of his colleagues on board the rig. The plaintiff further alleged that this state of affairs in the work environment generated so much apprehension in him that he might be sexually assaulted that he quit the job.

Title VII of the Civil Rights Act prohibits employers from discriminating against employees on grounds of sex, race, color, national origin, and religion. As a general principle, this statute applies to employers having fifteen or more employees. The employer could be a federal, state, or local government agency. The act equally applies to private and public schools, colleges and universities, and any organization that employs people in the furtherance of its activities.

Although Title VII makes it illegal to discriminate, the EEOC (U.S. Equal Employment Opportunity Commission) enforces the federal laws against some of the following: "unwelcome sexual advances, requests for sexual favors, and other verbal or physical conduct of a sexual nature constitutes sexual harassment when this conduct and other verbal or physical conduct explicitly or implicitly affects an individual's work performance, or creates an intimidating, hostile or offensive work environment."

In the years leading up to the *Oncale* case, there had been significant jurisprudence established in regard to sexual harassment cases under Title VII of the Civil Rights Act of 1964. However, there had not been a case with distinctive facts like the case under consideration. The peculiarity of the *Oncale* case is that both the aggrieved party and the alleged perpetrators of the harassing acts were males, but none of the parties was actually gay. Be that as it may, the decision in *Oncale* has become a key judgment for gay employees enduring harassment because of their sexual orientation.

Given the variety of ways in which sexual harassment occurs in the workplace, it becomes challenging to craft a definition that contemplates all possible manifestations. The *Oncale* case has generated much debate because it clarified who could be a victim or perpetrator of sexual harassment in the eyes of the law.

Alaba Oludare and Jude L. Jokwi Lenjo

See also: Equal Employment Opportunity Commission (EEOC); *Faragher v. City of Boca Raton*; Faragher-Ellerth Defense; Title VII of the Civil Rights Act of 1964

Further Reading

Ator, J. J. 1998. "Same-Sex Sexual Harassment after Oncale v. Sundowner Offshore Services, Inc: Overcoming the History of Judicial Discrimination in Light of the 'Common Sense' Standard." *American University Journal of Gender, Social Policy & the Law* 6(3): 583–614.

Chisolm, B. J. 2001. "The (Back)door of Oncale v. Sundowner Offshore Services, Inc.: Outing Heterosexuality as a Gender-Based Stereotype." *Law & Sexuality: Review Lesbian, Gay, Bisexual & Transgender Legal Issues* 31(1): 193–238.

Lester, T. 1999. "Protecting the Gender Nonconformist from the Gender Police—Why the Harassment of Gays and Other Gender Nonconformists Is a Form of Sex Discrimination in Light of the Supreme Court's Decision in Oncale v. Sundowner." *New Mexico Law Review* 29(1): 89–118.

Lussier, D. 1998. "Oncale v. Sundowner Offshore Services Inc. and the Future of Title VII Sexual Harassment Jurisprudence." *Boston College Law Review* 39(4): 937–963.

Ware, D. D., and B. R. Johnson. 1999. "Oncale v. Sundowner Offshore Services, Inc.: Perverted Behavior Leads to a Perverse Ruling." *Florida Law Review* 51: 489–509.

P

"Passing the Trash"

Sexual harassment and assault accusations in Hollywood generated the #MeToo Movement, and the resulting widespread media attention created heightened awareness of this problem in American society. Moreover, this surge in coverage of sexual abuse and misogyny in the United States also illuminated long-standing problems with sexual harassment and misconduct in various institutions that had previously escaped public notice. According to the most recent and accurate data by the U.S. Department of Education, more than 4.5 million K–12 students (9.6 percent of all students) experienced sexual misconduct by school employees. Most of the abuse was perpetrated by teachers, but other culprits included coaches, administrators, librarians, nurses, and other employees or volunteers working with K–12 students (Shakeshaft 2004).

Unfortunately, many of these victimizations came about as the result of a secretive administrative process known as "passing the trash." Passing the trash enables known abusers to "quietly" leave the school district in which they teach or work and seek employment elsewhere (Grant, Wilkerson, and Henschel 2018). The U.S. Government Accountability Office noted that, on average, a teacher abuser will be employed by three different school districts before being apprehended. A 2018 study examined 361 cases of sexual misconduct by school officials and revealed that one-third had more than one victim and, on average, were arrested for two sexual misconduct cases, with a range of one to nine charges.

COLLECTIVE BARGAINING AND NONDISCLOSURE

The failure to discipline sexual abusers is probably the most significant cause of the student sexual abuse/harassment cycle of passing the trash. Many sexual misconduct cases are not reported to the authorities; instead, they are handled informally and in secret by the school administration. When fellow educators are accused of sexual misconduct, school district officials may have a natural tendency to sympathize with their colleagues and enter into a settlement or a nondisclosure collective bargaining agreement in exchange for their resignation. The nondisclosure settlement agreement usually limits how much information the district can share with other school districts. These collective bargaining agreements often allow for "wiping" personnel files, so no disciplinary record remains once an abuser leaves the school.

School district officials will sometimes even provide positive (i.e., misleading) references to potential future employers to successfully pass the trash. The high-profile passing the trash case of school teacher Jason Fennes, for example, spurred

New Jersey to pass a law to end the practice. In 2017, Fennes was sentenced to a fourteen-year prison term for sexually abusing five students in two different schools. After being accused of molesting four young girls in 2010, Fennes reached an agreement with the school district and was quickly hired by another school, where he sexually abused another young girl. Fennes later admitted to having sexual relations with a fifteen-year-old student a decade earlier at yet another school.

Teachers unions, whose primary role is advocating for teachers and protecting their rights, often provide support for accused sexual abusers and participate in negotiating the passing the trash agreements. Most states have tenure statutes that protect public school teachers from termination. To terminate a tenured teacher, a school district must show just cause or a valid job-related reason for termination. School district officials fear potential lawsuits and other workplace problems initiated by the termination. Therefore, tenure is one of the most commonly cited factors that motivate school district officials to negotiate passing the trash agreements.

Another motive for entering passing the trash agreements is the potential stigma and criticism a school may face if the public learns that it hired a sexual abuser. Passing the trash allows for "self-preservation" of the school. When abusers are secretly passed off to other schools, the school's reputation, public image, and "clean" record are maintained—unless, of course, the abuser is caught and his or her complete work history comes under scrutiny.

LAWS PROTECTING STUDENTS

When children leave the supervision of their parents or guardians to go to school, the school employees take on the physical and legal roles of the parents/guardians, or in loco parentis (Latin for "in the place of a parent"). Therefore, specific federal guidelines were created to protect students while in school. Federal laws such as Title IX, the Child Abuse Prevention and Treatment Act (CAPTA) of 1974, the Adam Walsh Protection Act of 2006, and Erin's Law, a 2015 amendment to CAPTA, all require that public schools have policies in place to protect children from abuse. However, only one federal law, the Every Student Succeeds Act (ESSA) of 2015, specifically addresses the practice of passing the trash. ESSA includes a provision that bans aiding and abetting school employees accused of sexual abuse by requiring states to have specific laws that prohibit allowing a known sexual abuser to "quietly" leave a school district to seek employment elsewhere. The federal government does not have the authority to mandate, direct, or control state or district compliance with the laws. However, the federal government can indirectly pressure school districts to enforce these laws by withholding critical funding for schools that fail to implement these measures. For example, ESSA prevents schools that receive Title II (Preparing, Training, and Recruiting High-Quality Teachers and Principals) grants from helping a school employee obtain another job if that employee was terminated for sexual misconduct with a minor.

Although the ESSA is a step in the right direction for protecting students from sexual abuse and curbing passing the trash, further protections must be implemented at the state and local levels. Washington was the first state to pass a law prohibiting the practice of passing the trash. Since then, Oregon, Pennsylvania, Missouri, Nevada, Texas, and New Jersey have passed similar laws. The self-preservation of schools achieved by passing the trash is in direct opposition of *in loco parentis*. Laws and policies regarding sexual abuse and harassment must result in a cultural change as to how sexual abuse and harassment by school employees are viewed and handled, with an emphasis shift to the best interest of the students and not the best interest of the school.

STEPS TO STOP "PASSING THE TRASH"

Because of *in loco parentis*, teachers, coaches, and other school employees serve an important mentoring role for students, particularly those who most need attention and support. This can confuse the boundaries between inappropriate behavior and being a caring, supportive teacher or coach. School districts must provide training and support to faculty to help them recognize and navigate the fine line between maintaining strict professional boundaries when interacting with students while also providing emotional support for students when deemed necessary.

First, schools must have a zero tolerance sexual abuse and harassment policy in which any or all violations will result in some form of meaningful discipline. Second, schools must have clear written policies about the use of technology and social media—a common vehicle for sexual harassment—and provide specific guidelines for appropriate and inappropriate behavior from employees toward students. Such guidelines may include prohibiting school employees from being alone with students (e.g., giving students rides home, closing classroom doors, one-on-one tutoring). Third, prior to hiring, schools must perform a national fingerprint-based criminal background check and a complete evaluation of all prior employment experience. These two problems were noted in the Government Accountability Office 2010 report. However, background checks only uncover reported cases and will not detect cases that were dismissed or other court records, such as restraining orders. Therefore, all schools must have policies in place that have been implemented and sanctioned at the both the state and local levels that prohibit passing the trash deals and require truthful and accurate full-disclosure references from former employees.

Melanie Clark Mogavero

See also: Authority Figures; Equal Employment Opportunity Commission (EEOC); K–12 Education, Peer-to-Peer; #MeToo Movement; Nondisclosure Agreements; Sexual Harassment Training; Title IX

Further Reading

Bludworth, Carol. 1996. "Stop Passing the Trash: The Principal's Role in Confronting Sexual Abuse." *American Secondary Education* 25: 2–8.

Grant, Billie-Jo, S. Wilkerson, and M. Henschel. 2018. "Passing the Trash: Absence of State Laws Allows for Continued Sexual Abuse of K–12 Students by School Employees." *Journal of Child Sexual Abuse* 28(1): 84–104. https://doi.org/10.1080/10538712.2018.1483460.

Hobson, Charles, J. 2012. *Passing the Trash: A Parent's Guide to Combat Sexual Abuse/ Harassment of Their Children in School.* North Charleston, SC: CreateSpace Publishing.

Hogan, John C., and M. D. Schwartz. 1987. "In Loco Parentis in the United States, 1765–1985." *Journal of Legal History* 8: 260–274.

Maass, Allison. 2017. "'Passing the Trash': Teachers Accused of Sexual Abuse Aren't Always Unemployable." November 1. Accessed January 14, 2019. https://www.dnainfo.com/chicago/20171024/rogers-park/teachers-fired-by-cps-banned-from-charters-after-watchdog-report/.

Nance, Jason P., and P. Daniel. 2007. "Protecting Students from Abuse: Public School District Liability for Student Sexual Abuse under State Child Abuse Reporting Laws." *Journal of Law and Education* 36: 33–63.

Shakeshaft, Charol. 2004. *Educator Sexual Misconduct: A Synthesis of Existing Literature.* Washington, DC: U.S. Department of Education, Policy and Programs Studies Service. Accessed January 14, 2019. https://www2.ed.gov/rschstat/research/pubs/misconductreview/report.pdf.

Shakeshaft, Charol, and Audrey Cohan. 1994. "In Loco Parentis: Sexual Abuse of Students in Schools: What Administrators Should Know." *Administration and Policy Studies, Hofstra University* 1: 1–40.

Surface, Jeanne L., D. L. Stader, and A. D. Armenta. 2014. "Educator Sexual Misconduct and Nondisclosure Agreements: Policy Guidance from Missouri's Amy Hestir Student Protection Act." *The Clearing House* 87: 130–133.

U.S. Department of Education, Office of Civil Rights. 2001. "Revised Sexual Harassment Guidance: Harassment of Students by School Employees, Other Students or Third Parties." Accessed January 14, 2019. https://www2.ed.gov/about/offices/list/ocr/docs/shguide.pdf.

U.S. Government Accountability Office. 2010. "K–12 Education: Selected Cases of Public and Private Schools That Hired or Retained Individuals with Histories of Sexual Misconduct." Report to the Chairman, Committee on Education and Labor, House of Representatives. Washington, DC. December 2010. Accessed January 14, 2019. http://www.gao.gov/assets/320/313251.pdf.

U.S. Government Accountability Office. 2014. "Federal Agencies Can Better Support State Efforts to Prevent and Respond to Sexual Abuse by School Personnel." Report to the Ranking Member, Committee on Education and the Workforce, House of Representatives. Washington, DC. Accessed January 14, 2019. https://www.gao.gov/assets/670/660375.pdf.

Wright, Peggy. 2017. "Ex-Montville Teacher Gets 14 Years for Sexually Abusing Five Students." *Daily Record*, January 20. Accessed February 13, 2019. https://www.dailyrecord.com/story/news/crime/morris-county/2017/01/20/ex-montville-teacher-jason-fennes-sentenced/96683226/.

Pepe Le Pew

Pepe Le Pew is a cartoon character of an amorous skunk created by Warner Brothers in 1945. He was introduced alongside other Warner Brothers cartoons, such as Bugs Bunny, Looney Tunes, Tweety Bird, and Daffy Duck. Pepe is a narcissistic and deeply sexist character who does not care about or respect the feelings of the females he romantically pursues in the least. He has a misperception that all females want him, and he has no compunctions about forcing himself on them. He uses his skunk spray as a cologne, assuming it entices the female characters (portrayed as feminized cats) to him. Even when the female characters run away from him to escape his harassment, he assumes they are playing hard to get. In reality, most of the female characters are simply scared or annoyed by him.

Today, Pepe Le Pew's inappropriate behaviors are widely recognized as textbook examples of sexual harassment and misconduct. In the episode "Wild over You," for example, the female character dismisses Pepe Le Pew by running away from him. He continues to chase her (assuming that she is simply not noticing him); he does not respect her decision and continues to pursue a relationship without any regard for what she wants. This is just one episode that demonstrates how Pepe Le Pew's actions could be classified as sexual harassment.

The fact that Pepe Le Pew continued to chase females that ran from him introduced another level of harassment—stalking. Pepe Le Pew chases the females from the beginning of the episode until the end. At times he silently stalks the characters, following their every move without them noticing that he is present until he magically appears in front of them. Once he is near them, he harasses them until they give him the attention he is seeking. Even when Pepe Le Pew is hurt by rejection from the females, he continues to pursue them over and over again.

Pepe Le Pew may sound like a silly or insignificant show, but it earned an Academy Award in 1949 for Best Animated Short. According to critics, the enduring popularity of the character for the next few decades ensured that millions of young boys and girls would be exposed to the show's treatment of sexual harassment as a rich source of comedy material—and its message, conveyed in episode after episode, that the feelings of women are unimportant.

Pepe Le Pew was a popular but short-lived series that ended after only sixteen episodes, but reruns of the show were broadcast for many years beyond that. However, sightings of these original episodes on broadcast television are rare today. It is evident that Pepe Le Pew could be seen as offensive in the post-#MeToo world.

All in all, this generation is hyperaware of harassment. Warner Brothers created many iconic cartoons that have paved the way for other artists, but they cannot erase the history they created with Pepe Le Pew. Pepe Le Pew may have been able to get away with his behavior in the past with his shenanigans, but he is regarded today as a sort of cartoon mascot of sexual harassment and misogyny. As writer Richard Wright noted, "I watched these cartoons as a child, and way into my teens, as did many others way before the 80s. I don't think I thought it was right, or wrong. It was something more insidious. It was . . . normal." But as an adult living in the #MeToo era, Wright came to recognize that "Pepe Le Pew provided just one of many cues I received as a teen in the 80s that normalized rape culture and patriarchy" (Wright 2018).

Emmanuel Burgos and Gina Robertiello

See also: Hostile Work Environment; #MeToo Movement; Stalking

Further Reading

Levine, K. 2018. "Pepe Le Pew." *By Ken Levine* (blog), July 9. http://kenlevine.blogspot.com/2018/07/pepe-le-pew.html.

Thompson, K. 1998. "Ah Love! Zee Grand Illusion! Pepé Le Pew, Narcissism and Cats in the Casbah." In *Reading the Rabbit; Explorations in Warner Bros. Animation*, edited by Kevin Sandler, 137–153. New Brunswick, NJ: Rutgers University Press.

Wright, R. 2018. "Pepe Le Pew Is the Mascot of Sexual Harassment: A Retrospective on Growing Up with Rape and Consent Culture in 80s Pop Culture." Viva Media, March 28. https://viva.media/pepe-le-pew-is-the-mascot-of-sexual-harassment-a-retrospective-on-growing-up-with-rape-and-consent-culture-in-80s-pop-culture.

Plaza Hotel Plaintiffs

In August 2017, six women who would come to be known collectively as the Plaza Hotel Plaintiffs sued the Plaza Hotel in New York City for failing to address complaints about the sexual harassment they endured as employees at the hotel. The case was still pending as of 2020. Employer liability for sexual harassment that employees experience is dependent on several factors, including who is engaging in sexual harassment. The plaintiffs, six former and current employees, claim they were sexually harassed by supervisors and coworkers, that senior management did nothing to address the issue, and that they were retaliated against for reporting sexual harassment. The plaintiffs' complaint accuses the Plaza Hotel of promoting rape culture (an environment where rape is pervasive and normalized) by ignoring sexual harassment complaints made by female employees.

SPECIFIC ALLEGATIONS IN THE PLAZA HOTEL COMPLAINT

The Plaza Hotel Plaintiffs consist of Dana Lewis, Crystal Washington, Kristina Antonova, Veronica Owusu, Sergeline Bernadeau, and Paige Rodriquez. They are being represented by the Goodstadt Law Group. The plaintiffs have accused both senior management and coworkers of sexual harassment. They further complain that Plaza Hotel management has been made aware of sexual harassment on numerous occasions and that these complaints were ignored. They also said the hotel retaliated against women workers who have brought complaints.

In the complaint, Dana Lewis accuses a general manager of assaulting her in a coat check closet out of range of video cameras and of being subjected to inappropriate behavior during a performance review. Crystal Washington and Veronica Owusu both reported sexual harassment of a coworker to their supervisors and claim no action was taken by the Plaza Hotel. Two of the plaintiffs did not report sexual harassment by supervisors to the hotel's human resources department due to fear of losing their jobs, and one plaintiff claims that when she did complain to human resources, she was told to do her own investigation. The complaint lists several more instances of sexual harassment committed against each plaintiff and examples of how the Plaza Hotel failed to address their concerns.

According to these women, senior management knew about the sexual harassment, and in some cases even experienced it for themselves, yet they did nothing to stop the perpetrators. The plaintiffs also claim that senior management told them there was nothing that could be done and forced the plaintiffs to continue to work with their harassers. The plaintiffs also claim there were numerous instances of "tangible employment actions," including suspensions and false accusations from supervisors of workplace violations in retaliation for reporting the sexual harassment.

SEXUAL HARASSMENT AND DISCRIMINATION IN EMPLOYMENT

In the United States, sexual harassment is considered a form of sex discrimination. Sex discrimination and other forms of employment discrimination are covered under Title VII of the Civil Rights Act of 1964. The Civil Rights Act of 1964 is a federal law, and Title VII of the act outlaws discrimination in all aspects of employment, including hiring and firing, compensation, recruiting, and salary and benefits. This federal law applies to employers with fifteen or more employees. The U.S. Equal Employment Opportunity Commission (EEOC), officially established in 1965, is the federal agency in charge of investigating claims of workplace discrimination.

This means that sexual harassment has been illegal in the United States, in theory, for over fifty years. However, sex discrimination in employment was largely ignored by the U.S. government until the 1970s. It was not until 1977, when sexual harassment was determined to be a form of sex discrimination by U.S. courts and thus a violation of Title VII, that a large number of employers began paying attention to the issue. The EEOC officially established sexual harassment as a form of sex discrimination in 1986 due to the U.S. Supreme Court decision *Meritor Savings Bank v. Vinson*.

A series of subsequent Supreme Court cases established what constitutes sexual harassment and when employers are liable for sexual harassment that occurs in their business. There are two forms of sexual harassment that were originally recognized by the EEOC (and established by the Supreme Court): quid pro quo harassment and a hostile work environment. Quid pro quo harassment ("this for that") occurs when a supervisor requests an employee provide sexual favors or risk demotion, job loss, or other job-related consequences. For this type of sexual harassment to occur, the offender must have power over the employee's job, such as hiring, firing, or promotion. Thus, only a supervisor can commit quid pro quo sexual harassment, according to the EEOC and the Supreme Court.

The second type, hostile work environment, occurs when an employee is subjected to unwanted sexual comments or conduct that creates a hostile environment. A hostile work environment occurs when actions are severe enough or so persuasive that they interfere with an employee's job performance or create a work environment that is offensive or intimidating. Sexual harassment is not the only conduct that can create a hostile work environment. Comments and actions based on race, ethnicity, religion, and other characteristics legally protected by the U.S. government can also create a hostile work environment that is illegal according to U.S. law. However, employees who report sexual harassment must also show that the behavior was unwanted, a requirement that is not included for other hostile work environment complaints.

Over time, the usefulness of the two categories of sexual harassment, quid pro quo and hostile work environment, have been questioned. Instead, U.S. courts have focused on whether a "tangible employment action" has taken place against the employee, such as demotion, suspension, or firing. Whether a tangible employment action has taken place impacts what employees must prove when pursing sexual harassment cases against employers and whether employers are responsible (and automatically liable) for sexual harassment of their employees.

EMPLOYER RESPONSIBILITY

Are employers responsible when employees are sexually harassed? The answer provided by the U.S. Supreme Court is that it depends. It depends on who is engaging in sexual harassment (e.g., a supervisor, another employee, or a client), what happened because of sexual harassment (demotion, firing, etc.), and what the employer has done to address the issue. Employers are not automatically responsible when employees are subjected to sexual harassment. If a supervisor sexually harasses an employee and it leads to a detrimental effect on employment, a tangible employment action such as suspension, firing or demotion, the employer is automatically responsible for the harassment and may have to pay the employee significant monetary damages. If sexual harassment committed by a supervisor does not lead to a tangible employment action (no job loss, suspension, or demotion), the employer is still automatically responsible but may not have to pay the employee monetary damages if the employer can show two things: (1) the employer tried to prevent and address the behavior in a prompt manner (typically by having adequate policies in place on sexual harassment and how it is addressed and showing that this policy was followed) and (2) the employee did not take actions provided by the employer to prevent the behavior.

It is more difficult for employees to receive monetary damages when sexual harassment occurs from coworkers. The employer is not automatically responsible, as they are when supervisors engage in this conduct. The employee must show the employer knew about the sexual harassment or at least should have known. The employee must also show that the employer failed to try to prevent and address the sexual harassment in a prompt manner. An employer can also be responsible—but is not automatically liable—for sexual harassment conducted by customers or clients, also known as third-party sexual harassment. Again, the employee must show that the employer failed to try to prevent or address the issue. Employer responsibility for sexual harassment also depends on whether the victim and perpetrator are of opposite sexes or of the same sex. If same-sex harassment occurs, the employee must show the harassment occurred because of his or her sex.

SEXUAL HARASSMENT IN THE HOSPITALITY INDUSTRY

Some research suggests that sexual harassment in the hospitality industry (which includes a broad set of service occupations, such as hotels, restaurants, and recreation) is high compared to other industries. The prevalence of sexual harassment in this industry has been linked to employees working directly with customers and being responsible for ensuring customer satisfaction. The hotel industry also may have unique challenges in combating sexual harassment of its employees due to many employees working in both public and very private settings (such as private rooms).

Sexual harassment in hotels has been so pervasive that several cities have passed or are considering passing laws that require hotel workers to be provided with panic buttons. Hotel housekeepers are especially prone to being harassed or assaulted. Thus, workers in the hotel industry and the broader hospitality industry must contend with a work environment that can make sexual harassment difficult to address, as employers have less control over third-party harassment from customers. However, much of the research examining sexual harassment in this industry focuses on sexual harassment from customers. The complaint of the Plaza Hotel Plaintiffs does not accuse customers of sexual harassment, but supervisors and coworkers.

Season Hoard

See also: Hostile Work Environment; Power Dynamics; Quid Pro Quo; Sexual Harassment Training; *Time Magazine* "Silence Breakers"; Title VII of the Civil Rights Act of 1964

Further Reading

Cohen, S. 2016. "A Brief History of Sexual Harassment in America before Anita Hill." *Time*, April 11. http://time.com/4286575/sexual-harassment-before-anita-hill/.

Eller, M. E. 1990. "Sexual Harassment in the Hotel Industry: The Need to Focus on Prevention." *Journal of Hospitality and Tourism Research* 14(2): 431–440.

Grossman, J. L. 2016. "Protection against Sexual Harassment Is Alive and Well in the Sixth Circuit." *Scholarly Commons at Hofstra Law*, March 1. https://scholarly commons.law.hofstra.edu/cgi/viewcontent.cgi?article=1922&context=faculty _scholarship.

Guerrier, Y., and A. S. Adib. 2000. "'No, We Don't Provide That Service': The Harassment of Hotel Employees by Customers." *Work, Employment, & Society* 14: 689–705.

Katz, D. S., and A. L. Bess. 2018. "Current Status of Sexual Harassment Claims and Cases." District of Columbia Bar, January 17. https://www.americanbar.org/groups /litigation/committees/solo-small-firm/practice/2018/3-firm-policy-ideas-metoo -legislation/.

Lewis, Washington, Antonova, Owusu, Bernadeau, and Rodriguez v. Sahara Plaza LLC. 2017. https://iapps.courts.state.ny.us/nyscef/ViewDocument?docIndex= 5FFS9YqcINNaDEmHIoyURw==.

Raphelson, S. 2018. "Advocates Push for Stronger Measures to Protect Hotel Workers from Sexual Harassment." NPR, June 29. https://www.npr.org/2018/06/29/624373308 /advocates-push-for-stronger-measures-to-protect-hotel-workers-from-sexual -harass.

Popular Music

A great deal of popular music and music videos tend to have lyrics of a sexual nature. Within some songs and videos, references to females have been demeaning. Some of these even glorify sexual misconduct toward women. Research has confirmed that these sexist, misogynistic, and sometimes violent messages have influenced societal views toward females. Music can have a major impact on its listeners. In particular, adolescent attitudes about sexuality and gender are influenced by what they see and hear. Artists with varied experiences or orientation convey personal messages that may explain why females are portrayed and written about in such dissimilar ways. One of the more controversial or negative ways to illustrate the female identity is through sexual objectification. Sexual objectification is a point of view that asserts that the primary function for women is sexual in nature and that her essential value is predicated on her sexual desirability.

In nearly all musical genres, there is an excess of misogynistic lyrical content. Rap, hip-hop, rock, country, and pop music are all genres that have objectified females in dehumanizing, misogynistic ways. When young women accept the characterizations of women as subordinate and valued based on their sexual attractiveness and availability, they may also normalize other behaviors that correspond with misogynistic practices, such as coercion, aggression, and physical assault.

Many of these presentations went largely unnoticed or unchallenged by mainstream society for years. With the emergence of the #MeToo Movement, however, mass media and social media outlets have begun to highlight these sexist and sometimes proviolence messages within popular music and music videos, further drawing issues of sexual misconduct into the spotlight. Like many social movements, the #MeToo Movement has extended its influence to the music and video industries.

However, given the seemingly widespread acceptance of the message of the #MeToo Movement, there is an interesting paradox that has been exposed in music videos that represents women both favorably and unfavorably. From a feminist perspective, a sexualized or objectified representation of females is considered misogyny, whereas favorable representations are seen as philogyny.

Popular music is, by its very nature, music that is appealing to a broad audience. Popular music can often be about issues relevant to the time in which the music is produced and released. The lyrics (and the video portrayals of those lyrics) can be considered a form of poetry and artistic expression, in which the musical artists have creative freedom. This is also true for music videos. However, some of the music and video creations within popular music have been heavily criticized for their negative depictions of women and girls, including reducing them to objects of sexual desire. Sexual objectification is making a person into a commodity for sexual pleasure of another rather than seeing the individual for their humanistic characteristics. According to some critics, this genre of popular music sends misogynistic messages to society and contributes to sexual misconduct toward women.

The use of sexual objectification within popular music and music videos is not exclusive to male artists. It has been argued that female artists, and in particular female rappers, have sexually objectified themselves and used stereotypes of female sexuality to sell their music. The messages within the lyrics of such music have been argued by some to be detrimental to females because music may influence male attitudes toward the sexual objectification of females.

Some research has shown a negative impact on males' sexual attitudes toward females based on popular music and music videos. One study argued that the sexualization and objectification of women within the music videos leads to more male acceptance of interpersonal violence—and especially violence toward women (Aubrey, Hopper, and Mbure 2010). Another study found that females are more accepting of sexual harassment when they listen to sexualized pop music (Strouse, Goodwin, and Roscoe 1994). A third study found that exposure to sexual music increases attitudes that accept the sexual double standard (the idea that it is acceptable for males to engage in sexual behaviors but not acceptable for females) for both males and females (Zhang, Miller, and Harrison 2008).

However, critiques of music lyrics alone are not sufficient to address sexual misconduct within popular music. Both the #MeToo and Time's Up Movements have also called out artists who have been credibly accused of misogyny, sexual assault, or other forms of sexual misconduct. Famous musicians such as R. Kelly, Chris Brown, XXXTentacion, and the members of the band Red Hot Chili Peppers have all been accused of sexual violence toward women, ranging from sexual harassment to sexual assault and rape. Several music producers have also been accused of sexual misconduct toward female musicians.

Some female musicians have begun to use their music to address sexual misconduct within the music industry. Songs such as "Man Down" by Rhianna, "Praying" by Kesha, and "Til It Happens to You" by Lady Gaga are examples of popular songs that depict experiences of sexual misconduct.

In 2014, Kesha also alleged that record producer Lukasz Gottwald, better known as Dr. Luke, repeatedly subjected her to sexual abuse up to and including rape. Kesha sought a legal injunction to renege on her contact with Gottwald, thus enabling her to join another music label. But the courts ruled Kesha was obliged to produce music under Gottwald during the length of the contract. Gottwald then filed a defamation lawsuit against Kesha (which is still pending legal action at the time of this writing). Kesha's supporters contend that his lawsuit is intended as retaliation for Kesha's report of sexual misconduct within the workplace, but Gottwald and his supporters counter that the courts have ruled in his favor on multiple legal points during their long legal battle and that Kesha has dropped several of her claims. In February 2020, a New York judge ruled that Kesha had defamed Gottwald when she publicly claimed that he had raped singer Katy Perry—a claim that Perry categorically denied.

Since 2016, more famous artists have begun to make public statements about their experiences with sexual misconduct in the music industry. Yet, it continues to be argued that the industry has not held artists, producers, and other stakeholders accountable for their sexual misconduct or misogynistic or sexist treatment of female performers. Researchers argue that systematic change is slow. The emerging work of the #MeToo and Time's Up Movements is still being assessed in terms of the impact of change on popular music, and more time is needed to determine whether the movements and their supporters will be able to effectuate meaningful and enduring change in how popular music depicts women's sexuality.

It is difficult to determine the extent of the influence of the #MeToo Movement on the music video industry, but it is reasonable to expect that it would have an impact on the artists who compose the music or collaborate on the videos. This is evident in the music videos in which women are adored, rather than objectified. A true fondness or admiration for women, also known as philogyny, challenges the stereotype of misogyny. Rather than characterizing women in music videos as sexual objects, some music videos characterize women in a positive way. These alternative images seem to represent admiration for women as human beings equal to men and also fully capable of expressing their own sexuality on their own terms and not dictated by male perspectives. The greatest difference between these two depictions is the ability of women to control the message.

Because a music video is a cultural phenomenon, it makes sense that the #MeToo Movement has had a particular impact on the entertainment industry and is therefore likely to influence the music and music video mediums as well. This could explain why the messages are mixed. The mixed messages, or paradoxes, can be interpreted in different ways. The first explanation is that artists and producers believe their audiences embrace misogyny. or female objectification, and, therefore, they deliver that content. There is a second explanation for a different projection of females in music video, and that is feminism.

For example, Black American feminism arose from the need to address negative racial portrayals of Black girls and women in media. Those that are called hip-hop feminists constructed their identity based on the second wave of American feminism, which is the wave associated with the civil rights movement. If hip-hop feminists embrace an ideology that calls traditional treatment of females into question, it seems likely that this would affect the narratives of their music.

The narratives and images displayed in music video most likely result from the mindset and experiences of the artist. Therefore, the messages will differ, and this may explain why the counternarratives to misogyny are evident in some of today's music videos. Specifically, this indicates that rather than objectifying women in video portrayals, some video producers may actually promote women's rights and challenge sexual objectification. Those individual narratives (lyrics) and depictions also reinforce and represent many of the changing values and norms of modern society. While early hip-hop was ingrained in political and social consciousness that was dominated by male artists, there is an emerging group of women who may have been influenced by the second and third waves of feminism as well as the #MeToo Movement and its predominant message. What remains to be seen is whether the traditional power structures of this industry will support their alternative message.

Aimée X. Delaney and Beverly Ross

See also: Backlash against Allegations of Sexual Harassment and Assault; Gender Equality; Hostile Work Environment; Kelly, R.; Kesha (Kesha Rose Sebert, Ke$ha); #MeToo Movement; Music/Video Settings; Objectification of Women; Retaliation; Time's Up Movement

Further Reading

Abdurraqib, H. 2018. "Year in Music: The Slow Road to Music's #MeToo Moment." *Billboard.* https://www.billboard.com/articles/events/year-in-music-2018/8489958/metoo-movement-music-industry-year-in-music-2018.

Aubrey, J., and C. Frisbey. 2011. "Sexual Objectification in Music Videos: A Content Analysis." *Mass Communication and Society* 14(4): 475–501.

Aubrey, J. S., M. Hopper, and W. G. Mbure. 2010. "Check That Body! The Effects of Sexually Objectifying Music Videos on College Men's Sexual Beliefs." *Journal of Broadcasting & Electronic Media* 55: 360–379.

Henry, N., and A. Powell, A., eds. 2014. *Preventing Sexual Violence: Interdisciplinary Approaches to Overcoming a Rape Culture.* London; New York: Palgrave Macmillan.

Herd, D. 2015. "Conflicting Paradigms on Gender and Sexuality in Rap Music: A Systematic Review." *Sexuality and Culture* 19: 577–589.

Powers, A. 2017. "Songs That Say 'Me Too.'" NPR, October 17. https://www.npr.org/sections/allsongs/2017/10/17/558098166/songs-that-say-me-too.

Rentschler, C. A. 2014. "Rape Culture and the Feminist Politics of Social Media." *Girlhood Studies* 7(1): 65–82.

Segal, R. 2018. "Does Nicki Minaj Empower or Objectify Women?" The Perspective. https://www.theperspective.com/debates/entertainment/nicki-minaj-empower-objectify-women/.

Strouse, J. S., M. P. Goodwin, and B. Roscoe. 1994. "Correlates of Attitudes toward Sexual Harassment among Early Adolescents." *Sex Roles* 31: 559–577.

Tyree, T., and M. Jones. 2015. "The Adored Woman in Rap: An Analysis of the Presence of Philogyny in Rap Music." *Women's Studies* 44(1).

Weitzer, R., and C. E. Kubrin. 2009. "Misogyny in Rap Music: A Content Analysis of Prevalence and Meanings." *Men and Masculinities* 12(3): 3–29.

Zhang, Y., L. E. Miller, and K. Harrison. 2008. "The Relationship between Exposure to Sexual Music Videos and Young Adults' Sexual Attitudes." *Journal of Broadcasting & Electronic Media* 52: 368–386.

Zilles. C. 2018. "The #MeToo Movement Shows the Power of Social Media." Social Media HQ, May 3. socialmediahq.com/the-metoo-movement-shows-the-power-of-social-media/.

Pornography

The pervasiveness of pornography in the United States and much of the rest of the world in the 2020s is comparable perhaps only to the prevalence of sexual activity in art, myth, and social life in ancient Rome and Greece. Unlike antiquity, however, the mass availability of pornography today is linked inextricably to the emerging technologies of the twentieth century, and especially to the advent of the internet in the 1990s. The internet has ushered in an unprecedented level of accessibility, affordability, and anonymity to pornography. Private consumption has expanded, content has changed, and researchers know even less than in the past about personal and community effects of pornography.

In 2018, the six most visited pornography websites in the world all ranked in the top one hundred of all internet sites visited worldwide. Four of them (PornHub, Porn555, LiveJasmin, and Xvideos) ranked in the top fifty. In 2013, almost a third of all global internet traffic was porn related. What troubles many is the claim that much of the material accounting for the growth in online pornography is perceived to be depraved (such as legal depictions of bondage, sadomasochism, and incestuous role-playing that frequently sexualize the mistreatment of the female gender) or both evil *and* criminal (such as works of child pornography).

A social critique of pornography has continuously proved elusive. In a 1964 U.S. Supreme Court decision, pornography was defined by the phrase "I will know it when it when I see it." In today's world of online pornography, webpages move and morph almost overnight; content that is offensive one day is normalized the next. Evaluating pornography as a First Amendment issue or public harm concern is and always has been an exercise in hitting a moving target. Today, that target is moving at lightning speed. How did this dynamic develop and take hold?

A BRIEF HISTORY OF MODERN PORN

In addition to technological advances, mass-produced print pornography and progressive political movements during the 1960s paved the way for today's current, constant, and free supply of pornography. When Hugh Hefner published the first *Playboy* magazine in 1953, he strategically marketed it as glamorous and smart, helping to change porn images from something that only creepy, perverted men engaged in to a mainstream vice that might be found hanging on the walls of any male-dominated workplace. Social mores were changing, and by the late 1960s, liberal political movements had swept across the country. Eventually, publications that trafficked in more hardcore/explicit porn, such as *Penthouse* (1969) and *Hustler* (1974), joined the scene. By the late 1970s, what was once hidden, discreet, and hard to get just twenty years prior could be purchased with a few dollars at a local convenience store.

By the mid-1980s, this normalization of pornography experienced pushback. In 1986, a Commission on Pornography led by Attorney General Edwin Meese resulted in over eight thousand retailers pulling the magazines from their shelves. However, these efforts proved futile. Sales of pornographic magazines were already in steep decline, not because the market for them had waned but because consumption had shifted to more digitized mediums.

From 1996 to 2005, sales of pornography increased from $8 billion annually to $12 billion, with the bulk of this income generated from VHS and DVD sales. By 1996, income from adult film rentals alone had risen by $590 million over just ten years. Through this period, not surprisingly, production of adult videos sharply increased (and was increasingly centered in California following a 1989 state supreme court decision that ruled filmed sex was not prostitution). Compared to the landscape of both amateur and produced pornography today, this was a relatively benign time to be making porn.

By 2007, more than half of U.S. households had internet, and by 2013, more than half had smartphones. *Playboy* stopped publishing pictures of nude women in 2005 because, as their chief executive noted, "The onslaught of Internet pornography has made the nude images in Playboy passé. . . . You're now one click away from every sex act imaginable for free" (Bowerman 2015). In this ubiquitous, unregulated global zone, studios and the lucrative contracts they were once able to offer quickly became outdated. The new norm is for workers to be paid per sex act, and wages are in decline. However, with advances in technology and web streaming, there has been a marked increase in DIY (do-it-yourself) porn. Meanwhile, online pornography is filled with an ever-expanding menu of sexual bondage, sadomasochism, and brutality. To some, this is indicative of degradation and dehumanization; for others, it is merely an extension of sexual liberation begun in the 1970s.

VIOLENCE AND DEGRADATION IN MODERN PORN

Pornography that presents sexual bondage, dominance, submission, and sadomasochism (BDSM), such as Kink.com, is so popular today that James Franco, a well-known Hollywood actor, made *Kink* (2014), a documentary film about the site's content, mission, and participants. His film, which appeared at prestigious festivals such as *Sundance*, sought to depathologize the BDSM community. The extremely popular trilogy of books and films by E. L. James, *Fifty Shades*, has a different slant on BDSM. The protagonist's love interest suffers from sexually sadistic and dominating proclivities that are the result of personal trauma; he is eventually relieved of these darker desires through love. Regardless of what side of the BDSM argument you are on, in the world of online pornography, these types of behaviors are increasingly common and overwhelmingly directed at females. Depictions of women in these types of pornography sometimes portray them as enjoying their treatment, while others are shown in tears or showing expressions of pain or terror.

Many believe that the effects of aggressive or violent pornography are different from "traditional" pornography (e.g., erotica). Violent pornography is pornography that contains varying degrees of physically aggressive action, such as spanking, open-hand slapping, hair pulling, choking, or bondage. Researchers have examined how watching violent pornography affects behaviors ranging from how men act toward female partners in problem-solving (they are more dominant) to the extent to which it may make them more likely to become perpetrators of sexual violence. Younger males tend to be more vulnerable to imitating behaviors they see in porn, and women who watch more of it are more tolerant of male violence.

More recently, a distinct area of research has emerged to examine the onslaught of pornography that deals exclusively with degradation and dehumanization. Pornography that contains degradation typically includes nonnormative sex acts (e.g., fellatio intended to make the performer vomit, anal sex immediately followed by fellatio) and a target who has less status or power. Simulations of gang rape (sometimes referred to as "running a train," where a single female is penetrated in rapid succession by multiple men), forced public sex (a female is offered for sex to any stranger), and multiple simultaneous penetrations function to dehumanize the sexual object, who is most often a female. Researchers have related consumption of this type of pornography by men to increases in sexual harassment of women, increases in negative views of real-life female partners, and loss of compassion for female rape victims.

QUESTIONS OF HARM

Much of the controversy around pornography has always centered on the degree to which it denigrates females. Opposition to pornography based on community standards of decency (e.g., obscenity) is almost obsolete in today's porn climate. Since the "porn wars" of the 1970s, feminist scholars such as Catherine MacKinnon and Andrea Dworkin have viewed pornography as a political expression of male power that exploits the vulnerable and erodes consent. In today's climate of ubiquitous and unregulated porn, questions about how porn might contribute to detrimental attitudes, thoughts, and behaviors toward women and children have become of increasing concern.

The presentation of legally adult young women in pornographic material who are meant to appear underage has always been of concern. For this type of pornography, degradation is implicit in the legal status of the performers; they are not on equal footing, nor do they have the ability to consent. One study of the most popular adult videos found that at least 12 percent present girls as underage minors (Swaner et al. 2016). Childlike qualities of female performers are communicated in various ways, such as video titles that emphasize words and terms, such as "teen" and "barely legal," or the small size of the performers. Girls are dressed in outfits that children would wear (i.e., cotton underwear with rainbows and unicorns, the clichéd schoolgirl uniform). Storylines that include fear of parental supervision, encounters with babysitters, and arguments with teachers all communicate that the object of sexual pleasure is not yet of age. That the subject is not yet capable of independent choice seems to be a critical component in a film's erotic power.

SEX TRAFFICKING OF MINORS

The most visible and concrete public harm issue that has been related to the ubiquity of pornography today is the expansion of sex trafficking, especially of children and girls, so easily (and profitably) facilitated by internet pornography. While some popular commentators have interpreted a correlation between the rise of porn and decreases in rape and domestic violence as causal, other correlational observations to the rise of porn have received less attention. For instance, the rise of porn has also coincided with a sharp increase in the number of teenage girls who say they have engaged in anal sex. There has also been a steady increase in the number of minors who are sex trafficked. Although trends in sex trafficking are difficult to define, as victim protection laws change quickly, in the last five years, U.S. legislators in all but eight states have signed over two hundred anti-trafficking bills into law. Still, conclusive evidence regarding the relationship of ubiquitous pornography, especially the degrading types, to broader social issues and trends is largely unknown.

Anna King

See also: MacKinnon, Catharine A.; Objectification of Women in Movies, Books; Power Dynamics; Traditionally "Male" Workplaces

Further Reading

Baker, Berenice. 2013. "The Internet Wouldn't Exist without Porn." *New Statesman*, June 17. https://www.newstatesman.com/business/2013/06/internet-wouldnt-exist-without-porn.

Bowerman, Mary. 2015. "'Playboy' to Stop Publishing Nude Photos." *USA Today*, October 13. https://www.usatoday.com/story/money/2015/10/13/playboy-magazine-nude-pictures-internet-porn/73856022/.

Bridges, Ana J., Robert Wosnitzer, Erica Scharrer, Chyng Sun, and Rachael Liberman. 2010. "Aggression and Sexual Behavior in Best-Selling Pornography Videos: A Content Analysis Update." *Violence against Women* 16(10): 1065–1085.

Cooper, A. L. 1998. "Sexuality and the Internet: Surfing into the New Millennium." *Cyberpsychology & Behavior: The Impact of the Internet, Multimedia and Virtual Reality on Behavior and Society* 1(2): 187–193.

Dominique Roe-Sepowitz, James Gallagher, Kimberly Hogan, Tiana Ward, Nicole Denecour, and Kristen Bracy. 2017. "A Six-Year Analysis of Sex Traffickers of Minors: Exploring Characteristics and Sex Trafficking Patterns." Arizona State University and the McCain Institute for International Leadership. http://ssw.dtn.asu.edu/static/summary.pdf.

Finkelhor, David, Richard Ormrod, Heather Turner, and Sherry L. Hamby. 2005. "The Victimization of Children and Youth: A Comprehensive, National Survey." *Child Maltreatment* 10(1): 5–25.

Forrester, Katrina. 2016. "Making Sense of Modern Pornography." *New Yorker*, September 26. https://www.newyorker.com/magazine/2016/09/26/making-sense-of-modern-pornography.

Foubert, John D., and Ana J. Bridges. 2017. "Predicting Bystander Efficacy and Willingness to Intervene in College Men and Women: The Role of Exposure to Varying Levels of Violence in Pornography." *Violence against Women* 23(6): 692–706.

Friedersdorf, Conor. 2016. "Is Porn Culture to Be Feared?" *Atlantic*, April 7. https://www.theatlantic.com/politics/archive/2016/04/porn-culture/477099/.

Lo, Ven-Hwei, and Ran Wei. 2005. "Exposure to Internet Pornography and Taiwanese Adolescents' Sexual Attitudes and Behavior." *Journal of Broadcasting & Electronic Media* 49(2): 221–237.

MacKinnon, Catherine A. 2011. "Trafficking, Prostitution, and Inequality." *Harvard Civil Rights–Civil Liberties Law Review* 46: 271–309.

Smith, Aaron. 2013. *Smartphone Ownership—2013 Update*. Washington, DC: Pew Research Center, 1–12.

Stack, Steven, Ira Wasserman, and Roger Kern. 2004. "Adult Social Bonds and Use of Internet Pornography." *Social Science Quarterly* 85(1): 75–88. http://www.jstor.org/stable/42955928.

Swaner, Rachel, Melissa Labriola, Michael Rempel, Allyson Walker, and Joseph Spadafore. 2016. *Youth Involvement in the Sex Trade: A National Study*. New Work: Center for Court Innovation. https://www.ncjrs.gov/pdffiles1/ojjdp/grants/249952.pdf.

Tibbals, Chauntelle. 2017. "Book Review: Walter S. DeKeseredy and Marilyn Corsianos, Violence against Women in Pornography." *Theory in Action* 10(1): 108–113.

Verham, Zack. 2015. "The Invisibility of Digital Sex Trafficking in Public Media." *Intersect* 8(3): 1–12.

Wald, Matthew L. 1986. "'Adult' Magazines Lose Sales as 8,000 Stores Forbid Them." *New York Times*, June 16. https://www.nytimes.com/1986/06/16/us/adult-magazines-lose-sales-as-8000-stores-forbid-them.html.

Waxman, Olivia B. 2017. "'The Deuce' and the Real History of Why the Porn Industry Flourished in the '70s." *Time*, September 8. http://time.com/4923536/the-deuce-hbo-pornography-history/.

Power Dynamics

Power dynamics in an organizational setting is the way people at different levels of authority interact with subordinates to achieve desired outcomes. Oftentimes, the individual with greater authority uses his or her power to control or influence the behavior of others in the relationship. Generally, power dynamics in an organization can also be influenced by interpersonal differences, including gender, age, race, nationality, and socioeconomic status, that are recognized in wider society. Power dynamics influence the interactions of people, including the ways individuals process information, experience emotion, and respond to situations.

The more powerful people in the organization often focus on achieving their perceived goals with less concern about others in the relationship. In organizations with a high degree of lopsided power distribution, sexual harassment of subordinates is more likely to occur. Correspondingly, harassment is less likely to occur in settings where power is evenly distributed among the various demographic or socioeconomic status groupings. Thus, power grants an individual the ability to exercise control over other persons.

The workplace is supposed to afford a conducive environment for every worker in the organization to feel comfortable and free from the threat of sexual harassment, irrespective of their position in the organizational hierarchy. Research and news reports consistently find that employees with relatively more power or authority than their subordinates often unduly subject them to sexually unwelcome behaviors (sexual jokes and unwelcome touching). Victims of such treatment often feel pressure to comply with or at least endure such unwelcome behaviors to maintain favored status with the authority figure engaging in the abusive behavior, creating a quid pro quo of sorts.

According to the U.S. Equal Employment Opportunity Commission (EEOC) sexual harassment includes "unwelcome sexual advances, requests for sexual favors, and other verbal or physical conduct of a sexual nature . . . when this conduct explicitly or implicitly affects an individual's employment, unreasonably interferes with an individual's work performance, or creates an intimidating, hostile, or offensive work environment."

In most of the research on cases of workplace-related sexual harassment, women report a higher rate of victimization than men. Although men are considerably less threatened by sexual harassment behaviors than women, incidents of sexual coercion carried out by women in positions of power and authority have also been documented.

Title VII of the Civil Rights Act of 1964 provides the framework for litigating sexual harassment cases. The role of power dynamics in sexual harassment in the workplace cannot be overemphasized. Beginning with the case of *Meritor Savings Bank v. Vinson* (1986), the U.S. Supreme Court made sexual harassment an illegal form of discrimination, as such harassment creates a hostile work environment for the victim.

The U.S. Supreme Court also held in the case of *Faragher v. City of Boca Raton* (1998) that the city was liable to the respondent for sexual harassment because it had made no attempt to monitor its supervisors' behavior toward subordinates and for failing to circulate policy to all employees prohibiting sexual harassment. Similarly, in the case of *Burlington Industries v. Ellerth* (1988), the U.S. Supreme Court held that Burlington Industries was liable for the sexual harassment of a subordinate by a supervisor who created a hostile work environment for the employee.

Current U.S. jurisprudence insists that employers regularly review and circulate their sexual harassment policies to all employees—including policies designed to ensure that power dynamics in the organization do not provide fertile ground for such misconduct. Organizations should also incorporate anti–sexual harassment training for employees on a regular basis. Company regulations should emphasize a zero tolerance policy when it comes to sexual misconduct and should establish procedures for a thorough, fair, and impartial investigation process for any sexual harassment complaints. Any unwelcome behaviors should be addressed forthwith, and organizations should continually work toward gender equality and inclusion at all levels of the organization.

Alaba Oludare

See also: Equal Employment Opportunity Commission (EEOC); *Faragher v. City of Boca Raton*; Faragher-Ellerth Defense; *Meritor Savings Bank v. Vinson*; Quid Pro Quo; Title VII of the Civil Rights Act of 1964

Further Reading

Burlington Industries, Inc. v. Ellerth, 524 U.S. 742 (1998).

Chamberlain, H. L. J., M. Crowley, D. Tope, and D. T. Randy. 2008. "Sexual Harassment in Organizational Context." *Journal of Work and Occupations* 35: 262–295.

Faragher v. City of Boca Raton, 524 U.S. 775 (1998).

Hersh, J. 2011. "Gender Gaps in Families, Health Care, and Industry: Compensating Differentials for Sexual Harassment." *American Economic Review: Papers & Proceedings* 101(3): 630–634

Meritor Savings Bank v. Vinson (477 U.S. 57 (1986).

Predatory Sex Offenders

Predatory sex offenders are individuals who intentionally seek out or seize opportunities to have nonconsensual sex with their victims. When the term *sexual predator* was initially used in the 1920s by Federal Bureau of Investigation (FBI) director J. Edgar Hoover (1895–1972), it was narrowly conceptualized as an offender who habitually seeks out sexual situations in an exploitative manner. This popularized the image of sex offenders as primarily hunters searching for vulnerable victims who are unknown to the offenders. While predatory sex offenders may commit sexual assaults on victims who are unknown to the offender, decades of research have demonstrated that a disproportionate number of sex offenders seize opportunities to sexually assault or have nonconsensual sex with someone they know. Therefore, sexual predators can be broadly categorized into either opportunity-seeking or opportunity-seizing offenders.

OPPORTUNITY-SEEKING

Opportunity-seeking sexual predators are offenders who habitually seek out and participate in activities that will increase their opportunities to have nonconsensual sex with or sexually assault a victim. Such activities may include going to night clubs, parties, bars, public parks, shopping malls, or other densely populated locations where they might find potential victims. With night clubs, parties, or bars, the offender may be able to find suitable victims who are inebriated by alcohol or illicit drugs. At public parks, the offender may find a jogger running alone or an unattended child playing. These offenders may also troll neighborhoods looking for children or others to sexually assault. Increasingly, predatory sex offenders are using the internet to search for potential victims on various social networking sites. These offenders adopt various tactics, such as using a fake identity, to gain the trust of potential victims (often minors) before requesting sexually provocative or explicit photographs or arranging to meet in person in settings where the offender can sexually assault the victim.

OPPORTUNITY-SEIZING

Most predatory sex offenders are individuals who seize an opportunity to sexually assault a person with whom they have an ongoing relationship. These sex offenders are often family members, friends, lovers, neighbors, or others who are trusted by the victims or by the victims' parents or guardians. In fact, seven out of ten rapes reported to law enforcement are committed by perpetrators that are known to the victim. With juvenile victims, the perpetrator is known in approximately 93 percent of the reported cases according to the U.S. Bureau of Justice Statistics. These offenders often do not plan to sexually assault their victims in advance but will act spontaneously if an opportunity for sexual contact arises. Research has found that family members, friends, or others who have sexually assaulted a child in their care generally chose to sexually assault the child only moments before the act. They chose to take advantage of a situation that had increased the child's vulnerability, for instance, while changing the child's clothes, giving the child a bath, or under other vulnerable circumstances. Opportunity-seizing predators may also leverage positions of authority, such as employers, doctors, police officers, and politicians, to have nonconsensual or coerced sex with a vulnerable victim.

The underlying motivation for offenders to commit sex crimes varies. Most sex offenders commit their crime to exercise power and control over their victim. These offenders use sex as a weapon to dominate or denigrate another person or to resolve feelings of inadequacy and self-doubts. A statistically small number of sex offenders are sadistic, using some form of torture to inflict pain on their victims. These offenders gain sexual gratification from the act of causing pain to their victim rather than from sexual intercourse. The sadistic sex offender's crime is also more likely to result in death.

David A. Marvelli and Natalie Johns

See also: Authority Figures; Corrections System; Health Care Industry; Office/Workplace Settings

Further Reading

Beauregard, E., K. D. Rossmo, and J. Proulx. 2007. "A Descriptive Model of the Hunting Process of Serial Sex Offenders: A Rational Choice Perspective." *Journal of Family Violence* 22: 449–463.

Benoit, L., and J. Proulx. 2017. "An Opportunity View of Child Sexual Offending: Investigating Nonpersuasion and Circumstances of Offending through Criminological Lens." *Sexual Abuse a Journal of Research and Treatment* 30(7): 869–882.

Department of Justice, Office of Justice Programs, Bureau of Justice Statistics. 2017. *National Crime Victimization Survey* 2015–2016, Washington, DC.

Finkelhor, D. 2012. *Characteristics of Crimes against Juveniles.* Durham, NH: Crimes against Children Research Center.

Salter, A. C. 2003. *Predators: Pedophiles, Rapists, and Other Sex Offenders.* New York: Basic Books.

Presidential Scandals

Throughout the history of the United States, those who have sought and achieved the highest office in the land have weathered their share of scandals, including those involving some manner of sexual misconduct. Of those men elected to office, some were alleged to have engaged in sexual misbehavior prior to ascending to the presidency; others continued or initiated their misbehavior after assuming their role as president and, in some cases, were able to largely hide their conduct from the public while in office. Even if the misconduct in question was exposed, presidential denials could be very effective in swaying public opinion, and it is only with the hindsight of many years of historical investigation (and in some cases DNA analysis) that the truth behind the allegations has been revealed.

Many of these scandals involved prior or ongoing extramarital affairs. Both George Washington and Thomas Jefferson were alleged to have fathered children by slaves; it is considered an established fact by the Monticello Foundation and other organizations tasked with securing Jefferson's legacy that he indeed fathered children with Sally Hemings, one of his slaves, although at the time he admitted no intimate relationship with her.

Grover Cleveland ran for office on an image of moral respectability, but unseemly behavior from his past came to haunt him on the 1884 campaign trail once he became the Democratic Party's nominee, with "Ma, Ma, where's my Pa?" becoming the taunting rallying cry of his political rivals. He eventually admitted to having fathered a child out of wedlock (while outrageously slandering the reputation of the child's mother, Maria Halpin, by coloring her as a sexually promiscuous drunkard), and this admission neutralized the scandal. He was ultimately elected president in November 1884.

Warren Harding notoriously carried on an affair with Nan Britton while in office and eventually fathered a child with her. John F. Kennedy's extramarital dalliances are legendary, and Franklin Roosevelt, Dwight Eisenhower, and Lyndon Johnson are all alleged to have engaged in extramarital affairs before becoming president. None of these aforementioned incidents seriously threatened these men's ascent to the presidency or their ability to remain in office. There have been, however, more recent scandals involving presidential sexual misconduct that have undermined their respective administrations far more dramatically.

CLINTON SEX SCANDALS

Bill Clinton was elected as the forty-second president of the United States in November 1992 and assumed office in January 1993. He weathered multiple allegations of sexual impropriety during his political career. These allegations, which ranged from multiple claims of consensual sexual activity to accusations of sexual assault, spanned the period in which he served as governor of Arkansas (1979–1981 and 1983–1992), the two years he served as attorney general of Arkansas prior to his first term as governor, and both terms of his presidency (1993–2001).

Some of these alleged incidents involved consensual sexual activity. Former Arkansas state troopers claimed that when Clinton was governor, he had requested their assistance while they were on duty in not only arranging sexual assignations with a series of women but also hiding evidence of those encounters and actively deceiving his wife, Hillary Clinton, regarding these liaisons. These allegations came to be known in the news media as "Troopergate." A lengthy affair with Gennifer Flowers (one of his "Troopergate" paramours) predated his presidency but created a scandal when Flowers came forward with her story during Clinton's first presidential campaign. It did not derail his ambitions, however, and he ultimately was elected to office.

A subsequent affair with White House intern Monica Lewinsky resulted in dramatically different consequences, including impeachment and a Senate trial for perjury and obstruction of justice. There were also other accusations of sexual assault and nonconsensual contact. White House volunteer Kathleen Willey, for example, claimed that during Clinton's first year in office, he groped and forcibly kissed her when she met with him in the Oval Office to ask for assistance for her financially beleaguered husband. These allegations were ultimately scrutinized as part of a larger impeachment investigation coordinated by independent counsel Kenneth Starr; however, doubt was cast upon her credibility, and her claims gained little traction.

Juanita Broaddrick, a prospective volunteer for Clinton's first gubernatorial campaign, claimed he had raped her, but the allegations received little attention at the time or in the decades following and resulted in no formal legal consequences. Broaddrick was an Arkansas resident who had approached Clinton in 1978 about volunteering for his first gubernatorial campaign after he had visited the nursing home she owned and managed. He urged her to reach out to him to discuss the matter should she ever visit Little Rock, and when she later attended a conference in the city, she contacted him. He suggested they meet in her hotel room, where she alleged he overpowered and raped her. She did not report the incident to law enforcement but did share the story with several friends (who later corroborated her claims that she had told them about the alleged attack shortly after it supposedly occurred). Years later, just before Clinton announced his presidential bid, Broaddrick claimed he contacted her to apologize for his past behavior. She rejected the apology. As Clinton earned the Democratic Party nomination and eventually the presidency, the story remained under the radar. Although the allegations were widely circulated in political and media spheres, Broaddrick refused to meet with journalists.

Another woman, Paula Jones, made claims of unwanted groping and sexual solicitation similar to those leveled by Willey. Jones, an employee with the Industrial Development Commission of the State of Arkansas, was attending a conference in Little Rock in 1991 when she encountered then governor Clinton. He invited her to his suite, sending an Arkansas state trooper to escort her. She claimed that shortly after her arrival, Clinton propositioned her and then groped and attempted to kiss her. He also exposed himself to her as she was attempting to disengage from him.

Jones filed a lawsuit in federal court in May 1994 seeking damages for sexual harassment. Judge Susan Webber Wright issued a ruling later that year that a sitting president could not be the target of a lawsuit (and even if so, there was no evidence that Jones experienced any harm professionally because of the alleged encounter). As a result, the legal action was deferred indefinitely. Jones appealed this decision, and the U.S. Court of Appeals for the Eighth Circuit determined that the lawsuit could, in fact, continue; Clinton in turn appealed this ruling. The case was ultimately reviewed by the U.S. Supreme Court, which affirmed the decision of the Eighth Circuit (*Clinton v. Jones* 1997). The lawsuit was eventually settled for $850,000, with Clinton admitting no wrongdoing. It was, however, the lengthy paper trail associated with this lawsuit and the supporting documents, interviews, and sworn testimony (including from Clinton himself) that had accumulated over the years that ultimately produced grounds for impeachment and nearly resulted in Clinton's political undoing, specifically in relation to Clinton's association with Monica Lewinsky.

The Paula Jones lawsuit also brought Broaddrick's claims into the public spotlight. Although Broaddrick initially denied that she has been sexually assaulted by Clinton when interviewed by Jones's lawyers, she eventually recanted her denial. The allegations surfaced once again when Clinton was under investigation in relation to his possible impeachment (which was itself a consequence of Clinton's alleged acts of obstruction of justice and perjury in an attempt to hide his sexual relationship with White House intern Monica Lewinsky). After Clinton was acquitted of the charges levied against him during impeachment, an interview with Broaddrick aired on NBC in which she publicly discussed her claims for the first time. Clinton denied her account, and the story once again disappeared from public awareness—only to reemerge many years later, during the 2016 presidential race, when Hillary Clinton (Bill Clinton's first lady, who had since served as a U.S. senator and as secretary of state) was the Democratic nominee for the presidency.

Clinton's most famous extramarital relationship during his presidency was with a young White House intern named Monica Lewinsky. This affair became a defining moment of the second term of his presidency once details of their sexual encounters surfaced. Lewinsky, who by 1996 had been transferred from the White House to the Pentagon, had confided to Linda Tripp, her friend and coworker, that she had been engaging in an ongoing sexual affair with Clinton since 1995 (which ultimately ended in 1997). Tripp began secretly recording their conversations.

The ongoing Paula Jones lawsuit served as a catalyst for the pandemonium that was to come. Jones's lawyers had received an anonymous tip regarding a sexual relationship between Clinton and Lewinsky. In January 1998, they subpoenaed Lewinsky's testimony in the hope that she might provide information that would establish a pattern of harassment perpetrated by Clinton against women. Lewinsky signed a sworn affidavit in which she denied any kind of intimate relationship with Clinton. In a later conversation with Tripp, Lewinsky suggested that Tripp lie about her knowledge of the relationship if also asked to testify. Instead, Tripp (aware that Lewinsky had submitted an affidavit that contradicted her admissions in their conversations) turned over the taped conversations to independent counsel Kenneth Starr, who was in the process of investigating the Whitewater real estate scandal that predated Clinton's ascent to the presidency.

With Tripp's tapes in hand, Starr broadened his investigation to also examine Lewinsky's possibly perjurious statements regarding the Jones case—an investigation that reached dramatic levels of complexity when Clinton also provided a sworn statement in relation to the Jones lawsuit in which he denied any kind of sexual relationship with Lewinsky. This initiated an eight-month investigation involving numerous witnesses presented to a grand jury, including Lewinsky (who was promised immunity from prosecution); Lewinsky's mother, Marcia Lewis; Linda Tripp; Clinton's personal secretary, Betty Currie; multiple Secret Service agents; and Clinton himself.

Clinton, meanwhile, finally went public with his admission of an "improper physical relationship" with Lewinsky. Starr's investigation culminated with the release of the Starr Report in September 1998, which presented eleven impeachable offenses. After initiating an impeachment inquiry and completing a two-month investigation, the Republican-controlled U.S. House of Representatives voted to impeach Clinton on two articles of impeachment: perjury and obstruction of justice. Clinton vowed to stay in office, rejecting any suggestions that he resign, and in January 1999, the U.S. Senate began its impeachment trial. After three weeks, Clinton was acquitted of both charges by the Senate, which was also controlled by the Republicans. The bid to impeach Clinton was a failure, and his supporters accused the opposition of political gamesmanship. During the entirety of the impeachment process, nationwide polls indicated high levels of public approval of Clinton's performance as president, and the scandal did little to dim popular support of his administration.

TRUMP SEX SCANDALS

Donald Trump, who was elected as the forty-fifth president of the United States in 2016 and assumed office in January 2017, was an unconventional and controversial candidate Past presidents typically boasted an established track record of accomplishments in public service, serving in the military or in an elected or appointed governmental position, in particular; Trump had no such history. At the same time, he had enjoyed a level of celebrity unknown to any previous major-party candidate for office. He had been in the public eye since emerging in the 1980s as a seemingly wildly successful New York City–based builder and developer, and he had fashioned a public persona of immeasurable wealth and professional success. He lived his life in the public eye in a scope previously unknown to presidential candidates. Personal scandals involving multiple marriages and extramarital affairs were splashed across tabloids as well as mainstream media, and his entire life seemed open to public scrutiny.

After some serious financial setbacks, Trump achieved a career renaissance in the early 2000s as a reality-show producer and star of the successful television program *The Apprentice*. When he first announced his intention to seek the Republican nomination for the presidency for the 2016 election, few observers gave him any chance. But he cruised to the nomination with a bombastic campaign that mixed boasts about his business acumen with rhetoric about the United States' alleged immigration and crime woes that supporters found refreshingly candid and critics condemned as transparently untruthful and racist.

Trump's rival for the presidency in 2016 was Democratic nominee and former first lady Hillary Clinton. During the campaign, Trump resurrected Juanita Broaddrick's accusations with a series of tweets and invited three women who had accused Bill Clinton of sexual misconduct—Broaddrick, Kathleen Willey, and Paula Jones—as his guests to his second debate with Hillary Clinton. Broaddrick had at this point gone public with her support of Donald Trump in the upcoming election and had claimed that Hillary Clinton had been aware since the time of the alleged assault that her husband had raped her. Allegations of her husband's sexual misconduct had serious implications for Hillary Clinton's own presidential ambitions, and some observers believe that it may have been a factor in Trump's exceedingly narrow upset victory over Clinton (who lost in the Electoral College despite winning the popular vote by a margin of 2.9 million votes).

Soon after his presidency began, however, Trump was dogged by two interconnected scandals involving sexual impropriety and legally questionable efforts to hide his involvement. One of these involved former Playboy playmate Karen McDougal, who claimed to have had an ongoing sexual relationship with the married Trump beginning in 2006 and spanning into 2007. During the same time frame, Trump also engaged in a brief sexual affair with adult film actress Stephanie Clifford, known professionally as "Stormy Daniels." After Trump secured the Republican nomination in the summer of 2016, McDougal was offered $150,000 for exclusive rights to her story by American Media, Inc. (AMI), a company managed by David Pecker, who considered Trump a friend. AMI publishes the *National Enquirer* tabloid, which had endorsed Trump for president. AMI thus secured ownership of McDougal's account of her affair with Trump and could therefore deny access to the story to any other media outlet; at the same time, AMI's own publications ignored the story, and McDougal's allegations were effectively buried.

After initial denials, Trump's personal attorney, Michael Cohen, admitted in August 2018 to having arranged "hush money" payments of $150,000 and $130,000 to McDougal and Clifford, respectively, once Trump had been named the Republican nominee to protect Trump's candidacy and to "influence the election." There were questions regarding not only the legitimacy of the nondisclosure agreements implied in these payments but also the origins of the funds used to cover them. Cohen had originally claimed that payments were made from his own personal accounts, but he eventually testified under oath that he violated federal law by drawing from campaign funds to supply the payments, at the direction of Trump. Cohen eventually pleaded guilty to multiple charges stemming from his conduct regarding the hush money payments. Trump was not charged, and the scandal did not appear to immediately impact his presidency, although the events remained under investigation.

Miriam D. Sealock

See also: Authority Figures; Corrections System; Power Dynamics

Further Reading

Baker, Peter. 2015. "DNA Is Said to Solve a Mystery of Warren Harding's Love Life." *New York Times*, August 12. https://www.nytimes.com/2015/08/13/us/dna-is-said -to-solve-a-mystery-of-warren-hardings-love-life.html.

Harris, John. 2005. *The Survivor: Bill Clinton in the White House*. New York: Random House.

Palazzolo, John, and Michael Rothfeld. 2018. "Trump Lawyer Used Private Company, Pseudonyms to Pay Porn Star 'Stormy Daniels.'" *Wall Street Journal*, January 18. https://www.wsj.com/articles/trump-lawyer-used-private-company-pseudonyms -to-pay-porn-star-stormy-daniels-1516315731.

Posner, Richard. 2000. *An Affair of State: The Investigation, Impeachment and Trial of President Clinton*. Cambridge, MA: Harvard University Press.

Thompson, John. 2000. *Political Scandal: Power and Visibility in the Media Age*. Cambridge, UK: Polity Press.

Toobin, Jeffrey. 2000. *A Vast Conspiracy: The Real Story of the Sex Scandal That Nearly Brought Down a President*. New York: Random House.

Woodward, Bob. 2018. *Fear: Trump in the White House*. New York: Simon & Schuster.

Publishing

The contents of books and magazines have historically been cited as key factors in the objectification of women in American society. The objectification of women further leads to the acceptance of the poor treatment of women and may increase the rate of violence against them. It is important to examine the different forms of media, books, and magazines that then affect societal attitudes and can contribute to sexual harassment and violence against women. It is also important to identify solutions to decrease the number of women being sexually violated and victimized.

Objectification theory was created by Barbara Fredrickson and Tomi-Ann Roberts in 1997 as a way to understand the sexual objectification of women in society. The concept of the objectification of women can be explained in a sociocultural context in which sexually objectifying the female body—judging its appearance and desirability—equates to a woman's worth. This is done by speaking or thinking of women only in reference to their bodies, whether their whole body or specific fetishized body parts (e.g., breasts). We live in a culture that overly sexualizes the female body, and this objectification of women comes in different forms. These views are particularly cultivated in books, magazines, movies, and television.

Sexual objectification also intersects with women's sociocultural identities in other realms, such as race, ethnicity, socioeconomic status, sexuality, and class. For example, same-sex female relationships are increasingly sexualized, exploited, and used as male fantasies. Racially, the sexual objectification of African American women in slavery was used to create stereotypes and images of Black women as sexually aggressive savages. In contrast, Asian women have been portrayed as childlike, exotic, and submissive.

Many critics assert that both in the past and the present, the publishing industry (ranging from comic books to best-selling novels) has commonly presented women in ways that dehumanize them and objectify their appearance. Some comic books and teen novels include subjects or images that dehumanize women and objectify their appearance. Many of these pieces of literature include toxic masculinity and sexism because the female characters are given traits that represent a male's perspective on the most desirable female attributes (both in terms of appearance and behavior) and women's roles in society. The "damsel in distress" theme, for example, suggests that women cannot get out of anything by themselves and therefore need the aid of a man to solve their problems.

In recent years, the comic industry has taken a turn for the better with the introduction of Captain Marvel and other similar characters highlighting women's strength and the empowerment of women. In addition, the world of young adult (YA) literature has experienced a surge of works that condemn toxic masculinity, sexism, racism, and homophobia and the destruction that such attitudes wreak on individuals, families, communities, and society as a whole. In fact, works that celebrate "girl power" and racial equality have become pillars of the frontlists of many publishers.

The objectification of women is prominent through female representation in comic books in particular. Women are often shown as large breasted, small waisted, and long haired, and they are often drawn with extreme curves, long legs, and arched backs. These representations reflect an objectification status of oversexualized submission, and this can undermine the power of women in general. When using these models of women in comic books, editors and authors of the major comic book companies promote sex object heroines to their male-dominated audience.

One of the largest and most impactful way in which women are objectified is in literature. Some researchers suggest there is a continuation of genres of literature, and that view contributes to the belief that sexual objectification is a shared experience among women, no matter the age. But other literary works by women stand as clear criticism of the objectification and marginalization of women and of the patriarchal, misogynistic attitudes that pave the way for such treatment. *The Handmaid's Tale*, by Margaret Atwood, for example, is set in a dystopian patriarchal society that prohibits women from having a job, money, and basic rights. As fertility rates have dropped due to chemical poisoning, fertile women are collected and kept in homes with couples who desire a baby, where they are raped, impregnated by the husband, and then sent to the next family to do the same once the baby has been born. This novel shows a world in which women are owned by others, forced to abide by demoralizing and dehumanizing rules, and turned into sexual slaves.

The degree to which women are sexualized today in music videos, magazines, song lyrics, video games, and other forms of media and on television and the internet is unprecedented. In a 2015 congressional briefing, Dawn Hawkins, who serves as vice president of the National Center on Sexual Exploitation, asserted that "yesterday's pornography is today's mainstream media."

There is a growing list of negative consequences—physical, psychological, emotional, sexual, and cultural—when girls view or read this content. Several studies have suggested that the media plays a large role in shaping a woman's body image and that girls exposed to sexualizing media are more likely to experience negative feelings about their bodies.

Further, there are many advertisements that feature women in an objectified way. Advertisements depict sexual images of women that not only seek to attract the "male gaze" but also convey unrealistic expectations of the female body. It has been argued that the female identity in advertising is almost exclusively defined in terms of sexuality. In the case of women, this is largely due to their perceived lack of social power. Several companies targeting the male demographic continue to portray women as sexual objects. Alcohol commercials depict sexy, vulnerable women and implicitly suggest that if a man drinks that beer, he will get the girl. In industry after industry, the portrayal of male dominance over females is the most powerful and commonly employed advertising tool. Even clothing and food advertisements resort to these negative messages.

These images can perpetuate the belief that female victims contribute to their own difficulties with sexual harassment or assault. For example, some research studies indicate that women and men who have been exposed to the sexually objectifying images of women commonly found in mainstream media were significantly more accepting of rape myths. Media that sexually objectifies women have been accused by feminist scholars of even implicitly encouraging sexual assault and harassment. Experts have suggested that the more men are exposed to objectifying depictions, the more they will think of women as things that exist for men's sexual gratification—and that this dehumanizing perspective on women may then inform attitudes regarding sexual violence against women. Studies show that extended and persistent exposure to sexual objectification in advertisements and other media can make men more likely to express misogynistic and sexist attitudes, engage in sexual harassment, or champion sexist cultural attitudes in society. The hateful treatment toward women can perpetuate victim blaming and violence against women, leading some women to have skewed views on sex and relationships.

While it cannot be proven that there is a direct correlation between exposure to the objectification of women in books and media and the likelihood of people so exposed to engage in victim blaming, sexual assault, and other destructive behaviors, it is important to understand the impact that movies, music videos, television, books, and magazines can have on views of women. This can be very dangerous because the media is creating social stereotypes for women that can result in unhealthy social and physical habits in the long run. Objectification of women is common because the more the media has the power to use sexual content concerning women, the more audiences seem to acquire those habits and beliefs. The media is allowed to continue this behavior because the objectification of women is a successful marketing approach, judging from the sales and popularity of these different types of media.

The limited research on women's objectification contributes to the ignorance regarding its effect on sexual harassment and violence against women. While demonstrating the scope of the media and its reach, as well as real-world consequences of normalizing violence against women, more research on the objectification of women in the books and magazines published today is needed.

Brianna Robertiello, Sapphire Beverly, and Gina Robertiello

See also: Fashion Industry; News Media Coverage; Objectification of Women; Sexism; Victim Blaming

Further Reading

Calogero, R., S. Tantleff-Dunn, and J. Thompson. 2011. *Self-Objectification in Women.* Washington, DC: American Psychological Association.

Karsay, K., J. Knoll, and J. Matthes. 2017. "Sexualizing Media Use and Self-Objectification: A Meta-Analysis." *Psychology of Women Quarterly* 42(1): 9–28.

Nelson, K. 2015. "Women in Refrigerators: The Objectification of Women in Comics." *AWE: Women's Experience* 2: 73–74.

Papadaki, E. 2018. "Feminist Perspectives on Objectification." In *The Stanford Encyclopedia of Philosophy (Summer 2018 Edition)*, edited by E. N. Zalta. Accessed February 26, 2020. https://plato.stanford.edu/archives/sum2018/entries/feminism-objectification/.

Szymanski, D. M., L. B. Moffitt, and E. R. Carr. 2011. "Sexual Objectification of Women: Advances to Theory and Research." *Counseling Psychologist* 39(1): 6–38.

Quid Pro Quo

Quid pro quo is a Latin term that means "this for that." It is referred to when something of value is traded for something else of value. This powerful term has been used and interpreted in many different contexts. Its most common and fundamental usage refers to the mutual consideration that passes between two parties in a contractual agreement, confirming the agreement as valid and binding between the two concerned parties. However, it has been used in other contexts as well, including politics, the workplace, education, and housing. In politics quid pro quo generally refers to the use of political office for personal benefit. This typically includes instances where a candidate campaigning for election or an elected official promises or offers preferential treatment to those who make or have made large campaign contributions. Such acts are considered violations of the law and are prosecuted under the Hobbs Act, which makes it a felony for a public official to extort property under the power of office. The Hobbs Act prohibits the use of campaign contributions for promises of official actions or inactions. Former Illinois governor Rod Blagojevich was convicted under this act for attempting to obtain personal financial benefits in 2008 by leveraging his authority as governor to appoint a new senator to replace Illinois senator Barack Obama when he became president elect.

Movements such as #MeToo, #UsToo, and Time's Up have transformed today's work environment and provided a unique new meaning to sexual harassment, hostile workplace, and quid pro quo sexual harassment. Unlike a general hostile environment, quid pro quo harassment involves a supervisor in a position of power threatening an employee or promising advancement or bonuses in return for sexual favors. Currently, the most recognized types of sexual harassment in the workplace are quid pro quo and hostile work environment harassment.

Sexual harassment was first brought to court in cases involving women who had been fired after refusing sexual advances from their employers (*Barnes v. Costle*, 1977). This type of sexual harassment became defined as quid pro quo sexual harassment (meaning that a job, educational opportunity, or advancement in career is contingent upon some kind of sexual performance or favor). Initially, it was acknowledged that such behavior constitutes a violation of Title VII of the Civil Rights Act of 1964. This act "generally prohibits discrimination in the workplace but does not contain an express prohibition against harassment." Thus, as more cases and different types of harassment cases surfaced, labor and employment laws began recognizing the situation as a hostile work environment (see *Williams v. Saxbe*, 1976). In 1980, the Equal Employment Opportunity Commission (EEOC) identified quid pro quo as one type of sexual harassment and hostile work environment. In 1986, the U.S. Supreme Court recognized this distinction in *Meritor Savings Bank v. Vinson*.

Title VII of the Civil Rights Act of 1964, which generally prohibits discrimination in the workplace but does not contain an express prohibition against harassment, nonetheless remains the primary legal protection against quid pro quo and other types of sex-based harassment and discrimination. Meanwhile, the EEOC's guidelines state that unlawful "quid pro quo" conditions exist if submission to unwelcome sexual advances "is made either explicitly or implicitly a term or condition of an individual's employment" or if submission to unwelcome sexual advances "is used as the basis for employment decisions affecting such individual" (29 C.F.R. § 1604.11).

The Supreme Court has interpreted the statute to prohibit certain forms of harassment, including sexual harassment. Since the 1986 *Meritor Savings Bank v. Vinson* decision, the court has also established legal standards for determining when offensive conduct amounts to a Title VII violation. As interpreted in Title VII, quid pro quo in the workplace denotes contexts where sexual favors become a trading chip for securing or retaining employment. It is the most commonly recognized form of sexual harassment in the United States and adds a special meaning to the terms of employment by making it contingent upon the employee's compliance with the employer's request or demand for sexual favors. It is one of the terms used to explain when a person in authority (generally an employer or a supervisor), exerts his or her power to influence the outcomes for the employees in terms of employment (e.g., hiring, firing, promotion, or scheduling, among others) in return for sexual favors or advances.

Compliance and noncompliance to the request may have tangible effects on the person's employment. Such conditions may include implicit or explicit promises of favorable actions if the employee complies and threats of a poor job evaluation or firing or disciplining the employee if he or she objects and defies such advances. For example, the employer may say, "I will promote you if you sleep with me." Or an employer may propose to the applicant when he or she is interviewing for the job, "I will hire you if you sleep with me." The implicit threat in both of these statements is that "I won't promote/hire you if you don't sleep with me." Thus, it can be equated to a form of sexual blackmail. In such cases, getting a job, advancement in a career, and other workplace privileges are contingent on the employee's compliance to the superior's sexual advances. If noncompliance results in the superior retaliating against an employee, this also falls under the quid pro quo category. All these iterations of quid pro quo are prohibited and can be prosecuted under Title VII of the Civil Rights Act of 1964 (42 U.S. Code § 2000e–2).

The literature suggests that although the media primarily focuses on high-profile celebrities, harassment in the workplace is endemic. However, a close examination of news stories and court cases on harassment reveals that although quid pro quo is ubiquitous and has infiltrated all industries and workplaces, the majority of the incidents reported originate from places where there are significant disparities in power among employees, in the service industry, in businesses with a strong emphasis on customer service and client satisfaction, and in industries where there is tolerance or encouragement of alcohol consumption. Indeed, much of the news coverage surrounding sexual harassment allegations has focused on cases in the worlds of politics, entertainment, and news. But many harassment cases originate in retail and restaurant industries and corporate offices. The common feature of these locations is disparities in power, which creates an environment that is conducive to harassment.

Many scholars point to the 1991 hearings convened to consider the nomination of Clarence Thomas to the U.S. Supreme Court as the first time that Americans openly discussed the issue of sexual harassment. At those nationally televised hearings, law professor Anita Hill testified that she was the victim of sexual harassment by Thomas.

In recent years, a number of the high-profile sexual harassment allegations that have garnered attention have orbited around claims of quid pro quo harassment in the workplace. The charges filed against Harvey Weinstein, for example, revealed that he would often exploit his power as an influential producer in Hollywood to manipulate women into performing sexual acts in return for employment or promotion in his own company or in other companies throughout Hollywood. The women had only two choices: comply and get the job or promotion or refuse and lose the employment or promotion. Such extortion falls under quid pro quo harassment.

PREVALENCE OF QUID PRO QUO IN THE WORKPLACE

A 2018 study conducted by National Academies of Sciences, Engineering, and Medicine reported that an analysis of studies on sexual harassment since the 1980s demonstrated that sexual harassment remains widespread in workplaces and that, over the years, the rates of sexual harassment in workplaces have not significantly decreased. Another study by the School of Industrial and Labor Relations at Cornell University published in 2019 reported that approximately 11 percent of New Yorkers over the age of eighteen had experienced sexual harassment in which a superior at work tried to trade job benefits for sexual favors (12.2 percent were females, and 9.5 percent were male). Further, 50 percent of men and women who reported such harassment at work revealed that the experience impacted their work life, career advancement, or the ability to obtain, keep, or perform a job. The study also revealed that minorities were disproportionately affected by quid pro quo sexual harassment at work. About 14 percent of people of color and of Hispanic origin in New York State, versus 8.5 percent of non-Hispanic whites, said they had experienced quid pro quo workplace sexual harassment.

According to the Cornell University study, 83 percent of New Yorkers want public officials to do more to address the problems associated with sexual harassment. This indicates that the society is ready for change. On the legal side, existing laws have been modified, and new laws have been passed to address this issue. Still, some fundamental changes need to be brought about in our social norms and attitudes to truly control and prevent it.

Empirical evidence suggests that sexual harassment occurs when it is tolerated (when policies are not enforced and when incidents are not taken seriously). Employers thus need to set examples to show the behavior will not be tolerated.

Role models encourage behavior, so executives and superiors seeking to change social and workplace norms for the better need to take the focus off the victim and put the spotlight on the offender and his or her transgressions.

Suman Kakar

See also: *Barnes v. Costle*; Equal Employment Opportunity Commission (EEOC); Harvey Weinstein Scandal; Hill, Anita; *Meritor Savings Bank v. Vinson*; #MeToo Movement; Retaliation; Tailhook; Thomas, Clarence; Time's Up Movement; Title VII of the Civil Rights Act of 1964

Further Reading

Advocates for Human Rights. 2019. "Quid Pro Quo Sexual Harassment." Stop Violence against Women (STOPVAW), February. http://www.stopvaw.org/quid_pro_quo _sexual_harassment.

Back, J. C., and C. W. Freeman. 2018. *Sexual Harassment and Title VII: Selected Legal Issues*. Congressional Research Service. https://fas.org/sgp/crs/misc/R45155.pdf.

Chuck, Elizabeth. 2018. "#MeToo in Medicine: Women, Harassed in Hospitals and Operating Rooms, Await Reckoning." NBC News, February 20. https://www.nbcnews .com/storyline/sexual-misconduct/harassed-hospitals-operating-rooms-women -medicine-await-their-metoomoment-n846031.

Faragher v. City of Boca Raton, 118 S. Ct. 2275 (1998).

National Academies of Sciences, Engineering, and Medicine. 2018. *Sexual Harassment of Women: Climate, Culture, and Consequences in Academic Sciences, Engineering, and Medicine*. Washington, DC: National Academies Press.

Precious, T. 2019. "Study Polls New Yorkers on Workplace 'Quid Pro Quo' Sex Harassment." *Buffalo News*, February 13. https://buffalonews.com/2019/02/13/study-finds -more-than-1-in-10-new-yorkers-faced-workplace-quid-pro-quo-sexual-harassment/.

Schindler, S., M. A. Reinhard, D. Stahlberg, and A. Len. 2014. "Quid Pro Quo: The Effect of Individuals' Exchange Orientation on Prosocial Behavior and the Moderating Role of Mortality Salience." *Social Influence* 9(4): 242–254. https:/doi.org/10.1080 /15534510.2013.815132.

Quinn, Zoë (1987–)

Zoë Quinn is an independent and self-taught game developer who became well known in the gaming industry after the release of her interactive game *Depression Quest*. Quinn grew up as an only child in New York. She learned how to code in a six-week course on video game development in her early twenties. Quinn suffered from depression as a teenager, so after the course, she began to develop *Depression Quest*, a game that takes the player through a series of everyday life events where they have to make decisions to manage their depression. The goal of the game is to show others who suffer from depression that they are not alone.

The game was released to praise, but shortly thereafter, Quinn's ex-boyfriend made the ending of their relationship public in a now deleted blog post that he placed on two popular online video game sites. He made a variety of false allegations against Quinn, including that she had obtained positive reviews of her video games in exchange for sex. These postings made her a target of online mobs, death and rape threats, and the release of sensitive personal information about her and her family (called doxing). Over several months, Quinn was victimized to the point where she had to leave her home, and she had to cancel public speaking appearances due to safety concerns. In time, the attacks became less frequent, and Quinn now helps to run a nonprofit organization, Crash Override, that provides support and assistance to other victims of online harassment (Quinn 2017).

This online campaign would eventually lead to a global discussion on how to protect online users (especially women) from threats of physical and sexual violence. Quinn has also joined with other victims of online harassment, such as Anita Sarkeesian, to speak out about "the rising tide of online violence against women and girls" (Frank 2015). They have petitioned social media sites to update how they operate to deter online harassment and have encouraged countries to develop laws to enforce compliance and exact punitive actions against perpetrators.

Despite the continued online harassment of those speaking out against male domination in the gaming industry or in support of the inclusion of women, people of color, and nonbinary individuals, women like Quinn have helped create spaces of progress and empowered momentum for change. Major gaming companies have signed open letters condemning the behavior, and social media sites such as Twitter continue to update their policies to eliminate online harassment of its members.

Gamergate was initially the result of an angry ex-boyfriend and fueled by an online hate mob advocating the maintenance of the status quo, but a real pushback has now emerged to help make the gaming industry more open and welcoming to everyone.

Bryan M. Blaylock, Ellen Repeta, and Nadine Marie Connell

See also: Gamergate; Objectification of Women; Sarkeesian, Anita; Social Media

Further Reading

Frank, A. 2015. "Anita Sarkeesian, Zoe Quinn and More Take Aim at Cyber Harassment against Women." Polygon, September 25. Accessed February 1, 2019. https://www.polygon.com/2015/9/25/9399169/united-nations-women-cyber-violence-anita-sarkeesian-zoe-quinn.

Jason, Z. 2015. "Game of Fear: The Story behind GamerGate." *Boston Magazine*, February 23. Accessed February 1, 2019. https://www.bostonmagazine.com/news/2015/04/28/gamergate/.

Klepek, Patrick. 2017. "The Legacy of Feminist Frequency's Tropes vs Women Series." Waypoint, April 28. Accessed February 1, 2019. https://waypoint.vice.com/en_us/article/nzpkkw/the-legacy-of-feminist-frequencys-tropes-vs-women-series.

Quinn, Zoë. 2017. *Crash Override: How Gamergate (Nearly) Destroyed My Life, and How We Can Win the Fight against Online Hate*. New York: PublicAffairs.

R

Ramírez, Mónica (1977–)

Mónica Ramírez is a civil rights attorney, author, orator, and expert on gender equality. She is the daughter and granddaughter of migrant farmworkers from rural Ohio and has advocated for immigrants, women of her Latino community, women, and workers for over two decades. She is especially invested in ending gender-based violence in the workplace and wage equity. Ramírez is the founder of several major initiatives and projects, including Esperanza: The Immigrant Women's Legal Initiative of the Southern Poverty Law Center, the Bandana Project, and the Latina Impact Fund (LIF). She is the president of the board of the National Farmworker Women's Alliance and a board member for the National Latina Institute for Reproductive Health (NLIRH). Ramírez is also the deputy director for the Labor Council for Latin American Advancement (LCLAA).

Ramírez was an instrumental figure in starting the first national organization serving the interests of the country's seven hundred thousand migrant women farmworkers in the fight against workplace exploitation and sexual harassment. One of her well-known roles in the #MeToo Movement has been broadening the movement to include Latinos. Latina cultural beliefs about gender norms likely play a significant role in the prevalence of sexual harassment and violence in the agricultural industry, which employs a large number of workers of Latino heritage. She has consistently and publicly emphasized that many farmworker women do not report sexual assault on the job out of fear of retaliation, loss of work, and embarrassment. In many instances, women wear layers of bulky clothes to hide their bodies from potential predators.

In 2017, after numerous members of the entertainment industry made public accusations of sexual assault and harassment against famous Hollywood figures, Ramírez wrote a letter on behalf of Alianza Nacional de Campesinas, conveying support and solidarity from Latina farmworkers. After the letter was published in *Time* magazine, it went viral; as *Time* reported, Ramírez's "decades of working as an attorney in defense of farmworker women's rights had prepared her for this moment in history, and when she raised her voice, it was heard" (Time Staff 2017).

Ramírez's letter was regarded as the spark that led to the creation of the Time's Up Movement, in which women from all works of life, from farmworkers to Hollywood actresses, came together to demand justice and equality within their respective professions. Ramírez gained visibility as a leader within the movement, particularly in regard to ending sexual violence against female farmworkers. She stated in the article in *Time* magazine that "there is a need to make sure we're not

saying 'oh, yeah and this also happens to women working in low-paying industries, like farmworker women.'" She emphasized that everyday Latinas are heroes
in their own right and are making important contributions to the country. Ramírez
urges Americans to make a commitment to support and lift others up, building
community versus confrontation.

Tara A. Garrison

See also: Gender Equality; #MeToo Movement; Time's Up Movement; Workplace Gender
Diversity

Further Reading

Bauer, M., and M. Ramirez. 2010. *Injustice on our Plates: Immigrant Women in the US
    Food Industry*. Montgomery, AL: Southern Poverty Law Center.

Garcia, J. 2011. "Invisible behind a Bandana: U-Visa Solution for Sexual Harassment of
    Female Farmworkers." *University of San Francisco Law Review* 46: 855.

Paral, R. 2009. "The Unemployment and Immigration Disconnect: Untying the Knot,
    Part I of III." Washington, DC: Immigration Policy Center, American Immigra-
    tion Law Foundation. https://www.americanimmigrationcouncil.org/sites/default
    /files/research/Untying_the_Knot_Series_051909.pdf.

Ruffini, Karen. 2018. "Who Is Monica Ramirez? Laura Dern's Golden Globes Date Is An
    Advocate for Women." Elite Daily, January 7. https://www.elitedaily.com/p/who
    -is-monica-ramirez-laura-derns-golden-globes-date-is-advocate-for-women
    -7816153.

Shaw, E., A. Hegewisch, and C. Hess. 2018. *Sexual Harassment and Assault at Work:
    Understanding the Costs*. Institute for Women's Policy Research, October 15.
    https://ncvc.dspacedirect.org/handle/20.500.11990/1846.

Time Staff. 2017. "700,000 Female Farmworkers Say They Stand with Hollywood Actors
    against Sexual Assault." *Time*, November 10. https://time.com/5018813/farmworkers
    -solidarity-hollywood-sexual-assault/.

Rap Music

Misogyny is an expression of hatred for women that is derived from two Greek
words, *misos* and *gyne*, which mean "hatred" and "woman," respectively. Misogyny is the reduction of women to objects for men's use and abuse. Misogyny is
embedded in male-dominated systems and societies, linked to disrespect or disre-
gard for women, and evident in many areas of popular culture. One American
musical form that has become notorious for featuring misogynistic and demeaning lyrics toward women is rap.

Lyrics in many rap and hip-hop (an overlapping musical form closely associated with rap) songs refer to women in derogatory terms, using words that diminish and objectify them. Due to the negative nature of these words, the Federal
Communications Commission (FCC) has regulations preventing these words
from being played over public broadcasting. Altered or edited versions of the
songs can be heard on the radio, however, and of course uncensored versions are
widely available for listening or purchase online. Some rap music also perpetuates
stereotypes about Black women in particular, depicting the mammy (a U.S.

stereotype, especially prevalent in the South, for a Black mother), the family matriarch, the welfare mother, and the jezebel.

NETWORKED MISOGYNY

These negative, hostile messages in some rap music are part of a wider online digital environment that has been described as "networked misogyny" (Banet-Weiser and Miltner 2016). Other terms used to describe this phenomenon include *online hate*, *e-bile*, and *gender trolling*. Networked misogyny is the means through which hate groups and far-right movements mobilize and propagate their ideologies online. This is coordinated misogyny. There is a connection between misogyny and the concept of masculinity as often depicted online. The behavioral aspects of masculinity portrayed across social media include violence, aggression, lack of emotional openness, leadership, and dominance.

Misogyny is a widespread feature of Western culture that affects women's experiences at work, during leisure time, and in relationships and thus affects their aspirations. It is a cultural force that can be traced to the hatred of English women in brewing between ca. 1300 and ca. 1700 and their steady withdrawal from this trade. Women were very skilled in the brewery business and were hated for it. Misogyny is considered hate speech, and it rests on the premise of inequality between men and women.

Misogynistic lyrics are considered hateful and may contribute to woman-hating discourse among men. Warwick and Houghton (2017) argued that the appearance and portrayal of women in many music videos reflects similar power imbalances between men and women and emphasizes sexual objectification of women. They further reasoned that addressing the problem of misogyny in music must be seen beyond sexualization, which may be tackled through age ratings for music and related materials.

Misogyny in music causes cultural harm because music affects everyone in the society (Warwick and Houghton 2017). This has led to the linking of certain rap music lyrics to the objectification of women, domestic violence, and rape. Misogynistic ideology is prevalent in gangster rap music and serves to create stereotypes about Black women that normalize and glamorize oppressive ideas about women (Moody-Ramirez and Scott 2015).

It has been argued that misogyny in rap music can be understood to be more than a reflection of gender relations within Black communities. Instead, it can be seen as a reflection of institutionalized images of Blackness, strengthening stereotypes and creating a false sense of inclusion among makers and consumers in the production of the music.

MISOGYNISTIC RAP LYRICS

The elements of misogynistic lyrics often found in rap music include the presentation of the female body, the portrayal of women as witches and whores, the celebration of women's reproductive and domestic roles in popular music, and the portrayal and celebration of dominating masculinity. The lyrics also reflect hegemonic views on sexuality and ownership of women as property. The culture that emulates misogynistic rap music engages in domination of women. Critics contend that the messages contained in this music are damaging to both boys, who come to see toxic masculinity as something to be admired and emulated, and girls, who are taught to loath their authentic selves and embrace a scripted, diminished version of themselves. Nevertheless, there are female artists such as Beyoncé Knowles and Nicki Minaj who have created alter egos as vehicles for their artistry, probably as an attempt to resist and to profit from popular culture. As such, they feed men's fantasies while simultaneously presenting a vision of an empowered female.

As an introduction to lyrics that celebrate the sexual prowess of men, it has been argued that popular songs are vehicles for the display of masculine identities and that this mirrors sexual domination of women in society. The term *Ndezve varume izvi* is referenced when discussing these lyrics, literarily meaning "this is only for men." Therefore, trying to control or eliminate misogynistic lyrics in gangster rap music is challenging because the perpetrators are often considered and treated as celebrities. Similarly, some consumers of gangster rap music ignore the misogynistic lyrics and focus on the lyrical dexterity of the artist as well as broader social and political commentary in the music. This contributes to the appeal of this style of music. However, researchers express concern that continuous exposure to misogynistic lyrics influences attitudes about domestic violence and increases hostile and aggressive thoughts. Rap music promotes misogyny and makes it difficult for young people listening to this music to unlearn the values they pick up on from hearing it.

Bamidele Wale-Oshinowo, Olasunmbo Ayanfeoluwa Olusanya,
and Brianna Robertiello

See also: Discrimination; Gender Equality; Objectification of Women; Sexism

Further Reading

Banet-Weiser, S., and K. Miltner. 2016. "Masculinity So Fragile: Culture, Structure, and Networked Misogyny." *Feminist Media Studies* 16(1): 171–174.

Basham, Kelsey B. 2015. "Perspectives on the Evolution of Hip-Hop Music through Themes of Race, Crime, and Violence." Honors Theses. 270, Eastern Kentucky University.

Chiweshe, M. K., and S. Bhatasara. 2013. "Ndezve Varume Izvi: Hegemonic Masculinities and Misogyny in Popular Music in Zimbabwe." *Africa Media Review* 21(1&2): 151–170.

Corradi, C., C. Marcuello-Servós, S. Boira, and S. Weil. 2016. "Theories of Femicide and Their Significance for Social Research." *Current Sociology* 64(7): 975–995.

Cundiff, G. 2013. "The Influence of Rap/Hip-Hop Music: A Mixed-Method Analysis on Audience Perceptions of Misogynistic Lyrics and the Issue of Domestic Violence." *Elon Journal of Undergraduate Research in Communications* 4(1): 71–93.

Folami, A. N. 2016. "Hip Hop, the Law, and the Commodified Gangsta." 143–150. https://scholarlycommons.law.hofstra.edu/faculty_scholarship/802.

Gilman, M. E. 2014. "The Return of the Welfare Queen." *Journal of Gender, Social Policy and the Law* 22(2/2): 247–279.

Ging, D., and E. Siapera. 2018. "Special Issue on Online Misogyny." *Feminist Media Studies* 18(4): 515–524.

Hackett, L., and E. Crook. 2016. "Masculinity and Misogyny in the Digital Age." https://www.ditchthelabel.org/wp-content/uploads/2016/10/masculinity-and-misogyny-2016.pdf.

Harvey, A., and K. Leurs. 2018. "Networked (In)Justice: An Introduction to the #AoIR17." *Special Issue, Information, Communication & Society* 21(6): 793–801.

Jane, E. A. 2018. *Misogyny Online: A Short (and Brutish) History*. Melbourne, VIC, Australia: Sage, 1–3.

Jerald, M. Cs. 2018. "Respectable Women: Exploring the Influence of the Jezebel Stereotype on Black Women's Sexual Well-Being." Doctor of Philosophy Thesis, University of Michigan.

Kandra, X. 2015. "Gender and Video Games: How Is Female Gender Generally Represented in Various Genres of Video Games?" *Journal of Comparative Research in Anthropology and Sociology* 6(1): 171–193.

Loughnan, S., and M. G. Pacilli. 2014. "Seeing (and Treating) Others as Sexual Objects: Toward a More Complete Mapping of Sexual Objectification." *TPM* 21(3): 309–325.

Marwick, A. E., and R. Caplan. 2018. "Drinking Male Tears: Language, the Manosphere, and Networked Harassment." *Feminist Media Studies* 18(4): 543–559. https://doi.org/10.1080/14680777.2018.1450568.

Moody-Ramirez, M., and L. M. Scott. 2015. "Rap Music Literacy: A Case Study of Millennial Audience Reception to Rap Lyrics Depicting Independent Women." *Journal of Media Literacy Education* 7(3): 54–72.

Rebollo-Gil, G., and A. Moras. 2012. "Black Women and Black Men in Hip Hop Music: Misogyny, Violence and the Negotiation of (White-Owned) Space." *Journal of Popular Culture* 45(1): 118–132.

Richardson–Self, L. 2018. "Woman–Hating: On Misogyny, Sexism, and Hate Speech." *HYPATIA—A Journal of Feminist Philosophy* 33(2): 256–272.

Romanell, C. 2019. "Sour Beer at the Boar's Head: Salvaging Shakespeare's Alewife, Mistress Quickly." *Humanities* 8(6): 1–15.

Rosen, M. 2017. "A Feminist Perspective on the History of Women as Witches." *Dissenting Voices* 6(1): 21–31.

Sloan, J. 2017. "Sex Doesn't Matter? The Problematic Status of Sex, Misogyny, and Hate." *Journal of Language and Discrimination* 1(1): 61–82.

Tobias, E. S. 2014. "Flipping the Misogynist Script: Gender, Agency, Hip Hop and Music Education." *Action, Criticism, and Theory for Music Education* 13(2): 48–83.

Tucker B. 2013. "Musical Violence Gangsta Rap and Politics in Sierra Leone." *Current African Issues* 52: 1–64.

Warwick, B., and R. Houghton. 2017. "Age Restrictions on Music Videos—Sexism Solved?" http://eprints.lse.ac.uk/78703/1/Engenderings%20–%20Age%20restrictions%20on%20music%20videos%20–%20sexism%20solved_.pdf.

Wood, H. 2017. "Feminists and their Perspectives on the Church Fathers' Beliefs Regarding Women: An Inquiry." *Verbum et Ecclesia* 38(1): 1609–9982.

Rape, Abuse & Incest National Network (RAINN)

The Rape, Abuse & Incest National Network (RAINN) is the largest organization that advocates against and addresses sexual violence in the United States. RAINN's catalog of programs includes the National Sexual Assault Hotline; the

Safe Helpline through the Department of Defense (DoD); awareness, prevention, and education initiatives; training, consulting, and technology services to partner organizations, universities, and government agencies; assistance to victims and their families; and advocacy and public policy that promotes holding perpetrators of sexual violence accountable for their crimes.

THE NATIONAL SEXUAL ASSAULT HOTLINE

RAINN was founded in 1994 in Washington, DC, by Scott Berkowitz. Since its inception, the organization has assisted more than 2.7 million people affected by sexual violence. In pursuance of its mission, RAINN initiated the nation's first decentralized hotline for victims of sexual assault in 2008. The National Sexual Assault Online Hotline operates twenty-four hours a day and provides online crisis support to survivors via instant messaging, with service available in both English and Spanish. The telephone hotline (800-656-HOPE) partners with a network of over one thousand local affiliate organizations that enable RAINN hotline volunteers to reroute calls to local service providers based on the first six digits of the caller's phone number. Callers may also choose to enter the ZIP code of their current location for more accurate redirection. The National Sexual Assault Hotline, both online and via telephone, is RAINN's signature service.

The National Sexual Assault Hotline contributes to survivors' healing through the provision of confidential support from trained service providers. Assistance offered includes counseling, referrals to local legal and health facilities for services such as sexual assault forensic exams, local resources for therapeutic interventions to assist survivors in healing and trauma recovery, and referrals to more long-term support within the survivor's local region.

To become a RAINN National Sexual Assault Hotline affiliate organization, service providers from across the United States are vetted by RAINN to ensure that they meet various criteria. To apply to become a RAINN Hotline affiliate, service providers must operate their own 24/7 hotline for sexual violence survivors; offer services to anyone affected by sexual violence, irrespective of race, age, gender identity, or sexual orientation; and conduct thorough criminal background checks on anyone working or volunteering with the organization. RAINN includes vetted affiliated organizations in its national service provider referral database, which is available online (https://www.rainn.org/sexual-assault-service -providers). Affiliate organizations offer individual and group counseling, medical services and hospital accompaniment, legal advocacy, community and professional education, emergency shelter, and casework services.

LEADERSHIP, OUTREACH CAMPAIGNS, AND MEDIA PROFILE

RAINN's leadership consists of a five-member board of directors, all of whom, except president and founder Scott Berkowitz, serve one-year terms as independent voting members. As of March 2020, RAINN's board of directors consists of the following individuals: Scott Berkowitz (president and founder), Regan Burke (chairperson), Cybele Daley (treasurer), Katherine Miller (board member), and Tracy Sefl (secretary).

Since its founding, RAINN has been active in its public outreach. Musician Tori Amos was the organization's first spokesperson, and actress Christina Ricci has been national spokesperson since 2007 and is also a member of RAINN's National Leadership Council. Other notable members of the National Leadership Council include numerous high-profile individuals, such as actor Torrey DeVitto, actress Ashley Judd, singer/songwriter Kesha, and the managing director of the Child Rescue Coalition, E. Desiree Asher. RAINN utilizes the involvement of its National Leadership Council to collaborate with the entertainment industry to ensure depictions of sexual violence in film and television are objectively reflecting the true driving factors and circumstances in which such crimes arise as well as its consequences on survivors.

Utilizing the handle @RAINN, RAINN maintains a social presence on all major social media platforms. Through social media, RAINN disseminates information about services, highlights the work of its partner organizations, creates news content, and provides expert research and commentary on sexual violence news and stories. RAINN's social media presence is particularly significant during its annual RAINN Day, which is held in April to coincide with Sexual Assault Awareness and Prevention Month (SAAPM).

RAINN also maintains an active Speakers Bureau, which involves more than fifteen hundred survivors who speak with community members and the media about their experiences. Moreover, RAINN partners with colleges and universities to raise awareness and create a conversation about the issues of sexual violence prevention and recovery on campuses. Through RAINN's online Prevention Navigator, colleges and universities can find resources regarding on-campus sexual violence prevention programs.

ADVOCACY AND PUBLIC POLICY

RAINN engages in extensive advocacy and public policy efforts with state and national legislators to ensure critical services are available to sexual assault survivors and to challenge the way the United States prosecutes perpetrators. The key policy areas in which RAINN directs its resources include protecting children from sexual abuse, addressing sexual crime on cruise ships, promoting adequate compensation for victims, addressing the rape kit backlog, supporting the Sexual Assault Kit Initiative (SAKI), and making recommendations to lawmakers on statute of limitations laws.

Laurence Cobbaert

See also: National Sexual Assault Awareness and Prevention Month; Relationship Violence; Sexual Harassment Training; Statute of Limitations

Further Reading
Campbell, R., H. Feeney, G. Fehler-Cabral, J. Shaw, and S. Horsford. 2015. "The National Problem of Untested Sexual Assault Kits (SAKs): Scope, Causes, and Future

Directions for Research, Policy, and Practice." *Trauma, Violence, & Abuse* 18(4): 363–376. https://doi.org/10.1177/1524838015622436.

Finn, J., and P. Hughes. 2008. "Evaluation of the RAINN National Sexual Assault Online Hotline." *Journal of Technology in Human Services* 26(2–4): 203–222. https://doi .org/10.1080/15228830802094783.

Leonard, E. B. 2015. *Crime, Inequality, and Power.* New York: Routledge.

Rape, Abuse, and Incest National Network. Accessed March 3, 2020. https://www.rainn .org/.

Tannura, T. A. 2014. "Rape Trauma Syndrome." *American Journal of Sexuality Education* 9(2): 247–256. https://doi.org/10.1080/15546128.2014.883267.

Ratner, Brett (1969–)

American filmmaker Brett Ratner was born on March 28, 1969, in Miami, Florida. He has directed and produced several hit films that have resonated with audiences across the globe, bringing in more than $2 billion at the box office. His directorial credits include *The Family Man, Rush Hour, Money Talks, Rush Hour 2, Red Dragon, Hercules, X Men: The Last Stand,* and *Black Mass.* He also served as both executive producer and director of films such as *The Revenant, I Saw the Light,* and *Truth.* Ratner and James Packer partnered and formed RatPat Entertainment in 2013. RatPat Entertainment has cofinanced over fifty-two motion pictures that have exceeded more than $9 billion in box office receipts worldwide. Meanwhile, Ratner cultivated the persona of a Hollywood "playboy" by boasting about his sex life in public and attending many glitzy parties and other entertainment industry affairs.

In 2017, however, a dark cloud fell over Ratner and his perch among Hollywood's most successful and visible filmmakers when several women stepped forward and accused him of sexual misconduct and harassment. The women who made these allegations against him included Melanie Kohler (who later dropped a lawsuit against Ratner after he countersued alleging defamation), Olivia Munn, Natasha Henstridge, Ellen Page, Jaime Ray Neuman, and Katharine Towne. The events these women described varied in specific details and circumstances, but all of them alleged that he engaged in conduct that qualified as harassment or outright sexual assault. Newman, for example, described being on a plane with Ratner when he took the seat beside her and began describing sexual acts that he wanted them to perform on one another. Newman indicated that she was disturbed by the encounter to the point that she reported the incident to others, including her mother. Munn, meanwhile, asserted that the filmmaker masturbated in front of her without her consent, and Henstridge accused him of sexually assaulting her in his New York City apartment when she was a nineteen-year-old fashion model. For his part, Ratner categorically denied all the allegations against him.

The accusations against Ratner came at a time when the wider #MeToo movement had prompted a new level of scrutiny of sexual harassment and misogyny in the American entertainment industry. As a result, Ratner's career has experienced several setbacks, most notably the loss of a $450 million filmmaking contract with Warner Bros.

Deveon Treadway and Rochelle McGee-Cobbs

See also: Discrimination; #MeToo Movement; Movies, Depictions of Sexual Harassment

Further Reading

Engel, B. 2017. "Why Don't Victims of Sexual Harassment Come Forward Sooner?" Psychology Today, *The Compassion Chronicles* (blog), November 16. http://www.psychologytoday.com/us/blog/the-compassion-chronicles/201711/why-dont-victims-sexual-harassment-come-forward-sooner.

Kaufman, A., and Daniel Miller. 2018. "Six Women Accuse Filmmaker Brett Ratner of Sexual Harassment or Misconduct." *Los Angeles Times*, November 1. http://www.latimes.com/business/hollywood/la-fi-ct-brett-ratner-allegations-20171101-htmlstory.html.

Puente, M., and Cara Kelly. 2018. "How Common Is Sexual Misconduct in Hollywood?" *USA Today*, February 20. http://www.usatoday.com/story/life/people/2018/02/20/how-common-sexual-misconduct-hollywood/1083964001/.

Reeves v. C.H. Robinson Worldwide, Inc. (2010)

Reeves v. C.H. Robinson Worldwide, Inc., decided by the U.S. Court of Appeals for the Eleventh Circuit in 2010, is a disparate treatment sexual harassment case based on a hostile work environment claim. The main issue before the court was whether there was sufficient evidence to prove that a female employee was subjected to a hostile work environment when her male coworkers consistently used vulgar language, including gender-specific derogatory terms for women, on a daily basis but did not specifically direct the language toward her.

Ingrid Reeves worked for C.H. Robinson Worldwide, Inc., as a transportation sales representative in the company's office in Birmingham, Alabama. The office was an open style office with no walls, so Reeves could easily hear the conversations of her coworkers. Reeves worked with six men, including her immediate supervisor, in the sales office. The only other woman in the Birmingham office worked in a different area from Reeves. Reeves testified that her male coworkers used crude, vulgar language in the office on a daily basis and frequently listened to a crude morning radio show; on one occasion, a coworker also had a pornographic image of a nude woman on his computer.

Much of the language used by her male coworkers was not gender-specific, but the men did consistently refer to female colleagues (who worked in other offices) as "bitches," "whores," and "c***s." Furthermore, the men insulted the other Birmingham branch's female employee, Casey Snider, by referring to her as a "bitch" in front of Reeves (but not within Snider's hearing), and they openly discussed Snider's buttocks in front of Reeves. However, Reeves admitted that her coworkers never directed the vulgar and insulting language at or to her individually. There was no evidence presented that the men in the office ever called her any derogatory names.

Reeves complained to her immediate supervisor, who was the branch manager, about his use of the derogatory terms as well as the behavior of the other men, but the supervisor essentially told Reeves that that was the way it was and she had to get used to it. Reeves formally complained about the language in two evaluations, and she tried to set up meetings with two company executives; however, the executives did not address the issue. The company never did anything to address Reeves's complaints, and she resigned after nearly four years of working at C.H. Robinson Worldwide.

Reeves filed a Title VII sexual harassment lawsuit against her employer in the U.S. District Court for the Northern District of Alabama. Reeves's employer filed a motion for summary judgment asking the trial court to dismiss Reeves's case without a trial. The employer argued that the gender-specific vulgar language was not specifically addressed to Reeves, that the men had used such language even before Reeves started working in the office, and that the men also called each other "bitch" and "whore." The trial court granted the employer's motion and dismissed Reeves's lawsuit before it could go to trial. Reeves appealed to the Eleventh Circuit Court of Appeals.

The circuit court held that a reasonable jury could find that a meaningful portion of the alleged offensive conduct in the office contributed to conditions that were humiliating and degrading to women on account of their gender and therefore created a discriminatorily abusive work environment for Reeves. The court emphasized that the gender-specific derogatory language did not have to be specifically directed to the plaintiff and that she could prove a hostile work environment by showing severe or pervasive discrimination directed toward her protected group (women) even if she herself was not individually singled out for the offensive conduct.

Regarding the employer's argument that the men called each other the same names, the court pointed out that this made the situation worse because the men were using derogatory names for women to insult each other because "calling a man a 'bitch' belittles him precisely because it belittles women." Therefore, the appellate court reversed the trial court's grant of summary judgment and remanded the case for trial.

Elizabeth W. Marchioni

See also: Hostile Work Environment; Objectification of Women; Title VII of the Civil Rights Act of 1964; Traditionally "Male" Workplaces

Further Reading

Findley, Henry, Lee Vardaman, and Ping He. 2013. "A Hostile Sexual Harassment: A Legal Update." *Journal of Legal Issues and Cases in Business* 2: 1–12.

Gregg, Robert E. 2013. "It Was Just a Joke: Improper Comments and Practice Liability." *Journal of Medical Practice Management* 29(2): 124–127.

Novak, Monika Erpelo. 2012. "The Trouble with 'Bitch': Rethinking the Seventh Circuit's Approach to Causation in Sexist Harassment Cases." *Seventh Circuit Review* 8(1): 152–192.

Reeves v. C.H. Robinson Worldwide, Inc., 594 F.3d 798 (11th Cir. 2010).

Relationship Violence

Relationship violence has long been a significant social problem in the United States. For much of the country's history, however, this type of intimate partner violence—most frequently manifest in battering of wives and girlfriends by spouses and boyfriends—was tacitly accepted or treated as a shameful secret not fit for public discussion. In the 1980s, though, women's rights advocates spearheaded a drive to bring the different iterations of intimate partner violence out of the shadows and into the light, to give victims of relationship violence tools to escape, and to demand police intervention. These efforts have dramatically increased public recognition that relationship violence is never acceptable and that men and women who sexually abuse or physically injure their partners or children need to be stopped. Over time, the United States' understanding of relationship violence has also expanded to encompass more than just female victims and male offenders and to extend beyond the boundaries of the marital household.

The cost of criminal justice intervention, psychological assessment, training, and the economic challenges faced by victims, their families, their employers, and the criminal justice system total in the billions of dollars annually within the United States. These costs can have strong implications for government agencies and how they address the problem of relationship violence. However, the fear of dismantling marriages plagued with violence and separating children from violent parents is still a concern for some. Many still hold to the sanctity of a marriage or contend that keeping abusers who are the primary breadwinners in the workforce is an important factor to consider in any intervention.

CHARACTERISTICS OF RELATIONSHIP VIOLENCE

Relationship violence is usually exhibited in an intimate or familial relationship in which the abuser thrives on fear and intimidation to obtain power and control over the victim. Relationship violence affects both genders, though women are the most at risk. Moreover, it extends to heterosexual and same-sex couples who cohabitate, are married, or are current or former dating partners. Relationship violence is also sometimes broadly defined to include instances where children or parents are victims. Individuals who are faced with relationship violence encounter a perpetrator who inflicts violence in the form of physical abuse, sexual abuse, economic abuse, psychological abuse, and stalking.

Culture teaches us that some people are *entitled*, meaning they feel as though they have a legal right to make and enforce relationship and personal rules. Many victims who are economically dependent on their abusers or are raising children with them believe that there is no escape from their circumstances. The aggressor's life becomes priority. Within relationship violence, fear is the key component that destabilizes the victim. According to Lenore Walker, through a cycle of violence, many victims learn helplessness and give up, holding the belief that no one can save them. This has been supported and debated by the research community. In some cases, this results in post-traumatic stress disorder (PTSD), which numbs the individual psychologically and physically. PTSD is more likely to occur with victims who experience extreme and prolonged relationship violence.

As noted above, relationship violence can take many forms. Physical abuse can be exhibited in many ways, such as choking, punching, restraining, assaulting with a weapon, and purposefully abandoning the victim in unsafe places. These abuses may continue until the point of serious bodily harm or death. Stalking is unwanted verbal, written, or visual contact with a victim. Forms of stalking include hyperintimacy (excessive attempts to win over the victim), mediated contact (using technology to stay in touch with the victim), interactional contact (joining the same groups or showing up at the same places and trying to engage with the victim), surveillance, invasion, harassment and intimidation, and coercion and threat. In the worst cases, stalking can devolve from repeated attempts to win over the victim to kidnapping and assault. Stalkers exhibit these threatening behaviors at the victim's home, school, and place of employment and at social gatherings. Stalkers are often thought to be strangers or former intimates; however, they are often current intimate partners.

Sexual abuse can take many forms, including sexual control, sexual assault, coercive rape, and forcible rape. The act of rape has the intended purpose of degrading and intentionally hurting the victim. Intimate partner violence embraces all these components, including harassment and economic abuse. Each can be devastating to the victim. Psychological or emotional abuse involves demeaning and isolating the victim as well as causing the victim to live in fear. Additionally, research has revealed that children who are victims of emotional abuse can suffer more long-term effects. Finally, economic abuse often involves the abuser tightly controlling the money to control the victim and his or her activities and movement, even when the money is earned by the victim. This is typical in intimate partner violence and elder abuse.

PREVALENCE OF RELATIONSHIP VIOLENCE

Relationship violence affects millions of people in the United States each year. One in four women and one in ten men will be victims of intimate partner physical or sexual violence or stalking in their lifetime. However, males are four times more likely to report their victimization to the police because females are more likely to fear reprisals. Furthermore, females are more likely to experience severe physical violence.

According to the most recent National Intimate Partner and Sexual Violence Survey, 16 percent of females will be victims of intimate partner stalking in their lifetime. This figure is 5.8 percent for males. While intimate partner violence accounts for 15 percent of all violent crimes, news reports rarely cover this type of crime. Additionally, according to the National Intimate Partner and Sexual Violence Survey, 18.3 percent of all female victims and 8.2 percent of male victims are sexually victimized by an intimate partner, yet news reports typically focus on stranger rape. The National Center for Victims of Crime has demonstrated that women between the ages of eighteen and twenty-four are more likely to be sexually assaulted than any other age demographic. The National Crime Victimization Survey found that only 24.9 percent of these rapes are reported to the police. The fear of reporting relationship violence resonates in victims' fear of retaliation and lack of confidence in the criminal justice system.

There may be long-term effects of relationship violence as the victim attempts to recover from violent and psychological abuse. Women may experience miscarriages, migraines, sexually transmitted diseases, and physical disfigurement from their partners, and PTSD may occur. Additionally, victims may become suicidal, self-medicate with drugs or alcohol, or become socially dysfunctional. Men who are victims of relationship violence exhibit some of the same physical and mental experiences as women. Further, children who experience domestic violence often exhibit violence later in their lives; 45–70 percent of child abuse victims have also witnessed intimate partner violence. Furthermore, these children have higher rates of future victimization and report higher rates of trauma.

MEDIA PORTRAYALS OF RELATIONSHIP VIOLENCE

The media play a major role in shaping people's perception of violence. National and local news and social media provide most of our knowledge of crime and victimization. Research by Carlyle, Slater, and Chakroff (2008); Garcia; and others find that media, as a whole, reproduce media frames that define relationship violence as acceptable under certain circumstances, even inevitable, and that resolving the tensions responsible for triggering such violence is the responsibility of the victim. Additionally, while relationship violence is not commonly covered in the news, these stories are more likely to result in extreme injury or death. Social media and internet news allow people to receive and repost these definitions rapidly. According to social construction theory, individuals interpret what they see and hear, reproducing these values and beliefs about relationship violence. The high volume of news media produces a strong influence on people's exposure and interpretation, which exacerbates violence or the acceptance of violence. Media messages have short- and long-term effects that increase violence among men, women, and children.

Research has documented the extent to which violence permeates much of society's popular media. Children and adults alike often spend hours playing violent games on tablets, computers, cell phones, and game consoles. Research is mixed, however, on the connection between violent video games and other entertainment media and violent behavior. Some point to the socialization hypothesis in which gaming socializes children to be more aggressive, if not violent. Other research supports the selection hypothesis, which postulates that aggressive and violent youth are more likely to seek out and play violent games. One study found that children who play violent video games that are rated "Mature" are more likely to engage in cyberbullying. Some research suggests that children imitate the combat played in video games by punching, shoving, and in some cases assaulting inanimate objects. Moreover, as the child turns into an adult, the child carries these aggressions into his or her relationships.

Among the many crimes covered in the new media, incidents of relationship violence are the least likely to be covered—unless one or more members of the relationship are public figures. According to victim advocates, this relative absence of coverage conveys a misleading impression that relationship violence is a rarity. Some observers believe that this has changed somewhat with the emergence of the #MeToo Movement, but even there, sexual assault and harassment in the workplace, rather than in preexisting personal relationships, has attracted the most attention. Finally, researchers and advocates both note that rapists who commit acts of sexual violence against strangers tend to attract more media attention than those who sexually assault family members and friends.

RELATIONSHIP VIOLENCE AND THE LEGAL SYSTEM

Treatment of relationship violence by the criminal justice system also works to diminish its seriousness. Police often *unfound* or *defound* cases in which victims know their offenders. They determine that the crime did not occur (unfound) or did not occur to the extent reported by the victim (defound). The result in these cases is that victims of relationship violence do not receive the protection they need. The judicial system adds to this dysfunction with a judicial process that is often confusing and difficult to navigate, for example, when seeking a protection order.

In family court, a civil system, the presence of children in common to the couple makes processing more complicated for the victim. Prior to any judicial review, the victim must file charges and appear in court to pursue an order of protection for the abuse inflicted by the predator. However, such protection orders have limited effectiveness in restraining men and women consumed with rage. Prosecutors are also sometimes reluctant to pursue criminal charges against perpetrators of relationship violence because victims sometimes lose their will to proceed or charges are difficult to prove. As a result, many domestic violence charges get reduced to misdemeanor plea agreements. Although legislatures have made it easier to charge an offender in relationship violence cases, prosecutors' reliance on evidence-based prosecution still provides barriers for victims.

Relationship violence affects all groups within society and involves many forms of abuse. Human service agencies and members of the community need to be aware that each plays a part in facilitating relationship violence by ignoring symptoms and signs. News media play a strong part by providing biased narratives of the assailants and their victims, downplaying the occurrence while demonizing minorities. Victims need to be aware that they have a way out of any violent relationship. Social service organizations and domestic violence hotlines are available for anyone who is victimized by relationship violence. Finally, the justice community must reform some policies to strengthen its ability to hold predators accountable and help victims of relationship violence build healthier and safer lives.

Donald Dula and Venessa Garcia

See also: Marital Violence; #MeToo Movement; News Media Coverage

Further Reading

Alejo, K. 2014. "Long-Term Physical and Mental Health Effects of Domestic Violence." *Themis: Research Journal Justice Studies and Forensic Science* 2: 82–98.

Alvarez, A., and R. Bachman. 2017. *Violence: The Enduring Problem*. 3rd ed. Los Angeles: Sage Publications, Inc.

American Psychiatric Association. 2013. *Diagnostic and Statistical Manual of Mental Disorders: DSM-5*. 5th ed. Arlington, VA: American Psychiatric Association.

Carlyle, K. E., M. D. Slater, and J. L. Chakroff. 2008. "Newspaper Coverage of Intimate Partner Violence: Skewing Representations of Risk." *Journal of Communication* 58(1): 168–186.

Dittrick, C. J., T. T. Beran, F. Mishna, R. Hetherington, and S. Shariff. 2013. "Do Children Who Bully Their Peers Also Play Violent Video Games? A Canadian National Study." *Journal of School Violence* 12(4): 297–318.

Finkelhor, D., and H. Turner. 2015. "A National Profile of Children Exposed to Family Violence: Police Response, Family Response, and Individual Impact." *National Criminal Justice Reporting System.* https://www.ncjrs.gov/pdffiles1/nij/grants /248577.pdf.

Garcia, V., and S. G. Arkerson. 2018. *Crime, Media, and Reality: Examining Mixed Messages about Crime and Justice in Popular Media.* Lanham, MD: Rowman & Littlefield.

Garcia, V., and P. McManimon. 2011. *Gender Justice*: *Intimate Partner Violence and the Criminal Justice System.* Lanham, MD. Rowman & Littlefield.

Kaura, S. A., B. J. Lohman. 2007. "Dating Violence Victimization, Relationship, Satisfaction, Mental Health Problems, and Acceptability of Violence: A Comparison of Men and Women." *Journal of Family Violence* 22: 367–381.

Mallicoat, S. L. 2019. *Women, Gender, and Crime: Core Concepts.* Los Angeles: Sage Publications.

Modi, M. N., S. Palmer, and A. Armstrong. 2014. "The Role of Violence Against Women Act in Addressing Intimate Partner Violence: A Public Health Issue." *Journal of Women's Health* 23(3): 253–259.

Morgan, R. E., and B. A. Oudekerek. 2019. "Criminal Victimization, 2018." U.S. Department of Justice, Bureau of Justice Statistics. https://www.bjs.gov/content/pub/pdf /cv18.pdf.

National Center for Victims of Crime. 2018. "Crime and Victimization Fact Sheets: Sexual Violence." Office of Victims of Crime. https://ovc.ncjrs.gov/ncvrw2018/info _flyers/fact_sheets/2018NCVRW_SexualViolence_508_QC.pdf.

Reaves, B. 2017. "Police Response to Domestic Violence, 2006–2015." U.S. Department of Justice, Bureau of Justice Statistics. https://www.bjs.gov/content/pub/pdf /prdv0615.pdf.

Sinozich, S., and L. Langston. 2014. "Rape and Sexual Assault Victimization among College-Age Females, 1995–2013." U.S. Department of Justice, Bureau of Justice Statistics. https://www.bjs.gov/content/pub/pdf/rsavcaf9513.pdf.

Smith, S. G., X. Zhang, K. C. Basile, M. T. Merrick, J. Wang, M. Kresnow, and J. Chen. 2018. *The National Intimate Partner and Sexual Violence Survey: 2015 Data Brief.* Atlanta, GA: National Center for Injury Prevention and Control, Centers for Disease Control and Prevention. https://www.semanticscholar.org/paper/The -National-Intimate-Partner-and-Sexual-Violence-%3A-Smith-Zhang/ff5c19c69c3 92968ea23c62f58da43a68639a5cb.

Surette, R. 2015. *Media, Crime, and Criminal Justice: Images, Realities, and Policies.* 5th ed. Stamford, CT: Cengage Learning.

Walker, L. 1978. "Battered Women and Learned Helplessness." *Victimology* 2(3–4): 525–534.

Religious Organizations

Sexual abuse, child sexual abuse, and clerical abuse among religious organizations are not new phenomena in the United States, but public awareness of the issue is on the increase. Revelations of sexual abuse by priests in positions of authority have rocked the Catholic Church on several occasions over the last few decades, and many Evangelical and other Protestant communities have grappled with documented cases of sexual abuse and assault among their leadership as well. Insurance companies reported over 7,094 claims of sexual abuse against religious organizations between 1987 and 2007, which is an average of 260 sexual abuse claims per year. The suits resulted in a total of $87.8 million in compensation to victims (Denney, Kerley, and Gross 2018).

Many victims of sex abuse by clergy, particularly children, are likely to suffer from post-traumatic stress disorder (PTSD), depression, and the propensity to victimize others or be revictimized. The emotional effects of clergy abuse may include anger, self-blame, nightmares, shame, anxiety, mood swings, social anxiety, guilt, difficulty trusting oneself and others, and even promiscuity. Many of those abused within the church did not tell anyone about their encounters, and it affected their entire lives (Global Sisters Report 2019). Most who have reported the abovementioned lifelong effects have also explained that, for many years, they were too scared to come forward because the priest or rabbi or minister was not only the leader of their religious community but also a family friend. Many victims also feel embarrassed or confused about their faith because their victimizer is so closely associated with God and worship.

While instances of sexual abuse in the Roman Catholic Church have received the most extensive press coverage in recent times, many other religious organizations have grappled with scandals or allegations of sexual abuse, including various Protestant denominations, Jehovah's Witnesses, Muslims, Buddhists, and Scientologists (Trujillo 2019; Blair 2018).

In some cases, religious organizations have tried to keep allegations of child sexual abuse from reaching legal authorities, citing the belief that abusers can find penance and forgiveness in the church. Many victims' rights advocates contend that such stances are primarily grounded in concerns about the reputation and fiscal health of the church. They further assert that such churches are less likely to implement strategies to deal with these issues in terms of holding perpetrators accountable and ensuring justice and compensation for victims (Aljazeera 2014; Child's Rights International Network 2019).

The emergence of the #MeToo Movement has been cited by many researchers as a phenomenon that empowered many childhood victims to come forward many years later, as adults. The movement has also been credited with strengthening efforts to assist victims and punish offenders, regardless of the setting in which the abuse, harassment, or assault took place.

O. Oko Elechi and Ifeoma Okoye

See also: Authority Figures; Buddhism; Power Dynamics; Rape, Abuse & Incest National Network (RAINN); Retaliation

Further Reading

Aljazeera. 2014. "Vatican Criticized in Report on Child Abuse." January 15. https://www.aljazeera.com/news/europe/2014/01/vatican-criticised-report-child-abuse-201411592321951919.html.

Associated Press. 2019. "New Wave of Sexual-Abuse Lawsuits Could Cost Catholic Church More Than $4 Billion." MarketWatch, December 2. https://www.marketwatch.com

/story/new-wave-of-sexual-abuse-lawsuits-could-cost-catholic-church-over-4
-billion-2019-12-02.

Blair, L. 2018. "10 Notable Clergy Sex Scandals in 2017." *Christian Post*, February 5.
https://www.christianpost.com/news/10-notable-clergy-sex-scandals-in-2017
.html.

Child's Rights International Network. 2019. "End Sexual Violence in Religious Institutions." https://archive.crin.org/en/home/campaigns/end-sexual-violence-religious
-institutions.html.

Denney, A. S., K. R. Kerley, and N. G. Gross. 2018. "Child Sexual Abuse in Protestant
Christian Congregations: A Descriptive Analysis of Offense and Offender Characteristics." *Religions* 9(27): 1–13

Global Sisters Report. 2019. "Women Religious Shatter the Silence about Clergy Sexual
Abuse of Sisters." https://www.globalsistersreport.org/news/trends/women-religious
-shatter-silence-about-clergy-abuse-of-sisters.

Herbeck, D. 2019. "Does the Catholic Church Have Bigger Sex Problems Than Other
Religions?" *Buffalo News*, August 16. https://buffalonews.com/2019/08/16/does
-catholic-church-have-bigger-child-sex-abuse-problem-than-other-religions/.

Speckhardt, R. 2011. "The Religious Sex Abuse Epidemic." HuffPost, December 18.
https://www.huffpost.com/entry/religious-sex-abuse-epidemic_b_1008805.

Trujillo, Y. 2019. "Clerical Sexual Abuse: Religious Institutions Must Have a Pentecost
Moment and They Must Have It Now." Berkeley Center Georgetown. https://
berkleycenter.georgetown.edu/responses/clerical-sexual-abuse-religious
-institutions-must-have-a-pentecost-moment-and-they-must-have-it-now.

Zamzow, J. 2018. "Should Churches Handle Sexual Abuse Allegations Internally?" *Christianity Today*, February 2. https://www.christianitytoday.com/ct/2018/february-web
-only/should-churches-handle-sexual-abuse-investigations-internal.html.

Restaurant/Bar Industry

Sexual harassment has been described as a common problem in the food and beverage service industry. However, the issue received scant attention until after the
emergence of the #MeToo Movement in 2017, which in turn resulted in a celebrity
chef sexual harassment scandal. These events triggered a higher level of scrutiny
of working conditions in the restaurant and bar service sector than ever before,
and the myriad stories of sexual harassment and abuse revealed by that scrutiny
led to calls for major industry reforms.

Food and beverage services require physically and emotionally demanding
work. The bullying of subordinates in the high-pressure kitchen environment is
widely acknowledged in the stereotype of the short-tempered chef. Sexual harassment is also a type of bullying. These conditions are exacerbated in certain mar-
kets. Profit margins in many restaurants rely heavily on alcohol sales, resulting in
joint marketing strategies that exploit female sexuality. Courts have been lenient,
even recognizing gender as a "BFOQ," or bona fide occupational qualification,
that permits gender discrimination in hiring. Restaurant chains such as *Hooters*
and *Twin Peaks* have taken advantage of this to hire only female waitstaff and
outfit them in skimpy uniforms that make presentation of attractive female bodies
a central focus of the restaurant experience for patrons. Employee handbooks and

hiring documents at *Hooters* have even required "Hooter's Girls" to document their understanding that they are expected to interact with and entertain their customers and that sexual jokes will be part of that interaction and entertainment.

Semipornographic images of women and sexual innuendo were also used to bolster fast-food market share in the late 1990s and early 2000s. This approach was largely pioneered by Andrew Pudzer, the CEO of CKE Restaurants, the parent company of Carl's Jr. and Hardee's. Puzder's efforts on behalf of the restaurant industry earned him a nomination for labor secretary by President Donald Trump in 2017. (He later withdrew after he was criticized by Senate Republicans for past controversial comments about labor rights and for employing an undocumented immigrant housekeeper.) These efforts included opposition to raising the minimum wage, opposing the Affordable Care Act, and opposing abortion rights.

While serving as CEO of the National Restaurant Association from 1996 to 1999, Herman Cain was himself accused of sexual harassment. Cain denied the accusations, but a settlement was reached contingent on the complainant's signing of a nondisclosure agreement (NDA).

SOURCES OF HARASSMENT

Harassment primarily comes from coworkers and customers, but management also harasses workers at disproportionate rates compared to other workplaces. In 2014, a restaurant industry study found that 66 percent of 688 respondents reported incidents of harassment by management, 80 percent stated that they had been harassed by coworkers, and 78 percent said that customers has sexually harassed them. Employees who were female, transgender, or reliant on tips reported higher levels of harassment (Restaurant Opportunities Centers United 2014). Anecdotal evidence strongly suggests being an undocumented worker is also a factor. Similar patterns were reported in 2018 in the *Harvard Business Review*, with 76 female respondents reporting 226 incidents of sexual harassment over a three-month period. Of these incidents, 112 were by coworkers, 85 by customers, and 29 by managers.

The typical restaurant worker is a young female working under an older male manager. Women predominate in front-of-the-house positions—positions marked by direct interactions with patrons—as hostesses (86 percent), servers (70 percent), and bartenders (57 percent). Women also comprise 40 percent of cooks but only 19 percent of chefs and head cooks (Johnson and Madera 2018). Cooks and back-of-the-house employees, such as bussers, dishwashers, and kitchen help, are disproportionately minorities. One-fourth of the industry's workers are Hispanic, and one-fourth is foreign-born, according to U.S. Bureau of Labor Statistics (2018).

HIGH-PROFILE ALLEGATIONS AGAINST CELEBRITY CHEFS

Following the 2017 Harvey Weinstein scandal and the launch of the #MeToo Movement, four celebrity chef/restauranteurs admitted to sexual harassment and were forced to resign in quick succession from the companies that they had founded and led: John Besh, Ken Friedman, Charlie Hollowell, and Mario Batali.

On October 21, 2017, the New Orleans' *Times-Picayune* published an investigative report alleging that the city's resident celebrity chef, John Besh, and his business partner, Octavio Mantilla, both engaged in persistent sexual misconduct against their employees. Twenty-five employees charged that the two maintained a corporate and restaurant workplace culture of normalized sexual harassment against female employees at all levels, including verbal harassment and frequent unwanted touching. Besh stepped down from the company, which had twelve hundred employees but no human resources department, two days later.

Similarly, the *San Francisco Chronicle* made public long-standing allegations against Charlie Hallowell, the celebrity chef-owner of the flagship restaurant Pizzaiolo, in December 2017. After the *Chronicle* published its report, Hallowell apologized for his history of degrading sexual banter and unwelcome touching and kissing. He stepped away from operations at the company and left its management to his business partner, Richard Weinstein, who was subsequently also accused of sexual misconduct by other female employees.

At the Spotted Pig in New York's West Village, celebrity chef Ken Friedman was accused by multiple female employees of frequent sexual harassment and misconduct, including groping, requests for group sex and nude pictures, daily touching and kissing of employees, and tolerating other aggressive sexual misconduct toward female staff from guests, such as fellow celebrity chef Mario Batali. Employees even referred to an upstairs dining alcove as "the rape room." Friedman also stepped away from his company's daily operations and his television show in December 2017, though he retains his financial interests.

Mario Batali had been the media voice of Batali and Bastianich Hospitality Group, with its flagship restaurant, Babbo, located in Greenwich Village, New York City. In 2012, Batali's restaurants reached a $5.25 million settlement with restaurant staff for tip skimming. The financial misconduct had left Batali's reputation largely intact. However, in May 2017, eight women came forward in the wake of the #MeToo Movement to accuse Batali of sexual misconduct. Additional allegations were made in 2018. The Food Network, ABC, Target, and Las Vegas Sands Corps terminated business plans and contracts with Mario Batali in 2017 and 2018.

REFORMS

Only about 1.5 percent of the restaurant industry's employees are unionized. In 2017, restaurant union leadership itself suffered some disruption from resignations by sexual harassers. Like restaurants, union organizing involves tight deadlines, intense campaigns, and unusual working hours infused with a culture of machismo. The Service Employee International Union's vice president, Scott Cortney, and three other staff members were compelled to leave when the allegations of sexual misconduct came to light, as was Terry Stapleton of the AFL-CIO.

Unions as well as industry leaders have historically failed to address sexual harassment problems in the restaurant and hospitality industry and have even experienced it in their own ranks. However, feminist organizations such as the

Ms. Foundation and 9to5 have worked with Restaurant Opportunity Centers (ROC) in its efforts to document sexual harassment through such reports as *The Glass Floor* (2014); ROC has also used social media hashtags such as #NotOn-TheMenu to highlight sexual harassment as part of its larger efforts to organize workers, diners, and owners for overall wage and other reforms. Suggested reforms from ROC and other advocates include developing and enforcing anti-harassment policies, management training and bystander intervention training for all employees, a reporting mechanism that can bypass an immediate supervisor who harasses, protecting staff from customer harassment, and doing away with the tip credit. Clear and frequent communication of both anti-harassment policies and reporting procedures is also recommended.

In 2016, the Equal Employment Opportunity Commission (EEOC) released *A Report of the Co-Chairs of the Select Task Force on the Study of Sexual Harassment in the Workplace*. The EEOC report documents twelve risk factors for harassment, seven of which prevail in the restaurant industry: cultural and language differences, nonconforming workers, coarsened social discourse, young workers, power disparities, encouraging alcohol consumption, and high reliance on customer satisfaction. The EEOC does not publicly release sexual harassment data by industry. However, restaurant workers constitute a disproportionate share of filings. From this research, the EEOC released new guidelines on sexual harassment liability in the workplace, the "Proposed Enforcement Guidance for Unlawful Harassment," in January 2017 for public comment.

Meanwhile, some individual restaurant owners and managers are taking the initiative in combating sexual harassment in their facilities. For example, Oakland, California, restauranteur and chef Erin Wade discovered her male managers were dismissing staff concerns about inappropriate customer behaviors. Wade was already an innovator when she opened her restaurant, in Oakland, California, with 100 percent of her leadership team made up of women and people of color. Her mac and cheese restaurant, Homeroom, is where Wade invented a groundbreaking color-coded system to protect her staff against harassment by customers. Now known as Not on the Menu, her unique system was adopted as a recommended best practice by the EEOC and is used at restaurants and bars around the country (Sprayregen 2019). In a March 2018 *Washington Post* opinion piece, Wade described the color-coded system she implemented in 2011 for servers to indicate the level of harassment they were experiencing from customers: yellow for mild discomfort, orange for more objectionable behaviors, and red for unwelcome touching or other severe customer misconduct.

Cynthia Ninivaggi

See also: Batali, Mario; Equal Opportunity Employment Commission (EEOC); Groping; Harvey Weinstein Scandal; #MeToo Movement; Nondisclosure Agreements

Further Reading

Equal Opportunity Employment Commission. 2016. "A Report of the Co-Chairs of the Select Task Force on the Study of Sexual Harassment in the Workplace." https://www.eeoc.gov/june-2016-report-co-chairs-select-task-force-study-harassment-workplace.

Jayarumen, S. 2016. *Forked: A New Standard for American Dining.* Oxford: Oxford University Press.

Johnson, S. K., and J. M. Madera. 2018. "Sexual Harassment in the Restaurant Industry Is Pervasive: Here's What Needs to Change." *Harvard Business Review*, January 18. https://hbr.org/2018/01/sexual-harassment-is-pervasive-in-the-restaurant-industry -heres-what-needs-to-change.

Restaurant Opportunity Centers United, Forward Together. 2014. *The Glass Floor: Sexual Harassment in the Restaurant Industry*. New York: Restaurant Opportunities Centers United. https://chapters.rocunited.org/publications/the-glass-floor-sexual -harassment-in-the-restaurant-industry/.

Sprayregen, M. 2019. "Erin Wade Wants to Revolutionize the Restaurant Industry. Here's How She Already Has." *Forbes*, November 24. https://www.forbes.com/sites /mollysprayregen/2019/11/24/erin-wade-wants-to-revolutionize-the-restaurant -industry-heres-how-she-already-has/#254b29fb4151.

U.S. Bureau of Labor Statistics. 2018. "Labor Force Statistics from the Current Population Survey." https://www.bls.gov/cps/cpsaat11.htm.

Wade, E. 2018. "I'm a Female Chef. Here's How My Restaurant Successfully Dealt with Harassment from Customers." *Washington Post*, March 29. https://www.washington post.com/opinions/how-my-restaurant-successfully-dealt-with-harassment-from -customers/2018/03/29/3d9d00b8-221a-11e8-badd-7c9f29a55815_story.html.

Retaliation

Retaliation is defined by *Merriam-Webster* as "a course of conduct which annoys, threatens, intimidates, alarms, or puts a person in fear of their safety." It may be further defined as any form of unwanted verbal, nonverbal, or physical conduct of a sexual nature that creates an intimidating, hostile, degrading, or offensive environment. The act of retaliation has the same characteristics as revenge, in that it is enacted out of a sense of unfairness or perceived injustice, with the goal of evening the score. In the workplace, retaliation occurs when an employer takes an "adverse action" against an employee because he or she has exercised a "protected legal right." Many state and federal laws protect employees from employer retaliation.

Studies have shown that the desire for retaliation is quite high among people who are left offended by a personal interaction, specifically if the encounter results in a tarnished self-image. However, while wanting to retaliate is common, the actual act of retaliation is rare, in many cases because acting out against an individual in a social or professional setting can come at a cost. There have been high-profile court cases surrounding retaliatory harassment, including the recent allegations and legal action against movie producer Harvey Weinstein. Weinstein was accused of sexual misconduct, including assault, and of intimidating women to ensure their silence while threatening their careers. The allegations against him started a national conversation about sexual assault and harassment both inside and outside the workplace. Over the past decade, the Equal Employment Opportunity Commission (EEOC) has reported that "retaliation is the most common issue alleged by federal employees and the most common discrimination finding in federal sector cases. FY 2018 data show that retaliation continued to be the most frequently filed charge filed with the agency, followed by sex, disability and race" (EEOC 2019).

Harassment followed by retaliation leads to further complications surrounding sexual harassment as a whole. Some victims of sexual harassment are ostracized by their coworkers after disclosing their experiences, both knowingly and unknowingly. This prevents others from coming forward, as they fear a similar disconnection with their peers (Brown and Battle 2019). The #MeToo Movement, by nature, works against ostracism by creating a community around the shared experience of harassment, abuse, and assault and giving people the courage to make their stories public.

FORMS OF RETALIATION

Online retaliation involves harassment and denigration of an individual on social media, in newsgroups, in chat rooms, and via email. This harassment takes the form of obscene or derogatory comments focused on attributes such as a victim's gender, religion, race, nationality, or sexual orientation. The harassment can also intensify to include the theft and dissemination of a victim's digital photos, with the aim of causing anxiety and distress.

Power retaliation, or *power harassment*, describes harassment based on workplace politics. It can involve threats, psychological abuse, unwelcome attention, and bullying and sometimes forced activities that go outside the bounds of a given job description. Power harassment is considered illegal discrimination.

Psychological retaliation involves abuse that affects a person's mental well-being, including attacks meant to humiliate, intimidate, or scare. This type of retaliation is sometimes hard to see or prove, as there is little evidence beyond a victim's report or complaint. This type of retaliation can look like calculated bouts of intimidation, verbal bashing, or acts of aggression.

Community-based psychological retaliation takes the form of a group of people ganging up on an individual and using repeated, coordinated attacks that they know will negatively affect the victim. For example, Gamergate was a harassment campaign conducted in the world of video game creators and enthusiasts, primarily through the use of the hashtag #Gamergate. The controversy centered on issues of sexism and progressivism in video game culture and on the various forms of misogynistic retaliation and intimidation that were directed at women in the industry.

Tara A. Garrison

See also: Equal Employment Opportunity Commission (EEOC); Hostile Work Environment; Stalking

Further Reading

Berger, G. J. 1972. "Retaliatory Eviction in California: The Legislature Slams the Door and Boards Up the Windows." *Southern California Law Review* 46: 118.

Brown, S. E., and J. S. Battle. 2019. "Ostracizing Targets of Workplace Sexual Harassment before and after the #MeToo Movement." *Equality, Diversity and Inclusion: An International Journal* 39(1): 53–67.

Chen, H., A. Domenzain, and K. Andrews. 2016. "The Perfect Storm." Labor Occupational Health Program, May. https://lohp.berkeley.edu/the-perfect-storm/.

Gewin, V. 2015. "Social Behavior: Indecent Advances." *Nature* 519(7542): 251–253.

Kidd, Dustin, and Amanda J. Turner, 2016. "The #GamerGate Files: Misogyny in the Media." In *Defining Identity and the Changing Scope of Culture in the Digital Age*, edited by Alison Novak and Imaani J. El-Burki, 122. Hershey, PA: IGI Global.

Samnani, A., and P. Singh. 2012. "20 Years of Workplace Bullying Research." *Aggression and Violent Behavior* 17(6): 581–589. https://doi.org/10.1016/j.avb.2012.08.004

Zugelder, M. T., P. J. Champagne, and S. D. Maurer. 2007. "Dealing with Retaliation in All of Its Forms." *Journal of Individual Employment Rights* 12(3): 223–238.

Roiphe, Katie (1968–)

Katie Roiphe is an American author best known for writing the controversial *The Morning After: Sex, Fear & Feminism on Campus* (1993). Her expression of disbelief regarding women's claims of sexual victimization is a common obstacle for advocates of women's rights and social reformers. While a college student at Harvard University, the *New York Times Magazine* published a brief version of her opinion piece "Date Rape Hysteria" (1991), which was later republished in *Playboy* magazine. Riding a wave of backlash against the growing awareness of date rape led by conservative men such as Neil Gilbert, Roiphe, who is the daughter of Anne Roiphe, a prominent feminist, argued that the increasing attention to date rape, especially on college campuses, was nothing more than victim feminism run amok. Roiphe completed her PhD in literature at Princeton University in 1996 and has since published multiple books. She is currently a professor at New York University's Arthur L. Carter Journalism Institute.

INTERPRETING THE DATE RAPE CRISIS

Multiple research studies that asked large samples of women about sexual assault from a legal point of view have found that approximately one in four college women can expect to be the victim of sexual assault. Roiphe, however, asserted in nationally published essays in 1991 and 1993 that these statistics on rape are false. Based on her anecdotal experiences as an Ivy League undergraduate, Roiphe contended that female college students who said they were raped were just feeling guilty after engaging in drunken sex. In essence, they were "crying rape" and refusing to take responsibility for their choices.

Roiphe and her arguments about rape were quickly picked up and embraced by many major male-dominated news outlets during the 1990s. These news outlets used Roiphe's claims to run stories inquiring whether the rise in reports of sexual assault on campus and in other sectors of American society was no more than "date rape hype." The fulcrum of the controversy shifted from "how can this be?" to questions about the amount of responsibility that women should take for sexual activity once they have had alcohol.

Roiphe's critique also involved her observation that she personally did not hear her female friends on campus talking about rape. Critics of Roiphe countered that the nature of sexual assault is such that the majority of survivors do not disclose the crime. Survivors either know already or quickly find out that once they disclose their experience, they run the real risk of having their account questioned or not believed at all, and they begin to retreat into shame and silence. This dynamic is an integral element of the psychological damage that sexual assault can do.

Roiphe's critics have charged that she rose to prominence because she expressed an idea that was enormously advantageous to a patriarchal system of power. They claimed that a young, smart, female college student denying that date rape was a crisis was powerful because it seemed to fly in the face of self-interest. But detractors claimed that the attention that Roiphe received is best explained by the political agenda it served. From this point of view, her role in the issue of sexual assault, harassment, and misconduct is representative of the role of other proxies of patriarchal power. Roiphe, however, believes the perspective that she expressed forty years ago still holds true and is a product not of manipulation but of an accurate assessment of conditions.

At the height of the #MeToo Movement, *Harper's* magazine published an article by Roiphe harshly criticizing the #MeToo Movement itself. Prior to its publication, a rumor circulated that the intent of the article was for Roiphe to make public the name of a woman who initiated a crowdsourced dataset (the "Shitty Media Men list") for women in the media industry to share their stories and warn each other about men who engaged in sexually harassing behavior. Before the article was published, journalist Moira Donegan announced that she had created the list. She said that she did so because she became convinced that Roiphe intended to reveal her name in *Harper's*, which Roiphe denied. Once the disclosure was made by Donegan, however, Roiphe's article allegedly was revised considerably (Peiser 2018). Roiphe's central argument in the *Harper's* piece was that women who did not agree with the aims and spirit of the #MeToo Movement felt that they were being bullied into silence—a claim that was ridiculed by #MeToo supporters (Traister 2018).

Anna King

See also: Media Men's List; #MeToo Movement; SCREAM; Traister, Rebecca; Victim Blaming

Further Reading

Cantor, D., B. Fisher, S. Chibnall, R. Townsend, H. Lee, C. Bruce, and G. Thomas. 2017. *Report on the AAU Campus Climate Survey on Sexual Assault and Sexual Misconduct*. Rockville, MD: Westat.

Fisher, B. S., F. T. Cullen, and M. G. Turner. 2000. *The Sexual Victimization of College Women*. Washington, DC: National Institute of Justice, Bureau of Justice Statistics, U.S. Department of Justice.

Gonnerman, Jennifer. 1994. "The Selling of Katie Roiphe." *The Baffler*, no. 6 (December). https://thebaffler.com/salvos/the-selling-of-katie-roiphe.

Koss, M. P., C. A. Gidycz, and N. Wisniewski. 1987. "The Scope of Rape: Incidence and Prevalence of Sexual Aggression and Victimization in a National Sample of Higher Education Students." *Journal of Consulting and Clinical Psychology* 55(2): 162.

Peiser, Jacklyn. 2018. "'Media Men' List Creator Outs Herself, Fearing She Would Be Named." *New York Times*, January 10. https://www.nytimes.com/2018/01/10/business/media/a-feminist-twitter-campaign-targets-harpers-magazine-and-katie-roiphe.html.

Roiphe, Katie. 1993. *The Morning After: Fear, Sex, and Feminism on Campus.* Boston: Little, Brown & Co.

Roiphe, Katie. 2017. "The Other Whisper Network—How Twitter Feminism Is Bad for Women." *Harper's Magazine*, March. https://harpers.org/archive/2018/03/the-other-whisper-network-2/.

Traister, Rebecca. 2018. "No One Is Silencing Katie Roiphe." *The Cut*, February. https://www.thecut.com/2018/02/rebecca-traister-on-katie-roiphe-harpers-and-metoo.html.

Rose, Charlie (1942–)

Charlie Rose, a former television journalist, was terminated from his employment as a coanchor of *CBS This Morning* in November 2017 because of allegations of unwanted sexual advances by eight women.

Rose was born on January 5, 1942, to Margret and Charles Peete Rose Sr. and was raised in Henderson, North Carolina. From a young age, he assisted his parents with their tobacco farm and country store. A graduate of Duke University, with an undergraduate degree in history, Rose also holds a juris doctor from the Duke University School of Law.

From 1972 to 2017, Rose hosted several popular television programs, including his namesake *Charlie Rose* on PBS, *60 Minutes, 60 Minutes II, CBS News Nightwatch*, and *CBS This Morning.* Throughout his career, Rose had interviewed numerous high profile celebrities, authors, politicians, and other newsmakers, becoming a celebrity of sorts in his own rights.

Over these same years, Rose received numerous awards, including the National Museum's Vincent Scully Prize, which was bestowed on him based on his interviews of leaders in the architectural and design field. For his 2013 interview of President Bashar al-Assad of Syria, Rose received an Emmy Award and Peabody Prize.

Nonetheless, 2017 marked the end of his career in broadcast news and the cancellation of his top-rated *Charlie Rose* show. His downfall came on the heels of the #MeToo Movement, which exploded into the publish consciousness in late 2017 after actress Alyssa Milano encouraged her followers to use the hashtag #MeToo to spread awareness of sexual assault and harassment.

Accusations against Rose were leveled by several former employees and dated back to the 1990s. Rose was accused of making lewd telephone calls, groping women, and appearing naked in the presence of some of his accusers while at his home. After these initial allegations were made public, it was revealed that CBS executives had been warned over the course of thirty years about some of the allegations against Rose. In some instances, women claimed that they feared to report Rose's behavior due to his industry stature. At the time of the allegations, from the late 1990s to 2011, the ages of the women accusers ranged from twenty-one to thirty-seven.

After the allegations had surfaced, Rose apologized for his inappropriate behavior; however, he stated that he did not believe all the accusations against him were accurate. Rose claimed that he thought he had been pursuing women based on impressions that they shared a mutual attraction, but he may have eventually realized that he had been mistaken. Since the initial 2017 sexual misconduct revelations, investigators have interviewed numerous current and former employees under the condition of anonymity due to the fear of retaliation. As a result of these investigations, an additional twenty-seven women who worked with Rose at CBS or PBS emerged to claim that Rose had sexually harassed them at one time or another.

Rose filed a motion to have the sexual harassment lawsuit dismissed, claiming that his accusers were seeking to exploit the #MeToo Movement for financial gain. However, in December 2018, CBS and Rose reached financial settlements with three of his accusers, Sydney McNeal, Katherine Brooks Harris, and Yuquing Wei, who had filed their claims in New York State. Two of the accusers worked directly for Rose, and the other worked for CBS. Part of their claims charged retaliation by CBS for either firing or demoting them. At the request of the accusers, terms of the financial settlements are confidential.

Brian L. Royster

See also: Hostile Work Environment; #MeToo Movement; Sexual Harassment Training

Further Reading

Bauder, David. 2018. "As More Women Accuse Charlie Rose of Sexual Harassment, Some Say They Alerted CBS Managers." *PBS NewsHour*, May 3. Accessed January 10, 2019. https://www.pbs.org/newshour/arts/as-more-women-accuse-charlie-rose-some-say-they-alerted-cbs-managers.

Carmon, Irin, and Amy Brittain. 2017. "Eight Women Say Charlie Rose Sexually Harassed Them—with Nudity, Groping, and Lewd Calls." *Washington Post*, November 20. Accessed January 10, 2019. https://www.washingtonpost.com/investigations/eight-women-say-charlie-rose-sexually-harassed-them--with-nudity-groping-and-lewd-calls/2017/11/20/9b168de8-caec-11e7-8321-481fd63f174d_story.html.

Swenson, Kyle, and Samantha Schmidt. 2017. "Charlie Rose: The Rise and Plummet of a Man Who Preached 'Character' and 'Integrity.'" *Washington Post*, November 21. Accessed January 10, 2019. https://www.washingtonpost.com/news/morning-mix/wp/2017/11/21/i-am-by-nature-civil-the-rise-of-charlie-rose/.

S

Same-Sex Abuse

Sexual abuse is a deliberate act that entails undesired sexual behavior perpetrated by one person upon another. This unwanted sexual activity may involve use of force, threats of force, lack of consent from the victim, or preying on minors. All these forms of abuse can and do take a heavy emotional and psychological toll on victims. Sexual abuse can be found in both heterosexual and homosexual relationships. In recent decades, there has been a plethora of studies on lesbian, gay, bisexual, and transgender experiences of sexual abuse.

According to the Centers for Disease Control and Prevention (CDC), LGBTQ (lesbian, gay, bisexual, transsexual, queer) people experience sexual abuse at equal or higher rates than heterosexuals. Studies approximate that nearly one in ten LGBTQ victims of intimate partner violence (IPV) have experienced sexual assault and other sexual offenses from those partners The CDC has reported that 43.8 percent of lesbian women and 61 percent of bisexual women have experienced rape, physical violence, and stalking by an intimate partner in their lifetime. Comparatively, 26 percent of gay men and 37 percent of bisexual men have experienced rape, physical violence, and stalking by an intimate partner at some point in their lifetime (Walters, Chen, and Breiding 2013). This reveals that women in same-sex relationships are more likely to suffer sexual abuse from their intimate partners than men. Even within heterosexual relationships, women are more likely to experience sexual abuse than males.

According to the 2015 U.S. Transgender Survey, conducted by the National Center for Transgender Equality, 47 percent of transgender people experience sexual assault at some point in their lifetime. This same study also found that transgender minorities were at the highest risk of sexual assault; 65 percent of American Indian respondents, 59 percent of multiracial respondents, 58 percent of Middle Eastern respondents, and 53 percent of Black respondents reported being victims of sexual assault (James et al. 2016).

Same-sex sexual abuse may take different forms or be defined in different ways. Sexual assault refers to unwanted sexual activity by a same-sex intimate partner or nonpartner without the consent of the victim, for example, inappropriate touching, rape, or attempted rape. Rape refers to a type of sexual assault by a same-sex intimate partner or nonpartner that involves forceful insertion of a bodily organ or an object into the sex organ of the victim without his or her consent. And groping refers to unwanted touching of same-sex body parts, such as the breast, butt, or genitals.

Sexual harassment refers to an indecent act, repeated acts, or degrading remarks that relate to a person's sexuality performed by a person of the same sex on another with the intention of causing humiliation or sexual satisfaction. Use of technology refers to the use of digital photos, videos, apps, phone messages, emails, or social media by a same-sex partner or nonpartner to engage in unsolicited or nonconsensual sexual activities. Indecent exposure refers to a form of sexual violence that involves same-sex unwanted exposure of private parts. Sexual stalking refers to any behavior directed at a person of the same sex that reasonably places such a person in fear for his or her safety with intention to facilitate sexual advances.

The typical forms of same-sex sexual abuse are rape, sexual assault, sexual harassment, stalking, attempted rape, and technology-assisted sexual abuse. Considering the existence of same-sex sexual abuse, it is essential to engage in prevention strategies at the local, state, and national levels that are evidence-based and realistically achievable. There is also a need to create awareness, develop prevention strategies that will avert perpetration and victimization, and make resources easily available to victims.

Ifeoma Okoye and O. Oko Elechi

See also: Groping; Power Dynamics; Relationship Violence; Retaliation; Stalking

Further Reading

American Psychological Association. 2019. "Sexual Abuse." https://www.apa.org/topics/sexual-abuse/index.

Brown, T. N., and J. L. Herman. 2015. "Intimate Partner Violence and Sexual Abuse among LGBT People." The Williams Institute, UCLA School of Law. https://williamsinstitute.law.ucla.edu/publications/ipv-sex-abuse-lgbt-people/.

Centers for Disease Control and Prevention. 2010. "NISVS: An Overview of 2010 Findings on Victimization by Sexual Orientation." National Intimate Partner and Sexual Violence Survey (NISVS). https://www.cdc.gov/violenceprevention/pdf/cdc_nisvs_victimization_final-a.pdf.

James, S. E., Jody L. Herman, Susan Rankin, Mara Keisling, Lisa Mottet, and Ma'ayan Anafi. 2016. *The Report of the 2015 U.S. Transgender Survey.* Washington, DC: National Center for Transgender Equality.

Smith, S. G., J. Chen, K. C. Basile, L. K. Gilbert, M. T. Merrick, N. Patel, M. Walling, and A. Jain. 2017. *The National Intimate Partner and Sexual Violence Survey (NISVS): 2010–2012 State Report.* Atlanta, GA: National Center for Injury Prevention and Control, Centers for Disease Control and Prevention. https://www.cdc.gov/violenceprevention/pdf/NISVS-StateReportBook.pdf.

Walters, M. L., J. Chen and M. J. Breiding. 2013. *The National Intimate Partner and Sexual Violence Survey (NISVS): 2010 Findings on Victimization by Sexual Orientation.* Atlanta, GA: National Center for Injury Prevention and Control, Centers for Disease Control and Prevention.

Sarkeesian, Anita (1983–)

Anita Sarkeesian is a Canadian American self-identified feminist blogger. She is known for her critiques about how women are portrayed in digital media and the video game industry. In 2012, the feminist blogger produced a series of online videos titled *Tropes vs. Women in Video Games* on the internet site YouTube (Webber 2017). The series included eighteen episodes over a five-year period, from 2012 to 2017 (Klepek 2017). The series discussed how female characters in video games were mostly used as plot devices, either a princess to be saved or a prostitute to be used for sexual gratification and then beaten and murdered. Although the series received positive reviews, it led to online harassment that targeted her through all her social media accounts. Sarkeesian was eventually forced to flee her home and to cancel speaking events after threats on her and her family members' lives.

Sarkeesian has a bachelor's degree in communication from California State University and a master's degree in social and political thought from York University. She is the founder and CEO of her organization, Feminist Frequency, a website that continues to take a feminist perspective on women in pop culture. Since Gamergate, she has taken on a larger activist role in bringing awareness to the damages of online harassment and has partnered with Zoë Quinn's Crash Override organization. She was included in Time's 100 Most Influential People in 2015 (Wheaton 2015) and was awarded an honorary PhD from the Liberal and Performing Arts College of the New School in New York City in 2016 (The New School 2016).

Sarkeesian came to public prominence as a result of the so-called Gamergate scandal, which erupted after an ex-boyfriend of video game designer Zoë Quinn viciously attacked her on two popular online video game sites. Although Quinn was the original target of the online attack that would become Gamergate, Sarkeesian, along with other prominent female game designers and critics, became a target as a result of her own advocacy work in the industry.

Beyond the rape and death threats, the victims' personal information was also published online as well as the information of their family members. On several occasions, Quinn and Sarkeesian were forced to leave their homes, cancel public speaking appearances, and change personal information for fear of safety. This online campaign would eventually lead to a global discussion on how to protect online users from threats of physical and sexual violence, with both Quinn and Sarkeesian taking active roles in promoting responsibility at the level of internet sites (such as Twitter and YouTube) and individual behavior.

Despite the continued online harassment of those speaking out against male domination in the gaming industry or in support of the inclusion of women, people of color, and nonbinary individuals, women such as Sarkeesian, Quinn, and Brianna Wu have helped to create spaces of progress and empowered momentum for change. Major gaming companies have signed open letters condemning the behavior, and social media sites such as Twitter continue to update their policies to eliminate online harassment of its members. Gamergate was initially the result of an angry ex-boyfriend and fueled by an online hate mob advocating the maintenance of the status quo, but a real pushback has now emerged to help make the gaming industry open and welcoming to everyone.

Bryan M. Blaylock, Ellen Repeta, and Nadine Marie Connell

See also: Gamergate; Objectification of Women; Quinn, Zoë; Social Media

Further Reading

Frank, A. 2015. "Anita Sarkeesian, Zoe Quinn and More Take Aim at Cyber Harassment against Women." Polygon, September 25. Accessed February 1, 2019. https://www

.polygon.com/2015/9/25/9399169/united-nations-women-cyber-violence-anita
-sarkeesian-zoe-quinn.

Jason, Z. 2015. "Game of Fear: The Story behind GamerGate." *Boston Magazine*, April
28. https://www.bostonmagazine.com/news/2015/04/28/gamergate/.

Klepek, Patrick. 2017. "The Legacy of Feminist Frequency's Tropes vs Women Series."
Waypoint, April 28. Accessed February 1, 2019. https://waypoint.vice.com/en_us
/article/nzpkkw/the-legacy-of-feminist-frequencys-tropes-vs-women-series.

The New School. 2016. "Commencement 2016: Get To Know The Honorary Degree
Recipients." May 3. https://blogs.newschool.edu/news/2016/05/commencement
-2016-honorary-degree-recipients/.

Webber, J. E. 2017. "Anita Sarkeesian: 'It's Frustrating to Be Known As the Woman Who
Survived #Gamergate.'" *The Guardian*, October 16. Accessed March 1, 2019.
https://www.theguardian.com/lifeandstyle/2017/oct/16/anita-sarkeesian-its
-frustrating-to-be-known-as-the-woman-who-survived-gamergate.

Wheaton, W. 2015. "Anita Sarkeesian." *Time*, April 16. Accessed February 1, 2019. http://
time.com/collection-post/3822727/anita-sarkeesian-2015-time-100/.

Schneiderman, Eric (1954–)

Eric Schneiderman was the attorney general of New York for more than seven
years, from 2010 to 2018. During that time, he was a powerful Democratic player
in New York and a champion of the #MeToo Movement as well as a high-profile
legal foe to Donald Trump. His tenure as state attorney general came to an abrupt
end in May 2018, however, when the *New Yorker* magazine published a shocking
article detailing his allegedly violent and abusive behavior in a series of romantic
relationships. The article portrayed him as a powerful public official and formidable force within the #MeToo Movement (for actions such as suing accused sexual predator and moviemaking mogul Harvey Weinstein and forcefully fighting
for victims' rights) who in his private life engaged in nonconsensual sadism with
several partners. Since his fall from political grace, he has remained out of the
limelight, and it is unclear what the future holds for him.

Prior to 2018, Schneiderman was known as a foe to Wall Street banks during
the subprime mortgage crisis as well as a defender of women's rights, both as a
legislator and then, later, as attorney general. But he may have been best known
nationally as a thorn in the side of President Trump, with *Politico* magazine asking, "Will this man take down Donald Trump?" just a few months after Trump
took office.

The animosity between Trump and Schneiderman dated back to 2011, when
Schneiderman's office went after Trump University, pursuing it legally to drop the
"university" title. Schneiderman called the program fraudulent, as the university
had not received a charter to offer higher education and offered no degrees. Citing
false advertising, the company faced a slew of complaints from former customers
in multiple states (Helderman 2016). Despite a rancorous counteroffensive strategy as well as numerous assertions that he would never settle, Trump eventually
did settle the lawsuit filed by Schneiderman's office for $25 million shortly after
the 2016 election.

After the presidential election in 2016, Schneiderman focused his office's efforts to oppose the Trump administration on a host of topics, including fighting the initial "Muslim ban" and supporting "sanctuary cities" for immigrants, upholding net neutrality, and protecting women's reproductive rights from Trump administration attacks. Further, his office helped to set strategy among many other state attorneys general. On the relationship his office had to the Trump administration, Schneiderman stated, "We try to protect New Yorkers from those who would do them harm. The biggest threat to New Yorkers right now is the federal government, so we're responding to it." In the first year of Trump's presidency, the *New York Times* reported that Schneiderman's office had taken one hundred legal or administrative actions against Trump administration policies (Hakim and Rashbaum 2017).

Schneiderman's legacy, however, was permanently marred with the publication of an investigative report by Jane Mayer and Ronan Farrow in the *New Yorker* in May 2018. The story chronicled Schneiderman's alleged violence against women with whom he was in relationships. Several claimed he slapped them—hard—leaving bruises and causing long-lasting emotional and physical trauma. They described his escalating controlling and abusive behaviors, from belittling their careers to criticizing their weight and appearance. The women also cataloged a pattern of excessive drinking and misuse of prescription medications. Several women feared coming forward because they were afraid of Schneiderman's wrath. When one woman pulled away from the relationship, he reportedly warned her that "I am the law" (Mayer and Farrow 2018). Another woman declined to come forward because she believed Schneiderman was doing good legal work on the national stage and did not want to jeopardize it.

In response to the allegations, Schneiderman issued a denial and claimed he never assaulted anyone and that activity in his personal relationships may have been part of "role-playing and other consensual sexual activity." But he also submitted his resignation hours after the story published, saying that he felt the allegations would impede his ability to act effectively as attorney general.

The revelations of Schneiderman's violence against women felt like a betrayal to many women, given his strong advocacy for women's causes and particularly with his role in taking on accused sexual offender Harvey Weinstein. After his resignation, New York governor Andrew Cuomo appointed a special prosecutor to investigate Schneiderman's conduct. As of early 2019, it is unclear whether Schneiderman will face criminal charges or what the future holds for him, politically or personally.

Jennifer M. Balboni and Samyah Williams

See also: #MeToo Movement; Presidential Scandals

Further Reading

Freedlander, D. 2017. "Will This Man Take Down Donald Trump?" *Politico*, February 3. https://www.politico.com/magazine/story/2017/02/eric-schneiderman-donald-trump-new-york-214734.

Hakim, D. and W. Rashbaum. 2017. "New York's Attorney General in Battle with Trump." *New York Times*, December 26.

Helderman, R. 2016. "Trump Agrees to $25 Million Settlement in Trump University Fraud Cases." *Washington Post*, November 18. https://www.washingtonpost.com /politics/source-trump-nearing-settlement-in-trump-university-fraud-cases/2016 /11/18/8dc047c0-ada0-11e6-a31b-4b6397e625d0_story.html.

Mayer, Jane, and Ronan Farrow. 2018. "Four Women Accuse New York's Attorney General of Physical Abuse." *New Yorker*, May 7.

SCREAM (Students Challenging Realities and Educating against Myths)

SCREAM (Students Challenging Realities and Educating against Myths) is a student-based theater program at Rutgers University in New Jersey. It is an innovative peer education theater program that aims to educate students on how to prevent sexual assault in different venues. While entertaining and delivering educational information to the audience, SCREAM employs bystander intervention principles and promotes critical thinking.

Approximately twenty to thirty undergraduate students formed SCREAM Theater and SCREAM Athletes to raise awareness of sexual assault, domestic and dating violence, same-sex violence, stalking, peer harassment, and bullying. Since 1991, the interactive theater group has been performing nationwide, seeking to educate audiences on sexual assault prevention and bystander intervention. In 1992, expanding the SCREAM Theater model, a group of student athletes performed exclusively for athletic team members under the name SCREAM Athletes. They also produced a video—"Taking the Lead: SCREAM Athletes Step Up to Prevent Sexual Violence"—that was made available to other campuses.

SCREAM Athletes is committed to educating the athletic community on issues of interpersonal violence, such as sexual assault, dating violence, and sexual harassment. In collaboration with the Rutgers Intercollegiate Athletic Department, SCREAM Athletes performs for all freshman, sophomore, and junior student athletes at Rutgers, for university athletic trainers, for student athletes at colleges and high schools locally and nationwide, and at conferences. Every year, SCREAM Theater and SCREAM Athletes carry out around seventy performances to students at Rutgers, area high schools, other universities, and local and national conferences. SCREAM Theater also performs at Rutgers University's mandatory New Student Orientation for all first-year students.

Depending on the topic, SCREAM performances typically feature a fifteen- to thirty-minute skit addressing issues related to sexual assault in colleges, universities, high schools, workplaces, and different settings familiar to audiences. Skits are written, developed, performed and narrated entirely by Rutgers students. Skits are not limited to sexual assault, however. The troupe can also cover a wide range of topics, such as stalking, bullying, harassment, and the role of alcohol in sexual assault. Rutgers students can customize the scenario based on a community's or an organization's needs, and they occasionally use humor in the skits to catch the audience's attention.

Values clarification is a learning outcome of SCREAM Theater that helps students explore and recognize their most important values. Other elements of the SCREAM Theater and SCREAM Athletes programs are interactive question and answer sessions, followed by small group discussions facilitated by peer educators.

These are designed to allow students to express their emotions and build respect for different perspectives. In the question and answer sessions, the student actors remain in character. The facilitator and the audience members ask questions of the characters, who portray perpetrators, victims, and friends and family members. In this interactive session, the characters and the audiences educate each other about the differences between acceptable and unacceptable behaviors. In the discussion session, students evaluate their values and beliefs when they confront a perpetrator. Facilitated discussions seek to help audiences broaden their understanding of sexual assault and their role in the process of preventing it. The presentation concludes with the student actors introducing themselves to the audience, stating the purpose of their characters, and explaining how they became involved in the SCREAM Theater Project.

In 2014, the White House Task Force to Protect Students from Sexual Assault specifically cited the SCREAM program as an example of innovative and creative approaches to rally public support and understanding for combating sexual assault in its many forms. Other evaluations have also found that SCREAM has had a positive impact on public understanding of sexual assault and the willingness of attendees to actively intervene when they personally see episodes of sexual assault and harassment or recognize warning signs that someone may be in an abusive relationship.

Durmus Alper Camlibel

See also: Amateur Sports; College Campuses; Gender Equality; Groping; Power Dynamics; Relationship Violence; Sexism; Sexual Harassment Training; Stalking

Further Reading

Johnson, L., S. McMahon, and J. L. Postmus. 2014. "SCREAMing to Prevent Violence: A Model for Peer Educational Theater Programs." *Rutgers School of Social Work: Centers VAWC.* https://socialwork.rutgers.edu/centers/center-violence-against -women-and-children/research-and-evaluation/scream-ing-prevent-violence -overview.

Katz, J., and J. Moore. 2013. "Bystander Education Training for Campus Sexual Assault Prevention: An Initial Meta-Analysis." *Violence and Victims* 28(6): 1054–1067.

McMahon, S., C. T. Allen, J. L. Postmus, S. M. McMahon, A. Peterson, and M. L. Hoffman. 2014. "Measuring Bystander Attitudes and Behavior to Prevent Sexual Violence." *Journal of American College Health* 62(1): 58–66.

McMahon, S., J. L. Postmus, and R. A. Koenick. 2011. "Conceptualizing the Engaging Bystander Approach to Sexual Violence Prevention on College Campuses." *Journal of College Student Development* 52(1): 115–130.

McMahon, S., J. L. Postmus, C. Warrener, and R. A. Koenick. 2014. "Utilizing Peer Education Theater for the Primary Prevention of Sexual Violence on College Campuses." *Journal of College Student Development* 55(1): 78–85.

Sakai, K. 2000. "Scream Theater: A Student Surprises Herself by Joining Up." *About Campus* 5(2): 29–30.

Sexism

Sexism is defined as prejudgments or discrimination based on a person's gender. It is deeply ingrained in American culture. Women are treated differently than men, and this has real-world impacts. Daily sexism has become so normalized that its existence as an issue that needs redress remains largely invisible. Members of society have engaged in an unspoken social contract regarding sexism. As long as society agrees that extreme expressions of sexism (e.g., violent rape) are only committed by the mythical "bad man," then "we" are not a sexist society.

Unfortunately, this perspective is not based in reality. For example, studies have demonstrated that sexism contributes to gender-based inequities in income and career advancement. Research shows that fewer women are working in professional and managerial positions, that they are paid less than men when engaged in the same work, and that they are more likely to be working in lower-paying occupations. There is no evidence that industries have pay scales instructing employers to pay people differently based on gender. However, there are structural inequities built into our social system. Gender-based pay inequity exists and continues to occur, even in the face of laws crafted to combat this reality.

Employers have been criticized for making hiring and promotion decisions using what they think are gender-neutral criteria but that nonetheless exist in a wider cultural context that is deeply sexist. For example, women have long battled patriarchal notions that women are less competent than men and that the types of work that have historically been open to them are of less value than the work and careers of men. This treatment affects their workplace interactions and workplace politics, and it impacts the culture of the workplace environment and, ultimately, their overall career as well as marriage and legal rights.

A lot of sexism is unconscious, unintended, and unexamined, and it manifests itself in small ways. Referring to a woman as a "girl" is one example. If it feels wrong to call a grown man a "boy" but okay to call a grown woman a "girl," it might be because our culture is sexist. The details matter because together they weave a cultural fabric that dictates how we relate to each other. Victims often feel the offensive behavior is too "minor" to make a fuss. But the behaviors can include insults consisting of jokes or terms based on gender or devaluing women's views or voice by interrupting them. On some occasions, women will recall situations where a male restated what a woman said in order for the suggestion or comment to be heard.

Role stereotyping is common too; coworkers, employers, and even customers may state or think that a woman cannot do heavy lifting on the job, or, even more insulting, women are automatically assumed to be the note-takers in a meeting solely because of their gender. Others may comment on their perceived preoccupation with physical appearance, and some may think it is acceptable to make comments about how they dress or other aspects of their appearance. Women also run a greater risk of being labeled as emotional for behavior that, if it was displayed by a man, would be portrayed as indicative of strong or empathetic leadership. Finally, women in the workplace who are also raising children still encounter criticisms for "working outside of the home" that are rarely leveled against their male colleagues (Priestley 2019).

What can be done about these assumptions and situations? First, one should not sit back and put up with these generalizations, even if they are not directed at a particular person and even if you are not a female. Laughing at comments or even ignoring them will not make the culture of sexism go away. The goal is to stop it from happening by calling people out on the behavior. At a workplace, supervisors can hold discussions or meetings about the work men and women can do, and they should have equal access to flexible work schedules for all (so that women are not judged if they want to work from home occasionally). Employers must also recognize when gender stereotypes are being applied to assess performance or leadership roles. Mothers do take more time off work than men for the births of their children and for a longer length of time (eleven weeks for women versus one week for men). A Pew Research Center (2019) study found that 42 percent of women said they experienced gender discrimination at work versus 22 percent of men. It also found broad agreement that the country needs to continue making changes to give men and women equality (77 percent of women and 63 percent of men agreed with this statement).

The good news is that the situation has improved since the 1980s. But numbers have been stable for the last fifteen years or so. In 2018, Pew found that women earned 85 percent of what men earned in terms of median hourly earnings for full-time and part-time work in the United States (Pew Research Center 201). Meanwhile, data from the U.S. Census Bureau from 2017 indicated that women earn 80 percent of what men do. However, young women between the ages of twenty-five and thirty-four earn 89 percent of what men earn. The narrowing of the gap has been explained by measurable factors, such as gains women have made in educational attainment and work experience. However, it is negatively impacted by occupational segregation.

Interestingly, lifelong earnings have been affected by where you were born; for example, in the Deep South, the numbers are worse, and women born in more sexist places are more likely to marry and have their first child at a younger age. This fact then impacts future earning potential and career choices. For example, law and medicine, which are higher-paying careers, require long hours and lots of off-duty work; these factors might well diminish the number of women with children who go into those careers. Teaching, on the other hand, is a common career for women. Yet, even as teachers, there have long been different judgments and assumptions made about the quality of instruction that teachers provide based on their gender. Female teachers are judged as more empathic and better suited for teaching subjects in the humanities (i.e., language, art, music, and writing), but male teachers are stereotypically seen as being more intelligent and better suited to teach math and science.

Sexism shapes everything about women's experiences as long as we continue to support its invisibility. There is no doubt that significant progress has been made toward equality. However, sexism pervades everything in our culture and perpetuates significant harm. It took more than one hundred years for women to gain the right to vote in the United States. Women have gained access to other rights since then, though they were added piecemeal, and some are now at risk of being, in the long arc of history, very short-lived. Supporters of an Equal Rights Amendment assert that the failure to add such a provision to the U.S. Constitution is not just symbolic. They contend that such an amendment would broadly codify women's equality in all aspects of American life. Without it, the core problem is not addressed (Weiss 2018).

It is tempting to think that the facts will be enough. Even in this era of "alternative facts," many people still care about data and evidence. When it comes to sexism, the problem with facts is that even those who are moved by information of its existence do not know what to do next.

Pushing for meaningful social change is not an easy endeavor or a polite activity. Women were demeaned, harmed, and sometimes killed to gain suffrage. But gaining suffrage and other legal protections did not end sexism. To decrease sexism, society will need to change the underlying social issues that allowed it to happen in the first place.

Erin Scott and Gina Robertiello

See also: Gender Competency; Workplace Gender Diversity

Further Reading

Hooks, Bell. 2000. *Feminism Is for Everybody: Passionate Politics*. Boston: South End Press.

Manne, Kate. 2018. *Down Girl: The Logic of Misogyny*. Oxford: Oxford University Press.

Pew Research Center. 2019. "Gender Pay Gap Has Narrowed but Changed Little in the Past Decade." March 22. https://www.pewresearch.org/fact-tank/2019/03/22/gender-pay-gap-facts/.

Priestley, A. 2019. "Six Common Manifestations of Everyday Sexism at Work." Smart Company, July 10. www.smartcompany.com.au/people-human-resources/six-common-manifestations-everyday-sexism-work/.

Solnit, Rebecca. 2015. *Men Explain Things to Me*. Chicago: Haymarket Books.

Weiss, Elaine. 2018. *The Woman's Hour: The Great Fight to Win the Vote*. New York: Viking Penguin.

Sexual Harassment Training

Sexual harassment is the targeting of others with unwelcome sexual actions, sexual comments, or sexual gestures based on ones sexual orientation, gender, or gender expression. Although studies show sexual harassment among men is becoming more common, most victims of sexual harassment are women. Employment-related sexual harassment is a common problem among a wide range of professions, both in the United States and internationally, and can result in significant costs to both employers and their workers. In recognition of this vulnerability, many companies of all shapes and sizes and in a wide range of industries are rolling out new anti-harassment training programs or beefing up ones already in existence.

SEXUAL HARASSMENT IN THE WORKPLACE

Employers who allow sexual harassment to exist within the culture of their organizations may find that the costs of doing so are substantial and result in high employee turnover, increased absenteeism, higher risk of on-the-job accidents, and lower work productivity. Understandably, these issues can lead to a sharp decrease in overall organizational effectiveness as well as exposure to expensive litigation and legal penalties. Huge sums of money are spent annually by employers on sexual harassment litigation.

The costs to victims of employment-related sexual harassment are high in terms of both short- and long-term consequences. In addition to the psychological and physical stress brought on by the trauma of experiencing sexual harassment, victims are often further impacted by financial insecurity and worry over reduced job performance. Long-term assessments show that sexual harassment victims report being less satisfied with their jobs and are more likely to experience health problems.

The U.S. Equal Employment Opportunity Commission (EEOC) formally established sexual harassment as a form of sex discrimination in 1980. The EEOC defined *sexual harassment* as unwanted verbal or physical behavior of a sexual nature that "affects an individual's employment, unreasonably interferes with an individual's work performance or creates an intimidating, hostile or offensive work environment" (Equal Employment Opportunity Commission 1980, 74677). The EEOC also issued guidelines to assist employers in the implementation of workplace sexual harassment prevention policies and programs, in addition to clarifying conditions leading to employer liability as a result of insufficient training and prevention practices. The EEOC guidelines on workplace harassment have since been unanimously upheld in two U.S. Supreme Court decisions: *Meritor Savings Bank v. Vinson* (1986) and *Harris v. Forklift Systems, Inc.* (1993).

The number of litigated workplace sexual harassment and sex discrimination cases increased exponentially in the final decades of the twentieth century. In the years between 1990 and 2000 alone, the number of annual cases tripled. More recently, employment legal cases constitute 30 percent of the total U.S. civil litigation, with up to 25 percent of women employees having experienced some form of sexual harassment in the workplace (Burn 2019). In terms of timing, it has been theorized that there is an upsurge of sexual discrimination and harassment cases when employee layoffs occur during economic slowdowns. As a result of tightened budgets, employers may be tempted to reduce the scope of employee sexual harassment training just when risk exposure is at its highest (Johnson 2004).

PROGRAMS TO ADDRESS HARASSMENT

Most contemporary business organizations recognize sexual harassment as a serious workplace issue not only in terms of employee productivity but also in terms of public reputation and vulnerability to potentially costly litigation. As a result, they developed and implemented formal training programs to protect their organizations' effectiveness, improve employee satisfaction, and affect cost reduction. The annual cost to U.S. employers for sexual harassment training climbed to over $10 billion by the beginning of the 2010s (Goldberg 2011), and experts believe that the expense has increased in subsequent years. Proponents of this training also emphasize that there are significant business costs associated with allowing sexual harassment and other gender-based inequities in their operations, including lost productivity, increased employee turnover, legal costs if victims file lawsuits, and damage to public reputation.

In general, sexual harassment training teaches employees to recognize the types of speech and behaviors that constitute sexual harassment and misconduct and educates them on their responsibilities and options when confronted with workplace sexual harassment. Employees also receive valuable information regarding resources for providing victim support as well as the process for reporting grievances. Effective training programs protect employees by reducing victim blaming and fostering victim support from supervisors and peers (Bainbridge, Perry, and Kulik 2018).

The United States has been a leader in both the terms of the development of sexual harassment training programs and in examining their effectiveness. Policies in other countries, especially those in the European Union, have largely been shaped by those in the United States. EEOC guidelines specify that all employees should regularly attend training on the subject of workplace sexual harassment. U.S. federal employees are among the most likely group in the workforce to participate in sexual harassment training, with more than 75 percent having received training at some point; of these, 50 percent have done so within the previous year. Most of these workers report that training increased their sensitivity to the problem of sexual harassment as well as heightened their feelings of empathy toward their coworkers (Antecol and Cobb-Clark 2003).

Research on sexual harassment training and cognitive outcomes has confirmed that sexual harassment training programs serve to significantly increase employee understanding about the issue and its ramifications for individuals and companies alike. In particular, training promoting empathy toward sexual harassment victims has been found effective in fostering more positive attitudes and support toward targets of harassment. A comprehensive study that examined the impact of sexual harassment training's effectiveness on cognitive outcomes among fourteen empirical studies reported that training had a consistent significant and positive impact on knowledge attainment about sexual harassment (Roehling and Huang 2018).

With the proliferation of high-profile sexual harassment cases in the era of #MeToo, the problem of gender-based harassment, intimidation, and assault in workplace settings has shot to the forefront of the public consciousness. People who have been the targets of such attacks have become more aware of their civil rights, and many feel more empowered to demand justice.

With this cultural shift, the number of reported incidents has been increasing. Employers will need to be ready with effective training programs in place that educate their employees about sexual harassment in general as well as inform them of the anti-harassment policies within their particular organization. Additionally, employers should inform their workers about reporting procedures and provide support to targets of harassment. Finally, employers benefit when taking a proactive stance in preventing sexual harassment through conscious efforts to promote an organization-wide culture of civility and respect.

Angela R. Gover

See also: Equal Employment Opportunity Commission (EEOC); *Harris v. Forklift Systems*; *Meritor Savings Bank v. Vinson*; #MeToo Movement; Title VII of the Civil Rights Act of 1964

Further Reading

Antecol, H., and D. Cobb-Clark. 2003. "Does Sexual Harassment Training Change Attitudes? A View from the Federal Level." *Social Science Quarterly* 84(4): 826–842.

Bainbridge, H. T., E. L. Perry, and C. T. Kulik. 2018. "Sexual Harassment Training: Explaining Differences in Australian and US Approaches." *Asia Pacific Journal of Human Resources* 56(1): 124–147.

Burn, S. M. 2019. "The Psychology of Sexual Harassment." *Teaching of Psychology* 46(1): 96–103.

Equal Employment Opportunity Commission. 1980. "Discrimination because of Sex under Title VII of the Civil Rights Act of 1964, as Amended; Adoption of Final Interpretive Guidelines (29 C.F.R. Sec. 1604.1 1 et seq.)." *Federal Register* 45: 74676–74677.

Goldberg, C. B. 2011. "What Do We Really Know about Sexual Harassment Training Effectiveness?" In *Praeger Handbook on Understanding and Preventing Workplace Discrimination*, edited by M. A. Paludi, C. A. Paludi, Jr., and E. DeSouza, 45–48. Santa Barbara, CA: Praeger.

Johnson, M. W. 2004. "Harassment and Discrimination Prevention Training: What the Law Requires." *Labor Law Journal* 55(2): 119.

Roehling, M. V., and J. Huang. 2018. "Sexual Harassment Training Effectiveness: An Interdisciplinary Review and Call for Research." *Journal of Organizational Behavior* 39(2): 134–150.

Sixteen Candles

Sixteen Candles is a 1984 teen comedy-romance film that ranks among the best known of the coming-of-age films directed by John Hughes. *Sixteen Candles* was intended to be a classic love story featuring Sam, a teenage "girl next door" on the verge of her sixteenth birthday, getting the attention of Jake, the all-American popular boy. The premise of the story seemed like a fairy tale when the film was released, and it came to be regarded as one of the best-known offerings of 1980s pop culture.

However, watching *Sixteen Candles* in 2019, in the wake of the #MeToo Movement, was seen by many as a sobering, troubling experience. In 2019, *Sixteen Candles* was widely criticized for depicting and even glorifying rape culture, sexism, body shaming, and misogyny. According to many detractors, *Sixteen Candles* inadvertently shows how tolerant society was of rape culture—and how dismissive it was of female empowerment—in the 1980s. In 2018, Molly Ringwald (who played the role of Sam in the movie) stated in an interview in the *New Yorker* that when reflecting on the movie, it absolutely exemplified rape culture. There are several scenes involving sexual misconduct and the emotional abuse of characters that would not be positively received by modern moviegoing audiences.

The film has been condemned on a variety of fronts. For example, *Sixteen Candles* portrayed body shaming among the characters of the movie, usually for laughs. First, Sam's brother offers sneering comments on her bra size and about her physical features. Sam also receives heavy criticism from her grandparents, who spend more time analyzing her body than acknowledging the fact that it is her birthday. This scene is meant to be comical, but the statements made about her body by her grandparents play out as discouraging and disheartening.

Body image and the objectification of girls' bodies are recurring subjects throughout the film, including a scene that takes place in the locker room. In this scene, Sam and her best friend, Randy, make explicit and definite remarks about the body of another girl, Caroline. *Sixteen Candles* shows how normalized body shaming is among high school teenagers and the impact it can have on not only how a teenage girl perceives herself but also how she responds to the treatment of others. The movie clearly showed a picture of a male-dominated society, where body shaming and judgmental thoughts about a "girl's" appearance were prominently evident.

In many scenes, girls were objectified for no reason at all. This is shown in the treatment Caroline (Jake's girlfriend) accepts from Jake. When Jake's attention turns to Sam, he becomes coldheartedly mean toward Caroline, and yet her love for him remains unscathed; Jake remains seen as the perfect guy. *Sixteen Candles* did such a good job of painting Jake Ryan as an "ideal" that audiences overlooked the fact that he gave a drunk and unconscious Caroline over to another guy to "have fun with" because he no longer had interest in her. Jake not only treated Caroline as an object that could be given away; he also manipulated her into thinking the man she was going off to sleep with was in fact him.

When the film was released, this situation was not taken seriously, nor was it acknowledged as rape. During this time, rape was still widely believed in American culture to be something that could only occur at the hands of a stranger. Jake "gives" Caroline over to Ted, a character the movie simply named "the Geek." After they have sex, Ted takes a picture of himself next to Caroline's unconscious body while his friends praise him as "a legend." Ted was not ashamed, nor was he shamed or shunned for having sex with Caroline, who was drunk and incapable of giving consent. Instead, Ted is glamorized and earns the adoration of his friends. The movie also displayed homophobic attitudes as part of its efforts to get laughs, with members of the LGBT community ridiculed and demeaned at several different points.

Today, the movie's depiction of girls and women as objects to use for male enjoyment and gratification has been cited as a lesson of sorts. It shows how normalized these portrayals of rape culture in television and film have been over the years and how they still influence perceptions of males and females today.

M'Balu P. Bangura and Ariatu Sillah

See also: #MeToo Movement; Movies, Depictions of Sexual Harassment; Television

Further Reading

Bain, A. L. 2010. "White Western Teenage Girls and Urban Space: Challenging Hollywood's Representations." *Gender Place & Culture: A Journal of Feminist Geography* 10(3): 197–213.

Bartlett, A., K. Clarke, and R. Cover. 2019. "Flirting on Film: Boundaries and Consent, Visibility and Performance." In *Flirting in the Era of #MeToo*, 77–103. New York: Palgrave Macmillan.

Benfer, S. 2015. "Sixteen Candles, Rape Culture, and the Anti-Woman Politics of 2013." *Bitch Flicks*, July 8. Discus. August 14, 2015.

Carpenter, L. M. 1998. "From Girls into Women: Scripts for Sexuality and Romance in Seventeen Magazine, 1974–1994." *Journal of Sex Research* 35: 158–168.

Joyner, K., and E. O. Laumann. 2001. "Teenage Sex and the Sexual Revolution." In *Sex, Love, and Health in America: Private Choices and Public Policies*, edited by Edward O. Laumann and Robert T. Michael, 41–71. Chicago: University of Chicago Press.

Milkie, M. 1999. "Social Comparisons, Reflected Appraisals, and Mass Media: The Impact of Pervasive Beauty Images on Black and White Girls' Self Concept." *Social Psychology Quarterly* 62(2): 190–210.

Walsh-Childers, K. ed. *Sexual Teens, Sexual Media: Investigating Media's Influence on Adolescent Sexuality*. Mahwah, NJ: Lawrence Erlbaum Associates.

Social Media

One of the challenges in tackling harassment, particularly in the context of an intimate partner violent relationship, is addressing forms of abuse and harassment transmitted via social media, including but not limited to platforms such as Facebook, YouTube, Instagram, and Twitter. Even when the victims have managed to physically escape from their aggressors, the harassers may continue to reach out to menace them. Such harassment can continue unabated 24/7. Tracking software such as the "track my iPhone" mechanism can facilitate stalking, as the harassers will know where their targets are physically. Intentionally cruel messages can be left on Facebook walls for all to see. A sexually explicit revenge porn picture can easily be uploaded to social media, spreading quickly online and humiliating the victim. These are just some of the ways that social media has amplified the harm that can be wreaked on victims of harassment.

Every year, millions of individuals experience assault at the hands of current or former intimate partners. As reported by the Substance Abuse and Mental Health Services Administration, about one in four women and one in nine men indicate they have been physically abused (e.g., beaten up, slapped, punched, kicked, struck by household items or other projectiles, or had a weapon used against them) by an intimate partner during their lifetime. While most people typically think of intimate partner violence (IPV) in the context of a marriage (e.g., battered wives), relationship violence is not limited to just married couples and adult women.

Adolescent dating violence is also fairly common. According to the Centers for Disease Control and Prevention (2019), about one in eleven female adolescents and one in fifteen male teenagers had experienced physical violence from a dating partner during the prior year. The types of abuse are similar in both adult and adolescent IPV relationships and can include behaviors such as pushing, slapping, or shoving a partner against a wall. But it is not just physical abuse that is a problem. IPV can be verbal and psychological as well and may include threatening a partner, damaging his or her possessions, or insulting a partner in front of his or her friends. Although both males and females may inflict aggression and emotional pain on intimate partners, males typically cause more physical injury to their victims.

The use of text messaging and social media platforms such as Facebook, Twitter, YouTube, and Instagram has exploded in the past decade. This new form of communication is particularly popular with young people, so it stands to reason that adolescent relationship harassment and aggression often plays out over electronic forms of communication. A 2018 study from the Pew Research Center found that nearly 60 percent of American teenagers had experienced some online abuse, including being called offensive names, having false rumors spread about them, or being subjected to threats. One in four had been sent explicit sexual images they had not asked for. In dating relationships, online and in-person victimization often overlap, particularly psychological abuse. Other research has found technology-facilitated aggression against dating partners, specifically receiving menacing text messages, emails, or voicemail messages; being cursed at via cell phone; and being bothered on social media sites. There are gender differences in electronic harassment, with young females being victimized more and young males perpetrating more harassment against partners.

Researchers emphasize that when harassment is happening via social media and text messaging, it is likely happening in "real life" (in person) as well. As such, there are other factors to be considered that also contribute to IPV and harassment. Witnessing violence between one's parents or experiencing child abuse while growing up may contribute to an individual's later experiences with IPV firsthand, either as a victim or perpetrator. Gender is also a factor. Some research shows that among teenagers who date, male and female adolescents are equally likely to initiate violence against a romantic partner. Females who act aggressively in relationships may be reacting to violent male partners in order to defend themselves, and the violence by females may be less severe in terms of the likelihood of causing physical injury. Substance use, including alcohol, has also been linked to relationship violence, including dating violence among young people.

Finally, particularly with regard to adolescent dating violence, friends play an important role in teenage lives in general. Having friends also involved in dating violence, either as victims or perpetrators, is related to young people's personal experiences with dating violence. In fact, Arriaga and Foshee (2004) found that friends' dating violence more strongly influenced a youth than any relationship violence between the youth's parents. Other work by Foshee concluded that adolescents first find friends who have been victimized through dating violence and then go on to experience their own dating violence. Youth who are aggressive with their romantic partners may also behave that way with their friends.

Harassment and partner violence via social media do not happen in a vacuum. To the extent that individuals' cyber lives reflect their "real" lives, online harassment is likely happening in person as well and may include both physical and verbal/emotional mistreatment. As was mentioned, known risk factors include having witnessed or experienced violence and mistreatment in one's family while growing up; substance use, particularly alcohol; and friendships with others for whom aggression is also a factor. Professionals in a position to observe such things—doctors, nurses, teachers, and school counselors—should take steps to reach out to individuals they suspect are being harassed via social media or in real life, including asking questions specifically about IPV victimization via social media and text messages. Awareness should be raised at the societal level that although rudeness over social media may seem like the norm, it is not in fact an acceptable way to communicate and can be dangerous.

Connie Hassett-Walker

See also: Groping; Marital Violence; #MeToo Movement; Sexual Harassment Training; Stalking

Further Reading

Anderson, M. 2018. *A Majority of Teens Have Experienced Some Form of Cyberbullying.* Washington, DC: Pew Research Center. http://www.pewinternet.org/2018/09/27/a -majority-of-teens-have-experienced-some-form-of-cyberbullying/#fn-21353-1.

Arriaga, X., and V. A. Foshee. 2004. "Adolescent Dating Violence: Do Adolescents Follow in Their Friends', or Their Parents', Footsteps?" *Journal of Interpersonal Violence* 19(2): 162–184. https://journals.sagepub.com/doi/10.1177/0886260503260247.

Centers for Disease Control and Prevention. 2019. "Preventing Teen Dating Violence Factsheets." https://www.cdc.gov/violenceprevention/intimatepartnerviolence /teendatingviolence/fastfact.html.

Foshee, V. A., T. S. Benefield, S. T. Ennett, K. E. Bauman, and C. Suchindran. 2004. "Longitudinal Predictors of Serious Physical and Sexual Dating Violence Victimization during Adolescence." *Preventive Medicine* 39(5): 1007–1016. https://www .ncbi.nlm.nih.gov/pubmed/15475036.

Substance Abuse and Mental Health Services Administration. n.d. "Partners Address Domestic Violence and Homelessness." https://www.samhsa.gov/homelessness -programs-resources/hpr-resources/domestic-violence-homelessness.

Zweig, J., M. Dank, P. Lachman, and J. Yahner. 2013. *Technology, Teen Dating Violence and Abuse, and Bullying.* Washington, DC: Urban Institute, Justice Policy Center. https://www.urban.org/sites/default/files/publication/23941/412891-Technology -Teen-Dating-Violence-and-Abuse-and-Bullying.PDF.

Spacey, Kevin (1959–)

Kevin Spacey is a famous Hollywood actor, singer, and producer whose career was marked by numerous critically acclaimed performances—until serious allegations of sexual misconduct and assault derailed his movie and television careers.

Spacey was born on July 26, 1959, in South Orange, New Jersey. His family name is Fowler, which is the name all his siblings use as their surnames. Kevin, however, adopted the surname Spacey, which was his paternal grandmother's maiden name. He grew up in Southern California, where his family relocated when he was about four years old. His father was a technical writer and data consultant. One of his siblings described his father, Thomas Geoffrey Fowler, as a sexual and physical abuser. Kevin's father was also known to hold racist views and was a supporter of the Nazis.

Kevin graduated covaledictorian in 1977 from Chatsworth High School in Chatsworth, California. As a high school senior, he starred in the school's production of the *Sound of Music.* He also spent time at the Northridge Military Academy. He studied drama under Marian Seldes at the Juilliard School in New York City, where he also performed part-time as a stand-up comedian. Early professional acting roles included playing Henry VI during the New York Shakespeare Festival in 1981 and playing the role of Oswald in the production of Henrik Ibsen's *Ghosts* in his maiden Broadway performance.

Spacey's stage acting blossomed after he played Jamie in Jonathan Miller's production of Eugene O'Neill's *Long Day's Journey into Night* in 1986. However, he did not achieve stardom until earning an Academy Award for Best Supporting Actor for the crime thriller *The Usual Suspects* (1995) and the Academy Award for Best Actor for the film *American Beauty* (1999). He also won a Tony Award for Best Featured Actor in a Play for *Lost in Yonkers* (1991) as well as numerous other prestigious awards.

Spacey's career came crashing down, however, when he was accused of sexual misconduct. One of the first people to accuse him of sexual abuse was another Hollywood actor, Anthony Rapp. According to Rapp, he and Spacey were friends when both of them were performing on Broadway. At the time, Rapp was fourteen years old, and Spacey was twenty-six. The alleged incident that Rapp made public occurred in 1986. On the night in question, Rapp said that the older actor brought Rapp to his apartment, threw him on his bed, and proceeded to make sexual advances toward him. Rapp said that he was inspired to publicly air his allegations by the #MeToo Movement. Rapp said that wanted to add his voice to the movement and help highlight sexual misconduct by authority figures that had been shrouded in secrecy for so long.

Spacey apologized to Rapp on Twitter for his alleged sexual misconduct toward him, even though he claimed he had no recollection of the incident. He also seized the opportunity of the sexual allegation against him to publicly announce that he was gay. In response to his critics, he also added that just because he had not previously publicly announced that he was gay, it did not mean he was living a lie. Instead, he said that he chose to keep his sexual orientation private. Thirty other people have come out since Anthony Rapp and publicly accused Spacey of sexual misconduct, saying that they either witnessed or experienced sexual misconduct from the actor. Some of the allegations emphasize that he used his powerful celebrity status to take advantage of budding actors or young actors seeking career mentorship from him.

Another man who wanted to remain anonymous claimed that he and Spacey had a sexual relationship between 1983 and 1984, when he was fourteen years old and the actor was twenty-four. Spacey denied that this relationship ever occurred. The BBC further reported on November 1, 2017, that in 1985, Spacey had sought to establish a sexual relationship with a seventeen-year-old boy. Kate Edwards, who teaches performing arts in London, also claimed that Spacey made sexual advances toward her in 1986, when she was seventeen years old. She claimed that the encounter traumatized her for a long time.

Another sixteen-year-old boy named Justin Dawes claimed that, in 1988, Spacey invited him and another friend to his apartment, where he proceeded to show them gay pornography. BuzzFeed further reported that Mark Ebenhoch claimed that Kevin propositioned him in 1995 through another friend for a sexual relationship when they worked together on a project.

After the allegations started to come out, Mexican actor Roberto Cavazos accused Spacey of sexual harassing him while they were both working at the Old Vic Theatre in London. He said he was afraid to report the harassment at the time because of Spacey's stature in the entertainment world. Former workers at the Old Vic subsequently told the newspaper *The Guardian* that the London theater ignored their allegations of inappropriate sexual behavior against Spacey. Specifically, charges were made that when Spacey was the artistic director of the Old Vic Theatre between

2004 and 2015, he used his position there to sexually harass about twenty young actors at the theater. More recently, some of the victims of Spacey's alleged sexual assaults at the theater were advised to report their victimization to the police.

Movie director Tony Montana also alleged that, in 2003, when Montana was in his thirties, Spacey groped him in a bar. He said that the incident caused him to experience PTSD for over six months. BuzzFeed also reported that a journalist in London in his early twenties claimed that Spacey groped him repeatedly despite his protestations that he was in a committed relationship with a woman. Many other people, ranging from bartenders to other actors, also came forward with allegations that Spacey had harassed or groped them. In 2016, the teenage son of journalist Heather Unruh claimed that Spacey was pressuring him to attend a party with him. Unruh advised his son to file a police report against the actor for sexual harassment.

Many of the crew members who worked with Spacey on his hit Netflix television show *House of Cards* and at the Old Vic Theatre also alleged that Spacey regularly harassed them and thereby created a toxic work environment. Netflix subsequently fired Spacey from the show, and it appears that his film and television career is over. Many observers note that if it were not for the #MeToo Movement, Spacey's sexual harassment history might never have seen the light of day, and the victims of his sexual misconduct would have continued to suffer in silence.

Rochelle McGee-Cobbs and O. Oko Elechi

See also: Hostile Work Environment: #MeToo Movement; Quid Pro Quo; Sexism; *Time Magazine* "Silence Breakers"

Further Reading

Caplan, J. 2017. "Update: Kevin Spacey Breaks Silence over Sexual Harassment Scandal—Comes Out as Gay." *Gateway Pundit*, October 29. https://www.thegateway pundit.com/2017/10/update-kevin-spacey-breaks-silence-sexual-harassment -scandal-comes-gay/.

Miller, H. 2019. "Why Is Kevin Spacey in Baltimore While Awaiting Court Appearance on Assault Charges?" *Baltimore Sun*, January 2. Accessed April 14, 2019. https:// www.baltimoresun.com/features/baltimore-insider-blog/bs-fe-kevin-spaceys -baltimore-roots-explained-20190102-story.html.

Staff writer. 2017a. "Kevin Spacey Seeks Treatment as More Stars Face Harassment Claims." BBC News, November 2. Accessed April 14, 2019. https://www.bbc.co .uk/news/entertainment-arts-41843955.

Staff writer. 2017b. "Kevin Spacey Timeline: How the Story Unfolded." BBC News, July 18. Accessed April 14, 2019. https://www.bbc.com/news/entertainment-arts-41884878.

Victor, D. 2017. "Kevin Spacey Criticized for Using Apology to Anthony Rapp to Come Out." *New York Times*, October 30. Accessed April 14, 2019. https://www.nytimes .com/2017/10/30/arts/kevin-spacey-reaction.html.

Speier, Jackie (1950–)

U.S. representative Jackie Speier was born in May 1950 in San Francisco, California, to Nancy and Fred Speier. After earning a law degree from the University of California's Hastings College of Law in 1976, she joined the staff of Democratic congressman Leo Ryan, serving as his legal counsel. Spier accompanied Ryan in

November 1978 when he traveled to Jonestown, Guyana, to investigate allegations that hundreds of American citizens who had relocated to Jonestown at the urging of cult leader Jim Jones were being subjected to abuse and were in physical danger. During their visit, Ryan and his group were ambushed by Jones's followers in an attack that killed Ryan and four members of his delegation (including one cult member who begged to leave Guyana with the congressman). Spier was shot five times and did not receive medical aid for twenty-two hours. Meanwhile, Jones recognized that the attack on Ryan's group meant that Jonestown's days were numbered. He responded by orchestrating a mass suicide in Jonestown that claimed the lives of more than nine hundred cult members.

After recovering from the wounds she suffered in Guyana, Spier served eighteen years in the California State Legislature—first running for the California State Assembly in 1986 and then winning election to the California State Senate in 1998. She was elected to the U.S. House of Representatives in 2008, and as of 2020, she continues to represent California's Fourteenth District in Washington. A year prior to her successful run for Congress, Speier coauthored the book *This Is Not the Life I Ordered: 50 Ways to Keep Your Head above Water When Life Keeps Dragging You Down* and later released a revised version. In 2018, she published the book *Undaunted: Surviving Jonestown, Summoning Courage, and Fighting Back* to document her near-death experience during the Jonestown shooting.

Representative Speier, a member of the Democratic Party, is a supporter of the Women's Economic Agenda, an advocate for women's rights, and a cosponsor of the Pregnant Workers Fairness Act. In 2014, she hosted an entrepreneurial event for women called Ready, Set, SUCCEED. She has also sponsored or cosponsored several signature pieces of legislation. Every Congress since 2013, she has sponsored a bill removing the deadline for the ratification of the Equal Rights Amendment (HR Res 113—113th Congress, HR Res 51—114th Congress, and HR Res 53—115th Congress). During the 111th Congress, Representative Speier sponsored H.R. 1887, a bill that established the Presidential Commission on Women Act of 2009. The purpose of the legislation was to review the status of women in the nation and to assess the federal government's aid to and promotion of women. In 2011, Speier gave a personal account of her own abortion experience in a speech on the House floor opposing a proposal to reduce Title X funding for clinics that provide gynecological and other health services to women and families.

On November 15, 2017, Representative Speier introduced the ME TOO Congress Act, which would amend the Congressional Accountability Act of 1995 by providing procedures for the investigation and resolution of allegations against legislative employers. The bill also included protections against sexual harassment and required the updating of programs of sexual harassment prevention. Representative Speier has sponsored and introduced several other bills in the U.S. House of Representatives to protect women, minorities, and members of the LGBTQ community as well. This legislation includes the HALT Campus Sexual Violence Act, the Pink Tax Repeal Act, and Closing the Law Enforcement Consent Loophole Act of 2018. She was also instrumental in the creation of National Rosie the Riveter Day, which was first celebrated on March 21, 2018. Finally, she has joined with a wide range of Equal Rights Amendment supporters, from actresses Alyssa Milano and Patricia Arquette to Representative Carolyn Maloney (D-NY) and other congresswomen, to keep that proposed constitutional amendment in the public eye.

Charles Adams and Arelia Johnson

See also: Congress; #MeToo Movement; Milano, Alyssa; Sexual Harassment Training; Title IX

Further Reading

Congress.gov. 2018. "H.R.6568—Closing the Law Enforcement Consent Loophole Act of 2018." https://www.congress.gov/bill/115th-congress/house-bill/6568.

Huffman, Jared. 2017. "Lawmakers Introduce Bipartisan, Bicameral Resolution to Designate 'National Rosie the Riveter Day.'" huffman.house.gov/media-center/press-releases/lawmakers-introduce-bipartisan-bicameral-resolution-to-designate-national-rosie-the-riveter-day.

Speier, Jackie. 2015. "Congresswoman Speier Introduces Resolution to Allow for Ratification of the Equal Rights Amendment." May 14, 2015. https://speier.house.gov/2015/5/congresswoman-speier-introduces-resolution-allow-ratification-equal.

Speier, Jackie. 2018. *Undaunted: Surviving Jonestown, Summoning Courage, and Fighting Back*. New York: Little A.

Stalking

According to the National Institute of Justice (2007), the legal definition of stalking refers to the willful, malicious, and repeated pattern of behaviors and harassing of another person that threatens one's safety and produces fear in the targeted person.

The National Intimate Partner and Sexual Violence Survey (NISVS) estimates that in the United States, 1 in 6 women (16 percent, or 19.1 million) and 1 in 17 men (5.8 percent, or 6.4 million) have been stalked at some point in their lives, with the average first stalking encounter occurring prior to age eighteen for the victim. Women are also more likely to be targeted for cyberstalking—the practice of using electronic communications such as email, phones, and social media to harass and threaten someone with physical or emotional injury—than men. According to the NISVS, 14.3 percent of an estimated 2,618,000 women respondents and 9.4 percent of an estimated 607,000 men respondents have experienced cyberstalking during their lifetime. According to the same sources, when accounting for race and the past twelve months of stalking occurrences, Black respondents reported experiencing higher prevalence of stalking (5 percent for women and 2.9 percent for men) compared to white respondents (4 percent for women and 1.5 percent for men).

According to national experts, stalking activities include physically following targets from a distance; using cameras, listening devices, and other technology to spy on them; leaving unwanted gifts; showing up uninvited at the home, school, or workplace of the victim; and unlawful entry or damage to the property of targeted individuals. In addition, stalkers frequently make their victims aware that they have invaded their personal space. It is also common for stalkers to threaten violence against family, friends, and pets of victims and to bully them with unwanted excessive phone calls, texts, or voice messages.

Cyberstalking has added another layer of menace to many stalking cases. Harassment through media platforms such as Facebook, Twitter, and Instagram or electronic communication channels such as text or email is on the rise.

A 2017 summary published by the U.S. Department of Justice highlighted that victims of stalking tend to know their stalkers in some capacity. Although the full extent of the psychological damage of stalking on victims is a subject of continued research, it is well documented that stalking causes fear and substantial emotional distress. Even in instances when stalking ceases, the victim-survivor likely experiences distress in believing that the behavior will eventually resume.

LAWS COMBATING STALKING

The Violence Against Women Act (VAWA) of 1994 (P.L. 103-322) is the first U.S. federal policy intended to combat violence against women. Among other interventions, the VAWA Reauthorization Act of 2013 amended the Jeanne Clery Act, obligating educational institutions participating in federal financial aid programs to gather and publicly disclose statistics of stalking as well as domestic violence and dating violence.

While there remain widespread debates across social justice platforms on defining and measuring stalking, the progressive efforts of the Jeanne Clery Act set a precedent by the U.S. Department of Education. Continued preventative approaches are needed to deter stalking and reinforce guidelines to support designated representatives to safeguard victim-survivors from stalking (i.e., enforcing PPOs) and conducting timely and impartial investigations.

Personal protection orders (PPO) are court orders meant to stop acts of harassment, threats, or stalking. However, many cases of stalking tend to go unreported or underreported for fear of retaliation by the stalker or fear of not being believed by law enforcement. Distrust of law enforcement and skepticism about the effectiveness of the criminal justice system may also diminish the likelihood of reporting stalking activity.

Women's rights activists and law enforcement experts alike agree that the United States must do more to understand how frequently stalking occurs and to establish and enforce aggressive anti-stalking and anti-bullying policies. Experts also urge people to be diligent about protecting themselves by logging out of social media platforms, changing settings on social media pages to private, using strong passwords, and refusing social media friend requests from unknown persons. Victims are urged to seek support from family, friends, and within the school or workplace as well as from law enforcement. A communal response is required to eradicate stalking.

Selena T. Rodgers and Durrell Malik Washington Sr.

See also: Campus Accountability and Safety Act (CASA); Hostile Work Environment; Statute of Limitations

Further Reading

Centers for Disease Control and Prevention. 2018. "Preventing Stalking." https://www
.cdc.gov/violenceprevention/intimatepartnerviolence/stalking/fastfact.html.

Gill, A. 2018. "Survivor-Centered Research: Towards an Intersectional Gender-Based
Violence Movement." *Journal of Interpersonal Violence* 33: 559–562.

Logan, T. K., and Robert Walker. 2019. "The Impact of Stalking-Related Fear and Gender on
Personal Safety Outcomes." *Journal of Interpersonal Violence* (February 10): 1–23.

National Institute of Justice. 2007. "Overview of Stalking." October 24. https://nij.ojp.gov
/topics/articles/overview-stalking.

Sameer, H. 2018. "Cyberstalking." Cyberbullying Research Center, March 21. https://
cyberbullying.org/cyberstalking.

Smith, Sharon G., et al. 2018. *The National Intimate Partner and Sexual Violence Survey
(NISVS): 2015 Data Brief—Updated Release.* Atlanta, GA: National Center for
Injury Prevention and Control, Centers for Disease Control and Prevention.

U.S. Bureau of Justice Statistics. 2017. "Stalking." Office of Justice Programs. https://
www.bjs.gov/index.cfm?ty=tp&tid=973.

State Legislatures

Sexual harassment refers to unwanted sexual relations imposed by superiors on
subordinates at work or in other settings. Since the emergence of the #MeToo
Movement in 2017, there have been increased efforts to bring awareness of sexual
harassment and to adopt policies and laws to stamp out such behavior. Sexual
harassment can occur in many societal settings, but much of the reform focus has
been directed toward sexual harassment in the workplace, where most victims are
women. It was in this #MeToo environment of reform and of speaking out against
long-standing abuses by men in positions of power, that revelations of sexual
harassment in statehouses and state governments across the country finally came
to light.

In the wake of the rise of the #MeToo Movement, legislatures in many regions
of the country were embarrassed by news stories revealing rampant and systemic
patterns of sexual misconduct and harassment by lawmakers. *Politico* reported in
November 2017, for example, that "amid a flood of recent testimonials from female
legislators, staff and lobbyists, a portrait is fast emerging of male-dominated state
capitol cultures rife with sexual harassment and bereft of protections for victims,
where complaints from women frequently languish—or are outright ignored"
(Korecki, Marinucci, and Vielkind 2017).

As outrage over these revelations increased, legislators belatedly introduced
and supported several laws and regulations to address workplace sexual harassment in state legislatures. For example, in 2018 alone, over 125 pieces of legislation were introduced in thirty-two states. These states introduced legislation to
expel members, criminalize sexual harassment in the legislature, and mandate
harassment training within the legislature.

Most of the policies addressing sexual harassment in the statehouse are in their
early stages of development. Even though many of the policies and programs

designed to help eradicate sexual harassment within the statehouses are similar to other business policies and practices. There are subtle differences within the statehouses where specific policies have to be tailored to help address the different dynamics. For example, partisan political factors can add another layer of stigmatization or public scrutiny to the reaction of political constituents, lobbyists, news stations, and the general public to charges of sexual harassment in statehouses. These considerations can further complicate the decisions of victims of sexual misconduct and harassment to come forward. Furthermore, there are numerous reasons beyond victim publicity as to why individuals' decisions may be influenced regarding whether to report sexual harassment. Some of these reasons may include victims' fear regarding retaliation, political blackmail, or the notoriety generated by reporting sexual harassment, all of which can imperil one's career and economic security.

In 2018, over 170 women who work at the Washington State Capitol signed a letter demanding change. The letter came after women accused two former lawmakers of sexual misconduct. Other women at the capitol have also come forward and reported experiencing sexist comments and sexual harassment, such as unwanted advances, groping, inappropriate comments and jokes, and assault.

The case of Kirsten Anderson illustrates the changes brought forth by women working in statehouses across the nation. Anderson filed a sexual harassment lawsuit in October 2014 against her employer, the Iowa Senate, where she worked as a communications director. During this time frame, women comprised one-fifth of the Iowa Senate. Given the small percentage of women, the caucus had turned into an environment that allowed inappropriate and sexually discriminatory behavior. Instead of reporting incidents, male and female staff were quiet bystanders, even as they witnessed sexual innuendo and other inappropriate behavior exhibited by their male coworkers, supervisors, and state senators. However, several people admitted the reporting policies and procedures were outdated, in need of revision, and incomplete and that staff often lacked knowledge of steps to report sexual harassment incidents.

Anderson's case showed the extent to which sexual harassment and misconduct had become normalized in some statehouses. For instance, the first time Anderson reported the harassment, her supervisor offered her two options: (1) he could ask the individual to stop harassing her politely over coffee, or (2) she could file a complaint, but this would put a black mark on the accused employee's file, which would be disastrous to his career. As the acts became more egregious, Anderson and a female colleague reported the new incidents to a staff director. When nothing came of this and the harassment continued, Anderson reported the behavior to the Senate minority leader. The results were shocking; instead of taking steps to stop the sexual harassment, Anderson's superiors and other male staff harassed her.

Anderson explained that the work environment was a toxic space where derogatory and vile terms toward women had become commonplace. She stated that it started with referencing her as "one of the boys," where male colleagues felt comfortable to talk about women's body parts and comment on her appearance. The acts progressively became more intolerable as male staff asked her to view pictures of naked women on their computers and made sexually crude comments about female lawmakers.

After Anderson's unsuccessful attempts to file complaints, she was fired. She then sued the state for wrongful termination and sexual harassment in the workplace. She stated the lawsuit was no longer just about her own experience but that of all women in the workplace. Anderson's case ushered in long overdue reforms. Iowa's State Legislature reviewed and developed new training for employees. It also implemented new policies and procedures on the process to follow to report sexual harassment.

Future research on sexual harassment in state legislatures across the country will likely be influenced by shifting gender dynamics as well as the commitment of state political leaders to eradicate all forms of sexual harassment in the statehouses and detoxify workplace environments. Failure to cast a broad enough net to capture all forms of sexual harassment and provide solutions may result in some instances being driven further underground. It is essential that research is conducted to guide in developing policies to create an atmosphere where victims can report and receive the appropriate services and that no sexual harassment perpetrator is safe from identification and prosecution.

Suman Kakar, Brent Blakeman, and Wendy Dressler

See also: #MeToo Movement; Office/Workplace Settings; Time's Up Movement

Further Reading

Kirsten Anderson vs. The State of Iowa. Case No. LACL131321. August 2, 2017. http://cdn .radioiowa.com/wp-content/uploads/2017/08/170802-ST-BIS-Motion-for -JNOV.pdf.

Korecki, Natasha, Carla Marinucci, and Jimmy Vielkind. 2017. "Sexual Misconduct Allegations Rock Statehouses." *Politico*, November 5. https://www.politico.com/story /2017/11/05/sexual-misconduct-allegations-statehouses-244555.

National Conference of State Legislatures. 2019. "2018 Legislation on Sexual Harassment in the Legislature." February 11. http://www.ncsl.org/research/about-state-legislatures /2018-legislative-sexual-harassment-legislation.aspx.

"175 Women Demand Change to Culture, Sexual Harassment Policies at Washington Legislature." 2018. KNKX, March 1. https://www.knkx.org/post/175-women -demand-change-culture-sexual-harassment-policies-washington-legislature.

Statute of Limitations

A statute of limitations is a legal provision that limits the time in which a legal case can be brought. In criminal cases, statutes of limitations bar prosecution if a certain amount of time has passed from the date of the offense. In civil cases, such rules prevent a party from suing if the requisite time has elapsed after the harm occurred or was discovered. Time limits vary significantly from state to state and at the federal level for criminal offenses such as groping or rape, and they are notoriously short for civil harms such as sexual harassment. As a result, the pursuit of a claim may depend on where and in what circumstances an incident occurred, and claims that have merit may not ever be pursued by the justice system simply because the time limit for that particular alleged offense has expired. Many critics assert that short and arbitrary statute of limitations periods can contribute to a culture of impunity for legitimate sexual misconduct claims.

The purpose of statutes of limitations is to promote fairness and efficiency in the legal system. In theory, evidence is easier to obtain and more reliable if an incident recently occurred, and legislators traditionally assumed that legitimate victims come forward quickly. Time limits protect an accused innocent from defending against a claim in circumstances where memories have faded and witnesses are not available. Prohibiting the adjudication of so-called stale cases brings finality and reliability to the legal system. However, research demonstrates that in sexual misconduct cases, victims often do not report abuse immediately. They may fear physical, professional, or personal retaliation; be traumatized; or think they will not be believed. Moreover, institutions that fail to report abuse, deny claims, or "pass the trash" isolate victims, adding to delays. Reformers claim that state and federal legislators, who establish statutes of limitations, have historically not taken victims' considerations into sufficient account. Victim advocates argue that short statutes of limitations "place an overwhelming burden on victims and allow sexual predators to evade punishment" (Padawer 2018), contributing to the low prosecution rate in sexual assault cases.

Determining the time limit that applies to prosecuting an alleged crime is not easy. It depends on the type of offense and its classification, whether the victim reported the crime (in some jurisdictions, the time frame is shorter if the crime was not reported), whether the state allows an exception when DNA or other evidence is discovered, and whether the victim was a minor. In some states, for certain crimes, the time limit does not begin to run until the victim turns eighteen or becomes aware of injuries. Statutes of limitations are inconsistent from state-to-state and even within states across different areas of the law. A state may have a shorter time period for a civil tort claim (where the victim seeks financial compensation from the accused) as compared to a criminal claim (brought by prosecutors). There are no time limits, however, for some serious crimes (like homicide and acts of terrorism).

High-profile child sexual abuse cases, and more recently the #MeToo Movement, have led to reforms in dozens of states in which it was determined that existing statutes of limitations were an obstacle to pursuing abusers. Ten states have abolished time limits for the most serious sexual offenses, but some have a short time limit. Connecticut, for example, has a five-year time limit for aggravated sexual assault involving an adult victim. For employment discrimination, claims must be filed within 180 days of the last incident of harassment or relevant event (extended to 300 days depending on the state), shorter than limits in other civil areas. Time limits for tort claims related to violent incidents may be one or two years, and the time is not extended by a criminal or administrative case on the same issue.

Marny Requa

See also: Equal Employment Opportunity Commission (EEOC); #MeToo Movement; "Passing the Trash"; Rape, Abuse & Incest National Network (RAINN)

Further Reading

Crump, D. 2016. "Statutes of Limitations: The Underlying Principles." *University of Louisville Law Review* 54: 437–453.

Garner, B. A., ed. 2015. "Statute of Limitations." *Black's Law Dictionary*. 10th ed. St. Paul, MN: Thomson West.

Khorram, E. 2012. "Crossing the Limit Line: Sexual Abuse and Whether Retroactive Application of Civil Statutes of Limitations Are Legal." *UC Davis Journal of Juvenile Law & Policy* 16: 391–426.

Mizrahi, R. 2018. "Sexual Harassment Law after #MeToo: Looking to California as a Model." *Yale Law Journal Forum* 128: 121–151.

Padawer, R. 2018. "Should Statutes of Limitations for Rape Be Abolished?" *New York Times Magazine*, June 19.

Rape, Abuse & Incest National Network. 2018. "State by State Guide on Statutes of Limitations." Accessed August 6, 2018. www.rainn.org/state-state-guide-statutes -limitations.

U.S. Equal Employment Opportunity Commission. 2018. "Time Limits for Filing a Charge." Accessed August 7, 2018. https://www.eeoc.gov/employees/timeliness.cfm.

STEM Fields

In 2006, Tarana Burke coined the phrase *Me Too* in efforts to draw attention to women who have survived sexual violence as well as the frequency with which sexual harassment, assault, and other forms of abuse are tolerated in American society. Over a decade later, the #MeToo Movement emerged to lead a broad societal campaign against sexual harassment.

Campus sexual harassment first received meaningful research scrutiny back in 1957 when Clifford Kirkpatrick and Eugene Kanin published their study on "Male Sex Aggression on a University Campus." In 1987, Mary P. Koss, Christine Gidycz, and Nadine Wisniewski, conducted one of the largest scientific studies on campus sexual assault. Their research eventually morphed into the book *I Never Called It Rape* (1994) by Robin Warshaw.

STEM (science, technology, engineering, and math) faculty as well as social science and humanities faculty have been accused of engaging in acts of sexual harassment and gender discrimination not only against undergraduate students but also graduate assistants, adjunct faculty, and tenure-track faculty. Gender-based sexual harassment occurs in many forms and has a detrimental and lasting effect on colleges and universities.

Colleges and universities have based sexual harassment complaints, investigations, and disciplinary proceedings on protocols provided by Title IX and, in some cases, additional measures introduced by the institutions' legal and human resources departments. However, Title IX has experienced many changes in the past few years, and the emergence of the #MeToo Movement has increased pressure on school administrations to take strong actions to stamp out sexual harassment, sexual assault, and other forms of sexual misconduct on their campuses. However, some critics contend that new policy shifts and training modalities have failed to keep up with the changing landscape. They charge that too little is done to protect victims who file complaints from being subject to threats and intimidation by perpetrators and their allies on campus. These factors place survivors of harassment in difficult and potentially compromising positions that can permanently impact their lives and careers. Some recent efforts have been made within discipline-specific groups to help shift the atmosphere and behaviors on college campuses. However, there is still much more work to be done.

SEXUAL HARASSMENT AND STEM FACULTY

One of the chief areas of focus for activists seeking to address sexual misconduct in college and university settings concerns STEM (science, technology, engineering, and math) fields, which have historically been dominated by male students. In 2018, the National Academies of Sciences, Engineering, and Medicine commissioned a study based on data from two large universities to assist in evaluating harassment from faculty and staff. The results indicated at least one in five female science students experienced harassment from faculty or staff members. Although harassment policies (additional human resources protocols and Title IX) have been designed to provide legal assistance to educational institutions in order for them to provide clear access to procedures and an understanding of the processes for the victim and the offender. In addition, these policies have been designed to provide relevant guidance with reporting and with the court system. However, they have done little to change behaviors of those who commit egregious acts of gender or sexual harassment. Although early policies were drafted to consider rights of victims and suspected perpetrators and to balance needs for campuses, reinforcement of policies has been difficult, and recent ongoing changes to Title IX with the U.S. Department of Education has presented challenges. Recommendations were encouraged to implement policies, procedures, and guidelines to prevent sexual harassment in academia. Researchers concluded that sexual harassment issues in academia can no longer be viewed as simply "a few bad apples in the basket." The extent to which this has worked has been difficult to assess with the changing rules and guidelines for reporting.

Sexual harassment is a social and public health problem within the college and university systems. Gender and sexual harassment hurt constructive scientific research initiatives and work productivity and can damage careers permanently for both perpetrators and survivors. Students' (undergraduates and graduates) grades and academic performances suffer. As was discovered within the margins of colleges' and universities' STEM departments, harassment from faculty and academic administrators have ranged from unwanted sexual behaviors (in professor-student interactions, at academic conferences, etc.) to gender discrimination (with treatment of pregnant women, promotions within faculty, etc.) The major predictor of whether the STEM department had problems with sexual harassment, which resulted from findings of the National Academies study, was the organizational climate.

Additional studies have suggested that over 50 percent of women who work professionally within the sciences and math fields have experienced gender-based harassment and discrimination (Skelly 2017). There is also evidence to suggest other barriers exist not only for women but also for people of color. Many incidents and situations tend to occur outside the classroom, either in the field or lab environ-ment, in nontraditional, informal settings. "This informality breeds a sense of uncertainty, a blurring of lines between professional and personal" (Skelly 2017).

At the University of California, Berkeley, professor and astronomer Geoffrey Marcy was determined to be a serial harasser for over a decade. The result of the investigation was that he was only given a warning. Although there was denuncia-tion of the recommendation and he ultimately resigned, the institution was harshly criticized for its response. Elsewhere, critics contend that academic institutions and STEM departments have been slow to recognize the persistent problem and take stronger action against complaints.

California Institute of Technology (Caltech) suspended a professor in 2015 due to two specific complaints from graduate students based on Title IX and gender discrimination. After a lengthy investigation, the university suspended the ten-ured professor, and the committee defended taking its time to help ensure trans-parency of the proceedings and support the privacy of those involved. Caltech was applauded for its thoroughness and consideration to complainants. At the Univer-sity of Chicago, several female graduate students filed complaints against a biol-ogy professor for making unwanted sexual advances at an off-campus retreat. The professor left before any disciplinary actions were taken by the university.

Nonetheless, Title IX and sexual harassment accusations and scandals across American colleges and universities remain a prevalent issue. Unfortunately, the impact is significant in the area of STEM professorships and researchers. Efforts to recruit women to STEM fields are difficult, and retention rates are low. Women faced with these persistent problems as well as general gender discrimination often end up choosing other academic and career paths.

In February 2019, Texas A&M was approached by the National Science Foun-dation (NSF) to conduct a two-year "pan-disciplinary" study on sexual harass-ment issues within the STEM field, to be led by ethics expert Dr. Susan Fortney. Dr. Fortney and her team of investigators hope to not only do a comprehensive and extensive study on the topic across the United States but also to develop tools that institutions can implement to prevent harassment from occurring. Universities and colleges with STEM departments must address the sexually hostile environ-ments and prioritize creating a safe and secure environment for students, faculty, and staff of both genders to ensure proper ethical execution of research and sup-port for continued interest in the career pathways.

Cathryn Lavery

See also: Burke, Tarana; Gender Equality; #MeToo Movement; Sexual Harassment Train-ing; Title IX

Further Reading

Burke, T. 2018. "Founder of #MeToo Movement Talk (Speech)." AUSG Women's Initia-tive Award for Excellence in Activism. February 10, 2018. American University.

Diep, F. 2018. "How Academics in STEM Fields Are Combating Sexual Harassment." *The Week*, July 10. https://theweek.com/articles/781140/how-academics-stem-fields-are-combating-sexual-harassment.

Kirkpatrick, C., and E. Kanin. 1957. "Male Sex Aggression on a University Campus." *American Sociological Review* 22(10): 52–58.

Koss, M. P., C. A. Gidycz, and N. Wisniewski. 1987. "The Scope of Rape: Incidence and Prevalence of Sexual Aggression and Victimization in a National Sample of Higher Education Students." *Journal of Consulting & Clinical Psychology* 55(2): 162–170.

Mervis, J. 2016. "Caltech Suspends Professor for Harassment." *Scientific Community* 351(6270): 216. https:/doi.org/10.1126/science.351.6270.216.

Skelly, S. 2017. "Professor Becca Barnes, Fighting Sexual Harassment in STEM." *The Catalyst*, September 29. https://serc.carleton.edu/advancegeo/news/news/192162.html.

Strategic Harassment

Broadly defined, *harassment* is a form of discrimination that violates national laws such as the Title VII of the Civil Rights Act of 1964, Age Discrimination in Employment Act, and Americans with Disabilities Act. Conduct that could be seen as harassment is unwelcome and based on age, race, ethnicity, sex, and even disability. It becomes unlawful when the offensive behavior becomes a condition of employment or when it creates a work environment that is hostile (U.S. Equal Employment Opportunity Commission n.d.). Harassment can be broken down into subtypes, such as sexual and quid pro quo harassment, but a less visible type is specific to a work environment or territory. Otherwise known as strategic or territorial harassment, these are actions that are used to maintain privilege in workplace locations that are typically male-dominated (Martin 1996).

The #MeToo Movement has shed light on harassment in a general sense as well as on incidents of strategic harassment specifically. As more women enter the workforce, more harassment cases have come to the surface. In a study conducted around the time of the #MeToo Movement, researchers found that 38 percent of women surveyed had experienced harassment in the workplace (Stop Street Harassment 2018). This increase coincides with an increase in the percentage of women working outside the home, whether by choice or necessity (e.g., higher numbers of females have become the only means of support for families). In 2017, women were primary or sole earners for 40 percent of households with children under the age of eighteen. In male-dominated professions, especially in STEM occupations, women are still underrepresented (DeWolf 2017). But what drives strategic harassment?

A majority of strategic harassers commit it unconsciously and believe they are making innocent fun (Hendriksen 2017). The minority do so consciously to humiliate the victim. In the workplace, harassment can be used to intimidate and discourage women who try to work in male-dominated professions. These professions include the military, politics, and STEM professions such as mathematics, engineering, or computer science. This harassment can also be seen as a desire to protect occupational territory, where a woman may be seen as trying to take what men deem to be rightfully theirs or as a threat to their manhood (McLaughlin, Uggen, and Blackstone 2012). Harassment of the strategic variety can also be motivated by an actual or perceived power disparity between two people. This is more commonly seen in male-dominated professions.

Additionally, the vulnerable-victim hypothesis argues that men harass women because the latter are more vulnerable or underrepresented in some occupations (DeWolf 2017). This is also in line with threats to power, which explains that women in authority positions are more likely to be victims of harassment than both men and women in nonauthority positions (Yonack 2017). Lastly, Raewyn Connell's theory of hegemonic masculinity, first offered in 1987 and further refined in 2005, posits that society privileges one distinct gender stereotype and harassment is used as a tool to enforce appropriate female subordinate behavior and to punish female gender nonconformity. This is also in line with Susan Faludi's work indicating that harassment is connected with males' perceptions about the proper gender roles of a man in today's society (Faludi 1991). Thus, harassment may be used as a means of protecting a man's traditional dominance, gender roles, and economic status in American society.

Kaitlyn Brenna Hoover

See also: Equal Employment Opportunity Commission (EEOC); Quid Pro Quo; Sexual Harassment Training; Title VII of the Civil Rights Act of 1964

Further Reading

Chamberlain, L., Martha Crowley, Daniel Tope, and Randy Hodson. 2008. "Sexual Harassment in Organizational Context." *Work and Occupations* 35: 262–295.

Connell, R. W. 1987. *Gender and Power: Society, the Person, and Sexual Politics.* Stanford, CA: Stanford University Press.

Connley, C. 2017. *3 Psychologists Explain Why Men Harass Women in the Workplace.* https://www.cnbc.com/2017/11/20/3-psychologists-explain-why-men-harass -women-in-the-workplace.html.

DeWolf, M. 2017. *12 Stats about Working Women.* https://blog.dol.gov/2017/03/01/12-stats -about-working-women.

Faludi, S. 1991. *Backlash: The Undeclared War against American Women.* Manhattan, NY: Crown Publishing.

Hendriksen, E. 2017. *Four Psychological Traits of Sexual Harassers.* https://www .psychologytoday.com/us/blog/how-be-yourself/201711/four-psychological-traits -sexual-harassers.

Martin, B. 1996. "Sexual Harassment and Nonviolent Action." *Nonviolence Today* 48: 8–9.

McLaughlin, Heather, Christopher Uggen, and Amy Blackstone. 2012. "Sexual Harassment, Workplace Authority, and the Paradox of Power." *American Sociological Review* 77(4): 625–647. https://doi.org/10.1177/0003122412451728.

Stop Street Harassment. 2018. *2018 Study on Sexual Harassment and Assault.* http://www .stopstreetharassment.org/resources/2018-national-sexual-abuse-report/.

U.S Equal Employment Opportunity Commission. n.d. "Harassment." https://www.eeoc .gov/laws/types/harassment.cfm.

Willer, R. 2005. "Overdoing Gender: A Test of Masculine Overcompensation Thesis." Paper presented at the American Sociological Association Annual Meeting, Philadelphia, PA.

Yonack, L. 2017. "Sexual Assault Is about Power: How the #MeToo Campaign Is Restoring Power to Victims." *Psychology Today*, November 14. https://www.psychologytoday .com/us/blog/psychoanalysis-unplugged/201711/sexual-assault-is-about-power.

Street Harassment

Street harassment, a global phenomenon, is the most common form of sexual violence. Street harassment is often discussed interchangeably with sexual harassment. While sexual harassment usually occurs in the workplace, street harassment includes unwanted comments, unsolicited physical contact, catcalling, honking, whistling, exposing oneself, taunting with sexual demands, creating an unwelcome atmosphere charged with sexuality, and ogling in public and semipublic contexts, including the street, public transportation, parks, malls, and recreation venues. Overwhelmingly, although not exclusively, the perpetrators of street harassment are men, and the targets of street harassment are women. More often than not, the perpetrators of the harassment do not know the individuals they are harassing.

Many argue that street harassment is a collection of unwanted attention and actions meant to ensure existing systems of male dominance remain unchanged. Although less frequently discussed, a similar argument can be made for "straight" dominance, when gay men and nongender binary identifying individuals are targeted. The combination of a hostile atmosphere and physical danger maintain a society where the targets' status as subordinates remains and where their entry into and actions within spaces can be restricted and controlled. Research demonstrates that street harassment is more likely to invoke fear in the target when the aggressor is older, when the target of the harassment is alone, when the harassment occurs at night, when the harassment is persistent and the aggressor is in close physical proximity to the target, and when it includes touching.

Many women, gay men, and non-gender-binary-identifying individuals see street harassment as an unpleasant but common and unavoidable part of existence. Furthermore, research indicates that the more minority statuses one holds, the more likely one is to experience street harassment and that the street harassment of individuals who hold multiple minority statuses is different (it occurs more often and is more common) than those of individuals who possess a single minority status. Victims of street harassment can experience uneasiness and generalized anxiety, and many experience one or more symptoms of post-traumatic stress disorder (PTSD).

Perpetrators of street harassment have often claimed that their behavior is protected by laws assuring the right to free speech. Many times, perpetrators claim that their actions are complimentary and that the victims should interpret the actions as such.

In the 2000s, as knowledge and concerns about societal problems with sexual harassment grew, campaigns to combat street harassment gained greater prominence. These include Hollaback!, an international organization founded in 2005 with the aim of making public spaces safe for all individuals through bystander intervention training, advocacy training, and research. The organization Stop Street Harassment monitors the work of local groups attempting to combat street harassment worldwide. Street harassment has been banned in Peru and France and in some U.S. states and some areas of the Philippines.

Sarah F. Fischer

See also: Catcalls

Further Reading

Davis, Deirdre. 1994. "The Harm That Has No Name: Street Harassment, Embodiment, and African American Women." *UCLA Women's Law Journal* 4: 135–178.

Fileborn, Bianca. 2013. "Conceptual Understandings and Prevalence of Sexual Harassment and Street Harassment." Accessed January 31, 2019. https://aifs.gov.au/sites/default/files/publication-documents/rs6.pdf.

Vera-Gray, Fiona. 2017. *Men's Intrusion, Women's Embodiment: A Critical Analysis of Street Harassment.* New York: Routledge.

Swift, Taylor (1989–)

Taylor Swift is best known as one of the most famous American pop stars, but in 2017, she also made headlines when she related her own experiences as a victim of sexual harassment in a highly publicized civil trial.

Swift was born on December 13, 1989, in Reading, Pennsylvania. At a young age, she became interested in music and began performing in local theater productions. She moved to Hendersonville, Tennessee, a suburb of Nashville, with her family at the age of fourteen to pursue a music career. She signed with Big Machine Records in 2005 and released her first album, *Taylor Swift*, in 2006. Over the next eleven years, Swift released six studio albums, and she has won numerous awards and is one of the best-selling musical artists of all time.

On June 2, 2013, Swift held a "meet and greet" promotional event prior to a concert at the Pepsi Center in Denver, Colorado. During the meet and greet, David Mueller, a radio DJ for local station KYGO, and his girlfriend posed for a photo with Swift. Immediately following the photo, Swift approached her mother, Andrea, and told her that David Mueller had reached under her skirt and grabbed her butt during the photo. Swift's mother and other members of her team met with her radio promotions director prior to the concert to discuss the incident. Following that meeting, Swift's security team contacted Mueller and accused him of inappropriately touching Swift. Mueller was subsequently removed from the concert venue. The next day, a member of Swift's team contacted the vice president of KYGO regarding the incident, leading to the suspension of Mueller without pay and a formal investigation of Swift's allegations. When questioned about his behavior, Mueller denied touching Swift in an inappropriate way, but on June 4, 2013, he was fired from KYGO for violating a morality clause within his contract.

Mueller then filed a $3 million suit against Swift in September 2015, claiming that her false claims led to his termination and the loss of other business opportunities. A month later, Swift filed a countersuit claiming assault and battery and requesting $1. This amount was a symbolic gesture to demonstrate that he was guilty, despite the fact that she did not need (or want) his money. She just wanted to prove a point. In February 2016, Mueller also filed slander claims against Swift regarding the incident. Swift gave her initial deposition in July 2016, providing detailed information about what happened in 2013. In May 2017, Judge William Martinez determined that the case should go to a jury. The trial began on August 7, 2017.

During the trial, Swift provided detailed, straightforward testimony when questioned about the events of June 2, 2013. The content of her testimony—which effectively rejected all attempts by Mueller's lawyers to pin blame for the disc jockey's own behavior on Swift—and the strength she showed during the proceedings were applauded in the media and by many other organizations and individuals both in and out of the women's rights movement. After four hours of deliberation, the jury reached its decision, and Judge Martinez dismissed Mueller's claim of defamation as well as his suit against Swift as a result of the evidence submitted during trial, awarding Swift her $1 countersuit.

Since the trial ended, Swift has been praised for her willingness to be so open about such a personal incident. She has been credited with calling attention to the necessity of being vocal about sexual assault and harassment. She was also identified as one of the "Silence Breakers" in *Time* magazine's 2017 Person of the Year issue, which dealt specifically with women speaking out about sexual assault and harassment. Although Swift acknowledged that she had intentionally been out of the public eye during and after her trial, she gave her first interview since the trial to *Time*. During the interview, she spoke about the shame that victims often feel and how many times they are blamed for their victimization. She encouraged victims to report their sexual assault or harassment and called for changes in how society views perpetrators as well as victims of sexual harassment and assault.

On the one-year anniversary of her win in court, Swift addressed the crowd at a concert in Tampa, Florida. She thanked her fans and her personal support system for standing behind her and believing her when others did not. She has expressed a desire to help other victims who are not as fortunate as her and has been reported to have made donations to organizations that help defend sexual assault and harassment victims.

Darla D. Darno

See also: Music/Video Settings; *Time Magazine* "Silence Breakers"

Further Reading

Dockterman, Eliana. 2017. "'I Was Angry.' Taylor Swift on What Powered Her Sexual Assault Testimony," *Time*, December 6. Accessed October 10, 2018. http://time.com/5049659/taylor-swift-interview-person-of-the-year-2017/.

Stelloh, Tim. 2017. "Jury Sides with Taylor Swift in Sexual Assault Trial." NBC News, August 14. Accessed October 12, 2018. https://www.nbcnews.com/pop-culture/pop-culture-news/taylor-swift-sexual-assault-trial-heads-jury-n792636.

Zacharek, Stephanie, Eliana Dockterman, and Haley Sweetland Edwards. 2017. "*Time* Person of the Year 2017: The Silence Breakers." *Time*, December 18. Accessed October 10, 2018. http://time.com/time-person-of-the-year-2017-silence-breakers/.

T

Tailhook

For many, the word *Tailhook* is synonymous with sexual assault, harassment, scandal, leadership failure, and cover-up. The event to which it refers, an official U.S. military conference that degenerated into a frenzy of sexual assault, brought the issue of sexual abuse and harassment of women in the military to the attention of the American public. Newspapers and news broadcasts across the nation provided extensive coverage of the despicable acts that occurred as part of the 35th Annual Tailhook Symposium that took place at a Las Vegas, Nevada, Hilton on September 5–7, 1991. During this symposium, over one hundred U.S. Navy and Marine Corps aviators were accused of sexually assaulting eighty-three women and seven men, many of whom were fellow service members (Johnson 2015).

A tailhook, for which the Tailhook organization is named, is a retractable hook on the underbelly of the tail end of a carrier-based aircraft. It is designed to catch the arresting-gear cable when landing on the deck of an aircraft carrier, thereby bringing the aircraft to a controlled stop. Tailhook, the organization, is an internationally recognized lobbyist organization and a staunch supporter of aircraft carrier and sea-based aviation. According to its LinkedIn page, as a fraternal organization, its purpose is to foster, encourage, develop, study, and support the U.S. aircraft carrier community, its sea-based aircraft, and the associated military personnel. It also touts an instructional and public relations role in educating the public about the important role played by aircraft carriers and related aviation assets in defense of the United States and its interests abroad ("Tailhook Association" 2018).

The first Tailhook Symposium took place in 1956, at Rosario Beach, California. It then moved to San Diego for a few years before settling in Las Vegas in 1963. The notorious 35th Tailhook Symposium took place in 1991, during a national time of celebration. Operations Desert Shield and Desert Storm had just ended; patriotism was strong across the nation, and military morale was high. The symposium agenda was packed with relevant topics on naval operations, munitions effectiveness, advanced aircraft technology, and a series of roundtable discussions on relevant issues facing the service. Most of the talks focused on professional development and were designed to engage junior and senior officers in attendance in meaningful dialogue about the navy's future while also allowing time to socialize. The symposium turnout was near record-breaking, as two thousand service members were registered along with over twenty-five hundred civilian contractors. The conference also attracted various other navy, marine, air force, and army personnel interested in visiting the more than 170 display booths scattered throughout the hotel (Parks 1994, 90–92).

While professional activities and conduct ruled the day, social activities and less than professional conduct ruled the night. The Tailhook symposiums had a reputation built on sordid tales of parties that took place on Friday and Saturday nights. The 1991 symposium was no different. Those evenings were characterized by excessive alcohol drinking, vulgar language, fighting, indecent exposure, and property damage. What separated this Tailhook symposium from all others was the crossing of the line from male-versus-male horseplay to sexual harassment and sexual assault inflicted by mainly male military service members on their female peers, subordinates, and in one case, an underage civilian girl.

Most of the illicit and sexually abusive behavior took place on the Saturday night of the symposium and was concentrated in the hallway on the third floor of the hotel, where individual units established hospitality suites. Some units played pornographic films in their suites with senior officers present. As people circulated between the suites, the hallway became congested. Drinks were spilled, and food was trampled into the carpet. Movement through the hallway soon became difficult as people pushed their way through the narrow pathway that would open and close with the fluctuation of the crowd. It was down this hallway that the "gauntlet" was established. The gauntlet was a narrow passage leading down the hallway, now deliberately maintained as a challenge to anyone attempting to navigate its path. Both men and women "ran" through this narrow passage, despite being pushed, shoved, groped, grabbed, and pinched. Some of the runners seemed to relish the challenge of navigating the passage. Some ran the gauntlet numerous times, trying to collect unit patches as their reward.

As the night progressed, however, the touching, grabbing, and pushing became more aggressive, and a growing number of women became unwilling targets of drunken groping that crossed the line into sexual assault. Some have suggested the vicious targeting of women was the direct result of a female aviator asking a senior naval officer about the navy changing its policy on women aviators flying combat missions. This question and the ambiguous response caused the primarily male audience to voice their opposition to this possibility (Parks 1994, 91–92).

Although some of the women present did not seem to be alarmed by the behavior, numerous other women, both officer and civilian, were shaken and expressed feelings of humiliation and betrayal. Ironically, the navy had recently established a zero tolerance sexual harassment policy. One aviator could not allow this type of behavior to continue. Lieutenant Paula Coughlin, a navy aviator and aide to an admiral, immediately reported through her chain of command that she had been sexually assaulted. Simultaneously, several senior navy officers were disgusted by the behavior and were working to address the issue.

Despite immediately severing its ties with the Tailhook organization, the navy's internal investigative efforts, with significant oversight and interest from the Department of Defense and Congress, did not make much progress in the nine months following Lieutenant Coughlin's initial report. This perturbed Coughlin so much that in June 1992, she went public in an interview on ABC in which she described what happened to her during the 1991 Tailhook Symposium. Investigations continued for three years by various organizations both inside and outside the navy. In all, there were over seven separate investigations. It has been reported that almost half of the accused received some level of punishment. The secretary of the navy was fired, and other senior officers retired early. However, most 1991 Tailhook attendees were junior and mid-grade officers whose only guilt was attending the symposium. Most of these officers suffered career-ending penalties of guilt by association either immediately or later in their careers (Lancaster 1994).

The infamous 1991 Tailhook convention also drove the conversation about the role of women in the navy and the larger military to the national stage. On April 28, 1993, the secretary of defense lifted the combat exclusion policy, which allowed women to serve in any aviation occupational specialty. In 2013, the ban on women serving in combat was lifted. Finally, in 2016, Secretary of Defense Ash Carter opened every military combat occupational specialty to women (Beck 2016).

Unfortunately, Lieutenant Coughlin never received justice and felt abandoned and exposed by the navy. Her case was eventually dropped, citing the lack of evidence. She left the navy in 1994, after which time she continued to advocate for victims of sexual assault. In 2013, she wrote the blog post "It Is Time to Change the Culture of the Military and Change Attitudes about Sexual Assault" for the HuffPost. In the article, she asserts that not much has changed since 1991, especially regarding leadership and the power of the commander failing to take appropriate action concerning an allegation of sexual assault (Coughlin 2013).

Frank Hall

See also: Office/Workplace Settings; Sexual Harassment Training; Uniform Code of Military Justice

Further Reading

Beck, Robert L. 2016. "Tailhook Scandal Sets Stage for Gender Equality Fight." *San Diego Union-Tribune*, September 1. Accessed September 10, 2018. http://www.sandiegouniontribune.com/opinion/commentary/sdut-utbg-tailhook-navy-women-2016sep01-story.html.

Coughlin, Paula. 2013. "It Is Time to Change the Culture of the Military and Change Attitudes about Sexual Assault." HuffPost, November 20. Accessed September 10, 2018. https://www.huffingtonpost.com/paula-coughlin/military-sexual-assault_b_4312348.html.

Johnson, Dani. 2015. "We've Come a Long Way; Still Have a Ways to Go." U.S. Army, January 14. Accessed September 5, 2018. https://www.army.mil/article/141110/weve_come_a_long_way_still_have_a_ways_to_go.

Lancaster, John. 1994. "Jury Is Still Out on Tailhook Scandal's Effect on Navy Attitudes." *Washington Post*, February 17. Accessed September 10, 2018. https://www.washingtonpost.com/archive/politics/1994/02/17/jury-is-still-out-on-tailhook-scandals-effect-on-navy-attitudes/e3d4e15d-5960-4fab-9efc-dc99d6f3bfb3/.

Parks, W. Hays. 1994. "Tailhook: What Happened, Why & What's to Be Learned." *Proceedings*, 1st ser., 120, no. 9 (September): 90–92. Accessed September 7, 2018. https://www.usni.org/magazines/proceedings/1994/september/tailhook-what-happened-why-whats-be-learned.

"Tailhook Association." 2018. LinkedIn. Accessed September 6, 2018. https://www.linkedin.com/company/tailhook-association/.

Television

Television programming has changed since its inception in 1927. Since that time, technology has improved many aspects of television viewing, and television programming today hardly resembles its humble beginnings. In the early history of television, not every home possessed a television set. Television technology was new and expensive in yesterday's dollars. Today, practically every home across the United States boasts at least one television in the home. In addition, television programming capacity today is now in a "take with" mode far exceeding viewing capacity of yesterday. Couple this with the addition of streaming services, and programming is now available on multiple handheld devices for on the go viewing anywhere, anytime.

The global reach of television has had a profound impact on how relationships are viewed and what is considered normal behavior in American society. As programming evolved through the years, the depiction of relationships and how men and women interact with one another became a common and popular theme.

Television programming of yesteryear initially produced a limited scope of programs, most of which depicted relationships and families in traditional, conservative frameworks. Since the 1990s, however, television has increasingly broadcast positive depictions of many different relationships and families. It has also become more explicit in dealing with issues of sexual abuse and violence—even as other programming leans heavily into titillating sexual content.

Technology, combined with evolving story lines and vivid imagery, created a rich entertainment experience for the viewer that continues to evolve today. In 1996, President Bill Clinton signed legislation deregulating telecommunications, creating vast opportunities for broadcasters and cable companies. This change opened the door to myriad television viewing choices as well as intense competition between broadcast companies vying for the attention of television viewers.

As competition increased, programming developed various themes to shock, entrance, and enthrall viewers. Early programming was straightforward and centered on a simple story line. As television progressed, story lines became more complex, with content delving deeper into uncharted waters. Television programming, from inception, was considered family oriented, and themes were centered around variety shows or a family format. Early programming consisted of traditional family relationships comprised of traditional roles of a husband, wife, a child or two, and possibly a dog. The character June Cleaver (played by Barbara Billingsley) of *Leave It to Beaver* (which ran from 1957 to 1963) was one of the first women depicted in a major television role. Mrs. Cleaver played the role of the family matriarch, who spent her days in the home primarily caring for her family. This was typical of the era, as women portrayed on television were typically of a subordinate position. Rarely were women seen as leaders. Rather, women were seen as adjuncts to the males in the program. The *Mary Tyler Moore Show*, which aired from 1970 to 1977, was the first program to feature a woman as a lead character. The popular show followed the life of a single, working woman who fought to gain an equal footing in the workplace.

Early programming required little censorship. Material presented was cutting edge for the time period, however, and as time and technology progressed, television programming increasingly pushed the boundaries of acceptability and what was previously considered socially decent. The TV parental guidelines enacted January 1, 1997, provided a television content rating system in the United States to assist parents in understanding the content of programming to better protect children from inappropriate material. It was not uncommon for storylines to feature physical or sexual violence against women or to depict few female characters in roles without substance or depth. Women were commonly depicted in roles that were viewed as sensual and sexual for daytime programming. The focus in programming shifted again toward what women were not wearing, the overall attractiveness of the female character, and an "ideal" body type of 36-24-36. Female characters were frequently seen as objects in the story line as opposed to adding any substance to the plot.

As television programming progressed, female characters of substance continued to fade, giving way to the emergence of female characters endowed with physical attributes and dimensions regarded as widely desired by male viewers. "Pinup girls," "bimbos," and "blonde bombshells" were common terms used to describe female actors. Boundaries were pushed as more female characters were portrayed as objects or playthings, with the lead male character(s) in hot pursuit. Even in animated television shows, the male cartoon character Pepe Le Pew could be seen romping through scene after scene in constant pursuit of the noncompliant female object of his desire. Actresses such as Marilyn Monroe (1926–1962), Jayne Mansfield (1933–1967), Raquel Welch (1940–present), and Farrah Fawcett (1947–2009) achieved fame primarily for their sex appeal rather than their acting abilities.

In other programming, women were portrayed as confident but severely lacking in respect. On the long-running comedy *M*A*S*H*, for example, the only female lead character in the series, Margaret "Hot Lips" Houlihan (played by Loretta Swit (1937–present)) was subjected to a steady stream of sexual jokes by her male counterparts, who were portrayed as competent and confident. In the *All in the Family* series, the female character Edith Bunker (Jean Stapleton (1923–2013)) was portrayed as subservient to her husband, Archie Bunker (Carroll O'Connor (1924–2001)). Each week, viewers witnessed scenes in which Archie berated Edith for one action or decision for which he did not approve. Week to week, Edith could be seen trotting around the home, fetching Archie his meals, his newspaper, his coffee, or his beer.

In the most recent expansion of television programming, violence toward women has become a common plot device. Programs such as the *Law and Order* franchise, *The Newsroom*, *True Blood*, *Downton Abbey*, *Scandal*, *Greenleaf*, and *Game of Thrones* use the rape of women as centerpieces of storylines, and shows such as *Criminal Minds* are focused on acts of sexual violence against girls and women in gruesome detail.

The expansion of cable and streaming services introduced pornography as an on demand service. Nudity, violence, demeaning comedy, and other graphic activity is available on television directly through subscription to a cable service. In addition to this content, pornographic programming moved out of dark storefronts directly into the privacy of the viewer's home. Programs that depict various story lines of graphic sexual content, to the detriment of women, are available 24/7 with a renewable subscription service. As television viewing appetites changed, mainstream programming continued to blur the lines.

Television today has evolved to the point where practically any type of programming one wants is available and readily viewable—including shows that arguably glorify violence against women. Activists fighting to reduce sexual violence and harassment find this deeply troubling, given the impact that popular culture can have on societal attitudes. Many groups are mounting an offensive to change how women are depicted on television and to educate consumers on how these images can negatively impact relationships, families, and American society as a whole.

Lori Madison

See also: Gender Equality; Movies, Depictions of Sexual Harassment; Pepe Le Pew; Relationship Violence

Further Reading

Galdi, S., A. Maass, and M. Cadinu. 2013. "Objectifying Media: Their Effect on Gender Role Norms and Sexual Harassment of Women." *Psychology of Women Quarterly* 38(3): 2014.

Gottfried, J. A., S. E. Vaala, A. Bleakley, M. Hennessy, and A. Jordan. 2013. "Does the Effect of Exposure to TV Sex on Adolescent Sexual Behavior Vary by Genre?" *Communication Research* 40(1): 73–95. https://doi.org/10.1177/0093650211415399.

Selinger, Evan M. 2014. "Television." In *Ethics, Science, Technology, and Engineering: A Global Resource*, 2nd ed., Vol. 4, edited by J. Britt Holbrook, 341–345. Farmington Hills, MI: MacMillan Reference USA.

Thomas, Clarence (1948–)

Clarence Thomas is an associate justice of the Supreme Court of the United States. He was appointed to the court by President George H. W. Bush on October 23, 1991, and is presently the most senior member of the court. Judge Thomas is an African American man and was born on June 23, 1948, in Pin Point Georgia. He was the second oldest of three children. His father, M. C. Thomas, was a farm worker, and his mother, Leola Williams, was a domestic worker. Thomas graduated cum laude with a bachelor's in English literature from the College of the Holy Cross, Worcester, Massachusetts, in 1971. While there, Thomas cofounded a Black Student Association. Thomas completed his juris doctor (JD) in 1974 from Yale Law School.

In September 1974, Thomas was called to the Missouri Bar. He subsequently started work as the Missouri assistant attorney general. He was a legislative assistant from 1979 to 1981 in charge of energy matters at the Senate Commerce Committee. He was appointed the assistant secretary of education for the Office of Civil Rights at the U.S. Department of Education from 1981 to 1982. This was during the Reagan administration. He became chairman of the Equal Employment Opportunity Commission (EEOC) in 1982, and he served in that post until 1990.

President George H. W. Bush nominated Thomas to the U.S. Court of Appeals for the District of Columbia Circuit in October 1989. He was confirmed by the

Senate without controversy on March 6, 1990. Following the resignation of Justice Thurgood Marshall from the Supreme Court in 1991, Clarence Thomas was nominated by President George H. W. Bush to replace him. Justice Marshall was a popular liberal jurist of African descent. Before his retirement, he was the only African American justice on the Supreme Court.

ANITA HILL ALLEGATIONS

Thomas's Senate confirmation hearing turned into one of the most contentious in living memory. Although there were many interest groups opposed to Thomas's confirmation because of his conservative views and opposition to progressive ideals, it was the testimony of Anita Hill, who accused Thomas of sexual harassment, that posed the greatest threat to his confirmation. Hill (who as of 2020 is a professor of law and women's studies at Brandeis University) worked under Clarence Thomas both at the Department of Education and later at the EEOC. During Thomas's confirmation hearing, she came forward and testified that Thomas had sexually harassed her at both agencies. Hill claimed that Thomas tried to date her when she was his assistant. When Hill declined Thomas's advances, he developed other strategies in a bid to seduce her. According to Hill, Thomas brought up pornography and other sexually inappropriate subjects in conversation (including graphic boasts about his sexual prowess and large penis). She also described an instance where Thomas allegedly queried her about who put pubic hair into his bottle of Coke.

Hill provided four female witnesses to support her allegations against Thomas, but the Senate failed to grant them an opportunity to testify in support of her claims. Thomas denied all the allegations of sexual harassment leveled against him by Hill. Meanwhile, some of Thomas's supporters said that she was not a credible witness and accused her of seeking revenge because she had been spurned by Thomas. Some even alleged that she was delusional and politically motivated. After an extensive but often contentious debate, Clarence Thomas was confirmed by the Senate through a vote of 52–48. His confirmation is one of the narrowest margins of vote confirmation for a U.S. Supreme Court candidate.

OTHER ALLEGATIONS OF MISCONDUCT

Reporters who carried out their own investigations into the allegations of sexual misconduct by Thomas confirmed Hill's claim that Thomas had a pattern of discussing his experience with pornography with other female colleagues. While it is not a crime for an adult to watch pornography, this discovery strengthened Hill's allegation that Thomas frequently discussed pornographic scenes with her in a failed attempt to seduce her.

Lillian McEwen, a lawyer, said that she had dated Clarence Thomas during his days at the EEOC and Education Department. She too claimed that she had knowledge that Thomas regularly discussed scenes from pornography and other sexual talks with his colleagues in the office. McEwen had actually written to Senator Joe Biden (who at the time was in charge of the Thomas Senate confirmation hearing). However, Biden declined to bring her in to testify. Even though McEwen had volunteered to testify publicly before the Senate about Thomas's sexual misconduct as described by Anita Hill, she was not willing at the time to bring her case to the media.

McEwen said that she changed her mind about coming forward with her story after Clarence Thomas's wife, Ginni, called and left a message on Anita Hill's answering machine in October 2010. In the message, Ginni asked Anita Hill to apologize to her husband for telling a lie against him during his Senate confirmation hearing. According to McEwen, however, Hill's account of Thomas's behavior was consistent with her own experiences with him. She relayed instances when Thomas told her about his preferences for hiring women with big breasts and even on one occasion asked a female colleague about her bra size. Even though McEwen's interview was widely reported, Thomas and his supporters chose not to come after her. She believed this might be because McEwen had a lengthy romantic relationship with Thomas and might be in a position to produce other material evidence to support her allegation.

In October 2016, another woman lawyer came forward and publicly accused Thomas of sexual assault. Moira Smith, an attorney based in Alaska, recounted on Facebook her experience in 1999 when she encountered Justice Clarence Thomas at a dinner party as a twenty-four-year-old just starting her legal career. She and Thomas first exchanged pleasantries, but she asserted that as the evening wore on, he groped her multiple times and made a number of sexually suggestive remarks. Thomas denied ever groping Smith. In addition, as with earlier allegations made against Thomas, several women who have worked with the Supreme Court justice over the years praised his character and contended that the sexual harassment and assault claims made against him were politically motivated.

O. Oko Elechi and Ifeoma Okoye

See also: Hill, Anita; #MeToo Movement; Sexism; *Time Magazine* "Silence Breakers"

Further Reading

Abramson, Jill. 2018. "Do You Believe Her Now? It's Time to Reexamine the Evidence That Clarence Thomas Lied to Get onto the Supreme Court—and to Talk Seriously about Impeachment." *New York Magazine*, February 2018. http://nymag .com/intelligencer/2018/02/the-case-for-impeaching-clarence-thomas.html.

Carmon, I. 2014. "Anita Hill Talks Feminism, Sexual Harassment and Clarence Thomas." MSNBC, March 27. https://www.msnbc.com/msnbc/anita-hill-her-regrets-msna 294851.

Liptak, A. 2016. "It's Been 10 Years. Would Clarence Thomas Like to Add Anything?" *New York Times*, February 2. https://www.nytimes.com/2016/02/02/us/politics /clarence-thomas-supreme-court.html.

McCaskill, Nolan. 2016. "Woman Accuses Clarence Thomas of Groping Her at a Dinner Party in 1999." *Politico*, October 28. https://www.politico.com/story/2016/10 /clarence-thomas-accuser-moira-smith-230401.

Toobin, Jeffrey. 2014. "Clarence Thomas's Disgraceful Silence." *New Yorker*, February 21. http://www.newyorker.com/news/daily-comment/clarence-thomass-disgraceful -silence.

Time Magazine "Silence Breakers"

In 2017, *Time Magazine* named a group of American women, collectively described as "Silence Breakers," as the magazine's Person of the Year. The Silence Breakers are individuals who publicly spoke out about their experiences of being sexually harassed or assaulted, often by serial perpetrators in positions of power. Instead of staying silent, these Silence Breakers spoke out against their harassers, paving the way for other victims of these perpetrators to come forward with their own stories of harassment and assault. Some of these Silence Breakers were public figures or celebrities, although many were not. The article told these individuals' stories and talked about the outcomes of breaking the silence surrounding sexual harassment.

The cover of this issue of the magazine featured a photo of Ashley Judd, Susan Fowler, Adama Iwu, Taylor Swift, and Isabel Pascual. The article told these women's stories of sexual harassment and their experiences when they spoke out against the powerful men subjecting them to harassment. Ashley Judd was the first actress to publicly accuse Hollywood film mogul Harvey Weinstein of sexual harassment. After Judd told her story, multiple women in the entertainment industry came forward with their own stories of sexual harassment by Weinstein, leading to multiple lawsuits and Weinstein's eventual arrest for rape. Susan Fowler was an engineer for ride-sharing service Uber. After leaving her position with Uber, she wrote a blog post about the culture of sexual harassment at the company. This led to the resignation of Uber's CEO, Travis Kalanick, and the firing or resignation of twenty top-level employees at the company. Adama Iwu, a California lobbyist, wrote an open letter about the culture of harassment in California politics after being groped at a public event in view of multiple other attendees, none of whom intervened; 147 women signed the letter Iwu wrote. After writing the letter, Iwu founded We Said Enough, a digital platform to provide support to victims of sexual harassment.

Singer-songwriter Taylor Swift reported DJ David Mueller to his boss after he groped her during a photo public relations event. Swift's action led to Mueller's firing. Mueller denied the accusation and sued Swift for defamation; Swift countersued for a symbolic one dollar in damages and won. Isabel Pascual spoke about her experience of being sexually harassed and stalked at home by her harasser when she worked as a strawberry picker in California. Pascual's name was changed for the article to protect her family because her harasser threatened to hurt her family if she told anyone about his actions.

The sixth women on the cover of the "Silence Breakers" issue was an anonymous hospital worker who was sexually harassed by a hospital executive; only her arm was shown on the cover. The article explained that she is pictured as a representative of the women who have been sexually harassed but were unable to tell their stories.

Many other women who had emerged as Silence Breakers were discussed in the *Time Magazine* issue as well. Tarana Burke is a social activist who founded a group called Me Too to support survivors of sexual harassment and assault. Actress Alyssa Milano started a global movement when she tweeted "#metoo" on October 15, 2017. Within twenty-four hours, half a million people had retweeted the hashtag, exposing the scope of the problem of sexual harassment and assault. The movement spread around the world, with other countries creating their own hashtags. Sandra Muller, a French journalist, popularized the French hashtag "balance ton porc," meaning "expose your pig." People in countries across Europe, the Middle East, and Asia translated the #MeToo hashtag into their own languages, such as #yotambien (Spanish) and #ana_kaman (Arabic).

Other Silence Breakers highlighted in the special issue of *Time* included hospitality workers, journalists, and politicians. Juana Melara, a hotel housekeeper, told stories of constant sexual harassment by hotel guests. Another hospitality worker, Crystal Washington, sued the Plaza Hotel in New York for allowing a culture of harassment. Five other female employees joined her in the lawsuit. Washington could not afford to leave her job, so she was forced to see her harasser daily at work during the lawsuit. Social media manager Lindsey Reynolds reported a culture of harassment in the Besh Restaurant Group for which she worked. She filed a complaint with the U.S. Equal Employment Opportunity Commission (EEOC) that ultimately led to CEO Josh Besh stepping down from his position. Sandra Pezqueda, a dishwasher at a California resort, reported her supervisor for sexual harassment. He retaliated by cutting the number of hours she worked, effectively reducing her income. Pezqueda filed a lawsuit against the resort and won a monetary settlement.

In addition to the actresses and performers featured on the cover, multiple other individuals in the entertainment industry were named as Silence Breakers. Rose McGowan and producer Zelda Perkins were among the over eighty women who reported sexual harassment or assault by Harvey Weinstein. Actress Selma Blair reported her sexual assault by screenwriter and director James Toback after keeping it a secret for twenty years because of threats he made. Blair's report led to an investigation by the *Los Angeles Times*, during which thirty-eight other women accused Toback of harassment and assault. Eventually, over two hundred women came forward about their experiences of harassment and assault at Toback's hands. Fox News guest Wendy Walsh was one of the first women to report sexual harassment by journalist Bill O'Reilly. News anchor Megyn O'Kelly also reported sexual harassment by O'Reilly. The *New York Times* published an article about settlements reached by O'Reilly with women he had harassed, which played a role in O'Reilly's dismissal from Fox News. Kelly also reported harassment by Fox News CEO Roger Ailes, who eventually resigned after multiple women joined Kelly in accusing the network executive of sexual harassment.

Summer Zervos publicly accused Donald Trump of sexual harassment that occurred when she was a contestant on his reality show *The Apprentice*. Andrea Constand accused actor Bill Cosby of drugging and sexually assaulting her. After Constand's claims were made public, sixty women came forward with their own stories of being assaulted by Cosby. The famous actor was convicted of the assault against Constand and sentenced to three to ten years in prison. Blaise Godbe Lipman accused agent Taylor Grasham of sexual assault. The agency for which Grasham worked fired him, and the Los Angeles Police Department opened an investigation. Actor Terry Crews sued agent Adam Venit for sexual assault. After a settlement was reached, Venit resigned from the firm for which he worked.

Several women featured in the *Time* article reported harassment and assault by politicians. Oregon state senator Sara Gelser reported another state senator, Jeff Kruse, of sexual harassment. After an investigation, the statehouse pulled Kruse from his committees. Kruse eventually resigned from his position in the Senate. Leigh Corfman accused Alabama Senate nominee Roy Moore of sexually abusing her as a fourteen-year-old teenager. Eight more women came forward with their own stories of harassment and assault by Moore. These public accusations led to Moore's loss of the Senate race. Radio host Leeann Tweeden reported that Senator Al Franken of Minnesota groped her. Seven more women came forward with their stories of harassment and assault by Franken. As a result of these accusations, Franken resigned from his Senate seat.

Accusations of sexual harassment against politicians were not confined to the United States. Journalist Jane Merrick reported sexual harassment by British defense secretary Michael Fallon. Merrick was joined in her accusations by multiple other women. Fallon quit his Cabinet position after these accusations surfaced. Terry Reintke, a member of the European Parliament, reported a culture of harassment in European politics. Charity worker Bex Bailey reported being sexually assaulted at a Labour Party event; Bailey was told to not report the assault by another member of the Labour Party.

Other Silence Breakers include women such as entrepreneur Lindsay Meyer, who reported sexual harassment by venture capitalist Justin Caldbeck. Caldbeck resigned from his position after more women came forward with their own stories of harassment. Eight employees of the University of Rochester, including professors Celeste Kidd and Jessica Cantlon, sued the university for a culture of harassment—and of retaliation against victims when incidents of sexual harassment was reported. Art curator Amanda Schmitt sued *Artforum* publisher Knight Landesman for sexual harassment. She spoke in the article about the culture of harassment that was accepted in the art industry. Landesman stepped down from his position because of the lawsuit. An anonymous woman spoke of leaving her position as an office assistant because of sexual harassment. She felt she had to leave because there was nowhere to report the harassment, and she did not think she would be believed by other members of her small Native American community.

The *Time Magazine* article discussed the fact that many women who are sexually harassed do not speak out because of the fear that they will become known for being the victim of sexual harassment. The article recognized some of the women in history who spoke out against their harassment, despite a lack of public support for victims of sexual harassment. In 1975, for example, Carmita Wood accused her supervisor at Cornell University of sexual harassment. This led to the creation of the term *sexual harassment*. In 1991, Anita Hill accused U.S. Supreme Court nominee Clarence Thomas of sexual harassment. Although these women did not receive a great deal of support—and in some instances were vilified—they paved the way for the Silence Breakers of today.

Silence Breakers play an important role in changing culture. Breaking the silence about sexual harassment by serial perpetrators can empower other victims to come forward to speak about their own experiences of harassment and assault. In addition, when the Silence Breaker is a public figure, it makes other victims more likely to be believed when they come forward. The public outing of serial sexual harassers has led to a shift in societal focus from blaming victims and holding them responsible for preventing their own harassment to confronting perpetrators and holding them responsible for their actions. There have been wide-reaching ramifications for sexual harassment perpetrators as a result of Silence Breakers coming forward. Victims have brought civil lawsuits against their perpetrators and have won. Multiple top-ranking officials and other individuals in power have been forced to resign from their positions because they have been credibly accused of sexual harassment by multiple victims. Other perpetrators have faced criminal charges and legal punishments.

Policy changes have also been enacted as a result of the Silence Breakers coming forward. Many employers have begun to implement strict policies against sexual harassment as well as training for employees about what sexual harassment is and how to prevent it. States are enacting legislation against sexual harassment. At the federal level, the U.S. House and Senate have mandated sexual harassment training for members of Congress and staff.

Antonia Curtis

See also: Blair, Selma; Crews, Terry; Fowler, Susan J.; Iwu, Adama; Judd, Ashley; McGowan, Rose; #MeToo Movement; Milano, Alyssa; Swift, Taylor

Further Reading

Recupero, Patricia R. 2018. "The Notion of Truth and Our Evolving Understanding of Sexual Harassment." *Journal of the American Academy of Psychiatry and the Law* 46(1) (March): 23–30.

Skjelsbaek, Inger. 2018. "Silence Breakers in War and Peace: Research on Gender and Violence with an Ethics of Engagement." *Social Politics: International Studies in Gender, State & Society* 25, no. 4 (December): 496–520.

Zacharek, Stephanie, Eliana Dockterman, and Haley Sweetland Edwards. 2017. "*Time* Person of the Year 2017: The Silence Breakers." *Time*, December 18.

Time's Up Movement

The purpose of the Time's Up Movement is to bring awareness to the sexual violence and sexual harassment that women in the workplace experience and to provide solutions to combat these concerns. The movement was conceived in the fall of 2017 after a group of Hollywood stars—including Reese Witherspoon and Halle Barry—brought attention to the inequality of women in the entertainment industry. Time's Up was born out of the #MeToo Movement and the scandal surrounding Harvey Weinstein, an American film producer accused of sexual harassment and assault of women in the movie industry. The organization developed two main goals. First, Time's Up aims to prevent sexual harassment and abuse in the workplace. Second, the organization hopes to diversify the workforce by increasing the number of women and women of color in leadership positions.

This movement expanded outside of its Hollywood roots when the Alianza Nacional de Campesinas (a group of low-income farmworkers) wrote a letter of allegiance supporting Time's Up's mission. These farmworkers recognized that even though they worked in vastly different conditions, they shared a common experience with the women in Hollywood. These women experience the same feelings of hurt, shame, anger, and desperation that accompany sexual violence and harassment. This union of solidarity became the foundation of the Time's Up Movement, which formally launched on January 1, 2018.

Lisa Borders (1961–present) was initiated as the first president and CEO of Time's Up in October 2018 after serving as the vice president of global community affairs at Coca-Cola and as the president of the Women's National Basketball Association. Borders, considered a born politician by many scholars, received her education from Duke University. Soon after the start of the #MeToo Movement, she felt a calling to become involved in an organization that supported survivors of sexual harassment and inequality in the workplace. "I was being not just invited but encouraged—implored—to step forward and be part of this transformational change for women," Borders said (Desta 2018). Borders saw Time's Up as her opportunity to make a lasting impact and recognized the organization's substantial vision for change. During her first few months as president, she began by assessing both the successes and challenges of the organization (Time's Up 2018).

The Time's Up Legal Defense Fund is one of the best-known and most important aspects of the organization. Its aim is to provide resources and financial support to individuals who have undergone sexual harassment or retaliation in their workplace. *Sexual harassment* is defined as the "unwelcome sexual advances, requests for sexual favors, and other verbal or physical harassment of sexual nature" (Time's Up 2018). Harassment can also include nonsexual comments that are offensive toward an individual's sex in general. The fund is directed by the National Women's Law Center (NWLC), an advocacy group for women's rights directed by Sharyn Tejani (1968–present). Tejani works for the Department of Justice, and in her legal career, she specializes in issues regarding civil rights and women's rights.

The Legal Defense Fund serves two primary purposes: support individuals that need legal assistance and fund outreach grants. As of January 2019, this fund reached more than $22 million from numerous donors, including Hollywood stars, Time's Up's partners, and the general public, through sources such as GoFundMe (an online platform that allows individuals to raise money for a specific cause). The money was used to provide legal resources—including access to eight hundred attorneys across the country—to more than thirty-four hundred women from all fifty states. Two-thirds of the women supported through this fund fall into the low-income category. Along with legal support, eighteen outreach grants have utilized $750,000 to create and share educational materials that teach the public about their rights as well as the resources in place to support survivors (Time's Up 2018).

The organization and Hollywood stars gained media attention by shining light on the Time's Up movement through the 2018 Golden Globes "blackout" and the creation of the #AskMoreOfHim campaign. During the 2018 Golden Globe Awards, celebrities wore black to stand in solidarity against sexual harassment in the workplace. This sign of unity brought attention to the magnitude of the problem. Sophia Bush (1982–present), an American actress, said that the symbolism of the blackout was something the media could not ignore. The organization's prominence at the Golden Globes continued into the 2019 awards, when celebrities wore bracelets and ribbons, stating TIMESUP×2, to symbolize Time's Up's effort to double the number of women in leadership positions in multiple industries (Time's Up 2018).

Another effort by the Time's Up Movement was the initiation of the #AskMoreOfHim campaign by several male actors. David Schwimmer, Justin Baldoni, David Arquette, and Matt McGorry created the campaign to show support and solidarity with the Time's Up Movement and encourage men to use their power in society to campaign for an end to sexual harassment. In the initial letter that started the campaign, David Arquette and David Schwimmer concurred that men play an essential role in ending sexual harassment, as men are the primary abusers in most harassment situations. These aggressors blend in with the rest of society as friends, neighbors, coworkers, elected officials, and more. Arquette and Schwimmer asserted that men must hold one another accountable for their actions to create an environment of safety and security for people of all genders and sexualities. Thirty men signed this letter in support of launching the #AskMoreOfHim campaign. They vowed to hold themselves and those around them accountable for their actions to help prevent sexual harassment for women, men, and gender nonconforming individuals alike. The campaign provides resources and strategies for men to utilize to take action in their own communities (The Representation Project 2019).

The Time's Up Movement has been met with an outpouring of support, yet it has also received strong criticism. Critics of Time's Up argue that it is no more than a symbolic movement that will make relatively little or no impact in the lives of the women it strives to support. One media outlet criticized the movement for being hypocritical. The news source claimed that the Time's Up movement is merely a publicity stunt and that the women behind the movement continue to work for the rich and highly funded abusers within their industry (Clark 2018). Some Hollywood stars supported this viewpoint, claiming that the Golden Globes blackout was a symbol of "Hollywood fakery" because many of the women involved in the movement worked for Harvey Weinstein at one point or another in their careers. Additionally, this movement failed to incorporate Weinstein's accusers, who played a key role in the birth of the Time's Up movement (McGrath 2018).

Anna Doering

See also: Harvey Weinstein Scandal; #MeToo Movement; Sexual Harassment Training; Social Media

Further Reading

Clark, Corinne. 2018. "Hollywood's #TimesUp Movement Still Fails Young Women, Despite Buzz and Accolades." *Washington Examiner*, January 2. Accessed February 12, 2019, from https://www.washingtonexaminer.com/hollywoods-timesup -movement-still-fails-young-women-despite-buzz-and-accolades.

Desta, Yohana. 2018. "Lisa Borders, Time's Up's First President and C.E.O., Knows This Isn't Going to Be Easy." *Vanity Fair*, October 2. Accessed February 13, 2019. https:// www.vanityfair.com/hollywood/2018/10/lisa-borders-times-up-president-ceo.

McGrath, Rachel. 2018. "Rose McGowan Critiques Time's Up Movement, Singling Out Justin Timberlake." HuffPost, January 31. Accessed February 12, 2019. https://www.huffingtonpost.co.uk/entry/rose-mcgowanmes-up-justintimberlake_uk_5a71af5ae4b0a6aa4874f4d6.

The Representation Project. 2019. "#AskMoreOfHim." Accessed February 10, 2019. http://therepresentationproject.org/the-movement/askmoreofhim/.

Time's Up. 2018. "Time's Up." Accessed February 10, 2019. https://www.timesupnow.com/.

Title IX

Title IX is the revised comprehensive federal law amending the Civil Rights Act of 1964, which was originally signed by President Richard Nixon on June 23, 1972. Title IX (20 U.S.C. 1681 et seq.) mandated changes in American education by prohibiting discrimination on the basis of sex in any federally funded education program or activity. In addition to educational institutions such as colleges, universities, elementary and secondary schools, Title IX applies to any education or training program operated by an entity that receives federal financial assistance. This law speaks to all aspects of the educational program, including faculty employment, student recruitment, and admission; financial assistance; courses offered; facilities; programs or activities; athletics; and employment. It is also mandatory that these entities employ at least one Title IX coordinator.

As a civil rights statute, Title IX falls under the authority of the Office for Civil Rights (OCR) in the U.S. Department of Education, which has enforced racial discrimination laws since 1964. The law states the following: "No person in the United States shall, on the basis of sex, be excluded from participation in, be denied the benefits of, or be subject to discrimination under any educational program or activity receiving Federal financial assistance" (Cornell Law School's Legal Information Institute 2018).

The impetus for Title IX was the civil rights and feminist movements that took place in the late 1950s, 1960s, and early 1970s. In 1964, based on events in the 1950s and early 1960s, Congress passed the Civil Rights Act. This act mandated an end to discrimination in the areas of employment and public accommodation based on race, color, religion, sex, or national origin. However, the 1964 act did not prohibit sex discrimination against persons employed at educational institutions (Civil Rights Act of 1964 and the Equal Employment Opportunity Commission, n.d.). A parallel law, Title VII of the Civil Rights Act of 1964, prohibits discrimination in organizations, public or private, that are recipients of federal funds. Discrimination, in this regard, is based on race, color, and national origin, but sex is excluded. In 1965, a Presidential Executive Order 11246 was issued, prohibiting federally funded entities from denying employment on the basis of race, color, religion, or national origin. President Johnson amended this executive order by adding "sex" as one of the prohibited criteria for discrimination. This order became effective on October 13, 1968. The order was renamed Executive Order 11246 (Sept. 24, 1965) as amended by Executive Order 11375 (October 13, 1967) effective October 1968, marking the origin of Title IX. During the early 1970s, feminists again lobbied Congress to add sex as a protected class to prohibit discrimination in all federally funded educational programs. Title IX was thus enacted to fill this gap. A recent amendment to this order came on July 21, 2014, where "sex or national origin" was substituted for "sex, sexual orientation, gender identity, or national origin" (The American Presidency Project).

Title IX received legislative support from the 1976 amendments to the Vocational Equity Act of 1963. This act requires state recipients of federal funding for vocational education programs to eliminate all forms of sex bias, stereotyping, and discrimination in their programs. The amendments also affected the allocation of federal funds in other areas impacting the well-being of women. The amended law also required states to appoint "vocational education sex equity coordinators" responsible for developing vocational training and materials conducive to both males and females, making vocational training less segregated. Another relevant act, the Carl D. Perkins Act of 1984, allowed the administration of funds for programs geared toward eliminating discrimination based on sex and programs aimed at addressing the training needs of single parents and homemakers, who in most cases were female.

Title IX is more often recognized in connection with athletic programs and sports and has undergone specific changes in this regard. In addition to athletic programs and sports, Title IX is associated with campus sexual assault, but the Title IX amendments speak to the following ten areas:

1. Access to Higher Education for Women. Full access to higher education was not awarded to women until after the 1970s.

2. The Participation of Women in Sports. Prior to Title IX, girls were less likely to play sports, receive an athletic scholarship, or compete at elite levels in competitions.

3. Career Education for Women. Prior to Title IX ,girls were not permitted to participate in vocational courses deemed appropriate only for boys.

4. Education for Pregnant and Parenting Students. Prior to Title IX, a pregnant teenager was denied the opportunity to continue her education if she chose to continue with the pregnancy.

5. Equal Employment of Women in Higher Education. Prior to Title IX, women in education were relegated to the elementary and secondary levels and women's colleges, and they were not awarded tenure and earned less salary than male educators.

6. Equality in the Learning Environment. Prior to Title IX, the learning environment was geared toward fostering the education of males.

7. Involvement of Women in Math and Science. Prior to Title IX, girls were discouraged from participating in higher-level classes in the math and science fields.

8. Sexual Harassment. Prior to Title IX, "inappropriate" sexualized behaviors toward women were not recognized as such.

9. Standardized Testing. Prior to Title IX, standardized tests did not reflect the knowledge level and experiences of girls.

10. Technology. Prior to Title IX, computer technology and programming were geared toward the interest of males.

Sexual harassment was not the focus of the original law but was first recognized as a part of sex discrimination in 1977 by the DC Circuit Court of Appeals' decision in a Title VII case (American Association of University Professors 2016). Sexual harassment has since become an area of major concern. The standard definition of *sexual harassment*, as defined by the Equal Employment Opportunity Commission (EEOC) in 1980, is "the demand for sex in exchange for favorable treatment (quid pro quo) and the creation of an environment so infused with hostility, that it unreasonably interfered with an individual's ability to work" (American Association of University Professors 2016, 74). In 1981, the OCR, based on recommendations from the National Advisory Council on Women's Educational Programs, declared the sexual harassment protection under Title IX.

Sherill V. C. Morris-Francis

See also: Equal Employment Opportunity Commission (EEOC); Gender Equality; Quid Pro Quo; Title VII of the Civil Rights Act of 1964

Further Reading

American Association of University Professors (AAUP). 2016. "The History, Uses, and Abuses of Title IX." *2016 AAUP Bulletin*. https://www.aaup.org/file/TitleIXreport.pdf.

American Presidency Project. https://www.presidency.ucsb.edu.

"Civil Rights Act of 1964 and the Equal Employment Opportunity Commission." n.d. National Archives. Accessed October 10, 2018. https://www.archives.gov/education/lessons/civil-rights-act.

Cornell Law School's Legal Information Institute. 2018. "Compliance with Title IX of the Education Amendments of 1972," P.L. 92-318, 92-318, 20 U.S.C.S. section 1681 et seq. 20 U.S. Code § 1681—Sex. Accessed October 10, 2018. https://www.law.cornell.edu/uscode/text/51/40909.

Lyndon B. Johnson: Executive Order 11375—Amending Executive Order No. 11246. "Relating to Equal Employment Opportunity." American Presidency Project. Accessed October 10, 2018. https://www.presidency.ucsb.edu/documents/executive-order-11375-amending-executive-order-no-11246-relating-equal-employment.

National Archives Catalog, Civil Rights Act of 1964. https://catalog.archives.gov/id/1622796.

Schmuck, P. A., and R. Schmuck. 1985. "Administrative Strategies for Institutionalizing Sex Equity in Education and the Role of Government." In *Handbook for Achieving Sex Equity through Education*, edited by S. S. Klein, 91–94. Baltimore, MD: Johns Hopkins University Press. Accessed October 10, 2018. https://files.eric.ed.gov/fulltext/ED290810.pdf.

Section 703(a) (1), Civil Rights Act of 1964, Pub. L. No. 88-352, 78 Stat. 241, 255, As Amended Through P.L. 114-95, Enacted December 10, 2015). Accessed October 10, 2018. https://www.law.cornell.edu/uscode/text/26/703.

Stromquist, N. P. 1993. "Sex-Equity Legislation in Education: The State as Promoter of Women's Rights." *Review of Educational Research* 63(4): 379–407. Accessed October 10, 2018. https://doi.org/10.3102/00346543063004379.

Title VII of the Civil Rights Act of 1964

Title VII of the Civil Rights Act of 1964 (Title VII), as amended, protects employees from discrimination by their employers based on race, color, religion, sex, and national origin. The term *Title VII* refers to a specific section of the Civil Rights Act of 1964 that was passed by Congress. The Civil Rights Act has been amended several times since 1964 and now appears in the U.S. Code at Title 42, beginning at Section 2000(e). In addition to the protections under Title VII, other federal and state laws prevent discrimination based on other statuses, such as age, disability, or genetic information.

Under Title VII, employers with fifteen or more employees cannot discriminate against employees in hiring, firing, compensation, terms of employment, conditions of employment, or privileges of employment. Smaller employers who have fewer than fifteen employees are not subject to Title VII, but other state and federal discrimination laws do apply to smaller employers. In some situations, the protections under Title VII may overlap with protections under other federal or state laws. For instance, Title VII prohibits employers from paying men more than women and vice versa for equal work. In addition, the Equal Pay Act also prohibits pay discrimination.

In addition to passing Title VII, Congress created the U.S, Equal Employment Opportunity Commission (EEOC) to oversee, enforce, and administer the law. As part of its duties, the EEOC promulgated federal regulations that implement workplace discrimination laws and lay out the EEOC policies regarding its enforcement of employment discrimination laws. These regulations are found in the Federal Code of Regulations (CFR) and have the force of law.

The words "sexual harassment" do not appear in Title VII, and the EEOC did not originally include sexual harassment in its policies. That changed, however, in 1980 when the EEOC extended discrimination based on the employee's sex to include sexual harassment. The EEOC then issued guidelines as to what constitutes sexual harassment, which have been codified in the CFR.

In 1986, the U.S. Supreme Court ruled on its first sexual harassment case in its landmark decision *Meritor Savings Bank v. Vinson*, 477 U.S. 57 (1986). In its opinion, the court stated that sexual harassment is a violation of Title VII. Additionally, the court recognized and applied the EEOC's guidelines regarding sexual harassment. The court's affirmation of the EEOC's guidelines was critical because sometimes courts will not use regulations or guidelines created by government agencies if they believe the guidelines are invalid or unconstitutional. The court also held in *Meritor* that sexual harassment claims are not limited to claims for economic (monetary) loss.

Not all sexual conduct in the workplace, even between superiors and subordinates, is prohibited under Title VII. Sexually harassing conduct must be "unwelcome" and must be in the form of "sexual advances, requests for sexual favors, and other verbal or physical conduct of a sexual nature" (29 C.F.R. 1604.11). Furthermore, the employee alleging sexual harassment must demonstrate that "(1) submission to such conduct is made either explicitly or implicitly a term or condition of an individual's employment, (2) submission to or rejection of such conduct by an individual is used as the basis for employment decisions affecting such individual, or (3) such conduct has the purpose or effect of unreasonably interfering with an individual's work performance or creating an intimidating, hostile, or offensive working environment" (29 C.F.R. 1604.11).

The unwelcome sexual conduct described under sections 1 and 2 are what the courts describe as "quid pro quo" sexual harassment. In other words, the harasser is requesting sexual favors in return for something, such as a promotion or continued employment. The unwelcome sexual conduct described in section 3 constitutes what is known as "hostile work environment" harassment. On it webpage, the EEOC further states that "the conduct is severe or pervasive enough to create a work environment that a reasonable person would consider intimidating, hostile, or abusive." According to the EEOC, "offensive conduct may include, but is not limited to, offensive jokes, slurs, epithets or name calling, physical assaults or threats, intimidation, ridicule or mockery, insults or put-downs, offensive objects or pictures, and interference with work performance."

The standard of liability applied to the employer depends on the status of the person who allegedly sexually harassed the employee (plaintiff). If the accused harasser is a coworker, the plaintiff must prove the employer "knew or should have known" about the coworker's sexual harassment conduct. The employer can rebut this allegation by demonstrating that it took "immediate and corrective action" regarding the situation. However, if the alleged harasser was the plaintiff's supervisor, the employer faces a higher standard, which is called "strict liability." Strict liability means that the employer is liable regardless of whether it knew (or should have known) about the supervisor's conduct. Finally, employers may even be responsible for harassment by nonemployee third parties, such as customers, vendors, and others who sexually harass the employees. Just as with a coworker, the plaintiff will only prevail in his or her complaint if the plaintiff proves the employer "knew or should have known" about the third party's conduct.

Employees may not sue their employers for sexual harassment unless they first file a complaint with the EEOC. The EEOC will notify the employer of the claim and then investigate the employee's allegations. In some cases, the EEOC encourages the employee and employer to participate in mediation to try to settle the claim, but participation is not mandatory. In some cases, the EEOC will sue the employer directly if it determines that the employer violated Title VII. In other cases, the EEOC will not sue the employer, but it will provide the employee with a Notice of Right to Sue letter, which allows the employee his or her own lawsuit against the employer. The EEOC has up to 180 days to investigate the claim before it issues the Notice of Right to Sue, but it may issue it earlier.

Title VII also allows other employees (who were not themselves sexually harassed) to file a complaint if the employees were denied a benefit or opportunity because the benefit was given to another employee who submitted to the employer's request for sexual favors.

Elizabeth W. Marchioni

See also: Code of Conduct; Equal Employment Opportunity Commission (EEOC); Hostile Work Environment; *Meritor Savings Bank v. Vinson*; Quid Pro Quo

Further Reading

Frye, Jocelyn. 2017. "How to Combat Sexual Harassment in the Workplace." Center for American Progress, October 19. https://www.americanprogress.org/issues/women/news/2017/10/19/441046/combat-sexual-harassment-workplace/.

Lytle, Tamara. 2014. "Title VII Changed the Face of the American Workplace." *HR Magazine*, May 21. https://www.shrm.org/hr-today/news/hr-magazine/pages/title-vii-changed-the-face-of-the-american-workplace.aspx.

Meritor Savings Bank v. Vinson, 477 U.S. 57 (1986).

U.S. Equal Employment Opportunity Commission. n.d. "Facts about Sexual Harassment." Accessed January 8, 2020. https://www.eeoc.gov/eeoc/publications/fs-sex.cfm.

Tootsie

In 2019, women are standing up for themselves across the United States. The creation of the #MeToo Movement empowered women to speak out against sexual abuse and harassment. In Hollywood, many actresses came forward about incidents regarding sexual harassment that occurred as long as thirty years ago, which means for over thirty years, many of these men who held power in Hollywood had been participating in sexual misconduct without consequence.

Too often, sexual harassment and the mistreatment of women have been seen as a joke in mainstream media. Prominent male figures in the entertainment industry who have been accused of sexual harassment in the past have become more of a pop cultural referenced joke than a shunned sexual predator. The movie *Tootsie* has been frequently cited by critics as a prime example of the abuse of women in Hollywood being displayed on film—but not being portrayed as a serious issue that needed to be contained and condemned.

Released on December 17, 1982, *Tootsie* stars Dustin Hoffman in what screenwriter Sydney Pollock oversimplified as "the story of a guy who puts on a dress and by so doing becomes a better man." While Hoffman's character, Michael Dorsey, does become a better man by the end of the film, it is not simply because he puts on a dress. It is because he lived as a woman trying to make it in a deeply sexist Hollywood. The movie received ten Oscar nominations and is commonly referred to as one of the best comedic movies to date. However, watching *Tootsie* in the modern era—and especially after #MeToo—has been described by many woman as more vexing and outrageous than humorous.

Many of the scenes in *Tootsie* align all too well with the accounts told by the many actresses who have recently come forward with their stories. The plot begins with a struggling actor who decides to audition for a soap opera as a woman, Dorothy Michaels, after discovering from his agent that no one will work with him. As Dorothy, Michael immediately realizes how a woman is judged by her looks first and not her talent. When she is dismissed from the audition and told that she would not be a good fit, Dorothy delivers a powerful speech to the director, stating, "Yes, I think I know what y'all really want. You want some gross caricature of a woman. To prove some idiotic point, like, like power makes women masculine, or masculine women are ugly. Well shame on the woman who lets you do that."

Dorothy catches the attention of the female producer, who sees Dorothy as a confident, outspoken, and a passionate actress. Dorothy secures the role and instantly becomes aware of the harassment and unequal treatment the women on set receive. She becomes an unintentional feminist icon as she speaks up for the women on set and takes control of how her character is portrayed. In one scene, she insists that the director refer to her as Dorothy and not as "tootsie" or "sweetie" or "honey," as that is not her name and he calls all the men on set by their names. This is something that causes great shock to the rest of the cast and crew, who stand in awe as Dorothy storms off the set. Dorothy's strength inspires her fellow costar, Julie, whose character was deemed "the hospital slut," to also take control of her character and to reevaluate the way she lets herself be treated by men.

Tootsie provides insight into why actresses waited thirty or more years to come forward; they simply felt as though they would not have been heard. When Dorothy cleverly avoids kissing her costar (John Van Horn) during a scene, Van Horn forces a kiss on her after filming ends. Van Horn then simply walks off set, outwardly showing pride in his actions, and everyone on set carries on as if nothing had happened. Van Horn later goes to Dorothy's apartment to confess his feelings and persuade her to sleep with him. Despite Dorothy's forceful attempts to escape his grasp, the costar continues to force himself on Dorothy. The only thing that stops him from attempting to rape her is the entrance of Dorothy's roommate into the apartment, and Van Horn's erroneous assumption that this is her boyfriend. Van Horn then apologizes to Dorothy, not for his behavior but for not respecting the fact that she had a boyfriend. Although Dorothy denied his advances multiple times, her protests were ignored, and her clear attempt to escape his hold was not acknowledged or taken seriously until another man was present.

While Michael empowered women as Dorothy Michaels, it cannot be ignored that the confidence he possessed to fearlessly speak up for Dorothy and other women during this era was due to his male privilege. He felt confident in confronting inequalities for women because he was not a woman; his empowerment came from the fact that he was a man. Although *Tootsie* explores masculinity, sexuality, sexism, sexual harassment, and gender bias, among other issues, it also portrays these issues for comic effect and perpetuates the idea that a man is needed in for a woman to be heard. The movie somehow manages to highlight feminist themes while simultaneously keeping women in the shadows.

Tootsie has of an all-star cast, featuring Dustin Hoffman as Tootsie, Jessica Lange as Julie, and Bill Murray as Hoffman's roommate. The movie grossed $177 million, making it 1982's second-highest-grossing film after *E.T. the Extra-Terrestrial*. Despite the film's popularity and the fact that it drew attention to sexual misconduct in Hollywood, the sexual abuse and mistreatment portrayed in the film continued to play out in real life for over thirty years after the movie's release. Hoffman's character, Michael Dorsey, may have learned from the experience of playing a woman, but Hoffman himself may not have. In 2017, two women came forward and reported sexual harassment by Hoffman on the set of *Death of a Salesman* in 1985, three years after *Tootsie*.

M'Balu P. Bangura

See also: Hostile Work Environment; #MeToo Movement; Movies, Depictions of Sexual Harassment; Power Dynamics; Quid Pro Quo

Further Reading

Barbara, B. 2014. "Bill Cosby Raped Me. Why Did It Take 30 Years for People to Believe My Story?" *Washington Post*, November 13. https://www.washingtonpost.com /posteverything/wp/2014/11/13/bill-cosby-raped-me-why-did-it-take-30-years-for -people-to-believe-my-story/.

Higgins, B. 2019. "Hollywood Flashback: Dustin Hoffman Cross-Dressed for Success in 1982's Tootsie." *Hollywood Reporter*, April 26. https://www.hollywoodreporter .com/news/dustin-hoffman-cross-dressed-success-1982s-tootsie-1203828.

Holloway, D. 2017. "Dustin Hoffman Accused of Exposing Himself to a Minor, Assaulting Two Women." *Variety*, December 14. https://variety.com/2017/biz/news/dustin -hoffman-2-1202641525.

Victor, D. 2017. "How the Harvey Weinstein Story Has Unfolded." *New York Times*, October 18. Accessed May 14, 2019. https://www.nytimes.com/2017/10/18/business /harvey-weinstein.html.

Traditionally "Male" Workplaces

Many commentators and researchers have linked sexual harassment and misconduct to the persistence of male-dominated workplaces. The U.S. Department of Labor Women's Bureau has identified traditionally male workplaces as occupations whose total number of employees is not at least 25 percent female. Occupations such as aircraft pilots, firefighters, engineers (all types), police and sheriff's patrol officers, detectives and criminal investigators, information security analysts, software developers, and computer programmers are just some of the occupations that as of 2014, despite enormous gains in gender equality in the U.S. workforce over the last fifty years, are still male dominated. When workers separate into different occupations by gender, women face several challenges.

The reasons why almost a third of all men and women in the United States work in separate professions are complicated. Some argue that women are "naturally" disinterested or lack the necessary skills for male-dominated professions. Others identify a complex web of legislative history and socioeconomic factors that have shaped gender segregation at work.

It was not until the protections of Title VII of the Civil Rights Act of 1964 that employment discrimination based on sex (and race, color, creed, and national origin) was made illegal. Until then, a woman's ability to choose certain jobs was either prohibited or greatly restricted. Female employees could only work a certain number of hours in certain shifts in certain industries, and they had distinct physical regulations placed on what they could and could not do in the workplace. Many of these laws were passed at the start of the twentieth century, and their stated intent was protection (e.g., *Muller v. Oregon*, 1908). Multiple legal decisions cited women's importance to the state via their maternal role, their physical "frailty," and their inability to fully embrace their rights as grounds for different (unequal) treatment (protection) under the Fourteenth Amendment.

In practice, these laws put women at a competitive disadvantage. As part of the effort to include sex in the 1964 Civil Rights Act, congressional representatives argued that allowing different rules based on gender opened the door to abuse and exploitation of workers. Martha Griffiths (D-MI) noted that "most of the so-called protective legislation [for women] has really been to protect men's rights in better paying jobs." And Katharine St. George (R-NY) pointed out that many of the employment restrictions for women only applied "when the pay is higher . . . and the load, if you please, is lighter," and not, for instance, in regard to women working late at night cleaning offices (U.S. Congress 1964, 2580).

When Title VII passed into law, women gained an important new legal protection—and they used it. Lorena Weeks, a phone operator who was denied a promotion based on a Georgia law prohibiting women from lifting anything over thirty pounds, won a gender bias lawsuit against Southern Bell in 1969. The mother of three, whose daily work responsibilities as a phone operator already included lifting a thirty-four-pound typewriter (not to mention her domestic tasks, which undoubtedly included lifting small children), presented evidence that the promotion to "switchman" would actually require less lifting on her part, as switchmen used a dolly to move hardware. What it *did* include, however, was higher pay. As the roles of women in social life expanded, more and more women have taken advantage of equal opportunity and entered occupations that in the past had no females. However, the predicted gains have not yet materialized in the way that the crafters envisioned.

POST–EQUAL OPPORTUNITY CHALLENGES

First, males still far outnumber females in the most highly paid professions, such as financial managers, physicians, lawyers, and chief executives. Women continue to be overrepresented in the lowest-paying jobs, referred to as "pink collar" jobs, such as childcare workers, personal care aides, and cashiers. Researchers cannot explain this overrepresentation by a higher level of skill or educational attainment for men. When women do break into male-dominated fields, their wages are still lower than those of their male counterparts, and when a significant percentage of women enter an occupational field, the average pay for that profession declines. The number of women in the most lucrative senior leadership positions is low. In 1995, there were no women chief executive officers (CEOs) of Fortune 500 companies. In 2017, that figure stood at 6 percent (the highest ever), and in 2018, women accounted for 5 percent of the CEOs of those companies.

Second, social mores around a woman's role in domestic life have not changed. As Facebook CEO Sheryl Sandberg famously noted, "We need to live in a world where being a parent is not a full-time job for a woman and a part-time job for a man." Although certain aspects of the law have given women opportunities, the expectations that women bear the majority of domestic work have not. This type of seemingly peripheral social issue has a potentially large impact. As no human being can effectively be in two places at once, certain professions and leadership roles will effectively not be good long-term "choices" for women. Many call for effective legislation to help support parents economically, specifically mothers (e.g., subsidized childcare), to lighten the weight of these domestic responsibilities for women. Reformers argue that without change in this area, gender segregation in workplaces will continue.

Third, when women do succeed in male-dominated workplaces, it comes with risk—real, physical, and psychological risk. Men who work in male-dominated occupations tend to have views of women that put the women they work with in jeopardy of sexual harassment and assault. The men also tend to be the bosses. Women increasingly report these crimes, in addition to being subject to double standards for promotion, misogyny/sexism, and generally hostile work environments. Psychologists have noted that some men in these workplaces may view women as economic competitors and participate in such behaviors in an effort to reclaim "turf."

Whatever the reason, the risks to women of sexual harassment or assault in the U.S. military, on college campuses, and in industries such as sports, media, publishing, academia, restaurants, and tech have received renewed attention. As part of the #MeToo Movement, women from various fields have come forward, often breaking nondisclosure agreements (NDAs) to tell their stories. A common thread that emerges is that male-dominated workplaces often produce cultures where abuses of women's rights are normalized and meaningful discipline for violators is lacking.

Anna King

See also: College Campus; Discrimination; Equal Protection Clause; Factory and Manufacturing Settings; Gender Equality; Hostile Work Environment; #MeToo Movement; Military Settings; News Media Coverage; Nondisclosure Agreements; Publishing; Restaurant/Bar Industry; Title VII of the Civil Rights Act of 1964

Further Reading

Ansel, Bridget. 2017. "Do U.S. Women Choose Low-Paid Occupations, or Do Low-Paid Occupations Choose Them?" *Equitable Growth*, April 3.

Catalyst. 2018. "Quick Take: Women in Male-Dominated Industries and Occupations." August 23. Accessed February 14, 2019. https://www.catalyst.org/research/women-in-male-dominated-industries-and-occupations/.

Cohen, Philip. 2013. "The Problem with Mostly Male (and Mostly Female) Workplaces." The Atlantic, March 20.

Cooper, Marianne. 2017. "The 3 Things That Make Organizations More Prone to Sexual Harassment." *The Atlantic*, November 27.

Equitable Growth. 2017. "Fact Sheet: Occupational Segregation in the United States." October 3. Accessed February 22, 2019. https://equitablegrowth.org/fact-sheet-occupational-segregation-in-the-united-states/.

Groer, Annie. 2013. "Fifty Years of Feminism in 'Makers: Women Who Make America.'" *Washington Post*, February 25.

Kennedy, Joseph P. 1972. "Sex Discrimination: State Protective Laws since Title VII." *Notre Dame L. Rev.* 47(3): 514–549.

McGrew, Will. 2016. "Gender Segregation at Work: 'Separate but Equal' or 'Inefficient and Unfair.'" Equitable Growth, August 18.

"Muller v. Oregon, 208 U.S. 412 (1908)." n.d. Justia Law. Accessed February 27, 2019. https://supreme.justia.com/cases/federal/us/208/412/.

Pew Research Center's Social & Demographic Trends Project. 2018. "The Data on Women Leaders." Accessed February 22, 2019. http://www.pewsocialtrends.org/fact-sheet/the-data-on-women-leaders/.

U.S. Congress. *Congressional Record*. 88th Cong., 2nd session, 1964. Vol. 110, pt. 2.

U.S. Department of Labor, Women's Bureau. 2014. "Traditional and Nontraditional Occupations." https://www.dol.gov/agencies/wb/data.

Traister, Rebecca (1975–)

Rebecca Traister is a celebrated feminist, author, and journalist. Her award-winning articles and books have brought a great sense of awakening to women in the #MeToo Movement era and encouraged women to realize that their anger is a powerful emotion and does not always have to be internally damaging and suppressing. Rather, it can be a catalyst and used to bring on much-needed reform and change to uplift women. All her work focuses on the power of women.

Traister was born in 1975, and she was raised on a farm near Philadelphia, Pennsylvania. She attended Quaker High School and earned her undergraduate degree in American Studies from Northwestern University. Thereafter, she moved to New York City, where she started her career in journalism as an entry-level assistant at *Talk Magazine* and then as a fact checker and journalist at the *New York Observer*. From there, she briefly toiled as a gossip columnist and reporter on the film industry. In 2003, she moved to Salon.com, where she became known for writing on the social, political, and economic status of women from a feminist point of view. A National Magazine Award finalist, Traister continues to publish pieces in *Salon*. She also became a writer at large for *New York Magazine* and regularly contributes feature stories to such national publications as *Elle*, the *New Republic*, the *Nation,* the *New York Observer*, the *New York Times*, the *Washington Post*, *Vogue*, *Glamour*, and *Marie Claire*.

Traister has stated that a pivotal moment in both her personal and professional life came in 2000, when as a young reporter with the *New York Observer*, she spent several weeks trying to arrange an interview with Hollywood mogul Harvey Weinstein. She finally managed to track him down at a party he was hosting. However, her surprise arrival at the party infuriated Weinstein. The film producer flew into a rage, jabbed a finger into her chest, and then used coarse, misogynistic language to humiliate her. When one of her colleagues from the *Observer*, cameraman Andrew Goldman, intervened, Weinstein shoved Goldman down a set of stairs, causing head injuries to another female attendee. Weinstein then dragged him out of the party in a headlock. In this case, even though Weinstein had violently reacted to a journalist's questions and was clearly out of line, the *New York Post* dismissed Traister and Goldman as "pushy reporters," called Traister "the aggressor," and blamed Traister for infuriating Weinstein by asking inappropriate questions.

Basically, the *New York Post* blamed Traister for bringing the treatment she received on herself. This is a common social norm of victim precipitation, blaming women for making men angry and bringing violence on themselves. The *New York Times* quoted a Miramax official, who said that Traister's line of questioning "really wasn't appropriate" and had made Weinstein "upset." Weinstein's furious response, on the other hand, was treated as a "normal response" to allegedly inappropriate questioning.

This experience was a defining moment in Traister's career as a reporter and writer. Her subsequent writings—both in books and magazines—have encouraged women to realize and understand the hidden power of their anger and other emotions. She has demonstrated how women have historically endured atrocities and used their anger to bring the most extraordinary radical social changes in American history, such as abolition, suffrage, and the civil rights movement.

Traister won several awards for her work during the 2008 presidential election. Her writings on Hillary Clinton, Sarah Palin, Michelle Obama, the media's coverage of the candidates during the 2008 campaign from a feminist (and personal) perspective, and the role of women within the media have won her many accolades and encouraged many women to realize their untapped potential.

In 2012, Traister was honored with a Making Trouble/Making History Award from the Jewish Women's Archive, and in the same year, she received a Mirror Award for Best Commentary in Digital Media for two essays that appeared in *Salon* ("'30 Rock' Takes on Feminist Hypocrisy—and Its Own" and "Seeing 'Bridesmaids' Is a Social Responsibility") and one that appeared in the *New York Times* ("The Soap Opera Is Dead! Long Live the Soap Opera").

Traister's first book, *Big Girls Don't Cry* (2010), was a *New York Times* Notable Book of 2010 and the winner of the Ernesta Drinker Ballard Book Prize in 2012. She followed that up with *All the Single Ladies* (2016) and *Good and Mad: The Revolutionary Power of Women's Anger* (2018). Both of these works have sought to help women realize how their anger at always having been relegated to subservient or lesser positions in American culture and society can be used to uplift them and bring out change. She also uses these works to speak out about her belief that women do not have to assess their value in terms of how men see them or how they fit into patriarchal notions of what constitutes "proper" behavior for women. Finally, her works have urged women to be politically active in this #MeToo movement era to eradicate socially, politically, and economically embedded inequities that have maintained women's marginalized status for ages.

Traister continues motivating women to lift themselves up in all spheres: socially, politically, and economically. In addition to her books and articles, she is also invited to speak on feminism and its evolution in politics, media, entertainment, and society at large. She is a regularly invited speaker at prominent national events, such as the Early Money Is Like Yeast (EMILY's List) annual events, the National Association for the Repeal of Abortion Laws (NARAL) and the National Abortion Rights Action League (NARAL), and the Democratic National Convention events. She is often invited to speak at universities, town halls, and other conventions, conferences, and organizations and is a regular guest on national news networks.

Suman Kakar

See also: Harvey Weinstein Scandal; #MeToo Movement; Movies, Depictions of Sexual Harassment

Further Reading
Darozhkina, N. 2017. "Simplify Singlehood: Feminist Writer Rebecca Traister on the Power of Being Single." Blinkist Magazine, December 21. https://www.blinkist.com/magazine/posts/simplify-singlehood-rebecca-traister.

DeMarco, N. 2018. "Rebecca Traister Wants Women to Stay Furious." I-D, October 2. https://i-d.vice.com/en_us/article/j53vax/rebecca-traister-good-and-mad-kavanaugh -trump-metoo.

Live Wire Radio Podcast. 2016. "'Making History' with Rebecca Traister, Ruth Goodman and the Last Artful, Dodgr." Episode 150, March 11, 2016. https://radiopublic.com /live-wire-with-luke-burbank-GEA11G/s1!22f0f.

Marcotte, A. 2018. "We Know What [MAGA] Is Code For. It's Not Even a Secret." Salon, October 8. https://www.salon.com/2018/10/08/rebecca-traister-we-know-what-maga -is-code-for-its-not-even-a-secret/.

Traister, R. 2016. *All the Single Ladies: Unmarried Women and the Rise of an Independent Nation*. New York: Simon and Schuster.

Traister, R. 2018. *Good and Mad: The Revolutionary Power of Women's Anger*. New York: Simon and Schuster.

Truitt, J. 2011. "Slutwalk Redux with Rebecca Traister and Feministing Writers—Ladies We Have a Problem." Feministing.com, July 22. http://feministing.com/2011/07 /22/slutwalk-redux-with-rebecca-traister-and-feministing-writers/.

Wiener, J. 2018. "The Politics of Women's Anger: Rebecca Traister on Women's Activ-ism." *The Nation*, October 12. https://www.thenation.com/article/rebecca-traister -the-politics-of-womens-anger/.

U

Uniform Code of Military Justice

On May 1, 2018, the U.S. Department of Defense (DoD) released its *Annual Report on Sexual Assault in the Military* for fiscal year 2017. The report reflects a 10 percent increase across all services in reporting sexual assaults as compared to fiscal year 2016. Over sixty-seven hundred DoD employees reported being sexually assaulted in 2017, the largest number in one year since the DoD started tracking such data in 2006. In addition, the military received seven hundred separate sexual harassment complaints in 2017. The military handles sexual assaults and sexual harassment charges differently. Sexual assaults are considered a crime, whereas sexual harassment is a considered a violation of policy, specifically the Equal Opportunity (EO) policy. The data shows almost two-thirds of the sexual assaults were handled through the Uniform Code of Military Justice (UCMJ) and resulted in some form of disciplinary action (Gibbons-Neff 2018). Sexual harassment is not covered by a specific article of the UCMJ. The DoD, each military service, and each command have individual sexual harassment policies. Any violation of military policy could result in charges being brought under several general articles of the UCMJ.

Military justice is a legacy from the earliest organized forces. It focuses on two fundamental tenets: the ability to fight and win our nation's wars and to be an efficient, but fair, system for commanders to use to ensure good order and discipline. The foundation of military law is the Constitution of the United States. The Constitution states that Congress has the responsibilities to raise a military force and to make rules to regulate that force, and it establishes the president as commander in chief of all armed forces. Congress exercised its duties over military justice by enacting the UCMJ, the legislation contained in Title 10 of the U.S. Code, sections 801 through 946. The UCMJ was passed by Congress on May 5, 1950, and signed into law on May 31, 1951, by President Harry S. Truman. It is uniform in its application across all services and is meant to be a tool for commanders to use to maintain good order and discipline in the ranks (Uniform Code of Military Justice n.d-a, n.d.-b.).

In his role as commander in chief of the armed forces, the president of the United States has the legal responsibility of writing rules and regulations to implement military law through the publication of the *Manual for Courts-Martial* (MCM). The MCM provides guidance on the conduct of military courts, including providing guidelines for maximum punishments for violation of the articles of the UCMJ (www.military.com).

The UCMJ is a complete set of criminal laws that includes many crimes punished under civilian law (e.g., murder, rape, drug use, larceny, drunk driving), but it also punishes conduct that affects military good order and discipline, such as being absent without leave, failure to obey an order, and dereliction of duty. The specific articles of the UCMJ covering sexual assault are Article 120: Rape and sexual assault generally, Article 125: Sodomy, Article 134: General article covering anything that detracts from good order and discipline or brings discredit upon the armed forces, and Article 80: Attempts, meaning anything done to commit an offense.

In an agency-wide memorandum for Sexual Assault Awareness and Prevention Month, Secretary of Defense James N. Mattis wrote, "Preventing sexual assault is our moral duty. . . . By its nature, sexual assault is one of the most destructive factors in building a mission-focused military" (Ferdinando 2018, 1).

In response, the DoD enhanced the capabilities of the Sexual Assault Prevention and Response Office (SAPRO) to better represent the secretary of defense as the central authority charged "with preventing sexual assault in the military and facilitating recovery for survivors. As the authority for the Department, SAPRO unifies the prevention and response efforts of the Army, Marine Corps, Navy, Air Force, and National Guard by ensuring an equal emphasis on critical challenge areas and making best practices or lessons learned common across these Services" (United States Department of Defense: Sexual Assault Prevention and Response n.d.).

The approach is strategic as actions are guided through five critical areas: (1) prevention, establishing a climate that prevents sexual assault; (2) victim assistance, uncompromising in quality and commitment to survivors; (3) investigation, developing specifically trained investigators and prosecutors; (4) accountability: holding offenders accountable; and (5) assessment, learning and pushing progress forward.

The DoD has made progress in several areas, such as enacting fifty-four secretary of defense–directed SAPR initiatives since 2012, legislating seventy-one sections of law and over one hundred unique requirements, certifying 35,000 service men and women as sexual assault response coordinators and victim advocates, and training 2,000 special agents and prosecutors in advanced sexual assault investigations since 2009. It has 185 specially trained attorneys in place to help victims exercise their rights and navigate the justice system (United States Department of Defense: Sexual Assault Prevention and Response n.d.).

The current focus is on creating the 2017–2021 Sexual Assault Prevention Plan of Action, implementing the Retaliation Prevention and Response Strategy, executing the DoD Plan to Prevent and Respond to Sexual Assault of Military Men, and conducting assessments to measure the effectiveness of case management (United States Department of Defense: Sexual Assault Prevention and Response n.d.).

These are signs of progress, but the more significant problem of sexual assaults in the military remains. Researchers, lawmakers, and military leaders all state that the nation must come to grips with the magnitude of the problem of sexual assault and harassment and invest in finding best practice solutions to prevent the degradation of U.S. military readiness and morale. A solution will require significant attention from Congress, the Armed Services Committees, Appropriations

Committees, and military commanders and leaders at every level. Congress and defense leaders must support and fund the sexual assault prevention programs and initiatives, especially those showing signs of quantitative success. One such initiative focuses at the beginning of the military life cycle—basic training recruiting units—in which professional trainers engage recruits on tough topics such as military sexual assault to promote integrity and awareness from the outset of their military careers (Neiweem 2017).

Frank R. Hall

See also: Code of Conduct; Sexism; Sexual Harassment Training; Tailhook

Further Reading

Department of Defense. n.d. "Department of Defense: Sexual Assault Prevention and Response Office." Accessed August 17, 2018. http://sapr.mil/public/docs/press/SAPROOverviewSlickSheet_20160725.pdf.

Ferdinando, Lisa. 2018. "DoD Releases Annual Report on Sexual Assault in Military." U.S. Department of Defense, May 1. Accessed August 17, 2018. https://www.defense.gov/News/Article/Article/1508127/dod-releases-annual-report-on-sexual-assault-in-military/.

Gibbons-Neff, Thomas. 2018. "Reports of Sexual Assault in the Military Rise by 10 Percent, Pentagon Finds." *New York Times*, April 30. Accessed August 16, 2018. https://www.nytimes.com/2018/04/30/us/politics/sexual-assault-reports-military-increase.html.

Keller, Jared. 2018. "The Biggest Obstacle to the Pentagon's War on Sexual Assault: The Military Justice System." Pacific Standard, May 29. Accessed August 16, 2018. https://psmag.com/news/the-biggest-obstacle-to-the-pentagons-war-on-sexual-assault-the-military-justice-system.

Neiweem, Christopher. 2017. "Sexual Assault in the Military Is More Than a Political Problem." The Hill, March 9. Accessed August 17, 2018. http://thehill.com/blogs/pundits-blog/the-military/323197-sexual-assault-in-the-military-is-more-than-a-political.

Shalal-Esa, Andrea. 2012. "'Tailhook' Cleaned Up, but Top Marine See More Work to Stop Sex Assaults." Reuters, September 10. Accessed August 16, 2018. https://www.reuters.com/article/us-usa-marines-sexualassault/tailhook-cleaned-up-but-top-marine-sees-more-work-to-stop-sex-assaults-idUSBRE88913O20120910.

"Uniform Code of Military Justice." n.d-a. Accessed August 17, 2018. https://www.law.cornell.edu/uscode/text/10/subtitle-A/part-II/chapter-47.

"The Uniform Code of Military Justice (UCMJ)." n.d-b. Military.com. Accessed August 17, 2018. https://www.military.com/join-armed-forces/the-uniform-code-of-military-justice-ucmj.html.

United States Department of Defense: Sexual Assault Prevention and Response. n.d. https://www.sapr.mil.

Unions

Unions have served as the pillar for the employment sector for decades. Beginning with the National Labor Relations Act of 1935, unions have evolved into democratic organizations that act as an intermediary between their members and employers to advance social and economic interests. These interests include negotiating contracts for good wages and benefits and safe working conditions for their diverse memberships. According to the 2019 Bureau of Labor Statistics, 14.7 million wage and salary workers were members of unions in 2018, which is down 0.2 percent from the previous year. Highlights from the 2018 survey indicate that New York and Hawaii had the largest memberships. The same survey reported that unions were predominately comprised of the public sector and those who work in protective service occupations (e.g., police officers, firefighters, and game wardens), education, and librarianship. The majority of union members have always been—and continue to be—men.

Despite public support for organized labor, membership in unions has seen a steady decline during the past several decades across all occupations. Literature addressing union density—the percentage of workers in unions—attributes the decline of membership to steep funding cuts in governmental aid, weakening collective bargaining power, the inability to protect competitive wages, job dissatisfaction among workers, a peak in inequality, a decrease in solidarity, privileged ideologies, and perceptions of anti-union government administrations. While these factors may help explain some of the changes and trends in union membership, laws and legal decisions, such as the U.S. Supreme Court decision in *Janus v. AFSCME* (2018), have fundamentally transformed union practices.

JANUS V. AFSCME (AMERICAN FEDERATION OF STATE, COUNTY, AND MUNICIPAL EMPLOYEES)

Before *Janus v. AFSCME*, court decisions in several states required employees to meet financial obligations to contribute toward union expenditures (see *Abood v. Detroit Board of Education*, 431 U.S. 2009 1977). In the *Janus* case, however, plaintiff Mark Janus, an Illinois state public employee, rejected membership with AFSCME. He thus objected to "fair-share" fees that were deducted from his monthly paycheck and went to the union. In other words, exercising his free speech right, the plaintiff refused to pay fees that would be used by the union for lobbying activities and other political action—activities and actions that did not align with his own personal political beliefs. On June 27, 2018, the U.S. Supreme Court issued a 5–4 landmark decision in *Janus v. AFSCME*, overturning a four-year precedent giving power to public sector unions to exact agency fees from nonmembers, also referred to as "free riders." The Supreme Court ruled that the practice of imposing fees by AFSCME on Janus was unconstitutional.

Despite the opposition by many to the *Janus* ruling and concerns that it will drastically weaken and ultimately eliminate unions throughout the United States, unions who have elected to provide exclusive representation have an inherent duty to provide equal representation to all employees—fee payers (union members) and free riders (persons who benefit from union gains but do not pay dues)—alike. In addition to labor organizations, unions also represent employees in the federal government.

THE RIGHT TO UNION STEWARDSHIP: WEINGARTEN PROTECTION

It is anticipated that union representatives will be called upon to act on behalf of members as well as free riders in addressing complaints and grievances about workplace conditions, including workplaces with sexual harassment problems. Union literature also recognizes that harassers work in various roles, which include supervisors and may be extended to coworkers.

The right to union representation began with the landmark case *National Labor Relations Board v. J. Weingarten, Inc.*, in which the employee requested and was denied union representation during an investigatory interview. However, as mentioned previously, many employees do not work within unionized companies. Summarizing the U.S. Supreme Court decision, the Weingarten rights occur when (1) the employee requests representation (may be based on a complaint), (2) an interview is limited to situations where the employee reasonably believes the investigation will result in disciplinary action, or (3) the exercise of the right may not interfere with legitimate employer prerogative.

Although the Weingarten rights are practical in a union environment, concern arises when these rights are not afforded in the nonunion workplace. Policies are also less clear when both the harasser and victim-survivor are employees within the same workplace.

ORGANIZED LABOR'S RESPONSE TO THE #METOO MOVEMENT

Sexual harassment and assaults allegations have peaked in recent years. Insofar as sexual harassment is a form of sex discrimination, which violates Title VII of the Civil Rights Act of 1964, Weingarten rights are anticipated to become more pronounced in the workplace. Unions have an obligation to uphold the rights, dignity, and self-worth of all workers they represent. Both alleged harassers and alleged victim-survivors who are union members are encouraged to seek support from their unions initially. It is important to note that unions have a responsibility to ensure that the penalties incurred by harassers (such as suspension or termination) match the severity of the offense and to provide resources concerning grievances and arbitration. With the implementation of *Janus v. AFSCME* federal law, however, are unions equipped to expand and offer robust action to accommodate sexual harassment and assault cases?

SEXUAL HARASSMENT TRAINING GOALS

Insofar as collective bargaining has remained a central role for labor unions, anti-harassment activists and experts have urged organized labor to negotiate additional funding for preventive measures, stronger employer positions on sexual harassment, and increased anti-harassment compliance training. Advocacy groups and coalitions are encouraged to look to the Equal Employment Opportunity Commission (EEOC) to train managers and employees alike to recognize and defuse harassing behavior. Imperatives must also enforce serious penalties that help to deter future violation of the law.

Selena T. Rodgers

See also: Equal Employment Opportunity Commission (EEOC); Hostile Work Environment; Title VII of the Civil Rights Act of 1964

Further Reading

Abood v. Detroit Board of Education, 431 U.S. 209 (1977).

Bureau of Labor Statistics. 2019. "Union Members Summary." https://www.bls.gov/news .release/union2.nr0.htm.

Dawkins, Cedric. 2019. "Beyond Wages and Working Conditions: A Conceptualization of Labor Union Social Responsibility." *Journal of Business Ethics* 95: 129–143. https://doi.org/10.1007/s10551-009-0342-3.

DeSilver, Drew. 2018. "Most Americans View Unions Favorably, though Few Workers Belong to One." Pew Research Center, August 30. http://www.pewresearch.org /fact-tank/2018/08/30/union-membership-2/.

Herbert, William, A. 2007. "The History Books Tell It? Collective Bargaining in Higher Education in the 1940s." *Journal of Collective Bargaining in the Academy* 9(1): 1–40.

Hirsch, Barry T, and David A. Macpherson. 2016. "Union Membership and Coverage Database from the Current Population Survey." *Industrial and Labor Relations Review* 56(2): 349–354. https://doi.org/10.1177/001979390305600208.

Mellor, S., and L. M. Kath. 2016. "Union Revitalization: How Women and Men Officers See the Relationship between Union Size and Union Tolerance for Sexual Harassment." *Employee Responsibilities and Rights Journal* 28: 45–59. https://doi.org/10 .1007/s10672-015-9261-x.

Morgan, J. F., J. M. Owens, and G. M. Gomes. 2002. "Union Rules Intrude upon the Nonunion Domain: Workplace Investigations and the NLRB." *Employee Responsibilities and Rights Journal* 14(1): 33–43.

National Labor Relations Board v. J. Weingarten, Inc., 420 U.S. 251 (1975).

Stinglhamber, F., C. Gillis, C. P. Teixeira, and S. Demoulin. 2013. "To Be or Not to Be Unionized? A Question of Organizational Support and Identification." *Journal of Personnel Psychology* 12(2): 92–96. https://doi.org/10.1027/1866-5888/a000086.

Wright, S., and T. Moore. 2012. "Shifting Models of Equality? Union Equality Reps in the Public Services." *Industrial Relations Journal* 43(5): 433–447.

Vance v. Ball State University (2013)

In *Vance v. Ball State University,* the U.S. Supreme Court examined the question of who qualifies as a supervisor when an employee sues his or her employer under Title VII of the Civil Rights Act of 1964 for workplace harassment. *Vance,* which was decided in 2013, involved a claim of racial discrimination rather than sexual harassment, but the court's decision serves as precedent in all Title VII cases.

The question presented in *Vance* was important because in Title VII cases, the classification of the harasser as a supervisor versus a coworker determines what the plaintiff must prove to win his or her case. If the alleged harasser was the plaintiff's coworker, the employer is only liable if the employer was negligent in controlling the harassing employee's actions and the work environment. To prove negligence, the plaintiff claiming harassment must prove that the employer knew or should have known about the harassment and did not prevent or stop it.

However, if the harasser was the plaintiff's supervisor, the employer may be held strictly liable for the supervisor's harassment. *Strictly liable* means that the employer is liable for the supervisor's actions even if the employer was not negligent, so the plaintiff does not have to prove that the employer knew about the harassment. Therefore, Title VII harassment cases involving supervisors are often easier to prove then those involving coworkers.

Prior to the Supreme Court's decision in *Vance,* the lower federal courts had not reached a consensus as to what constitutes a supervisor for purposes of Title VII. Some circuit courts and the Equal Employment Opportunity Commission (EEOC) defined supervisor more broadly as someone having the ability to exercise significant direction over another's daily work. Other circuit courts defined it more narrowly as someone who has the power to hire, fire, demote, promote, transfer, or discipline the other employee. As there was a split among the lower courts, the Supreme Court accepted the case on appeal to decide the question of what constitutes a supervisor.

The case involved Maetta Vance, an African American woman who worked for Ball State University (BSU) as a catering assistant in BSU's Banquet and Catering division of Dining Services. Saundra Davis, who was white, also worked for BSU as a catering specialist in the same division as Vance. In Vance's complaint against BSU, she stated that Davis "gave her a hard time" by, among other things, glaring at her, slamming pots and pans, blocking her with a cart, and giving her weird looks. The employer and employee disagreed as to whether Davis was Vance's supervisor, but they both agreed that Davis "did not have the power to hire, fire, promote, transfer, or discipline Vance."

The court defined *supervisor* for purposes of strict vicarious liability under Title VII as "one who is empowered by the employer to take tangible employment decisions against the victim." The court further stated that such tangible employment decisions mean the power to "effect a significant change in employment status such as hiring, firing, failing to promote, reassignment with significantly different responsibilities, or a decision causing significant change in benefits."

The court held in a narrow 5–4 decision, carried by its conservative majority, that Davis was not Vance's supervisor under Title VII. The *Vance* court's definition of supervisor is now the controlling law in all Title VII cases throughout the country, including sexual harassment cases. It is important to note, as the court pointed out, that the *Vance* decision only applies to an employer's strict liability for the acts of supervisors. With regard to acts by coworkers who do not qualify as supervisors, plaintiffs can still win Title VII cases against their employers by proving that the employer acted negligently in controlling the work environment.

Elizabeth W. Marchioni

See also: Equal Protection Clause; Hostile Work Environment; Title VII of the Civil Rights Act of 1964

Further Reading

Freeman, Andrew. 2015. "A Bright Line, but Where Exactly: A Closer Look at Vance v. Ball State University and Supervisor Status under Title VII." *Lewis & Clark Law Review* 19: 1153.

Hirsch, Jeremy M. 2013. "Supreme Court's 2012–2013 Labor and Employment Law Decisions: The Song Remains the Same." *Employment Rights & Employment Policy Journal* 17: 157.

Vance v. Ball State University, 570 U.S. 421 (2013).

Vodanovich, Stephen J., and Chris Piotrowski. 2014. "What Constitutes the Definition of Supervisor in Workplace Harassment Cases?" *Journal of Instructional Psychology* 41(1–4): 97–99.

Victim Blaming

Victim blaming is the practice of holding a victim of a crime (or other harmful act) responsible for his or her own victimization. In the case of sexual assault, a nonvictim would attribute the crime to the victim's behavior (e.g., she walked home alone or she dressed immodestly), not to the perpetrator's own violent conduct. Some view analyzing the role of victims in their own victimization as a valid and legitimate area of inquiry. From this point of view, victim blaming is not only appropriate but also the only realistic way for one to avoid harm. Women who take responsibility for how their actions contribute to crimes against them can avoid such events; women who do not take responsibility deserve what they get. Camille Paglia, one of the most central proponents of this perspective, put it this way, "A girl who lets herself get dead drunk at a fraternity party is a fool. A girl who goes upstairs alone with a brother at a fraternity party is an idiot. Feminists call this 'blaming the victim.' I call it common sense" (Paglia 2017, 54).

Feminists and many others believe that blaming victims shifts the focus from the true cause of harm, the perpetrator. From this point of view, blaming victims is the dysfunctional product of nonvictims' instinct for self-protection (or a defense mechanism). When confronted with human injustice or suffering, the argument goes, blaming the victim functions to restore a feeling of safety and control (e.g., "I would not have acted the way that victim did, so I would not have been harmed"). It can also alleviate other anxieties that those events provoke, such as feelings of guilt and helplessness. For those working to prevent harm from this point of view, however, blaming victims for crimes that they are less or not at all responsible for presents an almost immovable obstacle. How, they ask, can change occur in a culture that refuses to look at the actual source of the problem?

RISING SCHOLARLY INTEREST IN VICTIM BLAMING

Scholarly attention to victim blaming did not begin with feminists or gender injustice but in the aftermath of the atrocities of World War II. Social science researchers struggled to understand how so many people could have been complicit in mass genocide against Jews in Germany and other European nations. Their hypothesis, based on a Freudian model of the unconscious, was that certain characteristics related to a fascist or authoritarian personality were responsible (Adorno et al. 1950). They identified "authoritarian aggression" as a dispositional tendency to engage in the projection of one's own insecurities and anxieties onto those who have less power (e.g., women, minorities); this process is part of the adherence to an externally imposed authority that defines acceptable norms. In sum, it is frightening and dangerous to blame an authority who is seen as capable of aggressive action (e.g., the Third Reich, the patriarchy) against accusers. For many, aligning with the source of that power offers relief from uncomfortable feelings as well as a possible escape from retaliation, if only temporarily. A witness to human cruelty or crime thus circumvents his or her own fear by symbolically "joining" the aggressor in their attack on what (or whom) is actually a powerless target.

Americans became more familiar with the phrase "blaming the victims" during the civil rights movement. For example, sociologist and U.S. senator Daniel Patrick Moynihan issued a report on ongoing poverty in African American communities that portrayed Black poverty as caused by deficits of values and character within Black culture rather than deep and corrosive currents of institutional racism in American society (Moynihan 1965). Psychologist William Ryan wrote *Blaming the Victim* (1971), which asserted that Black poverty was due to structural causes external to the community, namely, persistent, endemic, and multi-layered racism. His book was widely regarded as a direct and critical response to Moynihan's report. Ryan considered blaming people who had borne unjust persecution, discrimination, and human rights violations—for carrying collective scars of those abuses—to be irrational and morally abhorrent. His argument was that things like poverty were simply the logical consequences of structural injustice, not proof that negative outcomes such as poverty were deserved.

Researchers have coined the term *secondary victimization* to describe victim-blaming attitudes and the absence of policies that take victim trauma into account, especially for victims of sexual assault navigating the criminal justice system. Some research indicates that victims who experience law enforcement as unsympathetic are less likely to go forward with prosecution. In essence, critics argue that, too often, the very people who are supposed to be helping victims are part of a culture that believes that bad things happen to bad people. Melvin Lerner, who also began his work in the wake of social science research that asked, "How can ordinary people become complicit in the harm of others?" offers some insight. Lerner studied the readiness of people to deny external structural causes of injustice. He eventually developed the "just world theory," which attributes blaming victims to a cognitive bias best described as the need to believe that the world delivers fair outcomes, or that bad things only happen to people who deserve it.

DIFFERENT FORMS OF VICTIM BLAMING

Perhaps because practices such as blaming women for male sexual misbehavior (e.g., Eve made Adam do it) and even the offering up of sacrificial lambs to appease angry gods (e.g., scapegoats) go back to the days of Abraham, many believe that a propensity to blame victims, especially female ones, is endemic to the human condition. However, there is considerable evidence that victim blaming varies. Attractive women are more likely to be blamed for their own assault, as are women who have consumed drugs or alcohol, who knew the perpetrator, or who are believed to not have resisted strongly enough. Those with sexist beliefs are more likely to blame victims, and in cultures where gender inequality is high (e.g., Yemen, Pakistan), victim blaming is more pervasive.

At the same time, cultures move through periods where awareness and attention to the negative outcomes of victim blaming increase and then fade, even where progress and tradition seem to coexist. For instance, in the United States, a victim's movement that began in the 1970s eventually evolved to include the use of victim impact statements in court cases involving rape and sexual assault. In 2018, during the sentencing phase of the trial of USA Gymnastics doctor Larry Nassar, who had sexually abused hundreds of young female athletes under the guise of providing medical treatment, 204 victim impact statements were read aloud in court, and many were televised. For those seeking to rid the culture of victim blaming, the inclusion of voices and perspective into the national discussion was a high point.

Anna King

See also: Authority Figures; Discrimination; Gender Equality; Hill, Anita; Larry Nassar Scandal; Sexism; Thomas, Clarence

Further Reading

Adorno, Theodor W., Else Frenkel-Brunswik, Daniel J. Levinson, and R. Nevitt Sanford. 1950. *The Authoritarian Personality.* New York: Harper & Brothers.

Eigenberg, H., and R. Garland. 2008. "Victim Blaming." In *Controversies in Victimology,* edited by L. J. Moriarty, 21–36. Newark, NJ: Elsevier Press.

Gravelin, Claire R., Monica Biernat, and Matthew Baldwin. 2019. "The Impact of Power and Powerlessness on Blaming the Victim of Sexual Assault." *Group Processes & Intergroup Relations* 22(1): 98–115.

Grubb, A., and J. Harrower. 2009. "Understanding Attribution of Blame in Cases of Rape: An Analysis of Participant Gender, Type of Rape and Perceived Similarity to the Victim." *Journal of Sexual Aggression* 15: 63–81.

Kalra, Gurvinder, and Dinesh Bhugra. 2013. "Sexual Violence against Women: Understanding Cross-Cultural Intersections." *Indian Journal of Psychiatry* 55(3): 244–249.

Lepore, Jill. 2018. "The Rise of the Victims'-Rights Movement." *New Yorker*, May 14. https://www.newyorker.com/magazine/2018/05/21/the-rise-of-the-victims-rights-movement.

Lerner, M. J. 1966. "The Unjust Consequences of the Need to Believe in a Just World." In *Meeting of the American Psychological Association*. New York, September.

Loughnan, S., A. Pina, E. A. Vasquez, and E. Puvia. 2013. "Sexual Objectification Increases Rape Victim Blame and Decreases Perceived Suffering." *Psychology of Women Quarterly* 37: 455–461.

Moor, A. 2010. "She Dresses to Attract, He Perceives Seduction: A Gender Gap in Attribution of Intent to Women's Revealing Style of Dress and Its Relation to Blaming the Victims of Sexual Violence." *Journal of International Women's Studies* 11: 115–127.

Moynihan, Daniel Patrick. 1965. "The Negro Family: The Case for National Action (The Moynihan Report)." Office of Policy Planning & Research, U.S. Department of Labor. https://www.dol.gov/general/aboutdol/history/webid-moynihan.

Paglia, Camille. 2017. *Free Women, Free Men*. New York: Pantheon Books.

Patterson, Debra. 2011. "The Linkage between Secondary Victimization by Law Enforcement and Rape Case Outcomes." *Journal of Interpersonal Violence* 26(2): 328–347.

Pedersen, Sven H., and Leif A. Strömwall. 2013. "Victim Blame, Sexism and Just-World Beliefs: A Cross-Cultural Comparison." *Psychiatry, Psychology and Law* 20(6): 932–941.

Roberts, Kayleigh. 2016. "The Psychology of Victim-Blaming." *The Atlantic*, October 5. https://www.theatlantic.com/science/archive/2016/10/the-psychology-of-victim-blaming/502661/.

Ryan, William. 1976. *Blaming the Victim*. New York: Vintage Books.

Solnit, Rebecca. 2018. "The Brett Kavanaugh Case Shows We Still Blame Women for the Sins of Men." *The Guardian*, September 21. http://www.theguardian.com/commentisfree/2018/sep/21/brett-kavanaugh-blame-women-anita-hill-cosby-weinstein.

Violence Against Women Reauthorization Act of 2013

The original Violence Against Women Act (VAWA) became law in 1994 after receiving bipartisan support for its goals. Senator Joe Biden (D-DE) and Representative Louise Slaughter (D-NY) drafted the legislation together to help prevent and to respond appropriately to instances of sexual violence. VAWA also created the Office on Violence against Women, which was added to the Department of Justice under the Clinton administration.

VAWA has been reauthorized by Congress in 2000, 2005, and 2013. The 2013 reauthorization represented the conclusion of a lengthy ideological battle in 2012 (the legislation's originally intended reauthorization date) between Democrats and Republicans about the inclusion of other minority groups in VAWA's coverage. During the 2012 debates over VAWA reauthorization, critics took issue with the protections offered to same-sex couples and undocumented immigrants, even as supporters applauded the Obama administration's 2010 expansion of protections to include groups not previously covered by the legislation. Ultimately, the two sides came to an agreement to reauthorize VAWA.

Senator Patrick Leahy (D-VT) first introduced the 2013 iteration of the bill to Congress on January 22, 2013, and the bill became law on March 7, 2013. The 2013 reauthorization of VAWA included a number of new provisions. This particular reauthorization increased pro bono legal services for victims of sexual and domestic violence; improved available support services for victims; further protected marginalized victims, such as minors, immigrants, or victims residing on tribal lands; and amended the sections of the Jeanne Clery Disclosure of Campus Security and Campus Crimes Statistics Act (Clery Act). The VAWA-imposed amendments to Clery include increased awareness programs and educational initiatives to prevent sexual violence on college campuses.

Proponents of the law said that the 2013 VAWA reauthorization created broader support for all victims of sexual violence while providing even more support for those victims who may lack resources in their own communities or networks. Given the alarmingly high rates of sexual violence on college campuses (White House Task Force to Protect Students from Sexual Assault 2014, 2) and the even more alarming rates of underreporting of such instances (Fisher et al. 2003, 24), college students fit into this "under-supported victim" category.

Less than one year after the reauthorization of VAWA, the Obama administration created the White House Task Force to Protect Students from Sexual Assault. The task force issued its first report in April 2014 and echoed many of the goals and reforms contained in the most recent VAWA reauthorization. In its report, the task force references violence prevention, responding to and supporting victims, and effectively enforcing other existing legislation, such as the Clery Act and VAWA (White House Task Force to Protect Students from Sexual Assault 2014, 2–5).

VAWA has not been updated or amended since the 2013 reauthorization. The legislation expired in December 2018 in the middle of a government shutdown and was only reinstated for a short time in January 2019 with the assistance of short-term government spending legislation. Following the expiration of that bill, VAWA expired once again in February 2019. In April 2019, the Democratic-controlled House passed a VAWA reauthorization bill that included provisions extending protections to transgender individuals, but the legislation stalled in the Republican-controlled Senate. The current future of VAWA is uncertain, even as issues of sexual violence and violence against women remain nationwide problems in the United States.

Lindsay R. Davis

See also: Campus Accountability and Safety Act (CASA); Campus Sexual Violence Elimination Act (SaVE Act); College Campuses; Gender Equality; Sexism; Title IX

Further Reading

Fisher, B. S., Leah E. Daigle, Francis T. Cullen, and Michael G. Turner. 2003. "Reporting Sexual Victimization to the Police and Others: Results from a National-Level Study of College Women." *Criminal Justice and Behavior* 30(1): 6–38.

U.S. Department of Justice. 2019. "Office on Violence against Women." March. https://www.justice.gov/ovw.

Violence against Women Reauthorization Act of 2013, S.47, 113th Congress (2013–2014).

White House Task Force to Protect Students from Sexual Assault. 2014. "Not Alone: The First Report of the White House Task Force to Protect Students from Sexual Assault." U.S. Government Publishing Office, April. Accessed February 8, 2019. http://purl.fdlp.gov/GPO/gpo48344.

Women's March

The Women's March, a broad movement to support women's rights both in the United States and abroad, brought some four million Americans out to protest on January 21, 2017. Scheduled the day after President Donald Trump's inauguration, the march was meant to symbolize the resistance many had to his allegedly anti-woman policies as well as his record of remarks seen as insulting or misogynistic toward women. Considered to be the largest one-day demonstration in U.S. history, the genesis of this movement came from a retired attorney in Hawaii, Teresa Shook, who was distraught over the news of Donald Trump's victory in the 2016 presidential election. Stunned by this turn of events, one evening, she channeled her frustration by inviting some of her Facebook friends to protest in Washington, DC, the day after his inauguration. That evening, forty of her friends responded and then, in turn, passed on the invitation to others. By the next morning, ten thousand people had signed on, signaling a much bigger event than she could have ever imagined. Several others relayed similar stories: astronomical responses to invitations to protest. In total, there were at least 653 marches involving four million people in the United States and hundreds of thousands more abroad, involving protestors on every continent on the globe.

ORGANIZATION AND PLATFORM OF THE WOMEN'S MARCH

While the initial conception of the march may have been born out of frustration with Donald Trump's treatment of women and the incoming administration's expected policies, it was clear that it tapped into a broader wellspring of both political dissent and female solidarity. Within a short time, and in part because the movement grew exponentially, the early organizers ceded control to professional activists, who were brought in to establish a nonprofit agency with a mission and to iron out administrative and legal issues that accompany large-scale demonstrations. The primary organizers of the movement were Vanessa Wruble, Tamika D. Mallory, Carmen Perez and Linda Sarsour. The organization, also known as Women's March, coalesced around several specific themes, and by the time the march came around on January 21, 2017, the organizers had a clear policy platform and mission:

> The mission of Women's March is to harness the political power of diverse women and their communities to create a transformative social change. Women's March is a women-led movement providing intersectional education on a diverse range of

issues and creating entry points for new grassroots activists & organizers to engage in their local communities through trainings, outreach programs and events. Women's March is committed to dismantling systems of oppression through nonviolent resistance and building inclusive structures guided by self-determination.

This mission was then further explicated through the "Unity Principles," which outlined goals of "ending violence" and strongly endorsed "reproductive freedom, LGBTQIA rights, civil rights, worker's rights, disability rights, immigrant rights and environmental justice."

On January 21, 2017, the march descended on hundreds of cities across the country. The primary site, in Washington, DC, drew more than one million people. In addition to the high turnout in the streets, there were stories of those who could not physically march but found ways to participate. Patients in a cancer ward in a Los Angeles hospital reportedly marched the hallways inside the hospital, and hundreds of others who were physically disabled and could not make it out of their homes offered online support.

The march also drew many celebrities to protest, both as speakers and as citizens who wished to engage in the protest informally. At the largest rally, in Washington, DC, Angela Davis, Ashley Judd, Michael Moore, Maryum Ali, Scarlett Johansson, and Gloria Steinem were among the many speakers. Others were spotted on social media just attending the march and holding their own signs.

According to several sources, there was not a single arrest at any of the marches around the world: no skirmishes or eruptions of violence and no burned buildings or cars. In fact, several media outlets published accounts of marchers high-fiving the police along their route. And while many touted this as a sign that women knew how to protest peacefully, others pointed out that perhaps the police response was different when facing a crowd of largely white women. Many observers pointed out that crowds of color, such as Black Lives Matter (BLM) protests, did not receive the same reception from law enforcement. To the contrary, BLM protests and demonstrations against police violence against people of color were often met with riot gear from the outset.

Some critics criticized the "whiteness" of the Women's March crowds, asserting that the march needed to not only have more representation from women of color and from LGBTQ communities but also that it should have focused more on minority groups' long-standing issues of oppression (e.g., immigration reform, legal protection for those who identify as LGBTQ). Others pointed out that women of color had been fighting for women's rights for some time, and when the march took off, they felt their concerns were dismissed or overlooked. They further pointed out that although the march had a markedly anti-Trump atmosphere, a majority of white women in the United States had voted for Trump, providing a key demographic in his electoral win. Some critics questioned whether when people associated with the march asserted women's rights were human rights, they were more narrowly focusing on *white* women's rights. Further, some people of color felt betrayed by white women.

Still, even for critics, the success of the day was hard to argue: the expanse of the women marching in solidarity for women's rights from the United States and Europe all the way to Iceland and Antarctica was powerful. With no violence or arrests to speak of, critical conservative media outlets such as Fox News were left to focus on the litter left behind by protesters. Others criticized what they saw as the vulgarity of the "p***y hats" worn by many participants. Nevertheless, there was much less backlash to the Women's March than to other similar recent protests, such as Black Lives Matter.

SYMBOLS AND SIGNS

The march was rich with signs and symbols of female power. Without question, the dominant symbol of the Women's March were pink "p***y hats." The hats were knitted with twin peaks, to symbolize cat ears. At least in part, the hats were a symbol of defiance toward President Trump's vulgar comments made on a hot mic while taping for *Access Hollywood* years earlier: "You know, I'm automatically attracted to beautiful [women]—I just start kissing them. It's like a magnet. Just kiss. I don't even wait. And when you're a star, they let you do it. You can do anything. . . . Grab 'em by the p***y. You can do anything."

The disclosure of these audiotapes shook the political world just a few weeks before the 2016 election, and many felt this would be the final nail in a scandal-ridden presidential campaign. Of course, those folks who thought no candidate could survive such endorsements of outward misogyny and sexual assault were wrong; perhaps as a result, the Women's March (and the p***y hats, in particular) became a vehicle for many women to remind Trump and the wider Republican Party of what he said and to declare that they were not going to stand for the normalization of sexual assault.

The hats quickly emerged as a clear visual representation of feminine power. Pictures of the Women's March vividly show the sea of pink that was present that day. Even making the hats became a moment of bonding and connection over the cause: media outlets covered many stories where local stores ran out of pink yarn due to the surge in demand. Many women who could not make it to a march—for medical reasons or otherwise—contributed by knitting the hats and distributing them to friends or strangers.

Along with the hats, the march was awash in a sea of signs—many funny with biting wit and others expressing fierce anger or deep sadness. Other signs indicated that the female gender was up for the challenge of opposing an administration seen by many marchers as corrupt and misogynistic: "Fight like a girl" or "Feminazis against actual Nazis." Some signs drew parallels to history, alluding to Japanese American citizens who had been forcibly interned by the government during World War II or Jewish Americans who had lived in concentration camps in Europe. These signs pointed out the dangers of past historical figures who peddled fear and xenophobia, clearly implying their creators' views that Trump had engaged in similar behavior during the campaign. These signs often had messages of "Never again" or "History is watching."

Celebrated artists also contributed their work for distribution. Shepard Fairy created a series of iconic posters depicting women of color and proclaiming, "We the People Are Greater Than Fear," "We the People Defend Dignity," and "We the People Protect Each Other." These signs were ubiquitous and have subsequently become a common symbol for the march and the greater movement. While there was a diversity of messages on these signs, the overarching message was that women would not relinquish their rights, and they would not be quietly relegated to secondary citizens.

LEGACY OF THE MARCH

Just days after the event in January 2017, many wondered whether the march would be a powerful cultural moment or a burgeoning political movement. Since then, scholars generally agree that the march was the beginning of *something*, although historians will likely disagree about precisely what that is. At the very least, the Women's March can be viewed as the kickoff event for an era of sporadic—but sometimes large scale—marches and protests demonstrating opposition to President Trump's policies. The first of these happened within a week of the Women's March, when President Trump and his administration enacted an executive order that outlined a wide-scale effort to suspend immigration temporarily and bar refugees from multiple heavily Muslim countries. Within a short time, protests erupted at airports across the country where immigrants and refugees were being detained. Shortly thereafter, large protests were held in Washington, DC, and New York, with smaller protests in many other cities. Other protests sprang up in various cities around Martin Luther King Day marches as well as around issues of democracy, racism, immigration policies, and abortion rights.

While none of these protests approached the scope of the initial Women's March, many have observed that the country's willingness to protest policies has substantially increased. The Trump era has become an era of persistent protest within the United States, with some observers describing it as a period of social upheaval not seen since the civil rights movement in the 1960s.

While mobilization in the streets has occurred in record numbers, mobilization on the ballot is another piece of the march's legacy. In 2018, a record number of women (mostly Democrats) ran in elections for the House of Representatives and Senate, and most of these women were not incumbents. Many of these women won their bids for elected office as well. The 116th Congress that began its work in January 2019 included a record 102 women in the House, more than 23 percent of that chamber's total membership, and 25 women in the Senate, a quarter of that chamber's total. This type of mobilization—both in elections and on the streets—proves that women and women's issues are now a formidable force within in the U.S. political landscape.

ME TOO/TIME'S UP

The Women's March harnessed an energy among women and their male allies to demand change. Without question, it was this foundation that provided fertile ground for the next major historical development in women's history in the United States: the #MeToo Movement. Brought on by the dozens of allegations of sexual abuse by Harvey Weinstein, the powerful filmmaking mogul, the #MeToo hashtag spread far and wide. Although #MeToo had existed prior to 2017—primarily as a vehicle for women of color and LGBTQ who had been victimized—the hashtag quickly went viral and gained mainstream recognition. The disclosures became contagious; from average citizens to celebrities, women came forward to claim their experiences. The message behind #MeToo was that women would stand together, support one another, and shed any shame they may have felt in the past. *Time Magazine* later named the "Silence Breakers" to be the Person of the Year for 2017.

2018 WOMEN'S MARCH

In 2018, a second Women's March took place in dozens of cities across the country. Although it did not have the same expanse of the inaugural Women's March, it still drew between 1.8 million and 2.6 million participants and again featured few arrests or documented incidents of violence.

Despite increasing awareness of women's issues and a series of high-profile disclosures of sexual harassment and violence that have ousted several powerful men since the first march, the movement itself has experienced significant setbacks. In particular, the confirmation of Justice Brett Kavanaugh in September 2018 to the U.S. Supreme Court, even after several credible accusations of sexual assault (including the testimony of Dr. Christine Blasey Ford before Congress), was seen by many #MeToo activists as a blow to their efforts to create a more equitable and fair society. Still, the energy harnessed by the march is not likely to dissipate any time soon.

Jennifer M. Balboni and Samyah Williams

See also: #MeToo Movement; *Time Magazine* "Silence Breakers"

Further Reading

Brooks, David. 2017. "After the Women's March." *New York Times*, January 24.

Chenowith, E., and J. Pressman. 2017. "This Is What We Learned by Counting the Women's Marches." *Washington Post*, February 7.

Holloway, S. T. 2018. "Why This Black Girl Will Not be Returning to the Women's March." HuffPost, January 19. Accessed January 10, 2019. https://www.huffingtonpost.com/entry/why-this-black-girl-will-not-be-returning-to-the-womens-march_us_5a3c1216e4b0b0e5a7a0bd4b.

"Our Mission." The Women's March. Accessed January 10, 2019. https://womensmarch.com/mission-and-principles.

Sparks, G., and A. Grayer. 2018. "256 Women Won House and Senate Primaries, a Huge New Record." CNN, September 17. Accessed January 10, 2019. https://www.cnn.com/2018/09/16/politics/house-women-update-september/index.html

Zacharek, S., E. Dockterman, and H. Sweetland Edwards. 2017. "Person of the Year: The Silence Breakers." *Time Magazine*, December 18. Accessed January 10, 2019. http://time.com/time-person-of-the-year-2017-silence-breakers/.

Wood, Carmita (1931–)

Sexual harassment law was shaped by the battle of Black women during the civil rights era of the 1960s and 1970s. Carmita Wood, who was born and raised in Cayuga Lake, New York, was a pioneering figure in the battle against sexual harassment in the American workplace, and her example was an inspiration to the #MeToo Movement as it is known today.

In 1975, Wood was a forty-four-year-old single mother of four who served as an administrative assistant to Boyce McDaniel, a renowned nuclear physicist who had worked on the Manhattan Project before becoming director of Cornell University's Laboratory of Nuclear Sciences (Jackson 2018). McDaniel constantly made Wood feel uncomfortable at work. He stood too close to her, pressed his body against her, and touched her in unwelcome ways. Wood also stated that McDaniel would "shake his crotch" at her while opening his mail. At an office Christmas party, McDaniel cornered Wood in an elevator and kissed her on the mouth without her consent. From that point, Wood took the stairs in an attempt to avoid being trapped by McDaniel again. Wood developed chronic back and neck pain as well as tingling in her right thumb. At this time, there was no cultural conversation—let alone legal framework—addressing the harassment she was experiencing. Instead, countless women quietly endured unwanted advances, sexual innuendo, and other forms of harassment on the job because they had no other recourse other than to leave their job.

In 1974, one year prior to Wood's experience with McDaniel, journalist Lin Farley was teaching a course in the Human Affairs Program at Cornell titled Women and Work. After speaking with the women enrolled in her class, Farley noted that almost all her students had left or been fired from a job as a result of sexual harassment perpetrated by male colleagues or supervisors. In addition, she noted that the women in her class seemed empowered by having the opportunity to share their experiences. Once women had a safe space to share about their harassment, they formed a community around their stories, one that connected students of all races, classes, and marital statuses.

Wood ultimately requested a transfer to another department, and when it did not go through, she quit. She temporarily left to go out of town for rest. Upon her return, she applied for unemployment insurance. When the claims investigator asked why she had quit, she was at a loss for words to describe the embarrassment and shame she had experienced at McDaniel's hands. Wood told the investigator that her reasons for leaving were personal. As a result, the investigator denied her claim for unemployment benefits. Wood then turned to other women employees at Cornell University for help. That decision had enduring implications for women across the United States, as it served as the catalyst for changes in workplace relations between men and women and outdated ideas about propriety.

Although Carmita Wood lost her appeal, Cornell did place her in another campus job. Working alongside activists from Cornell's Human Affairs Office, many of whom were galvanized by Lin Farley's class and others, and civil rights lawyers such as Eleanor Holmes Norton—who was, at the time, New York City's commissioner of human rights—Wood helped form Working Women United (WWU). The group shed light upon the pervasive sexual harassment they were seeing in their workplaces and held "speak-outs" to form a community around the problem. Norton drafted an anti–sexual harassment clause for affirmative action agreements, a precursor to the sexual harassment guidelines she would issue in 1980 as chair of the U.S. Equal Employment Opportunity Commission (EEOC).

Working Women United disbanded just one year later; however, individual women associated with WWU continued to raise funds for research and create robust networks of attorneys and advocates with the aim of solidifying sexual harassment as a criminal offense. After more than a decade, in a landmark 1986 decision, the U.S. Supreme Court ruled that sexual harassment is illegal, as it violates federal law against sex discrimination in the workplace.

Tara A. Garrison

See also: Equal Employment Opportunity Commission (EEOC); Farley, Lin; #MeToo Movement; Norton, Eleanor Holmes; Title VII of the Civil Rights Act of 1964

Further Reading

Jackson, D. L. 2018 "'Me Too': Epistemic Injustice and the Struggle for Recognition." *Feminist Philosophy Quarterly* 4(4): 1–19.

Maloney, C. 2016. "From Epistemic Responsibility to Ecological Thinking: The Importance of Advocacy for Epistemic Community." *Feminist Philosophy Quarterly* 2(2): 7.

Romdenh-Romluc, K. 2016. "Hermeneutical Injustice: Blood-Sports and the English Defense League." *Social Epistemology* 30(5–6): 592–610.

Workplace Gender Diversity

Gender diversity in the workplace has been linked to numerous positive outcomes. Greater gender diversity in the workplace has been associated with less sexual harassment, greater business profits, and even higher employee satisfaction. Thus, workplace gender diversity has the potential to improve the workplace environment for employees and employers. Yet, gender diversity in the workplace remains difficult to attain, especially in particular industries and professions. Although the United States and other countries have made inroads in increasing gender diversity in employment, several occupations and workplaces remain highly segregated between men and women. This segregation contributes to both gender inequality and inequality for people of color in the United States.

How can a healthier workplace environment be created, not just for women but for all employees? Some point to gender occupational segregation (disproportionality in the occupations held by women and men) as an explanation for several persistent gender inequities in the workforce. There are two types of occupational segregation: horizontal segregation (men and women disproportionally hold different occupations at the same level) and vertical segregation (women disproportionately hold lower-ranking occupations). Vertical segregation is also known as the glass ceiling, where women are frequently able to attain and hold low or middle management positions but have trouble breaking through to upper management.

IMPACT

How does this impact gender diversity in the workplace? Occupational segregation leads to male- and female-dominated occupations in the labor market and fewer women in higher level positions, such as senior management. For instance, in the United States, women held over 70 percent of the jobs in education and nursing in 2017, while over 75 percent of firefighter and law enforcement jobs were filled by men (U.S. Census Bureau 2018). Women also held fewer than 25 percent of corporate board seats at S&P 500 companies in 2018 (Catalyst 2019).

Male-dominated occupations (occupations where women comprise 25 percent or less of the workforce) are linked to several issues, including the pay gap (differences in the average annual salary between men and women), differences in running for political office, and experiences with gender discrimination. Male-dominated occupations have been linked to a workplace culture that presents numerous challenges for women, including increased problems with sexual harassment, insufficient mentoring of women employees, and pervasive gender stereotypes.

Women working in male-dominated occupations, both in private business and government occupations such as law enforcement, report experiencing more sexual harassment than men in these same occupations and women in occupations that are female dominated. Women in male-dominated occupations may leave the industry as a result of the workplace environment, exacerbating gender issues, such as the pay gap. Thus, occupational segregation creates less gender diverse occupations, and male-dominated workplaces are associated with a workplace environment that is challenging and potentially hostile for women.

OCCUPATIONAL INTEGRATION

One potential way of creating a healthier workforce environment is to increase levels of occupational integration (so that women and men constitute about 50 percent of an occupation) of the U.S. workforce. It is argued that this would improve several gender inequality issues, including the gender pay gap. Occupational integration should also create greater diversity in the workforce and lead to more gender diversity in U.S. workplaces, thus reducing sexual harassment and gender discrimination in employment. Gender diversity in the workplace has not only been linked to reduced sexual harassment and gender discrimination in employment, but some studies have also found that gender diversity leads to higher profits, better recruitment and retention of talented employees, better employee performance, and higher employee satisfaction.

However, for gender diversity and occupational integration to change the workplace environment, some argue that *where* integration occurs in the workplace is equally important. To reduce gender discrimination and sexual harassment, many experts emphasize that increased gender diversity is needed in management and supervisory positions. In other words, vertical occupational segregation must be reduced. This presents a challenging problem, as women's representation in management, and especially in top-level management (e.g., corporate boards, chief executives), remains well behind men, and women of color are particularly rare in top corporate positions. It is also argued that increasing women in management positions and senior management positions is important for increasing gender diversity, as these women serve as role models for other women in the industry.

INCREASING GENDER DIVERSITY IN THE WORKFORCE

Although there is wide agreement that increasing gender diversity in the workforce would reduce sexual harassment and gender discrimination and promote a healthier work environment, strategies for accomplishing that goal vary. Although women's labor force participation and occupational integration has increased in both the United States and European countries since the 1960s, progress on full integration has been slow. Some countries have elected to use a "fast-track" philosophy to get more women in senior-level management positions. Several European countries have instituted gender quotas (a required or voluntary mechanism for increasing the number of women in an organization) for company corporate boards. The success of gender quotas depends on several factors, perhaps most notably whether the effort includes an adequate enforcement mechanism so that companies who do not meet the desired standard of gender diversity and professional growth for women receive stiff penalties.

In 2018, California became the first and only U.S. state to implement a gender quota for corporate boards. Using gender quotas to increase gender diversity on corporate boards is not without criticism, as some have expressed concerns over qualified candidates and reverse discrimination (favoring underrepresented groups). Other suggestions for increasing gender diversity in workplaces include reducing pay gaps between men and women, including more women in the hiring process, and more robust mentoring of current women employees.

Season Hoard

See also: Gender Equality; Power Dynamics; Sexism; Sexual Harassment Training; STEM Fields; Traditionally "Male" Workplaces

Further Reading

Badal, S. B. 2014. "The Business Benefits of Gender Diversity." Gallup, January 20. https://www.gallup.com/workplace/236543/business-benefits-gender-diversity.aspx.

Bertrand, M., S. E. Black, S. Jensen, and A. Lleras-Muney. 2019. "Breaking the Glass Ceiling? The Effect of Board Quotas on Female Labour Market Outcomes in Norway." *Review of Economic Studies* 86: 191–239.

Catalyst. 2019. "Pyramid: Women in S&P 500 Companies." https://www.catalyst.org/knowledge/women-sp-500-companies.

Hegewisch, A., M. Phil, H. Liepmann, J. Hayes, and H. Hartmann. 2010. "Separate and Not Equal? Gender Segregation in the Labor Market and the Gender Wage Gap." Institute for Women's Policy Research. https://iwpr.org/iwpr-issues/employment-and-earnings/separate-and-not-equal-gender-segregation-in-the-labor-market-and-the-gender-wage-gap/.

Lonsway, K. A., R. Paynich, and J. N. Hall. 2013. "Sexual Harassment in Law Enforcement: Incidence, Impact, and Perception." *Police Quarterly* 16: 177–210.

Parker, K. 2018. "Women in Majority-Male Workplaces Report Higher Rates of Gender Discrimination." Pew Research Center, March 7. http://www.pewresearch.org/fact-tank/2018/03/07/women-in-majority-male-workplaces-report-higher-rates-of-gender-discrimination/.

U.S. Census Bureau. 2018. "Occupation by Sex for Civilian Employed Population 16 Years and Over." *2013–2017 American Community Survey 5 Year Estimates.*

https://sites.wp.odu.edu/MapsRUS/wp-content/uploads/sites/1329/2019/07
/occupations_Tangier_2017-4.pdf.

Weeden, K. A., M. Newhart, and D. Gelbgiser. 2018. "State of the Union 2018: Occupational
Segregation." Stanford Center on Poverty and Inequality. https://inequality.stanford
.edu/sites/default/files/Pathways_SOTU_2018_occupational-segregation.pdf.

Wynn, Steve (1942–)

Steve Wynn was born as Stephen Alan Weinberg on January 27, 1942, in New Haven, Connecticut, to Zelma Wynn and Michael Weinberg, who was an enterprising bingo parlor operator. Michael Weinberg changed the family's name from "Weinberg" to "Wynn" when Steve was only six months old. His successful business plummeted, however, and he became addicted to gambling and lost most of his wealth. These setbacks contributed to his encouragement to his sons, Steve and Kenneth, to excel in their education and pursue stable professions. Steve Wynn attended a private school for boys, Manlius, and graduated in 1959. After graduating from high school, he pursued his college degree at the University of Pennsylvania. In 1963, while attending school, his father died while undergoing open heart surgery. Wynn managed to graduate with a BA in English literature despite his family's severe financial difficulties—a result of the gambling debts left after the death of his father.

As a young man, Wynn considered a career in law. At age twenty-one, though, he gave up a slot at Yale Law School to carry on the family business. Working diligently, he transformed the long-struggling family business and expanded it into a money-making business. Over decades, Wynn became one of the leading hotel and casino moguls in the United States.

Wynn has played a major role in the construction and operation of prestigious hotels in Atlantic City and Las Vegas, including the Mirage, Treasure Island, the Golden Nugget, and the Bellagio. He also played an integral role in the expansion of the Las Vegas Strip in the 1990s. Wynn married Elaine Pascal, twice, from 1963 to 1986 and again from 1991 to 2010. They have two children, Gillian Wynn Early and Kevyn Wynn. In 2011, Steven Wynn married Andrea Danenza Hissom.

Wynn came under intense public scrutiny following serious sexual assault allegations leveled against him by four women who were employees of Wynn Resorts Each case occurred in different years: 2005, 2006, 2008, and 2011. As reported by the Massachusetts Gaming Commission, Wynn Resorts' executives were responsible for covering up decades of misconduct allegations from dozens of women against Wynn. It was alleged that Wynn Resorts had maintained a culture of secrecy and that victims of sexual misconduct and harassment were terrified to file sexual harassment complaints against the billionaire because they believed such actions would be useless due to his political connections and tremendous wealth.

Before the revelations of the cover-up became public, there were several reports from women who quietly agreed to financial settlements for the alleged harassment (and worse) that they had endured at Wynn's hands. In one report, a woman told a supervisor that she had been raped by Wynn and became pregnant in 2005. She alleged that Wynn assaulted her in a massage room that was connected to his office. The report indicated that the case led to a $7.5 million settlement in 2005. In a deposition, Wynn claimed that he and the woman had consensual intercourse after the women rubbed his leg and placed her hand up his shorts. There was another report made by a woman who claimed she was compelled to resign from her job in Las Vegas after engaging in unwanted sexual intercourse with Wynn. This case settled for $975,000 in 2006.

There have been numerous claims of sexual misconduct against Wynn since these cases were settled. Dozens of employees of Wynn Resorts alleged that Wynn made unwelcome sexual advances or committed acts of indecent exposure. There have also been reports of him compelling employees to engage in unwanted sexual intercourse.

In late January 2018, Wynn resigned as campaign finance chairman of the Republican National Committee, and early the following month he resigned as chairman and chief executive of Wynn Resorts. Both of these resignations came in the wake of the publication of a *Wall Street Journal* investigation that documented allegations from several women about harassment or sexual assaults that Wynn had committed against them. Wynn denied the allegations of sexual misconduct, saying that "the idea that I ever assaulted any woman is preposterous." He also stated, "We find ourselves in a world where people can make allegations, regardless of the truth, and a person is left with the choice of weathering insulting publicity or engaging in multi-year lawsuits" (Berzon et al. 2018).

In April 2019, Jennifer Marietta-Westberg, who is employed by Cornerstone Research as a senior economist providing financial consulting and expert testimony in phases of complex litigation and regulatory proceedings, indicated that, since 2014, Wynn Resorts has made "the strongest and swiftest response" in distancing itself from the CEO and making major changes to its board of directors. According to a Massachusetts Gaming Commission 2019 report, there are indications that, for years, "a limited group of executives and employees in [a] position of authority" had knowledge of the sexual misconduct allegations against Wynn but did not adhere to company sexual harassment or employee grievance policies in place to handle the complaints. The investigation also revealed that company executives made "affirmative effort" to conceal the sexual allegations against Wynn. According to the Massachusetts Gaming Commission report, Wynn Resorts was fined $20 million in February 2019 for not responding properly to allegations of sexual misconduct against Wynn.

Since the #MeToo Movement and the publicized details about Wynn's behavior, there have been several changes at Wynn Resorts. Wynn stepped down as CEO, the executive board added three female members, Wynn Resorts expanded and implemented training for every employee to prevent sexual misconduct, and the company formed a "special committee" to investigate sexual misconduct allegations within the company.

Tony McClendon and Rochelle McGee-Cobbs

See also: Hostile Work Environment; #MeToo Movement; Quid Pro Quo; Sexism

Further Reading

Berzon, Alexandra, Chris Kirkham, Elizabeth Bernstein, and Kate O'Keeffe. 2018. "Dozens of People Recount Pattern of Sexual Harassment by Las Vegas Mogul Steve Wynn." *Wall Street Journal*, January 27. Accessed January 16, 2020. https://www.wsj.com/articles/dozens-of-people-recount-pattern-of-sexual-misconduct-by-las-vegas-mogul-steve-wynn-1516985953.

CNN. 2019. "Wynn Resorts Executives Concealed Sexual Misconduct Accusations against Steve Wynn Gaming Regulators Say." April 15. https://www.cnn.com/2019/04/03/us/wynn-resorts-massachusetts-gaming-commission/index.html.

Ferrara, David. 2018. "Second Massage Therapist Files Lawsuit against Steve Wynn." March 1. Accessed February 1, 2020. https://www.reviewjournal.com/business/casinos-gaming/second-massage-therapist-files-lawsuit-against-steve-wynn/.

Goldstein, Matthew, Tiffany Hsu, and Kenneth P. Vogel. 2018. "Stephen Wynn, Casino Mogul, Accused of Decades of Misconduct." *New York Times*, January 26. Accessed April 16, 2019. https://www.nytimes.com/2018/01/26/business/steve-wynn-sexual-misconduct-claims.html.

Summers, Marivic Cabural. 2018. "RNC Finance Chairman Steve Wynn Resigns Amid Sexual Misconduct Allegations." USA Herald, January 27. Assessed April 17, 2019. https://usaherald.com/rnc-finance-chairman-steve-wynn-resigns-amid-sexual-misconduct-allegations/.

WSLS-TV. 2018. "Exec Concealed Sexual Misconduct Accusations against Steve Wynn." Accessed April 17, 2019. https://www.cnn.com/2019/04/03/us/wynn-resorts-massachusetts-gaming-commission/index.html.

About the Editor
and Contributors

EDITOR

GINA ROBERTIELLO, PhD, is a full professor in the Department of Criminal Justice at Felician University in Lodi, New Jersey. She is the author of more than thirty publications in the areas of policing, domestic violence, restorative justice, and crisis intervention. She is the author of *Police and Citizen Perceptions of Police Power* (2204) and *The Use and Abuse of Police Power in America* (ABC-CLIO, 2017). Dr. Robertiello received her BS in administration of justice from Rutgers University (New Brunswick, NJ), and her MA and PhD from Rutgers University (School of Criminal Justice, Newark, NJ). She teaches courses in research methods, victimology, criminology, juvenile delinquency, and deviance and is an FYE instructor. She is a textbook reviewer, a manuscript reviewer, a member of a number of advisory boards, and a volunteer for many organizations, especially those that support her Italian heritage. She resides in New Jersey and enjoys participating in activities with her husband and three children as well as reading at the beach and jogging every day.

CONTRIBUTORS

CHARLES ADAMS is a criminologist who focuses on social inequality, police misconduct, and racial injustice. Currently, he is the chair of the Department of Behavioral Sciences and Human Services at Bowie State University.

HASAN AKIN, MSc, is a researcher and a former diplomat. He is the founder, owner, and chief trainer of the ATILIM Martial Arts Organization.

AJARATU ALGHALI received her BA in psychology from Montclair State University with a business minor and is working on her MA at the College of New Jersey in Clinical Mental Health Counseling. She hopes to bring awareness to the importance of mental health services for individuals from marginalized communities.

JENNIFER M. BALBONI is a professor of criminal justice at Curry College in Milton, Massachusetts. Her areas of interest include criminal justice policy and reform as well as and restorative justice.

M'BALU P. BANGURA is an experienced civil rights investigator and Baltimore City's first equity specialist. She considers herself an inequity eliminator and has spent her academic and professional career as a social justice advocate, promoting diversity, equity, and inclusion for all.

GARY L. BERTE is an assistant professor at Springfield College. He has a BS from Westfield State College, an MS from American International College, and an EdD from the University of Massachusetts.

SAPPHIRE BEVERLY graduated with a bachelor's in criminal justice and minor in sociology. She hosted, coordinated, and planned the Leaders 4 Diversity Conference at Tarleton State University, presented at numerous conferences, and is working on a MS degree in criminology at Texas A&M University. Her area of interest is on the effectiveness of sex trafficking aftercare policies in the United States.

ROBERT L. BING III is a professor of criminology and criminal justice at UT Arlington. He is the author of four books. His research areas include race and crime, organizational politics in the courtroom, and issues in higher education.

BRENT BLAKEMAN is a PhD student and teaching assistant at Florida International University. His research focuses on collecting and using quantitative data to better understand human trafficking from an empirical perspective.

CHASTITY BLANKENSHIP, PhD, is an assistant professor of social science in the Department of Criminology at Florida Southern College. She has published nearly twenty articles and book chapters on race, class, and gender issues within the criminal justice system.

BRYAN M. BLAYLOCK is a former combat veteran who served ten years in the U.S. Marine Corps, from 2006 to 2017. He received his BA in criminology in 2019 from the University of Texas at Dallas. He will be starting law school in the fall of 2020.

STEVEN BLOCK is an associate professor at Central Connecticut State University in the Department of Criminology and Criminal Justice. His academic interests include victimless crimes and interpersonal violence.

KWAN-LAMAR BLOUNT-HILL, JD, is the director of research and data analytics for the Kings County (Brooklyn) District Attorney's Office and is completing his PhD in criminal justice at the City University of New York Graduate Center/ John Jay College of Criminal Justice.

ANGELO BROWN is a PhD student in criminal justice and criminology at Washington State University. His research interests are comparative criminal justice and criminal justice policy.

MICHELLE J. BUDIG, PhD, is the vice provost for faculty development and a professor of sociology at the University of Massachusetts–Amherst. Her research interests include labor market inequalities, wage penalties for paid and unpaid caregiving, work-family policy, and nonstandard employment.

EMMANUEL BURGOS graduated from Felician University with a degree in criminal justice. His area of interest is law enforcement.

DURMUS ALPER CAMLIBEL, PhD, is an assistant professor of criminal justice at University of Wisconsin, Oshkosh. He teaches courses in policing, criminal justice policy, crime prevention, terrorism, and narcotic drugs. His research currently focuses on law enforcement stress, inmate violence, opioid addiction, and ethnic conflict.

MARY-PAULA CANCIENNE is an assistant professor of theology and religious studies at Georgian Court University in New Jersey.

MYRNA CINTRON is an associate professor in the Department of Justice Studies in the College of Juvenile Justice & Psychology at Prairie View A&M. She has over twenty years' teaching experience. Her broader research and teaching interests include minorities in the criminal and justice systems.

DANIEL N. CLAY is currently an assistant professor at Elmira College in the Departments of Criminal Justice and Legal Studies. He holds a master of science in crime and justice studies from Suffolk University (2015), a juris doctor from Suffolk University Law School (2015), and a master of laws in international criminal law and justice from the University of New Hampshire School of Law (2016).

LAURENCE COBBAERT, B. Psych., M. Phil., is a research assistant in the School of Social Sciences at the University of Adelaide, Australia.

NADINE MARIE CONNELL is an associate professor in the School of Criminology and Criminal Justice at Griffith University, Queensland, Australia. She received her PhD from the University of Maryland at College Park. Her research interests include school violence, juvenile delinquency prevention, program and policy evaluation, and capital punishment.

GEORGE E. COROIAN JR., JD, PhD, is an assistant professor of criminal justice in the Department of Social Sciences and Public Administration at West Virginia University–Institute of Technology. He holds a PhD in criminology from Indiana University of Pennsylvania and a JD from Ohio Northern University College of Law, and he is a licensed attorney. Further, he has law enforcement experience.

GEMINI CREASON-PARKER obtained her MS and MA at Northeastern State University. She is pursuing a PhD in sociology at Texas A&M.

GORDON A. CREWS is the chair and Keith A. Ferguson Endowed Professor in criminal justice at the University of Texas Rio Grande Valley. His publications include referred journal articles and books dealing with juvenile and K–12 school violence, occult/satanic involvement and youth, and various law enforcement and correctional issues.

ANNE CROSS holds a PhD in sociology from Yale University, and directed the Women's Studies program at the University of Wisconsin–Stout. She currently serves as a professor of criminal justice at Metropolitan State University and is a cheerleading coach where the team cheers for the hockey team within the Minneapolis Public Schools.

ANTONIA CURTIS conducts research on maternal incarceration, including research on the outcomes of participation in prison bonding and parenting programs for incarcerated mothers and their children as well as research on sexual assault prevention and advocacy, including research on culture, attitudes, values, and beliefs surrounding sexual violence.

JEFFREY CZARNEC is the associate dean of the Department of Criminal Justice at SNHU Global as well as an academic consultant and program/faculty developer. He is a retired police officer, having served twenty-three years with the City of Manchester, New Hampshire, Police Department.

DARLA D. DARNO is an assistant professor of criminal justice within the Department of Sociology, Social Work & Criminal Justice at East Stroudsburg University.

LINDSAY R. DAVIS, EdM, is a current doctoral student in the Simmons School of Education and Human Development at Southern Methodist University, with an expected graduation date of May 2021.

AIMÉE X. DELANEY, PhD, is an associate professor of criminal justice at Worcester State University. Her research focuses on family and community violence and the victimization of youth. Her work has been published in *Criminal Justice Review*, *Contemporary Perspectives in Family Violence*, and the *Encyclopedia of Community Corrections*. Prior to academia, Dr. Delaney worked in the criminal and juvenile justice systems, including as a special investigator for sexual assault of youth.

SERHAT DEMIR is a researcher and a former police chief. He holds the title of sifu in the martial arts system.

CAROLYN DENNIS is contributing criminal justice faculty at Walden University. Her background includes over twenty-five years in academia. She is a former adult probation/parole officer, and she is a qualitative and quantitative researcher with several publications.

ANNA DOERING is an undergraduate student at the University of South Dakota studying criminal justice. Her research experience has focused on sexualized violence.

WENDY DRESSLER holds a BS in criminal justice from San Jose State University, an MA from John Jay College of Criminal Justice, and a PhD in international crime from Florida International University. Her professional experience includes fifteen years of reentry program compliance and management. Her research interests include the nexus of drug trafficking, human trafficking, and terrorism and the effects of drug trafficking on children.

DONALD DULA is an adjunct professor at Essex County College in Newark, New Jersey, and a retired law enforcement professional. He is a member of the National Society of Leadership and Success and serves as president of C.O.I.N.S (Correctional Officers in Neighborhood and Schools). Currently, he is a doctoral candidate in public policy and administration at Walden University.

JENNIFER EDWARDS received a PhD in sociology from Oklahoma State University in 2004. She currently serves as a professor of sociology, the coordinator of the BA degree in sociology, and the coordinator of the MS degree in criminal justice at Northeastern State University. Her areas of specialization include intergroup conflict, the relationship between ritual behavior and power, and criminology.

O. OKO ELECHI is a professor in the Criminal Justice Department at Mississippi Valley State University. He received his PhD from Simon Fraser University, Canada. He also holds two degrees from the University of Oslo, Norway.

THERESA FANELLI is an assistant professor at Felician University. She earned a BA in psychology and an MA in applied behavior analysis and in research and experimental design, with specialization in Pavlovian and Skinnerian conditioning. She is a (retired) special agent for the Federal Bureau of Investigation.

LAURA FINLEY is a professor of sociology and criminology at Barry University in Miami, Florida. She is the author, coauthor, or editor of thirty books and numerous book chapters and journal articles. In addition, Dr. Finley is actively involved in many human rights and social justice organizations.

SARAH F. FISCHER earned her PhD from American University. She is an assistant professor of criminal justice at Marymount University in Arlington, Virginia.

ASHLEY FUNDACK, PhD, is an assistant professor of criminal justice at Cecil College. Her affiliations include the American Society of Criminology, the

Academy of Criminal Justice Sciences, the Baltimore City Human Trafficking Collaborative and the HT Public Awareness Committee, the InfraGard Maryland Chapter, the Maryland Crime Prevention Association, and the Northeastern Association of Criminal Justice Sciences. She is also a member of the Victim Services Providers Network of Maryland and is a member of the board of directors of the Baltimore Child Abuse Center.

VENESSA GARCIA is an associate professor of criminal justice at New Jersey City University. She received her PhD in sociology from the SUNY University at Buffalo. Dr. Garcia's research focuses on oppressed groups but mainly on women as officials, criminals, and victims. She has published research articles in these areas in various journals, including *Deviant Behavior, Children and Youth Services Review, Journal of Criminal Justice, Police Practice and Research: An International Journal*, and the *Journal of Contemporary Criminal Justice*.

TARA A. GARRISON earned her MS in administration of justice and security from the University of Phoenix and her PhD from Walden University. She continues her research in criminal justice and mental health issues. She is the author of the Garrison deviance conformity theory.

ANGELA R. GOVER is a professor of criminology and criminal justice in the School of Public Affairs at the University of Colorado Denver. Her areas of research include intimate partner violence, gender and crime, crime victimization/victimology, personal protection orders, domestic violence offender treatment, and law enforcement officers' perceptions of intimate partner violence.

FRANK R. HALL is an associate professor in the Homeland Security Master's Program at Northwestern State University. He is a retired Army Intelligence colonel with twenty-eight years of active duty, four deployed in combat.

CONNIE HASSETT-WALKER previously worked as a research associate at the Violence Institute of New Jersey (Rutgers University) and for thirteen years was an associate professor of criminal justice at Kean University. She joined the faculty at Norwich University, Department of Justice Studies and Sociology, in July 2020.

SEASON HOARD received her MA and PhD in political science from Washington State University (WSU). She is an associate professor in the Division of Governmental Studies and Services and the School of Politics, Philosophy and Public Affairs at WSU. Her areas of interest are gender equality policy, applied research methods, and comparative public policy.

LISA BELL HOLLERAN, PhD, is an assistant professor of criminal justice at St. Edward's University in Austin, Texas. Her research focus is juror decision-making in capital cases, mitigation and aggravation, veteran's treatment court, and incarcerated mothers.

KAITLYN BRENNA HOOVER is currently working on her PhD at Florida State University, with a research focus on mental health and substance use.

MELISSA INGLIS, PhD, is an assistant professor of criminal justice and the Col. Tom A. Thomas Endowed Chair at East Central University. She holds an expertise in victimology and rural justice issues.

SHAUNTEY JAMES earned her PhD from Western Michigan University and a JD from Thomas Cooley Law School. She is an assistant professor at Penn State Harrisburg.

NATALIE JOHNS is a graduate student at George Mason University, where she is pursuing an MS in criminal justice. She received her BS in psychological science from the University of Mary Washington.

ARELIA JOHNSON is a doctoral student at Howard University. She is earning a degree in sociology and criminology with a concentration in gender and sexuality.

CHERYL LAURA JOHNSON earned her bachelor of arts degree in sociology from Elon University and her master's in criminal justice at Radford University. She obtained a certificate in crime analysis and is currently working on her dissertation at the University of Cincinnati.

JUDE L. JOKWI LENJO is an assistant professor of criminal justice at Wiley College, Marshall, Texas. Dr. Jokwi Lenjo has practiced law for many years, and his research interests include wrongful convictions, terrorism, and policing.

SUMAN KAKAR, PhD, is a professor of criminology and criminal justice at Florida International University. Her research interests focus on human trafficking, sexual harassment, child abuse, domestic violence, race relations, and immigration issues. She has published extensively on these issues. She provides workshops on human trafficking and race relations.

SEBRENA KEARNS is a social worker at the Jewish Association Serving the Aging (JASA). She completed her field placement at the Master of Social Work Program at the City University of New York, York College, and is a recent master of social work graduate from SUNY, Stony Brook University.

POCO KERNSMITH is a professor and PhD program director in the School of Social Work at Wayne State University. Her current research focuses on the etiology and prevention of violence in families and intimate relationships, with particular focus on the gendered context of perpetration of violence. Her research also includes policy approaches for the prevention and treatment of violence.

ANNA KING, PhD, is an associate professor in the Department of Criminal Justice, Anthropology, Sociology and Human Rights at Georgian Court University in New Jersey.

CATHRYN LAVERY, PhD, is a professor of criminal justice and a graduate coordinator at Iona College. Her research interests focus on sexual harassment and Title IX, human trafficking, campus crime, officer wellness, and community-based corrections issues.

LORI MADISON is a criminal justice professional from Michigan who is pursuing a doctorate at the University of Phoenix in management and organizational leadership. Lori began her law enforcement career in 1986, retiring in 2009. Lori currently instructs criminal justice administration capstone courses at the University of Phoenix.

ELIZABETH W. MARCHIONI, JD, is an associate professor of law and justice studies at Wesley College in Dover, Delaware. She teaches courses in legal studies and criminal justice and is the director of the Legal Studies Program, an American Bar Association–approved program. She also serves as the college's pre-law advisor.

ERZULIE VICA MARS is the associate director of student development and the coordinator for numerous social justice events at York College of the City University of New York (CUNY). She holds a master of science in education in higher education administration (MSEd-HEA) from CUNY Baruch College.

DAVID A. MARVELLI is a supervisor at the FBI and an adjunct professor for John Jay College of Criminal Justice and the University of Mary Washington. He received his PhD from Rutgers University.

TONY MCCLENDON is a sophomore majoring in criminal justice and minoring in sociology at Mississippi Valley State University. He is currently enlisted in the U.S. Army Reserves as a mechanic and plans on pursuing graduate studies in criminal justice

ROCHELLE MCGEE-COBBS received her PhD in juvenile justice from Prairie View A&M University, in Prairie View, Texas, in 2015. She is an associate professor and undergraduate coordinator for the Department of Criminal Justice at Mississippi Valley State University. In addition, she has published scholarly articles and papers in professional academic journals and anthologies.

MELANIE CLARK MOGAVERO is an assistant professor of criminal justice at Georgina Court University. Her primary research areas include sexual offending, sex offender policy, and vulnerable populations in the criminal justice system.

SHERILL V. C. MORRIS-FRANCIS, PhD, MSW, BSW, is an associate professor and graduate coordinator in the Department of Criminal Justice and the director of academic assessment at Mississippi Valley State University. Her research interests include program implementation and evaluation, minorities and the juvenile justice system, school factors and delinquency, and juvenile mental health issues.

LAUREN MOTON, MS, is a doctoral student in criminal justice at the City University of New York Graduate Center/John Jay College of Criminal Justice, and has a master of science in criminal justice from Bowling Green State University. She is currently researching women in policing, police legitimacy, sexual minorities, human trafficking, and sex work.

CYNTHIA NINIVAGGI, PhD, BCBA, is the director of women's studies and an associate professor of anthropology in the Department of Criminal Justice, Anthropology, Sociology, and Human Rights at Georgian Court University.

JAMES RANDALL NOBLITT earned his PhD in clinical psychology from the University of North Texas. He is a clinical psychologist licensed in the state of Texas and a professor of clinical psychology at the California School of Professional Psychology at Alliant International University in Los Angeles. He is the author of several books and articles, most of which address the psychological consequences to women and child victims of physical, emotional, and sexual assault.

PAMELA PERSKIN NOBLITT earned a BA in psychology from Dallas Baptist University. She is an advocate for children and women who have been subjected to physical, emotional and sexual abuse since 1986. She was honored by the Eckerd's Foundation as one of Eckerd's 100 Women of 2000 for her advocacy, and she presented at the United Nations Commission on the Status of Women Annual Conferences from 2009 through 2017 along with her husband and coauthor, Randy Noblitt.

IFEOMA OKOYE is an assistant professor of criminal justice at Virginia State University. Her research and teaching interests revolve around quantitative analysis, idiographic and nomothetic research, terrorism and counterterrorism, and legal aspects of justice administration.

ALABA OLUDARE is an assistant professor of criminal justice at the Mississippi Valley State University. Dr. Oludare has practiced law for many years, and her research interests include cybercrime, terrorism, violence reduction, gangs, prisons, policing, and restorative justice.

OLASUNMBO AYANFEOLUWA OLUSANYA, PhD, is from the University of Lagos, Nigeria, and an employment relations and human resource management specialist with a focus on informal economy, entrepreneurship, labor economics, and development studies. She is a research member of the ARUA Centre of Excellence for Unemployment and Skills Development, University of Lagos, Nigeria.

NOEL OTU holds a PhD from Florida State University and is an associate professor of criminal justice at the University of Texas Rio Grande Valley.

STACEY B. PLICHTA, ScD, CPH, is a full professor of health policy and management at the City University of New York (CUNY) Graduate School of Public Health and Health Policy. She has been conducting research and publishing in the area of women's health for over twenty years.

ELLEN REPETA is a graduate student at the University of Texas at Dallas studying criminology. She is working on her thesis on human trafficking, with an emphasis in sex trafficking.

MARNY REQUA is an associate professor and chair of the Department of Criminal Justice, Anthropology, Sociology, and Human Rights at Georgian Court University in New Jersey.

BRIANNA ROBERTIELLO attended the University of Tampa, where she was a writer for *The Odyssey*, and Felician University, where she graduated with a degree in journalism. She is a freelance writer for the Vicinity Media Group as well as *VUE* magazine, both in New Jersey.

SELENA T. RODGERS is an associate professor and founding director of the Master of Social Work Program at the City University of New York, York College, where she examines the well-being of Black women through an intersectional disciplinary, theoretical, and structural lens with particular attention to various forms of violence. She earned her master's degree in social work from Syracuse University and a PhD from Adelphi University's School of Social Work.

BEVERLY ROSS teaches undergraduate- and graduate-level conflict resolution and criminology courses at California University of Pennsylvania. Ross holds master's degrees in forensic psychology and sociology and a PhD in international psychology.

BRIAN L. ROYSTER is currently an assistant professor at Saint Peter's University in Jersey City, New Jersey, where teaches numerous criminal justice and sociology courses. He has attained an EdD in education leadership management and policy, an EdS in administration and supervision, and a MA in education from Seton Hall University. He also holds a MS in criminal justice from New Jersey City University and a BA in sociology from Montclair State.

ERIN SCOTT, Esq., has been working on domestic violence and sexual assault issues since volunteering as a rape crisis counselor in 1990. She is the executive director at the Family Violence Law Center in Oakland, sits on the board of directors of UnCommon Law, and is a former board member of the California Partnership to End Domestic Violence and the Family Violence Appellate Project. She received a BA from Swarthmore College and a JD from New York University School of Law.

MIRIAM D. SEALOCK is a professor in the Department of Sociology, Anthropology and Criminal Justice at Towson University. Her research primarily focuses on criminology theory and decision-making within the criminal justice system and includes published works on the subjects of police discretion, general strain theory, and the prevention and treatment of juvenile delinquency and drug use.

CATHIE PERSELAY SEIDMAN is a former assistant district attorney. She has an MA in criminal justice from the Rutgers University School of Criminal Justice and is a full professor of criminal justice at Hudson County Community College.

MEGAN CALLAHAN SHERMAN has been a practicing social worker for twenty years. She is a licensed clinical social worker and certified clinical social work supervisor. Currently, Dr. Sherman serves as the chairperson and assistant professor of social work at Georgian Court University, where she is also the program director of the bachelor of social work program.

ARIATU SILLAH earned her bachelor's degree at William Paterson University in criminal justice with a minor in sociology, and her MS is in criminal justice. She is a recent graduate of New Jersey City University's Graduate Criminal Justice Program. Her research focused on human trafficking and sex crimes.

FRANCESCA SPINA, PhD, is the chair of the Criminal Justice Department at Springfield College. Her research interests include gender and crime, race and justice, and criminal justice policy reform.

DEVEON TREADWAY is a senior at Mississippi Valley State University who is double majoring in English and criminal justice.

BAMIDELE WALE-OSHINOWO is a lecturer at the Faculty of Business Administration, University of Lagos, Nigeria. Her broad teaching and research interests are in the areas of entrepreneurship and strategic management. Prior to joining the academia, Bamidele worked in the industry for over eight years in Nigeria in the areas of relationship management and financial and business advisory services. She has a PhD, MBA, MSc, and BSc.

DURRELL MALIK WASHINGTON SR. is a PhD student in the School of Social Service Administration at the University of Chicago and a graduate research assistant and teaching assistant at the Pozen Family Center for Human Rights Lab. His research focuses on the intersections between juvenile justice and systems of care to understand patterns of incarceration in urban neighborhoods; he received his MA in social work from Columbia University.

SAMYAH WILLIAMS recently graduated from Curry College with a bachelor's degree in criminal justice and is planning to attend law school in the near future.

Index

Note: Page numbers in **bold** indicate the location of main entries.